SOCIALISM AND AMERICAN LIFE

D0169065

PRINCETON STUDIES

IN AMERICAN CIVILIZATION

Number 4

SOCIALISM
AND
AMERICAN
LIFE

EDITORS: DONALD DREW EGBERT

AND STOW PERSONS

BIBLIOGRAPHER: T. D. SEYMOUR BASSETT

VOLUME 2

BIBLIOGRAPHY:

DESCRIPTIVE AND CRITICAL

PRINCETON, NEW JERSEY

PRINCETON UNIVERSITY PRESS

1952

*Publication of this book has been aided by a grant from the
Princeton University Research Fund*

Printed in the United States of America
by Princeton University Press, Princeton, New Jersey

PREFACE

THE function of this selective and critical bibliography is to map the subject; it therefore belongs both in the field of historiography and in the category of guides to the literature of socialism. In preparing it, a many-sided approach was deliberately chosen, largely because of the very nature of socialism itself which has meant many things to many people throughout a long history. But the subject was approached in this way for another reason, namely, the belief of the authors that such an approach offered the best chance for achieving a relatively high degree of objectivity despite such a highly controversial theme.

Titles were selected for inclusion on the basis of one or more of the following five standards: (1) the importance of a given title for understanding the particular group with which it deals; (2) its ability to stand as a representative and typical sample; (3) in some cases, its unusual characteristics which indicate the breadth of the movement as a whole; (4) its quality as a signpost for scholarship in a part of the field; or (5) its relevance and importance under other generally accepted canons of scholarship. In the case of a choice between editions, either the first edition or the one considered most accessible to American readers has ordinarily been included.

In spite of this broad basis of choice, and in spite of the length of the bibliography, it nevertheless represents a high degree of selectivity—and necessarily so because of the enormous amount that has been written on the subject of socialism. Perhaps some idea of that amount can most easily be conveyed to the reader by mere mention of the fact that one of the chief bibliographies in the field, Josef Stammhammer's *Bibliographie des Socialismus und Communismus* (Jena, 1893-1909), which does not attempt to cover nearly so wide a range of material as the present book, consists of three good-sized volumes and yet does not go beyond 1908.

In an effort to increase the usefulness of the bibliography, it has been organized in a somewhat unusual way. Each section of it has been made into a short essay in which the nature and history of the particular aspect of socialism under consideration is discussed. These bibliographical essays are arranged in Parts corresponding roughly to the arrangement of the essays in Volume 1. Each Part consists of a section of General Reading covering the whole area to which the Part is devoted, followed by a series of short essays on specific related topics generally recognized as important to any discussion of socialism. The General Reading of each Part not only covers a wider field than any single topic, but also serves to call attention to various issues not otherwise covered in any topic.

v

Throughout the volume the bibliography of American socialism is treated not in isolation, but in relation to European sources and parallels. Wherever studies on a particular aspect of American socialism, and sometimes also on its European parallel, are lacking, an attempt has been made to fill the gap in the following way. In such cases the General Reading includes references to parts of works dealing generally with the subject of the section but not specifically with socialism, or else to parts of works dealing generally with socialism but only indirectly with the specific field of knowledge in question. This is especially true of PARTS III and VI. The selections included in the General Reading have been chosen also with regard to the needs of readers unfamiliar with the subjects treated in greater detail in the Special Topics. For this reason selections from several standard treatises on socialism recur throughout the General Reading sections, and users already familiar with the main outlines of the subject will prefer to turn to the more specialized topical essays.

PART I, although basically on European socialism, is focused particularly upon those elements of European socialism which have most influenced socialism in the United States. However, in order to show the antiquity, diversity, spread, and interrelations of socialist movements, some discussion of socialism in certain other regions is included. In general, PART I is weighted in favor of titles dealing with socialism in France, Germany, and Great Britain not only because of the influential roles these countries have played in the history of socialism, but also because their languages are widely understood by Americans. Collected in this Part are the essential works of Marx and Engels and of their outstanding successors and opponents, although repetition of some of these titles in later Parts could not be avoided. The section on Russia is generally limited to a selection of the relatively few items available in English translations both because of the fact that—since so few Americans read Russian—the influence of Russian works has been felt chiefly through translations, and because so many items published in Russia are not easily available in this country.* The specialist can find many of them, however, in the excellent Russian collections at the libraries of the University of California, the University of Chicago, the Russian Institute at Columbia University, Harvard University, the Hoover Library on War, Revolution, and Peace at Stanford University, the Yale University Library, and especially the Library of Congress and the New York Public Library.

* When Slavic authors' names have been transliterated into English in several different ways, or when they appear differently in different works, for the sake of simplicity a single uniform spelling, easily located in the index, has ordinarily been followed in this bibliography. This system of transliteration has not been used for a few famous names already widely known to Americans under a different spelling. In such cases the spelling given in *Webster's Biographical Dictionary* is normally followed.

PART II provides what can be considered a minimum of the literature essential for an understanding of socialism in the United States, as well as a sampling of the numerous groups not treated in the special topics. It also includes references to important movements, particularly the labor movement, which at times have been more or less related to socialism.

The remaining Parts, dealing analytically with socialism in more direct relation to specific fields of knowledge, repeatedly emphasize the continuing interpenetration of the American and the foreign phases of the socialist movements, and in many matters, also, the strong dependence of American socialism on European precedent and example. For this reason, the reader will find that it is not possible to dismiss the European contribution entirely after PART I.

It should be noted that the bibliography is not limited solely to the subject of socialism itself. As the title of these volumes indicates, we have chosen to cast this study of socialism against the background of the ideals and institutions of nonsocialist America. This perspective has influenced the choice of bibliographical material throughout. It has provided the explicit criteria for the selection of references in PART III, and elsewhere has required the inclusion of many references to American capitalism, individualism, and democracy as they oppose or interact with socialism. Although it was manifestly even less possible to provide an exhaustive bibliography on the central features of the American tradition than on socialism itself, it seemed desirable to include at least a few references which would seek to indicate and treat the key points where these complexes of ideas and institutions parallel and supplement, or conflict with, each other.

It is true that this general arrangement and content (like all others suggested while the project was being planned) are necessarily somewhat arbitrary. They also require some repetition in spite of a considerable number of cross references; at the same time, considerations of space and cost obviously made it impossible to repeat in every case titles pertinent to more than a single aspect of socialism. However, every effort has been made to overcome these difficulties both by means of careful organization and by means of clear expositions in the brief essays which accompany each section of the bibliography. During the seven years this book has been in preparation, preliminary drafts of the bibliography twice served as the basis for year-long seminars conducted for selected college seniors, and the preliminary drafts were carefully revised on the basis of this experience. As a result, it is hoped that the bibliography will prove useful to the general reader, while at the same time serving also as an introduction and guide for the specialist in those aspects of the subject which he has not yet investigated in detail.

While the bibliography is primarily limited to books, serials, pamphlets, and articles—in short, to matter already in print—a few important works in manuscript or in progress are cited. The location of major manuscript collections is mentioned, and the available guides to their contents are listed. The task of analyzing such collections critically and in detail has, however, been left to their custodians and other specialists particularly qualified to deal with them. Although the references to printed matter have been systematically made only to July 1948, the titles of some important books published through 1950 have been added since the manuscript of this book first went to press in the spring of 1950. A few items to be published in 1951 have also been cited.

The bibliography is in a real sense a cooperative undertaking. Its form was determined, and the basic work on PARTS I, II, III, and VI carried out, by the three original directors of the project, Professors David Bowers (d. 1945), Stow Persons, and Donald Egbert. In PART I the General Reading and half the special topics were drafted by Mr. Bowers, the remaining topics by Mr. Persons; in PART II, the General Reading by Messrs. Egbert and Bowers, the topics by Egbert, Persons, and Bowers; PART III by Bowers and Persons; and PART VI by Egbert except for topics 7-10, which were contributed in a shorter version by Professor Willard Thorp. A first draft of the General Reading, PART IV, "The Economics of Socialism," was submitted by Miss Virginia Buckner, but the final version is very largely by the hand of Professor T. D. S. Bassett. In his capacity as research associate and bibliographer of the Special Program in American Civilization at Princeton University during over two years between 1946 and 1948, Mr. Bassett wrote PARTS IV and V, and revised and expanded the remainder of the bibliography, so that major credit for preparing this volume in its present form is his. Nearly all of the numerous revisions were typed by Mrs. Helen Wright and the final draft thoroughly checked by Dorothy Reuss Persons. Both Mrs. Wright and Mrs. Persons made many helpful suggestions for changes and revisions in the entire book, which could hardly have been produced without their expert assistance.

Every effort was made throughout to secure the advice of libraries and specialists. Special acknowledgment must be made of the indispensable and unstinted aid furnished by the staff of the Princeton University Library, as well as by those in charge of the collections and reference service of the New York Public Library, the Library of Congress, and the Dartmouth College Library. Valuable assistance by conference and correspondence was received from the contributors to Volume 1 in the form of ideas for the organization and treatment of the materials, additional references, and review of sections of the bibliography. Special thanks are also due to Robert A. Alexander, Arthur E. Bestor, Jr., Cyril E. Black,

Reinhold Niebuhr, Max Nomad, Edmund Silberner, John Spargo, Marion Tinling, and Bertram D. Wolfe for their critical reading of sections of the typescript and their suggestions.

Although it is impossible to recognize adequately in every case the aid received from countless sources, the following persons should be mentioned for help generously given: Frederick B. Adams, Jr., Theodor W. Adorno, Arthur E. Albrecht, Raymond E. Bassett, Catherine Bauer, Mrs. Valentine Bill, Richard P. Blackmur, Mrs. Roger Butterfield, Gilbert Chinard, Edward S. Corwin, Leo Crespi, Edward Devereux, Mrs. E. V. Deyo, William Ebenstein, Frank D. Graham, Philip K. Hitti, Milton W. Hamilton, Henrik F. Infield, A. Leland Jamison, Dorothy A. Koch, Leon Kramer, Algernon Lee, Alpheus T. Mason, Oskar Morgenstern, Boris I. Nicolaevsky, Frederick I. Olson, Aaron M. Orange, David A. Shannon, J. Benjamin Stalvey, Fred Thompson, Margaret Farrand Thorp, Jacob Viner, J. P. Warbasse, and R. D. Welch.

The contributions of the following persons, institutions, and organizations are also gratefully acknowledged: Peter Stuck, Amana Society; Clarence S. Brigham, American Antiquarian Society; Boston Public Library; Carl Schurz Memorial Foundation, Philadelphia; University of Chicago Library; Columbia University Library; Cornell University Library; *Fourth International*; Library of the Franklin Institute, Philadelphia; Harvard College Library; International Publishers; William J. Petersen, The State Historical Society of Iowa; *Jewish Frontier*; Labor Zionist Organization of America; Poale Zion; University of Michigan Library; Library of the Workingmen's Institute, New Harmony, Ind.; Dorothy C. Barck, New-York Historical Society; New York State Library, Albany; Forbes Library, Northampton, Mass.; Ellen Lord, University of Omaha Library; Harrop Freeman, Pacifist Research Bureau; S. K. Stevens, state historian, Pennsylvania Historical Commission; Historical Society of Pennsylvania; University of Pennsylvania Library; Peoples Songs, Inc.; Pioneer Publishers; Socialist Labor Party; Eaton Memorial Library, Tufts College; University of Utah Library; Vassar College Library; University of Wisconsin Library; Workers Socialist Party; and Yale University Library.

The staff of the Princeton University Press has been most helpful throughout. The unfailing cooperation of Mr. Datus C. Smith, Jr., Director of the Press, and of Mr. Allan Wendt, its editor for this book, is especially appreciated.

DONALD DREW EGBERT AND STOW PERSONS, *Editors*

T. D. SEYMOUR BASSETT, *Bibliographer*

Princeton, New Jersey
August 1, 1951

CONTENTS · VOLUME 2

PART I

The World Setting of American Socialism

For discussion in Volume 1 relevant to this Part (PART I) of the Bibliography, see especially Chapters 1 and 2.

General Reading

THE history of socialism in America, although conditioned by indigenous forces and assuming forms peculiar to itself, is still largely an outgrowth of a movement implicit in Western civilization and owes much of its inspiration to foreign writers and philosophies. To understand American socialism, therefore, it is essential to consider it first against the background of its European complements.

In Europe itself socialism has had a long history, assuming many different forms and presenting problems of a special order. Originating, as far as its modern form is concerned, in medieval times (Topic 1), it became a recurrent phenomenon in early modern history appearing in connection with such great social upheavals as the Reformation, the Cromwellian revolution in England, and the French Revolution of 1789 (Topic 2). And growing even stronger in the nineteenth century it assumed, under the leadership of Marx, an international form, creating as its special organs the First, Second, Third, and Fourth Internationals (Topics 3 and 4). In the latter period, also, it exfoliated in many different directions depending upon the different stages of economic and political development of the countries in which it appeared. Thus, in England and Germany, where the political tradition was legalistic rather than revolutionary, it assumed the so-called "gradualist" forms of Fabian socialism, guild socialism, "orthodox" Marxism, and revisionism (Topic 9). Similarly, in such countries as France and Russia, where the political tradition was revolutionary, it assumed the more violent forms of syndicalism and bolshevism (Topic 8).

But in whatever form it has appeared, it has always stood in sharp contrast to the capitalist system which it would replace (Topic 5) and has often found itself associated with such other revolutionary movements opposed to capitalism as anarchism and fascism (Topic 10). For this reason it has been subject to severe criticisms of varying kinds (Topic 6) and has in defense sought to graft itself upon such important established institutions as religion and science (Topic 7).

Since it is impossible to cover the whole of the complicated history of socialism in Europe in detail, the most we can hope for here is a quick survey of the movement in its pre-Marxian, Marxian, and post-Marxian phases. Major European contributions on specific aspects of socialism, such as socialist theories of imperialism or stratification, will be referred to in later sections. See first H. W. Laidler, *Social-Economic Movements* (New York, 1944, 828 pp.), Pt. I (except chap. 11), and Pt. II; H. J. Laski, *Communism* (New York, 1927, 256 pp.), chap. 2; and *Manifesto of the Communist Party* (1848; ed. by Engels; London, 1888, 31 pp., and many other editions). E. H. Carr, *Studies in Revolution* (London, 1950, 227 pp.), a series of essays originally published anonymously in the *Times* (London) *Literary Supplement*, has especially good chapters on Marxian socialism, including Leninism and Stalinism, as well as on the *Communist Manifesto*, Saint-Simon, Proudhon, Sorel, and Russian radical thought of the nineteenth century.

1. General Histories of European Socialism

Because of the scope of the subject none of the overall histories of European socialism is entirely satisfactory. For balance and synthesis, the best short surveys by western Europeans are Félicien Challaye, *La Formation du socialisme; de Platon à Lénine* (Paris, 1937, 192 pp.), Alexander Gray, *The Socialist Tradition, Moses to Lenin* (London, 1946, 523 pp.), and N. I. Mackenzie, *Socialism; a Short History* (London, 1949, 192 pp.). Also see Élie Halévy, *Histoire du socialisme européen* (Paris, 1948, 367 pp.). Max Beer, *Allgemeine Geschichte des Sozialismus und der sozialen Kämpfe* (6th ed., Berlin, 1929, 789 pp.), is the product of a life-long student of socialism, but admittedly nothing but an extended outline. The five parts have been published separately in English under the following titles: *Social Struggles in Antiquity* (London, 1922, 222 pp.); *Social Struggles in the Middle Ages* (London, 1924, 215 pp.); *Social Struggles and Socialist Forerunners* (London, 1924, 224 pp.); *Social Struggles and Thought (1750-1860)* (London, 1925, 218 pp.); lastly, *Social Struggles and Modern Socialism* (London, 1925, 224 pp.). Also summary are Georg Adler, *Geschichte des Sozialismus und Kommunismus von Plato bis zur Gegenwart* (2nd ed., Leipzig, 1920, 281 pp.)—which analyzes socialism first in relation to the philosophical and religious ideals of antiquity and the Middle Ages and then in relation to the naturalistic ideals of the present—and H. W. Laidler, *A History of Socialist Thought* (1927), revised and reissued as *Social-Economic Movements* (New York, 1944, 828 pp.). In many respects Laidler's history is the most useful although it emphasizes Marxian socialism at the expense of pre-Marxian socialist thought, and omits Chartism. Karl Kautsky and others cooperated in a work of high scholarly standards, *Die Vorläufer des neueren Sozialismus* (*Die Geschichte des Sozialismus in Einzeldarstellungen*, Vol. 1; Stuttgart, 1895, 2 vols. in 1): I, *Von Plato bis zu den Wiedertäufern*; II, *Von Thomas More bis zum Vorabend der französischen Revolution*. Alfred Sudre, *Histoire du communisme; ou, Réfutation historique des utopies socialistes* (1849; 5th ed., Paris, 1856, 487 pp.), is an avowed polemic against all utopians from Plato to Proudhon, but is comprehensive and readable. Charles Gide, *Communist and Co-operative Colonies* (1928; tr. by E. F. Row; New York, 1931, 222 pp.), although often superficial and incomplete, is interesting for its coverage of such little-known socialist experiments as the Jesuit republics of Paraguay. See also J. J. Thonissen, *Le Socialisme depuis l'antiquité jusqu'à la constitution française du 14 janvier 1852* (Louvain, 1852, 2 vols.), J. Löser, *Führer durch die soziale Frage des Altertums, des Mittelalters, und der Neuzeit bis gegen Ende des 19. Jahrhunderts* (Karlsruhe, 1895, 172 pp.); H. P. G. Quack, *De Socialisten: personen en stelsels* (Amsterdam, 1899-1901, 6 vols.), which devotes only one volume to the period before 1800 and emphasizes Holland; and F. D. Nieuwenhuis, *De geschiedenis van het socialisme* (Amsterdam, 1901-1902, 3 vols.), by a Dutch anarchist.

For surveys of utopian socialism see Mary Hennell, *An Outline of the Various Social Systems and Communities . . . Founded on the Principle of Co-operation* (London, 1844, cxiv, 252 pp.), or J. O. Hertzler, *The History of Utopian Thought* (New York, 1923, 321 pp.). A. E. Bestor, Jr., "The Evolution of the Socialist Vocabulary," *Journal of the History of Ideas,* ix (June 1948), pp. 259-302, is a comprehensive essay on the invention and development of a large family of socialist and anarchist terms, and the changes in their meaning, with references (p. 277 and note 95) to studies on the origin of the word "socialism," such as Carl Grünberg, "Der Ursprung der Worte 'Sozialismus' und 'Sozialist'," in *Archiv für die Geschichte des Sozialismus und der Arbeiterbewegung,* ii (1912), pp. 372-379. See also the definition by Émile Durkheim, "Définition du socialisme," *Revue de métaphysique et de morale,* xxviii (July/Sept.-Oct./Dec. 1921), pp. 479-495, 591-614.

For DICTIONARIES, HANDBOOKS, AND ENCYCLOPEDIAS of socialism, see A. C. A. Compère-Morel, *Grand dictionnaire socialiste du mouvement politique et économique, national et international* (Paris, 1924, 1057 pp.); *Encyclopédie socialiste, syndicale et coopérative de l'Internationale ouvrière* (published under the direction of Compère-Morel; Paris, 1912-1921, 12 vols.); Charles Vérecque, *Dictionnaire du socialisme* (Paris, 1911, 502 pp.); Carl Stegmann and Hugo Lindemann (C. Hugo, pseud.), *Handbuch des Socialismus* (Zurich, 1897, 878 pp.); W. D. P. Bliss, *A Handbook of Socialism* (New York, 1895, 291 pp.); and A. S. Rappoport, *Dictionary of Socialism* (London, 1924, 271 pp.), all of which are now somewhat dated and, the last mentioned in particular, not always accurate. For a more recent handbook in English, consult Louis Wasserman, *Modern Political Philosophies and What They Mean* (Philadelphia, 1944, 287 pp.). See also *Handwörterbuch der Staatswissenschaften* (4th ed., ed. by Ludwig Elster and others; Jena, 1923-1929, 8 vols. and supp.); *Internationales Handwörterbuch des Gewerkschaftswesens* (ed. by Ludwig Heyde and others; Berlin, 1930-1932, 2 vols.); Ludwig Elster, ed., *Wörterbuch der Volkswirtschaft* (4th ed., Jena, 1931-1933, 3 vols. in 5), especially "Sozialistische Ideen und Lehren, i: Sozialismus und Kommunismus," by Carl Grünberg and Henryk Grossmann, iii, pp. 272-341;

and the *Encyclopaedia of the Social Sciences* (E. R. A. Seligman, editor-in-chief; New York, 1930-1935, 15 vols.), for introductory articles on communism and socialism, with their cross references and bibliographies.

For BIBLIOGRAPHIES AND SOURCE MATERIAL, see especially Josef Stammhammer, *Bibliographie des Socialismus und Communismus* (Jena, 1893-1909, 3 vols.); also Eugène Hatin, *Bibliographie historique et critique de la presse periodique française* (Paris, 1866, 660 pp.), essential for early socialist periodicals; Michel Ralea, *Révolution et socialisme; essai de bibliographie* (Paris, 1923, 80 pp.); Ernst Drahn, *Bibliographie des wissenschaftlichen Sozialismus, 1914 bis 1922* (Berlin, 1923, 160 pp.); *Die Welt des Sozialismus; eine Zusammenstellung der wichtigsten sozialistischen Literatur* (Leipzig, 1927, 120 pp.); Zürich, Zentralbibliothek, *Revolutionäres Schrifttum 1789-1925: Katalog zweier 1932/33 erworbener Bibliotheken* (Zurich, 1933, 78 pp.); and Édouard Dolléans and Michel Crozier, *Mouvements ouvrier et socialiste; chronologie et bibliographie; Angleterre, France, Allemagne, États-Unis (1750-1918)* (Paris, 1950, 381 pp.). *Archiv für die Geschichte des Sozialismus und der Arbeiterbewegung* (Leipzig, 1911-1930), is the best of the socialist periodicals for bibliography, reviews, and source materials.

2. History of Socialism in Different Periods

On socialism in ANTIQUITY the standard work is Robert von Pöhlmann, *Geschichte der sozialen Frage und des Sozialismus in der Antiken Welt* (1893-1901; 3rd ed. by F. Oertel, Munich, 1925, 2 vols.). Valuable material is also contained in Salvatore Cognetti de Martiis, *Socialismo antico* (Turin, 1889, 632 pp.); Edgar Salin, *Platon und die griechische Utopie* (Munich, 1921, 287 pp.); and Karl Kautsky, *Foundations of Christianity* (tr. from 13th German ed.; New York, 1925, 480 pp.), a Marxian interpretation of the historical role of Jesus and the origins of the Christian church. Both Ernst Troeltsch, *The Social Teaching of the Christian Churches* (tr. by Olive Wyon; New York, 1931, 2 vols.), and C. J. Cadoux, *The Early Church and the World* (Edinburgh, 1925, 675 pp.), deal with the primitive Christian attitude toward social and secular problems. Troeltsch has extended footnote criticisms of sources and interpretation, and a full bibliography. On the socialistic aspects of a specific heresy, see, for example, M. von Nathusius, *Zur Charakteristik der Cirkumcellionen des 4. u. 5. Jahrhunderts in Afrika* (Greifswald, 1900, 38 pp.), and F. Martroye, "Une tentative de révolution sociale en Afrique; Donatistes et circoncellions," *Revue des questions historiques*, LXXVI (Oct. 1904), pp. 353-416, LXXVII (Jan. 1905), pp. 5-53. A unique example of communism in the Middle East is the Zoroastrian heresy of Mazdak, briefly countenanced by the Sassanid king Qubād I (A.D. 488-531) but crushed by his successor. See A. E. Christensen's account, *Le Règne du roi*

Kawādh I et le communisme Mazdakite (Copenhagen, 1925, 127 pp.). Ernst Faber, *Die Grundgedanken des alten chinesischen Socialismus; oder, Die Lehre des Philosophen Micius* (Elberfeld, 1877, 102 pp.), analyzes socialistic ideas in ancient China.

Background material on socialism in the MEDIEVAL and EARLY MODERN PERIOD may be found in R. W. and A. J. Carlyle, *A History of Mediaeval Political Theory in the West* (Edinburgh, 1903-1936, 6 vols.); G. M. Trevelyan, *England in the Age of Wycliffe* (New York, 1899, 380 pp.); and R. H. Tawney, *The Agrarian Problem in the Sixteenth Century* (London, 1912, 464 pp.). For the beginnings of capitalism in the Renaissance and Reformation period, see references to Weber, Sombart, Tawney, and others in Topic 5. The socialist tendencies of the same period are the subject of Karl Kautsky's classic study, *Communism in Central Europe in the Time of the Reformation* (tr. by J. L. and E. G. Mulliken; London, 1897, 293 pp.). See also Ernst Bloch, *Thomas Münzer als Theologe der Revolution* (Munich, 1922, 297 pp.); Engels' own history, *The Peasant War in Germany* (tr. by M. J. Olgin; New York, 1926, 191 pp.); Émile Dermenghem, *Thomas Morus et les utopistes de la renaissance* (Paris, 1927, 282 pp.); and W. B. Guthrie, *Socialism before the French Revolution* (New York, 1907, 339 pp.). For other titles see Topics 1 and 6.

For socialism AFTER 1700 see Hector Denis, *Histoire des systèmes économiques et socialistes* (Paris, 1904-1907, 2 vols.). Denis deals with socialist economic theory chiefly in relation to the eighteenth-century beginnings of British classical economics. Of the many histories of socialism in the nineteenth century probably the best account, though highly critical, is Werner Sombart, *Socialism and the Social Movement* (tr. with intro. and notes by M. Epstein; London, 1909, 319 pp.). The tenth German edition was published under the title, *Der proletarische Socialismus* (Jena, 1924, 2 vols.). A later brief account is Paul Louis, *Cent cinquante ans de pensée socialiste* (new ed., Paris, 1947, 261 pp.). S. F. Markham, *A History of Socialism* (New York, 1931, 328 pp.), also stresses socialism as a social movement and usefully reprints in full the Gotha Programme of 1875 and the Erfurt Programme of 1891. See also Thomas Kirkup, *A History of Socialism* (5th ed. rev. and largely rewritten by E. R. Pease; London, 1920, 490 pp.); F. J. C. Hearnshaw, *A Survey of Socialism* (London, 1928, 473 pp.); and such centennial volumes as Robert Aron, ed., *De Marx au marxisme, 1848-1948* (Paris, 1948, 319 pp.), and George Woodcock, ed., *A Hundred Years of Revolution, 1848 and After* (London, 1948, 286 pp.). R. C. K. Ensor's anthology, *Modern Socialism as Set Forth by Socialists in Their Speeches, Writings and Programmes* (3rd ed., New York, 1910, 396 pp.), is a useful handbook of socialist thought in the nineteenth century.

For systematic introductions to Marxian and post-Marxian socialism

7

consult especially R. N. C. Hunt, *The Theory and Practice of Communism; an Introduction* (London, 1950, 231 pp.), and—more advanced, and written from a Marxian point of view—Rudolf Schlesinger, *Marx: His Time and Ours* (London, 1950, 440 pp.).

For the relation of democracy to socialism in Europe see the Marxian historical account of Arthur Rosenberg, *Democracy and Socialism* (New York, 1939, 369 pp.), the analysis of S. P. Orth, *Socialism and Democracy in Europe* (New York, 1913, 352 pp.), and references in Topic 9. F. A. Hermens, *Democracy or Anarchy? A Study of Proportional Representation* (Notre Dame, Ind., 1941, 447 pp.), is a world-wide investigation, published by the *Review of Politics*, of a device for representing minority groups. The book includes useful figures on the growing number of socialist deputies in national parliaments since the late nineteenth century. Recent studies of labor and its relation to socialism include the symposium edited by H. A. Marquand, *Organized Labour in Four Continents* (New York, 1939, 518 pp.); W. A. McConagha, *Development of the Labor Movement in Great Britain, France and Germany* (Chapel Hill, N.C., 1942, 199 pp.); A. F. Sturmthal, *The Tragedy of European Labor, 1918-1939* (New York, 1943, 389 pp.), and H. W. Laidler, *Labor Governments at Work* (New York, 1948, 23 pp.). Laidler's essay is limited to postwar developments in the British Commonwealth and Scandinavia. For an introduction to periodicals published just before World War II see *La Presse socialiste; la presse des partis affiliés à l'Internationale Ouvrière Socialiste* (Brussels, 1939, 63 pp.), the Labor and Socialist International *Bulletin*, Ser. 4, No. 2, in French, English, and German. For those published just after, see Giulio Muratore, "Marxist Journals in the Europe of Today," *Science & Society*, xi (Winter 1947), pp. 69-75. W. Z. Foster, *The New Europe* (New York, 1947, 128 pp.), is the official American communist interpretation of 1945-1947 developments.

Noteworthy collective biographies are Max Adler, *Wegweiser* (5th ed., Vienna, 1931, 389 pp.), including twelve thinkers from Rousseau to Marx; and Max Nomad, *Rebels and Renegades* (New York, 1932, 430 pp.), and *Apostles of Revolution* (Boston, 1939, 467 pp.). Nomad's interpretive sketches of nineteenth- and twentieth-century radicals are based on the assumption that the subjects preferred power to principles. The autobiography of Angelica Balabanoff, *My Life as a Rebel* (New York, 1938, 324 pp.), illustrates both by the account of her personal relations with European Marxist leaders and by her point of view the surviving internationalism of the twentieth-century movement.

3. History of Socialism in Different Countries, etc.

After the French Revolution the history of European socialism falls into three distinct chronological periods for which different nations in turn have provided the international leadership. For about the first sixty years after the revolution—the so-called utopian period the European socialist movement had its principal center in France and turned for intellectual guidance to the great French socialist "trinity," Saint-Simon, Fourier, and Proudhon. During the next period—roughly 1870-1917—socialist hegemony passed to Germany where, under the influence of the German Social Democratic Party, socialism was firmly established on the basis of a Marxism evolutionary and revisionist in tendency. Finally, with the Russian Revolution of October 1917,* European socialism entered upon its third phase: revolutionary Marxian communism. International socialism came to be associated with the Third, or Communist, International and with Soviet Russia, its preponderant member. In the third period, democratic socialism continued to gain numerical strength, with the alternate cooperation and hostility of both democratic reformers and communists. In the twenties, social democrats often held precarious power with the help of groups less radical. After Hitler, and again immediately after World War II, they combined with communists in coalition governments. The independent victory of the British Labour Party in 1945 marked Britain as a major stronghold of the gradualists, but did not signalize the revival of the Labor and Socialist International. With British and other postwar socialist governments, national interests took precedence over the international claims of socialism. In spite of its avowed internationalism, the history of modern socialism tends to break down into the history of socialism in particular countries and requires study from this point of view for full understanding.

A. France. The most comprehensive history of socialism in France is *Histoire socialiste* (*1789-1900*) published in twelve volumes between 1901 and 1908 at Paris under the general editorship of Jean Jaurès. This work, however, is highly uneven in quality and should be supplemented by such other overall accounts as Paul Louis, *Histoire du socialisme en France* (5th ed., Paris, 1950, 432 pp.); and the German historian Lorenz von Stein, *Geschichte der sozialen Bewegung in Frankreich von 1789* (1850; new ed. by G. Salomon, Munich, 1921, 3 vols.). For other general histories of French socialism see Celestin Bouglé, *Socialismes français: du "socialisme utopique" à la "democratie industrielle"* (Paris, 1932, 200 pp.), a study of the background and continuing influence of Saint-Simon, Fourier, and Proudhon; and J. Delevsky, *Les Antinomies socialistes et l'évolution du socialisme français* (Paris, 1930, 529 pp.), which professes to discover in French socialism certain antinomies such as that between absolute freedom and absolute equality and traces the influence of these antinomies from the beginning of French socialism to the present. Marcel Prélot,

---

* November 1917 in our calendar.

9

L'Évolution politique du socialisme français, 1789-1934 (Paris, 1939, 302 pp.), emphasizes the period since 1872. Samuel Bernstein, *The Beginnings of Marxian Socialism in France* (New York, 1933, 229 pp.), and the articles by the same author in *Science & Society*, e.g., "Babeuf and Babouvism," II (Winter 1937-Spring 1938), pp. 29-57, 166-194; "Jules Guesde, Pioneer of Marxism in France," IV (Winter 1940), pp. 29-56, and "The Paris Commune," V (Spring 1941), pp. 117-147, constitute an American Marxist interpretation of the movement to 1900 and a critique of the most significant literature. Compare the French work by Roger Garaudy, *Les Sources françaises du socialisme scientifique* (Paris, 1948, 286 pp.).

For socialism in the French Revolution, see H. J. Laski, "The Socialist Tradition in the French Revolution," in *The Social & Political Ideas of Some Representative Thinkers of the Revolutionary Era* (ed. by F. J. C. Hearnshaw; London, 1931, 251 pp.), chap. VIII; Alfred Espinas, *La Philosophie sociale du xviiie siècle et la révolution* (Paris, 1898, 412 pp.); and the extensive literature on Babeuf and "Babouvisme," references to which are given in Topic 2 below. Background material on the socialist ideas of the eighteenth century may also be found in André Lichtenberger, *Le Socialisme au xviiie siècle* (Paris, 1895, 471 pp.), which dwells particularly on socialist ideas of eighteenth-century French literature; and in both Hans Girsberger, *Der utopische Sozialismus des 18. Jahrhunderts in Frankreich* (Zurich, 1924, 253 pp.), and André Lecocq, *La Question sociale au xviiie siècle* (Paris, 1909, 126 pp.).

For French socialism between 1800 and 1848, see, for the utopians, references to Fourier, Considérant, and Cabet in Topic 2 below, and to Proudhon in the General Reading on anarchism below. The most general treatments of the utopian schools are Sébastien Charléty, *Histoire du Saint-Simonisme (1825-1864)* (1896; new ed., Paris, 1931, 386 pp.); Henri Louvancour, *De Henri de Saint-Simon à Charles Fourier* (Chartres, 1913, 452 pp.); Hubert Bourgin, *Fourier; Contribution à l'étude du socialisme français* (Paris, 1905, 617 pp.); Louis Blanc's own history of the period, *The History of Ten Years, 1830-1840* (London, 1844-1845, 2 vols.); and W. L. Sargant, *Social Innovators and Their Schemes* (London, 1858, 468 pp.), a spirited criticism of the utopian group by an English contemporary. John C. Wahlke of Amherst College is preparing a study of the political theories of Fourier and Saint-Simon as related to those of their contemporaries. For special aspects of the socialist movement during the period 1830-1848, see Georges Morange, *Les Idées communistes dans les sociétés secrètes et dans la presse sous la monarchie de juillet* (Paris, 1905, 169 pp.); H. J. Hunt, *Le Socialisme et le romantisme en France; étude de la presse socialiste de 1830 à 1848* (Oxford, 1935, 399 pp.); the more inclusive *Histoire du Parti républicain en France de 1814 à 1870* (1900; new ed., Paris, 1928, 431 pp.), by G. J. Weill; and D. O. Evans,

Le Socialisme romantique; Pierre Leroux et ses contemporains (pref. by Édouard Dolléans; Paris, 1948, 262 pp.). Evans started with the purpose of tracing Leroux's purely literary influence upon Sainte-Beuve, Victor Hugo, and Georges Sand, and broadened his investigation to put Leroux's thought into its historical and philosophical setting. The excellent annotated bibliography, pp. 239-260, includes a chronological list of Leroux's writings.

The writings of Claude Henri de Saint-Simon have been published as *Oeuvres de Saint-Simon & d'Enfantin* (Paris, 1865-1878, 47 vols.). Saint-Simon combined the older religious impulses toward social equality in the spirit of primitive Christianity with the rationalistic social analysis of the Enlightenment. Rather than make a religion of socialism, as the Marxians were to do, he felt compelled to reinforce his socialism of equal opportunity with traditional religion. See also the study by the sociologist of religion, Émile Durkheim, *Le Socialisme; sa définition, ses débuts, la doctrine saint-simonienne* (ed. by M. Mauss; Paris, 1928, 352 pp.). For appraisals of Saint-Simon and his theories consult Georges Weill, *Un Précurseur du socialisme: Saint-Simon et son oeuvre* (Paris, 1894, 247 pp.); L. H. Jenks, "Henri de Saint-Simon," in *Essays in Intellectual History* (New York, 1929, 359 pp.), pp. 221-240; and E. S. Mason, "Saint-Simonism and the Rationalisation of Industry," *Quarterly Journal of Economics*, xLV (Aug. 1931), pp. 640-683. Saint-Simon's influence in socialist thought is assessed in H. R. d'Allemagne, *Les Saint-Simoniens 1827-1837* (Paris, 1930, 453 pp.); Georges Weill, *L'École saint-simonienne* (Paris, 1896, 319 pp.); Sébastien Charléty, *Histoire du saint-simonisme, 1825-1864* (cited above); and E. M. Butler, *The Saint-Simonian Religion in Germany* (Cambridge, Eng., 1926, 446 pp.). A contemporary guide to the literature of the Saint-Simonians is Henri Founel, *Bibliographie saint-simonienne . . . de 1802 au 31 décembre 1832* (Paris, 1833, 130 pp.).

For the Revolution of 1848 and its origins, see Karl Marx, *The Class Struggles in France (1848-50)* (1850; ed. by C. P. Dutt; intro. by F. Engels; New York, 1934, 159 pp.); Pierre Quentin-Bauchart, *La Crise sociale de 1848, les origines et la révolution de février* (Paris, 1920, 326 pp.); Suzanne Wassermann, *Les Clubs de Barbès et de Blanqui en 1848* (Paris, 1912, 248 pp.); and the *Collection du Centenaire de la Révolution de 1848* (Paris, 1948), containing pamphlets on Marx, Proudhon, Blanc, Blanqui, Sue, the national workshops, etc. Michel Collinet, *La Tragédie du marxisme; du Manifeste communiste à la stratégie totalitaire* (Paris, 1948, 337 pp.), an historical summary critical of later developments in Marxism, is especially useful for its account of Marx's point of view toward the Revolution of 1848 and the Commune. On Louis Blanc and the national workshops, see Blanc, *Organisation du travail* (1839; 9th

11

ed. enl., Paris, 1850, 240 pp.; English tr. of earlier eds., 1848 and 1911), and Émile Thomas, *Histoire des ateliers nationaux* (Paris, 1848, 395 pp.). These have been reprinted with the title, *The French Revolution of 1848 in Its Economic Aspect* (Oxford, 1913, 2 vols.), by J. A. R. Marriott, whose introduction was reissued separately as *The Right to Work* (Oxford, 1919, 97 pp.). See also Blanc, *Le Socialisme; droit au travail* (2nd ed., Paris, 1848, 107 pp.); J. A. Blanqui, *Des classes ouvrières en France pendant l'année 1848* (Paris, 1849, 2 pts. in 1 vol.); Édouard Renard, *La Vie et l'oeuvre de Louis Blanc* (Toulouse, 1922, 192 pp.), and *Bibliographie relative à Louis Blanc* (Toulouse, 1922, 24 pp.); and Hermann Pechan, *Louis Blanc als Wegbereiter des modernen Sozialismus* (Jena, 1929, 136 pp.). How Blanc's proposals were sabotaged is told by D. C. McKay in *The National Workshops* (Cambridge, Mass., 1933, 191 pp.).

The standard monograph on the period following 1848 is G. J. Weill, *Histoire du mouvement social en France, 1852-1924* (3rd ed., Paris, 1924, 512 pp.). An early French account of the Paris Commune, translated into many languages and into English by Eleanor Marx Aveling, is P. O. Lissagaray, *History of the Commune of 1871* (1876; London, 1886, 500 pp.). The best non-Marxian treatments in English are Frank Jellinek, *The Paris Commune of 1871* (New York, 1937, 447 pp.), and E. S. Mason, *The Paris Commune, an Episode in the History of the Socialist Movement* (New York, 1930, 386 pp.). Mason challenges the usual socialist claim that the 1871 revolution had proletarian origins. For the Marxian interpretation, and for studies of the Commune's relation to the First International, see Topic 3.

French socialism since 1870 is surveyed by A. B. Zévaès, *Le Socialisme en France depuis 1871* (Paris, 1908, 353 pp.), and *Le Socialisme en France depuis 1904* (Paris, 1934, 186 pp.). Gaëtan Pirou, *Les doctrines économiques en France depuis 1870* (Paris, 1925, 204 pp.), contrasts French socialist and capitalist economic thought before World War I. Jessica Peixotto, *The French Revolution and Modern French Socialism* (New York, 1901, 409 pp.), compares the principles of the beginning and close of the nineteenth century. See also *Revue socialiste* (Paris, 1885-1914, 1946-   ). Of the biographical material on the period through World War I, A. B. Zévaès, *Jules Guesde (1845-1922)* (Paris, 1928, 209 pp.), and H. R. Weinstein, *Jean Jaurès; a Study of Patriotism in the French Socialist Movement* (New York, 1936, 200 pp.), are notable. The writings of Jaurès have been edited by Max Bonnafous, *Oeuvres* (Paris, 1931-1939, 9 vols.), and sample essays can be read in English as translated by Mildred Minturn, *Studies in Socialism* (New York, 1906, 197 pp.). A collective appraisal by such leaders as Jouhaux and Vandervelde is *Jaurès par ses contemporains* (Paris, 1925, 217 pp.).

The Popular Front period is treated from different points of view in

Jean Jacoby, *Le Front populaire en France et les égarements du socialisme moderne* (Paris, 1937, 139 pp.); Leon Trotsky, *Whither France?* (tr. by J. G. Wright and H. R. Isaacs; New York, 1936, 160 pp.); Maurice Thorez, *France To-day and the People's Front* (tr. by Emile Burns; New York, 1936, 255 pp.); and in the authorized biography by Geoffrey Fraser and Thadée Natanson, *Léon Blum, Man and Statesman* (Philadelphia, 1938, 330 pp.). For the best general history of the French Communist Party see Gérard Walter, *Histoire du Parti communiste français* (Paris, 1948, 390 pp.). See also Thorez' autobiography, *Son of the People* (tr. by Douglas Garman; New York, 1938, 237 pp.); and Louis Aragon, *L'Homme communiste* (Paris, 1946, 246 pp.). Another prominent French communist, Roger Garaudy, has written *Le Communisme et la morale* (Paris, 1945, 127 pp.), a useful statement of the Marxist position. The rivalry of communist, syndicalist, and reformist factions in the trade unions is documented by H. W. Ehrmann, *French Labor from Popular Front to Liberation* (New York, 1947, 329 pp.). For the period of German occupation see A. J. Liebling's compilation of materials on the French Resistance, 1940-1944, *The Republic of Silence* (New York, 1947, 522 pp.); also Angelo Rossi, *A Communist Party in Action* (tr. by Willmoore Kendall; New Haven, Conn., 1949, 301 pp.), a somewhat abridged translation of Rossi's *Physiologie du Parti communiste français* (Paris, 1948, 512 pp.), which treats the activities of the French Communist Party during 1940-1943, and is written under a pseudonym by an anonymous former Franco-Italian communist. The situation immediately after liberation is indicated by Alfred Spire, *Inventaire des socialismes français contemporains* (2nd ed., Paris, 1946, 223 pp.), Léon Blum, *For All Mankind* (1945; tr. by W. Pickles; New York, 1946, 186 pp.); and Léo Moulin, *Socialism of the West* (tr. by Alfred Heron; London, 1948, 336 pp.), abridged from the French version, which essays "a new socialist humanism." Additional periodical sources are *Cahiers du bolchévisme* (Paris, 1924-), communist theoretical organ, *Lutte de classes* (Paris, 1928-1933), *Revue marxiste* (Paris, 1929), and *Critique sociale* (Paris, 1931-1934).

B. GERMANY. Partial bibliographies of socialism in Germany have been compiled by the communist Ernst Drahn: *Führer durch das Schrifttum des deutschen Sozialismus* (2nd ed., Berlin, 1920, 75 pp.), a list of books in print at the end of 1919, and "Zur Quellenkunde einer Pressegeschichte der Sozialisten (Marxisten) Deutschlands," *Jahrbücher für National-ökonomie und Statistik*, Ser. 3, Vol. 77 (Feb.-Mar. 1930), pp. 225-239, 393-409. The best of the older general histories is Franz Mehring, *Geschichte der deutschen Sozialdemokratie* (12th ed., Stuttgart, 1922, 4 vols.), while among the more comprehensive of recent histories is

Richard Lipinski, *Die Sozialdemokratie von ihren Anfängen bis zur Gegenwart* (Berlin, 1927-1928, 2 vols.). The best of the histories in English are W. H. Dawson's companion volumes: *German Socialism and Ferdinand Lassalle* (2nd ed., London, 1891, 300 pp.), a biographical history of German socialism in the nineteenth century; and *Bismarck and State Socialism* (London, 1890, 171 pp.), an analysis of German social legislation between 1870 and 1890. For a brief, older historical sketch in English, see Bertrand Russell's little-known interpretation, *German Social Democracy* (London, 1896, 204 pp.). Evelyn Anderson, *Hammer or Anvil; the Story of the German Working-Class Movement* (London, 1945, 207 pp.), enjoys a mid-twentieth-century perspective in reviewing German labor politics from Bismarck's antisocialist law to the accession of Hitler. Charles Andler, *Les Origines du socialisme d'état en Allemagne* (Paris, 1897, 495 pp.), is an able intellectual history of the origin and development in Germany of socialist doctrines of right, property, rent, etc. See also the reports of the annual congresses of the German socialist parties.

For the beginnings of socialism in Germany before 1848, see Hermann Buddensieg, *Die Kultur des deutschen Proletariats im Zeitalter des Frühkapitalismus* (Lauenberg, 1923, 178 pp.), and Bruno Bauer, *Die bürgerliche Revolution in Deutschland seit dem Anfang der deutsch-katholischen Bewegung bis zur Gegenwart* (Berlin, 1849, 295 pp.). Paul Wentzcke has collected references on the German uprisings of 1848, "Bibliographische Beiträge zur Geschichte des deutschen Sozialismus in der Bewegung von 1848," *Archiv für die Geschichte des Sozialismus und der Arbeiterbewegung*, xi (1923), pp. 196-214. The most detailed studies by a contemporary are by Bernhard Becker, *Die deutsche Bewegung von 1848 und die Gegenwärtige* (Berlin, 1864, 2 pts.), and *Die Reaktion in Deutschland gegen die Revolution von 1848* (Vienna, 1869, 491 pp.). A chemistry professor, K. G. Winkelblech (Karl Marlo, pseud.), wrote a federalist work calling for the nationalization of land and other productive property, *Untersuchungen über die Organisation der Arbeit; oder, System der Weltökonomie* (1850-1859; 2nd ed., Tübingen, 1884-1886, 4 vols.). Marlo criticized, on the premises of natural-rights philosophy, both liberalism and communism, but his work was virtually unknown for years after his death in 1865. The literature on Ferdinand Lassalle— the father of the German Social Democratic Party—and his influence is extensive. Lassalle's works have been edited by Eduard Bernstein, *Gesammelte Reden und Schriften* (Berlin, 1919-1920, 12 vols.), and his correspondence with Marx, Rodbertus, and others by Gustav Mayer, *Nachgelassene Briefe und Schriften* (Stuttgart, 1921-1925, 6 vols.). His significance both as a reformer and as a precursor of social democracy is described in Bernstein, *Ferdinand Lassalle as a Social Reformer* (tr. by

Eleanor Aveling; New York, 1893, 192 pp.), and in Bernhard Harms, *Ferdinand Lassalle und seine Bedeutung für die deutsche Sozialdemokratie* (Jena, 1909, 128 pp.). The standard life is Georg Brandes, *Ferdinand Lassalle* (New York, 1911, 230 pp.); see also David Footman, *The Primrose Path; a Life of Ferdinand Lassalle* (London, 1946, 251 pp.). For Marx's critique of Lassallean socialism, see PART IV, below. For an example of the purely ethical type of socialism characteristic of the period just before the rise of the social democracy consult *Die heilige Geschichte der Menschheit* (Stuttgart, 1837, 346 pp.), an anonymously published work by Moses Hess. Hess, who was responsible for Engels' and indirectly Marx's conversion to communism, is the subject of Theodor Zlocisti's biography, *Moses Hess, der Vorkämpfer des Sozialismus und Zionismus, 1812-1875* (2nd ed., Berlin, 1921, 441 pp.), and Auguste Cornu, *Moses Hess et la gauche hégélienne* (Paris, 1934, 120 pp.). Also see the article by Edmund Silberner, "Moses Hess: From Assimilation to Zionism," which will be published in *Historia Judaica*, XIII, Pt. 2. Silberner is the author of a forthcoming bibliography, *Moses Hess, an Annotated Bibliography* (Burt Franklin Bibliographical Series, No. 4; New York), to be published in 1951.

The later "orthodoxy" and "revisionism" of the Social Democratic Party is the subject of Topic 9. Albert Bovenschen traces the evolution of party doctrine between 1891 and 1919 in *Die Grundsätze und Forderungen der Sozialdemokratie in ihren geschichtlichen Entwicklung am Erfurter Programm und an der deutschen Revolution dargestellt* (Berlin, 1920, 296 pp.), as does Sigmund Rubinstein, *Romantischer Sozialismus: ein Versuch über die Idee der deutschen Revolution* (Munich, 1921, 417 pp.). For the Spartakus group—the revolutionary segment of the Social Democratic Party which tried to seize power during the revolution of 1918—see the writings of Franz Mehring, Klara Zetkin, and (especially) of Rosa Luxemburg and Karl Liebknecht. Articles by Liebknecht and Mehring are published in L. C. Fraina, *The Social Revolution in Germany* (Boston, 1919, 108 pp.). Of particular interest in this connection are Luxemburg, *Reform or Revolution* (1899; tr. by Integer [Herman Jerson]; New York, 1937, 53 pp.); and *The Crisis in the German Social-Democracy* (published under the pseudonym "Junius" at Berne in 1916; New York, 1919, 128 pp.), which condemned the failure of the Social Democratic Party to oppose the war, and predicted—as in fact happened—that this failure would eventually destroy the socialist movement in Germany. Luxemburg's authorship of the Junius pamphlet is still questioned. Her *Gesammelte Werke* (Berlin, 1923-1928, Vols. 3-4, 6) include *Gegen den Reformismus, Gewerkschaftskampf und Massenstreik*, and *Die Akkumulation des Kapitals*, classics on economic and political problems taken up in PART IV. The only published biography

15

in English up to World War II was Paul Frölich, *Rosa Luxemburg* (London, 1940, 336 pp.), but the MS dissertation of C. E. Rothwell, *Rosa Luxemburg and the German Social Democratic Party* (Stanford University, Calif., 1938, 662 leaves), is available in microfilm. Zinoviev and Trotsky, *Karl Liebknecht und Rosa Luxemburg* (Petrograd, 1920, 32 pp.), written after the latter two were shot, emphasize the significance of the Spartacist leaders for revolutionary socialism everywhere. Arthur Rosenberg, *A History of the German Republic* (tr. by I. F. D. Morrow and L. M. Sieveking; London, 1936, 350 pp.), deals at length with social democracy from 1918 to 1930; O. K. Flechtheim, *Die Kommunistische Partei Deutschlands in der Weimarer Republik* (Offenbach, 1948, 294 pp.), is an important contribution, with excellent bibliography. *The Lesson of Germany* (New York, 1945, 222 pp.), by Gerhart Eisler and others, is a communist post-mortem, while Ruth Fischer, *Stalin and German Communism; a Study in the Origins of the State Party* (Cambridge, Mass., 1948, 687 pp.), is an anticommunist analysis by a former Spartacist. Abundant source material on German socialism in general may be found in the files of the official organ of the Social Democratic Party, *Neue Zeit* (Stuttgart, 1883-1923), especially for the nineteenth century (see its Index, 1883-1902). *Gesellschaft* (Berlin, 1924-1933) expressed social democratic views; *Sozialistische Monatshefte* (Berlin, 1897-1933), which superseded *Sozialistische Akademiker* (Berlin, 1895-1896), revisionist; and *Kommunistische Arbeiter-Zeitung* (Berlin, 1919-1933; title varies), those of the Third International.

C. ENGLAND. The best general history of socialism in England is Max Beer, *A History of British Socialism* (1912; New York, 1940, 2 vols. in 1), which carries the story of English socialism from the medieval period to 1939. A. B. Ulam, *The Philosophical Foundations of English Socialism*, to be published by the Harvard University Press in 1951, is announced as an exploration of the sources, aims, and methods of British socialism and the welfare state. For the period preceding the French Revolution, see the references to the Digger movement in Topic 2 below, and, in addition, H. M. Hyndman, *The Historical Basis of Socialism in England* (London, 1883, 492 pp.), whose early chapters give a summary account of the period as a whole.

For a general account of British socialism in the nineteenth century, see G. D. H. Cole, *A Short History of the British Working Class Movement, 1789-1937* (London, 1938, 3 vols. in 1), and the same author's *British Working Class Politics, 1832-1914* (London, 1941, 320 pp.). With Raymond Postgate he has covered the last two centuries in *The British People, 1746-1946* (New York, 1947, 600 pp.). For the early part of the century see such histories of Chartism as R. G. Gammage, *History of the*

Chartist Movement, 1837-1854 (rev. ed., Newcastle-on-Tyne, 1894, 438 pp.), Édouard Dolléans, *Le Chartisme, 1830-1848* (Paris, 1912-1913, 2 vols.), and J. L. LeB. and Barbara Hammond, *The Age of the Chartists, 1832-1854* (London, 1930, 386 pp.); also such specialized studies as Esther Lowenthal, *The Ricardian Socialists* (New York, 1911, 105 pp.), an analysis of the economic and social theory of William Thompson, John Gray, Thomas Hodgskin, and John Francis Bray; and R. F. Wearmouth, *Methodism and the Working-Class Movements of England, 1800-1850* (London, 1937, 289 pp.). For the aftermath of Chartism at the middle of the century, see F. E. Gillespie, *Labor and Politics in England, 1850-1867* (Durham, N.C., 1927, 319 pp.).

Background material for the development of British socialism in the latter part of the century may be found in Ralph Fox, *The Class Struggle in Britain in the Epoch of Imperialism* (London, 1932-1934, 2 vols.), a study of English economic history since 1880 from the point of view of Lenin's theory of imperialism. Édouard Guyot, *Le Socialisme et l'évolution de l'Angleterre contemporaine (1880-1911)* (Paris, 1913, 543 pp.), carefully analyzes socialist tendencies in the British labor movement, the British cooperative movement, the Liberal Party, and in the history of recent British social thought. This period is also covered briefly in R. H. Tawney, *The British Labor Movement* (New Haven, Conn., 1925, 189 pp.), a short account designed for American readers, and in Sidney Webb, *Socialism in England* (1889; 2nd ed., New York, 1893, 136 pp.), a description of the socialist organization and socialist tendencies in Britain at the turn of the century. Note also the *Autobiography* of John Stuart Mill (1873; new ed., New York, 1924, 221 pp.), whose theories were tending toward socialism at his death; and H. M. Hyndman, *The Record of an Adventurous Life* (New York, 1911, 422 pp.). Edward Carpenter states in his autobiography, *My Days and Dreams* (London, 1916, 340 pp.), that *Towards Democracy* (1883; New York, 1912, 507 pp.) contains the core of his mystical nondoctrinaire ideas on anarchism, sex, the arts, and civilization. The literature about William Morris, who attracted Carpenter to socialism, can be found in Margaret Grennan, *William Morris, Medievalist and Revolutionary* (New York, 1945, 173 pp.). Also see Volumes 16, 22, and 23 of Morris' *Collected Works* (London, 1910-1915, 24 vols.). And see PART VI, General Reading, for Morris' writings on the arts and socialism. A socialist best seller at the turn of the century was the tract of Robert Blatchford, editor of the *Clarion, Merrie England* (London, 1894, 210 pp.). For further references consult H. S. Foxwell, "Bibliography of the English Socialist School," in Anton Menger, *The Right to the Whole Produce of Labour* (tr. by M. E. Tanner; London, 1899, cxviii, 271 pp.), pp. 189-267. References to the rise of Fabian and guild socialism are in Topic 9.

The British Labour Party of the twentieth century has been a federation, many of whose member organizations have been socialist. J. K. Hardie, *From Serfdom to Socialism* (London, 1907, 130 pp.), expresses the evangelical rather than Marxist orientation of its early days. C. F. Brand, *British Labour's Rise to Power* (Stanford University, Calif., 1941, 305 pp.), six studies on the period from 1914 to 1923, includes an introduction on nineteenth-century trade-union background and a concluding chapter on the continuing fight with the Communist Party. Fenner Brockway, *Socialism over Sixty Years; the Life of Jowett of Bradford (1864-1944)* (London, 1946, 415 pp.), contains autobiographical material on the Independent Labour Party leader. See also H. W. Lee and Edward Archbold, *Social-Democracy in Britain; Fifty Years of the Socialist Movement* (London, 1935, 288 pp.); G. D. H. Cole, *A History of the Labour Party from 1914* (London, 1948, 516 pp.); and Herbert Tracey, ed., *The British Labour Party* (London, 1948, 3 vols.). For an American criticism and evaluation of the accomplishments of the Labour government, consult R. A. Brady, *Crisis in Britain; Plans and Achievements of the Labour Government* (Berkeley, Calif., 1950, 730 pp.). A communist account of communist-socialist strife is Thomas Bell, *Pioneering Days* (London, 1941, 316 pp.). William Gallacher, *Revolt on the Clyde* (London, 1936, 301 pp.), is the autobiography of the first communist elected to Parliament. Douglas Hyde, *I Believed* (New York, 1950, 312 pp.), is the autobiography of a former member of the British Communist Party who was news editor of the London *Daily Worker*, but who left the party and became a Roman Catholic. Hyde has also written *The Answer to Communism* (London, 1949, 79 pp.), a brief exposé of communist theory and methods.

Franz Linden calls attention to the decline in militancy of the Labour Party in *Sozialismus und Religion; Konfessionssoziologische Untersuchungen der Labour Party, 1929-1931* (Leipzig, 1932, 178 pp.). For typical British socialist utopias between the two world wars see Sidney and Beatrice Webb, *A Constitution for the Socialist Commonwealth of Great Britain* (London, 1920, 364 pp.); G. R. Mitchison, *The First Workers' Government; or, New Times for Henry Dubb* (London, 1934, 528 pp.); and *Britain without Capitalists; a Study of What Industry in a Soviet Britain Could Achieve* (London, 1936, 474 pp.), by a group of economists, technicians, and scientists. Noteworthy for the Popular Front period are D. E. McHenry, *The Labour Party in Transition, 1931-1938* (London, 1938, 320 pp.), and also George Orwell, *The Road to Wigan Pier* (London, 1937, 264 pp.).

Orwell's study of socialism and English character, *The Lion and the Unicorn* (London, 1941, 126 pp.), and *Labour's Aims in War and Peace* (London, 1940, 153 pp.), by C. R. Attlee and other prominent party members, express the British socialist attitude in World War II. For the temper of the seceding British communists after the Russo-German accord, see *The Betrayal of the Left* (London, 1941, 324 pp.), edited by Victor Gollancz. John Strachey, *Socialism Looks Forward* (New York, 1945, 153 pp.), and the articles by Margaret Cole and others, "British Labor Sets Its Course," *Antioch Review*, VI (Summer 1946), pp. 167-234, express the British socialists' view of their postwar opportunities. Ivor Thomas, a Labour M.P. from 1942 to 1948, became a Conservative in 1949 and published *The Socialist Tragedy* (London, 1949, 254 pp.), in which he argues that both socialism and communism seek to establish a state monopoly destructive of individual liberties. The sharp and sometimes telling criticism in Christopher Hollis, *The Rise and Fall of the Ex-Socialist Government* (London, 1947, 131 pp.), expresses the conviction of a Conservative Roman Catholic Member of Parliament that socialism leads to the managerial state. Compare the more comprehensive, critical but pro-Laborite conclusions of Francis Williams, *Socialist Britain* (New York, 1949, 278 pp.). *Socialization in Great Britain*, a résumé with comparison to Europe, published by the Pacifist Research Bureau (Ithaca, N.Y., 1947, 11 pp.), contains useful bibliographical notes. Noah Barou, *British Trade Unions* (London, 1947, 271 pp.), discusses the role of labor in recent British socialism.

For periodical sources, see the reports of the annual conferences of the Labour Party (London, 1901-), *Social-Democrat* (London, 1897-1911), superseded by the *British Socialist* (London, 1912-1913), organ of the Social Democratic Federation; *Socialist* (Glasgow, 1902-1924), organ of the Socialist Labour Party; *Socialist Review* (London, 1908-1934), organ of the Independent Labour Party; *New Statesman and Nation* (London, 1913-), left-wing laborite; and the communist *Labour Monthly* (London, 1921-).

D. RUSSIA. The enormous literature about the history of socialism in Russia is necessarily referred to in this bibliography in several places. Below are a few samples dealing with the period before 1917—except for the writings of the Bolshevik leaders—and general histories and surveys of the U.S.S.R. A good introductory essay, covering from the eighteenth century to 1933, with references, is Hans Kohn, "Russian Revolution," *Encyclopaedia of the Social Sciences*, XIII, pp. 474-493. The history and theory of the revolutionary bolshevism which seized power in 1917 is sampled in Topic 8; its domination of the Comintern in Topic 4; the contrasts between capitalist and Soviet society in Topic 5; and Russian anarchism in the General Reading below, and in Topic 10. Some topical material appears in later Parts.

Ludwik Kulczycki, *Geschichte der russischen Revolution* (Gotha, 1910-

1914, 3 vols.), and Konni Zilliacus' briefer *The Russian Revolutionary Movement* (London, 1905, 366 pp.), both begin with the Russian revolution of 1825. For a study of the Russian émigrés in the middle years of the nineteenth century see E. H. Carr, *The Romantic Exiles* (London, 1933, 391 pp.). David Hecht, *Russian Radicals Look to America, 1825-1894* (Cambridge, Mass., 1947, 242 pp.), is a monograph illustrating the interest in the United States shown by six non-Marxian leaders (Aleksandr Herzen, Nikolai Ogarev, Mikhail Bakunin, Nikolai Chernyshevsky, Petr Lavrov and Nikolai Chaikovsky). M. M. Laserson, *The American Impact on Russia—Diplomatic and Ideological—1784-1917* (New York, 1950, 441 pp.), includes discussion of the interest of early Russian radicals, such as Herzen and Chernyshevsky, in the American revolutionary tradition. The writings of Chernyshevsky, a leader of the Narodnik (Populist) movement, influenced Balkan socialists and Jules Guesde in France toward Marxism. The "nihilistic" wing of the movement, less important than its notoriety suggests, is the subject of S. M. Kravchinsky (Stepnyak, pseud.), *Underground Russia; Revolutionary Profiles* (tr. from Italian; 2nd ed., New York, 1885, 320 pp.), David Footman, *Red Prelude; the Life of the Russian Terrorist Zhelyabov* (New Haven, Conn., 1945, 267 pp.), and the novels of Turgenev, particularly *Fathers and Sons*, and Dostoevsky, particularly *The Possessed*, also translated as *The Demons*. T. G. Masaryk, *The Spirit of Russia* (1913; tr. by E. and C. Paul; New York, 1919, 2 vols.), centering on Dostoevsky, is still one of the best treatments of Russian social thought. A Russian Orthodox personalist interpretation of the background of bolshevism is found in N. A. Berdyaev, *The Origin of Russian Communism* (New York, 1937, 239 pp.).

Probably the most important of the early Marxian socialists in Russia was G. V. Plekhanov, whose *Fundamental Problems of Marxism* (ed. by D. B. Goldendach [Ryazanov, pseud.]; tr. by E. and C. Paul; London, 1929, 145 pp.) still remains a Marxian classic whose influence on such later Russian Marxists as Lenin was very great. The standard history of the Russian social democracy (from which the more revolutionary Bolsheviks under Lenin split off), is *Geschichte der russischen Sozialdemokratie* (tr. by Alexander Stein; Berlin, 1926, 340 pp.), by Y. O. Martov, one of the early Menshevik leaders of the party, with a supplement by Theodor Dan on Russian social democracy after 1908. See also the special monograph by Alfred Levin, *The Second Duma; a Study of the Social-Democratic Party and the Russian Constitutional Experiment* (New Haven, Conn., 1940, 414 pp.).

As one of the two most powerful states to emerge from World War II, Russia has been the subject of more publications than ever before. The unfavorable interpretations listed below, apart from their basic criticism of communism, emphasize the conservative methods and aims of an oppressive oligarchy and discount its achievements. The sympathetic accounts hold that no such growth could have been accomplished without communist rule, and accept more or less of the avowed Soviet program.

For an introduction to the literature see Philip Grierson, *Books on Soviet Russia, 1917-1942; a Bibliography and a Guide to Reading* (London, 1943, 354 pp.), critically annotated and arranged topically. This bibliography, chiefly restricted to books in English, has been continued by Grierson under the title "Books and Pamphlets on Russia," *Slavonic and East German Review*, xxiv (Jan. 1946), pp. 133-147; xxv (Apr. 1947), pp. 508-517; xxvi (Apr. 1948), pp. 512-518; xxvii (May 1949), pp. 556-562; and xxviii (Apr. 1950), pp. 486-492. An outstanding attempt to reach objectivity, with more sympathy than condemnation, is Rudolf Schlesinger, *The Spirit of Post-War Russia; Soviet Ideology, 1917-1946* (London, 1947, 187 pp.). H. J. Laski, *Communism* (New York, 1927, 256 pp.), and Arthur Rosenberg, *A History of Bolshevism from Marx to the First Five Years' Plan* (tr. by I. F. D. Morrow; London, 1934, 250 pp.), are still good histories of the early period. Isaac Deutscher, *Soviet Trade Unions; Their Place in Soviet Labour Policy* (London, 1950, 156 pp.), is a reasonable statement of a single important problem. The essays of E. H. Carr, *The Soviet Impact on the Western World* (New York, 1947, 113 pp.), by a British historian, evaluate Soviet influences fairly. For the official interpretation, see the *History of the Communist Party of the Soviet Union* (New York, 1939, 364 pp.), and the varying editions of Stalin's selected speeches and writings, e.g., *Leninism* (New York, 1942, 479 pp.). The publication of his collected works under the title *Sochineniya* was begun in Moscow in 1946. The complete proceedings of the Moscow trials of 1936-1938, in which communists claim they scotched a Fascist-Trotskyist plot to overthrow the Soviet state, while their enemies claim Stalin purged his remaining rivals, has been published in three lengthy volumes by the People's Commissariat of Justice: *Report of Court Proceedings, the Case of the Trotskyite-Zinovievite Terrorist Centre* (Moscow, 1936, 180 pp.); *Report of Court Proceedings in the Case of the Anti-Soviet Trotskyite Centre* (Moscow, 1937, 580 pp.); *Report of Court Proceedings in the Case of the Anti-Soviet "Bloc of Rights and Trotskyites"* (Moscow, 1938, 799 pp.). Among the periodicals in English with scholarly contributions on Russia are the *Slavonic and East European Review* (London, etc., 1922- , title varies), the *American Slavic and East European Review* (Menasha, Wis., 1945-), the *American Review on the Soviet Union* (New York, 1938-), published by the American-Russian Institute, and *Soviet Studies* (Oxford, Eng., 1949-). See also *Monde slave* (Paris, 1917-1918, 1924-1938), *A Digest of the Krasnyi Arkhiv (Red Archives); a Historical Journal of the Central Archive Department of the U.S.S.R.* (Cleveland, Ohio, 1947-), *Soviet Press Translations* (Seattle,

Wash., 1946-), and *Current Digest of the Soviet Press* (Washington, D.C., 1949-).

Among the favorable books written by outsiders during the twenties are *Russia after Ten Years* (New York, 1927, 96 pp.), a report of an American trade-union delegation to the Soviet Union; and the more detailed report of the delegation's technical advisers, *Soviet Russia in the Second Decade* (ed. by Stuart Chase and others; New York, 1928, 374 pp.). Later English accounts include the communist interpretations of Pat Sloan, e.g., *Soviet Democracy* (London, 1937, 288 pp.). S. N. Harper, *The Russia I Believe In* (Chicago, 1945, 279 pp.), is a memoir by a sympathetic American who often visited Russia between 1902 and 1941. See also Harper, *The Government of the Soviet Union* (New York, 1938, 204 pp.), one of the few studies on the subject in English; Louis Fischer's autobiography, *Men and Politics* (New York, 1941, 672 pp.); T. A. Taracouzio, *War and Peace in Soviet Diplomacy* (New York, 1940, 354 pp.); Max Beloff, *The Foreign Policy of Soviet Russia, 1929-1941* (London, 1947-1949, 2 vols.); and F. L. Schuman, *Soviet Politics at Home and Abroad* (New York, 1946, 663 pp.). Earl Browder, former American Communist Party leader, propounds his thesis of American-Soviet commercial cooperation in *War or Peace with Russia* (New York, 1947, 190 pp.). The selection of documents by B. J. Stern and Samuel Smith, *Understanding the Russians* (New York, 1947, 246 pp.), omits foreign policy and history.

Most of the unfavorable treatments below were written by Russian émigrés. Menshevik criticism is found in D. J. Dallin, *The Real Soviet Russia* (rev. ed., New Haven, Conn., 1947, 325 pp.), an analysis of the new classes of the Soviet Union, and also in the *New Leader* (New York, 1924-), a social democratic periodical long opposed to Stalinism, especially in articles by R. R. Abramovitch. The pamphlet by Norman Thomas and Joel Seidman, *Russia—Democracy or Dictatorship?* (New York, 1939, 71 pp.), represents the American Socialist Party position. Most important among the numerous Russian commentaries of Victor Serge is *Russia Twenty Years After* (tr. by Max Shachtman; New York, 1937, 298 pp.), written before the author abandoned Trotskyism for democratic socialism. See also *The Russian Enigma* (1938; tr. by F. G. Renier and Anne Cliff; London, 1940, 304 pp.), by the Croat Trotskyist Anton Ciliga, which suggests the theory of bureaucratic collectivism; and G. P. Maksimov, *The Guillotine at Work; Twenty Years of Terror in Russia (Data and Documents)* (Chicago, 1940, 624 pp.), an anarcho-syndicalist indictment published by the Chicago section of the Alexander Berkman Fund. The thesis that the Bolshevik upheaval interrupted Russian social and industrial progress, but that a conservative reaction has stabilized Soviet society, is advanced by N. S. Timasheff of Fordham

University in *The Great Retreat; the Growth and Decline of Communism in Russia* (New York, 1946, 470 pp.). The claim that socialism no longer exists in Russia is also made by Max Eastman, *Stalin's Russia and the Crisis in Socialism* (New York, 1940, 284 pp.), and Arthur Koestler, *The Yogi and the Commissar* (New York, 1945, 247 pp.). Of the books attacking forced labor in Russia, *The New Slavery* (Garden City, N.Y., 1947, 271 pp.), by Hoffman Nickerson, is useful primarily for its list of sources (pp. 243-261). *Slave Labor in Russia* (Washington, 1949, 179 pp.), a report of the A.F.L. to the United Nations, and D. J. Dallin and B. I. Nicolaevsky, *Forced Labor in Soviet Russia* (New Haven, Conn., 1947, 331 pp.), are better informed.

E. OTHER EUROPEAN COUNTRIES AND THE BRITISH DOMINIONS. The socialism in other European countries was a mixture of communism, social democracy, and syndicalism characteristic of the parties of the four major powers. In eastern Europe and the Balkans, where agrarian reformers were strong and the situation was complicated by anti-Semitism, weak, hounded, gradualist parties arose. These were overwhelmed by the communists as a result of World War II. In POLAND the movement was divided between a Jewish *Bund* and a Gentile section of the Second International. Elehard Esse, "Socialistes polonais et russes," *Humanité nouvelle*, IV (1899), pp. 434-450, is a sample article on the late nineteenth century, with bibliographical notes. For further references, see Zanna Kormanowa's guide to the literature, *Materjały do bibljografji druków socjalistycznych na ziemiach polskich w latach 1866-1918* (Warsaw, 1935, 374 pp.), with 4,000 titles. A. L. Strong, *I Saw the New Poland* (Boston, 1946, 280 pp.), reports the victory of communism. Socialism in RUMANIA was promoted first by the Jewish proletariat. B. Liber, "Ioan Nadejde; Socialism in Rumania in the Nineteenth Century," *Modern Quarterly*, V (Winter 1930-1931), pp. 467-482, sketches the betrayal of socialism there by its principal leader, and I. C. Atanasiu, *Pagini diu istoria contimporană a României, 1881-1916; Vol. I, Mișcarea socialistă, 1881-1900* (Bucharest, 1932, 448 pp.), is a detailed monograph. Otto Kuusinen, *The Finnish Revolution; a Self-Criticism* (London, 1919, 30 pp.), Oscar Jászi, *Revolution and Counter-Revolution in Hungary* (1923; tr. by E. W. Dickes; London, 1924, 239 pp.), and Klara Fetter, *Republic and Soviet in Hungary*, scheduled for publication by the Hoover Institute and Library, deal with communist uprisings in FINLAND and HUNGARY. *Bibliografie socialismu (soupis knih i revuálních, časopiseckých a novinářských članků) 1932* (Prague, 1933, 51 pp.), contains references to socialism in CZECHOSLOVAKIA, and the Czechoslovak Social Democratic Workers Party has published an official history, *The Evolution of Socialism in Czechoslovakia* (Prague, 1924, 45 pp.). Maurice Hindus, *The*

Bright Passage (Garden City, N.Y., 1947, 370 pp.), interprets the position of the revived country before the communist coup of 1948 as a bridge between eastern and western Europe. Published since the communist rise to control is Guy Braibant, *La Planification en Tchécoslovaquie* (Paris, 1949, 160 pp.). An anticommunist study of YUGOSLAVIA is R. H. Markham, *Tito's Imperial Communism* (Chapel Hill, N.C., 1947, 292 pp.). For Tito also see George Bilainkin, *Tito* (London, 1949, 287 pp.); Stephen Clissold, *Whirlwind; an Account of Marshal Tito's Rise to Power* (London, 1949, 245 pp.); and H. F. Armstrong, *Tito and Goliath* (New York, 1950, 309 pp.), which deals with Tito's struggle with Stalin as does Jan Yindrich, *Tito v. Stalin* (London, 1950, 215 pp.). Armstrong's book is especially important because it discusses "Titoism" and its implications in all the Russian satellite countries. Sample studies of communism in the Russian sphere are S. L. Sharp, *Nationalization of Key Industries in Eastern Europe* (Washington, 1946, 80 pp.), H. A. Lehrman, *Russia's Europe* (New York, 1947, 341 pp.), and Vernon Van Dyke, "Communism in Eastern and Southeastern Europe," *Journal of Politics*, IX (Aug. 1947), pp. 355-391, a condensed version of a report by the Yale Institute of International Studies. Sharp and others of the research staff of the Foundation for Foreign Affairs have published studies of socialist developments since World War II in the foundation's periodical, *American Perspective* (Washington, 1947-).

The small countries of the west and north followed the German and British patterns. Industrialized BELGIUM played a role in the democratic socialist movement out of proportion to its size. Two early histories are Louis Bertrand, *Histoire de la démocratie & du socialisme en Belgique depuis 1830* (Brussels, 1906-1907, 2 vols.), and *Le Socialisme en Belgique* (Paris, 1898, 515 pp.), by Jules Destrée and Émile Vandervelde, the compromiser of the Second International. See also Vandervelde, *Le Parti ouvrier belge, 1885-1925* (Brussels, 1925, 503 pp.); Joseph Devalte, *Histoire du mouvement socialiste belge* (Brussels, 1931, 55 pp.); Henri de Man, *Herinneringen* (2nd ed., Antwerp, 1941, 265 pp.); and Xavier Le Grand, *Le Socialisme belge et les problèmes d'aujourd'hui* (Brussels, 1935, 185 pp.). For an introduction to social democracy in HOLLAND see the party organ, *Socialistische Gids* (Amsterdam, 1916-1938), superseded by *Socialisme en Democratie* (Amsterdam, 1939-1940). AUSTRIA was the home of the Vienna International and controlled by social democrats much of the time between the fall of the Hapsburgs and the rise of Dollfuss. Its socialist history is treated in Ludwig Brügel, *Geschichte der österreichischen Sozialdemokratie* (Vienna, 1922-1925, 5 vols.); Karl Schwechler, *Die österreichische Sozialdemokratie* (2nd ed. rev., Graz, 1907, 210 pp.); Otto Bauer, *The Austrian Revolution* (tr. and abr. by H. J. Stenning; London, 1925, 287 pp.); and Julius Deutsch, *The Civil*

War in Austria (tr. by D. P. Berenberg; Chicago, 1934, 78 pp.). For SWITZERLAND, see *Geschichte der sozialistischen Ideen in der Schweiz* (Zurich, 1931, 228 pp.), by Robert Grimm, a leader of the Zimmerwald movement's left wing; and Willy Bretscher and Ernst Steinmann, eds., *Die sozialistische Bewegung in der Schweiz, 1848-1920* (Berne, 1923, 160 pp.), which emphasizes the war period. The communist view of IRELAND's dependent status is set forth in R. W. Fox, *Marx, Engels and Lenin on Ireland* (New York, 1940, 47 pp.).

A general report which includes the position of labor parties in Scandinavia is B. A. Arneson, *The Democratic Monarchies of Scandinavia* (New York, 1939, 244 pp.). On DENMARK see E. E. Wiinblad and Alsing Anderson, *Det Danske Socialdemokratis Historie, fra 1871 til 1921* (Copenhagen, 1931, 2 vols.), and *Social Denmark; a Survey of the Danish Social Legislation* (ed. by *Socialt Tidsskrift*; Copenhagen, 1945, 475 pp.). Socialists in NORWAY are treated in J. E. Nordskog, *Social Reform in Norway; a Study of Nationalism and Social Democracy* (Los Angeles, 1935, 184 pp.), and in Finn Moe, *Does Norwegian Labor Seek the Middle Way?* (New York, 1937, 40 pp.), a brochure published by the League for Industrial Democracy. The beginnings of social democracy in SWEDEN are covered in detail by the monographs of John Lindgren, *Det Socialdemokratiska arbetarpartiets uppkomst i Sverige, 1881-1889* (Stockholm, 1927, 349 pp.), and G. H. Nordström, *Sveriges social-demokratiska arbetareparti under genombrottsåren, 1889-1894* (Stockholm, 1938, 934 pp.). For further titles see Nordström's bibliography, pp. 900-930. Bjarne Braatoy, *The New Sweden, a Vindication of Democracy* (New York, 1939, 172 pp.), sketches recent developments.

In three British dominions democratic socialism kept pace with the movement in the mother country. For AUSTRALIA an early study is A. J. J. St. Ledger, *Australian Socialism; an Historical Sketch of Its Origin & Developments* (London, 1909, 365 pp.). A recent book on NEW ZEALAND is Walter Nash, *New Zealand, a Working Democracy* (New York, 1943, 335 pp.). The growth of the Cooperative Commonwealth Federation in CANADA, the subject of several current research projects, is outlined by national officers of the party, David Lewis and Frank Scott, in *Make This Your Canada; a Review of C.C.F. History and Policy* (Toronto, 1943, 223 pp.). Igor Gouzenko, *The Iron Curtain* (New York, 1948, 279 pp.), combining autobiography with an exposé of Soviet espionage in Canada, has been filmed.

In ITALY and Spain the struggles of communist, social-democratic, anarchist, and syndicalist groups hampered the socialist movement and led to fascism. Not only the Italian industrial workers but also large sections of the peasantry and intelligentsia before World War I were radicals or radical sympathizers. Robert Michels, *Storia critica del movimento socialista italiano dagli inizi fino al 1911* (Florence, 1926, 463 pp.), is the best account of the early period. See also the other work by the same author, *Sozialismus und Fascismus als politische Strömungen in Italien* (Munich, 1925, 2 vols.); Giuseppe Andriani, *Socialismo e comunismo in Toscana tra il 1846 e il 1849* (Rome, 1921, 60 pp.); Alfredo Angiolini and Eugenio Ciacchi, *Socialismo e socialisti in Italia* (Florence, 1919, 256 pp.); and Giulio Aquila, *Die italienische sozialistische Partei* (St. Petersburg, 1922, 46 pp.), the last a Comintern publication. See also Napoleone Colajanni, *Il socialismo: Appunti* (Catania, 1884, 396 pp.), published as Volume 1 of a work entitled *Il socialismo e sociologia criminale*; Filippo Turati, *Socialismo e scienza; a proposito di un nuovo libro di N. Colajanni* (Como, 1884, 30 pp.), by an early leader, and G. Mariotti's biography, *F. Turati* (Florence, 1947, 364 pp.). The *Avanti* (Paris, etc., 1897-), was the official socialist party organ. With the reconquest of Italy the left wing emerged stronger but strife was as bitter as ever.

Socialism in SPAIN met the obstacles common to the less industrialized parts of Europe: governmental repression, ecclesiastical hostility, and provincial separatism. For its growth up to the abolition of the monarchy in 1931 see Matías Gómez Latorre, *El socialismo en España* (Madrid, 1918, 272 pp.), a collection of articles carrying the story only to 1886; J. J. Morato's biography of the founder of the Spanish socialist party, *Pablo Iglesias Posse* (Madrid, 1931, 256 pp.), and his description of the party's situation at the close of World War I, *El partido socialista obrero* (Madrid, 1918, 320 pp.), and Fernando de los Ríos y Urruti, *El sentido humanista del socialismo* (Madrid, 1926, 416 pp.). *Documentos socialistas* (Madrid, 1935, 330 pp.), expresses the points of view of Indalecio Prieto and other socialists of the Republican period. Andrés Nin, Catalan communist theorist, translator of Soviet writings, and representative on the Red International of Trade Unions, later liquidated as a Trotskyist, compares the Catalan autonomy movement with others, chiefly in the Soviet Union, in *Els moviments d'emancipació nacional* (Badalona, 1935, 238 pp.). Among the many reports of observers and participants in the Spanish Civil War, Franz Borkenau, *The Spanish Cockpit* (London, 1937, 303 pp.), is the best contemporary analysis of the complex party relationships in the Loyalist coalition during the war. Edwin Rolfe, *The Lincoln Battalion* (New York, 1939, 321 pp.), emphasizes the part played by American communists and adventurers in the international brigades. Alvarez del Vayo, *Freedom's Battle* (tr. by E. E. Brooke; New York, 1940, 381 pp.), calls nonintervention a Franco-British mistake but defends his acquiescence in that policy while Republican foreign minister.

F. JEWS AND SOCIALISM. The question of the Jews and socialism was long before Hitler an emotion-distorted issue. This subject is treated at length by Edmund Silberner in a forthcoming volume, *Socialism and the Jews (1800-1914)*, with bibliographical references whose focus is the western European socialist attitude toward Jews. As part of his studies Silberner is in the course of publishing several important articles, including "Friedrich Engels and the Jews," *Jewish Social Studies*, xi (1949), pp. 323-342; "Pierre Leroux's Ideas on the Jewish People," *ibid.*, xii (1950), pp. 367-384; also the following to be published in 1951, "Moses Hess: From Assimilation to Zionism," *Historia Judaica*, xiii, Pt. 2; and "Ferdinand Lassalle: From Maccabeanism to Jewish Anti-Semitism," *Hebrew Union College Annual*. See also Louis Massoutié, *Judaïsme et marxisme* (Paris, 1938, 218 pp.). Bernard Lazare, *Antisemitism; Its History and Causes* (1894; New York, 1903, 384 pp.), is a general survey from the point of view of a French radical. In 1951 the Syracuse University Press is publishing S. N. Schwarz, *Jews in the Soviet Union*.

One of the peculiar alliances of nationalism and Marxism is the Poale Zion, or Jewish Labor Zionist movement. (See PART IV, Topic 3, for the attitude of American radicals on the Jewish question, and PART IV, Topic 6, for brief reference to Poale Zion and cooperatives.) Arising in central Europe in the late nineteenth century it spread wherever Zionism spread. The location of the homeland remained a subject of controversy until 1909. Standard works on the movement in general are Herz Burgin, *Die Geschichte fun der yiddisher arbeiter Bewegung* (New York, 1915, 935 pp.), in Yiddish; and Volume 3 of the Yiddish Scientific Institute's *Historishe Shriftn* (Warsaw, 1929-1939, 3 vols.). Poale Zion's pamphlet *Vozzvanie k evreiskoi molodezhi* [*An Appeal to Jewish Youth*] (London, 1901, 16 pp.), became virtually the official manifesto of Poale Zion. Its leader, Ber Borochov, considered Zionism to be "the only answer to the economic and historic needs of the Jewish people." See his materialist interpretation, *The National Question and the Class Struggle* (1905), published in his *Nationalism and the Class Struggle; a Marxian Approach to the Jewish Problem* (New York, 1937, 205 pp.). The early essay of Nachman Syrkin, *The Jewish Problem and the Jewish Socialist State* (1898), printed in Syrkin's *Essays on Socialist Zionism* (New York, 1935, 64 pp.), expresses the views of the idealist and cooperative wing of the movement.

Other European socialists generally opposed the yearnings of the Jews in the *Galut* for a home in Palestine. The social democratic outlook on Zionism can be found in Marc Jarblum, *The Socialist International and Zionism* (tr. by Maximilian Hurwitz; New York, 1933, 32 pp.). The main thesis of the communists up to the end of World War II, as expressed in such books as Avrahm Yarmolinsky, *The Jews and Other Minor Nationalities under the Soviets* (New York, 1928, 193 pp.), was that the Soviet

Union guaranteed to foster national cultures. In 1928, Birobidjan, an area somewhat larger than Palestine in the Russian Far East, was set aside for "contiguous Jewish colonies." Here, the communists claimed, was a Jewish refuge independent of capitalist imperialism. See also the work of the Belgian Trotskyist Abram Léon, *Conception materialiste de la question juive* (Paris, 1946, 169 pp.), which is to be published in English translation by *Fourth International*, the American Shachtmanite Trotskyist monthly.

Jewish labor socialism developed comprehensive cooperatives in Palestine and distinctive union principles. On the *Kvutza*, see H. F. Infield, *Cooperative Living in Palestine* (New York, 1944, 192 pp.), which has a good bibliography, pp. 181-186; Maurice Pearlman, *Adventure in the Sun* (London, 1947, 177 pp.); and Meyer Levin's novel, *My Father's House* (New York, 1947, 192 pp.). For labor organization and general comments see the Poale Zion report to the Brussels congress of the Labor and Socialist International by Walter Preuss, *The Jewish Labour Movement in Palestine* (Berlin, 1928, 89 pp.); Abraham Revusky, *The Histadrut (General Federation of Jewish Labor in Palestine), a Labor Commonwealth in the Making* (New York, 1938, 96 pp.); the League for Labor Palestine publication edited by Samuel Duker, *New Social Forms and Cooperative Palestine* (New York, 1944, 96 pp.); S. Levenberg, *The Jews and Palestine* (London, 1945, 402 pp.); and Samuel Kurland, *Cooperative Palestine; the Story of Histadrut* (New York, 1947, 276 pp.).

Socialism in the less industrialized parts of the world was insignificant until after 1900, and its twentieth-century development was virtually ignored in the United States until World War II. Then, as the United States examined its increased world interests, a flood of news summaries reported the almost universal collectivist trend. The growing revolutionary movements in these parts had religious, nationalist, democratic, authoritarian, and socialist elements in varying degrees, with a common anti-imperialist face. The contemporary publications concerning this vast theater of social action are too partisan, incomplete, and lacking in perspective to warrant selective citation here. Examples on Latin America and the Far East will indicate the scope of the trend.

G. LATIN AMERICA. There is no comprehensive study of all types of socialism in Latin America, and studies covering a single type or a single country are few and largely untranslated. A good deal of fragmentary information can be found in the publications of international labor organizations, the four Internationals (see below Topics 3 and 4), in the Marxian press of Europe (see above) and of the United States (see PART II, General Reading, pp. 104-105, and Topics 9-12), and in the reports and abundant publications of the various Latin American labor, socialist, anarchist, and communist movements. Given the attitude of many current Latin American governments toward socialism and the inaccessibility of a large part of the literature in the United States, it is extremely difficult to include with accuracy a fully representative selection of the material.

Socialism was a foreign importation to Latin America, as it was to the United States, and many parallels can be drawn. The segregated and theocratic religious communities of the United States had several characteristics in common with the collectivism of the Jesuit missions in Paraguay. French secular utopianism existed in southern South America contemporaneously with the Associationist movement in the United States. Radical groups were divided throughout the New World along anarchist, social democratic, communist, and Trotskyist lines, and even the I.W.W. had a Latin American following. In both the Americas the first Marxians were found among the urban immigrants. Both sought to recruit the underprivileged races, although in a largely colored region dominated by whites there has been less emphasis on racial appeal than one might expect.

In contrast to the similarities of North American and Latin American socialist development, striking differences arose from such conditions as the larger proportion of Indian and Negro population in Latin America, the dominance of the Roman Catholic Church, the prevalence of dictatorship, and the economy of high profits, low wages, large estates, and foreign control. Latin American socialism tended to emphasize Indian interests along the cordillera, to minimize its anticlericalism, to merge with the other opposition to caudillos, to capitalize upon the anti-imperialist and nationalist sentiment, and often to dominate organized labor.

For collectivism in pre-Columbian and colonial times, see, for example, *Geschichte und Kultur des Inkareiches* (Amsterdam, 1937, 208 pp.), by the German anthropologist and socialist Heinrich Cunow; and two studies of the Jesuit reductions in Paraguay, 1607-1767, *A Vanished Arcadia* (London, 1901, 294 pp.), by the British socialist R. B. Cunninghame Graham, and Pablo Hernández, S.J., *Misiones del Paraguay: Organización social de las doctrinas Guaraníes de la Compañía de Jesús* (Barcelona, 1913, 2 vols.).

Probably the outstanding Latin American secular utopian was Esteban Echeverría, Argentine poet and exile during the dictatorship of Rosas. He combined the romantic and Christian socialist ideas of Saint-Simon and Pierre Leroux with the democratic liberalism of Mazzini in *Dogma socialista* (ed. by Alberto Palcos from the Montevideo edition of 1846; La Plata, 1940, xcvi, 596 pp.). A. M. Giménez, *Los precursores del socialismo en la República Argentina* (Buenos Aires, 1917, 29 pp.), and F. J.

Legón, ed., *Doctrina política de la Asociación de Mayo* (Buenos Aires, 1939, 481 pp.), comment on the theories of Echeverría and other pre-Marxians. See also J. C. Jobet Búrquez, *Santiago Arcos Arlegui y la Sociedad de la igualdad; un socialista utopista chileno* (Santiago de Chile, 1942, 213 pp.). Two foreign attempts to found experimental colonies in the late nineteenth century were the Italian anarchist settlement, Cecilia, in Brazil, and the post-Associationist cooperative colony of Topolobampo, in Mexico. References to Cecilia are found in Max Nettlau, *Bibliographie de l'anarchie* (Brussels, 1897, 294 pp.), p. 216, and to Topolobampo in L. L. and Jessie Bernard, "The Late Utopistic Phase of Social Science: the Albert Kimsey Owen Group," in *Origins of American Sociology* (New York, 1943, 866 pp.), pp. 359-371.

The anarchists have been active in Latin America since the days of the First International, and have published thousands of pamphlets and books, and numerous periodicals. Among the leaders of the contemporary anarchist movement, the Spaniard Diego Abad de Santillán is an authority on the Argentine movement. See, for example, his *La F.O.R.A.—Ideología y trayectoria del movimiento obrero revolucionario en la Argentina* (Buenos Aires, 1933, 312 pp.). Abad de Santillán's biography, *Ricardo Flores Magón, el apóstol de la revolución social mexicana* (Mexico, D.F., 1925, 131 pp.), deals with one of the two anarcho-syndicalist brothers whose trial before World War I received sympathetic publicity in such radical journals as *Mother Earth*. See also the works of the Peruvian Manuel González Prada, *Horas de lucha* (1908; 2nd ed., Callao, 1924, 362 pp.), and *Anarquía* (3rd ed., Santiago de Chile, 1940, 174 pp.); and Eduardo Ghitor, *La bancarrota del anarco-sindicalismo; hacia un movimiento sindical revolucionario de masas en América Latina* (Montevideo, 1932, 53 pp.). A useful summary in English is S. F. Simon, "Anarchism and Anarcho-Syndicalism in South America," *Hispanic American Historical Review*, xxvi (Feb. 1946), pp. 38-59.

Democratic socialist parties have been strongest in Argentina, Chile, Uruguay, Brazil, and Ecuador. The only survey is R. J. Alexander, *Labor Parties of Latin America* (New York, 1942, 47 pp.), which includes the Aprista and similar movements. Most important in Argentina, the Socialist Party has published *Anuario socialista* (Buenos Aires, 1928-1946), and its publishers, La Vanguardia, have brought out the works of the first party leader, *Obras completas de Juan B. Justo* (Buenos Aires, 1930-1938, 5 vols.). Justo is said to have been the first translator of Marx's *Das Kapital* into Spanish, and is regarded as one of the leading theorists among Latin American Marxians. La Vanguardia and Editorial Claridad have also published the works of such Argentine socialists as Alfredo Palacios, Nicolas Repetto, Enrique Dickman, Americo Ghioldi, and Juan B. Solari. The first period (1896-1914) in the history of the Argentine party is covered in Jacinte Oddone, *Historia del socialismo argentino* (Buenos Aires, 1934, 2 vols.). This should be supplemented by such party publications as *36 años de vida socialista* (Buenos Aires, 1932, 62 pp.), issued by Federación Socialista de la Capital; *Problemas argentinos; planes socialistas para su solución* (Buenos Aires, 1938, 122 pp.), containing speeches by Jacinto Oddone and other leaders at the 24th congress of the party; and *35° congreso nacional del Partido socialista—informes y proposiciones* (Buenos Aires, 1946, 65 pp.), which discusses the party's attitude toward the Peronista movement. The Partido Democrático was the first socialist party in Chile, but grew conservative and was supplanted by more powerful working-class parties. For the temper of late nineteenth-century radicalism consult N. F. Torres, *Radicalismo chileno; su origen, su historia, su programa, sus tendencias, su porvenir y sus enemigos* (Coquimbo, Chile, 1896, 205 pp.), and for general political developments see Edmundo Montecinos Rozas, *Apuntaciones para el estudio de la evolución de los partidos políticos chilenos y de su proyección jurídica* (Santiago de Chile, 1942, 118 pp.). See also J. C. Jobet Búrquez, *Los fundamentos del marxismo* (2nd ed., Santiago de Chile, 1940, 112 pp.), and Oscar Schnake Vergara, *Política socialista* (Santiago de Chile, 1938, 96 pp.), both socialist publications. J. R. Stevenson, *The Chilean Popular Front* (Philadelphia, 1942, 155 pp.), is one of the very few special studies in English. One random sample of democratic socialist publication elsewhere is Luis Maldonado Estrada, *Bases del Partido socialista ecuatoriano* (Quito, 1938, 80 pp.).

A movement closely allied to the democratic socialist parties of Latin America is the Peruvian Apra (Alianza Popular Revolucionario Americana), now called Partido del Pueblo. Its founder and chief spokesman, Víctor Raúl Haya de la Torre, at first sought to unite "Indo-America" politically against North American imperialism. Samples of his prolific writings are *¿A donde va Indoamérica?* (2nd ed., Santiago de Chile, 1935, 280 pp.), and *El antimperialismo y el Apra* (2nd ed., Santiago de Chile, 1936, 216 pp.). With the rise of nazism, Haya modified his position, partly because of the good neighbor policy and Latin American need for foreign capital to develop industry and diversify agriculture, and partly because Yankee imperialism became the lesser evil compared with totalitarian racism. After World War II the Apristas became the major opposition in Peru and briefly joined a coalition administration. *La defensa continental* (2nd ed., Buenos Aires, 1942, 234 pp.) and its continuation, *Y después de la guerra ¿que?* (Lima, 1946, 249 pp.) develop his changed views under changing conditions. His leadership and program are described in F. Cossió del Pomar's biography, *Haya de la Torre, el indoamericano* (Mexico, D.F., 1939, 291 pp.). Parties similar to the

Apristas exist in Venezuela (Acción Democrática), Cuba (Partido Autén-tico), and in some other countries.

Perhaps no Marxian group has published so much in Latin America as the communists, but as in the United States, there have been few theorists. For general reference on the period before the Popular Front strategy, see *Los partidos comunistas de América del Sur y del Caribe y el movimiento sindical revolucionario* (Barcelona, 193[?], 61 pp.), and sections devoted to Latin America in international communist publica-tions. Stephen Naft, "Fascism and Communism in South America," *For-eign Policy Reports*, XIII (Dec. 15, 1937), pp. 225-236, is very useful. Developments since 1937 with emphasis on the postwar situation are sketched in Martin Ebon, *World Communism Today* (New York, 1948, 536 pp.), pp. 297-339, with bibliography, pp. 511-512. Perhaps the leading theorist—but never technically a party member and at one period con-demned as a "racial chauvinist"—was the long-exiled José Carlos Mariá-tegui. His most important work, applying Marxism to the Peru of the 1920's, was *7 ensayos de interpretación de la realidad peruana* (2nd ed., Lima, 1943, 273 pp.). See also the volume of selected writings, edited by Manuel Moreno Sánchez, *José Carlos Mariátegui* (Mexico, D.F., 1937, 133 pp.). Biographies of other communist leaders include Fernando Alegría, *Recabarren* (Santiago de Chile, 1938, 162 pp.), on Luis E. Recabarren Serrano, founder of the Chilean Communist Party, and *Luis Carlos Prestes; the Struggle for Liberation in Brazil* (New York, 1936, 39 pp.). Leading subjects of communist propaganda are economic democracy, patriotism, and attacks on competing leftists. For examples refer to L. C. Prestes, *Os comunistas na luta pela democracia* (Rio de Janeiro, 1945, 45 pp.); Francisco Calderío (Blas Roca, pseud.), *¡Al combate! ¡Por la economía y el bienestar popular!* (Havana, 1946, 77 pp.); and the works of such leaders as Rodolfo Ghioldi, editor of the Argentine communist daily, *La Hora*; Gerónimo Arnedo Alvarez, the Argentine party's secretary-general; Julio Arevalo and Carlos Contreras Labarca.

The Trotskyists have been as microscopic in Latin America as in the United States, but unlike their North American colleagues they have published almost no theoretical publications. Exceptions are their brief superiority over the Stalinists during the depression in Chile, and the strength of their Partido Obrero Revolucionario in the Bolivian miners' federation. See the publications issued by the Trotskyist faction of the communists reviewing their behavior under the Ibáñez dictatorship in Chile (1927-1931), *Hacia la formación de un verdadero partido de clase* (Santiago de Chile, 1933).

Writings on the Latin American labor movement contain information on its penetration by radical groups. R. J. Alexander of Rutgers University has a general survey in progress, expanding his pamphlet for the Fabian Society, *Labour Movements in Latin America* (Research Series, No. 122; London, 1947, 24 pp.). The leading Latin American scholar in the field is Moisés Poblete Troncoso, the Chilean labor economist, who has published the only general book on the subject, *El movimiento obrero latinoamericano* (Mexico, D.F., 1946, 296 pp.). For special studies of single countries, see Poblete Troncoso, *Labor Organizations in Chile* (Washington, 1928, 41 pp.), *La organización sindical en Chile* (Santiago de Chile, 1926, 191 pp.); the volume on Argentine labor by Diego Abad de Santillán cited above, and later studies by M. S. Casaretto and Alfredo Fernández; Francisco Alexandre, *Teoría e pratica do sindicalismo* (2nd ed., Rio de Janeiro, 1941, 182 pp.); and M. R. Clark's excellent *Organized Labor in Mexico* (Chapel Hill, N.C., 1934, 315 pp.). One offshoot of the Peronista movement, the Partido Laborista, is headed by the deputy Cipriano Reyes, whose book, *¿Que es el laborismo?* (Buenos Aires, 1946), indicates the disillusionment and hopes of some of the more socialistic elements among the Peronistas.

Mexican labor has felt only such communist influence as the government would allow, and the administrations since the revolution, although in some ways "socialist," have developed no coherent body of socialist theory and no socialist political party. For lack of any published study in English, see H. K. Geiger, *The Communist Party of Mexico* (MS senior thesis, School of Public and International Affairs, Princeton University, 1947, 94 pp.), and its bibliography. Deep insight into the meaning of the Mexican Revolution is exhibited in Frank Tannenbaum, *Peace by Revolution* (New York, 1933, 316 pp.). A later study of its significance is Manuel Hübner, *México en marcha* (Santiago de Chile, 1936, 676 pp.). Rafael Ramos Pedrueza, *La lucha de clases a través de la historia de México* (1934; 2nd ed. rev. and enl.; Mexico, D.F., 1936, 294 pp.), is a Marxian history comparable in point of view to the superior work of Caio Prado, Jr., and Gilberto Freyre in Brazilian history, where Negroes as well as Indians furnished the exploited labor. The temper of the Cárdenas "New Deal" of the late thirties, which expropriated oil, pushed the distribution of the *haciendas* to the *peons*, and took Calles' six-year plan seriously, is represented by Nathaniel and Sylvia Weyl, *The Reconquest of Mexico; the Years of Lázaro Cárdenas* (New York, 1939, 394 pp.); the writings of Vicente Lombardo Toledano, for example, *Un viaje al mundo del porvenir* (Mexico, D.F., 1936, 159 pp.) on the U.S.S.R.; Clarence Senior, *Democracy Comes to a Cotton Kingdom; the Story of Mexico's La Laguna* (Mexico, D.F., 1940, 56 pp.); and *The Mexican Government's Six Year Plan, 1934 to 1940* (Mexico, D.F., 1934, 84 pp.), published by the Partido Nacional Revolucionario.

H. THE FAR EAST. Socialism in the Far East has come to power in mainland China; has powerful minority adherents in India and southeast Asia; and was crushed in Japan, to reappear under American occupation. On China, see Mousheng Lin, *Men and Ideas; an Informal History of Chinese Political Thought* (New York, 1942, 256 pp.), for background. For three different points of view on the rise of the communists see: A. L. Strong, *China's Millions; the Revolutionary Struggles from 1927 to 1935* (New York, 1935, 457 pp.), and Leon Trotsky, *Problems of the Chinese Revolution* (tr. by Max Shachtman; New York, 1932, 432 pp.), opposing communist views; and Edgar Snow, *Red Star over China* (rev. ed., New York, 1938, 520 pp.). A popular biography of the chief Chinese communist is Robert Payne, *Mao Tse-tung: Ruler of Red China* (New York, 1950, 303 pp.). A. K. Wu, a former Chinese Nationalist diplomat, discusses, in *China and the Soviet Union* (New York, 1950, 434 pp.), Sino-Russian relations from 1618-1950, including the relations of the Chinese communists with Russia. The Hoover Institute and Library will publish R. C. North's study in progress, *Political Tactics in Soviet Policy toward China, 1917-1947*; while the Harvard University Press is issuing *Chinese Communism and the Rise of Mao*, by B. I. Schwartz of Harvard's Russian Research Center. In 1951 the Research Center will also publish *Documentary History of Chinese Communism*, by Conrad Brandt, Schwartz, and John K. Fairbank. A communist interpretation of India is R. P. Dutt, *The Problem of India* (New York, 1943, 224 pp.). Jawaharlal Nehru's writings, such as his autobiography, *Toward Freedom* (New York, 1941, 445 pp.), reveal the degree of sympathy entertained for socialist and communist ideology by the Congress Party leader. For early twentieth-century socialism in Japan, see Sen Katayama, *The Labor Movement in Japan* (Chicago, 1918, 147 pp.), originally intended for the *International Socialist Review*; and *The Socialist and Labour Movement in Japan* (Kobe, 1921, 145 pp.), by "an American sociologist," published by the *Japan Chronicle*.

4. Marx and Engels

No complete edition of the writings of Marx (1818-1883) and Engels (1820-1895) exists, but the Marx-Engels-Lenin Institute of Moscow has undertaken such an edition, *Karl Marx, Friedrich Engels; historisch-kritische Gesamtausgabe, Werke, Schriften, Briefe* (Moscow, etc., 1927-1935, Abt. I, 7 vols. in 8; Abt. III, 4 vols.). The volumes published thus far include the writings of Marx and Engels up to 1848 and all the known correspondence between Marx and Engels, 1844-1883. The early volumes, edited under the direction of D. Ryazanov [D. B. Goldendach], are best. This will long remain the standard edition, as it is taken directly from the central manuscript repository. It provides elaborate supplementary aids to research, with some inaccuracies inevitable in so monumental an undertaking. The Russian edition of Marx and Engels, *Sochineniya* (Moscow, 1928-), which had progressed as far as Volume 29 in 1946; *Letopisi marksizma* (Moscow, 1926-1930?); and *Arkhiv marksa i engelsa* (Moscow, 1924-), all contain materials not found elsewhere. International Publishers has three convenient collections for English readers: their *Marxist Library*, their edition of Marx's and Engels' *Selected Works* (ed. by C. P. Dutt; New York, 1936-1937, 2 vols.), and *Karl Marx and Friedrich Engels: Selected Correspondence, 1846-1895* (tr. and ed. by Dona Torr from the German ed. by Vladimir Adoratsky; New York, 1942, 551 pp.). A useful guide to the important titles in these collections is in Vernon Venable, *Human Nature: the Marxian View* (New York, 1945, 217 pp.), pp. 215-217, cited in this work in other places. From time to time Marxist publishers have compiled topical extracts, as, for example, Engels, *The British Labour Movement* (New York, 1940, 47 pp.). An earlier collection is Franz Mehring's edition, *Aus dem literarischen Nachlass von Karl Marx, Friedrich Engels, und Ferdinand Lassalle* (Stuttgart, 1902, 4 vols.). See also *Marx's Selected Essays* (tr. by H. J. Stenning; London, 1926, 207 pp.), containing a translation of *Zur Judenfrage*.

The most famous of Marx's writings were concerned with political economy directly. *A Contribution to the Critique of Political Economy* (1859; tr. by N. I. Stone; Chicago, 1904, 314 pp.), is particularly notable for its study of monetary theory and its classic statement of historical materialism. The great bible of the movement, unread by many socialists and even less read by nonsocialists, is *Capital, a Critique of Political Economy: Volume I, The Process of Capitalist Production* (1867; ed. by Engels and tr. from 3rd German ed. by Samuel Moore and Edward Aveling; Chicago, 1906, 869 pp.); *Volume II, The Process of Circulation of Capital* (1885; ed. by Engels and tr. from 2nd German ed. by Ernest Untermann; Chicago, 1907, 618 pp.); *Volume III, The Process of Capitalist Production as a Whole* (1894; ed. by Engels and tr. from 1st German ed. by Ernest Untermann; Chicago, 1909, 1048 pp.). C. H. Kerr & Co. have reprinted this edition (Chicago, 1925-1926, 3 vols.), and a new translation of Volume i appeared soon after, *Capital; a Critique of Political Economy; the Process of Capitalist Production* (tr. from Engels' 4th German ed. of 1890 by E. and C. Paul; New York, 1929, 927 pp.). The Moore-Aveling translation of Volume i has been frequently abridged and reprinted. *Theorien über den Mehrwert* (1905-1910; 4th ed., Stuttgart, 1921, 3 vols. in 4), was edited by Karl Kautsky from Marx's manuscript material for what would have formed the fourth volume of *Capital*. Marx's address to the general council of the First International in 1865, *Value, Price and Profit* (ed. by E. M. Aveling;

Chicago, 1908?, 128 pp.), and *Wage-Labor and Capital* (1849; intro. by Engels; rev. tr., Chicago, 1935, 59 pp.), with other central selections, has been conveniently reprinted in *The Essentials of Marx* (1926; ed. by Algernon Lee; 2nd ed., New York, 1946, 185 pp.).

The *Manifesto of the Communist Party*, by Marx and Engels (1848; ed. by Engels; London, 1888, 31 pp., and many other editions), is the classic statement both of the Marxian theory of history and of the differences between Marxian and other socialisms of the day. In two other joint works Marx and Engels attempted to distinguish their point of view from that of the Young Hegelians, in whose circle Marx had once moved: *Die heilige Familie; oder, Kritik der kritischen Kritik; gegen Bruno Bauer & Consorten* (Frankfurt-am-Main, 1845, 335 pp.), and *Die deutsche Ideologie; Kritik der neuesten deutschen Philosophie in ihren Repräsentanten, Feuerbach, B. Bauer und Stirner, und des deutschen Sozialismus in seinen verschiedenen Propheten*, written in 1845-1846, first published in full in Marx-Engels' *Gesamtausgabe*, Abt. i, Vol. v (Moscow, 1933, 706 pp.). Parts 1 and 3 have been published in English as *The German Ideology* (tr. by W. Lough and C. P. Magill; London, 1938, 214 pp.). *The Poverty of Philosophy* (1847; tr. by Harry Quelch with preface by Engels; Chicago, 1910, 227 pp.) is Marx's reply to Proudhon's chief economic work, *Système des contradictions économiques*. Engels used Marx's notes on Lewis Morgan's anthropology in *The Origin of the Family, Private Property, and the State* (1884; tr. by Ernest Untermann; Chicago, 1905, 217 pp.; or, ed. tr. from 4th [1934] Moscow ed. by Alick West and rev. by Dona Torr; London, 1941, 216 pp.), an attempt to apply historical materialism to primitive communism. Marx wrote chapter 10 in Pt. 2 of *Herr Eugen Dühring's Revolution in Science*, often referred to as the *Anti-Dühring* (first published in the Leipzig *Vorwärts*, 1877; tr. by Emile Burns and ed. by C. P. Dutt; New York, 1935, 364 pp.), Engels' defense of historical materialism against the attacks of the German socialist Dühring. *Socialism, Utopian and Scientific* (tr. by Edward Aveling; London, 1892, 117 pp.), consists of three chapters from the *Anti-Dühring* revised. See also Engels, *Dialectics of Nature* (tr. and ed. by Clemens Dutt with preface and notes by J. B. S. Haldane; New York, 1940, 383 pp.).

Marx and Engels also commented extensively on their contemporary society. The American edition of Engels, *The Condition of the Working Class in England in 1844* (1845; tr. by F. K. Wischnewetsky; New York, 1887, 199 pp.), includes Engels' 1887 preface on the American labor movement. Engels, *Revolution and Counter-Revolution; or, Germany in 1848* (ed. by E. M. Aveling: London, 1896, 148 pp.), was originally published in the *New York Tribune*, 1851-1852, in a series of articles which Engels wrote for Marx. For Marx's foreign correspondence on the French disturbances of 1848 and 1871 and the Crimean War, see *The Class Struggles in France (1848-50)* (1850; cd. by C. P. Dutt with intro. by Engels; New York, 1934, 159 pp.); *The Eighteenth Brumaire of Louis Bonaparte* (1852; tr. by E. and C. Paul; London, 1926, 192 pp.); *The Civil War in France* (1871; intro. by Engels; New York, 1940, 96 pp.); and *The Eastern Question* (1853-1856; ed. by E. M. and E. Aveling; London, 1897, 656 pp.). The reports of both Marx and Engels are reprinted in *The Civil War in the United States* (1861-1862; ed. with intro. and notes by Richard Enmale; New York, 1937, 325 pp.), and *Revolution in Spain* (1854-1873; New York, 1939, 255 pp.). *Critique of the Gotha Programme* (1891; ed. by C. P. Dutt; New York, 1938, 116 pp.) consists of Marx's notes on the compromise agreement with the Lassallean socialists. Some of the above titles concerned with political economy are further discussed in PART IV, General Reading, pp. 249-250.

The best biographies of Marx and Engels are Franz Mehring's great life, *Karl Marx* (tr. by Edward Fitzgerald; New York, 1935, 608 pp.), and Gustav Mayer, *Friedrich Engels* (The Hague, 1934, 2 vols.), rewritten for English-speaking readers and translated by G. and H. Highet (New York, 1936, 332 pp.). See also the brief sketch by D. B. Goldendach (Ryazanov, pseud.), *Karl Marx and Friedrich Engels* (tr. by Joshua Kunitz; New York, 1927, 224 pp.); Engels' sketch in *Handwörterbuch der Staatswissenschaften* (4th ed.), VI, pp. 496-503, edited with bibliography by Ernst Drahn; and the article, "Marks i marksizm," in *Bolshaya sovetskaya entsiklopediya*, XXXVIII (1938), cols. 157-240. Edmund Wilson, *To the Finland Station* (New York, 1940, 509 pp.), Pt. 2, although inadequate on the theoretical side, gives an evocative account of Marx's and Engels' personal relations to each other and to Lassalle, Bakunin, and other contemporaries. Marx has received more attention from biographers than Engels. Karl Korsch, *Karl Marx* (London, 1938, 247 pp.), and D. B. Goldendach (Ryazanov, pseud.), ed., *Karl Marx: Man, Thinker, and Revolutionist; a Symposium* (tr. from Russian and German by E. and C. Paul; New York, 1927, 282 pp.), deserve mention as most favorably biased; B. I. Nicolaevsky and Otto Maenchen-Helfen, *Karl Marx; Man and Fighter* (tr. by Gwenda David and Eric Mosbacher; Philadelphia, 1936, 391 pp.), as a social democratic interpretation; and Leopold Schwarzschild, *The Red Prussian; the Life and Legend of Karl Marx* (tr. by Margaret Wing; New York, 1947, 422 pp.), as the most violently unfavorable, although well documented. See other lives by Max Beer, Isaiah Berlin, E. H. Carr, H. J. Laski, Wilhelm Liebknecht, Achille Loria, R. W. Postgate, Otto Rühle, and John Spargo. *Friedrich Engels, der Denker* (Basel, 1945, 371 pp.), is important especially for its bibliography of works by and about Engels.

The best treatments of the historical background of Marx's leading ideas are found in Eduard Bernstein, *Zur Geschichte und Theorie des Socialismus* (2nd ed., Berlin, 1901, 426 pp.); Charles Andler's great commentary, in his edition of *Le Manifeste communiste* (Paris, 1901, 2 vols.); Franz Grégoire, *Aux Sources de la pensée de Marx: Hegel, Feuerbach* (Louvain, 1947, 204 pp.); and Auguste Cornu, *Karl Marx, l'homme et l'oeuvre; de l'hégélianisme au matérialisme historique (1818-1845)* (Paris, 1934, 427 pp.). See also the comments in H. J. Laski's edition, *Communist Manifesto, Socialist Landmark; a New Appreciation Written for the Labour Party* (London, 1948, 171 pp.). Sidney Hook, *From Hegel to Marx* (New York, 1936, 335 pp.), like Cornu, traces Marx's early intellectual development in relation to the thought of Hegel, Strauss, Bruno Bauer, Arnold Ruge, Max Stirner, Moses Hess, and Feuerbach. It is inadequate, however, in failing to give a proper sense of the general historical background of the group, and in overemphasizing what Hook claims to be the "instrumentalist" aspect of Marx's work.

The expository and critical books dealing with Marxism are almost endless; the following few items are only samples. One of the first treatments of Marxian economic theory in English—soon superseded—was H. M. Hyndman, *The Economics of Socialism* (Boston, 1921, 286 pp.). W. H. Emmett, *The Marxian Economic Handbook* (London, 1925, 350 pp.), and Karl Kautsky, *The Economic Doctrines of Karl Marx* (tr. by H. J. Stenning; New York, 1936, 252 pp.), are in effect commentaries on the first volume of *Capital*. Others are *Engels on Capital* (tr. and ed. by L. E. Mins; New York, 1937, 147 pp.); L. A. Leontyev, *Marx's Capital* (tr. by E. G. Kazakevich; New York, 1946, 160 pp.); and A. D. Lindsay, *Karl Marx's Capital* (London, 1925, 128 pp.). The outstanding argument against Marxian economics, based on the premises of the Austrian school, is that of Eugen von Böhm-Bawerk. See especially his classic *Capital and Interest, a Critical History of Economical Theory* (tr. by William Smart; London, 1890, 431 pp.), and Rudolf Hilferding's rebuttal, *Boehm-Bawerk's Criticism of Marx* (tr. by E. and C. Paul; Glasgow, 192[?], 94 pp.). Other criticisms are M. I. Tugan-Baranovsky, *Modern Socialism in Its Historical Development* (tr. by M. I. Redmount; London, 1910, 232 pp.); Ludwig von Mises, *Socialism* (1922; tr. by J. Kahane; New York, 1936, 528 pp.); and W. J. Blech (Blake, pseud.), *An American Looks at Karl Marx* (New York, 1939, 746 pp.; published also under the title *Elements of Marxian Economic Theory*). Blake describes and defends Marxian economic views in detail, and although often discursive, is valuable as a general handbook. G. D. H. Cole, *The Meaning of Marxism* (London, 1948, 302 pp.), a substantially rewritten version of *What Marx Really Meant* (New York, 1934, 309 pp.), is a good simplified introduction, with comments on social changes since Marx's death. *A Centenary of Marxism* (ed. by Samuel Bernstein and others; New York, 1948, 196 pp.), being Vol. 12, No. 1 of *Science & Society*, is a sample of the numerous publications and special editions of Marxian periodicals commemorating the centennial of the *Communist Manifesto*. More extended selections from the literature on Marxian political and economic theory are given in PART IV.

The philosophical setting of the doctrine of historical materialism is provided by F. A. Lange, *History of Materialism* (1866; 3rd ed., tr. by E. C. Thomas; London, 1890, 3 vols.), criticized by Marxians for not emphasizing the importance of the class struggle in the historical process. Sympathetic expositions are Antonio Labriola, *Essays on the Materialistic Conception of History* (tr. by C. H. Kerr; Chicago, 1904, 246 pp.); N. I. Bukharin, *Historical Materialism; a System of Sociology* (1921; tr. from 3rd Russian ed.; New York, 1925, 318 pp.); and *A Textbook of Marxist Philosophy* published by the Leningrad Institute of Philosophy and prepared under the direction of M. Shirokov (tr. by A. C. Moseley; rev. and ed. by John Lewis; London, 1937, 399 pp.). Rudolf Stammler, *Wirtschaft und Recht nach der materialistischen Geschichtsauffassung* (5th ed., Berlin, 1924, 706 pp.), and Benedetto Croce, *Historical Material- ism and the Economics of Karl Marx* (tr. by C. M. Meredith; New York, 1914, 188 pp.), are unsympathetic. Other titles on historical materialism are found in PART III, and on its relation to the arts in PART VI, General Reading, pp. 426-434. For further material on Marxism, see R. L. Prager, booksellers, Berlin, *Marx, Engels, Lassalle; eine Bibliographie des Sozialismus* (Berlin, 1924, 3 pts.); Werner Sombart, "Ein Beitrag zur Bibliographie des Marxismus," *Archiv für Sozialwissenschaft und Sozialpolitik*, xx (1905), pp. 413-430; Ernst Drahn, *Marx-Bibliographie* (2nd ed., Berlin, 1923, 30 pp.); and the article, "Die Literatur über Marx, Engels und über Marxismus seit Beginn des Weltkriegs," *Marx-Engels Archiv*, i (1925), pp. 467-549, compiled by E. Czóbel and P. Hajdu.

5. Anarchism

As with the literature of socialism proper, only works representing the extensive literature on anarchism can be cited here. Max Nettlau, *Bibliographie de l'anarchie* (Brussels, 1897, 294 pp.), and *Encyclopédie anarchiste* (ed. by Sébastien Faure; Paris, 193[?]-1934, 4 vols.), provide further references and interpret the subject broadly. Paul Eltzbacher's anthology, *Anarchism* (tr. by S. T. Byington; New York, 1908, 309 pp.), ranges from Godwin to Kropotkin and Tucker. For short introductory commentaries, see Karl Diehl, "Anarchismus," *Handwörterbuch der Staatswissenschaften* (4th ed.), i, pp. 276-292; E. V. Zenker, *Anarchism; a Criticism and History of the Anarchist Theory* (New York, 1897, 323 pp.); and Rudolf Rocker, *Anarcho-Syndicalism* (London, 1938, 158 pp.). The references in Topics 10, 3, and 8 distinguish socialism from anarchism, treat their rivalry in the First International, and their contributions to syndicalist development respectively. The early classic of the movement, William Godwin, *Enquiry Concerning Political Justice and Its Influence on Morals and Happiness* (1793; ed. by F. E. L. Priestley; Toronto, 1946, 3 vols.), stood almost alone for over half a century. Then, with the appearance of Proudhon, Max Stirner, and Bakunin, anarchism became a well-developed and active revolutionary creed.

Proudhon was not only the father of modern European anarchism but at the same time a founder of international socialism. His thought is perhaps best summarized in his three famous works: *What Is Property?* (1840-1841; tr. by Benjamin Tucker; New York, 189[?], 457 pp.); *Système des contradictions économiques; ou, Philosophie de la misère* (Paris, 1846, 2 vols.), Volume 1 of which has been translated into English as *System of Economical Contradictions* (tr. by Benjamin Tucker; Boston, 1888, 469 pp.); and *General Idea of the Revolution in the Nineteenth Century* (1851; tr. by J. B. Robinson; London, 1923, 302 pp.). These works outline Proudhon's scheme for cooperative workers' banks as a first step toward the perfect society, and his equalitarian and anarchistic conception of how the ideal society should be organized. Karl Diehl, in *P. J. Proudhon, seine Lehre und sein Leben* (Jena, 1888-1896, 3 vols.), describes these doctrines and analyzes them exhaustively. Proudhon's general conception of society and the social process is discussed in C. C. A. Bouglé, *La Sociologie de Proudhon* (Paris, 1911, 333 pp.). An American analysis is Shi Yung Lu, *The Political Theories of P. J. Proudhon* (New York, 1922, 153 pp.). For recent biographies see Henri de Lubac, *The Un-Marxian Socialist; a Study of Proudhon* (tr. by R. E. Scantlebury; New York, 1948, 304 pp.), and Édouard Dolléans, *Proudhon* (Paris, 1948, 528 pp.). Also see Dolléans and J. L. Puech, *Proudhon et la Révolution de 1848* (Paris, 1948, 77 pp.).

In contrast to Proudhon's "mutualist" anarchism, which called not only for equality but for mutual cooperation, Stirner defended an anarchism of the most individualistic type, in which the individual rejects not only social coercion but moral standards as well. The philosophic backgrounds of Stirner's position is traced by Victor Basch, in *L'Individualisme anarchiste, Max Stirner* (Paris, 1904, 294 pp.), back to Hegel, Schelling, and ultimately, Kant.

Communist anarchism or anarcho-communism recognizes the existence of a class struggle in which the workers must first be victorious before anarchism can be ushered in. Bakunin and Kropotkin represent this theory at its best. Bakunin's most important writing was done during the period 1867-1872, when he contested Marx's leadership of the European radical movement, especially in the First International. No collection of his complete works has been published, but selections are available in the French edition by Max Nettlau and James Guillaume, *Oeuvres* (Paris, 1895-1913, 6 vols.); in the German edition by Erwin Rholfs and Nettlau, *Gesammelte Werke* (Berlin, 1921-1924, 3 vols.); and in the Russian editions, *Sobranie sochineny i pisem* (ed. by Y. M. Steklov; Moscow, 1934-1935, 4 vols.), and *Izbrannye sochineniya* (Petersburg, 1920-1922, 5 vols.). The latter contains Bakunin's *Gosudarstvennost i anarkhiya* [*Statism and Anarchy*] (1873; Petersburg, 1922, 254 pp.). Of these writings, *God and the State* (tr. by B. R. Tucker; Boston, 1883, 52 pp.; also New York, 1916?, 86 pp.), was best known in the United States and most widely translated in Europe. See also *Correspondance de Michel Bakounine; lettres à Herzen et à Ogareff, 1860-1874* (ed. by Mikhail Dragomanov; tr. by M. Stromberg; Paris, 1896, 383 pp.). For Bakunin's writings in German see Ernst Drahn, "Versuch einer Bakunin-Bibliographie von Schriften, die in Deutschland und in deutscher Sprache erschienen," in the Berlin *Aktion*, XIII (June 15, 1923), cols. 299-301. The important works of Kropotkin include: *The Conquest of Bread* (London, 1913, 298 pp.); *Fields, Factories and Workshops* (rev. ed., New York, 1913, 477 pp.); *Mutual Aid; a Factor of Evolution* (Harmondsworth, Eng., 1939, 278 pp.); *The Great French Revolution, 1789-1793* (tr. by N. F. Dryhurst; New York, 1927, 2 vols.); and *Memoirs of a Revolutionist* (Boston, 1930, 502 pp.). The autobiography originally appeared in the *Atlantic Monthly*, 1898-1899. See also George Woodcock and Ivan Avakumovič, *The Anarchist Prince; a Biographical Study of Peter Kropotkin* (London, 1950, 464 pp.).

For other important works on anarchism in nineteenth-century Europe see Élisée Reclus, *L'Évolution, la révolution et l'idéal anarchique* (2nd ed., Paris, 1898, 296 pp.), and Max Nettlau, *Der Anarchismus von Proudhon zu Kropotkin . . . 1859-1880* (Berlin, 1927, 312 pp.), and *Anarchisten und Sozialrevolutionäre . . . 1880-1886* (Berlin, 1931, 409 pp.). In the twentieth century, Juan Montseny y Carret (Federico Urales, pseud.) has been an outstanding leader of the strong Spanish movement. See his *Mi Vida* (Barcelona, 1931, 3 vols.), and for an introduction to recent Italian anarchism, Errico Malatesta, *Scritti* (Geneva, 1934-1936, 3 vols.). In Germany, Proudhon's principles were carried on by John H. Mackay, who rediscovered Stirner and borrowed from American libertarians. His novels, *The Anarchists* (tr. by George Schumm; Boston, 1891, 305 pp.), and the more autobiographical *Der Freiheitsucher; Psychologie einer Entwickelung* (Berlin, 1920, 260 pp.), and his poems have given their most artistic expression to the individualist anarchist theories. See also his biography, *Max Stirner, sein Leben und sein Werk* (1898; 2nd rev. ed., Treptow, 1910, 298 pp.), and his *Gesammelte Werke* (Treptow, 1911, 8 vols.). Max Plowman's letters, published as *Bridge into the Future* (ed. by D. L. S. Plowman; London, 1944, 787 pp.), constitute the most important expression of the English pacifist community movement. Both varieties of anarchism waned after World War I, but after World War II both Berdyaev's personalism and J. P. Sartre's existentialism showed some of the characteristics of Stirner's egoism, according to Herbert Read, "Max Stirner," *Adelphi*, xxii (Apr.-June 1946), pp. 107-110.

Special Topics

Topic 1. Socialism in Medieval Society

SOCIALISTIC theories and practices spring from many of the most fundamental ideals and institutions of Western culture. In fact, socialism in forms recognizable in the twentieth century is far older than the individualistic capitalism of our own day. Although our survey commences with the medieval period we find that medieval men themselves in their religious and social thinking were influenced in part by traditions derived from Hebraic and Classical antiquity. The equalitarian implications of Christian teaching, for instance, were universally recognized. So were the socialistic consequences of the humanistic ethical speculations of the Classical world embodied in such a masterpiece as Plato's *Republic.* These traditions were partially merged in the current theories of natural law derived both from Roman imperial administration and from the writings of the Stoics.

In the minds of its members medieval society established itself upon a compromise between ideally conceived natural and Christian equality and the practical requirements of status and order in an agrarian and feudal society. Religious and secular authorities devoted their major efforts to the maintenance of this balance. To the extent that the dynamics of change disrupted the balance we find critics and reformers, whether in the interest of justice, salvation, or trade, proposing modifications of the established order. It is those modifications tending toward forms of socialism which especially concern us. Following the collapse of the Roman Empire the growth in power and wealth of the Roman Catholic Church seemed to many a standing contradiction of the spirit of the teaching of its founder. These critics, usually of the lowest social classes, recalled the communism of the primitive church—or of the time of Adam, when man delved and Eve span. The church itself, to a limited extent, encouraged a communistic life in order to reduce to a minimum the worldly cares of those who sought monastic retirement for spiritual contemplation. Social changes also tended to disrupt the balance of classes, and to the extent that the breakdown of the manorial system in the later Middle Ages dispossessed the peasants, revolts were encouraged which might take a communist form. Finally, with the growth of towns and the perfection of the guild system new forms of social cooperation appeared which were to have considerable consequences for subsequent socialist thought.

The following selected readings provide a preliminary orientation for the problem of the balance between individualism and communalism in the Middle Ages: Albert Hyma, *Christianity, Capitalism and Commu-*

nism (Ann Arbor, Mich., 1937, 303 pp.), pp. 1-40, 91-105; Bede Jarrett, *Mediaeval Socialism* (1914; London, 1935, 94 pp.), pp. 5-41; *The Rule of Saint Benedict* (tr. by Gasquet; London, 1909, 130 pp.), chaps. 2, 3, 5, 48, 57; Max Beer, *A History of British Socialism* (New York, 1940, 2 vols. in 1), I, pp. 29-47, and *Social Struggles in the Middle Ages* (tr. by H. J. Stenning; London, 1924, 215 pp.), pp. 149-207; Karl Kautsky, *Communism in Central Europe in the Time of the Reformation* (tr. by J. L. and E. G. Mulliken; London, 1897, 293 pp.), pp. 2-77.

No attempt is made here to mention general histories of the Middle Ages or to indicate general works which touch incidentally upon socialistic practices or ideas. A general statement of social doctrines, centered upon the teachings of the church but including heretical socialist variants, may be found in Bede Jarrett, *Social Theories of the Middle Ages, 1200-1500* (London, 1926, 280 pp.). He discusses in chapter 5 the theological bases for the ideas of property. Changes in economic life, which tended to transform the whole medieval system, are indicated for England in W. J. Ashley, *An Introduction to English Economic History and Theory* (New York, 1893-1894, 2 vols.), I, "The Middle Ages." A brief statement of the importance of medieval guilds as a background for modern guild socialism is made by E. R. Adair, "Economics," in F. J. C. Hearnshaw, ed., *Mediaeval Contributions to Modern Civilization* (London, 1921, 267 pp.), pp. 232-254. Histories of the guilds which have attracted the attention of guild socialists are G. F. Renard, *Guilds in the Middle Ages* (tr. by Dorothy Terry; ed. with intro. by G. D. H. Cole; London, 1919, 139 pp.), and Charles Gross, *The Gild Merchant* (Oxford, 1890, 2 vols.). Niles Carpenter, *Guild Socialism; an Historical and Critical Analysis* (New York, 1922, 350 pp.), discusses (pp. 39-50) the revival of interest in medieval civilization among certain British circles in the nineteenth century which contributed to the growth of the guild socialist movement. Guild socialists who have been particularly influenced by their study of the medieval guilds are A. J. Penty, *The Restoration of the Gild System* (London, 1906, 103 pp.); G. D. H. Cole, *Guild Socialism; a Plan for Economic Democracy* (New York, 1921, 202 pp.); and S. G. Hobson, *National Guilds* (ed. by A. R. Orage; London, 1914, 370 pp.), containing the substance of essays originally published in the *New Age* in 1912-1913. The interest of an anarchist in medieval social conditions is seen in Petr Kropotkin, "Mutual Aid in the Mediaeval City," *Nineteenth Century*, XXXVI (Aug.-Sept. 1894), pp. 183-202, 397-418, where Kropotkin contrasts the cooperative life of the rising city with the disorder of the surrounding countryside.

The vast literature on the medieval heretical socialist movements can only be summarized. Ignaz von Döllinger, *Beiträge zur Sektengeschichte des Mittelalters* (Munich, 1890, 2 vols.), deals with early gnostic and

Manichaean heretics in his first volume and devotes the second to documents and commentary on the Waldensians and Cathari. E. B. Bax, *Rise and Fall of the Anabaptists* (London, 1903, 407 pp.), is an account of that movement by an English socialist, while Josef Beck, ed., *Die Geschichts-Bücher der Wiedertäufer in Österreich-Ungarn* (Vienna, 1883, 654 pp.), is an edition of sources. John Horsch, *The Hutterian Brethren, 1528-1931* (Goshen, Ind., 1931, 168 pp.), recounts the history of a German sect some of whose members settled in America. Gustav Schmoller, "Zur Geschichte der national-ökonomischen Ansichten in Deutschland während der Reformations-Periode," *Zeitschrift für die gesammte Staatswissenschaft*, XVI (1860), pp. 698-706, discusses the communistic ideas of the Anabaptists. Socialistic ideas in the Middle Ages were rarely worked out in great precision. For instance, G. M. Trevelyan, *England in the Age of Wycliffe* (New York, 1899, 380 pp.), questions (pp. 197-198) Max Beer's thesis that the program of Wycliffe's followers was essentially socialistic. For further material see the *Brief List of References on the Communism of the Middle Ages as Found outside the Catholic Church* (Washington, 1922, 4 pp.) prepared by the division of bibliography of the Library of Congress.

Topic 2. Socialism from the Sixteenth to the Nineteenth Century

Since the Reformation the major periods of socialist activity have been associated with the great political and economic upheavals which have occurred roughly every hundred years since the seventeenth century. The Puritan revolution of 1640-1660 witnessed the appearance of a small but distinct communist sect, the Diggers. Although their leader, Gerrard Winstanley, cloaked his doctrines in religious language and was in fact concerned mainly with securing the social conditions requisite to salvation, the student can perceive the impetus given to social radicalism by changes in English society, especially the enclosure movement. Stimulated by the convulsions of revolution, English speculative thought in the seventeenth century formulated theories of natural law, compact, and primitive equality conceived in naturalistic terms but strangely parallel to the doctrines of medieval schoolmen, that have exerted profound influence upon subsequent liberal and socialistic thinkers. These notions were taken up and expressed in various forms by English, French, and German reformers of the eighteenth and nineteenth centuries. Socialism began to assume its modern forms as the society it criticized was transformed by the spread of the industrial revolution from England to the Continent.

The tenets of central figures in England and on the Continent are concisely revealed in: *The Works of Gerrard Winstanley* (ed. by G. H. Sabine; Ithaca, N.Y., 1941, 686 pp.), Intro., pp. 1-5, 58-70; D. O. Wagner, ed., *Social Reformers* (New York, 1939, 749 pp.), pp. 181-212; and R. T. Ely, *French and German Socialism in Modern Times* (New York, 1883, 274 pp.), pp. 53-203.

In addition to Sabine's edition of Winstanley's writings, other works dealing with the radical fringe of the Puritan revolutionary movement are Eduard Bernstein, *Cromwell & Communism; Socialism and Democracy in the Great English Revolution* (tr. by H. J. Stenning; London, 1930, 287 pp.); L. H. Berens, *The Digger Movement* (London, 1906, 259 pp.); G. P. Gooch, *English Democratic Ideas in the Seventeenth Century* (2nd ed., Cambridge, Eng., 1927, 315 pp.). Social tensions were largely concealed beneath religious problems in the seventeenth century, as W. S. Hudson indicates in "Economic and Social Thought of Gerrard Winstanley," *Journal of Modern History*, xviii (Mar. 1946), pp. 1-21. See also Christopher Hill, "The English Civil War Interpreted by Marx and Engels," *Science & Society*, xii (Winter 1948), pp. 130-156.

In the following century social critics appeared both in England and in France who attacked the prevailing order out of consideration for abstract ideas of justice, equality, and humanity. For a brief treatment of Wallace, Spence, Godwin, and Hall see Max Beer, *A History of British Socialism* (New York, 1940, 2 vols. in 1), i, pp. 84-87, 101-142. The French socialists Morelly, Boissel, Saint-Just, Mably, and Barnave are discussed in W. B. Guthrie, *Socialism before the French Revolution* (New York, 1907, 339 pp.), chaps. 6-8. For more extended treatment see André Lichtenberger, *Le Socialisme au XVIIIᵉ siècle* (Paris, 1895, 471 pp.). The following monographs treat socialist aspects of the revolution: Daniel Guérin, *La Lutte de classes sous la Première République; bourgeois et 'bras nus' (1793-1797)* (Paris, 1946, 2 vols.); André Lichtenberger, *Le Socialisme et la Révolution française* (Paris, 1899, 316 pp.); *Essays on the French Revolution*, by Thorez, Duclos, and other French communists first issued in *Cahiers du communisme*, 1939 (tr. by William Zak; ed. with intro. by T. A. Jackson; London, 1945, 211 pp.); E. B. Bax, *The Last Episode of the French Revolution; Being a History of Gracchus Babeuf and the Conspiracy of the Equals* (London, 1911, 271 pp.); René Montgrenier, *Gracchus Babeuf* (Paris, 1937, 79 pp.); F. Buonarroti, *Buonarroti's History of Babeuf's Conspiracy for Equality* (tr. by J. B. O'Brien; London, 1836, 454 pp.); Gérard Walter, *Babeuf, 1760-1797, et la conjuration des Égaux* (Paris, 1937, 262 pp.); and F. N. Babeuf, *La Doctrine des Égaux* (ed. by Albert Thomas; Paris, 1906, 96 pp.). Excerpts from Babeuf's writings have been edited with an introduction by M. Dommanget, *Pages choisies de Babeuf* (Paris, 1935, 330 pp.). For the influence of Babeuf see Georges Sencier, *Le Babouvisme après Babeuf* (Paris, 1912, 348 pp.). A recent biography by David Thomson,

The Babeuf Plot (London, 1947, 123 pp.), traces the subject's influence on later socialists and their theories.

Nineteenth-century socialists before Marx often criticized existing conditions as incisively and realistically as the Marxians. In their proposals for reconstruction, the utopians, filled with anger at the status quo, optimistically minimized the difficulties of the social situation. They had too easy a faith in appeals to the virtuous instincts of men, the revolutionary effects of proper education, the power of suggestion by the example of successful small communistic groups, or the sustaining force of revitalized religion. They sought to avoid conflict; the Marxians took it for granted and sought to exploit it. General sources and studies include Arnold Ruge, *Briefwechsel und Tagebuchblätter . . . 1825-1880* (ed. by Paul Nerrlich; Berlin, 1886, 2 vols.), I (1825-1847); Friedrich Muckle, *Die Geschichte der sozialistischen Ideen im 19. Jahrhundert* (Leipzig, 1909, 2 vols.), I, published later as *Die grossen Sozialisten* (4th ed., Leipzig, 1920, 2 vols.), I; Louis Reybaud, *Études sur les réformateurs* (7th ed., Paris, 1864, 2 vols.), I, containing studies of Saint-Simon, Fourier, and Owen.

The leading English utopian was Robert Owen, who put great faith in the regenerative power of education and environment. For the most important writings of the first period of his activity (1812-1821) see Robert Owen, *A New View of Society & Other Writings* (Everyman's Library, No. 799; intro. by G. D. H. Cole; London, 1927, 298 pp.), especially *A New View of Society* (1813-1814), pp. 1-90, and *Report to the County of Lanark* (1820), pp. 245-298. Owen's autobiography up to 1822, *The Life of Robert Owen* (London, 1857-1858, Vol. 1-1A), was republished (New York, 1920, 352 pp.) without the supplementary volume of 1858. In his early essays, Owen's utilitarian and rationalist assumptions are apparent, especially in his emphasis upon the inculcation of the hedonistic view that individual happiness depends upon the recognition of and dedication to the general welfare. For the literature on Owen and Owenism in the United States, see PART II, Topic 5. Returning from the United States, Owen looked for the solution to the social problem through trade unions and cooperatives (1828-1834). Notable in his third period was his *Outline of the Rational System of Society* (1830; London, 1831, 4 pp., and many other eds.), and *Lectures on the Marriages of the Priesthood of the Old Immoral World, Delivered in . . . 1835* (4th ed., Leeds, 1840, 92 pp.), a work later singled out for unfavorable criticism by the Fourierists in order to distinguish themselves from Owen's unorthodoxy. His interest in communities revived with the failure of his Grand National Consolidated Trades Union and was expressed in *The Book of the New Moral World* (1836-1844; 1st American ed., New York, 1845, 264 pp.; French ed., tr. and abr. Paris, 1847,

72 pp.); and *A Development of the Principles and Plans on Which to Establish Self-Supporting Home Colonies* (London, 1841, in three sections, 79, 47, 12 pp.), a detailed plan stressing the inequality of rich and poor published and circulated by the Home Colonization Society, affiliated with the Owenite community at Harmony Hall. *The Revolution in the Mind and Practice of the Human Race* (London, 1849, 171 pp.), was a vigorous restatement, the core of which could be found in his 1830 *Outline*. During the 1850's Robert Owen published profusely on spiritualism. The standard life by Frank Podmore, *Robert Owen, a Biography* (London, 1906, 2 vols.), contains a full bibliography of his published works, Volume 2, pp. 655-667. See also the inaccurate but extensive guide to materials by and about Owen issued by the National Library at Aberystwyth, Wales, *A Bibliography of Robert Owen, the Socialist, 1771-1858* (2nd ed., Aberystwyth, 1925, 90 pp.), and the lists in G. D. H. Cole, *The Life of Robert Owen* (2nd ed., London, 1930, 349 pp.), pp. 337-342. All of Owen's biographers tend to overemphasize his early career. W. L. Sargant, *Robert Owen and His Social Philosophy* (London, 1860, 446 pp.), is largely biographical and uncritical, as is *The Life, Times and Labours of Robert Owen* (2nd ed., ed. by W. C. Jones; London, 1895, 443 pp.), by Owen's associate, Lloyd Jones. The principal periodicals with which Owen was connected were the *Economist* (London, 1821-1822); *London Co-operative Magazine* (London, 1826-1830, title varies); *New Moral World* (London, etc., 1834-1846), with a regular section on the history of communities; and *Robert Owen's Journal* (London, 1850-1852).

Titles dealing with the British communities at Orbiston, Scotland, which lasted only a few weeks in 1826, and Harmony Hall, Queenwood, England, are Alexander Cullen, *Adventures in Socialism: New Lanark Establishment and Orbiston Community* (Glasgow, 1910, 329 pp.), and G. J. Holyoake, *A Visit to Harmony Hall!* (London, 1844, 27 pp.). Among the English equalitarians more radical than Owen who influenced him during the 1820's were William Thompson, author of *An Inquiry into the Principles of the Distribution of Wealth* (London, 1824, 600 pp.), and *Practical Directions for the Speedy and Economical Establishment of Communities* (London, 1830, 265 pp.); and John Gray, who wrote *A Lecture on Human Happiness* (1825; London, 1931, 72 pp., 16 pp.), and *The Social System; a Treatise on the Principle of Exchange* (Edinburgh, 1831, 374 pp.). The Philadelphia edition of Gray's *Lecture* (1826) was used in the constitution of the Valley Forge, Pa., Owenite community. Samples of the mass of polemics for and against Owenism are J. Hamilton, *Owenism Rendered Consistant with Our Civil and Religious Institutions* (London, 1825, 38 pp.), and *The Human Eccaleobion; or, The New Moral Warren* (London, 1842, 48 pp.). See also James Bonar, "Robert

Owen," *Economic History,* III (Jan. 1934), pp. 93-128, an imaginary dialogue which discusses Owen's secular utopianism with reference to Bentham, Malthus, and Marx; and F. M. Page, "Robert Owen and the Early Socialists," in *The Social & Political Ideas of Some Representative Thinkers of the Age of Reaction & Reconstruction, 1815-1865* (ed. by F. J. C. Hearnshaw; London, 1932, 219 pp.), chap. 5. A. E. Bestor, Jr.'s recent work, *Backwoods Utopias: The Sectarian and Owenite Phases of Communitarian Socialism in America, 1663-1829* (Philadelphia, 1950), compares Owen's theory with Fourier's in the early part of his book.

Charles Fourier developed his utopianism much more fully than did Saint-Simon (see PART I, General Reading, pp. 10-11). The millennium would be introduced through the organization of social units called phalanxes in which the "passions" would for the first time achieve harmonious development. Fourier's *Oeuvres complètes* (2nd ed., Paris, 1841-1845, 6 vols.) include only three of his longer writings, and nearly all of his work remains untranslated. Hubert Bourgin, *Étude sur les sources de Fourier* (Paris, 1905, 98 pp.), and E. Silberling, *Dictionnaire de sociologie phalanstérienne; guide des oeuvres complètes de Charles Fourier* (Paris, 1911, 459 pp.), serve as guides to others. Charles Fourier, *Oeuvres choisies* (ed. by Charles Gide; Paris, 1890, 232 pp.), is translated by Julia Franklin as *Selections from the Works of Fourier* (London, 1901, 208 pp.). Contemporary commentaries and elaborations of Fourierist theory are found in *Phalange* (Paris, 1832-1849, title varies); in Édouard de Pompery, *Théorie de l'association et de l'unité universelle de C. Fourier* (Paris, 1841, 384 pp.); Zoé Gatti de Gamond, *Fourier et son système* (5th ed., Paris, 1841-1842, 384 pp.), a popularized version; V. P. Considérant, *Destinée sociale* (Paris, 1834-1844, 3 vols.); and two works translated by the American Associationist F. G. Shaw: Mathieu Briancourt, *The Organization of Labor and Association* (1845; New York, 1847, 103 pp.), and Charles Pellarin, *Life of Charles Fourier* (2nd ed., New York, 1848, 236 pp.). An English apology was Hugh Doherty's *False Association and Its Remedy* (London, 1841, 167 pp.). Two contemporary descriptions of a modified phalanx in France are J. B. A. Godin, *Social Solutions* (1871; tr. by Marie Howland; New York, 1887, 326 pp.), by the founder, and Bernhard Becker, *Karl Fourier; Nebst einem Anhang: Der Social-Palast oder das Familistere in Guise* (Braunschweig, 1874, 93 pp.). See also the University of Geneva thesis by Léon Dunand, *Le Familistère de Guise* (Geneva, 1933, 179 pp.). The course of the Fourierist school is traced by Adolphe Alhaiza, second editor of *Rénovation,* one of its later organs, in *Historique de l'École Sociétaire fondée par C. Fourier* (Paris, 1894, 152 pp.). E. S. Mason in "Fourier and Anarchism," *Quarterly Journal of Economics,* XLII (Feb. 1928), pp. 228-262, finds that Owen and Fourier had a common source in natural law and the contractual view of society; that Fourier had none of Owen's understanding of mechanized industry but based his system on agricultural hand-labor. The most detailed biography is Hubert Bourgin, *Fourier* (Paris, 1905, 617 pp.), a doctoral thesis by a Marxian socialist. Bourgin's characterization of Fourier as a petty-bourgeois reactionary is modified by Maurice Lansac, *Les Conceptions méthodologiques et sociales de Charles Fourier; leur influence* (Paris, 1926, 144 pp.), which emphasizes the theoretical relationships between Fourierism and Marxism. See also August Bebel, *Charles Fourier, sein Leben und seine Theorien* (1888; 3rd ed., Stuttgart, 1907, 271 pp.). This relationship is recognized and receives a variety of comment by J.-M. Jeanneney, "Les Disciples de Fourier et la révolution de 1848," *Revue des sciences politiques*, LVI (Jan.-Mar. 1933), pp. 91-110; Adolphe Alhaiza, *Vérité sociologique, gouvernementale et réligieuse; succinct résumé du sociétarisme de Fourier comparé au socialisme de Marx* (Paris, 1919, 79 pp.); Morris Friedberg, *L'Influence de Charles Fourier sur le mouvement social contemporain en France* (Paris, 1926, 180 pp.); Werner Wessel, *Charles Fourier als Vorläufer der modernen Genossenschaftsbewegung* (Bergisch-Gladbach, 1929, 75 pp.); Auguste Pinloche, *Fourier et le socialisme* (Paris, 1933, 195 pp.); and Aníbal Ponce, *Dos hombres: Marx, Fourier* (Mexico, D.F., 1938, 63 pp.). For his relation to other movements see Charles Gide, *Fourier, précurseur de la coopération* (Paris, 1924, 204 pp.), and F. Armand and R. Maublanc, *Fourier* (Paris, 1937, 2 vols.), which incorporates Armand's earlier treatment of the connections between Proudhon and Fourierism. Consult Georges Sourine, *Le Fouriérisme en Russie; contribution à l'histoire du socialisme russe* (Paris, 1936, 127 pp.), as a sample study indicating the spread of the movement.

The romantic socialism of the contemporary writer Étienne Cabet is expressed in his classic utopian novel, *Voyage . . . en Icarie* (Paris, 1840, 2 vols. in 1), translated into German as *Reise nach Ikarien* (Paris, 1847, 541 pp.), and into Spanish as *Viaje por Icaria, Aventuras de lord Carisdall* (Barcelona, n.d., 2 vols.). Parts appeared in English in the *Popular Tribune* (Nauvoo, Ill., 1851). His other writings are polemical and reveal an identification of communism with "true" Christianity common to the rest of the French utopians. Jules Prudhommeaux, *Icarie et son fondateur, Étienne Cabet* (Paris, 1907, 688 pp.), which has a good bibliography and is the standard monograph on the Icarian movement, devotes one-third of the volume—pp. 1-200, also published separately as *Étienne Cabet et les origines du communisme icarien* (Nîmes, 1907, 218 pp.)—to its European phases. Cabet wrote a great deal besides his utopian novel. For years he was editor of *Populaire* (Paris, 1833-1835, 1841-1851), and in addition was a prolific pamphleteer. Among the works which cast particular light on his ideas are *Histoire populaire de la Révolution française de 1789 à 1830* (Paris, 1839-1840, 4 vols.; also later editions), not, however, important in the historiography of the revolution; *Comment je suis communiste et Mon credo communiste* (1841; 5th ed., Paris, 1847, 31 pp.), first published as two separate pamphlets; and *Le Vrai christianisme suivant Jésus-Christ* (Paris, 1846, 636 pp.). Biographies of Cabet include that published by *Populaire*, Cabet's journal, *Biographie de M. Cabet* (Paris, 1846, 112 pp.); Henry Carle and J. P. Beluze, *Biographie de Étienne Cabet, fondateur de l'école icarienne* (Paris, 1861-1862, 192 pp.); and Félix Bonnaud, *Cabet et son oeuvre* (Paris, 1900, 198 pp.). See also the following sketches: André Lichten-berger, "Cabet, Étienne," *Encyclopaedia of the Social Sciences*, III (1930), pp. 131-132; A. Crié, "Cabet," *La Grande encyclopédie*, VIII (1889), pp. 595-596; and A. Isambert, "Cabet," *Nouvelle biographie générale*, VIII (1855), cols. 20-25. Georges Bourgin, "Materialen zur Geschichte des Cabetismus unter dem zweiten Kaiserreiche," *Archiv für die Geschichte des Sozialismus und der Arbeiterbewegung*, IV (1914), pp. 466-478, publishes and comments on sources connected with the Second Empire's repression of the Icarians, and Cabet's trial for embezzlement of the funds collected for the American colony.

The General Reading discusses Louis Blanc under French socialism, Pierre Joseph Proudhon under anarchism, and Ferdinand Lassalle under German socialism.

Topic 3. ʽThe First and Second Internationals

The first International Workingmen's Association was formed in London in 1864. Its purpose was to promote the interests of labor through exchange of information between the member organizations in various countries leading to concerted international action. Its chief historic importance, however, lay in the fact that it became one of the agencies for the dissemination of Marxian doctrines throughout Europe. Groups affiliating with the International represented such divergent theories as liberal trade unionism, the cooperative "mutualism" of Proudhon, Lassalle's social democratic program, besides orthodox Marxism. Its activities were therefore confined to organizational propaganda, the raising of funds to assist strikers, and the dissemination of information. The International was doomed to failure by the conflicting views of its members, by the bitter struggle between Marx and Bakunin, and by its support of the Paris Commune of 1871, which alienated the trade unionists. The final rupture between the followers of Marx and Bakunin occurred in 1872, when the Marxists voted to transfer the headquarters of the International from London to New York in order to remove the threat of anarchist control. The Bakuninists then established their own International, but both wings quietly expired by 1878.

The Second or Socialist International was formed in 1889, the significant portion of its career terminating with the outbreak of war in 1914. Under the leadership of German socialists Marxian doctrines dominated the International, the communist-anarchism derived from Bakunin being excluded in 1896. During the active years of the Socialist International the divergent tendencies in Marx's teachings became fully developed in several schools of thought, each claiming true inspiration from Marx. Karl Kautsky's exposition of traditional Marxism did not prevent his followers from dividing on the question of parliamentary reforms in relation to the coming proletarian revolution. More fundamental was the split between orthodox socialists and the Bernstein revisionists who rejected the idea of "the" revolution in favor of social reforms secured by collaboration with liberal and progressive groups. Finally, Fabians, trade unionists, and syndicalists remained strong in England, France, and the United States. In spite of these divisions, however, the years before World War I witnessed the steady growth of socialist strength in Europe. It was already apparent that socialism in the major countries profited in part from liberal nationalism, and the International was unable to take a strong stand on the war issue. With few exceptions the outbreak of war found large majorities in each national socialist party supporting their respective governments. The International, although it maintained official existence, ceased to be a body of any importance.

A view of the aims and histories of the first two Internationals and the various socialist doctrines represented in them can be derived from L. L. Lorwin, *Labor and Internationalism* (New York, 1929, 682 pp.), pp. 29-59, 63-96, 134-146; Y. M. Steklov, *History of the First International* (tr. by E. and C. Paul; New York, 1928, 463 pp.), pp. 13-78, 248-254, 304-321; and R. P. Dutt, *The Two Internationals* (London, 1920, 92 pp.), pp. 49-54.

Documentary material relating to the First International has been collected by L. E. Mins, ed., *Founding of the First International: a Documentary Record* (New York, 1937, 96 pp.). Among other items this collection includes Marx's "Address and Provisional Rules of the Workingmen's International Association." Steklov (cited above) contains extensive references to the sources on the annual congresses of the International and literature not mentioned below. The Marx-Engels-Lenin Institute has begun the publication, with commentary and indices, of the reports of the congresses with *Londonskaya konferentsiya Pervogo Internatsionala* (Moscow, 1936, 345 pp.). Reflecting the anarchist point of view is the compilation of James Guillaume, *L'Internationale: documents et souvenirs, 1864-1878* (Paris, 1905-1910, 4 vols.). Oscar Testut has written several books, such as *L'Internationale et le jacobinisme au ban de l'Europe* (Paris, 1872, 2 vols.). The most entertaining account is that by R. W. Postgate, *The Workers' International* (London, 1920, 125 pp.). Other general histories are Gustav Jaeckh, *Die Internationale* (Leipzig, 1904, 236 pp.); Edmond Villetard, *History of the International* (tr. by S. M. Day; New Haven, Conn., 1874, 259 pp.); and Arne Ording, *Den Første Internasjonale* (Oslo, 1936, 370 pp.). Arthur Müller-Lehning, "The International Association (1855-1859); a Contribution to the Preliminary History of the First International," *International Review for Social History*, III (1938), pp. 185-286, discusses the correspondence and activities of Polish, German, and French refugees in London cooperating with former Chartists. For background, see also V. N. Cherkezov, *Précurseurs de l'Internationale* (Brussels, 1899, 144 pp.), and Theodore Rothstein, "The Forerunners of the International," in his book, *From Chartism to Labourism* (New York, 1929, 365 pp.), pp. 124-181. Gaspare Ambrosini, *Marx, Mazzini e l'internazionale socialista* (Campobasso, 1917, 35 pp.), calls attention to the connections between the First International and the internationalist democratic movement.

The story of the Paris Commune, a crucial event for the Workers' International, was told by Karl Marx, *The Civil War in France* (1871; intro. by Engels; New York, 1940, 96 pp.). Georges Bourgin, author of *Histoire de la Commune* (Paris, 1907, 191 pp.), points out in "La Lutte du gouvernement français contre la Première Internationale," *International Review for Social History*, IV (1939), pp. 39-138, that the relation between the First International and the Commune, assumed ever since to be intimate, has not yet been critically examined. He illustrates with documents the efforts of Foreign Minister Jules Favre to persuade other powers to attack the International, and the course of the punitive bill introduced by Thiers in the National Assembly. M. A. Fabre, *Vie et mort de la Commune, 1871* (Paris, 1939, 253 pp.), based upon court-martial papers in the Ministry of War archives, is, on the other hand, convinced that the First International was responsible for the uprising. In this connection see Samuel Bernstein, "The First International on the Eve of the Paris Commune," *Science & Society*, v (Winter 1941), pp. 24-42. An account of Bakunin's conflict with Marx is contained in Fritz Brupbacher, *Marx und Bakunin* (Munich, 1913, 199 pp.). The followers of Proudhon, with whom the Marxists came into conflict, derived their "mutualist" doctrines chiefly from P. J. Proudhon, *De la capacité politique des classes ouvrières* (Paris, 1865, 455 pp.). For the role of Proudhonism in the International see J. L. Puech, *Le Proudhonisme dans l'Association internationale des travailleurs* (Paris, 1907, 247 pp.). A French socialist of considerable influence in the early days of the International was Auguste Blanqui, who is believed to have inspired Marx's theory of the dictatorship of the proletariat. See E. S. Mason, "Blanqui and Communism," *Political Science Quarterly*, XLIV (Dec. 1929), pp. 498-527. For his major writings see L. A. Blanqui, *La Patrie en danger* (Paris, 1871, 359 pp.); *L'Armée esclave et opprimée* (Paris, 1880, 35 pp.); and *Critique sociale* (Paris, 1885, 2 vols.). The standard biography is Gustave Geffroy, *L'Enfermé* (rev. ed., Paris, 1926, 2 vols.). See also Maurice Dommanget, *Blanqui* (Paris, 1923, 96 pp.), and Neil Stewart, *Blanqui* (London, 1939, 352 pp.). Blanqui's influence in France is described by Charles da Costa, *Les Blanquistes* (Paris, 1912, 69 pp.).

A general account of the Socialist International is Josef Lenz, *Rise and Fall of the Second International* (New York, 1932, 285 pp.). Sample reports of individual congresses are *Protokoll des Internationalen Arbeiter-Congresses zu Paris . . . 14. bis 20. juli 1889* (Nürnberg, 1890, 133 pp.); J. M. Davidson, *Anarchist Socialism v. State Socialism at the London International Labour Congress (1896)* (London, 1897?, 24 pp.), reprinted from the English socialist periodical, *Clarion*; Augustin Hamon, *Le Socialisme et le Congrès de Londres* (Paris, 1897, 280 pp.); and Daniel De Leon, *Flashlights of the Amsterdam International Socialist Congress, 1904* (New York, 1904?, 150 pp.). The classic expression of Marxism in the Second International is Karl Kautsky, *The Class Struggle (Erfurt Program)* (tr. by W. E. Bohn; Chicago, 1910, 217 pp.), the program accepted by the German social democrats in 1891.

Since the nationalism of the sections destroyed the Socialist International when World War I broke out, references in the General Reading to the socialism of different European countries are pertinent here. Representative of the large volume of literature on the dilemma of the International at the outbreak of war written by contemporaries and prominent members of the International are Émile Vandervelde's collection of anti-German speeches and open letters, *La Belgique envahie et le socialisme international* (Paris, 1917, 234 pp.); the first section of Henri de Man, *The Remaking of a Mind* (New York, 1919, 289 pp.); A. W. Humphrey, *International Socialism and the War* (London, 1915, 167 pp.), based on English newspapers; and Omer Boulanger, *L'Internationale socialiste a vécu* (Paris, 1915, 312 pp.). See also the documentary collection of Alfred Rosmer, *Le Mouvement ouvrier pendant la guerre* (Paris, 1936, 588 pp.). W. E. Walling, ed., *The Socialism of To-day* (New York, 1916, 642 pp.), and *The Socialists and the War* (New York, 1915, 512 pp.), source books, and *Socialism as It Is* (New York, 1912, 452 pp.), together constitute an American's sanguine interpretation of socialist prospects and an unconscious epitaph for the Second International. For the conclusions of later scholars see Merle Fainsod, *International Socialism and the World War* (Cambridge, Mass., 1935, 238 pp.), and Austin Van der Slice, *International Labor, Diplomacy, and Peace, 1914-1919* (Philadelphia, 1941, 408 pp.). V. I. Lenin, *The War and the Second International* (London, 1931, 63 pp.), and the Menshevik

P. B. Akselrod, *Die russische Revolution und die sozialistische Internationale* (ed. by I. G. Tsereteli and V. S. Voitinsky; Jena, 1932, 205 pp.), treat the background and earliest stages of the Third International in its relation to the Second.

The Labor and Socialist International was essentially a different institution, maintaining the old organization after World War I, and holding several conferences up to 1933. See *The Moscow Trial and the Labour and Socialist International* (London, 1931, 47 pp.), compiled by its secretariat, and Heinrich Ehrlich, *The Struggle for Revolutionary Socialism* (tr. by Haim Kantorovitch and Anna Bercowitz; New York, 1934, 62 pp.), a report on the conference of 1933 in Paris. R. R. Abramovitch, "Towards Reconstitution of the International: Underlying Issues," *Modern Review*, i (Sept. 1947), pp. 516-524, discusses the alternatives faced by the Labor and Socialist International in relation to communist power in Europe after World War II.

Topic 4.   The Third and Fourth Internationals

The Third International grew out of the Russian Revolution and the Zimmerwald movement of socialists who denounced the World War as imperialist. In three conferences (Zimmerwald, 1915; Kienthal, 1916; Stockholm, 1917) the Left came under the leadership of Lenin, and through the movement's continuing International Socialist Commission at Berne and later at Stockholm maintained contact until replaced by the Communist International in 1919. With the prestige of a successful revolution, the Bolsheviks dominated the Comintern from the start. The original purpose of the Comintern was to promote world proletarian revolution. To that end it called on Socialist parties to purge their membership of liberal nationalists and reformist elements, break with the Second International, and agitate, legally or illegally, among the soldiers, farmers, and industrial workers.

The divisions and internal conflicts which had troubled the earlier Internationals plagued the communists also. The Trotskyist Left was expelled in 1928 over issues of Soviet economic development, the Chinese Revolution, and Anglo-Russian relations. After Trotsky's exile from Siberia to Istanbul in 1929, the Left opposition sought to remain a faction of the Comintern. By appeal to its executive committee and through propaganda the opposition hoped to change the majority policy. The Right deviation of 1929, following Bukharin, first set up an all-inclusive International Bureau of Revolutionary Socialist Unity at London in 1933. The Left opposition would not participate and later lost to the London Bureau the Spanish and Dutch Trotskyist adherents of popular fronts. In 1934 the Trotskyist International Communist League united with Dutch and German groups in a call for the organization of a new international. Schism continued, but the factions of eleven countries organized the Fourth International in Switzerland in September 1938. The London Bureau broke up before World War II. With the death of Trotsky in 1940 and the progress of World War II the movement, never comparable in power to the Comintern, lost focus. As Trotsky's prediction of revolution in one or more economically advanced European countries failed to materialize, Trotskyists of no one country had the preponderance to enforce democratic centralism in ideology or practical politics. Meanwhile the Comintern was successively an instrument of revolution, Russian factional struggles, and Russian foreign policy until its formal dissolution in 1943. Communist representatives announced on October 5, 1947, the formation of a voluntary organization, with headquarters in Belgrade (moved to Bucharest in 1948), to exchange information and coordinate Communist Party policy in nine European countries. While the Cominform (i.e., Information Bureau of the Communist and Workers Parties) did not have the binding legislative authority among Communist parties that the Third International had, as its differences with Yugoslav communists in the summer of 1948 indicated, it publicly reemphasized the internationalist aspect of communism.

The readings below bring out in short compass the splits and changes of policy of the Third International, following new developments in Russian and world history; the relation of the Trotskyist program for permanent world revolution to the original Comintern platform; and some of the differences and similarities in the organization of the two internationals.

On the Third International see Franz Borkenau, *The Communist International* (London, 1938, 442 pp.), pp. 22-56, 161-181, 296-318, 413-429; Martin Ebon, *World Communism Today* (New York, 1948, 536 pp.), especially for developments and new leaders since Borkenau wrote, for its sketches of communism in minor countries, and for its bibliography, pp. 499-515; O. A. Pyatnitsky, *The Twenty-one Conditions of Admission into the Communist International* (New York, 1934, 32 pp.), pp. 27-32; and Georgi Dimitrov (general secretary of the Comintern executive committee), *The United Front: the Struggle against Fascism and War* (New York, 1938, 287 pp.), pp. 262-269. On the Fourth International see Ann Vincent, "How the Fourth International Was Conceived," *Fourth International*, v (Aug. 1944), pp. 243-246, which covers the period from the first meetings with Trotsky at Paris in 1930 to August 1933; J. G. Wright, "Trotsky's Struggle for the Fourth International," *Fourth International*, vii (Aug. 1946), pp. 235-238; *The Death Agony of Capitalism and the Tasks of the Fourth International* (New York, 1946, 64 pp.), the transitional program adopted by the founding conference; and "Only Victorious Socialist Revolutions Can Prevent the Third World War!"

the manifesto of the Brussels Conference of 1946, which is available in the *Militant*, x (May 11, 1946), pp. 1-2, 7.

Studies of the war situation from which the Bolsheviks rose to power are found in O. H. Gankin and H. H. Fisher, *The Bolsheviks and the World War; the Origin of the Third International* (Stanford University, Calif., 1940, 856 pp.), which includes a comprehensive critical bibliography of monographs and periodicals (pp. 729-770). See also the general studies of the Socialist International cited in Topic 3 above. Of these Lenz's ends with the sixth world congress in 1928 and was endorsed by the Comintern. The Zimmerwald movement is summarized by Austin Van der Slice, *International Labor, Diplomacy, and Peace, 1914-1919* (Philadelphia, 1941, 408 pp.), pp. 49-56. The Hoover War Library has in progress a documentary study of the establishment of the Comintern and its first congress, to be called *The Bolsheviks and World Revolution; the Organization of the Third International*, a sequel to Gankin and Fisher.

The so-called Two and a Half International, composed of the left wing of the Second, is discussed in Lenz and Lorwin, cited in Topic 3, and in a Comintern document, *The Second and Third Internationals and the Vienna Union* (London, 1922, 94 pp.). See also Otto Bauer, *Bolschewismus oder Sozialdemokratie?* (Vienna, 1920, 120 pp.), and Karl Radek's reply, *Theorie und Praxis der 2½ Internationale* (Hamburg, 1921, 56 pp.). *The New Communist Manifesto of the Third International* (Glasgow, 1919, 12 pp.), constituted the Bolshevik call to world revolution, followed in 1920 by the twenty-one conditions cited above in Pyatnitsky. *The I.L.P. and the 3rd International* (London, 1920, 64 pp.), contains the questions submitted by the British Independent Labour Party delegation to the executive committee of the Comintern, its reply, and comments on the I.L.P. course. A Labour Party pamphlet of the united front period, *The Communist Solar System; the Communist International* (London, 1933, 23 pp.), calls attention to front organizations controlled by the Comintern. For information on some of these, see Willi Münzenberg, *Solidarität; zehn Jahre Internationale Arbeiterhilfe, 1921-1931* (Berlin, 1931, 527 pp.), and Andrés Nin, *Las organizaciones obreras internacionales* (Madrid, 1933, 205 pp.).

Miscellaneous publications issued by the executive committee and various reports and documents of the seven world congresses held at Moscow between 1919 and 1935 have been published in English translations. The bibliography of Philip Grierson, *Books on Soviet Russia (1917-1942)* (London, 1943, 354 pp.), pp. 131-152, provides an introduction to the sources. See especially the handbook, *The Communist International between the Fifth & the Sixth World Congresses, 1924-8* (London, 1928, 508 pp.), for the organization of the executive committee, the

International Control Commission, and reports from national sections. *Communist International* (Leningrad, New York, etc., 1919-1940), and *International Press Correspondence, English Edition* (Vienna, London, 1921-1938) continued as *World News and Views* (1938-1941), official organs published in several languages, are full of day-to-day events in the development of the Comintern. See also *Unter dem Banner des Marxismus* (Vienna, Berlin, 1925-1935), international commun'st theoretical journal. The publication of the recently organized Cominform is *For a Lasting Peace, for a People's Democracy* (Bucharest, etc., 1947-), published weekly in several languages. The official "Programme of the Communist International," in Emile Burns, *A Handbook of Marxism* (New York, 1935, 1087 pp.), pp. 963-1042, was a draft by Bukharin and Stalin approved by the world congress of 1928, superseding the work of the previous six years. Trotsky's elaborate critical comment on this draft, accompanying an appeal for reinstatement, first published in its entirety in German in 1929, is best available in English as *The Third International after Lenin* (tr. by J. G. Wright; intro. by Max Shachtman; New York, 1936, li, 357 pp.). *Blueprint for World Conquest* (Washington, 1946, 263 pp.), with an introduction by W. H. Chamberlin, reprints in full the essential Comintern documents of 1920 and 1928.

For a complete case history on the failure of communist propaganda in a major industrial center of a major power during the noncollaborationist period of the Comintern, 1929-1935, see H. D. Lasswell and Dorothy Blumenstock, *World Revolutionary Propaganda; a Chicago Study* (New York, 1939, 393 pp.). The material is analyzed in terms of channels, techniques, volume, and environmental and psychological facilitations and restrictions. Samples of ultraconservative alarmist literature on bolshevism are N. H. Webster, *World Revolution, the Plot against Civilization* (London, 1921, 327 pp.), and Hamilton Fish, *The Challenge of World Communism* (Milwaukee, Wis., 1946, 224 pp.) and *The Red Plotters* (New York, 1947, 103 pp.). Webster finds Jews and Freemasons at the bottom of bolshevism, and Fish asserts that Stalinist pressure for world revolution has actually increased since the dissolution of the Comintern. More substantial and still hostile is Ypsilon (pseud.), *Pattern for World Revolution* (Chicago, 1947, 479 pp.). The Infantry Journal Press has republished as *Communism; Its Plans and Tactics* (Washington, 1949, 102 pp.), the report of a subcommittee of the U.S. House Committee on Foreign Affairs, originally entitled *The Strategy and Tactics of World Communism*. "Historicus" (believed to be George A. Morgan, first secretary of the United States embassy at Moscow), concludes in "Stalin on Revolution," *Foreign Affairs*, xxvii (Jan. 1949), pp. 175-214, that Stalin ultimately intends world revolution, but not for another fifteen or twenty years. A French attack is Pierre Dominique (pseud.), et al., *Bilan du communisme* (Paris, 1937, 212 pp.), which includes sections on propaganda methods. Trotskyist accounts of the Comintern are C. L. R. James, *Wo ld Revolution, 1917-1936; the Rise and Fall of the Communist International* (London, 1937, 429 pp.), and Leon Trotsky, *The First Five Years of the Communist International*, I (1924; tr. and ed. by J. G. Wright; New York, 1945, 374 pp.; Vol. 2 is forthcoming).

The prolific writings of Tro sky, prime exponent of permanent world revolution, repeat the central ideas of the Fourth International. R. D. Warth, "Leon Tro sky; Writer and Historian," *Journal of Modern History*, xx (Mar. 1948), pp. 27-41, is a critical b bliographical essay emphasizing Trotsky's history of the Russian Revolution. Representative titles are *The Pe manent Revolution* (tr. with intro. by Max Shachtman; New York, 1931, xlviii, 157 pp.), an exposition of Trotsky's own thesis that to endure the socialist revolution must be world-wide, and that each stage of the revolution must be built on the preceding one until the class society is liquidated; *Stalinism and Bolshevism: Concerning the Historical and Theoretical Roots of the Fourth International* (New York, 1937, 29 pp.); and *The New Course* (New York, 1943, 265 pp.). *The Founding Conference of the Fourth International* (New York, 1939, 127 pp.) deals directly with its organization. *Byulleten oppozitsii (bolshevikov-lenintsev)* (Paris, etc., 1929-1941) edited by Trotsky's son, Leon Sedov, until his death in 1938, was the chief Trotskyist international organ.

Manifestos, theses, and resolutions adopted by the executive committee, the European secretariat, and the national sections are printed in the *Fourth International* (New York, 1940-), theoretical organ of the American Trotskyists. See for example II (Oct. 1941), pp. 229-231, in defense of the Soviet Union; v (May 1944), pp. 148-149, on the war position of the British Trotskyist fusion party; v (Oct. 1944), pp. 299-307, on the Indian question; vi (Mar., May 1945), pp. 78-86, 150-154, on changing the imperialist war into civil war and setting transitional goals; and vii (June 1946), pp. 169-187, on the international conference in Belgium, April 1946. The *Manifesto . . . on the Imperialist War and the Proletarian Revolution* was published as a pamphlet (New York, 1940, 47 pp.).

The Shachtmanite faction of the American Trotskyists split off in 1940 because it did not view Russia as a workers' state to be defended. Yet it considered its Workers Party a proponent of the Fourth International although this party was rejected by the 1946 conference. In May 1949 the Workers Party became the Independent Socialist League. The Cannonite Socialist Workers Party did not formally affiliate with the Fourth International because of the Voorhis Act barring parties with foreign or international allegiance. The *New International*, the Workers Party organ taken from the Cannonites has published such documents as "Capitalist Barbarism or Socialism," x (Oct. 1944), pp. 329-352, by German Trotskyists in exile, which predicts world rule by one monopoly capitalist country and outlines the function of the Fourth International opposition. Shachtman, *ibid.*, x (May 1944), pp. 135-137, indicates that the Italian section took his position on Russia. Felix Morrow of the Socialist Workers Party minority which some years ago joined the Workers Party, in his "On the Tempo in Europe," xII (Feb. 1946), pp. 49-53, calls for transitional aid to European democracies since Trotsky's last prediction of European revolution failed to materialize.

Topic 5. *Socialism and Capitalism*

Socialism and capitalism represent distinct but historically inseparable tendencies of Western civilization. Although capitalism has played much the more dominant role—at least in the modern period—the socialist ideal has always been present and has exhibited an independent vitality of its own. Formulated as a rule of the primitive Christian church and preserved as an organizing principle of the monastic order, the ideal survived the rise of capitalism to become in our own day a serious competitor to capitalism. Nevertheless, the respective developments of the capitalist and socialist ideals have always been intimately interrelated. Each has gone through approximately the same intellectual evolution, first attaching itself to the ethical sanctions of Christianity and then later repudiating these for a more secular and even materialistic philosophical basis. And each has also influenced the other either by setting itself up in opposition—as in the "red scare" of contemporary capitalism and in the Marxian doctrine of the class struggle—or by borrowing from each other—as in the case of Marx's development of classical economics.

But although historically interrelated, capitalism and socialism are fundamentally antithetical. In their modern form, each analyzes personality and society in terms of basically different needs and potentialities, and each prescribes, accordingly, a completely different institutional schematization and quite different codes of personal behavior. This contrast exists, moreover, not only in theory but in practice, and it is with the contrasts in practice that we shall be concerned here. Taking as its focal point the type of individual and the type of social philosophy each system tends to encourage, materials are selected to provide a basis for describing, contrasting, and evaluating the personal and social standards of the hypothetically ideal capitalist and the hypothetically ideal communist. For an analysis of the ideal businessman, see Werner Sombart, *The Quintessence of Capitalism: a Study of the History and Psychology of the Modern Business Man* (tr. and ed. by M. Epstein; New York, 1915, 400 pp.), chaps. 1, 4, 7, 8, 11, 12; and for an analysis of the ideal Communist Party member in Soviet Russia, see Sidney and Beatrice Webb,

Soviet Communism: a New Civilisation? (London, 1935, 2 vols.), I, pp. 339-353, 373-376, 401 407; II, pp. 1017-1143.

All important modern analyses of capitalism take their positions in the light of the investigations of Marx. The most suggestive and probably the most important sociological and historical studies in this succession are those of Max Weber, Ernst Troeltsch, R. H. Tawney, and Werner Sombart. Marx's thesis, stripped of the qualifications some Marxians find, posed ideology as the by-product of institutions and defined capitalism as a system of productive relations developed independently of human direction. Weber, while he had considerable respect for Marx, emphasized rather the *Geist* or spirit of Protestantism as producing capitalism. His earliest statement of this thesis is *The Protestant Ethic and the Spirit of Capitalism* (tr. by Talcott Parsons; London, 1930, 292 pp.). Troeltsch, in *The Social Teaching of the Christian Churches* (tr. by Olive Wyon; New York, 1931, 2 vols.), accepted Weber's point of view and carried it into a more intensive study of Christian history. Tawney, in *Religion and the Rise of Capitalism* (London, 1926, 339 pp.), asserted that Protestantism did not *create* the capitalist *Geist*, but merely prepared the way for it. Sombart, in a long series of studies, *Die Juden und das Wirtschaftsleben* (Leipzig, 1911, 476 pp.), *Der Bourgeois* (Munich, 1913, 540 pp.), *Der moderne Kapitalismus* (Munich, 1928, 3 vols. in 6), brilliantly recapitulated in his article, "Capitalism," *Encyclopaedia of the Social Sciences*, III, pp. 195-208, pointed out that Catholicism, Judaism, and even nonreligious factors were also important. *Modern Capitalism* will shortly be available in a complete English translation by K. F. Geiser. Sombart's work constitutes one of the most massive sociological analyses of capitalism to appear in our time. Among other books criticizing Weber's thesis as oversimplified are H. M. Robertson, *Aspects of the Rise of Economic Individualism* (Cambridge, Eng., 1933, 223 pp.), and Lujo Brentano, *Die Anfänge des modernen Kapitalismus* (Munich, 1916, 199 pp.). Amintori Fanfani, on the other hand, denied any intimate relationship between modern Christianity and the rise of capitalism in *Catholicism, Protestantism, and Capitalism* (London, 1935, 224 pp.).

An older analysis of capitalist culture which does not follow Weber is found in Thorstein Veblen, *The Theory of the Leisure Class* (New York, 1899, 400 pp.), *The Theory of Business Enterprise* (New York, 1904, 400 pp.), and *The Engineers and the Price System* (New York, 1921, 169 pp.). H. J. Laski, *The Rise of Liberalism; the Philosophy of a Business Civilization* (New York, 1936, 327 pp.), and Miriam Beard, *A History of the Business Man* (New York, 1938, 779 pp.), are general histories of business and its points of view. The preeminent English Marxist economist is Maurice Dobb, whose *Studies in the Development of Capitalism* (London, 1946, 396 pp.) analyzes certain aspects in the light of the labor theory of value.

No comparably objective literature exists on the sociological analysis of the socialist culture of Soviet Russia, the chief country where socialism has achieved complete power. Probably the best over-all account in English is that of Sidney and Beatrice Webb, cited above, which undertakes a complete and detailed survey in a sympathetic and often uncritical spirit. Less comprehensive critical accounts are W. H. Chamberlin, *Russia's Iron Age* (Boston, 1934, 400 pp.), Eugene Lyons, *Assignment in Utopia* (New York, 1937, 658 pp.), and Harry Best, *The Soviet Experiment* (New York, 1941, 120 pp.). The symposium edited by Margaret Cole, *Twelve Studies in Soviet Russia* (London, 1933, 282 pp.), maintains a generally favorable bias with some individual objections. Ella Winter, *Red Virtue; Human Relationships in the New Russia* (New York, 1933, 332 pp.), J. F. Hecker, *Moscow Dialogues* (London, 1933, 284 pp.) and *The Communist Answer to the World's Needs* (London, 1935, 322 pp.), and Hewlett Johnson, *The Soviet Power* (New York, 1940, 352 pp.), are frankly laudatory. Trotsky, *Problems of Life* (tr. by Z. Vengerova; New York, 1924, 114 pp.), discusses the public morals of the period under Lenin, and *The Soviet Comes of Age* (London, 1938, 337 pp.) contains studies by Soviet officials and citizens on Russian economics, politics, and culture. A comprehensive study is projected by Joseph K. Folsom, comparing the social organization and cultures of the United States, Great Britain, France, and the U.S.S.R. For titles on specific features of Soviet society see PARTS IV-VI.

General criticisms of socialism are Max Weber, *Der Sozialismus* (Vienna, 1918, 36 pp.), Victor Cathrein, *Socialism* (tr., rev., and enl. by V. F. Gettelmann, S.J.; New York, 1904, 424 pp.), and Adolf Weber, *In Defense of Capitalism* (tr. by H. J. Stenning; London, 1930, 128 pp.). Albert Hyma, *Christianity, Capitalism, and Communism* (Ann Arbor, Mich., 1937, 303 pp.), is a suggestive investigation of the historical interrelationships of the three movements. General comparisons of the economic aspects of capitalism and socialism began as early as John Carruthers, *Communal and Commercial Economy* (London, 1883, 334 pp.). Other comparisons are Otto Bauer, *Kapitalismus und Sozialismus nach dem Weltkrieg* (Vienna, 1931, 226 pp.); A. C. Pigou, *Socialism versus Capitalism* (London, 1937, 138 pp.); Eugen Varga, *Two Systems: Socialist Economy and Capitalist Economy* (tr. by R. P. Arnot; New York, 1939, 268 pp.); and J. A. Schumpeter, *Capitalism, Socialism, and Democracy* (New York, 1942, 381 pp.). Oscar Newfang, *Capitalism and Communism; a Reconciliation* (New York, 1932, 278 pp.), emphasizes similarities and argues for a long unhampered trial of both systems. C. A. Peters has compiled a manual, *American Capitalism vs. Russian*

Communism (New York, 1946, 305 pp.), with a useful selected bibliography (pp. 289-305).

Topic 6.   Literary Utopias and Socialist Utopianism

As one proposal for social change, socialism has been called utopian both on the ground that its analysis of existing social conditions is unrealistic and that the means it proposes for attaining its goals are impractical. Utopia means "nowhere" in Greek, and was related in the mind of Sir Thomas More, who coined the word, to *eutopia*, "the good place." These three connotations came to apply to the tradition of dialogues, essays, and narratives called utopias: their mythical nature, their perfection, and their disregard for or relatively unscientific treatment of given conditions and means. The opponents of socialism sought to defeat it by identifying it with these literary utopias. It is ironical to see Marxians since Engels using the utopian label to discredit the non-Marxian socialists.

The sociological research led by Karl Mannheim, showing Marxian influence in his class theory and in his attitude toward science and religion, both broadened and complicated the utopian concept. Trying to give it objective meaning, Mannheim applied the term to aspects of any theoretical system insofar as it is based on myth rather than evidence and logic.

Originally, Mannheim states, the primitive mythical mind of man created symbolic substitutes to escape from frustrating reality. As civilization developed, these myths became mixed with a progressively enlarged ingredient of science. As long as such myths have continued to motivate action, they have taken two forms, according to the class alignment of the believer. The ruling classes have used them as "ideologies" to stabilize the existing society. The subject masses, especially in times of economic or political disintegration, have converted them as "utopias" into subversive social doctrines. Mannheim uses "utopia" to denote both the myth-oriented system in general and the proletarian form in particular. Outbreaks of the utopian spirit were strongest in such troubled times and places as the Israel of the prophets; the Athens of the Peloponnesian wars; the Roman Empire at the time of Jesus; at the breakdown of European feudalism; and during the industrial revolution. During such crises, myth was a collectivizing force, conservative with the rulers and radical with the masses. New phases of social reality, the results of utopian collective action, paradoxically revealed the practical side of utopianism.

Rather than emphasize the invidious use of "utopian" as a slogan, profitable investigation could be undertaken to discern: (1) the myth-oriented and the science-oriented elements in socialist and utopian analyses of their contemporary societies; (2) whether the means of social change advocated are compatible with these analyses; and (3) whether the goals are in keeping with human and institutional potentialities and with proposed transitional programs. As a general introduction to such study read Karl Mannheim, "Utopia," *Encyclopaedia of the Social Sciences*, xv, pp. 200-203, which summarizes the main ideas in his *Ideology and Utopia* (tr. by Louis Wirth and Edward Shils; New York, 1936, 318 pp.), pp. 173-236; J. O. Hertzler, *The History of Utopian Thought* (New York, 1923, 321 pp.), pp. 257-314; and Georges Sorel, "Y a-t-il de l'utopie dans le marxisme?" *Revue de métaphysique et de morale*, vii (Mar. 1899), pp. 152-175.

The Marxian view that ideas and ideals reflect class interest is found in Friedrich Engels, *Socialism, Utopian and Scientific* (tr. by E. Aveling; London, 1892, 117 pp.), a section of his *Anti-Dühring*. For further references see General Reading, pp. 34-39 on Marx and Engels, PART III on historical materialism, and PART V on the sociology of knowledge and the psychology of socialism. The utopian element is, of course, prominent in the religious socialism treated in Topics 1, 2, and 7. For Marxian eschatology see Henri de Man, *The Psychology of Socialism* (tr. from 2nd German ed. by E. and C. Paul; New York, 1927, 509 pp.), especially pp. 97-194; and PART IV, Topic 12, on the classless society. Gertrud Hermes, *Die geistige Gestalt des Marxistischen Arbeiters und die Arbeiterbildungsfrage* (Tübingen, 1926, 331 pp.), a penetrating analysis of popular Marxism, points out that the irreligious proletariat has unconsciously reproduced many phases of traditional Christian thought, including the eschato'ogical Armageddon of "the final conflict" of classes. K. R. Popper, *The Open Society and Its Enemies* (rev. ed., Princeton, N.J., 1950, 732 pp.), is a notable analysis of the historical struggle between social science and social myth. Popper comments with decreasing emphasis on Plato, Hegel, and Marx as primarily responsible for hampering the development of rational social thought.

European literary utopias of major importance include Plato's *Republic*, More's *Utopia* (1516), Andreae's *Christianopolis* (1619), Campanella's *City of the Sun* (1623), Bacon's *New Atlantis* (1627), Harrington's *Oceana* (1656), Hertzka's *Freeland* (1890), Morris' *News from Nowhere* (1891), and H. G. Wells' *A Modern Utopia* (1905). C. B. Renouvier, *Uchronie (l'utopie dans l'histoire)* (1876; 2nd ed., Paris, 1901, 412 pp.), curiously transforms the utopian pattern by sketching the development of European civilization as it might have happened. This highly selective list should be supplemented by reference to Emilie Schomann, *Französische Utopisten des 18. Jahrhunderts und ihr Frauenideal* (Berlin, 1911, 192 pp.), pp. 8-20, which lists most of the important French, German, English, Italian, Spanish, Scandinavian, and Russian utopias; and Jerome Davis' table in his *Contemporary Social Movements* (New York, 1930, 901 pp.), pp. 64-68, which adds more.

General surveys of literary and socialist utopias usually confine themselves to the major examples. Lewis Mumford, *The Story of Utopias* (New York, 1922, 315 pp.), like Hertzler's sociological analysis cited above, rejects in part the Marxian evaluation. Mumford distinguishes types according to their emphasis on contemporary society, on the transition, or on the ultimate state. An early summary in England, covering from More to Marx, is by the Christian socialist Moritz Kaufmann, *Utopias; or Schemes of Social Improvement* (London, 1879, 267 pp.). Other English accounts are Paul Bloomfield, *Imaginary Worlds* (London, 1932, 283 pp.), and Harry Ross, *Utopias Old and New* (London, 1938, 252 pp.). For Continental points of view, see A. Gehrke, *Communistische Idealstaaten* (Bremen, 1878, 46 pp.); Friedrich Kleinwächter, *Die Staatsromane* (Vienna, 1891, 152 pp.); Giovanni de Castro, *Vecchie utopie* (Milan, 1895, 312 pp.); André Lichtenberger, *Le Socialisme utopique* (Paris, 1898, 277 pp.); E. H. Schmitt, *Der Idealstaat* (Berlin, 1904, 232 pp.); and Aleksander Swiętochowski, *Utopie w Rozwoju Historycznym* [*Utopias in Historical Development*] (Warsaw, 1910, 347 pp.). The selection of Ernst Bloch in *Freiheit und Ordnung; Abriss der Sozial-Utopien* (New York, 1946, 189 pp.) is unusually comprehensive and classifies the nineteenth-century utopians according to their centralist or decentralist tendencies. Martin Buber, *Paths in Utopia* (tr. by R. F. C. Hull; London, 1949, 152 pp.), seeks to show that the utopians had a much truer perception of the conditions necessary for the fulfillment of the socialist ideal than the Marxians. Other recent surveys of literary utopias from antiquity to the present are M. L. Berneri, *Journey through Utopia* (London, 1950, 339 pp.), and Raymond Ruyer, *L'Utopie et les utopies* (Paris, 1950, 293 pp.).

Concerning special aspects of utopias, education is the subject of Joseph Prys, *Der Staatsroman der 16. und 17. Jahrhunderts und sein Erziehungsideal* (Würzburg, 1913, 165 pp.), and Gildo Massó, *Education in Utopias* (New York, 1927, 201 pp.). Wolfgang Simon, *Die englische Utopie im Lichte der Entwicklungslehre* (Breslau, 1937, 89 pp.), discusses the influence of evolutionary ideas after 1870; Schomann's work, cited above, deals with the position of women; Fritz Gerlich, *Der Kommunismus als Lehre vom tausendjährigen Reich* (Munich, 1920, 275 pp.), and A. Dietsch, *Das tausendjährige Reich* (Aarau, 1844?, 95 pp.), with millennialism; and Fernando Vida Nájera, *Estudios sobre el concepto y la organización del estado en las "Utopias"* (Madrid, 1928, 458 pp.), and Gerhard Ritter, *Machtstaat und Utopie; vom Streit um die Dämonie der Macht seit Machiavelli und Morus* (3rd-4th ed., Munich, 1943, 194 pp.), with political theory.

Of the individual utopias, none has received such intensive study as More's. Karl Kautsky, *Thomas More and His Utopia* (1888; tr. by H. J. Stenning; New York, 1927, 250 pp.), is still a good introduction to More's realistic analysis of early modern capitalism but fails to put More into his historical setting. A. E. Morgan, *Nowhere Was Somewhere* (Chapel Hill, N.C., 1946, 234 pp.), argues that More derived the outlines of Utopia from his knowledge of Inca society and concludes with a favorable discussion of the utopian concept as the catalyst of social evolution. See also S. A. Zavala, *La "Utopía" de Tomás Moro en la Nueva España y otros estudios* (Mexico, D.F., 1937, 60 pp.), and R. A. Ames, *Citizen Thomas More and His Utopia* (Princeton, N.J., 1949, 230 pp.), a three-dimensional analysis of the author, the times, and the book.

Topic 7. *Religious and Scientific Socialism*

Since the eighteenth century, socialist thought has tended to divide roughly into religious and scientific schools so called. Examples of socialist thinking inspired by essentially religious or secular motives can of course be found in earlier times, but with the humanistic tendencies of the Enlightenment and especially with the self-ascribed scientific rigor of Marxism the distinction becomes more clearly drawn. All pre-Marxian socialists thought of themselves as expressing the true essence of Christianity, and the sectarians among them were definitely religious by the strictest construction of the term. Marxians themselves have been the group to insist most vehemently on the importance of the distinction. Such thoroughgoing materialists as Engels and Lenin have written philosophical treatises to reaffirm Marx's teaching that his system was a scientifically verifiable analysis of the laws of historical process. One hundred years after Marx the distinction between scientific and religious socialism seems much less clear than the Marxians conceived it to be. On the one hand the older Christian dichotomy between nature and the supernatural has often tended to become slurred over in a more recent emphasis on divine immanence which enables Christian social thinkers to take a position similar to that of many secularists. On the other hand, recent critics especially have questioned the scientific rigor of Marxism, and have laid bare the utopian, ethical, and even religious elements present in characteristic Marxian thinking. In the nineteenth century, however, the division between the two schools of thought was usually clear and significant.

What passed for Christian socialism in the nineteenth century appears today to be a pale moral intention based on righteous indignation at the conditions of industrial labor, and often a yearning for a return to medieval Christian communalism. The leaders were as vague about the new society that their church should foster as they were vehement against both the failures of existing society and the nonreligious efforts to find a solution. Their ideas varied between guild socialism and reformism. Men like Kingsley and Maurice in England and Ketteler and Huber in Germany were often political conservatives who looked to the existing state and its aristocracy for a partnership with the church in paternalistic measures. Their constructive efforts, therefore, were in the direction of workmen's cooperatives and reconciliation of industrial conflict. At the same time they struggled within their churches for ecclesiastical reforms. Catholics combated anticlericalism and sustained the influence of the Papacy.

The subject, divided chronologically, is concerned with (a) the nineteenth-century contrasts between Christian social movements and Marxian socialism, and (b) twentieth-century developments. For the nineteenth century the focus is on England, France, Germany, and the Papacy, while the modern problem resolves itself into an examination of the Soviet attitude toward religion, the religion of communism, and the later developments in European religious socialism. As an introduction to these subdivisions read Will Herberg, "The Christian Mythology of Socialism," *Antioch Review*, III (Spring 1943), pp. 125-132.

A. NINETEENTH CENTURY. The classic expression of Marxian materialism is Friedrich Engels, *Herr Eugen Dühring's Revolution in Science* (1877; tr. by Emile Burns and ed. by C. P. Dutt; New York, 1935, 364 pp.). For essential passages read excerpts in Emile Burns, *A Handbook of Marxism* (New York, 1935, 1087 pp.), pp. 240-256, 299-301. E. B. Bax, *The Religion of Socialism* (3rd ed., London, 1891, 177 pp.), pp. 48-53, 92-99, states the English Marxian criticism of the current Anglican socialism and discriminates between the religious and nonreligious aspects of his own creed. Further references to the Marxian attitude toward religion are cited in PART V, Topic 9. Rev. S. D. Headlam, et al., *Socialism and Religion* (London, 1908, 87 pp.), "Christian Socialism," pp. 5-26, and Rev. Moritz Kaufmann, *Christian Socialism* (London, 1888, 232 pp.), pp. xi-xviii, 1-34, present the Anglican point of view. Kaufmann's book is the only comparative study of nineteenth-century European Christian socialism, but it overstates the importance of Lamennais in France and is an illustration of the fuzziness of most of English Christian socialist thought. G. C. Binyon's *The Christian Socialist Movement in England* (London, 1931, 238 pp.) is the standard work on English Christian socialism, and in it (pp. 143-154) the Guild of St. Matthew, criticized by Bax, is fitted into its minor place in the movement. M. B. Reckitt, *Maurice to Temple* (London, 1947, 245 pp.), supplements Binyon on a century of the social movement in the Church of England.

Excerpts from W. E. von Ketteler, *Die Arbeiterfrage und das Chris-*

tenthum (3rd ed., Mainz, 1864, 212 pp.), translated in D. O. Wagner, ed., *Social Reformers* (New York, 1939, 749 pp.), pp. 272-287, provide an introduction to the social thinking of a prominent German Catholic bishop who pioneered in the Social Catholic movement. The effect of Pope Leo XIII's encyclical, *Rerum novarum* (May 15, 1891), which confirmed the social ideas of Ketteler and French Catholics like Count Albert de Mun, is evaluated in P. T. Moon's survey, *The Labor Problem and the Social Catholic Movement in France* (New York, 1921, 473 pp.), pp. 157-193.

The relation of nineteenth-century socialism to Christianity is exemplified by four titles dealing with German Marxism. Reinhart Seeger, *Friedrich Engels; die religiöse Entwicklung des Spätpietisten und Frühsozialisten* (Halle, 1935, 207 pp.), discusses how Christianity and socialism came to separate. The view that the socialist workers should be the core of the church was expressed by C. Boruttau, *Religion und Sozialismus* (Leipzig, n.d., 64 pp.), written in 1869. See also Joseph Dietzgen, *Die Religion der Sozialdemokratie* (6th ed., Berlin, 1903, 48 pp.), written about the same time, and Ferdinand Goldstein, *Urchristentum und Sozialdemokratie* (Zurich, 1899, 191 pp.). Sample accounts of the Christian attitude toward property are Ludwig Felix, *Der Einfluss der Religion auf die Entwicklung des Eigenthums* (Leipzig, 1889, 388 pp.), and the anonymous *Histoire de la communauté des biens dans l'antiquité et dans l'ère chrétienne* (Nancy, 1866, 2 vols.).

On the English Christian socialist movement, C. E. Raven, *Christian Socialism, 1848-1854* (London, 1920, 396 pp.), is standard for the early period. Bibliographies are found in Lujo Brentano, *Die christlich-soziale Bewegung in England* (2nd ed. enl., Leipzig, 1883, 124 pp.), pp. 75-78, and E. R. A. Seligman, "Owen and the Christian Socialists," *Political Science Quarterly*, I (June 1886), pp. 206-249. Charles Kingsley (1819-1875), the literary propagandist of the movement, has received much more attention than the founder, J. M. Ludlow, or its leader, F. D. Maurice. Its London weekly organ was *Politics for the People* (1848) succeeded by the *Christian Socialist* (1850-1851) with an interval between when a series, *Tracts on Christian Socialism*, was published. Kingsley's novels, *Alton Locke* (London, 1850, 2 vols.) and *Yeast* (New York, 1851, 292 pp.), discuss the predicaments of the city tailor and the farm laborer. Mrs. Charles Kingsley (Frances Eliza Grenfell) in *Charles Kingsley; His Letters and Memoirs of His Life* (1877; London, 1901, 2 vols.) idealizes her husband; Bishop C. W. Stubbs, *Charles Kingsley and the Christian Social Movement* (London, 1899, 199 pp.), is more judicious. *Social Morality* (1869; London, 1893, 414 pp.), is a sample of Maurice's prolific writings, and *The Life of Frederick Denison Maurice, Chiefly Told in His Own Letters* (New York, 1884, 2 vols.) is edited by his son, Frederick Maurice. For Maurice's beliefs see A. R. Vidler, *The Theology of F. D. Maurice* (Toronto, 1949, 248 pp.); A. M. Ramsey's *F. D. Maurice and the Conflicts of Modern Theology* (announced for 1951; Cambridge, Eng.); and H. G. Wood, *Frederick Denison Maurice* (Cambridge, Eng., 1950, 170 pp.). Among other studies in English nineteenth-century Christian socialism are the following: H. U. Faulkner, *Chartism and the Churches* (New York, 1916, 152 pp.); William Blissard, *The Ethic of Usury and Interest; a Study in Inorganic Socialism* (London, 1892, 194 pp.); W. H. Abraham, *The Studies of a Socialist Parson* (Hull, 1892, 220 pp.); Rev. William Nicholas, *Christianity and Socialism* (London, 1893, 220 pp.); A. V. Woodworth, *Christian Socialism in England* (London, 1903, 208 pp.); and Conrad Noel, *Socialism in Church History* (London, 1910, 284 pp.). C. P. McEntee, *The Social Catholic Movement in Great Britain* (New York, 1927, 312 pp.), describes the group around Cardinal Manning (1808-1892). The Socialist Quaker Society published *Tracts* (London, 1898-1901, 2 nos.).

Besides the work of Kaufmann and Moon on the French Social Catholic movement cited above, see the following: Hugues Félicité Robert de Lamennais (1782-1854), *Paroles d'un croyant; Le Livre du peuple; . . . De l'esclavage moderne* (Paris, 1937, 355 pp.), a reprinting of several essays written in the 1830's; Charles Périn, *Le Socialisme chrétien* (Paris, 1879, 74 pp.); Paul Ribot, *Du rôle social des idées chrétiennes* (Paris, 1879, 2 vols.); Joseph Félix, S.J., *Christianisme et socialisme* (Paris, 1879, 359 pp.); Henri Joly, *Le Socialisme chrétien* (Paris, 1892, 336 pp.); and Count Albert de Mun, *Ma vocation sociale; souvenirs de la fondation de l'Œuvre des cercles catholiques d'ouvriers (1871-1875)* (Paris, 1909, 254 pp.).

In Germany the Catholic tradition is represented by Franz von Baader (1765-1841), Bishop Ketteler (1811-1877), and Wilhelm Hohoff (1848-1923). Hohoff made extended and repeated efforts to reconcile Catholic and Marxian doctrines. See, for example, his reply to Bebel, *Christenthum und Sozialismus* (Hottingen-Zurich, 1887, 16 pp.), *Die Bedeutung der Marxschen Kapitalkritik* (Paderborn, 1908, 338 pp.), and two historical studies, *Protestantismus und Socialismus* (2nd ed. rev., Paderborn, 1883, 226 pp.) and *Der Revolution seit dem sechszehnten Jahrhundert im Lichte der neuesten Forschung* (Freiburg im Breisgau, 1887, 759 pp.). See Baader's *Sämmtliche Werke* (Leipzig, 1850-1860, 16 vols. in 9), and Fritz Werle, ed., *Franz Baader und sein Kreis* (Leipzig, 1924, 304 pp.), a collection of letters. Ketteler, *Die grossen socialen Fragen der Gegenwart* (Mainz, 1849, 92 pp.), was looked upon as his Church's answer to the *Communist Manifesto*. See also his *Soziale Schriften* (Essen, 1908, 117 pp.); J. J. Laux (George Metlake, pseud.), *Christian Social Reform; Program Outlined by Its Pioneer, William Emmanuel, Baron von Ketteler*

(Philadelphia, 1912, 246 pp.), which includes extracts from Ketteler's otherwise untranslated writings; and Albert Franz, *Der soziale Katholizismus in Deutschland bis zum Tode Kettelers* (Munich, 1914, 259 pp.). See also Heinrich Pesch, S.J., *Liberalismus, Socialismus und christliche Gesellschaftsordnung* (2nd ed., Freiburg, 1898-1901, 3 vols. in 5).

The Protestant social movement began with Victor Aimé Huber (1800-1869), an aristocratic former Catholic who longed for Christian reunion. See his *Sociale Fragen* (Nordhausen, 1863-1869, 7 pts. in 1 vol.), and *Ausgewählte Schriften über Socialreform und Genossenschaftswesen* (ed. by K. Munding; Berlin, 1894, cxviii, 1204 pp.). Other Protestant contributors to the movement were the conservative anti-Semitic Adolf Stöcker, *Christlich-sozial Reden und Aufsätze* (Bielefeld-Leipzig, 1885, 526 pp.), and Paul Göhre, *The Evangelical-Social Movement in Germany* (1896; abridged tr. by J. E. K. Shuttleworth; London, 1898, 236 pp.).

Three books dealing with both Protestant and Catholic socialism are Rudolf Todt, *Der radikale deutsche Socialismus und die christliche Gesellschaft* (Wittenberg, 1877, 479 pp.), August Erdmann, *Die christliche Arbeiterbewegung in Deutschland* (2nd ed., Stuttgart, 1909, 718 pp.), and Ernst Adam, *Die Stellung der deutschen Sozialdemokratie zu Religion und Kirche (bis 1914)* (Gelnhausen, 1930, 130 pp.). A view of socialism which tends to fuse the secular and religious traditions is expressed in Werner Sombart, *Socialism and the Social Movement* (tr. by M. Epstein; London, 1909, 319 pp.).

F. S. Nitti, *Catholic Socialism* (tr. from 2nd [1891] Italian ed. by Mary Mackintosh; London, 1911, 432 pp.), and Eduardo Soderini, *Socialism and Catholicism* (tr. by R. Jenery-Shee; London, 1896, 342 pp.), are examples of Italian writings in this field. The circumstances surrounding Pope Leo XIII's attitudes on socialism and the Social Catholic movement are discussed in Soderini's *Il pontificato di Leone XIII* (Milan, 1932-1933, 3 vols.). See also *The Great Encyclical Letters of Pope Leo XIII* (New York, 1903, 580 pp.), influential against scientific socialism, and J. C. Husslein, *The Christian Social Manifesto* (Milwaukee, Wis., 1931, 328 pp.). For echoes of Christian socialism in Hispanic America, see Zorobabel Rodríguez (1839-1901), *Tratado de economía política* (Valparaiso, 1894, 434 pp.). This Chilean scholar is the subject of several monographs, e.g., S. B. Rodríguez, *Malthus, Z. Rodríguez y el socialismo cristiano* (Quillota, Chile, 1906, 71 pp.).

B. TWENTIETH CENTURY. A convenient collection of Lenin's thoughts on religion scattered through his writings has been published separately under the title, *Religion* (London, 1931?, 56 pp.). From the great quantity of religious writings on the relation of communism and Christianity read N. A. Berdyaev, *The Origin of Russian Communism* (New

York, 1937, 239 pp.), pp. 191-229. The author (1874-1948) was a former Bolshevik well versed in Russian intellectual history and a prolific but sometimes obscure writer on the problems of religion and philosophy. For the English Protestant point of view read John Macmurray, *Creative Society* (New York, 193[?], 113 pp.), pp. 74-113. John Spargo, *Marxian Socialism and Religion* (New York, 1915, 187 pp.), pp. 127-179, surveys sketchily the relations between socialist parties and the churches before World War I. Wilhelm Schneemelcher and W. Liese summarize the Protestant and Catholic movements with emphasis on Germany in "Christlich-soziale Bestrebungen," *Handwörterbuch der Staatswissenschaften* (4th ed.), III, pp. 174-196.

V. I. Lenin, *Materialism and Empirio-Criticism* (*Collected Works*, XIII; tr. by David Kvitko and Sidney Hook; New York, 1927, 342 pp.; excerpts in Burns, *A Handbook of Marxism*, pp. 634-673), is the classic twentieth-century expression of the ideas in the earlier *Herr Eugen Dühring's Revolution in Science* of Engels. Karl Kautsky, *Foundations of Christianity* (tr. from 13th German ed.; New York, 1925, 480 pp.), and Heinrich Cunow, *Ursprung der Religion und des Gottesglaubens* (Berlin, 1913, 164 pp.), were much used as antireligious propaganda in the early Soviet period, but later were rejected as dangerous because—among other things—Cunow employed Taylor's theory of animism and Kautsky connected early Christianity with the movement of the Roman proletariat. Serge Bolshakoff, *The Christian Church and the Soviet State* (New York, 1942, 75 pp.), enumerates fifteen concessions to Christianity and the Christian church. The Roman Catholic N. S. Timasheff, however, in *Religion in Soviet Russia, 1917-1942* (New York, 1942, 171 pp.), insists that these were only minor concessions, since religious liberty is a hollow shell without free speech and a free press. Earlier pro-Soviet writings are J. F. Hecker, *Religion and Communism; a Study of Religion and Atheism in Soviet Russia* (London, 1933, 302 pp.), by an American sociologist who defends the Soviet Union against the Orthodox Church, but who would like to preserve the ethics of Christianity in communism; and E. Yaroslavsky, *Religion in the U.S.S.R.* (New York, 1934, 64 pp.).

Writings on the relation of communism and Christianity became numerous during the Popular Front period, when both movements found a common enemy in fascism. Religious writers had taken up the problem before, particularly in Germany, as in the series of pamphlets, *Christentum und soziale Frage* (Munich, 1919-1921, 7 nos.), by Georg Merz and others. Paul Tillich, *The Religious Situation* (tr. by H. Richard Niebuhr; New York, 1932, 182 pp.), called socialism the religious "manifestation of the human situation in our own time." *Christianity and the Social Revolution*, edited by John Lewis and others (New York, 1936, 526 pp.), took up socialism in historical Christianity, the orthodox Marxist view of Christianity, and fascism as the common enemy. A collection of essays originally in the *Spectator* and edited by H. W. Harris, *Christianity and Communism* (Oxford, 1937, 77 pp.), presented the conflicting views of Dean Inge, John Strachey, Joseph Needham, and others. Among the socialist or communist treatments of the subject in the decade after 1932 were J. M. Murry, *The Necessity of Communism* (London, 1932, 136 pp.) and *The Necessity of Pacifism* (London, 1937, 132 pp.); Kenneth Ingram, *Christianity—Right or Left?* (London, 1937, 207 pp.); Benjamin Davies, *The New Social Order* (London, 1937, 93 pp.); and Roger Lloyd, *Revolutionary Religion; Christianity, Fascism and Communism* (London, 1938, 191 pp.). Murry warned that socialism without the pacifist Christian ethic would be barren; Ingram and Davies found the two movements compatible; and Lloyd avowed that only Christianity could maintain both national dignity and a community without classes. For titles published just after World War II, see Joseph Needham's essays, *History Is on Our Side; a Contribution to Political Religion and Scientific Faith* (New York, 1947, 226 pp.), and Alexander Miller, *The Christian Significance of Karl Marx* (London, 1946, 127 pp.), both by Anglicans and both favorable to communism.

For the continuation of the milder Christian socialist movement in England and on the Continent, see for England: G. C. Binyon, *The Christian Faith and the Social Revolution* (London, 1921, 88 pp.); M. B. Reckitt, *Faith and Society; a Study of the Structure, Outlook and Opportunity of the Christian Social Movement in Great Britain and the United States of America* (London, 1932, 467 pp.), and a collection of essays edited by the same author, *Prospect for Christendom; Essays in Catholic Social Reconstruction* (London, 1945, 255 pp.); and *Christianity and Social Order* (New York, 1942, 93 pp.) by the late Archbishop William Temple. *Prospect for Christendom* is a product of the Anglo-Catholic group. Harold Robbins, *The Sun of Justice* (London, 1938, 160 pp.), is an essay on Roman Catholic social doctrine. It holds that Catholicism is incompatible with the industrial development of society since industrialism denies the doctrine of human responsibility. H. G. Wood, an English Friend, attacks Marx's ethics of revolution, historical materialism, and the class struggle in *Christianity and Communism* (New York, 1933, 149 pp.), and defends the traditional British cooperative idea and the co-existence of public and private property.

For the Social Catholic movement, see the discussion of French Catholic trade-union problems in J. Zirnheld, *Cinquante années de syndicalisme chrétien* (Paris, 1937, 275 pp.), and E. Delaye, *Éléments de morale sociale inspirée des principes chrétiens* (Paris, 1939, 198 pp.). Zirnheld was president of the Confederation Française des Travailleurs Chrétiens. P. T. Moon, *The Labor Problem and the Social Catholic Movement in*

France (New York, 1921, 473 pp.), is of course standard for the period through World War I. French reactions to communism are found in Gérard Walter, *Histoire du communisme*, Vol. 1 (Paris, 1931, 623 pp.), which asserts the Judaeo-Christian roots of communism; also Robert Honnert, *Catholicisme et communisme* (Paris, 1937, 158 pp.), and François Mauriac and others, *Le Communisme et les chrétiens* (Paris, 1937, 265 pp.), both concerned with "la main tendue," the Popular Front tactics of the Comintern. Mexican publications include Mateo Solana y Gutiérrez, *La raíz mística del comunismo* (Oaxaca, 1933, 119 pp.), and Eduardo Iglesias, *Catolicismo y comunismo* (Mexico, D.F., 1939, 272 pp.). See also N. A. Berdyaev, *Christianity and Class War* (tr. by Donald Attwater; London, 1933, 123 pp.).

Works by Swiss and German writers represent the continued participation of Protestants and Catholics in the social democratic program. Johannes Kaster, *Die christlich-sozialen Ideen und die Gewerkschaftsfrage* (M.-Gladbach, 1922, 69 pp.), deals primarily with the Catholics. *They Must, or God and the Social Democracy* (ed. by R. W. Weeks; Chicago, 1908, 232 pp.), by the Reformed Church pastor in Zurich, Hermann Kutter, was also summarized with other essays in *Social Democracy; Does It Mean Darkness or Light?* (pref. by Richard Heath; Letchworth, Eng., 1910, 175 pp.). Kutter's Swiss disciple, Leonhard Ragaz, carried on the tradition of liberal, pacifist, Christian socialism in *Dein Reich komme* (3rd ed., Zurich, 1922, 2 vols.), and *Von Christus zu Marx; von Marx zu Christus* (Wernigerode, 1929, 203 pp.).

Topic 8. Marxian Socialism and Its Revolutionary Forms: Syndicalism and Communism

No single interpretation of Marxism is acceptable to all Marxians. This is in part attributable to the complex social and ideological changes which have taken place since the death of Marx and which have often forced upon even his most devoted disciples the necessity of compromise. It is also in part attributable to Marx himself. Writing, as he so frequently did, with different audiences and different situations in mind, it was inevitable that he should not always achieve complete consistency, or at least complete clarity, in the statement of his principles.

But whatever the causes, the Marxist movement has always been highly factional in character, particularly on the question of tactics. Among such Marxists who conceived the collapse of capitalism as still remote and far off, the tendency has been toward gradualism, reformism, and even revisionism, with exclusive reliance placed upon the associated peaceful methods of mass education and conventional parliamentary procedures. Among those Marxists, on the other hand, who feel the decline of capitalism imminent, emphasis has fallen upon the use of force as exemplified both in the general strike and in the seizure of governmental power by coups d'état. In recent years this revolutionary type of Marxism has been most spectacularly embodied in the syndicalist movement and in the emergence of twentieth-century communism.

Syndicalism is the revolutionary creed evolved between 1894 and 1914 by the two powerful French trade-union federations, the Fédération des Bourses du Travail and the Confédération Générale du Travail. Partly as a result of the infiltration of anarchist teachings, and partly expressive of the French workers' contempt for the orthodox French Marxist parties which had failed to provide adequate revolutionary leadership, syndicalism, although Marxist in orientation, departed from the orthodox view in three particulars: first, in its distrust of intellectualism, socialist intellectualism particularly; second, in its repudiation of all forms of political action; and third, in its proposal to decentralize control in the future classless society by vesting power federatively in local *syndicats* or trade unions. The second was its most striking characteristic since, under the leadership of Fernand Pelloutier, Émile Pouget, Georges Sorel, Hubert Lagardelle, and others, it abandoned all hope of achieving its ends through political association, and recommended, instead, such direct acts of violence against the capitalist system as the general strike, boycotts, and industrial sabotage. This was a "correction" of Marxism, syndicalists argued, justified by the new revolutionary situation.

Unlike syndicalism, twentieth-century communism does not eschew political methods but recognizes the need for political and nonpolitical methods alike. Originating about 1903 as a left-wing movement in the Second International, and finding its clearest expression in the writings of Lenin and in the program of the Third International, which Lenin helped found, communism argues that the rate of decline of capitalism has been increased by its present imperialistic form and that it is the task of Marxian leadership both to accelerate that decline by any means at its disposal and to prepare the workers, organizationally and ideologically, for a revolutionary seizure of the state. Also unlike syndicalism, communism emphasizes the need for a constant theoretical analysis of the immediate economic and political situation. And, finally, although like syndicalism in envisaging the classless society as in the end a voluntary association, unlike syndicalism it argues both for a preliminary stage of dictatorship by the proletariat and for the continuance of a centralized control of production even after the classless society has been ushered in.

Neither syndicalism nor communism has succeeded in maintaining its original revolutionary fervor. After the leftist persecutions which followed immediately upon World War I, syndicalism either disappeared altogether—as in Italy—or became more moderate in tone—as happened in France, for example, after the more revolutionary trade unions seceded from the C.G.T. in 1922 to affiliate with the Communist International. And after the Stalinist turn of 1924-1928 led to the rejection of Trotsky's conception of permanent revolution in favor of Stalin's principle of building socialism in one country, the various communistic parties outside of Russia tended to become local agencies of Soviet foreign policy or mere opponents of that policy.

The literature presented below, however, treats the two movements at their zenith rather than in their decline. The selection provides evidence of the relationship between them with particular regard to their conception of the class struggle and its eventual outcome, as well as evidence of the grounds each had for repudiating the tactics of the other. For background, see Sidney Hook, *Towards the Understanding of Karl Marx* (New York, 1933, 347 pp.), chaps. 3-7, inclusive, and II. W. Laidler, *Social-Economic Movements* (New York, 1944, 828 pp.), chaps. 22, 23, 24, which describe the historical origin of the two movements. For syndicalism, see, in addition, chaps. 1 and 4 of Georges Sorel's classic defense of "direct actionism," *Reflections on Violence* (tr. by T. E. Hulme; London, 1915, 299 pp.), which was originally published in the *Mouvement socialiste* in 1906 and has appeared since in at least nine French editions; and for communism, Joseph Stalin, "The Foundations of Leninism," in *Leninism* (London, 1940, 667 pp.), pp. 1-38, 58-71, which, although written from Stalin's own point of view, summarizes the basic tenets of revolutionary communism. Julien Steinberg, ed., *Verdict of Three Decades* (New York, 1950, 634 pp.), is an anthology of the literature of individual revolt against Soviet communism.

The following histories of the syndicalist movement in France are the best accounts in English and supplement one another chronologically: L. L. Lorwin, *Syndicalism in France* (2nd ed., New York, 1914, 229 pp.); Pierre Monatte and others, *Left Wing Trade Unionism in France* (London, 1922, 129 pp.); D. J. Saposs, *The Labor Movement in Post-War France* (New York, 1931, 508 pp.); and M. R. Clark, *A History of the French Labor Movement (1910-1928)* (Berkeley, Calif., 1930, 174 pp.). Additional material, however, may be found in Mlle. Kritsky, *L'Évolution du syndicalisme en France* (Paris, 1908, 426 pp.), a documentary history written from the syndicalist point of view; Paul Louis, *Histoire du mouvement syndical en France (1789-1910)* (3rd ed., Paris, 1920, 282 pp.), originally published in 1911, also written from the syndicalist point of view; Georges Moreau, *Essai sur les théories et l'histoire du syndicalisme ouvrier en France* (Paris, 1925, 355 pp.); and Georges Lefranc, *Histoire du mouvement syndical français* (Paris, 1937, 471 pp.). For a history of the movement at the height of its power outside as well as in France, see Paul Louis, *Le Syndicalisme européen* (Paris, 1914, 310 pp.). Other general studies are André Tridon, *The New Unionism*

(New York, 1913, 198 pp.); Édouard Dolléans, *Histoire du mouvement ouvrier* (Paris, 1936-1939, 2 vols.), II (1871-1936); and Michel Ralea, *L'Idée de révolution dans les doctrines socialistes* (Paris, 1923, 400 pp.). Werner Sombart, *Socialism and the Social Movement* (tr. by M. Epstein; London, 1909, 319 pp.), chap. 5, analyzes the general origins of syndicalism. Ernst Drahn, "Syndikalismus," *Handwörterbuch der Staatswissenschaften* (4th ed.), VII, pp. 1186-1193, has a good bibliography.

For some of the best statements of the syndicalist position, see Georges Sorel, *La Décomposition du marxisme* (Paris, 1908, 64 pp.), which points to the disintegration of political Marxism and the need for a revision of Marx in syndicalist terms. The same author's *L'Avenir socialiste des syndicats* (Paris, 1901, 88 pp.), first published in *L'Humanité nouvelle*, Mar.-May 1898, is an attack on the intellectual as a social parasite. Writings by and about Sorel are listed in Paul Delesalle, "Bibliographie sorélienne," *International Review for Social History*, IV (1939), pp. 463-487. Sorel's letters to this bibliographer, also an important syndicalist, are published as *Lettres à Paul Delesalle, 1914-1921* (Paris, 1947, 238 pp.). Recent commentaries on Sorel's place in the syndicalist movement are Jacques Rennes, *Georges Sorel et le syndicalisme révolutionnaire* (Paris, 1936, 187 pp.); Victor Sartre, *Georges Sorel; élites syndicalistes et révolution prolétarienne* (Paris, 1937, 307 pp.); and J. de Kadt, *Georges Sorel; het einde van een mythe* (Amsterdam, 1938, 192 pp.). Other statements by intellectuals who wrote for the syndicalist *Mouvement socialiste* (Paris, 1899-1914) are Édouard Berth, *La Fin d'une culture* (Paris, 1927, 222 pp.), an examination of the theory of history; the same author's *Guerre des états ou guerre des classes* (Paris, 1924, 440 pp.), and Hubert Lagardelle and others, *Syndicalisme et socialisme* (Paris, 1908, 64 pp.). Émile Pouget, who came to the movement from anarchism, attacked reformism and justified the use of sabotage in *Le Sabotage* (Paris, 1911?, 68 pp.; English tr., Chicago, 1913, 108 pp.). Pouget and Émile Pataud discussed syndicalist methods in *Comment nous ferons la révolution*, translated by C. and F. Charles as *Syndicalism and the Co-operative Commonwealth* (Oxford, 1913, 240 pp.).

For critiques of syndicalism, see J. R. Macdonald, *Syndicalism: a Critical Examination* (Chicago, 1913, 74 pp.), John Spargo, *Syndicalism, Industrial Unionism and Socialism* (New York, 1913, 243 pp.), and, especially, J. A. Estey's excellent analysis, *Revolutionary Syndicalism: an Exposition and a Criticism* (London, 1913, 212 pp.). J. W. Scott, *Syndicalism and Philosophical Realism: a Study in the Correlation of Contemporary Social Tendencies* (London, 1919, 215 pp.), is an unconvincing but still suggestive attempt to link the direct action philosophy of syndicalism with the epistemological realism of Bergson, Meinong, and Russell. For the history, analysis, and evaluation of the general strike, see W. H. Crook, *The General Strike* (Chapel Hill, N.C., 1931, 649 pp.), Hubert Lagardelle, ed., *La Grève générale et le socialisme: enquête internationale, opinions et documents* (Paris, 1905, 423 pp.), a collection of essays by prominent socialists of widely differing opinions, and Rosa Luxemburg, *Grève générale; parti et syndicats* (Brussels, 1936, 77 pp.).

The literature of revolutionary communism is so extensive and partisan that nothing like a complete listing or an adequate evaluation can yet be made. The introductory selection below, however, will be helpful. In the *Encyclopaedia of the Social Sciences* see Maurice Dobb's brief summary of the basic principles of communism, "Bolshevism," ii, pp. 623-630, and L. L. Lorwin's description of the national sections of the Comintern, "Communist Parties," iv, pp. 87-95. In *Handwörterbuch der Staatswissenschaften* (4th ed.), Supp., see H. J. Seraphim, "Bolshewismus," pp. 200-239, and "Lenin," pp. 678-685. R. W. Postgate, *The Bolshevik Theory* (New York, 1920, 240 pp.), is one of the first sympathetic accounts by an Englishman of what Leninist communism involves and how it differs from syndicalism, orthodox Marxism, and other related theories. Also see William Gallacher, *The Case for Communism* (Harmondsworth, Eng., 1949, 208 pp.), by a leading British communist.

The most important works of the Russian revolutionaries themselves are by Lenin. *Imperialism* (1916), a critique of the imperialist phase of capitalism in its relation to the rate of capitalist decline, and *The State and Revolution* (1917), a reformulation of the Marxian theory of the proletarian revolution, have both been issued in a number of editions by various publishers, e.g., *Imperialism; the State and Revolution* (New York, 1927, 225 pp.) by Vanguard, and by International, *State and Revolution* (New York, 1932, 103 pp.) and *Imperialism; the Highest Stage of Capitalism* (New York, 1939, 128 pp.). In this connection see *New Data for V. I. Lenin's Imperialism*, Eugen Varga and L. A. Mendelson, eds. (New York, 1939, 322 pp.). One should also read Lenin's speeches and writings of 1914-1917, Volumes 18-21 in the authorized translation, not yet completed by International Publishers, of his *Collected Works* (New York, 1927-). The Marx-Engels-Lenin Institute has published the collected works in Russian, *Sochineniya* (1st ed., with title *Sobranie Sochineny*, Moscow, 1920-1925, 25 vols.; 2nd ed., 1926-1932, 30 vols.; 3rd ed., 1928-1937, 30 vols.; 4th ed., 1941- , in progress); publication of a German translation of the Russian edition was begun in Berlin in 1926 but has not been completed. See also the English translation of Lenin's *Selected Works*, including a biography by V. G. Sorin and a study of Leninism by V. Adoratsky (in Vol. i) (New York, 1935-1938, 12 vols.), and *Essentials of Lenin* (London, 1947, 2 vols.).

Biographies of the leader include *Memories of Lenin* (tr. by E. Verney from 2nd Russian ed.; New York, 1930, 2 vols.), by his wife,

N. K. Krupskaya; the Marx-Engels-Lenin Institute official life, *Vladimir I. Lenin* (New York, 1944, 288 pp.); Leon Trotsky, *Lenin* (New York, 1925, 216 pp.); Valeriu Marcu, *Lenin* (tr. by E. W. Dickes; New York, 1928, 412 pp.); and David Shub, *Lenin* (Garden City, N.Y., 1948, 438 pp.). For Lenin's relationship to the Third International, see Topic 4, above, and for Lenin's activities before the revolution, see G. Zinoviev, *Histoire du parti communiste russe* (Paris, 1926, 192 pp.). See also Christopher Hill, *Lenin and the Russian Revolution* (New York, 1950, 245 pp.), and Ernst Drahn, *Lenin . . . eine Bio-Bibliographie* (2nd ed. rev. and enl.; Berlin, 1925, 80 pp.).

Examples from the works of other important founders of Soviet communism are Trotsky, *Dictatorship vs. Democracy* (New York, 1922, 191 pp.); *Our Revolution; Essays on Working-Class and International Revolution, 1904-1917* (ed. and tr. by M. J. Olgin; New York, 1918, 220 pp.); and *My Life* (New York, 1930, 599 pp.); N. I. Bukharin and E. A. Preobrazhensky, *The A B C of Communism* (tr. by E. and C. Paul; London, 1922, 422 pp.); and O. A. Pyatnitsky, *Memoirs of a Bolshevik* (New York, 1933, 224 pp.), which covers the period 1896-1917.

A central issue in Soviet history, fought principally between Trotsky and Stalin, was world revolution versus socialism in one country. Boris Souvarine, *Stalin; a Critical Survey of Bolshevism* (tr. by C. L. R. James; New York, 1939, 690 pp.), is a highly factual, although anti-Stalinist, account of the subsequent break in the communist leadership between Trotsky and Stalin after Lenin's death. I. Deutscher, *Stalin; a Political Biography* (Oxford, Eng., 1949, 568 pp.), is less hostile than Souvarine. Trotsky, *Stalin* (2nd ed., ed. and tr. by Charles Malamuth; New York, 1946, 516 pp.), and his important work, *The History of the Russian Revolution* (tr. by Max Eastman; New York, 1936, 3 vols. in 1), express the thesis of the defeated faction. See especially Appendix ii, Vol. iii of the history, which charges that socialism in one country is not in the communist tradition, and pp. 422-434 of the biography, which attempts to outline all three major theories of the Russian Revolution. Stalin's reply may be found in "The Foundations of Leninism," in *Leninism* (London, 1940, 667 pp.), especially pp. 72-83; "The October Revolution and the Tactics of the Russian Communists," *ibid.*, pp. 86-117; and the pamphlet by Zinoviev, Stalin, and Kamenev, *Leninism vs. Trotskyism* (New York, 1925, 76 pp.). Eventually the bitter conflict between Stalin and Trotsky resulted in Trotsky's death: L. A. Sánchez Salazar and Julián Gorkin, *Murder in Mexico* (tr. by P. Hawley; London, 1950, 235 pp.), purports to be the real story of Trotsky's assassination by a Stalinist agent, written by the ex-head of the secret service of the Mexican police and by an anti-Stalinite, non-Trotskyite socialist. The international implications of the debate on socialism in one country are discussed in Topic 4.

Other interpretations of the 1917 Revolution are often as valuable for revealing the attitude of the author and his group as in describing the events themselves. Rosa Luxemburg's essay, *The Russian Revolution* (tr. by B. D. Wolfe; New York, 1940, 56 pp.), for example, expresses the revolutionary view of the German Spartacists. See also Klara Zetkin, *Um Rosa Luxemburgs Stellung zur russischen Revolution* (Hamburg, 1922, 224 pp.). A. J. Sack, *The Birth of the Russian Democracy* (New York, 1918, 527 pp.), is noteworthy as an example of the Russian Information Bureau's propaganda, and W. Z. Foster, *The Russian Revolution* (Chicago, 1921, 155 pp.), exhibits the American communist view. John Reed, *Ten Days That Shook the World* (New York, 1919, 371 pp.), is the report of an enthusiastic American eye-witness, mostly about the Petrograd Soviets. The judgment of the head of the provisional government during the three and a half months before the Bolshevik Revolution is found in A. F. Kerensky's basic memoirs, *The Crucifixion of Liberty* (New York, 1934, 406 pp.), and that of the social revolutionaries in V. M. Chernov, *The Great Russian Revolution* (New Haven, Conn., 1936, 466 pp.). Alexander Berkman and Emma Goldman, communo-anarchists deported from the United States, went to Russia and subsequently reported their loss of faith in the revolution. See Goldman, *My Disillusionment in Russia* (Garden City, N.Y., 1923, 242 pp.) and *My Further Disillusionment in Russia* (Garden City, N.Y., 1924, 178 pp.). For other American comments see those of the sociologist, E. A. Ross, *The Russian Soviet Republic* (New York, 1923, 405 pp.), Waldemar Gurian, *Bolshevism; Theory and Practice* (New York, 1932, 402 pp.), which includes an analysis of the revolutionary background from a Roman Catholic standpoint, and the succinct but oversimplified essay on the Bolshevik elite by Rudolf Sprenger, *Bolshevism; Its Roots, Role, Class View and Methods* (New York, 1940, 48 pp.). B. D. Wolfe, in a three-volume work, only one volume of which, *Three Who Made a Revolution* (New York, 1948, 661 pp.), has appeared, analyzes the revolution through the perspective of its three principal leaders: Lenin, Trotsky, and Stalin. An earlier history of the revolution is W. H. Chamberlin, *The Russian Revolution, 1917-1921* (New York, 1935, 2 vols.). In England, E. H. Carr is writing a history of Soviet Russia, Volume 1 of which is *The Bolshevik Revolution, 1917-1923* (London, 1950, 430 pp.). See also these documentary collections: F. A. Golder, *Documents of Russian History, 1914-1917* (tr. by E. Aronsberg; New York, 1927, 663 pp.); James Bunyan and H. H. Fisher, comps., *The Bolshevik Revolution, 1917-1918* (Stanford University, Calif., 1934, 735 pp.); and Bunyan, *Intervention, Civil War, and Communism in Russia, April-December, 1918* (Baltimore, 1936, 594 pp.). Ivan Knizhnik published *Chto chitat po obshchestvennym naukam: Sistematichesky ukazatel kommunisticheskoi i marksistskoi literatury* (Leningrad, 1924, 491 pp.), a bibliography of 10,000 titles covering only the first seven years of the Soviet Union (1917-1923).

Topic 9. Marxian Socialism and Its Evolutionary Forms: the Guild Socialists, Fabians, and Social Democrats

As noted above, not all Marxists have been revolutionary in outlook. Even in Marx's own day, many of his followers inclined to the view that socialism is a matter of evolution rather than revolution and that the use of such peaceful methods of change as education, political action within the legal framework of the state, and agitation for progressive social legislation were in the long run more effective in realizing socialist ends than the use of force. This, for example, was the controlling viewpoint of the Second International, which dominated socialist theory and practice between 1889 and 1914.

But evolutionary no less than revolutionary Marxism developed many different types of programs. In England, for example, it manifested itself (1) in Fabianism—which argues that socialism is inevitable and that as man becomes progressively more enlightened socialism will be voted in by stages—and (2) in guild socialism—which, with its distrust of the state and its ideal of decentralized economic control vested wholly in locally organized industrial and agricultural "communes," constitutes a nonrevolutionary equivalent of syndicalism (see Topic 8 above). But it was in Germany that the theory of parliamentary or evolutionary socialism achieved its clearest and most subtle statement. This was in the so-called "orthodox" Marxism of Kautsky and Hilferding, and in the revisionist school of Eduard Bernstein.

"Orthodox" Marxism was gradually evolved by the German social democracy which, after the agreement on the Erfurt Programme of 1891, accepted the Marxian theory of the class struggle and the view that socialism is possible only through proletarian revolt and dictatorship. But the revolutionary impetus of this movement was curbed in two ways: by a gradual change in its definition of social revolution, and by a gradual change in the conception of the role of socialism itself in the class struggle. The classic pattern of the French Revolution implied the need of violence, but the social democrats gradually substituted a definition of revolution scarcely distinguishable from evolution. According to Marx, socialist leadership involved full participation with the proletariat in the class struggle, as well as an intellectual understanding of the conflict. Since the social democrats assumed that revolutions, though inevitable, could not be hurried, they dropped Marx's activism and retained only the conception of socialism as a purely theoretical science seeking to understand rather than to direct the class struggle.

These tendencies were finally completed and rationalized in the revisionism of Bernstein, who called for a complete rethinking of socialist teachings on the ground that in modern times the class struggle has grown less rather than more acute. As against "orthodox" Marxism, accordingly, the revisionist school urged that all notion of revolution be dismissed and that socialism devote itself entirely to programs of immediate reform. The temper of the school is best summarized in Bernstein's own words that "the movement means everything, the final end nothing."

Of the many aspects of the various gradualist schools of thought, only two are treated below in any detail: guild socialism and the "orthodox" Marxism of Kautsky. The writings of these schools are selected to stress their differing ideas of revolution and the future socialist society. For background, read H. W. Laidler, *Social-Economic Movements* (New York, 1944, 828 pp.), chap. 23, and Sidney Hook, *Towards the Understanding of Karl Marx* (New York, 1933, 347 pp.), chaps. 3 and 4. For guild socialism, read, in addition, G. D. H. Cole, *Guild Socialism: a Plan for Economic Democracy* (New York, 1921, 202 pp.), chaps. 1, 2, 3, 10, 11; and for "orthodox" Marxism, Ernst Drahn, "Sozialdemokratie," *Handwörterbuch der Staatswissenschaften* (4th ed.), VII, pp. 510-566, with bibliography; and Karl Kautsky, *The Social Revolution* (tr. by A. M. and M. W. Simons; Chicago, 1905, 189 pp.).

For additional material on guild socialism, see Topic 1. N. H. Carpenter, *Guild Socialism; an Historical and Critical Analysis* (New York, 1922, 350 pp.), is an excellent description of the historical relationship of guild socialism to Marxism, syndicalism, and the medievalism of Ruskin and Morris, combined with a searching analysis of the value and feasibility of a socialist commonwealth along guild lines; see also M. B. Reckitt and C. E. Bechhofer, *The Meaning of National Guilds* (New York, 1918, 452 pp.), particularly "Problems and Policy," pp. 341-444. S. G. Hobson, *National Guilds* (London, 1914, 370 pp.), is one of earliest and best statements of guild principles. G. R. S. Taylor, *The Guild State; Its Principles and Possibilities* (London, 1919, 153 pp.), describes guild socialism in terms of its three basic principles of functionalism, self-management, and decentralization. J. N. Figgis, *Churches in the Modern State* (London, 1913, 265 pp.), is important for its early influence in confirming the antistate tendency of the movement; while both Léon Duguit, *Law in the Modern State* (New York, 1919, 247 pp.), and Ramiro de Maeztu, *Authority, Liberty, and Function* (London, 1916, 288 pp.), are similarly important in originally conditioning the guild emphasis on function. For a bibliography of guild socialism and a critical sketch of the movement, see N. H. Carpenter, "The Literature of Guild Socialism," *Quarterly Journal of Economics*, XXXIV (Aug. 1920), pp. 763-776. For a criticism of contemporary capitalism from the guild point of view, see R. H. Tawney, *The Acquisitive Society* (New York, 1920, 188 pp.), and G. D. H. Cole, *Chaos and Order in Industry* (London, 1920, 292 pp.). S. G. Hobson, *National Guilds and the State* (London, 1920, 406 pp.), is a criticism of Cole's guild theory from the point of view of a fellow guildsman. A later expression of Hobson's views is *The House of Industry; a New Estate of the Realm* (London, 1931, 113 pp.). See also Hobson, *Pilgrim to the Left; Memoirs of a Modern Revolutionist* (New York, 1938, 303 pp.). A. R. Orage's principal writings have been edited by Herbert Read and Denis Saurat, *Selected Essays and Critical Writings* (London, 1935, 216 pp.). A study of Penty published at the Catholic University of America is E. J. Kiernan, *Arthur J. Penty; His Contribution to Social Thought* (Washington, 1941, 158 pp.).

The standard history of Fabian socialism, which preceded and survived guild socialism, is E. R. Pease, *The History of the Fabian Society* (2nd ed., London, 1925, 306 pp.), which describes the sources of the movement, the founding of the Fabian Society in 1884, and its members and activities. Material on the history of Fabianism, however, may also be had in G. B. Shaw, *The Fabian Society: Its Early History* (Fabian Tract 41; London, 1899, 30 pp.); G. D. H. Cole, *The Fabian Society, Past and Present* (Fabian Tract 258; London, 1942, 23 pp.); Margaret Cole, *Beatrice Webb* (London, 1945, 197 pp.), and *The Webbs and Their Work* (London, 1949, 304 pp.); and in such autobiographies as Beatrice Webb's two volumes, *My Apprenticeship* (New York, 1926, 442 pp.), and *Our Partnership* (New York, 1948, 543 pp.); and those of the orthodox Marxist, H. M. Hyndman, *The Record of an Adventurous Life* (New York, 1911, 422 pp.), and *Further Reminiscences* (London, 1912, 545 pp.). Also see Margaret Cole, *Growing Up into Revolution* (London, 1949, 224 pp.).

Since the Fabian Society has always tended to stress education and research, its literary output has been voluminous, too voluminous to list completely. But *Fabian Essays* (1889; jubilee ed., New York, 1949, 289 pp.), by G. B. Shaw and others, and the long series of *Fabian Tracts* (now numbering over 250), which was begun in 1884, afford both a sense of the gradualist temper of the movement and a record of its interests and achievements. G. B. Shaw, *The Intelligent Woman's Guide to Socialism and Capitalism* (London, 1928, 494 pp.), is typical of the Fabian Society's efforts at popularizing socialism; while the recent publication of the society's International Bureau, *When Hostilities Cease* (London, 1943, 124 pp.), a collection of papers on relief and reconstruction by Julian Huxley, H. J. Laski, and others, illustrates the society's many contributions to public issues of immediate moment. Leon Trotsky, *Whither England?* (New York, 1925, 191 pp.), offers a criticism of the movement from the point of view of revolutionary Marxism. See also

G. D. H. Cole, *Fabian Socialism* (London, 1943, 172 pp.), and two conflicting interpretations of Shaw, William Irvine, "George Bernard Shaw and Karl Marx," *Journal of Economic History*, VI (May 1946), pp. 53-72, and E. J. Hobsbawm, "Bernard Shaw's Socialism," *Science & Society*, XI (Fall 1947), pp. 305-326. Max Beer, *Fifty Years of International Socialism* (London, 1935, 239 pp.), contains the observations of a socialist long resident in England on the gradualist outlook which developed in revolutionary exiles exposed to English socialist habits of compromise and restraint. See also E. B. Bax, *Reminiscences and Reflexions* (New York, 1920, 283 pp.).

The background of both "orthodox" Marxism and revisionism center largely in the history of the German social democracy, of which the most authoritative account is that given in Franz Mehring, *Geschichte der deutschen Sozialdemokratie* (12th ed., Stuttgart, 1922, 4 vols.). Mehring should be supplemented, however, with Eduard Bernstein, *Die Geschichte der Berliner Arbeiter-Bewegung* (Berlin, 1907-1910, 3 vols.), a documentary history of the labor movement in Berlin after 1848, and Paul Kampffmeyer, *Changes in the Theory and Tactics of the (German) Social Democracy* (tr. by W. R. Gaylord; Chicago, 1908, 164 pp.), a short history of the early ideological struggles within the party. Material may also be had from August Bebel, *Aus meinem Leben* (Stuttgart, 1910-1914, 3 vols.; first two vols. tr. under the title, *My Life*; London, 1912, 343 pp.), the autobiography of one of the founders of the Social Democratic Party; and from R. T. Ely's brief history, *French and German Socialism in Modern Times* (New York, 1883, 274 pp.), particularly chaps. 9-16.

The greatest theorist of "orthodox" Marxism was Karl Kautsky, for many years (1890-1917) the editor of *Neue Zeit*, and one of the outstanding socialist scholars of his day. His analysis and exposition of the Erfurt Programme, *Das Erfurter Programm*, translated by W. E. Bohn as *The Class Struggle* (Chicago, 1910, 217 pp.), is a Marxian classic and should be read in this connection. But the true temper of "orthodox" Marxism is best revealed in its polemics, first against the revisionists, and later against bolshevism. For the former, see: Kautsky, *Bernstein und das Sozialdemokratische Programm: eine Antikritik* (Stuttgart, 1899, 195 pp.), and L. B. Boudin, *The Theoretical System of Karl Marx in the Light of Recent Criticism* (Chicago, 1907, 286 pp.), which also defends Marxism against the attack of Böhm-Bawerk. For the "orthodox" Marxist attack upon bolshevism, see, among others: Kautsky, *The Dictatorship of the Proletariat* (1918; tr. by H. J. Stenning; Manchester, Eng., 1919, 149 pp.), which criticized the concept of the dictatorship of the proletariat and drew forth Lenin's sharp reply, *The Proletarian Revolution and Renegade Kautsky* (1918; New York, 1934, 110 pp.); and the same author's *Terrorism and Communism: a Contribution to the Natural History of Revolution* (tr. by W. H. Kerridge; London, 1920, 234 pp.), which condemns the linkage of terrorism with communism on the basis of an historical examination of the French Revolution and of the Paris Commune of 1871. Wilhelm Liebknecht, *Socialism: What It Is and What It Seeks to Accomplish* (1894; tr. by M. W. Simons; Chicago, 1897, 64 pp.), was an influential pamphlet among American socialists.

The great spokesman for revisionism was Eduard Bernstein, and its classic expression, Bernstein's *Die Voraussetzungen des Sozialismus und die Aufgaben der Sozialdemokratie* (Stuttgart, 1899, 188 pp.; tr. by Edith Harvey as *Evolutionary Socialism*; New York, 1909, 224 pp.). This attacks, among other things, Marx's theory of the concentration of capital and his theory of the disappearance of the middle class. See also Eugen von Böhm-Bawerk, *Karl Marx and the Close of His System* (tr. by A. M. Macdonald; London, 1898, 221 pp.). For other expressions of revisionism, see: V. G. Simkhovitch, *Marxism versus Socialism* (New York, 1913, 298 pp.); and for a brief history of the "orthodox"-revisionist controversy, see H. W. Laidler, *Social-Economic Movements* (New York, 1944, 828 pp.), chaps. 19-21.

Topic 10. Marxian Socialism, Anarchism, and Fascism

Marxian socialism is often confused with other revolutionary movements of the Left and Right, and with none more often, perhaps, than anarchism and fascism. The confusion with anarchism dates back roughly to the First International (1864-1876), with which both Marx and the great anarchist leader, Bakunin, were associated, and over the policies of which they eventually quarreled and divided. The confusion has also been abetted by the fact that although many anarchists have repudiated the use of force (cf. Tucker's "individualistic anarchism" and Tolstoy's "Christian anarchism," which go no further than to urge "passive resistance"), the most widely publicized anarchist group—the so-called "anarcho-communists"—accepts the Marxian theory of the class struggle and has on occasion aligned itself with Marxism. The more recent confusion of Marxian socialism with fascism and nazism has also been conditioned by two historical factors: by the fact that many Fascist leaders—among them Mussolini himself—were once Marxians; and by the fact that Marxism as embodied in the political structure of the U.S.S.R. has tended to assume a totalitarian form.

Yet neither confusion is justified. As distinct from anarcho-communism, Marxism recognizes the need for political and not merely economic methods in the successful prosecution of the class struggle, and envisages as its supreme end a classless society whose economic life is to be organized not about the local community (as anarchism demands) but around a national, and ultimately international, central planning and producing authority. Similarly, in contrast to fascism, Marxism repudiates both the *Führer prinzip* and the permanent division of society into employers and employees. Titles are cited below which contribute to an understanding of these differences, with particular reference to their implications for the Marxist, anarchist, and Fascist conceptions of the individual, property, and the state. For fascism and Marxism, see first C. E. M. Joad, *Guide to the Philosophy of Morals and Politics* (London, 1938, 816 pp.), chaps. 16 (pp. 605-663) and 17 (pp. 664-700, 713-724); and for anarchism: P. A. Kropotkin, "Anarchism," in *Encyclopaedia Britannica* (11th ed.), I, pp. 914-919, or Oscar Jászi, "Anarchism," in *Encyclopaedia of the Social Sciences*, II, pp. 46-53, and Paul Eltzbacher, *Anarchism* (tr. by S. T. Byington; New York, 1908, 309 pp.), chap. 6.

Besides the material on the relation of Marxism to anarchism noted in the General Reading, see the standard histories of the First International (Topic 3 above) and also the following works. E. H. Carr's biography, *Michael Bakunin* (London, 1937, 501 pp.), particularly Book 5, describes Bakunin's struggle with Marx for the control of the First International. A German treatment is Max Nettlau, *Michael Bakunin* (London, 1896-1900, 3 vols.). A popular sketch of Bakunin, Nechayev, and "Land and Freedom" (an organization of Russian social revolutionaries led by Bakuninist anarchists) appears in *History of Anarchism in Russia* (New York, 1937, 127 pp.), by E. Yaroslavsky, who holds the communist thesis that anarchism cannot overthrow capitalism and build socialism. B. P. Hepner, *Bakounine et le panslavisme révolutionnaire* (Paris, 1950, 320 pp.), is a volume of essays in which are discussed not only Bakunin and Panslavism but, among other things, the influence of French precept and practice upon revolutionary thinkers in Russia. Robert Hunter, *Violence and the Labor Movement* (New York, 1914, 388 pp.), is a brief critical history of the philosophy of terrorism in labor relations since 1850, with particular emphasis upon the role of terrorism in anarcho-communism. See also Bertrand Russell's comparative study, *Proposed Roads to Freedom: Socialism, Anarchism, and Syndicalism* (New York, 1919, 218 pp.); Jean Grave, *L'Anarchie; son but, ses moyens* (Paris, 1899, 332 pp.) and *Le Mouvement libertaire sous la 3e République* (Paris, 1930, 311 pp.); and F. D. Nieuwenhuis, *De geschiedenis van het socialisme* (Amsterdam, 1901-1902, 3 vols.), and *Van christen tot anarchist; Gedenkschriften* (Amsterdam, 1910, 600 pp.), by the Dutch anarchist leader. Luigi Fabbri, *Lettere ad un socialista* (Florence, 1914, 222 pp.), reprints of letters in the anarchist periodical, *Pensiero*, criticizes prewar Italian socialism. The same author's *Dittatura e rivoluzione* (Ancona, 1921, 373 pp.) is an anarchist analysis of the historical and theoretical problems of social revolution and the dictatorship of the proletariat, with special attention to bolshevism. Fabbri's study of his teacher's theories is *Vida y pensamiento de Malatesta* (tr. by D. Abad de Santillán; Barcelona, 1938, 332 pp.). For Marxian criticism of anarchism see: Marx, *The Poverty of Philosophy* (tr. by Harry Quelch; Chicago, 1910, 227 pp.), a reply to Proudhon's *Système des contradictions économiques, ou, Philosophie de la misère*; Eugen Dietzgen, *Ein Beitrag zur Aufklärung über Anarchismus und Socialismus* . . . (New York, 1896, 32 pp.); G. V. Plekhanov, *Anarchism and Socialism* (1894; tr. by E. M. Aveling; Chicago, 1908, 148 pp.), which deals mainly with Stirner, Proudhon, and Bakunin, and interprets anarchism as "bourgeois utopianism"; and Armand Cuvillier, *Proudhon* (Paris, 1937, 278 pp.), a Marxian study of Proudhon. P. A. Kropotkin, *The Conquest of Bread* (London, 1913, 298 pp.), particularly chaps. 11, 12, and 13, is an anarchist criticism of Marxism. Karl Diehl, *Über Sozialismus, Kommunismus und Anarchismus* (1906; 2nd ed., Jena, 1911, 492 pp.), is a comprehensive critical survey by a leading anti-Marxian scholar. Victor Cathrein, *Durch Atheismus zum Anarchismus; ein lehrreiches Bild aus dem Universitätsleben der Gegenwart* (1895; 2nd ed., Freiburg im Breisgau, 1900, 193 pp.), attacks anarchism from the Roman Catholic point of view. G. B. Shaw, *The Impossibilities of Anarchism* (Fabian Tract 45; London, 1903, 27 pp.), is a Fabian critique. By way of contrast see Oscar Wilde, *The Soul of Man under Socialism* (Boston, 1910, 63 pp.). This expresses the completely voluntarist and individualist view of "socialism" and thus illustrates the confusion of the two movements with each other.

For additional material on the relation of Marxism to fascism see Henri de Man, *Sozialismus und Nationalfascismus* (Potsdam, 1931, 61 pp.); G. S. Counts and others, *Bolshevism, Fascism and Capitalism* (New Haven, Conn., 1932, 274 pp.); Joseph Shaplen and David Shub, eds., *Socialism, Fascism, Communism* (New York, 1934, 239 pp.); Albert Weisbord's comparative study, *The Conquest of Power: Liberalism, Anarchism, Syndicalism, Socialism, Fascism, and Communism* (New York, 1937, 2 vols.); and Eduard Heimann, *Communism, Fascism, or Democracy?* (New York, 1938, 288 pp.). Compare the personal, anti-Marxian views of Werner Sombart, *A New Social Philosophy* (tr. and ed. by K. F. Geiser; Princeton, N.J., 1937, 295 pp.), which appeared in German as *Deutscher Sozialismus*, with the Hitler brand of national socialism. R. P. Dutt, *Fascism and Social Revolution* (rev. ed., New York, 1935, 318 pp.), or his *Fascism* (Allahabad, 1943, 129 pp.), and John Strachey, *The Menace of Fascism* (New York, 1933, 272 pp.), are summaries of the economic causes of fascism. Other writings on the question of whether fascism is a late stage of capitalism or a new nonsocialist society are included in PART IV, Topic 1. Luigi Fabbri (1877-1935), disciple of Errico Malatesta and popular in Spanish and Latin American anarchist groups, discusses Italian fascism in *Camisas negras; estudio crítico histórico del origen y evolución del fascismo, sus hechos y sus ideas* (Buenos Aires, 1934, 275 pp.). A Brazilian analysis, disregarding anarchism, is Egydio Hervé, *Democracia-liberal e socialismo entre os extremos: integralismo e comunismo* (Porto Alegre, 1935, 206 pp.). José Garcia Pradas, *Antifascismo proletario* (Madrid, n.d., 173 pp.), contains many lead articles from the Madrid anarcho-syndicalist daily during the first two years of the Spanish Civil War concerning theory, policy, and tactics. For Fascist criticism of Marxism, see Mussolini, *Fascism: Doctrine and Institutions* (Rome, 1935, 313 pp.), pp. 7-42; and Hitler, *Mein Kampf* (complete and unabr. tr., New York, 1939, 1003 pp.), *passim.* For the view that fascism is a logical development of Marxism, see F. A. Hayek, *The Road to Serfdom* (Chicago, 1944, 250 pp.), particularly chap. 12.

PART II
Types of American Socialism

For discussion in Volume 1 relevant to this Part (PART II) of the Bibliography, see especially Chapters 3, 4, 5, and 6; also 7 and 14.

General Reading

SOCIALISM in the United States continued the same diverse tendencies found in European socialism, as the general literature indicates. Detailed topical investigation of the important American manifestations of these tendencies reveals how American types copied or diverged from their European prototypes. Chronologically, religious communism tended to precede secular, and communitarian socialism tended to precede Marxian socialism, both in the United States and Europe.

Religious communism developed a number of distinct and sometimes contradictory characteristics. Groups of pietistic origin preferred to withdraw from the wicked world; other groups, such as the Oneida Community, were forced to separate from their neighbors because of their tabooed sexual practices. German pietists were cut off by language and customs, and therefore failed to grow after the original migrations. Communitarians who received impetus from revivalism lost strength as this religious manifestation declined, especially among such groups as the Shakers, whose celibacy made the conversion of new members essential. In those groups where celibacy was not practiced, the educational problem of maintaining the original communistic spirit was equally crucial. Religious communists, even those most withdrawn from the world, showed a striking harmony with their times. They reacted to the currents of the antislavery movement, the peace movement, spiritualism, mental or faith healing, and dietary reform, but inevitably in their own distinct way. Emphasis on agriculture or industry did not follow doctrinal lines, since doctrine was only incidentally concerned with economics. The Shakers and the Oneida Perfectionists manufactured surpluses for sale outside their communities, while the German pietists and Mormons were primarily self-sufficient farmers. As the German groups declined, and their power to satisfy their own needs dwindled, they, too, traded extensively with the world.

Secular socialism, both utopian and Marxian, was contemporary with the industrial revolution. Owenism was a product of the first stages of British industrialism, and Associationism, of the first widespread reaction to the American factory system and its cyclical maladies. Marxism, on the other hand, did not develop an American following until capitalism had collected large groups of predominantly immigrant workers in the cities. The secular socialism which expected to spread its ideas by pointing to the successful experience of pilot projects originated contemporaneously with the Romantic movement. It professed to be guided by a science of society, but the science of the day was just beginning to shake

91

off religious and philosophical a priori principles. Marxism developed in an America dominated by popular pragmatism and a faith in the technical applications of science. The followers of Owen, Fourier, and Cabet, although they practiced the democracy of discussion and cooperative responsibility, tended to slight the problems of governing large heterogeneous populations, and to attract individualist and Christian anarchists. Only with Marxism did some varieties of American socialism deliberately enter politics.

Two characteristics of nineteenth-century American socialism should be kept in mind in approaching its literature. (1) The rank and file, certainly, and often the leaders could not be clearly labeled with any degree of precision. Communitarians, beyond their willingness to make over settlements or build them on the frontier, could be found on both sides of almost every issue—political, economic, social, and religious. Marxians, united in their efforts to organize labor, differed on methods of emphasis, and over just as wide a field. Anarchists opposed the state, but developed all sorts of hybrid positions with respect to political, economic, or propagandist action. Within these three groups, prominent members often fitted the specifications for two of them equally well. (2) Schism—the perennial threat to any organization—occurred from New Harmony to the formation of the Socialist Party, but much less virulently than in the succeeding half century. Despite internal inconsistencies of the membership and the conflicts of leadership, the religious communists suffered scarcely any splits; Fourierism was a loose federation of all kinds of reformers; Lassalleans and Marxians cooperated, though grudgingly, for over twenty-five years.

Communitarian socialism has been emphasized, in spite of its comparative unimportance today, because this type reached its fullest expression in the United States, and illustrates certain peculiarly American characteristics. The very fact that most of these communitarian types of socialism chose the United States for their settlements reflects a long-standing and widespread European tendency. America has been conceived as the land where dreams could come true and ideas could most likely be fulfilled. This tendency has affected both European and American psychology.

As an introduction, H. W. Laidler, *Social-Economic Movements* (New York, 1944, 828 pp.), although it does not include the American religious communisms, offers excellent summaries and bibliographies of other varieties of American socialism; see especially pp. 100-117, 577-601. For the main currents of the communitarian movements, compare J. H. Noyes, *History of American Socialisms* (Philadelphia, 1870, 678 pp.), pp. 21-58, 93-132, 193-250, 411-563, 595-672; Charles Nordhoff, *The Communistic Societies of the United States* (New York, 1875, 439 pp.), pp. 11-301,

333-339, 385-418; W. A. Hinds, *American Communities* (rev. ed., Chicago, 1902, 433 pp.), pp. 20-249; and V. F. Calverton, *Where Angels Dared to Tread* (Indianapolis, Ind., 1941, 381 pp.), pp. 127-350. For the principal developments of Marxian socialism and its working-class background, compare Nathan Fine, *Labor and Farmer Parties in the United States, 1828-1928* (New York, 1928, 445 pp.), pp. 88-362; Morris Hillquit, *History of Socialism in the United States* (5th ed., New York, 1910, 389 pp.), pp. 193-365; R. T. Ely, *The Labor Movement in America* (3rd ed., New York, 1890, 399 pp.), pp. 209-294; Anthony Bimba, *The History of the American Working Class* (New York, 1927, 360 pp.), pp. 199-356; Lillian Symes and Travers Clement, *Rebel America; the Story of Social Revolt in the United States* (New York, 1934, 392 pp.), pp. 99-378; and P. S. Foner, *History of the Labor Movement in the United States* (New York, 1947, 576 pp.), pp. 219-248, 297-496.

1. General Histories of American Socialism

The best volumes devoted specifically to the general history of American socialism in both its Marxian and non-Marxian phases are Morris Hillquit, *History of Socialism in the United States* (5th ed., New York, 1910, 389 pp.), and *Rebel America; the Story of Social Revolt in the United States* (New York, 1934, 392 pp.), by Lillian Symes and Travers Clement. Hillquit wrote before the important developments which took place during and after World War I. Symes and Clement write in entertaining style but pass over the early religious communities in a few paragraphs. Even their treatment of Owenism and Fourierism is cursory. C. A. Madison, using the biographical method and a popular style, underlines the connections between nineteenth- and twentieth-century leaders and between reformists and revolutionaries in *Critics & Crusaders* (New York, 1947, 572 pp.).

Most of the histories of socialism as a world movement, listed in PART I, contain material on the United States. R. E. Westmeyer, *Modern Economic and Social Systems* (New York, 1940, 604 pp.), contains good but very brief summaries of both religious and secular American socialist thought. *Social Democracy Red Book* (Terre Haute, Ind., 1900, 133 pp.), a campaign handbook edited by Frederic Heath and published as No. 10 in the Debs Publishing Company's Progressive Thought Series, contains articles on the nineteenth-century American movement, on Brisbane as an agitator, and other information on socialism. F. B. Adams, *Radical Literature in America* (Stamford, Conn., 1939, 61 pp.), contains an introductory sketch (pp. 5-35) with emphasis on the pre-Marxians, followed by the annotated catalogue of an exhibition of books held at the Grolier Club which attempts to illustrate the entire subject. See also John Macy, *Socialism in America* (Garden City, N.Y., 1916, 249 pp.);

Jerome Davis' useful volume, *Contemporary Social Movements* (New York, 1930, 901 pp.), which omits the American communitarians; and Savel Zimand, *Modern Social Movements* (New York, 1921, 260 pp.). D. O. Wagner, *Social Reformers* (New York, 1939, 749 pp.), contains extracts from the writings of both communitarian and Marxian leaders whose disciples were active or influential in the United States, with comments.

2. *Communitarian Socialism*

There is much historical material on the background of the chief American socialist communities. In PART I, the utopian aspects of this background are discussed in Topic 6; Owenism, Fourierism, and Icarianism in Topic 2; and the Anabaptist background of pietism in Topic 1. In the standard histories of utopias, J. O. Hertzler, *The History of Utopian Thought* (New York, 1923, 321 pp.), concentrates almost entirely on European thought, and Lewis Mumford, *The Story of Utopias* (New York, 1922, 315 pp.), pp. 113-169, deals sketchily with the American phases. The best general survey of communistic settlements, Charles Gide, *Communist and Co-operative Colonies* (1928; tr. by E. F. Row; New York, 1931, 222 pp.), devotes pp. 89-154, 174-175, and 203-208 to colonies in the United States. For bibliography, however, which Gide's book lacks, see the various surveys of American socialist communities cited below, particularly Nordhoff and Hinds; and Ralph Albertson, "A Survey of Mutualistic Communities in America," *Iowa Journal of History and Politics*, xxxiv (Oct. 1936), pp. 375-444.

A brief summary is included with other material in A. F. Tyler, *Freedom's Ferment* (Minneapolis, Minn., 1944, 608 pp.), pp. 68-224. A superficial but satisfactory introduction to the subject is V. F. Calverton, *Where Angels Dared to Tread* (Indianapolis, Ind., 1941, 381 pp.). Robert Liefmann, *Die kommunistischen Gemeinden in Nordamerika* (Jena, 1922, 95 pp.), is good on early American socialisms. Another and earlier survey in German, with emphasis on the Fourierists, is Heinrich Semler, *Geschichte des Socialismus und Communismus in Nordamerika* (Leipzig, 1880, 394 pp.). François Sagot's dissertation, *Le Communisme au Nouveau Monde* (Dijon, 1900, 235 pp.), gives a rapid summary of communities in the United States in Pt. 2, pp. 117-186, with bibliography. "The 'Labor' Literature," in Joseph Dorfman, *The Economic Mind in American Civilization* (New York, 1946-1949, 3 vols.), ii, pp. 637-695, contains summaries of various radical theories contemporary with the secular utopian experiments. J. L. Blau, ed., *Social Theories of Jacksonian Democracy; Representative Writings of the Period, 1825-1850* (New York, 1947, 383 pp.), reproduces documents useful for understanding the historical background of these movements.

94

Perhaps the best treatment of most of the early American communities is still Charles Nordhoff, *The Communistic Societies of the United States* (New York, 1875, 439 pp.). Nordhoff visited a very large number himself when many were still flourishing. Another book containing excellent first-hand material, and published by the founder of one of the most important communities, is J. H. Noyes, *History of American Socialisms* (Philadelphia, 1870, 678 pp.). Noyes took a large part of his material from a manuscript collection (now in the Yale University Library) left by A. J. Macdonald, who had visited many of the communities and corresponded with others. Another early survey, also by a member of the Oneida Community, is W. A. Hinds, *American Communities* (1878; 3rd ed., Chicago, 1908, 608 pp.). E. S. Wooster, a twentieth-century communitarian, with much the same purpose as Noyes and Hinds, reviewed the experience of the past in *Communities of the Past and Present* (Newllano, La., 1924, 156 pp.). For brief general summaries see also E. S. Bates, *American Faith; Its Religious, Political and Economic Foundations* (New York, 1940, 479 pp.), pp. 355-399; E. T. Clark, *The Small Sects in America* (Nashville, Tenn., 1937, 311 pp.), pp. 162-197; D. W. Douglas and K. D. Lumpkin, "Communistic Settlements," *Encyclopaedia of the Social Sciences*, iv (1931), pp. 95-102; G. W. Noyes, ed., *John Humphrey Noyes; the Putney Community* (Oneida, N.Y., 1931, 393 pp.), pp. 151-169; R. B. Taylor, "Communistic Societies of America," *Encyclopaedia of Religion and Ethics*, James Hastings, ed., iii (1911), pp. 780-787; F. A. Bushee, "Communistic Societies in the United States," *Political Science Quarterly*, xx (Dec. 1905), pp. 625-664; C. M. Skinner, *American Communes; Practical Socialism in the United States* (Brooklyn, 1901, 38 pp.); Alexander Kent, "Cooperative Communities in the United States," U.S. Department of Labor *Bulletin*, vi (July 1901), pp. 563-646; and C. E. Robinson (C. R. Edson, pseud.), "Communism," forty brief illustrated articles, sixteen of them on the Shakers, in Volumes 23-26 (Jan. 1891-Apr. 1894) of the *Manufacturer and Builder*, for which the author was advertising manager. Alexandre Holynski, "Le Communisme en Amérique," twelve articles in *Revue socialiste*, xii-xvi (Sept. 1890-Sept. 1892), depends heavily on American secondary accounts for his first four sections on the German pietists and Swedes, but writes of the Shakers at Watervliet from first-hand knowledge gained during a four months' visit in 1842-1843, and of the Icarians on the basis of a visit to Nauvoo in 1855. A few American communitarian groups are dealt with in T. D. Woolsey, *Communism and Socialism* (New York, 1880, 309 pp.). A history of utopian communities in America from 1680 to 1880 by Mark Holloway, entitled *Heavens on Earth*, is announced for publication in 1951 by the Turnstile Press, London, and Library Publishers, New York.

As samples of the many groups otherwise omitted from this bibliography, see for other German groups, L. E. Deets, *The Hutterites; a Study in Social Cohesion* (Gettysburg, Pa., 1939, 64 pp.); J. J. Sessler, *Communal Pietism among Early American Moravians* (New York, 1933, 265 pp.); R. J. Hendricks, *Bethel and Aurora; an Experiment in Communism as Practical Christianity, with Some Account of Past and Present Ventures in Collective Living* (New York, 1933, 324 pp.); and C. A. Hawley, "A Communistic Swedenborgian Colony in Iowa," *Iowa Journal of History and Politics*, xxxiii (Jan. 1935), pp. 3-26. M. A. Mikkelsen, *The Bishop Hill Colony; a Religious Communistic Settlement in Henry County, Illinois* (Baltimore, 1892, 80 pp.), and Sivert Erdahl, "Eric Janson and the Bishop Hill Colony," *Illinois State Historical Society Journal*, xviii (Oct. 1925), pp. 503-574, deal with the Swedish Jansonists. For native New England experiments, see Adin Ballou, *History of the Hopedale Community* (ed. by W. S. Heywood; Lowell, Mass., 1897, 415 pp.); F. B. Sanborn, *Bronson Alcott at Alcott House, England, and Fruitlands, New England (1842-1844)* (Cedar Rapids, Iowa, 1908, 103 pp.). C. A. Sheffeld, ed., *History of Florence, Massachusetts; Including a Complete Account of the Northampton Association of Education and Industry* (Florence, Mass., 1895, 250 pp.), publishes many of the now lost records of the semi-Fourierist Northampton Association. A study utilizing local sources and relating the Association to the conditions of the period and the locality is A. E. McBee, *From Utopia to Florence; the Story of a Transcendentalist Community in Northampton, Mass., 1830-1852* (Northampton, Mass., 1947, 77 pp.). The New England influence in John A. Collins' semi-Owenite community at Skaneateles, New York, can be seen in *The Social Pioneer, and Herald of Progress* (Boston, 1844, 96 pp.). Collins was a member of the committee of the Boston Social Reform Convention of 1844, which drafted this pamphlet in order to promote the Skaneateles project. The extensive writings of Thomas Low Nichols, who tried Fourierism at the North American Phalanx, positivism and anarchism at Modern Times, Long Island, and founded the "Memnonia" colony at Yellow Springs, Ohio, illustrate the crosscurrents of reform which affected the socialist communities. See the fictionalized account of Nichols and his wife, Mary S. Gove, by Grace Adams and Edward Hutter, *The Mad Forties* (New York, 1942, 294 pp.), especially pp. 166-185, 248-260, 271-294, on their relations with various communitarians.

Among those studies which attempt to include all communist colonies within a single state, see M. E. McIntosh, "Co-operative Communities in Wisconsin," *Wisconsin State Historical Society Proceedings, 1903*, li (1904), pp. 99-117; W. V. Pooley, *The Settlement of Illinois from 1830 to 1850* (Madison, Wis., 1908, 309 pp.), chap. 13; Joseph Eiboeck, *Die Deutschen von Iowa und deren Errungenschaften* (Des Moines, Iowa,

1900, 799 pp.), pp. 95-117; and K. W. McKinley, "A Guide to the Communistic Communities of Ohio," *Ohio State Archaeological and Historical Quarterly*, XLVI (Jan. 1937), pp. 1-15. The survival of Associationist ideas after the Civil War is indicated in E. B. Bassett (Beta, pseud.), *The Model Town; or, The Right and Progressive Organization of Industry for the Production of Material and Moral Wealth* (Cambridge, Mass., 1869, 104 pp.).

3. Marxian Socialism

The history of Marxian or labor socialism in the United States is intimately bound up with the development of the American trade-union movement and with the effort to build an American labor party. American trade-union groups have usually followed the policy of "pure and simple" unionism, eschewing political action of their own and rejecting in particular any formal alliance with political parties of the Left. Marxian socialism, because of its proletarian slant, has always sought to ground itself in the labor movement, either by "boring from within" or by creating socialist trade unions of its own through the policy of "dual unionism." For this reason material on the general history of scientific socialism is to be found not only in such standard texts on socialism as Hillquit's (see p. 93 above), but in the standard histories of labor itself. In this connection, see the treatment of labor and politics in J. R. Commons and others, *History of Labour in the United States* (New York, 1918-1935, 4 vols.), particularly I, Pts. 2 (1827-1833) and 4 (1840-1860); II, pp. 203-234, 269-300 (late nineteenth century); and IV, pp. 169-286, 386-402, 412-432, 525-561 (twentieth century to 1920); together with the excellent bibliographies in II, pp. 541-587, and IV, pp. 639-661. For additional source material on the political tendencies of labor between 1820 and 1880, with special reference to socialism, see also Commons and others, eds., *A Documentary History of American Industrial Society* (Cleveland, 1910-1911, 10 vols. and supp.), particularly V, VII, and IX. About 130 boxes and 183 volumes of materials assembled by the American Bureau of Industrial Research in the preparation of these publications are in the manuscript division of the Wisconsin Historical Society. For details consult *Guide to the Manuscripts of the Wisconsin Historical Society* (Madison, Wis., 1944, 290 pp.), edited by the curator, Alice Smith. P. S. Foner, *History of the Labor Movement in the United States from Colonial Times to the Founding of the American Federation of Labor* (New York, 1947, 576 pp.), is the first half of a comprehensive study. Foner accepts some of the historical conclusions of Commons, but substitutes the Marxian for the institutional approach. Although based upon extensive additional research, the volume is not sufficiently critical of its evidence. N. J. Ware's two books, *The Industrial Worker,*

1840-1860 (Boston, 1924, 249 pp.), and *The Labor Movement in the United States, 1860-1895* (New York, 1929, 409 pp.), are still useful.

Additional but briefer histories dealing with the relation between the rise of trade unions and the growth of scientific socialism include: Anthony Bimba, *The History of the American Working Class* (New York, 1927, 360 pp.), particularly chaps. 21, 27, 29, and 31; and Nathan Fine, *Labor and Farmer Parties in the United States, 1828-1928* (New York, 1928, 445 pp.). Bimba's history is more interpretative and is itself written from a Marxian point of view, while Fine's account is more factual. They are, however, equally valuable. F. E. Haynes, *Social Politics in the United States* (Boston, 1924, 414 pp.), treats of the various utopian and Marxian groups in the general context of American progressivism. See also James Oneal, *The Workers in American History* (4th ed., New York, 1921, 208 pp.), and C. Legien, *Aus Amerikas Arbeiterbewegung* (Berlin, 1914, 203 pp.).

For an analysis of the different types of American trade-union ideologies, see P. K. Crosser's *Ideologies and American Labor* (New York, 1941, 221 pp.), which classifies these types as "paternalistic," "liberalistic," and "revolutionary"; and for an analysis of socialist trade-union tactics, see D. J. Saposs' excellent *Left Wing Unionism: a Study of Radical Policies and Tactics* (New York, 1926, 192 pp.).

The following titles deal with the background and history of American Marxism at different periods: before 1848, from 1848 to 1876, and after 1876.

A. BACKGROUNDS BEFORE 1848. For the non-Marxian backgrounds in militant trade unionism before 1848, see the accounts of such early labor parties as the Workingmen's Party of New York in Commons, *History of Labour in the United States*, I, pp. 167-332, and in F. T. Carlton, "The Workingmen's Party of New York City: 1829-1831," *Political Science Quarterly*, XXII (Sept. 1907), pp. 401-415; and writings on early radicals who rejected the communitarian solution in favor of the method of propaganda and labor politics (see PART IV, General Reading, p. 237). See also, for the labor struggles of this period, A. M. Simons, *Social Forces in American History* (New York, 1920, 325 pp.), particularly chap. 17 on the period 1824-1836.

B. THE PERIOD OF ORGANIZATION, 1848-1876. The period between the European uprisings of 1848, which sent radical exiles to the United States, and the founding of the first enduring Marxian party in 1876 reflected the current struggles of the European socialist movement. Followers of Lassalle, Marx, and the earlier communitarians fought inconclusively for the leadership of the weak American movement. Proudhonian propaganda is represented by C. A. Dana, *Proudhon and His Bank of the People*, and W. B. Greene, *Mutual Banking*, both published in 1849 and reprinted in *Proudhon's Solution of the Social Problem* (ed. by Henry Cohen; New York, 1927, 225 pp.). For the persistence of the Owenite, Fourierist, and Icarian movements, see Topics 5, 6, and 7 below.

The influence of these latter groups gradually yielded to hybrid socialist ideologies, partly communitarian, reformist, and religious, and partly Marxian. The thought of such figures as Wilhelm Weitling (1808-1871), John Francis Bray (1809-1897), and William H. Sylvis (1828-1869) illustrates this trend.

Weitling's three principal works are *Die Menschheit; wie sie ist und wie sie sein sollte* (1838; 2nd ed., Berne, 1845, 54 pp.), *Garantien der Harmonie und Freiheit* (Vevey, Switzerland, 1842, 264 pp.; published as *Lehre vom Sozialismus und Communismus*, New York, 1879, 288 pp.; new ed. with biographical sketch by Franz Mehring, Berlin, 1908, lii, 268 pp.), and *Das Evangelium eines armen Sünders* (Berne, 1845, 133 pp.). A German immigrant to the United States in 1846, Weitling was influenced in equal degree by his Christian background, his study of Babeuf, Saint-Simon, and other French socialists, and by his personal contact with Marx. He showed Marxian influence in his organization of the Arbeiterbund in New York in 1850. On the other hand he agitated for an exchange bank, attempted to prove that socialism is compatible with Christianity, and brought the support of his labor league in 1852-1853 to Heinrich Koch's German colony of Communia in Iowa. Weitling's significance as a transitional figure is made clear in Ernst Barnikol, *Weitling, der Gefangene und seine "Gerechtigkeit"* (Kiel, 1929, 280 pp.), and in Max Adler, *Wegweiser* (2nd ed., Stuttgart, 1919, 248 pp.), pp. 143-155. See also C. Meitzel, "Wilhelm Weitling," *Handwörterbuch der Staatswissenschaften* (4th ed.), viii, pp. 984-985, with bibliography; Emil Kaler, *Wilhelm Weitling; seine Agitation und Lehre im geschichtlichen Zusammenhange* (Hottingen-Zurich, 1887, 104 pp.); F. C. Clark, "A Neglected Socialist," *Annals of the American Academy of Political and Social Science*, v (Mar. 1895), pp. 718-739; F. Caillé, *Wilhelm Weitling; théoricien du communisme, 1808-70* (Paris, 1905, 100 pp.); Hans Mühlestein, "Marx and the Utopian Wilhelm Weitling," *Science & Society*, xii (Winter 1948), pp. 113-129; C. F. Wittke, *The Utopian Communist; a Biography of Wilhelm Weitling, Nineteenth-Century Reformer* (Baton Rouge, La., 1950, 327 pp.); and the editorials in Weitling's own publication, *Republik der Arbeiter* (New York, 1850-1855). In 1853, Weitling obtained a clerkship in the Castle Garden office of the Bureau of Immigration, and soon after retired from the labor and socialist movements.

Sylvis, a founder of the International Molders Union, is most important for his leadership of the National Labor Union (1866-1872), a predecessor of the Knights of Labor and the A.F.L., and for his recognition of the need for labor cooperation on an international scale. As one of the first native Americans having a direct connection with the First International, and as an organizer of the North American Federation of the International Workingmen's Association, the forerunner of the Socialistic Labor Party, Sylvis belongs with the early American Marxists. In his concern for producers' cooperatives and currency reforms, however, he was a predecessor of the populists. Jonathan Grossman, *William Sylvis, Pioneer of American Labor* (New York, 1945, 302 pp.), supplements with information from union records and contemporary periodicals the memorial volume by J. C. Sylvis, *The Life, Speeches, Labors, and Essays of William H. Sylvis* (Philadelphia, 1872, 456 pp.). Also consult Charlotte Todes, *William H. Sylvis and the National Labor Union* (New York, 1942, 128 pp.).

The ideas of Bray, Chartist and Ricardian socialist, reflect the shift in emphasis from community experiment to the political activities of labor. Bray is known chiefly for his pamphlet, *Labour's Wrongs and Labour's Remedy* (1839; facsm. repr., London, 1931, 216 pp.), written toward the end of his twenty years in England as a printer and labor leader (1822-1842). Acknowledging his debt to Owen and showing strong Associationist influences, Bray called for the abolition of private property, the co-partnership of labor and capital as insurance against strikes and the class struggle, and for the provision for social security. He also wrote, just before he left for America, a utopian satire which was never published, and in the United States, an attack on spiritualism (1855), a defense of secession (1864), an attack on orthodox theology (1879), an unpublished autobiography, and a running commentary on the labor movement in letters to labor journals. He was active in the American Labor Reform League, the Knights of Labor, and the Greenback and People's parties. M. F. Jolliffe has announced that he is preparing for publication Bray's complete works, samples of which he reproduces with a biographical sketch in his article, "John Francis Bray," *International Review for Social History*, IV (1939), pp. 1-38.

The most decisive conflict of the period, led on both sides by German-American labor, was between the Lassallean emphasis on politics and the dual Marxian emphasis on economic as well as political action by the working class. The Workingmen's Party of the United States was formed in 1876 from a union of the two groups. Commons' *History of Labour in the United States*, II, pp. 203-234, recounts the controversy between 1873 and 1876, and pp. 269-300, the continued strife between the same groups as factions within the Socialist Labor Party, successor to the

Workingmen's Party in 1877. Samples from the extensive literature on the radical element among the German-Americans are Ernest Bruncken, *German Political Refugees in the United States during the Period from 1815-1860* (Chicago, 1904, 59 pp.), and K. P. Heinzen, *Teutscher Radikalismus in Amerika* (Boston, 1867-1879, 4 vols. in 3).

No study of this stage in the development of American Marxism is complete without reference to the work of the German-American leaders, especially Joseph Weydemeyer (1818-1866), Joseph Dietzgen (1828-1888), and Friedrich A. Sorge (1828-1906). Weydemeyer, among the first of the Forty-eighters, edited the two weekly issues of *Die Revolution* in New York in January 1852. Unable to maintain regular publication, he brought out a special volume of the journal in May 1852, consisting of the first edition of Marx, *The Eighteenth Brumaire of Louis Bonaparte*. A good biography, which is forced by the paucity of sources to deal more with his times than his life, is Karl Obermann, *Joseph Weydemeyer; Pioneer of American Socialism* (New York, 1947, 160 pp.). Dietzgen is noteworthy because he developed his own theory of dialectical materialism independently of Marx and Engels. He spent two *Wanderjahre* in America, arriving at the age of twenty-one in June 1849, but most of his theory was evolved during his mature life in Germany. He spent the last four years of his life (1884-1888) writing and editing socialist papers in the United States. Most of Dietzgen's philosophical writings have been translated in *Some of the Philosophical Essays . . . by Joseph Dietzgen* (tr. by Max Beer and Theodore Rothstein; Chicago, 1906, 362 pp.), and *The Positive Outcome of Philosophy* (rev. tr. by W. W. Craik; Chicago, 1928, 430 pp.). A biographical sketch by his son, Eugen, originally published in *Neue Zeit*, XIII, Pt. 2 (Aug. 28, 1895), pp. 721-726, was included in each of the above volumes in revised and expanded form. See also G. Bammel, "Joseph Dietzgen," *Revue marxiste*, No. 3 (Apr. 1, 1929), pp. 295-316, or Henriette Roland Holst, *Josef Dietzgens Philosophie* (ed. by Eugen Dietzgen; Munich, 1910, 91 pp.).

Scholars have called F. A. Sorge—for most of his American career (1852-1906) a Hoboken music teacher—the first American Marxist. A friend of Marx himself, Sorge arrived in the United States a year after Weydemeyer, and at once became active in the labor movement. He was eventually appointed general secretary of the First International after the removal of its headquarters to New York in 1871. There is no biography of Sorge, although records of his secretariat are in the manuscript division of the Wisconsin Historical Society, and the New York Public Library has his collection of pamphlets and letters. Most of these letters, edited by Sorge, were published as *Briefe und Auszüge aus Briefen von Joh. Phil. Becker, Jos. Dietzgen, Friedrich Engels, Karl Marx u. A. an F. A. Sorge und Andere* (Stuttgart, 1906, 422 pp.). His reminiscences of the 1848 revolution and his four years of European exile were published under the title, "Erinnerungen eines Achtundvierzigers," *Neue Zeit*, xvii, Pt. 2 (Apr. 19-June 21, 1899), and a brief obituary appeared in the same journal, xxv, Pt. 1 (Oct. 31, 1906), pp. 145-147. Sorge wrote for the socialist German-language press, and his pamphlet, *Socialism and the Worker* (New York, 1876, 20 pp.), was frequently reprinted.

Mention should be made of other leading German-American socialists: the Alsatian, Adolf Douai, early advocate of kindergartens and author of *Better Times!* (Chicago, 1877, 32 pp.), and *Heinzen; wie er ist; eine Anklageschrift* (New York, 1869, 16 pp.); Dr. Abraham Jacobi and A. Cluss, who defended Weydemeyer against the followers of Weitling in 1853; Dr. Edmund I. Koch, contemporary of Weitling who circulated Blanquist literature in New York; Conrad Conzett; and A. Conrad. These and others are discussed in W. F. Kamman, *Socialism in German American Literature* (Philadelphia, 1917, 124 pp.), the best account of the role of the German-American press in promoting socialism. Outstanding among these papers were the *Sociale Republik* (New York, 1858-1860), the *Arbeiter-Union* (New York, 1866-1870), edited by Douai, and *Deutsche Pionier* (Cincinnati, Ohio, 1869-1887).

The best account of this period of organization as a whole, and of the succeeding period to the turn of the century, is given in Sorge, "Die Arbeiterbewegung in den Vereinigten Staaten," a history of American labor between 1850 and 1891, with additional notes covering 1892-1895, which appeared as a series of consecutive articles in *Neue Zeit*, ix, Pt. 1, to xiv, Pt. 1 (1890-1895), and in Russian translation as *Rabochee dvizhenie v Soedinennykh Shtatakh* (St. Petersburg, 1907, 298 pp.). See also B. D. Wolfe, *Marx and America* (New York, 1934, 32 pp.), a criticism of the tactics of the early German socialists from the point of view of their influence on subsequent policies of American socialism. Hermann Schlüter, *Die Anfänge der deutschen Arbeiterbewegung in Amerika* (Stuttgart, 1907, 214 pp.), on the period to about 1870, is particularly useful on the role of the German trade unions and the contribution of Weitling. For the latter part of the period, see Schlüter's account of the declining years of the First International, *Die Internationale in Amerika* (Chicago, 1918, 527 pp.), and his monograph on the attitude of class-conscious labor in Europe and the United States toward American Negro slavery, *Lincoln, Labor and Slavery* (New York, 1913, 237 pp.).

C. MARXIAN SOCIALISM AFTER 1876. The history of American Marxism after 1876 becomes identical with the history of Marxian parties: the Socialistic (later called Socialist) Labor Party (1877-), the Socialist Party (1901-), the Communist Party (1919-) with its Left and Right oppositions, and the I.W.W. (1905-). References to these parties are collected in Topics 8-11. R. T. Ely, *The Labor Movement in America* (3rd ed., New York, 1890, 399 pp.), is excellent in its description and appraisal of the background and policies of leftist groups in the early 1880's, and complements Sorge's history mentioned above. Ely's collection on labor and socialism is at the John Crerar Library in Chicago, which also has materials on socialism in its Gerritsen collection.

Other contemporary descriptions and appraisals represent significant points of view. The Yale prize essay by the nonsocialist H. A. James, *Communism in America* (New York, 1879, 86 pp.), is concerned primarily with the newly-formed Socialistic Labor Party, but also evaluates socialism in general. T. E. Brown, *Studies in Modern Socialism and Labor Problems* (New York, 1886, 273 pp.), is particularly valuable for its large bibliography, pp. 234-268. Edward and E. M. Aveling, *The Working-Class Movement in America* (2nd ed., London, 1891, 239 pp.), is useful chiefly for its first-hand impressions of socialists and labor leaders met during the authors' lecture tour of 1886. W. J. Kerby, *Le Socialisme aux États-Unis* (Brussels, 1897, 244 pp.), a University of Louvain dissertation, shows the interrelations of socialistic and reformist movements in the period 1876-1896. The prominent liberal clergyman Charles H. Vail defends the socialist movement in *Modern Socialism* (New York, 1897, 179 pp.). August Sartorius von Walterhausen, *Der moderne Socialismus in den Vereinigten Staaten von Amerika* (Berlin, 1890, 422 pp.), includes the labor movement, with some discussion of anarchism. American Jewish socialist activities up to World War I are included in Herz Burgin, *Die Geschichte fun der yidisher arbeiter Bewegung* (New York, 1915, xliii, 935 pp.), which deals first with the Jewish labor movement in Russia and England. Reasons for the failure of socialism in the United States to reach the proportions of the mass movement it had already achieved in Germany are suggested in Werner Sombart, *Warum gibt es in den Vereinigten Staaten keinen Sozialismus?* (Tübingen, 1906, 142 pp.).

Collateral movements cooperated with socialism at times during these years, but at other times opposed it. For an introduction to the single-tax movement, see Henry George, Jr., *The Life of Henry George* (New York, 1904, 2 vols.), also G. R. Geiger, *The Philosophy of Henry George* (New York, 1933, 581 pp.), and titles cited in PART IV, Topic 8. The outstanding student of the "Nationalism" of Edward Bellamy, likewise related to socialism, is A. E. Morgan, author of *Edward Bellamy* (New York, 1944, 468 pp.), and *The Philosophy of Edward Bellamy* (New York, 1945, 96 pp.). The biography includes an extensive bibliography, pp. 425-439. The *Nationalist* (Boston, 1889-1891) was the organ of the movement. Topic 13 below deals with the contemporary Christian socialist movement, and Topic 12 with anarchism.

For the period after 1900, Volumes 1 and 2 of *Revolutionary Radicalism* (Albany, N.Y., 1920, 4 vols.), the report of the New York State Legislature Joint Committee Investigating Seditious Activities, are valuable both for their reprinting of socialist documents now difficult to procure and for their editorial comment reflecting American public opinion at the time of the "red scare" of 1919. (The findings of this committee are usually known as the Lusk Report.) For the same reasons, U.S. Congress, House, Special Committee to Investigate Communist Activities, *Investigation of Communist Propaganda: Hearings . . . 71st Cong., 2d Sess.* (Washington, 1930, 6 pts. in 19 vols.), is useful for leftist activity of the late 1920's, and the hearings and other publications of the House Committee on Un-American Activities are helpful for the next two decades. For a sample of the Committee's conclusions see its booklet, *100 Things You Should know about Communism Series* (Washington, 1949, 128 pp.), a combined edition of six of its pamphlets.

Equally important sources are the socialist and liberal journals both here and abroad: *Neue Zeit* (Stuttgart, 1883-1923), *Archiv für die Geschichte des Sozialismus und der Arbeiterbewegung* (Leipzig, 1911-1930), *Revue socialiste* (Paris, 1885-1914, 1946-), *Social-Democrat* (London, 1897-1911) superseded by the *British Socialist* (London, 1912-1913), *Socialist Review* (London, 1908-1934), *International Socialist Review* (Chicago, 1900-1918), *Labor Age* (New York, 1913-1933, title varies), *World Tomorrow* (New York, 1918-1934, title varies), *Nation* (New York, 1865-), *Masses* (New York, 1911-1917) superseded by the *Liberator* (New York, 1918-1924), and others listed in Topics 8-10. *Foreign Nationality Groups in the United States* (Washington, 1943, 185 pp.), a handbook prepared by the foreign nationalities branch of the Office of Strategic Services, includes information on socialist and communist organizations concerned with European or Near Eastern politics and their foreign-language press. See also Edward Silvin, *Index to Periodical Literature on Socialism* (Santa Barbara, Calif., 1909, 45 pp.), which lists about 1,200 titles.

Other important sources are the biographies and autobiographies of such prominent socialist, I.W.W., and communist leaders as Debs, Haywood, Hillquit, William Z. Foster, Ella Reeve Bloor, and others, many of whom were at different times members of different radical factions and parties (see Topics 8-12). See also W. R. Browne, *What's What in the Labor Movement; a Dictionary of Labor Affairs and Labor Terminology* (New York, 1921, 577 pp.), and Solon De Leon, ed., *The American Labor Who's Who* (New York, 1925, 374 pp.).

Within the triangle bounded by Stalinist, Trotskyist, and De Leonist positions, a number of tiny sects not included in the Topics have flourished enough since World War I to publish their attacks and counter-attacks. The Workers Socialist Party was organized in Detroit in 1916 with a nucleus from the Socialist Party of America, and since then has been affiliated with the Socialist Parties of the British Empire. Its doctrinaire Marxism is, if anything, more rigid than that of the Socialist Labor Party. It published the *Socialist* (New York, 1929-1938) irregularly, and took over the *Western Socialist* (Winnipeg, 1933-1939; published jointly by the Canadian and American branches from Oct. 1939 through Apr. 1941; Boston, 1941-) after it was banned in Canada. The Proletarian Party of America, a fragment thrown off by the Socialist Party in its reaction to bolshevism, has maintained a pro-Soviet but anti-communist line similar to the Trotskyists'. See its organ, *Proletarian* (Detroit, Chicago, 1918-1931) superseded by *Proletarian News* (Chicago, 1932-), and the writings of John Keracher, national secretary of the party and chief stockholder in C. H. Kerr & Co., Chicago publishers, e.g., *Proletarian Lessons* (Chicago, n.d., 62 pp.). Splits among Marxian radicals during the depression and in regard to World War II created several other organizations publishing these organs: *Industrial Unionist* (New York, 1932-1940, Apr.-May 1941), issued by the United Workers of America; *Labor Power* (New York, 1934-1935), by the American Labor Party; *Labor Power* (New York, 1939-1941), first two numbers as *New Industrial Unionist*, by the Socialist Union Party, and not connected with either of the foregoing; the Proletarian Group *Bulletin* (New York, 1936-1937) superseded by its *Proletarian Outlook* (New York, 1938-1940); *Labor Front* (New York, 1934-1939), by the League for a Revolutionary Workers' Party; and *Bulletin* (New York, 1937-), first called *In Defense of Bolshevism*, edited by George Spiro (George Marlen, pseud.), of the ex-Trotskyist Leninist League, U.S.A.

Of special interest are the explorations and stock-takings of independent and Marxian socialists after World War II in their centennial issues of periodicals commemorating the *Communist Manifesto*, and such series as "The Future of Socialism," *Partisan Review*, xiv (Jan./Feb.-Sept./Oct. 1947), five articles by Sidney Hook, Granville Hicks, A. M. Schlesinger, Jr., George Orwell, and Victor Serge; and "New Roads in Politics," *Politics*, ii (Dec. 1945) to iii (Nov. 1946).

Special Topics

THE specific examples of American socialism which best illustrate those major phases distinguished in the general literature —the religious and secular communitarians and the Marxists— have been developed as special topics.

From literally hundreds of religious communist groups, only four major examples have been selected as illustrative of the chief types. The religion of the first two types was pietistic. Members of these groups sought personal salvation through voluntary withdrawal from the world. A very large proportion of these groups in the United States, including the earliest examples of them, grew out of German pietism. Topic 1 describes the literature relating to three characteristic examples of German origin: the Ephrata Cloister, the Inspirationists, and the Rappites. Topic 2 introduces the extensive writings about the Shakers, pietists of English origin who throughout their long and unusually successful history have aroused particular interest and controversy in the United States. The next two types—although religiously motivated like the pietistic groups—were to a larger degree forced into communism and withdrawal from general society by their unusual, and to outsiders, offensive customs. These groups are the Mormons (Topic 3) and the Oneida Community (Topic 4).

The second major phase of American socialism includes those communities whose allegiance was to the beliefs of no particular sect, and whom their contemporary opponents called antireligious. Only three of the most important examples have been chosen from a large number. Europeans founded these three movements, but the communities set up in the United States under their influence varied from the plans of the founders. Variations occurred even though two founders came to this country to superintend the first colonies. The influence of Robert Owen (Topic 5), particularly in the settlement at New Harmony, Indiana, was followed by that of Charles Fourier (Topic 6) on a group of "Phalanxes" such as the North American Phalanx near Red Bank, New Jersey, and later by that of Étienne Cabet (Topic 7) in the Icarian communities. Followers of these European socialists organized communities to set an example of the good life—and incidentally the good economy—which they hoped society at large would gradually imitate. Insofar as these communities emphasized the economic aspects of social life, they helped pave the way for Marxian socialism, but such economic emphasis was not nearly so fundamental for them as for the Marxians.

Although socialist communities are still being established, the varieties of American socialism which have deliberately sought to influence economic and political life without withdrawal into communities constitute the chief phase since the close of the nineteenth century. The direct participation of these groups in local, national, and international affairs has, wherever possible, taken the form of political parties, trade-union organizations, and sometimes cooperatives of producers or consumers. The developing industrial revolution, with its expanding class of factory wage earners, offered this type of socialism a much larger clientele.

Three party groups of Marxian origin or inspiration have been of particular importance in America: the Socialist Labor Party (Topic 8), the Socialist Party (Topic 9), and the Communist Party (Topic 10) with its Trotskyist and other schismatic groups. All of these party organizations still exist. The major conflicts between them arise chiefly from their different attitudes toward labor and labor unions, toward affiliation with international socialism, and toward the concept of revolution.

The last two topics concern socialistic movements which do not fit any of the three main phases of American socialism. The Industrial Workers of the World (Topic 11), although they did not favor community building, also refused to form a party, and concentrated on the direct economic action of one big labor union. The connections are tenuous, but the I.W.W. reflects, in spite of its native characteristics, the similar manifestations of French syndicalism. The various forms of American anarchism (Topic 12) likewise eschewed politics. Christian socialism (Topic 13), an ethical reaction to Marxian economic materialism, developed later in the United States than its European counterpart, because of the later appearance of industrialism and Marxism.

State socialism, Fabian socialism, and guild socialism—varieties of socialism important abroad and mentioned in PART I—have all to some degree affected American thought, but for the most part indirectly. Although special topics are not devoted to them here, some of them will be referred to in later Parts.

Topic 1. Ephrata, Amana, and the Rappites

The fundamental concern of these German Protestant pietists was individualistic, emphasizing the direct communication of the individual with God. Communal organization, however, was necessary for survival in a wicked world, and could be justified by the belief of the members of these groups in the equality of individuals before God, independent of the intervention of a priestly hierarchy. Yet such an organization has normally been established and maintained by a single powerful personality, or series of personalities, believed by disciples to have the gift of prophecy. Under the leadership of the prophet the members of each group have tended to withdraw from society, partly because of the unfriendly attitude of their neighbors, but particularly because of their acceptance of the gulf between church and worldly governments. (In contrast, the Mormons, for example, exhibit the Calvinistic tendency to subject state to church.)

These pietistic groups, believing this world merely a preparation for the world to come, have tended to be millennialist. Because they have conceived the wickedness of the world to be rooted particularly in the flesh, they have tended to adopt celibacy—though this was not so true in Amana. All three groups started with a base of self-sufficient agriculture and crafts, but during their decline, their ties with the economy of the world outside grew stronger.

A comparison of the three groups may be obtained from the following introductory material: for Ephrata, see V. F. Calverton, *Where Angels Dared to Tread* (Indianapolis, Ind., 1941, 381 pp.), pp. 43-68; and Redmond Conyngham, "An Account of the Settlement . . . at Ephrata . . . to Which Is Added a Short History . . . by the Late Rev. Christian Endress," *Memoirs of the Historical Society of Pennsylvania*, II, Pt. 1 (1827), pp. 133-153. For Amana, see C. F. Noe, "A Brief History of the Amana Society 1714-1900," *Iowa Journal of History and Politics*, II (Apr. 1904), pp. 162-187. For the Rappites, see V. F. Calverton, *Where Angels Dared to Tread*, pp. 69-85; and J. A. Bole, *The Harmony Society* (Philadelphia, 1904, 176 pp.), pp. 65-142. Charles Nordhoff, *The Communistic Societies of the United States* (New York, 1875, 439 pp.), an excellent first-hand discussion, covers both the Inspirationists of Amana (pp. 25-59) and the Rappites or Harmonists (pp. 63-95).

EPHRATA. The most complete bibliography on the community at Ephrata, Pennsylvania, which developed around Conrad Beissel in the late 1720's, is *The Ephrata Cloisters; an Annotated Bibliography*, published by the Carl Schurz Memorial Foundation (Philadelphia, 1944, 139 pp.). E. E. Doll has compiled a critical list of printed "Sources for the History of the Ephrata Cloisters," pp. 3-81, and A. M. Funke, a chronological list of 89 Ephrata imprints, 1745-1794, pp. 83-126—altogether 452 titles. Other bibliographical guides are listed on pp. 77-81; see also Emil Meynen, *Bibliographie des deutschtums der kolonialzeitlichen Einwanderung in Nordamerika* (Leipzig, 1937, 636 pp.), pp. 108-111. The fundamental book on anything having to do with Ephrata is J. F. Sachse, *The German Sectarians of Pennsylvania, 1708-1800; a Critical and Legendary History of the Ephrata Cloister and the Dunkers* (Philadelphia, 1899-1900, 2 vols.). Somewhat discursive, it is particularly good in its treatment of the background of German pietism in this country. For the period before the founding of Ephrata see Sachse, *The German Pietists of Provincial Pennsylvania . . . 1694-1708* (Philadelphia, 1895,

504 pp.). In his article, "A Unique Manuscript by Rev. Peter Miller (Brother Jabez), Prior of the Ephrata Community," Pennsylvania-German Society, *Proceedings and Addresses . . . 1910*, xxi (1912), pp. 69-113, Sachse has reproduced selected writings of Conrad Beissel, the founder of Ephrata, as they were translated by Peter Miller for Benjamin Franklin. Briefer but more critical than Sachse is O. W. Seidensticker's excellent monograph, *Ephrata, eine amerikanische Klostergeschichte* (Cincinnati, Ohio, 1883, 141 pp.). This is included in Seidensticker's *Bilder aus der deutsch-pennsylvanischen Geschichte*, in Carl Schurz, ed., *Geschichtsblätter, Bilder und Mittheilungen aus dem Leben der Deutschen in Amerika* (New York, 1884-1886, 2 vols.), ii, pp. 167-250, a manuscript English translation of which is in the Germantown Historical Society. Seidensticker's only work in English on Ephrata is "A Colonial Monastery," *Century Magazine*, xxiii (Dec. 1881), pp. 209-223. The most recent pamphlets and books devoted solely to Ephrata are A. M. Aurand, Jr., *Historical Account of the Ephrata Cloister* (Harrisburg, Pa., 1940, 24 pp.), and S. G. Zerfass, *Souvenir Book of the Ephrata Cloister* (Lititz, Pa., 1921, 84 pp.), the latter by a preacher at the Cloister and the son of a former manager of the community.

W. C. Klein, *Johann Conrad Beissel, Mystic and Martinet, 1690-1768* (Philadelphia, 1942, 218 pp.), is the best recent source on the life of the founder of Ephrata, and contains a select, critical bibliography on the Cloister (pp. 207-211). For the early history of Ephrata—which was so widely known that it was mentioned by Voltaire in his *Philosophical Dictionary* (New York, 1901, 10 vols.), iii, pp. 169-170—an important contemporary document written at Ephrata itself is *Chronicon Ephratense*, first published in 1786 in German by two lay brothers, Lamech and Agrippa, and translated by Dr. J. M. Hark with the title, *Chronicon Ephratense, a History of the Community of Seventh Day Baptists at Ephrata, Lancaster County, Penn'a* (Lancaster, Pa., 1889, 288 pp.). Delegates from the Cloister participated in the first three of seven conferences of the Congregation of God in the Spirit, a meeting of Pennsylvania German churches in 1742, whose proceedings (each conference has a separate title) were published by Benjamin Franklin (Philadelphia, 1742, 120 pp.). P. C. Croll has translated and edited the report of the third, which contains a statement of the Ephrata position, "The Oley Conference," *Lutheran Quarterly*, lvi (Jan. 1926), pp. 84-108. Israel Acrelius, head of the Swedish churches in America, in his *A History of New Sweden* (1759; tr. by W. M. Reynolds; Philadelphia, 1876, 458 pp.), published in the *Memoirs* of the Historical Society of Pennsylvania, xi, pp. 373-401, reports temperately and in detail a day's visit to the Ephrata Cloister in the summer of 1753, including his theological discussions with Peter Miller. Ezechiel Sangmeister, *Leben und Wandel des in Gottruhen-*

den und seligen Bruders Ezechiel Sangmeister, weiland ein Einwohner von Ephrata (Ephrata, Pa., 1825-1827, 4 vols.), which is based on Sangmeister's violently critical eighteenth-century letters and notes, and has been used as a source by later writers, is noteworthy as the partial forgery of the printer Joseph Bauman. Other accounts of early Ephrata include Jacob Duché, *Observations on a Variety of Subjects* (Philadelphia, 1774, 241 pp.), pp. 66-85; F. R. Diffenderffer, "Ephrata Community 125 Years Ago," Lancaster County Historical Society, *Historical Papers and Addresses*, III (Sept. 1898), pp. 3-13; also his "The Ephrata Community 120 Years Ago as Described by an Englishman," *ibid.*, IX (Jan. 1905), pp. 127-146. Still another and somewhat misleading account of early Ephrata is that by William Fahnestock, "An Historical Sketch of Ephrata," *Hazard's Register of Pennsylvania*, xv (Mar. 14, 1835), pp. 161-167, partially reprinted in I. D. Rupp, *An Original History of the Religious Denominations at Present Existing in the United States* (Philadelphia, 1844, 734 pp.).

Other books and articles that may be consulted on Ephrata are: Writers' Program, Pennsylvania, *Pennsylvania Cavalcade* (Philadelphia, 1942, 462 pp.), pp. 249-258; M. G. Brumbaugh, "An Outline for Historical Romance," Pennsylvania German Society *Proceedings and Addresses . . . Oct. 12, 1928*, XXXIX (1930), pp. 13-24; *History of the Church of the Brethren of the Eastern District of Pennsylvania* (Lancaster, Pa., 1915, 670 pp.), pp. 32-43; P. E. Gibbons, *"Pennsylvania Dutch," and Other Essays* (3rd ed. rev., Philadelphia, 1882, 427 pp.), pp. 138-172; Franz Löher, *Geschichte und Zustände der Deutschen in Amerika* (Cincinnati, Ohio, 1847, 544 pp.), pp. 55, 119-124; E. M. Williams, "The Monastic Orders of Provincial Ephrata," in H. M. J. Klein and E. M. Williams, eds., *Lancaster County, Pennsylvania, a History* (New York, 1924, 4 vols.), I, pp. 384-476; Franklin Ellis and Samuel Evans, *History of Lancaster County, Pennsylvania* (Philadelphia, 1883, 1101 pp.), pp. 836-843; I. D. Rupp, *History of Lancaster County* (Lancaster, Pa., 1844, 528 pp.), pp. 211-234, 293-295, 444-445; see also two popular magazine articles, E. W. Hocker, "A Plain People," *Era*, XI (Apr. 1903), pp. 347-366, and Howard Pyle, "A Peculiar People," *Harper's New Monthly Magazine*, LXXIX (Oct. 1889), pp. 776-785. Of these brief secondary accounts, E. M. Williams'—although unsympathetic—is probably the best.

The influence of Ephrata spread into other colonies: see J. E. Jacoby, *Two Mystic Communities in America* (Paris, 1931, 104 pp.), pp. 1-51, which mentions a group led by an Englishman, Israel Seymour, who founded an extension of Ephrata in South Carolina.

For further bibliography on Ephrata, dealing with art, architecture, and music, see PART VI.

AMANA. The Inspirationists, a German pietist group founded in 1714, had some influence on Beissel, founder of Ephrata. They settled Ebenezer, now a suburb of Buffalo, in 1843 and started moving in 1855 to Iowa, where they planted the seven villages of the Amana Society. The chief historian of Amana is Bertha M. Horack Shambaugh, who has written numerous books and articles on the community. See particularly her *Amana That Was and Amana That Is* (Iowa City, Iowa, 1932, 502 pp.), which includes her earlier volume, *Amana, the Community of True Inspiration* (Iowa City, Iowa, 1908, 414 pp.). For articles by the same author see "Amana—In Transition," *Palimpsest*, xvii (May 1936), pp. 149-184; "Amana," *ibid.*, ii (July 1921), pp. 193-228; and "Amana the Church and Christian Metz the Prophet," *Midland*, i (Aug. 1915), pp. 249-257.

Writings on Amana by members of the community itself include: Christian Metz, *Historische Beschreibung der Wahren Inspirations-Gemeinschaft* (Buffalo, N.Y., 1863, 189 pp.), a work by the leader of the group; also, a pamphlet issued by the Amana Society (after Amana had abandoned complete religious communism and become a cooperative in 1932) entitled *Seven Villages Practicing Modified Capitalism* (Amana, Iowa, 1936, 16 pp.).

Of the older discussions of Amana by outsiders, that of Charles Nordhoff (cited above) is the best. See also B. M. H. Shambaugh, "Amana Society," *Encyclopaedia of Religion and Ethics*, James Hastings, ed., i (1908), pp. 358-369; Albert Shaw, "Coöperation in the Northwest," Johns Hopkins University *Studies in Historical and Political Science*, vi (1888), pp. 350-359; W. R. Perkins and B. L. Wick, *History of the Amana Society* (State University of Iowa *Publications: Historical Monograph, No. 1*; Iowa City, Iowa, 1891, 94 pp.); the illustrated article by R. T. Ely, "Amana; a Study of Religious Communism," *Harper's Monthly Magazine*, cv (Oct. 1902), pp. 659-668; and W. A. Hinds, *American Communities* (3rd ed., Chicago, 1908, 608 pp.), pp. 301-326.

Later discussions include: V. F. Calverton, *Where Angels Dared to Tread* (Indianapolis, Ind., 1941, 381 pp.), pp. 111-116; A. F. Tyler, *Freedom's Ferment* (Minneapolis, Minn., 1944, 608 pp.), pp. 130-132; while interesting material on Amana and the Amana Society as it is today can be found in various places in the Federal Writers' Project guidebook, *Iowa* (New York, 1941, 583 pp.), issued in the American Guide Series. There have been a number of recent magazine articles on Amana, many of them stimulated by the fact that in 1932 financial decline forced the Amana communities to form an economic cooperative in which the religious and economic administrations were made separate. Among these articles may be mentioned the following: G. Schulz-Behrend, "The Amana Colony," *American-German Review*, vii (Dec. 1940), pp. 7-9, 38; M. L. Bach, "Amana—The Glory Has Departed,"

Christian Century, LII (Aug. 28, 1935), pp. 1083-1086; Peter Stuck, "Amana Protests," *ibid.*, LII (Sept. 25, 1935), p. 1212, which is a sharp reply to Bach's article by the secretary of the Amana Society; also M. M. Rice, "Eighty-nine Years of Collective Living," *Harper's Monthly Magazine*, CLXXVII (Oct. 1938), pp. 522-527; A. M. Smith, "The Amana Community," *Commonweal*, XXVII (Nov. 5, 1937), pp. 42-43, the record of a visit to Amana in 1896; and N. A. Crawford, "Communism Goes Broke in Iowa," *American Magazine*, CXLII (Nov. 1946), pp. 44-45, 104, 106-108.

An extensive manuscript collection on the Inspirationists exists at Amana. From the Ebenezer and Amana presses have appeared numerous publications including the articles of incorporation of the Amana Society and the bylaws of the society. For a time the society published annual yearbooks entitled *Jahrbücher der Wahren Inspirations-Gemeinden* (Vols. 1-2 published in Germany, n.p., 1842; Vols., 3-21, Ebenezer, N.Y., 1849-1863; Vols. 22-58, Amana, Iowa, 1866-1884). Various religious books, mostly of a mystical nature, hymnbooks, catechisms, etc., have also been issued and some of them are listed in the bibliography for PARTS III and VI.

THE RAPPITES OR HARMONISTS. Most of the bibliographical material deals with the last settlement of the Rappites, Economy, Pennsylvania, founded in 1825. A few books concentrate on their second home in Harmony, Indiana (1815-1825), with reference to their successors, the Owenites, while the original colony at Harmony, Pennsylvania (1803-1815) has received only the most cursory treatment. The most thorough work on the Harmonists, and the only one to do justice to their formative years, is that of Karl J. Arndt. The manuscript of his first volume (approximately 800 pp.) is available to scholars at the Pennsylvania Historical Commission in Harrisburg, pending publication. Short illustrated articles by Arndt have been published in the *American-German Review*. "The Life and Mission of Count Leon," VI (June 1940), pp. 5-8, 36-37; (Aug. 1940), pp. 15-19, describes the interloper who caused dissension at Economy. "George Rapp's Petition to Thomas Jefferson," VII (Oct. 1940), pp. 5-9, 35, concerns Rapp's request to move his colony from Harmony, Pennsylvania, to Indiana Territory. Jacob Zundel, a Rappite who became a Mormon, is the subject of "The Harmonists and the Mormons," x (June 1944), pp. 6-9, while "The Harmonists and the Hutterians," x (Aug. 1944), pp. 24-27, tells of a group of Russian immigrants who considered settling at Tidioute, Pennsylvania, on Harmony Society lands, rather than continuing to South Dakota.

The autobiographical account of the last trustee, J. S. Duss, *The Harmonists; a Personal History* (Harrisburg, Pa., 1943, 425 pp.), is particularly valuable for the period 1862-1905 and on the difficulties he experienced in closing the community's financial affairs. His address, published as *George Rapp and His Associates (The Harmony Society)* (New Harmony, Ind., 1914, 67 pp.), calls attention to Rappite contributions to the nation, both before and after the death of their first leader. Almost the only other published description by a Harmonist is *Die Colonie, oder die Harmoniten zu Oeconomie im Staate Pensylvanien* (Birsfelden, 1848), sometimes attributed to Father Rapp. An older general study is the University of Pennsylvania doctoral thesis by J. A. Bole, *The Harmony Society; a Chapter in German American Culture History* (Philadelphia, 1904, 176 pp.), reprinted, with illustrations and a partial list of the books in the Harmony Library, from *German American Annals*, N.S., ii (May-Nov. 1904). Aaron Williams, *The Harmony Society at Economy, Penn'a.* (Pittsburgh, Pa., 1866, 182 pp.), revised after its original publication in the *Pittsburgh Commercial*, deals particularly with Rappite ideals. Briefer accounts, mostly on Economy, include: *The Harmony Society in Pennsylvania* (Philadelphia, 1937, 38 pp.), by the Federal Writers' Project of Pennsylvania; Writers' Program, Pennsylvania, *Pennsylvania Cavalcade* (Philadelphia, 1942, 462 pp.), pp. 279-289; A. M. H. Gormly, "Economy—a Unique Community," *Western Pennsylvania Historical Magazine*, i (July 1918), pp. 113-131; W. A. Hinds, *American Communities* (3rd ed., Chicago, 1908, 608 pp.), pp. 69-98; Joseph Bausman, *History of Beaver County, Pennsylvania* (New York, 1904, 2 vols.), ii, pp. 1004-1030; W. G. Davis, "The Passing of the Rappists," *Gunton's Magazine*, xxv (July 1903), pp. 20-26; R. L. Baker, "Description of Economy, Beaver County, Pennsylvania," Historical Society of Pennsylvania *Memoirs*, iv, Pt. 2 (1850), pp. 183-187; Franz Löher, *Geschichte und Zustände der Deutschen in Amerika* (Cincinnati, Ohio, 1847, 544 pp.), pp. 258-269; and Karl Knortz, *Amerikanische Lebensbilder* (Zurich, 1884, 208 pp.), chap. 4.

Few early travelers failed to visit the Rappites or make favorable reports. John Melish, *Travels through the United States of America* (Philadelphia, 1818, 648 pp.), pp. 320-333, is one of the few accounts of Harmony, Pennsylvania, which the author visited in 1810. One of the best contemporary accounts of Harmony, Indiana, is the record of a visit in February 1821 by John Woods, "Two Years' Residence in the Settlement on the English Prairie in the Illinois Country," *Early Western Travels*, R. G. Thwaites, ed., x (Cleveland, Ohio, 1904), pp. 312-314. Woods's account was originally published in London in 1822. See also Thomas Hulme, "A Journal Made during a Tour in the Western Countries of America, September 30, 1818-August 7, 1819," *ibid.*, x (1904), pp. 50, 53-61; George Courtauld, *Address to Those Who May Be Disposed to Remove to the United States of America* (London, 1820, 40 pp.), dedicated to Father Rapp; "Diary of William Owen from November 10, 1824, to April 20, 1825," ed. by J. W. Hiatt, Indiana Historical Society *Publications*, IV (1906), pp. 52-56 (on Father Rapp's preparations at Economy), and pp. 71-134 (Harmony, Ind.); and William Hebert, *A Visit to the Colony of Harmony in Indiana . . . Recently Purchased . . . for the Establishment of a Society of Mutual Co-operation* (London, 1825, 35 pp.). For descriptions of Economy, Pennsylvania, during its most prosperous period, among the most detailed of many travelers' journals are Bernhard, Duke of Saxe-Weimar, *Travels through North America, during the Years 1825 and 1826* (Philadelphia, 1828, 2 vols. in 1), II, pp. 159-166; Maximilian, Prince of Wied, "Travels in the Interior of North America, 1832-1834," *Early Western Travels*, R. G. Thwaites, ed., XXII (Cleveland, 1906), pp. 139-143; J. S. Buckingham, *The Eastern and Western States of America* (London, 1842, 3 vols.), II, pp. 205-236; and W. A. Passavant, "A Visit to Economy in the Spring of 1840," *Western Pennsylvania Historical Magazine*, IV (July 1921), pp. 144-149.

Consult the *Dictionary of American Biography*, XV, pp. 383-384, and *Allgemeine deutsche Biographie*, XXVII (1888), pp. 286-290, for the life of George Rapp. The early parts of G. B. Lockwood, *The New Harmony Movement* (New York, 1905, 404 pp.), and Marguerite Young, *Angel in the Forest; a Fairy Tale of Two Utopias* (New York, 1945, 313 pp.), pp. 19-77, deal with the Harmonists chiefly as background for their treatment of the Owenites at New Harmony. See also Jacob Schneck and Richard Owen, *The Rappites; Interesting Notes about Early New Harmony; George Rapp's Reform Society* (Evansville, Ind., 1890, 17 pp.); and J. C. Andressohn, ed., "Twenty Additional Rappite Manuscripts," *Indiana Magazine of History*, XLIV (Mar. 1948), pp. 83-108. For the curious details of Count Leon's transactions at Economy, see C. G. Koch, *Lebenserfahrungen* (Cleveland, Ohio, 1871, 411 pp.).

Related to the Rappites, but more extreme in their individualism and in denouncing both church and state, were the Separatists of Zoar, a group not considered in any detail here. The chief books on the settlement at Zoar include G. B. Landis, "The Society of Separatists of Zoar, Ohio," American Historical Association, *Annual Report . . . 1898* (1899), pp. 163-220; E. O. Randall, *History of the Zoar Society* (2nd ed., Columbus, Ohio, 1900, 105 pp.), reprinted from *Ohio Archaeological and Historical Quarterly*, VIII (July 1899), pp. 1-105; and C. R. Dobbs, *Freedom's Will; the Society of the Separatists of Zoar* (New York, 1947, 104 pp.).

Topic 2. The Shakers

Like the groups of German origin discussed in Topic 1, the Shakers, too, were pietists, but developed out of English Quakerism and—remotely—out of the French Camisards. Their founder, Mother Ann Lee, came to America in 1774. As pietists, they have shown many of the same general characteristics as the German groups (see Topic 1). A special topic is devoted to the Shakers, however, because of the unusually long and successful life of the group, and particularly because it aroused such great and widespread interest and discussion.

Much more than the pietists of German origin, the Shakers were affected by, and influenced, other contemporary religious movements, especially revivalism and spiritualism, and the relation of this fact to their success should be studied more carefully than it has been. Furthermore, since the converts to Shakerism were mainly native Americans of English Protestant stock, Shakerism was strongly affected by a Calvinist heritage.

The Shakers awakened widespread and persistent interest, as the enormous literature by and about them indicates. Particularly at first, their dissident religious views aroused hostility, which in turn called forth Shaker apologies. Throughout their history their celibate life and peculiar observances attracted attention and comment, and elicited defense. Their business integrity and orderly behavior went far toward winning tolerance and favor, and their unique contributions in arts and crafts earned them a new group of enthusiasts in the twentieth century.

E. D. Andrews has in manuscript a history of Shakerism with the tentative title, *The Shaker Communities in America,* and as part of his extensive research is working on a separate, annotated bibliography. Until his history is published, the account of the two Shakeresses, Anna White and Leila Taylor, *Shakerism; Its Meaning and Message* (Columbus, Ohio, 1904, 416 pp.), especially pp. 13-80, and the popular treatment by the non-Shaker M. F. Melcher, *The Shaker Adventure* (Princeton, N.J., 1941, 319 pp.), especially pp. 1-83, 120-135, 227-265, will provide the best balanced introduction to the subject. The best of the shorter eyewitness accounts of an earlier generation is still that of Charles Nordhoff in *The Communistic Societies of the United States* (New York, 1875, 439 pp.), pp. 115-256, for Nordhoff himself visited fourteen of the eighteen Shaker communities then in existence.

The best published bibliography, E. C. Winter, "Shaker Literature in the Grosvenor Library; a Bibliography," *Grosvenor Library Bulletin,* xxii (June 1940), pp. 66-119, lists (p. 69) the principal collections of Shakeriana. C. C. Adams, "The New York State Museum's Historical Survey and Collection of the New York Shakers," *New York State Museum Bulletin,* No. 323 (Mar. 1941), pp. 77-141, is thoroughly illustrated with photographs of Shaker furniture and architecture from Watervliet and New Lebanon, and also contains (pp. 123-128) a list of the principal collections of Shaker documents. The largest collection, in the library of the Western Reserve Historical Society at Cleveland, Ohio, includes—among many other documents—1,800 printed items and 3,000 volumes of manuscripts. The Library of Congress has the next largest collection, founded upon the private collection of John P. MacLean. This consists of about 500 titles, while the Grosvenor Library itself has 388 items listed, including periodical articles. For the collection of the New York Public Library, see "List of Works in the New York Public Library Relating to Shakers," New York Public Library *Bulletin*, VIII (Nov. 1904), pp. 550-559. A third large bibliography is J. P. MacLean, *A Bibliography of Shaker Literature with an Introductory Study of the Writings and Publications Pertaining to Ohio Believers* (Columbus, Ohio, 1905, 71 pp.). The list in Nordhoff (cited above), pp. 421-428, is still useful.

For more than a century, the Shakers wrote and published general statements of their principles and previous history which are indispensable sources. Joseph Meacham, *A Concise Statement of the Principles of the Only True Church According to the Gospel of the Present Appearance of Christ* (Bennington, Vt., 1790, 24 pp.), their first published expression of belief, was also one of the few Shaker publications in the twentieth century (Mt. Lebanon, N.Y.? 1900, 16 pp.). The so-called "Shaker Bible," *The Testimony of Christ's Second Appearing*, by B. S. Youngs (Lebanon, Ohio, 1808, 600 pp.), a spiritual history up to the coming of Mother Ann Lee, is probably the most important single volume issued by the Shakers. There were several editions. Ann Lee published nothing herself, but *Testimonies of the Life, Character, Revelations and Doctrines of Our Ever Blessed Mother Ann Lee and the Elders with Her* (collected by Rufus Bishop and rev. by S. Y. Wells; Hancock, Mass., 1816, 405 pp.) is a major source on the founder and disciples. A second edition was revised by G. B. Avery (Albany, N.Y., 1888, 302 pp.). See also *Testimonies Concerning the Character and Ministry of Mother Ann Lee* (ed. by S. Y. Wells; Albany, N.Y., 1827, 178 pp.); F. W. Evans, *Ann Lee (the Founder of the Shakers), a Biography* (4th ed., Mt. Lebanon, N.Y., 1858, 187 pp.); and H. C. Blinn, *The Life and Gospel Experience of Mother Ann Lee* (East Canterbury, N.H., 1901, 264 pp.). Elder Evans told his own story, *Autobiography of a Shaker, and Revelation of the Apocalypse* (Mt. Lebanon, N.Y., 1869, 162 pp.). The description of a Shaker novitiate in M. A. Doolittle, *Autobiography of Mary Antoinette Doolittle . . . Prior to Becoming a Member of the Shaker Community* (Mt. Lebanon, N.Y., 1880, 48 pp.), indicates the care with which the Shakers chose their members. Among other important Shaker sources are included *The Constitution of the United Societies of Believers (Called Shakers)* (comp. by Richard McNemar; Watervliet, Ohio, 1833, 138 pp.); the periodical, *The Manifesto* (Shakers [Watervliet], N.Y., and Shaker Village [East Canterbury], N.H., 1871-1899; title varies); also sample regulations issued during the period of decline, *Authorized Rules of the Shaker Community; Given for the Protection and Guidance of the Members in the Several Societies* (Mt. Lebanon, N.Y., 1894, 16 pp.), and *Supplementary Rules of the Shaker Community* (Mt. Lebanon, N.Y., 1894, 4 pp.). Other sources devoted primarily to Shaker doctrine are cited in the General Reading of PART III, pp. 181-182.

Ex-Shaker accounts of their experiences within the United Society are by the nature of their authors' position critical. In general, the later they appeared, the more friendly their attitude. One of the best is the sympathetic account of Hervey Elkins, *Fifteen Years in the Senior Order of Shakers* (Hanover, N.H., 1853, 136 pp.). Probably the earliest attack is that of the Baptist preacher who was among the first distinguished converts, Valentine Rathbun, *An Account of . . . a New and Strange Religion* (Providence, R.I., 1781, 23 pp., seven other imprints), betraying anti-British sentiment. Comparable to this is Amos Taylor, a ten-months' member, *A Narrative of the Strange Principles, Conduct and Character of the People Known by the Name of Shakers* (Worcester, Mass., 1782, 23 pp.). Two critics who show increasing violence in each work are James Smith, author of *Remarkable Occurrences Lately Discovered among the People Called Shakers; of a Treasonous and Barbarous Nature* (Paris, Ky., 1810?, 24 pp.) and *Shakerism Detected . . . by the Dispositions of Ten Different Persons Living in . . . Kentucky and Ohio* (Paris, Ky., 1810, 44 pp.); and Mary Dyer, who wrote *A Portraiture of Shakerism* (Concord, N.H., 1822, 446 pp.) and *The Rise and Progress of the Serpent from the Garden of Eden to the Present Day; with a Disclosure of Shakerism* (Concord, N.H., 1847, 268 pp.). Thomas Brown, originally a Quaker, and a Shaker from 1798 to 1805, offered his moderate appraisal, *An Account of the People Called Shakers; Their Faith, Doctrines and Practice* (Troy, N.Y., 1812, 372 pp.), to the Shakers for correction before publishing—an offer they declined. Three later and decidedly unfriendly testimonies are John Woods, *Shakerism Unmasked* (Paris, Ky., 1826, 84 pp.); William Haskett, *Shakerism Unmasked* (Pittsfield, Mass., 1828, 300 pp.); and David Lamson, *Two Years' Experience among the Shakers* (West Boylston, Mass., 1848, 212 pp.).

The following are typical Shaker documents upholding the Shakers against attack: B. S. Youngs, *Transactions of the Ohio Mob, Called in the Public Papers "An Expedition against the Shakers"* (Miami Co., Ohio, 1810, 11 pp.), republished in *Ohio Archaeological and Historical Quarterly*, xxi (Oct. 1912), pp. 403-415; Richard McNemar, *Shakerism Detected <a Pamphlet Published by Col. James Smith . . .> Examined and Refuted* (1st ed., Lebanon, Ohio, and Lexington, Ky., 1811; reprinted Watervliet, Ohio, 1833, 12 pp.); *The Other Side of the Question* (Cincinnati, Ohio, 1819, 164 pp.), a volume which was compiled by Richard

McNemar and others; *A Review of Mary M. Dyer's Publication Entitled "A Portraiture of Shakerism"* (Concord, N.H., 1824, 70 pp.); *Investigator; or, a Defence of the Order, Government & Economy of the United Society Called Shakers* (Lexington, Ky., 1828, 47 pp.). Not issued by the Shakers is the factual *Report of the Examination of the Shakers of Canterbury and Enfield before the New-Hampshire Legislature at the November Session, 1848* (Concord, N.H., 1849, 100 pp.).

A Shaker village was on the itinerary of nearly every early nineteenth-century traveler. Since Mt. (New) Lebanon and Niskyuna (Watervliet) were near the Albany route which they usually took, and since here was the birthplace and center of Shakerism, these Families monopolized the publicity. The following accounts have been selected on the basis of the fame of the visitors or the extent of their comments. Timothy Dwight of Yale never stopped at Mt. Lebanon but passed by often, inquired of the neighbors, and in 1783 had engaged in a theological argument with Elder Meacham at Chicopee, Massachusetts. Part of his account in *Travels in New-England and New-York* (New Haven, Conn., 1821-1822, 4 vols.), III, pp. 149-169, is based on that of the ex-Shaker Thomas Brown, cited above. The visit of Robert Owen's party to Niskyuna on their first trip to New Harmony in November 1824 is recorded in "Diary of William Owen," ed. by J. W. Hiatt, Indiana Historical Society *Publications*, IV (1906), pp. 9-15. G. W. Pierson, *Tocqueville and Beaumont in America* (New York, 1938, 852 pp.), pp. 178-179, describes how the pair were nonplussed at a Shaker meeting at Niskyuna in 1831. C. D. Arfwedson, *The United States and Canada, in 1832, 1833, and 1834* (London, 1834, 2 vols.), I, pp. 83-106, considered his hosts "peaceable, industrious, and unhappy religious victims" (p. 103). Andrew Bell (A. Thomason, pseud.), *Men and Things in America* (London, 1838, 296 pp.), pp. 79-99, is generally favorable. J. S. Buckingham, who visited Niskyuna, includes considerable background material in *America; Historical, Statistic, and Descriptive* (London, 1841, 3 vols.), II, pp. 352-405. Harriet Martineau, *Society in America* (New York, 1837, 2 vols. in 1), I, pp. 310-315, is critical of the Family at Hancock, Massachusetts. C. G. B. Daubeny, *Journal of a Tour through the United States and in Canada* (Oxford, 1843, 231 pp.), pp. 18-24, visited Mt. Lebanon during a time of revival in 1837. In addition, Horace Greeley, "A Sabbath with the Shakers," *Knickerbocker*, XI (June 1838), pp. 532-537; Capt. Frederick Marryat, *A Diary in America* (Philadelphia, 1839, 2 vols. in 1), I, pp. 61-64; and Charles Dickens, *American Notes and Pictures from Italy* (Everyman's Library; London, 1907, 430 pp.), pp. 212-215, indicate the period of peak interest. Fredrika Bremer, *The Homes of the New World* (tr. by Mary Howitt; New York, 1858, 2 vols.), I, pp. 556-571, II, p. 598, was able to note the unchanging character of

Shaker institutions and habits by returning to Mt. Lebanon two years after her first visit in 1850, and comment on the women's life at Canterbury, New Hampshire (II, pp. 573-580). See also Emory Holloway, "Walt Whitman's Visit to the Shakers," *Colophon*, Pt. 13 (Spring 1930), a twelve-page account of a visit to Mt. Lebanon.

The pamphlet by Catharine Allen of the North Family at Mt. Lebanon, *A Full Century of Communism; the History of the Alethians Formally Called Shakers* (Pittsfield, Mass., 1897, 16 pp.), was the only late historical writing by a Shaker, except White and Taylor cited above. Besides the other general histories of Shakerism cited at the beginning of this topic, and sections of the works mentioned in the General Reading, PART II, pp. 94-95, there are a number of shorter accounts by non-Shakers. E. F. Dow, author of *A Portrait of the Millennial Church of Shakers* (Orono, Me., 1931, 52 pp.), comes from a Shaker background. C. E. Robinson, *A Concise History of the United Society of Believers Called Shakers* (East Canterbury, N.H., 1893, 134 pp.), a revision of a series of sixteen articles published in the *Manufacturer and Builder*, XXIII-XXIV (1891-1892), under the pseudonym of C. R. Edson, although it met the approval of Elder H. C. Blinn of the Canterbury Family, was not written at that community's request, nor was the author a Shaker. See also the abstract of Daryl Chase's University of Chicago 1936 doctoral thesis, *The Early Shakers; an Experiment in Religious Communism* (Chicago, 1938, 22 pp.); Stuart Hodgson, "An American Communist Experiment," *Contemporary Review*, CXLIV (Sept. 1933), pp. 320-328; J. M. Phillippi, *Shakerism, or, The Romance of a Religion* (Dayton, Ohio, 1912, 133 pp.); W. H. Dixon, *New America* (3rd ed., Philadelphia, 1867, 495 pp.), pp. 301-346; B. J. Lossing, "The Shakers," *Harper's New Monthly Magazine*, xv (July 1857), pp. 164-177; and an anonymous volume, actually by Benjamin Silliman, entitled *Peculiarities of the Shakers, Described in a Series of Letters from Lebanon Springs* (New York, 1832, 116 pp.).

The following deal with the history of individual Shaker communities or with communities in a given region. For New Lebanon, see Berton Roueché, "A Small Family of Seven," *New Yorker*, XXIII (Aug. 23, 1947), pp. 46-57; the first Shaker number of the *Peg Board*, IV, No. 3 (June 1936), published by the Lebanon School, New Lebanon, New York; and the Darrow School prospectus entitled *Darrow* (New Lebanon, N.Y., 1940, 50 pp.). For the New England communities in their early days, consult F. B. Sanborn, "The Original Shaker Communities in New England," *New England Magazine*, N.S., XXII (May 1900), pp. 303-309, which quotes letters written by William Plumer in 1782 and 1783. For the community at Harvard, Massachusetts, see H. E. O'Brien, *Lost Utopias* (Boston, 1929, 62 pp.); and C. E. Sears, *Gleanings from Old*

Shaker Journals (Boston, 1916, 298 pp.). *The Memorial of the Society of People of Canterbury, in the County of Rockingham, and Enfield, in the County of Grafton, Commonly Called Shakers* (n.p., 1818, 13 pp.), contains material relevant to those communities, as well as general doctrine. *Life*, xxvi (Mar. 21, 1949), pp. 142-148, prints illustrations of the East Canterbury community. W. R. Cross, *The Burned-over District: the Social and Intellectual History of Enthusiastic Religion in Western New York, 1800-1850* (Ithaca, N.Y., 1950, 383 pp.), includes some discussion of the Shakers at Sodus Bay.

For various western Shaker communities and their leaders, consult: Julia Neal, *By Their Fruits; the Story of Shakerism in South Union, Kentucky* (Chapel Hill, N.C., 1947, 279 pp.); Elizabeth Coombs, "Brief History of the Shaker Colony at South Union, Kentucky," *Filson Club History Quarterly*, xiv (July 1940), pp. 154-173; D. M. Hutton, *Old Shakertown and the Shakers* (Harrodsburg, Ky., 1936, 67 pp.); and especially J. P. MacLean's series of sketches of western Shakers in *Ohio Archaeological and Historical Quarterly*, including the following: "The Society of Shakers; Rise, Progress and Extinction of the Society at Cleveland, O.," ix (July 1900), pp. 32-116, republished separately at Columbus, Ohio, 1901; "The Shaker Community of Warren County," x (Jan. 1902), pp. 251-304; "Mobbing the Shakers of Union Village," xi (July 1902), pp. 108-133; "Shaker Mission to the Shawnee Indians," xi (Oct. 1902), pp. 215-229; "Origin, Rise, Progress and Decline of the Whitewater Community of Shakers Located in Hamilton County, Ohio," xiii (Oct. 1904), pp. 401-443. For MacLean's papers on Ohio Shakers, see also his *Shakers of Ohio: Fugitive Papers Concerning the Shakers of Ohio* (Columbus, Ohio, 1907, 415 pp.). For writings by and about Richard McNemar, a central figure in western Shakerism, see especially his collections of articles from contemporary journals, *A Review of the Most Important Events Relating to the Rise and Progress of the United Society of Believers in the West* (Union Village, Ohio, 1831, various pagings); *The Kentucky Revival . . . with a Brief Account of . . . Shakerism . . . in Ohio and Kentucky* (Cincinnati, Ohio, 1807, 119 pp., and other editions) by the same author; and J. P. MacLean, *A Sketch of the Life and Labors of Richard McNemar* (Franklin, Ohio, 1905, 67 pp.).

Shakerism drew strength from revivalism, Quakerism, and spiritualism. Most important was the Kentucky revival, treated by Richard McNemar (cited above), and J. P. MacLean, *The Kentucky Revival and Its Influence on the Miami Valley* (Columbus, Ohio, 1903, 45 pp.), reprinted from the *Ohio Archaeological and Historical Quarterly*, xii (July 1903), pp. 242-286. Examples of successful recruiting from the Society of Friends are shown in the works of Thomas Brown (cited above) and Jane Knight, *Brief Narrative of Events Touching Various Reforms* (Albany,

N.Y., 1880, 29 pp.). Jane Knight was raised a Quaker and joined the Shakers in 1826. For Shakerism's relationship with spiritualism, see H. C. Blinn, *The Manifestation of Spiritualism among the Shakers* (East Canterbury, N.H., 1899, 101 pp.), and F. W. Evans, *New England Witchcraft and Spiritualism* (Mt. Lebanon, N.Y., n.d., 8 pp.). It is worth noting that Elder Evans was a younger brother of George Henry Evans, the land reformer.

Other aspects of Shakerism are discussed in PARTS III-VI.

Topic 3. The Mormons

The Mormons were the largest religious group in America whose social organization at times exhibited the degree of coordination entitling them to be included in this survey of American socialism. This topic makes no effort to cover the history of the Mormons in its entirety, but is restricted to the cooperative and socialistic phases of Mormon group life. Two experiments in what may roughly be called socialism were attempted, and the reading deals primarily with the second of these experiments. The very size of the Mormon group presented problems not faced by the other communistic religious groups. The presence of the Mormons on the frontier constituted a national political and social problem throughout the middle of the nineteenth century, a problem naturally intensified by the practice of polygamy. Their rapidly growing numbers also tended to weaken the cohesive force of personal attachment to their leaders, although persecution and a sense of union in peculiar doctrines to some degree held the Mormons together. Finally, the wealth and importance of the society they created served as a magnet to draw the swiftly moving frontier with its engulfing tide of "gentiles" who would ultimately modify and corrupt the faith of the Saints.

Mormon theology and religious teaching fostered a curious combination of spiritual and worldly ideals which set the framework for social practices at once individualistic and cooperative to a singular degree. The prevailing social-economic doctrines of the Saints were far less radical than those of the other socialistic religious communities, and their experiments with communism were justified by their leaders only under the stress of unusual circumstances. Cooperation in economic and social enterprises had been customary for obvious reasons since the days of Joseph Smith and it was developed to its highest point in the Mormon state of Deseret. More thoroughgoing communism was inaugurated in the settlements at Kirtland, Ohio, and at Independence, Missouri, as a result of revelations vouchsafed to Smith in 1832. The failure of these first attempts did not dissuade Brigham Young from reverting many years later to the authority of Smith in inaugurating a "Second United Order of Enoch" in 1874. Young seems to have hoped that a closer organization of his people would avert the perils of disintegration which he feared in the steady encroachments of the gentiles. Thus the Mormon venture in communism appears to have been in part a defensive measure designed to hold the faithful together. It is significant that the United Order was voluntary. Those who wished to enter it surrendered their property to the church, receiving back from the bishop in stewardship such part of it as the authorities believed the former owners could manage and use in the general interest. The Mormons were, without knowing it, emphasizing one of the fundamental social justifications of American capitalism.

The following selections emphasize the significance of this experiment in communism as an effort to hold the Mormons together in Utah. G. O. Larson, *Prelude to the Kingdom; Mormon Desert Conquest* (Francestown, N.H., 1947, 327 pp.), by an orthodox Mormon, is the only comprehensive and documented survey of Mormon cooperation in its broadest aspects, but fails to relate the subject sufficiently to general American history. E. J. Allen, *The Second United Order among the Mormons* (New York, 1936, 149 pp.), is a somewhat fuller account of the narrower theme of the United Order in Utah. W. J. McNiff, *Heaven on Earth; a Planned Mormon Society* (Oxford, Ohio, 1940, 262 pp.), is the best general social history of the Utah phase of Mormonism, with many references to manuscript and other sources. See also Nels Anderson, *Desert Saints; the Mormon Frontier in Utah* (Chicago, 1942, 459 pp.), in particular his chapter, "Economy of Faith and Plenty," pp. 361-389, and his bibliographical references. For the broader aspects of the Mormons' associative life, see Hamilton Gardner, "Cooperation among the Mormons," *Quarterly Journal of Economics*, xxxi (May 1917), pp. 461-499, and E. E. Ericksen, *The Psychological and Ethical Aspects of Mormon Group Life* (Chicago, 1922, 101 pp.), pp. 49-55.

A good bibliography of early materials is in the *Bulletin* of the New York Public Library, xiii (Mar. 1909), pp. 183-239, which includes the collection of William Berrian, but has little on either United Order. The only author to treat both phases of the United Order is Hamilton Gardner, in his discerning article, "Communism among the Mormons," *Quarterly Journal of Economics*, xxxvii (Nov. 1922), pp. 134-174. B. H. Roberts, *A Comprehensive History of the Church of Jesus Christ of Latter-Day Saints* (Salt Lake City, Utah, 1930, 6 vols.), expresses the Mormon attitude in his brief references (i, p. 243) to Joseph Smith's disapproval of Rigdon's communists at Kirtland, and to the law of consecration as stewardship and not communism (i, chap. 20). He dismisses the second experiment in a short section (v, pp. 484-489) which includes the rules drawn up for members of the order and source references.

Joseph Smith, *The Doctrine and Covenants of the Church of Jesus*

Christ of Latter-Day Saints (Salt Lake City, Utah, 1911, 542 pp.), contains in section 82 the revelation to Smith concerning the establishment of the United Order, or "greater law"; section 119 is a similar revelation regarding the "lesser law" of tithing which replaced the First United Order until the time should be ripe for its restoration. A special study of the First United Order of Enoch (1831-1834) is by the Mormon, J. A. Geddes, *The United Order among the Mormons (Missouri Phase)* (New York, 1922, 172 pp.). This contains (pp. 19-21) a discussion of possible socialist influences upon Joseph Smith, and discounts that of Sidney Rigdon's followers, a communistic Campbellite group at Kirtland, Ohio, which largely joined the Mormons. Rigdon's career after he failed to receive the mantle of the martyred prophet, like that of other seceders, is even more obscure. The Order of Enoch among the followers of J. J. Strang at Beaver Island, Michigan, is referred to in M. M. Quaife, *The Kingdom of Saint James* (New Haven, Conn., 1930, 284 pp.), pp. 71-78, 139-140. C. R. Marks discusses another Mormon "communistic" settlement under Charles B. Thompson in "Monona County, Iowa, Mormons," *Annals of Iowa*, Ser. 3, VII (Apr. 1906), pp. 321-346.

Brigham Young's pronouncements on economic matters have been gathered in *Discourses of Brigham Young* (ed. by J. A. Widtsoe; 2nd ed., Salt Lake City, Utah, 1926, 760 pp.), especially the following passages: "Tithing, the United Order," pp. 269-281; "Unity and Co-operation," pp. 433-445; "Thrift and Industry," pp. 446-467; "Wealth," pp. 468-488. The chief source of these addresses of Young is the *Journal of Discourses* (Liverpool, Eng., 1854-1885, 26 vols.), a compilation of addresses by the Mormon leaders. The best biography of Brigham Young is M. R. Werner, *Brigham Young* (New York, 1925, 478 pp.), pp. 418-441 of which deal with the Second United Order, which Werner ascribed to Young's effort to avert religious and economic dissensions. A popular account of the Orderville community (1874-1885)—the only town to maintain the United Order beyond the first two years—may be found in the chapter entitled "Arcadian Village" of Wallace Stegner's book, *Mormon Country* (New York, 1942, 362 pp.), pp. 108-127. See also the observations of a visitor on "family communism" at Kingston and Orderville in P. S. Robinson, *Sinners and Saints* (Boston, 1883, 370 pp.), pp. 208-215, 219-234. A Berlin doctoral dissertation by A. E. Wilson, "Gemeinwirtschaft und Unternehmungsformen im Mormonenstaat," *Jahrbuch für Gesetzgebung Verwaltung und Volkswirtschaft*, XXXI (1907), pp. 1003-1056, traces the supplanting of "communism" and cooperation by capitalism among the Mormons as the gentiles moved into Utah.

D. D. Lum, *Social Problems of To-Day; or, The Mormon Question in Its Economic Aspects; a Study of Co-operation and Arbitration in Mormondom, from the Standpoint of a Wage-Worker* (Port Jervis, N.Y.,

1886, 91 pp.), is probably the best brief contemporary account of Mormon associative enterprise by a gentile. Lum had been a government official in Utah and was later active in the labor and anarchist movements. The illustrated article by Glen Miller, a former U.S. marshal in Utah, "The Mormons; a Successful Coöperative Society," *World's Work,* v (Dec. 1902), pp. 2881-2894, emphasizes the Church's paternalistic control over a wide range of business activities, as does the much briefer but more specific reference in R. T. Ely's general sketch, "Economic Aspects of Mormonism," *Harper's Monthly Magazine,* cvi (Apr. 1903), pp. 667-678. The chief Mormon cooperative, Zion's Coöperative Mercantile Institution, is described in A. G. Warner, "Three Phases of Coöperation in the West," American Economic Association *Publications,* ii (Mar. 1887), pp. 106-119.

Topic 4. The Oneida Community

In the history of Christian thought the promise of perfection implicit in the doctrine of salvation has more than once served social radicals who have used it to justify their unorthodox social and individual behavior. In America the great revivals of the 1820's and 1830's provided the occasion for the widespread appearance of perfectionist doctrines which found their source in Methodism and in the free-will teachings of N. W. Taylor of Yale. The communistic tradition of primitive Christianity suggested, although it did not necessitate, the socialized community as the natural expression of social perfection. It was not surprising, therefore, that theological perfectionism was to be found a characteristic ingredient of American religious communism. It received its most spectacular expression in the Bible Communists of Oneida.

The Perfectionists of the Oneida Community, like the Mormons, would in any event have been forced to form separate settlements because of the dislike aroused among their neighbors by their unusual sexual practices. As in the case of the Mormons, too, pressure from outside eventually forced the group to abandon these practices. Unlike the Mormon leaders, however, and, indeed, unlike the leaders of most of the other communistic groups already discussed, John Humphrey Noyes (1811-1886), the head of the Oneida Community, made a thorough study of previous American socialisms in an effort to find out the reasons for their success and failure. One result of his investigation was that the Oneida Community made much more effort to adapt itself to an industrial era than did the other groups. And although as a religious community it declined when its distinctive customs were abandoned, as a manufacturing community its industries have been successful to this day—as the wide sale of Community Plate in particular still attests.

The following selections describe the success of the Oneida Community in an industrial age and the abandonment of its communism. The leader, J. H. Noyes, in *History of American Socialisms* (Philadelphia, 1870, 678 pp.), pp. 614-645, traces its history to about the time the stirpicultural experiment was started. The best description by an outsider is still that of Charles Nordhoff in *The Communistic Societies of the United States* (New York, 1875, 439 pp.), pp. 257-301. See especially pp. 3-18, 125-193, in Pierrepont Noyes, *My Father's House; an Oneida Boyhood* (New York, 1937, 312 pp.), the reminiscences of an executive of the Oneida Community, Ltd., who was brought up in the Children's House and discusses the Perfectionists, the Community, and the leader. See also the summary in V. F. Calverton, *Where Angels Dared to Tread* (Indianapolis, Ind., 1941, 381 pp.), pp. 254-287.

A few years after the publication of Noyes's *History of American Socialisms* one of his followers, W. A. Hinds, published a somewhat similar study, *American Communities* (Oneida, N.Y., 1878, 176 pp.), which was twice enlarged and republished. Hinds, too, gave considerable space to the Perfectionists (1908 ed.), pp. 152-231. Another member of the group, Allan Estlake, devoted an entire volume to it: *The Oneida Community; a Record of an Attempt to Carry Out the Principles of Christian Unselfishness and Scientific Race-Improvement* (London, 1900, 158 pp.). Other descriptions, issued by the Community itself, include the *Hand-book of the Oneida Community* (Wallingford, Conn., 1867, 71 pp.; Nos. 2-[3] published at Oneida, N.Y., 1871, 1875), and *The Oneida Community* (Oneida, N.Y.?, 1865, 32 pp.). Also see the historical summary by W. D. Edmonds, *The First Hundred Years, 1848-1948* (n.p., 1948, 75 pp.).

Brief discussions of the group include J. E. Jacoby, *Two Mystic Communities in America* (Paris, 1931, 104 pp.), "A Strange Fellow, a Perfectionist; The Oneida Community," pp. 53-104; and Gilbert Seldes, *The Stammering Century* (New York, 1928, 414 pp.), pp. 174-197.

For Noyes's life see especially R. A. Parker's detailed and sympathetic biography, *A Yankee Saint; John Humphrey Noyes and the Oneida Community* (New York, 1935, 322 pp.). The period of Noyes's life at his family home in Putney, Vermont, beginning with the circumstances surrounding his departure from Ithaca in the fall of 1837 and ending with the transfer of the Community to Oneida in 1848, are recorded from Perfectionist publications and correspondence, and connected by an editorial narrative in *John Humphrey Noyes; the Putney Community* (Oneida, N.Y., 1931, 393 pp.), edited by G. W. Noyes. See also the interpretation of Russell Blankenship, "The Perfectionism of John Humphrey Noyes in Relation to Its Social Background," University of Washington *Abstracts of Theses*, II (1937), pp. 537-541. And consult W. R. Cross, *The Burned-over District: the Social and Intellectual History of Enthusi-*

astic Religion in Western New York, 1800-1850 (Ithaca, N.Y., 1950, 383 pp.), *passim.*

John Humphrey Noyes himself wrote prolifically on his beliefs. In addition to his *American Socialisms,* cited above, his most important early statements of doctrine are contained in *The Berean, a Manual for the Help of Those Who Seek the Faith of the Primitive Church* (Putney, Vt., 1847, 504 pp.), a collection of articles written by Noyes in the previous twelve years. *Male Continence* (Oneida, N.Y., 1872, 32 pp.) describes the sexual practice of the Community before it decided to raise children, and *Essay on Scientific Propagation* (Oneida, N.Y., 1875?, 32 pp.) outlines the essentials of stirpiculture. See also *Home-Talks* (ed. by Alfred Barron and G. N. Miller; Oneida, N.Y., 1875, 358 pp.); and numerous articles in the various periodicals of the Perfectionists. Noyes's other works on theology are discussed in PART III, pp. 182-183.

Other members of the Community wrote important books and pamphlets. W. A. Hinds mentions in his *American Communities* (1902 ed., p. 147, footnote) that he himself compiled the pamphlet *Mutual Criticism* (Oneida, N.Y., 1876, 96 pp.) which deals with a method of promoting social health and harmony in the Community. Other pamphlets and books by members of the Community indicating interests and beliefs of the members include: Alfred Barron, *Foot Notes; or, Walking as a Fine Art* (Wallingford, Conn., 1875, 330 pp.); and H. H. Skinner, *Oneida Community Cooking; or, A Dinner without Meat* (Oneida, N.Y., 1873, 51 pp.). In connection with its animal-trap industry, the Community edited *The Trapper's Guide,* by Sewell Newhouse and others (1865; 3rd ed., New York, 1869, 215 pp.; twelve editions to 1914). When the Oneida Community became a joint-stock company it published the *By-laws of the Oneida Community, Limited* (Community, N.Y., 1881, 40 pp.). *Table Ways of Today, Prepared by Community Plate* (Oneida, N.Y., 1930, 39 pp.) is a brochure advertising the table-silver industry developed after the abandonment of communism.

The Perfectionists issued periodicals from 1834 through 1879, either edited principally by Noyes or under his guidance. These were the *Perfectionist* (New Haven, Conn., 1834-1836, last four numbers called the *New Covenant Record*); the *Witness* (first three numbers, Ithaca, N.Y., 1837; then Putney, Vt., 1838-1846; title changed Feb. 15, 1843 to the *Perfectionist* and in Mar. 1844 to the *Perfectionist and Theocratic Watchman*); *Free Church Circular* (Putney, Vt., 1846-1847; Oneida Reserve, N.Y., 1848-1851; Vols. 1-2 called the *Spiritual Magazine*); *Circular* (Brooklyn, N.Y., 1851-1854; Oneida, N.Y., 1855-1864; Mt. Tom [Wallingford], Conn., 1864-1868; Oneida, N.Y., 1868-1876, called *Oneida Circular,* 1871-1876); and the *American Socialist* (Oneida, N.Y., 1876-1879). Frequency of issue and subtitle varied, with longest gaps during the early transfers from one place of publication to another.

A fundamental doctrine of Noyes's theology which stirred up particular discussion and opposition until abandoned in 1879, was that of "complex marriage," or as his enemies called it, "free love." In 1837 one of Noyes's disciples sent a letter by Noyes which gave his theory of marriage—a letter intended for private circulation only—to a Perfectionist named Theophilus Gates. Gates aroused a storm of comment by printing the letter in the second number of his publication, *Battle-Axe and Weapons of War*, of which three numbers were issued at Philadelphia in June, July, and December 1837, and a fourth in August 1840. For Gates's life see C. C. Sellers, *Theophilus, the Battle-Axe: a History of the Lives and Adventures of Theophilus Ransom Gates and the Battle-Axes* (Philadelphia, 1930, 67 pp.). The eugenic and gynecological effects of complex marriage were the subject of considerable scientific and medical discussion. Dr. T. R. Noyes, son of John Humphrey Noyes, issued a *Report on the Health of Children in the Oneida Community* (Oneida, N.Y., 1878, 8 pp.). E. Van de Warker published "A Gynecological Study of the Oneida Community," *American Journal of Obstetrics and Diseases of Women and Children*, xvii (Aug. 1884), pp. 785-810; A. N. McGee discussed "An Experiment in American Stirpiculture," *American Anthropologist*, iv (Oct. 1891), pp. 319-325; also discussed by H. H. Noyes and G. W. Noyes, "The Oneida Community Experiment in Stirpiculture," in *Scientific Papers of the Second International Congress of Eugenics* (Baltimore, Md., 1923, 2 vols.), i (*Eugenics, Genetics and the Family*), pp. 374-386.

Attacks on Noyes and his communities in general, and on free love in particular, were numerous. They include Rev. Hubbard Eastman, *Noyesism Unveiled* (Brattleboro, Vt., 1849, 432 pp.), and the very sharp but interesting attack in J. B. Ellis, *Free Love and Its Votaries; or, American Socialism Unmasked* (New York, 1870, 502 pp.), pp. 29-350. The publicity provided by W. H. Dixon in *New America* (3rd ed., Philadelphia, 1867, 495 pp.), pp. 387-424, and *Spiritual Wives* (London, 1868, 2 vols.), ii, pp. 1-185, was the most devastating because the temper of Dixon's comments had almost the detachment of the cultural anthropologist. He revealed his bias against the unorthodox theology and sexual practices of the Perfectionists in subtle ways, and his readers could not fail to interpret his accounts as hostile. Dixon had free access to Oneida records and took advantage of permission to interview members. J. H. Noyes replied to his critics and to Dixon in particular in *Dixon and His Copyists: a Criticism of the Accounts of the Oneida Community* (Wallingford, Conn., 1871, 40 pp.; also 2nd ed., 1874, 39 pp.). The attacks which removed Noyes and his followers from Vermont did not prevent them from maintaining a colony at Putney from 1852 to 1857.

A popular magazine account contemporary with the heyday of Oneida socialism is I. G. Reed, "The Oneida Community of Free Lovers," *Frank Leslie's Illustrated Newspaper*, xxx (Apr. 2, 1870), pp. 38-39. Two recent and valuable articles on the Oneida Community, "Children of the Kingdom," Pts. 1 and 2, written by Carl Carmer, appeared in the *New Yorker*, xii (Mar. 21, 1936), pp. 26-36; (Mar. 28, 1936), pp. 36-54, and were reprinted in *Listen for a Lonesome Drum* (New York, 1936, 381 pp.), pp. 138-164. See also the article by C. N. Robertson (a direct descendant of John Humphrey Noyes), "The Oneida Community," *New York History*, xxx (Apr. 1949), pp. 131-150.

Topic 5. Owen and New Harmony

One of the more significant reactions to the growth of industrialism in the early nineteenth century was the socialist movement led by the British industrialist Robert Owen (PART I, Topic 2). His success in rehabilitating the lives of his employees at New Lanark encouraged Owen in his belief that the wider application of his principles would solve the social problems attendant upon industrialism and introduce a new era of social harmony and human progress. Owen's thought united an acute and realistic analysis of the ills of contemporary society with a blithely optimistic faith in a millennial future to be introduced through his relatively simple panaceas. His central idea was education, based upon the hypothesis that any character can be inculcated in the proper social environment upon the blank slates of infants' minds. Education, particularly the development of the psychological attitudes of cooperativeness and mutuality, was the keynote of Owen's communitarianism, in the United States no less than in his own country. He was not content to experiment in the character formation of children, but illogically continued his tireless propaganda, among the prominent and the obscure, from the moment he first arrived in New York.

His concern for economic questions was secondary, and his treatment of them, for all his industrial experience, unsure and fluctuating. The depression following Waterloo he had ascribed to lack of mass purchasing power, caused by the antisocial practices of laissez-faire economy. As a benevolent capitalist he began gropingly with a program of subsistence agriculture for the unemployed. Gradually he came to conceive of agriculture and industry as equally necessary to a community. A few years before his first visit to the United States he saw his own class turning its back on him, and came more and more under the influence of such radicals as John Gray and William Thompson.

An opportunity to put his theories into practice came to Owen in 1824-

1825. He bought the Rappite village of Harmony, Indiana, and invited all interested persons to join him in his social experiment. The most exhaustive history of the New Harmony experience, set in the broad framework of European and American communitarian philosophy, is contained in A. E. Bestor, Jr., *Backwoods Utopias: the Sectarian and Owenite Phases of Communitarian Socialism in America, 1663-1829* (Philadelphia, 1950, 288 pp.). This contains a comprehensive bibliographical essay (pp. 245-268), including critical descriptions of the principal Owenite sources. See also R. A. Hurst, "The New Harmony Manuscript Collections," *Indiana Magazine of History*, xxxvii (Mar. 1941), pp. 45-49, which describes the collection of 14,000 pieces at the library of the Workingmen's Institute at New Harmony, Indiana. The chief source for Owenite propaganda, for the communities (1825-1827), for Owen's trip to America in 1828-1829 to obtain a Mexican grant for another experiment, and for political activities of Robert Dale Owen and Frances Wright, is the *Free Enquirer* (New Harmony, Ind., 1825-1828; New York, 1829-1835; Vols. 1-3 [1825-1828] as the *New-Harmony Gazette*).

Selected sources on American Owenism in the 1820's contain a whole spectrum of opinion. The first native published expression of the movement was the anonymous pamphlet attributed to the New York apothecary, Cornelius C. Blatchly, *An Essay on Common Wealths* (New York, 1822, 64 pp.). The author, founder, and moving spirit of the New York Society for Promoting Communities, included in the pamphlet an original essay, "The Evils of Exclusive and the Benefits of Inclusive Wealth," extracts from Owen's *New View of Society*, and Melish's account of the Harmonists. The pamphlet exhibited the cross-fertilization of American religious and European secular communitarianism with hitherto independent American speculation. The peak of Owen's initial propaganda campaign is represented by his two speeches before Congress, *A Discourse on a New System of Society, as Delivered . . . on the 25th of February, 1825* (Washington, 1825, 20 pp.) and *A Discourse on a New System of Society, as Delivered . . . on the 7th of March, 1825* (Washington, 1825, 26 pp.). The "Diary of William Owen from November 10, 1824, to April 20, 1825," ed. by J. W. Hiatt, Indiana Historical Society *Publications*, iv (1906), pp. 1-134, documents, from the point of view of Owen's twenty-two-year-old son, both the first tour of principal cities, and the history of New Harmony in transition from Rappite to Owenite control. "The Diaries of Donald Macdonald, 1824-1826," *ibid.*, xiv (1942), pp. 145-379, with an introduction by C. D. Snedeker, provide further evidence by a British soldier in Owen's party on Owen's first and second trips to New Harmony. A. E. Bestor, Jr.'s review of this publication in *New York History*, xxiv (Jan. 1943), pp. 80-86, supplies partial editorial comment on the diary. Macdonald's silence on the state of affairs at New Harmony in 1826 testifies to his disillusion-ment. The disillusionment of the upper-class Pears family, prominent in the community, is explicit in "New Harmony, an Adventure in Happiness; Papers of Thomas and Sarah Pears," ed. by T. C. Pears, Indiana Historical Society *Publications*, xi (1933), pp. 1-96. On the other hand, C. C. Pelham, ed., "Letters of William Pelham Written in 1825 and 1826," in Harlow Lindley, ed., *Indiana as Seen by Early Travelers* (Indianapolis, Ind., 1916, 596 pp.), pp. 360-417, reflects the enthusiasm of one of the oldest members, who nevertheless withdrew to a farm where he died just before the experiment was abandoned. Lindley also reprints other observations by Bernhard, Duke of Saxe-Weimar (pp. 418-437), who spent a week at New Harmony in 1826; by William Herbert, "A Visit to the Colony of Harmony in Indiana" (pp. 327-352), a portion of which outlines Owenite plans; and from "Diary and Recollections of Victor Colin Duclos" (pp. 536-548), by a pupil at Maclure's schools near Philadelphia and at New Harmony. At the extreme left was Paul Brown, who criticized Owen for not being a communist, for mismanagement, and for his theory of character formation in *Twelve Months in New-Harmony* (Cincinnati, Ohio, 1827, 128 pp.).

Sample documents relating to other Owenite communities are W. P. Fox, "The Kendal Community," *Ohio Archaeological and Historical Publications*, xx (1911), pp. 176-219, which consists of the constitution, reports of meetings, and final accounting of the community, May 1826-Jan. 1829; and the hostile pamphlet by James M'Knight, *A Discourse Exposing Robert Owen's System, as Practised by the Franklin Community at Haverstraw* (New York, 1826, 20 pp.). A. J. G. Perkins and Theresa Wolfson, *Frances Wright; Free Enquirer* (New York, 1939, 393 pp.), pp. 123-207, relates the misfortunes of the Nashoba experiment (1825-1828), with extensive undocumented quotations from the correspondence of participants, visitors, and critics. W. R. Waterman, *Frances Wright* (New York, 1924, 267 pp.), is an earlier life. See also O. B. Emerson, "Frances Wright and Her Nashoba Experiment," *Tennessee Historical Quarterly*, vi (Dec. 1947), pp. 291-314. Typical of outside criticism of Owenism in general is W. L. Fisher, *An Examination of the New System of Society by Robert Owen, Showing Its Insufficiency* (Philadelphia, 1826, 86 pp.).

Among the older secondary accounts, that of J. H. Noyes, *History of American Socialisms* (Philadelphia, 1870, 678 pp.), pp. 30-92, provides from the Macdonald manuscript the most information on lesser communities and on Owen's later career in the United States. Noyes appends (pp. 93-101) useful remarks on Owenite connections with later movements. Robert Dale Owen's reminiscences, *Threading My Way; Twenty-Seven Years of Autobiography* (London, 1874, 332 pp.), pp. 209-267, contain somewhat inaccurate memories of New Harmony. This section was first published as two articles in the *Atlantic Monthly*, xxxii (Aug.-Sept. 1873), pp. 224-236, 336-348. R. W. Leopold's biography, *Robert Dale Owen* (Cambridge, Mass., 1940, 470 pp.), pp. 19-46, the best brief summary, emphasizes the second year, after Robert Dale Owen had arrived from New Lanark, and mentions Owen's failure to provide wise or competent leadership at New Harmony. The most extended account before Bestor is G. B. Lockwood, *The New Harmony Movement* (New York, 1905, 404 pp.), enlarged from Lockwood's earlier study, *The New Harmony Communities* (Marion, Ind., 1902, 282 pp.). Lockwood handled competently, if not penetratingly, the evidence then available. See also the brief treatments in Frank Podmore, *Robert Owen* (London, 1906, 2 vols.), i, pp. 285-346, and G. D. H. Cole, *The Life of Robert Owen* (2nd ed., London, 1930, 349 pp.), pp. 239-251, Nora Fretageot's illustrated guidebook, *Historic New Harmony* (new ed., Mt. Vernon, Ind., 1923, 66 pp.), and the illustrations in "Life Visits New Harmony," *Life*, xix (Sept. 17, 1945), pp. 133-139. A "fairy tale" of Owen's experiment is contained in the latter part of Marguerite Young, *Angel in the Forest* (New York, 1945, 313 pp.), a combination of research and fiction.

The educational and scientific importance of New Harmony outweighed its significance as a social experiment, and in this phase of its activity William Maclure was an outstanding participant. A. E. Bestor, Jr., "Education and Reform at New Harmony; Correspondence of William Maclure and Marie Duclos Fretageot," Indiana Historical Society *Publications*, xv (1948), pp. 285-417, is the essential source. The first Pestalozzian teacher whom Maclure brought to the United States was Joseph Neef, who had published, before he became a New Harmony schoolmaster, *Sketch of a Plan and Method of Education* (Philadelphia, 1808, 168 pp.) and *The Method of Instructing Children Rationally, in the Arts of Writing and Reading* (Philadelphia, 1813, 338 pp.). Maclure's political and economic ideas, based, like Owen's, upon his idea of education, but more radical than Owen's, were published in *Opinions on Various Subjects* (New Harmony, Ind., 1831-1838, 3 vols.), articles mostly reprinted from the *Disseminator* (New Harmony, 1828-1835, title varies). A sketch of Maclure's life by S. G. Morton may be found in pamphlet form, *A Memoir of William Maclure* (Philadelphia, 1841, 37 pp.), or in the *American Journal of Science*, xlvii (Apr.-June 1844), pp. 1-17. Maximilian, Prince of Wied, spent the winter of 1832-1833 with some of the Owen family and the scientists who had remained in New Harmony after the community failed. His record, "Travels in the Interior of North America, 1832-1834," in *Early Western Travels*, R. G. Thwaites, ed. (Cleveland, Ohio, 1906), xxii, pp. 163-197, deals primarily with the natural history of the region which these scientists were studying. For a biography of one of that group, see H. B. Weiss and G. M. Ziegler,

Thomas Say; Early American Naturalist (Springfield, Ill., 1931, 260 pp.). See also C. A. Browne, "Some Relations of the New Harmony Movement to the History of Science in America," *Scientific Monthly*, XLII (June 1936), pp. 483-497.

Following the failure of New Harmony, Robert Dale Owen returned from a trip to England and joined Frances Wright in the nascent working-class movement, while his father, after one more attempt, was drawn into the British labor movement. Robert Owen, *Address . . . by Robert Owen, at a Public Meeting . . . in . . . Philadelphia . . . To Which is Added, An Exposition of the Pecuniary Transactions between That Gentleman and W. M'Clure* (Philadelphia, 1827, 39 pp.), airs the differences between the two leaders. See Frances Wright, "The People at War," *Free Enquirer*, III (Nov. 27, 1830), p. 38, also quoted partially in J. R. Commons and others, eds., *A Documentary History of American Industrial Society* (Cleveland, Ohio, 1910-1911, 10 vols. and supp.), V, pp. 178-181; and pp. 208-270, in Perkins and Wolfson's biography of Frances Wright cited above. A characteristic American reaction to this point of view is L. S. Everett, *An Exposure of the Principles of the "Free Inquirers"* (Boston, 1831, 44 pp.). *Robert Owen's Opening Speech, and His Reply to the Rev. Alex. Campbell . . . to Prove That the Principles of All Religions Are Erroneous. . . . Also, Mr. Owen's Memorial to the Republic of Mexico, and a Narrative of the Proceedings Thereupon* (Cincinnati, Ohio, 1829, 226 pp.) is the most outspoken and extended expression in the United States of Owen's views on religion. Campbell's version of this meeting is cited in PART V, Topic 9. It goes far toward explaining why, aside from the paramount reason that New Harmony had failed, American communitarians preferred Fourierism to Owen's competing propaganda in the 1840's. Commons, *Documentary History*, VII, pp. 152-182, samples this propaganda.

Topic 6.   The Associationists (Fourierists)

Just as the economic depression in England after the Napoleonic wars had stimulated the thinking of Robert Owen, so the panic and depression of 1837 in the United States provided the background for a group of social critics who rejected the individualist economy and many of the social institutions founded upon it. Their inspiration came from Europe, and their doctrines were largely derivatory, but to a much greater extent than the first American Owenite movement twenty years before, the leadership and personnel of the new movement were native in origin. To a considerable extent the Fourierists felt the compulsion to modify the received doctrine in conformity with American conditions.

The Associationists derived their ideas from the Frenchman Charles Fourier (see PART I, Topic 2). Like Robert Owen, Fourier (1772-1837) was impressed with the waste and inefficiency of capitalism, but emphasized the evils of commerce more than those of industry. Like Owen also, Fourier had lived through the era of the French Revolution and Napoleon, and sought a social solution that did not appeal to violence. He was disturbed by such social consequences of the system as class conflict, intolerable industrial working conditions, and the widening extremes of poverty and plenty. These conditions were to be found in America, but in less exaggerated forms. The American Fourierists pointed to the contradiction between the humanitarian and Christian social teachings and the selfish or immoral practices of prevailing economic life. In contrast to Owen and some of his followers many of the Associationists were ardent Christians who imparted to the movement something of an evangelical fervor. They atoned for their orthodoxy in this respect, however, by advocating a communal and cooperative way of living in an age when the individual home was still the paramount social unit in America.

The Associationists proposed to form productive and social units called phalanxes in which labor, talent, and capital would receive a decreasing share of the proceeds. Here was a compromise between communism and capitalism in which stockholders would realize a limited profit from the associated activities. The economies and pleasures of "attractive industry" would enable the individual member of the phalanx to live cheaply and in an atmosphere of harmonious association with other producers who in the larger acquisitive society could be viewed only as hostile competitors.

This topic deals chiefly with the organization and history of the Fourierist movement and its most important phalanxes. (Other aspects will be dealt with in PARTS III-VI.) The pioneer propagandist for American Association was Albert Brisbane. See the most influential of Brisbane's writings, *Association; or, A Concise Exposition of the Practical Part of Fourier's Social Science* (New York, 1843, 80 pp.), especially pp. 3-18, 30-51, 71-73. On the Associationist colonies, see in particular J. H. Noyes, *History of American Socialisms*, pp. 233-250 (Sylvania Phalanx), 411-448 (Wisconsin Phalanx), 449-511 (North American Phalanx); and the sympathetic treatment of the Fourierist phase of Brook Farm community in J. T. Codman, *Brook Farm; Historic and Personal Memoirs* (Boston, 1894, 335 pp.), pp. 25-45, 79-100, 101-125.

A. E. Bestor, Jr., of the University of Illinois has written comprehensively of American Fourierism, with elaborate bibliographical essays and references. But until his study is published the only general account, however cursory, is in J. H. Noyes, *History of American Socialisms*, pp. 181-563. Noyes quoted at length from the manuscripts of A. J. Macdonald, now in the Yale University Library. Macdonald interviewed many participants and collected their literature. Maurice Buchs, a French student, has written a doctoral dissertation, *Le Fouriérisme aux États-Unis; contribution à l'étude du socialisme américain* (University of Paris, 1948, 220 pp.). C. A. Madison, *Critics & Crusaders* (New York, 1947, 572 pp.), pp. 83-133, gives a layman's account of the "utopian" climate of opinion, with sketches of Margaret Fuller and Albert Brisbane. See also A. M. Schlesinger, Jr., *The Age of Jackson* (Boston, 1945, 577 pp.), pp. 361-368, and N. P. Gilman, "The Way to Utopia," *Unitarian Review*, xxxiv (July 1890), pp. 48-66.

Fourier's doctrines were circulated through his American disciples. In addition to Brisbane's pamphlet just cited, his *Social Destiny of Man; or, Association and Reorganization of Industry* (Philadelphia, 1840, 480 pp.), and Parke Godwin, *A Popular View of the Doctrines of Charles Fourier* (New York, 1844, 120 pp.), were the most widely read expositions of Associationism. *Albert Brisbane, a Mental Biography, with a Character Study by His Wife, Redelia Brisbane* (Boston, 1893, 377 pp.), traces Brisbane's travels in search of "a just and wise organization of human society," and tells how Fourier's system satisfied him and the changes it underwent in his hands. A critical evaluation of this source, and others for Brisbane, is appended to A. E. Bestor's article, "Albert Brisbane, Propagandist for Socialism in the 1840's," *New York History*, xxviii (Apr. 1947), pp. 128-158. This includes citations to periodicals for which Brisbane wrote, ms collections, and passing references in published books. Other bibliographical information is found in the footnotes. The first Fourierist publication in the United States was the pamphlet *Two Essays on the Social System of Charles Fourier, Being an Introduction to the Constitution of the Fourienne Society of New York* (New York, 1838, 24 pp.).

Several periodicals were established to popularize Fourierism, of which the *Present* (New York, 1843-1844), and the *Phalanx* (New York, 1843-1845) continued as the *Harbinger* (New York and Boston, 1845-1849), were the most important not only for the propaganda of the movement, but also for the controversy with non-Fourierist utopians and other critics and for reports on Fourierist settlements. Brook Farm under its Fourierist constitution published the *Harbinger* until June 1847. The American Union of Associationists, formed that year, then assumed the responsibility. The *Spirit of the Age* (New York, 1849-1850), edited by W. H. Channing, continued to issue Fourierist propaganda. An account of the aims of this union, with a report of its first general convention and other materials on local Fourierist societies, is found in J. R. Commons and others, eds., *A Documentary History of American Industrial Society* (Cleveland, Ohio, 1910-1911, 10 vols. and supp.), vii, pp. 185-206. This collection contains (vii, pp. 240-284) contemporary accounts of several

Associations not included in Noyes's *American Socialisms*. The *New York Tribune* and contemporary magazines such as the *Dial* and the *United States Magazine and Democratic Review* contain articles by such participants and sympathizers as Brisbane, Orestes A. Brownson, Elizabeth P. Peabody, Charles Sears, Parke Godwin, and Emerson. A summary of the Greeley-Raymond debate on socialism is found in Charles Sotheran, *Horace Greeley and Other Pioneers of American Socialism* (New York, 1915, 349 pp.), pp. 192-218. Sotheran's uncritical, extravagant, and jumbled book, first published in 1892, attempts to establish the native American tradition of the socialism of his time. Greeley's autobiography, *Recollections of a Busy Life* (New York, 1868, 624 pp.), contains sections (pp. 144-158, 497-527) on his socialist efforts and ideas including his own modification of the Fouricrist creed; and "The Social Architects—Fourier," in *Hints towards Reforms* (New York, 1850, 400 pp.), pp. 272-299, is one of his often repeated lectures.

During its Fourierist period Brook Farm was the spearhead of the movement, yet this later phase has received little attention. A. E. Bestor, Jr., plans to publish the principal official records of the Brook Farm Association, a selection of documents dealing with other phalanxes and with expressions of Associationist theory, and an extensive bibliography. Until the Brook Farm records are published they are available in the Massachusetts Historical Society. A few selections have appeared, such as the excerpts from George Ripley's scrapbooks in Clarence Gohdes, "A Brook Farm Labor Record," *American Literature*, i (Nov. 1929), pp. 297-303. See also the *Constitution of the Brook Farm Association* (2nd ed., Boston, 1844, 20 pp.); and Zoltán Haraszti, "Brook Farm Letters," *More Books*, xii (Feb.-Mar. 1937), pp. 49-68, 93-114. Lindsay Swift, *Brook Farm, Its Members, Scholars and Visitors* (New York, 1900, 303 pp.), devotes but eighteen pages (263-281) to the Brook Farm Phalanx, for which the author had little sympathy. M. D. Orvis, *Letters from Brook Farm, 1844-1847* (ed. by A. L. Reed; Poughkeepsie, N.Y., 1928, 191 pp.), reveals the difficulties of the communal life as seen by one thoroughly imbued with the ideal. In Codman, *Brook Farm* (cited above), pp. 259-335, are inquiries, replies, and comments, mostly from the later period. G. B. Kirby, *Years of Experience* (New York, 1887, 315 pp.), and Margaret Fuller, *Memoirs* (Boston, 1852, 2 vols.), with parts by Emerson, J. F. Clarke, and W. H. Channing, are sample autobiographies of a former member and a well-wisher. O. B. Frothingham, *George Ripley* (Boston, 1882, 321 pp.), pp. 166-198, discusses Ripley's leadership during the last three years. G. W. Cooke, *John Sullivan Dwight* (Boston, 1898, 297 pp.), deals with Dwight as a teacher at Brook Farm and as a music critic bringing prestige to the *Harbinger*. Dwight outlined his theory of education in A *Lecture on Association in Its Connection with Education*

(Boston, 1844, 22 pp.). J. H. Wilson, *The Life of Charles A. Dana* (New York, 1907, 544 pp.), pp. 33-60, 517-534, describes Dana as Greek and German teacher, laborer, and later trustee and secretary of the community. Rev. V. F. Holden's Catholic University dissertation, *The Early Years of Isaac Thomas Hecker (1819-1844)* (Washington, 1939, 257 pp.), devotes more space (pp. 91-150) than other lives of Father Hecker to his six months as a spiritually unsettled student at Brook Farm. Recent reviews of the Brook Farm endeavor are Zoltán Haraszti, *The Idyll of Brook Farm* (Boston, 1937, 46 pp.), and Katherine Burton, *Paradise Planters, the Story of Brook Farm* (London, 1939, 336 pp.). Haraszti emphasizes the relation of the Association to the hard times following 1837. Katherine Burton's extensive use of dialogue based on documents results in a cross between imaginative fiction and history. She is more concerned with the community's transcendentalism than its Fourierism.

The monographic literature on other Fourierist settlements is not large. A defense prepared by the phalanx near Red Bank, New Jersey (1843-1855), *Exposé of the Condition and Progress of the North American Phalanx; in Reply to the Inquiries of Horace Greeley, and . . . the Criticisms of Friends and Foes* (New York, 1853, 28 pp.), is a valuable source. See also Fredrika Bremer's sympathetic observations and criticism based on two brief visits in 1849 and 1851, in her travel diary, *The Homes of the New World* (tr. by Mary Howitt; New York, 1858, 2 vols.), I, pp. 75-85, and II, pp. 611-624; the account by an acknowledged leader of the community, Charles Sears, *The North American Phalanx* (Prescott, Wis., 1886, 18 pp.); and N. L. Swan, "The North American Phalanx," Monmouth County [N.J.] Historical Association *Bulletin*, I (May 1935), pp. 35-65. On the settlement (1844-1850) at present-day Ripon, Wisconsin, which departed more from Fourierist principles but alone achieved material success, see S. M. Pedrick, "The Wisconsin Phalanx at Ceresco," State Historical Society of Wisconsin, *Proceedings . . . 1902* (1903), pp. 190-226; and Joseph Schafer, "The Wisconsin Phalanx," *Wisconsin Magazine of History*, XIX (June 1936), pp. 454-474. The part played by Warren Chase, the principal leader in this venture, is also described in his anonymous autobiography, *The Life-Line of the Lone One* (1857; 5th ed., Boston, 1868, 310 pp.; ten "editions" to 1888), pp. 113-130. P. D. Jordan has a brief note, "The Iowa Pioneer Phalanx," in *Palimpsest*, XVI (July 1935), pp. 211-225. The Fourierists at Sodus Bay (formerly a Shaker community) are mentioned in W. R. Cross, *The Burned-over District: the Social and Intellectual History of Enthusiastic Religion in Western New York, 1800-1850* (Ithaca, N.Y., 1950, 383 pp.).

The last Fourierist enterprise, and the only one with French rather than American leadership and personnel, was Victor Considérant's colony at Reunion, near Dallas, Texas, 1855-1875. Considérant interested Albert

Brisbane in his Société de Colonisation Européo-Américaine au Texas, and after a trip to the state published the glowing promotional tracts, *Au Texas* (Paris, 1854, 194 pp.) and *The Great West; a New Social and Industrial Life in Its Fertile Regions* (New York, 1854, 60 pp.). The second edition of *Au Texas* (Brussels, 1855, 334 pp.) contained a constitution and plans for settlement as well as a description. Texan antagonism to the foreigners called forth Considérant's defense, *European Colonization in Texas; an Address to the American People* (New York, 1855, 38 pp.), and further propaganda, *Du Texas; premier rapport à mes amis* (Paris, 1857, 80 pp.); but forced the abandonment of the colony's Fourierist features. Considérant withdrew to San Antonio long before its final liquidation, and later returned to France. Among the posthumous accounts of the venture see Eusibia Lutz, "Almost Utopia," *Southwest Review*, XIV (Spring 1929), pp. 321-330.

Contemporary critiques of Fourierism were generally based on orthodox religious doctrine. The weak phalanxes in the Rochester area were particularly vulnerable to the attack of D. C. McLaren, *Boa Constrictor, or Fourier Association Self-Exposed as to Its Principles and Aims* (Rochester, N.Y., 1844, 32 pp.), essentially an alarmist review of Brisbane on Association. From another religious point of view, Hosea Ballou, II, a leading Universalist, commented unfavorably on Brisbane's *Concise Exposition* and Godwin's *Popular View* in "Fourierism and Similar Schemes," *Universalist Quarterly and General Review*, II (Jan. 1845), pp. 52-76. J. H. Fairchild, professor of languages at the Oberlin Collegiate Institute and later president of Oberlin College, reviewed the same pamphlets from the standpoint of Finneyite perfectionists in the *Oberlin Quarterly Review*, I (Nov. 1845), pp. 224-245. See also the curious poem by H. P. Harring, *Harro Harring's Episteln an die Fourieristen* (New York, 1844, 31 pp.).

Topic 7. The Icarians

Like the Owenite communities and the Fourierist phalanxes, the Icarian settlements, too, grew out of the ideas and writings of a celebrated European socialist leader, Étienne Cabet (see PART I, pp. 50-51). Cabet's famous utopian novel, *Voyage . . . en Icarie* (Paris, 1840, 2 vols. in 1; five editions in eight years), was the direct inspiration of the Icarian communities. Like Robert Owen, Cabet himself came to this country to establish a communistic utopia of a nonsectarian nature. When the attempts of an advance group to prepare a settlement in Texas failed, the first Icarian colony was established in 1849 at the abandoned Mormon settlement of Nauvoo, Illinois. Disputes among the Icarians, the first during the regime of Cabet himself, resulted in the withdrawal of minorities who established new communities, in turn split by dissension. As a result, successive colonies were established at Cheltenham, near St. Louis, Missouri; near Corning, Iowa; and at Cloverdale, Sonoma County, California. All, like the original settlement, eventually failed as communist societies.

Since the Icarians are the one group considered in PART II who were directly inspired by a utopian novel, the best approach to the subject is to read that novel, *Voyage en Icarie* (3rd ed., Paris, 1845, 600 pp.), especially pp. 1-51, and compare the blueprint with actual Icarian practices in the United States. The most thorough and accurate description of the American experiments, based fully on a critical evaluation of the widest range of sources then available, is in Jules Prudhommeaux, *Icarie et son fondateur, Étienne Cabet; contribution à l'étude du socialisme expérimental* (Paris, 1907, 688 pp.), pp. 201-608. This section had been published the year before as *Histoire de la communauté icarienne* (Nîmes, 1906, 483 pp.). For the general reader, Mrs. Marion Tinling, a former editor of the *Huntington Library Quarterly*, is preparing a briefer volume. A résumé of Prudhommeaux may be found in Charles Gide, *Communist and Co-operative Colonies* (1928; tr. by E. F. Row; New York, 1931, 222 pp.), pp. 132-154; and from a different point of view, W. A. Hinds, "The Icarians," in his *American Communities* (3rd ed., Chicago, 1908, 608 pp.), pp. 361-396, is still useful.

Prudhommeaux's volume, just cited, pp. xiii-xl, is still the best bibliographical source for the extensive material on Icaria and Cabet. The numerous periodicals growing out of factional disputes are listed, pp. xxxviii-xl. See also the list of imprints on Cabet in Georges Andrieux, *Importants livres et manuscrits relatifs aux Amériques . . . vente à Paris . . . les 18 et 19 juin 1934* (Abbeville, 1934, 129 pp.), pp. 101-104, and Paul Chéron, *Catalogue général de la librairie française au xixᵉ siècle* (Paris, 1856-1859, 3 vols.), II, cols. 500-505.

For the general background of Étienne Cabet's activities in France, consult PART I, pp. 50-51. S. A. Piotrowski, *Étienne Cabet and the Voyage en Icarie* (Washington, 1935, 158 pp.), discusses Cabet's social theory as expressed principally in the novel, with some bibliographical items not in Prudhommeaux.

Of Cabet's writings on the Icarian settlements in the United States the most important is *Colony or Republic of Icaria in the United States of America, Its History* (Nauvoo, Ill., 1852, 19 pp.). This had two editions in French (Paris, 1854, 60 pp.; Paris, 1855, 95 pp.). The "History and Constitution of the Icarian Community," *Iowa Journal of History and Politics*, xv (Apr. 1917), pp. 214-286, is a translation of the second Paris edition by Thomas Teakle. Relevant to Cabet's plans for his settlement is *Ce que je ferais si j'avais 500,000 dollars* (Paris, 1854, 30 pp.; German and English translations, Nauvoo, Ill., 1854). See also *Colonie icarienne;*

situation dans l'Iowa (Paris, 1853, 8 pp.); *Colonie icarienne aux États-Unis d'Amérique; sa constitution, ses lois, sa situation matérielle et morale, après le premier semestre 1855* (Paris, 1856, 239 pp.); and *Colonie icarienne; guerre à mort de l'opposition contre le cit. Cabet, fondateur et président d'Icarie et mémorable séance de la nuit du 12 au 13 mai 1856* (Nauvoo, Ill., 1856, 72 pp.).

Internal controversies were responsible for numerous pamphlets by J. P. Beluze, head of the Icarian propaganda bureau in Paris, and by members of the opposition party, as well as by Cabet. Beluze wrote *La Colonie icarienne à Saint Louis* (Paris, 1857, 24 pp.); *Organisation du travail dans la communauté icarienne* (Paris, 1857, 23 pp.); and edited *Contrat social, ou Acte de Société de la communauté icarienne; lois sur l'admission* (Paris, 1857, 46 pp.). An important early statement by the opposition is contained in *Adresse des icariens de Nauvoo au citoyen Cabet; protestation de quelques dissidents et réponse du citoyen Cabet* (Paris, 1851, 16 pp.). At Corning, Iowa, the dispute between the "Old" and "Young" Icarians produced the brochure for the latter group, *Realization of Communism: Brief History of Icaria; Constitution, Laws and Regulations of the Icarian Community* (Icaria [Corning], Iowa, 1880, 42 pp.).

Eyewitness accounts by sometime members or visitors are found in A. Holynski, "Cabet et les icariens," *Revue socialiste*, xiv-xvi (Nov. 1891, Jan.-Apr., Sept. 1892), based on a visit in 1855 and secondary American sources, and Frédéric Olinet (Job, pseud.), *Socialisme: Voyage d'un Autunois en Icarie, à la suite de Cabet* (Autun, 1898, 180 pp.). The Macdonald MSS at Yale contain a long section on the Icarians' first year at Nauvoo, but no American writer has yet fully exploited them. J. H. Noyes, *History of American Socialisms*, omitted the Icarians entirely, and Charles Nordhoff, *The Communistic Societies of the United States*, pp. 333-339, depended to a large extent upon his own observations at the Corning community.

Albert Shaw, *Icaria; a Chapter in the History of Communism* (New York, 1884, 219 pp.), was the first general survey, devoted almost entirely to the American communities. Shaw's findings were used extensively by the German social democrat Heinrich Lux in *Étienne Cabet und der ikarische Kommunismus* (Stuttgart, 1894, 294 pp.), and in the earlier pamphlet by Adolf Hepner, *Die Ikarier in Nordamerika; eine Warnung vor communistischen Colonialgründungen* (New York, 1886, 38 pp.). Also for a German-reading audience was H. F. Albrecht, *Gegenwart und Zukunft* (Philadelphia, 1873, 24 pp.), which theorized upon the best associative life and translated in a supplement a pamphlet by Cabet on the social organization of Icaria.

Short articles on Nauvoo include Mrs. I. G. Miller, "The Icarian Community of Nauvoo, Illinois," Illinois State Historical Society *Transactions . . . 1906*, pp. 103-107; Felicie Cottet Snider, "A Short Sketch of the Life of Jules Leon Cottet, a Former Member of the Icarian Community," in the same society's *Journal*, vii (Oct. 1914), pp. 200-217; and S. B. Barnes, "An Icarian in Nauvoo," *ibid.*, xxxiv (June 1941), pp. 233-244. On the Iowa Icarians, Marie Ross, *Child of Icaria* (New York, 1938, 147 pp.), is the memoir (1864-1895) of the daughter of a founder, editor, and president, A. A. Marchand. See also Charles Gray, "The Icarian Community," *Annals of Iowa*, Ser. 3, vi (July 1903), pp. 107-114; R. A. Gallaher, "Icaria and the Icarians," *Palimpsest*, ii (Apr. 1921), pp. 97-112; and Herman Hausheer, "Icarian Medicine," *Bulletin of the History of Medicine*, ix (Mar.-May 1941), pp. 294-310, 401-435, 517-529. Jules Leroux's personal publication expressing Christian socialism, *L'Étoile du Kansas* (Neuchatel, Kan., 1873-1876; later called *L'Étoile du Kansas et de l'Iowa*, Corning, Iowa, 1877-1880; and *L'Étoile des pauvres et des souffrants*, Saint-Helena, Calif., 1881-1883), contains information both about the French exiles and immigrants connected with the First International and—especially for the period 1876-1881—about the Corning Icarians.

In Arsène Sauva, author of *Icarie* (Corning, Iowa, 1877, 12 pp.), and Alcander Longley, the link between communitarian and Marxian socialism is plain. Longley wrote *Communism; the Right Way and the Best Way for All to Live* (St. Louis, Mo., 1880, 108 pp.), *What Is Communism?* (2nd ed., rev. and enl., St. Louis, Mo., 1890, 424 pp.), and edited the *Communist* (preliminary number, Corning, Iowa, 1867; St. Louis, 1868-1885), continued as the *Altruist* (St. Louis, etc., 1885-1917). Sauva, and several others who joined the Icarians in the 1870's, had participated in the Paris Commune of 1871 and in the First International. They helped establish close connections with the Franco-American socialists of the cities. Longley, although he stayed only a few months at Corning, was for sixty years an indefatigable promoter of communities and a member of the Socialistic Labor Party.

Topic 8. The Socialist Labor Party

The Socialist Labor Party, founded in 1877 and still in existence, was the first American Marxist party of any consequence to survive more than a few years. It is also one of the most important of these parties not only because it was the foremost American socialist party up to 1905, or even because it produced in the person of Daniel De Leon one of the few first-rate American socialist theoreticians, but also, in a negative sense, because its long history of internal conflicts set the original pattern for the schismatic and factionalist tendencies that have bedeviled the American socialist movement ever since.

For the first fifteen years of existence known as the Socialistic Labor

Party, and more often called by its German title, *Sozialistische Arbeiter-Partei*, it was rent by internal struggles between the Lassallean and Marxian factions which had originally joined to create it (see General Reading above). The Lassalleans, representing the right wing of the party and committed to a program purely political—and even that purely opportunistic—had captured the national committee of the party as early as 1877. Although they managed to retain control of the party organization until 1889 and during this period were even able to throw some of the party's support to such purely progressive and nonsocialist political movements of the period as the Greenback movement of 1880 and the single-tax campaign of 1886, they were able to do so only over bitter internal opposition. Thus in 1877, when the Lassallean element first came to power, Sorge and many of the trade-union factions (the revolutionary wing which placed primary emphasis upon militant unionism) withdrew in protest to form, first, the International Labor Union in 1878, and, in 1881, the American Federation of Labor. The latter, under the leadership of Adolf Strasser and Samuel Gompers, quickly submerged its original revolutionary socialist ideals in the "practical" policy of "pure and simple" unionism. The same pattern of schism was repeated in 1881 when the remaining militant factions—one syndicalist in tendency (under the leadership of Parsons and Spies) and the other anarchist in tendency (under Most)—withdrew to affiliate with the anarchist "Black International" of London on the basis of the famous anarchist *Pittsburgh Manifesto* of 1883.

During the 1890's, however, the party purged itself of its remaining influential Lassallean element and, rejuvenated by the leadership of Daniel De Leon, who joined the party in 1886 and became influential in 1890, entered upon the most aggressive and successful period of its history. In fact, the present party dates its founding from the advent of De Leon's leadership. Under him it attempted to transform itself from a predominantly German radical organization into an Americanized Marxian movement. It repudiated both its own earlier tendency to political reformism and also at the same time the "pure and simple" unionism of the A.F.L. It evolved a revolutionary program of its own which, although emphasizing militant trade unionism as primary, called for political action as well. In opposition to the A.F.L. it organized the Socialist Trade and Labor Alliance in 1895 and participated in the organization of the I.W.W. in 1905. Both of these organizations were committed to revolution rather than reform and the latter called for the organization of labor along industrial rather than craft-union lines. After 1894, the party withdrew from all affiliation with progressive and populist movements and ever since has supported only its own candidates for public office and its own platform for an immediate revolutionary conversion to an industrial democracy.

The decline of the party dates from the split of 1900 when, under the leadership of Morris Hillquit, those party members who resented the autocratic discipline imposed by De Leon and who, in opposition to De Leon's policies, were both friendly to the A.F.L. and gradualistic or evolutionary in their political attitude, broke away to form the Socialist Party. This decline was accelerated by the death of De Leon himself in 1914 with the result that the party today, although still retaining its revolutionary orientation, has become so diminished in numbers that its main activity is now restricted to agitation of a purely educational character.

An outline of the party at its zenith can be constructed from Morris Hillquit, *History of Socialism in the United States* (5th ed., New York, 1910, 389 pp.), pp. 193-278, 294-301. Arnold Petersen, *Revolutionary Milestones* (New York, 1931, 31 pp.), carries the story down to 1930. De Leon's writings set the tone of party doctrine. *Reform or Revolution* (New York, 1919, 32 pp.), an address given on January 26, 1896, defends revolutionary Marxism. *The Burning Question of Trades Unionism* (1904; New York, 1921, 43 pp.), discusses the relation of organized labor to socialism. *Socialist Reconstruction of Society*, originally entitled *The Preamble of the Industrial Workers of the World* (1905; New York, 1938, 64 pp.), De Leon's "gloss" on the I.W.W. manifesto of 1905, describes the relation of socialist trade unionism and socialist politics, with remarks at the end recommending a soviet type of organization of society after the revolution. These and other pamphlets have been bound together by the New York Labor News Co., party publishers, under the title, *Speeches and Editorials* (New York, n.d., 2 vols.). As De Leon's principal contribution relates primarily to economic and political theory, see PART IV for treatment of each title in its specific context. Other aspects of his thought are also mentioned in PARTS III and V.

Source material on the history of the party as a whole may be found in the published *Proceedings* of its usually quadrennial national conventions since 1879 (Vols. 2, 4, 8, 11-14 never published). Two other important documents of this sort are *Platform, Constitution and Resolutions, together with a Condensed Report of the Proceedings of the National Convention . . . 1879* (Detroit, Mich., 1880, 11, 50 pp.), and the *Proceedings of the First Convention of the Industrial Workers of the World . . . June 27-July 8, 1905* (New York, 1905, 616 pp.). The State Historical Society of Wisconsin at Madison has a valuable but largely unclassified manuscript collection, consisting of letters mostly to De Leon, and reports of locals, as well as miscellaneous published material, 1889-1907. See also the first English-language organ, *National Socialist*

(Cincinnati, Ohio, 1878), replaced by the *Socialist* (Chicago, 1878-1879), 69 numbers in all; the files of the *New Yorker Volkszeitung* from 1878 to 1900; and those of the official English-language organ, the *People* (New York, 1891- ; weekly, 1891-1900; daily and weekly editions, 1900-1914, entitled the *Daily People* and the *Weekly People*; weekly, 1914- , entitled the *Weekly People*), edited, 1892-1914, by De Leon. The *Volkszeitung* supported the Socialist Party after 1900. There were numerous ephemeral journals in several languages published in the interest of the party, such as the party organ, *Sozialist* (New York, 1885-1892), edited in 1885 by Joseph Dietzgen.

The history of the Socialistic Labor Party before De Leon has been comparatively neglected. The following selections from its pamphlet literature at this period indicate a decidedly different orientation from the one De Leon gave it: the pamphlet by the editor of the *New Yorker Volkszeitung*, Alexander Jonas, *Reporter und Sozialist; ein Gespräch über Ziele und Wege des Sozialismus* (New York, 1884, 46 pp.), an imaginary interview of a socialist by an American newspaperman; *Socialism and Anarchism; Antagonistic Opposites* (New York, 1886, 11 pp.), No. 6 of the party's Socialistic Library; and I. M. Van Etten and others, *The Socialist Labor Party in New York; a Criticism* (New York, 1892, 19 pp.), evidence of the fight within the party to control its press. J. R. Buchanan, *The Story of a Labor Agitator* (New York, 1903, 460 pp.), by a populist who joined the party briefly in 1887, contains expressions, *passim*, of his low opinion of the leadership, and greater sympathy for the Chicago anarchists. See also the references in the General Reading on Marxism after 1876, and J. E. Gourley, *A Survey of Available Material on Socialism in the '90's* (New York, 1932?, 10 pp.).

One of the best descriptions of the party at this time is R. T. Ely, *The Labor Movement in America* (3rd ed., New York, 1890, 399 pp.), chaps. 8-11, which deal with its relation to the contemporary anarchist movement. Ely also reprints (pp. 366-370) the party platform in full. J. R. Commons and others, *History of Labour in the United States* (New York, 1918-1935, 4 vols.), II, *passim*, discusses the role of the party in the general context of the labor movement. Typical of the conservative tendencies of the party at this time are Laurence Gronlund, *The Co-operative Commonwealth* (1884; rev. and enl. ed., Boston, 1890, 304 pp.) and *Our Destiny, the Influence of Socialism on Morals and Religion* (London, 1891, 170 pp.), which are also important for their attack on Spencerian individualism, at that time the philosophic bulwark of American capitalistic apologetics. Gronlund himself was a party officer who had earlier been an Icarian and who later was to help found the American Fabian Society. Alice Sotheran, a friend of Gronlund and wife of Charles Sotheran, describes the latter's political activities and expulsion from the

143

party in her introduction to his posthumously published work, *Horace Greeley and Other Pioneers of American Socialism* (New York, 1915, 349 pp.). See also Eugen Dietzgen, "Die sozialistische Parteibewegung in den Vereinigten Staaten," *Neue Zeit*, xviii, Pt. 1 (Oct. 18, 1899), pp. 111-118; Emil Liess, *Was ist Sozialismus? Sieben Vorträge* (San Francisco, 1899, 117 pp.); and Salvatore Cognetti de Martiis, *Il socialismo negli Stati Uniti d'America* (Turin, 1891, 303 pp.).

The only history of the party which could be called general is Henry Kuhn and O. M. Johnson, *The Socialist Labor Party during Four Decades, 1890-1930* (New York, 1931, 126 pp.). The book is defective, however, in its sketchy treatment of the development of Socialist Labor Party doctrine and in its almost exclusive concentration, particularly in the section written by Kuhn, on the question of party finance and defections from the party line. Petersen's *Revolutionary Milestones* (cited above) is far more useful. Both these histories by party members, however, should be supplemented by the accounts given in Nathan Fine's *Labor and Farmer Parties in the United States, 1828-1928* (New York, 1928, 445 pp.), and in Hillquit, *op.cit.*, which, although generally unfriendly in approach, describes not only the internal affairs of the party but takes greater cognizance of the place of the party in the socialist movement as a whole. For the role of the party in the founding of the I.W.W. see Topic 11.

There is no full length biography of De Leon but material on his life, particularly in his party relationships, is to be found in the two long biographical sketches: Henry Kuhn, "Reminiscences of Daniel De Leon" and Rudolf Katz, "With De Leon since '89," both of which are included in *Daniel De Leon: the Man and His Work* (4th ed., New York, 1934, 136, 186 pp.), a symposium first issued by the party in 1919. Further material of a reminiscent sort may be found in many of the biographies and autobiographies of former associates of De Leon who later abandoned the Socialist Labor Party. References to these biographies and autobiographies are given in Topics 9-11 below. For appreciations or evaluations of De Leon's significance as a social thinker and party leader see: Louis Fraina, "Daniel De Leon," *New Review*, ii (July 1914), pp. 390-399; L. G. Raisky, *Daniel De Leon, the Struggle against Opportunism in the American Labor Movement* (New York, 1932, 36 pp.); J. B. Stalvey, *Daniel De Leon: a Study of Marxian Orthodoxy in the United States* (unpublished doctoral dissertation in political science, University of Illinois, 1946; abstract published, Urbana, Ill., 1946, 21 pp.); and Arnold Petersen, *Daniel De Leon: Social Architect* (New York, 1941, 313 pp.), the last of which seeks to analyze De Leon's thought and work as a whole. Stalvey's ms thesis includes an extensive bibliography. See also the ms list compiled by J. C. Borden, Jr., for the Columbia School of

Library Service, *A Bibliographical List of the Writings of Daniel De Leon Issued by the Socialist Labor Party of America from 1892 to 1936* (New York, 1936, 45 leaves).

Since De Leon's death the leading theorist and spokesman for the party has been Arnold Petersen, national secretary since 1914. Petersen is the author of numerous pamphlets and books, some of which have been cited above. His *Karl Marx and Marxian Science* (New York, 1943, 189 pp.), defends his party's version of Marxism against American and British critics. He attacks the Communist Party in several tracts, such as *Proletarian Democracy vs. Dictatorships and Despotism* (New York, 1932, 63 pp.), *Burlesque Bolshevism; American "Communism" as an Auxiliary of Capitalism* (New York, 1934, 63 pp.), and W. Z. Foster, *Renegade or Spy?* (New York, 1932, 40 pp.), and with O. M. Johnson, *The Virus of Anarchy; Bakuninism vs. Marxism* (New York, 1932, 30 pp.). The communists repaid in kind, e.g., M. J. Olgin, *Capitalism Defends Itself through the Socialist Labor Party* (New York, 1932, 40 pp.). See also the national executive committee's *Manifesto of the Socialist Labor Party to the Working Class of America; Changing Tides around the Rock of Gibraltar* (New York, 1920, 41 pp.).

Topic 9.   The Socialist Party

In contrast to the Socialist Labor Party, from which it split off in 1900, the Socialist Party has been reformist in character and more democratic in its organization. Until the 1930's it continued to follow its original trade-union policy of supporting—though always with some reservations—nonsocialist labor organizations such as the A.F.L., no matter how conservative their programs and leadership, and until the same period it continued to advocate an evolutionary rather than a revolutionary conversion to socialism and to support progressive as well as socialist candidates for public office. Similarly, although the party leadership has at times acted autocratically, the party structure itself has never been frozen into the rigid hierarchical form characteristic of other leftist groups. And its requirements for admission to party membership have been less narrowly conceived than those of other socialist parties.

Formed originally out of a fusion of right-wing dissidents in the S.L.P. with the Social Democratic Party of America (a western socialist group organized by Debs, Berger, and others in 1898), its reformist and democratic character contributed to the rapid growth of the party between 1901 and 1912. Its membership rose from 10,000 to 118,000 and the votes cast for socialist presidential candidates increased proportionately from 100,000 to 900,000. Declaring that "The Socialist Party does not strive to substitute working class rules for capitalist class rules but . . . to free all humanity from class rule" (*Platform for 1908*), and restricting its immediate demands to mere reforms of the economic and political system, the party was able to enlist in its support not only orthodox socialists but also many of the heterogeneous elements remaining from progressive movements of the past, such as Greenbackers, populists, and even Social Gospelers. The result was a mass party, particularly strong in the West, which was prepared to sacrifice discipline for numbers and revolutionary aims for immediate political success. Evidence that this policy paid off is shown in the fact that in 1912 there existed throughout the country no less than 56 socialist mayors, over 300 socialist aldermen, a number of socialist state legislators, and one socialist congressman in the House of Representatives. However, this "rising tide of socialism"—as it was then called—was stopped short in the next decade. The party had not been as successful as its members and opponents believed, and suffered from the same external pressures which slowed down contemporary progressivism. Internal causes were first, the expulsion of its revolutionary syndicalist wing in 1912-1913; next, the party's official opposition to the war, which not only alienated the conservative membership of the party itself but led to the trial and imprisonment of such important party leaders as Eugene V. Debs and Victor Berger; and, finally, the Russian Revolution, which encouraged the left wing of the party to demand a more militant party program and, when this was not forthcoming, to secede from the party in 1919 to form the Communist Party.

From these blows the party never fully recovered, although during the twenties it helped to organize and support the La Follette ticket in the presidential race of 1924, and during the thirties experienced a brief resurgence of militancy signalized by the admission of a few hundred Trotskyists to party membership. But neither of these ventures amounted to much. The effort to build a mass party on the La Follette movement collapsed as soon as the campaign itself was over. The union with the Trotskyists a decade later caused the right wing of the party to withdraw in protest and to form the Social Democratic Federation in 1936, and the Trotskyists themselves were expelled the following year. The most recent split in the party occurred in 1941. When the party opposed American participation in the war, still more members withdrew to enter the Union for Democratic Action, and in the presidential election of 1944 Thomas received only 80,000 votes. In 1947 negotiations were pursued toward reunion with the Social Democratic Federation. Nevertheless, Thomas became so discouraged that at the national convention he even urged (though unsuccessfully) that the party give up all political activities and restrict itself to education.

Nathan Fine, *Labor and Farmer Parties in the United States, 1828-1928* (New York, 1928, 445 pp.), pp. 184-323, provides historical background, and Norman Thomas, *America's Way Out; a Program for Democracy*

(New York, 1931, 324 pp.), pp. 116-308, is a typical statement of more recent Socialist Party philosophy.

Many of the official party records before World War I have disappeared: the largest collection, covering the period 1901-1938, is in the Duke University Library, while later files are still at party headquarters. The Duke collection consists of 95,000 items and twenty-three volumes, and is fullest between 1915 and 1932. The Debs collection in the library of the Rand School of Social Science consists chiefly of scrapbooks, periodicals, and pamphlets; Morris Hillquit's correspondence is sealed in the possession of his widow, Mrs. Vera Hillquit of New York; and the Berger papers are held by his daughter, Mrs. Doris Hursley of Beverly Hills, California, and not available to scholars at present. Additional Berger correspondence (1910-1919) is available at the Milwaukee County Historical Museum, with the other records of the Wisconsin Socialist Party, mostly for the 1930's. Debs, Hillquit, and Berger, of course, figure prominently in the Duke collection.

There is no comprehensive bibliography of Socialist Party literature, but the principal monographs cited below contain reading lists. The catalogues and lists of C. H. Kerr & Co., socialist cooperative publishers, e.g., *What to Read on Socialism* (Chicago, 1910, 60 pp.), and the *Appeal Book Catalog* (Girard, Kan., 1915, 144 pp.) issued by the *Appeal to Reason*, are useful for the early period, although many of their references are elusive. The League for Industrial Democracy and its predecessor have issued suggestions for reading from time to time, such as H. W. Laidler, *Study Courses in Socialism* (New York, 1919, 32 pp.).

Printed source material may be found in the *Proceedings* of the party's national conventions, particularly those of 1912, 1919, and 1936, when the party took decisive action with regard to syndicalism, union with the Comintern, and admission of Trotskyists. See also the "campaign handbooks" and such pamphlet series as *Progressive Thought* (Terre Haute, Ind., 1899-1901), a monthly serial of the Social Democratic Federation issued by the Debs Publishing Company; the *Pocket Library of Socialism* (Chicago, 1899-1908?, 60 pts.), published by Kerr; the *Rip-Saw Series*, including No. 20, James Oneal, *Sabotage, or Socialism vs. Syndicalism* (St. Louis, Mo., 1913, 32 pp.), and others by A. W. Ricker, H. G. Creel, K. R. O'Hare, H. M. Tichenor, and Oscar Ameringer; and the *New Appeal Socialist Classics* (ed. by W. J. Ghent; Girard, Kan., 1916, 12 pts. of 64 pp. each).

The Socialist Party press is a major published source. The most important German-language socialist paper, the daily *New Yorker Volkszeitung* (New York, 1878-1932), with its weekly, *Vorwärts* (New York, 1878-1932), was superseded by the weekly *Neue Volkszeitung* (New York, 1932-). The English-language dailies were the *Chicago Daily Socialist*

(Chicago, 1901-1912, title varies) and the *New York Call* (New York, 1908-1923), whose title changed to the *New York Leader* (New York, 1923). The *New Leader* (New York, 1924-) followed Social Democratic Federation policy from 1936 to 1945; and the *Call* (New York, 1935- , title varies) took its place as a New York socialist paper. The *Milwaukee Leader* (Milwaukee, Wis., 1911-1939) was an influential daily edited by Victor Berger. Periodicals published in the interests of the party have from time to time appeared in other languages, such as *Neie Welt* (New York, 1912-1922?, title varies), *Idisher Kempfer* (Philadelphia, New York, 1906-1920?), and *Idisher Kemfer* (New York, 1923- , title varies, organ of Poale Zion), in Yiddish; and *Proletario* (New York, Philadelphia, 1897-1946), in Italian, an I.W.W. organ. The *Jewish Daily Forward* (New York, 1897-) in its early years was sympathetic. See the sketch of its history by Victor Erlich, "Jewish Labor and the 'Daily Forward,'" in the *Modern Review*, ɪ (Sept. 1947), pp. 533-542. The monthly *International Socialist Review* (Chicago, 1900-1918), which absorbed the *Comrade* (New York, 1901-1905); the party's official *Monthly Bulletin* (Chicago, 1904-1913) and its successors, the *Party Builder* (1912-1914), the *American Socialist* (1914-1917), the *Eye Opener* (1912-1920), and the *New Day* (1920-1922); and the *Socialist Review* (New York, 1932-1940, title varies), were the principal theoretical organs of the party although the first was published independently. After World War II the *Modern Review* (New York, 1947-) was started by the American Labor Conference on International Affairs, with a democratic socialist policy. In the West, the *Vorwärts* (Milwaukee, Wis., 1882-1924?), the *Appeal to Reason* (Girard, Kan., 1895- , title varies; 1929- , as *American Freeman*), and, in a limited sphere, *Wilshire's Magazine* (Los Angeles, 1900-1915), published by an unorthodox millionaire socialist, were influential before World War I, and the *American Guardian* (Oklahoma City, Okla., 1914-1942; 1914-1931 as *Oklahoma Leader*), between wars. *A Trip through the Appeal* (Girard, Kan., 1904, 32 pp.), W. J. Ghent, "'The Appeal' and Its Influence," *Survey*, xxvɪ (Apr. 1, 1911), pp. 24-28, and G. A. England, *The Story of the Appeal* (Girard, Kan.?, 1917, 307 pp.), are sources for the early history of this sensational and widely circulated paper and its socialist clientele. An independent monthly with a notable group of writers was the *Masses* (New York, 1911-1917), which started as an organ for cooperatives, absorbed the socialist *New Review* (New York, 1913-1916), and was killed by government opposition to its antiwar articles. It was succeeded by the *Liberator* (New York, 1918-1924). *Labor Age* (New York, 1913-1933, title varies), the *News-Bulletin* (New York, 1922-1932, called *L.I.D. Monthly*, 1929-1932), and miscellaneous pamphlets have been published by the League for Industrial Democracy and its predecessor, the Intercollegiate Socialist Society. See also the annual *American Labor Year Book* (New York, 1916-1932), published by the Rand School of Social Science.

Hillquit, *History of Socialism in the United States* (5th ed., New York, 1910, 389 pp.), Pt. 2, chaps. 4 and 5; Symes and Clement, *Rebel America* (New York, 1934, 392 pp.), Pt. 3, *passim*; and Fine (cited above) taken together cover the Socialist Party to 1934. These may be supplemented, moreover, by I. A. Kipnis, *The American Socialist Party, 1897-1912* (Ph.D. thesis, University of Chicago, 1950; available on microfilm), as well as by such studies of the party in its municipal strongholds as H. G. Stetler, *The Socialist Movement in Reading, Pennsylvania, 1896-1936* (Storrs, Conn., 1943, 198 pp.), and D. W. Hoan, *City Government; the Record of the Milwaukee Experiment* (New York, 1936, 365 pp.). Stetler analyzes the bases of Socialist Party support, and Hoan points with pride to improvements in city government while he was the socialist mayor. See also Marvin Wachman, *History of the Social-Democratic Party of Milwaukee, 1897-1910* (*Illinois Studies in the Social Sciences,* xxviii, No. 1; Urbana, Ill., 1945, 90 pp.). F. I. Olson is preparing a study of the Milwaukee socialists from 1897 to 1941. Isador Ladoff, in *The Passing of Capitalism and the Mission of Socialism* (Terre Haute, Ind., 1901, 160 pp.), issued by the Debs Publishing Company on the eve of the organization of the Socialist Party, speaks for the evolutionary, political, and rationalistic socialism of the Social Democratic Party, against the anarchists, the Socialist Labor Party, and the Christian socialists. A Rand School publication by August Claessens, *The Democratic Way of Life* (New York, 1940, 30 pp.), interprets the slogan of the French Revolution in terms of the 1937 declaration of principles of the Social Democratic Federation, printed at the end of the pamphlet. The party's 1940 election campaign is investigated in H. R. Penniman, *The Socialist Party in Action; the 1940 National Campaign* (unpublished Ph.D. thesis, University of Minnesota, 1942).

Party history is also reflected in the pamphlets and books published officially or by party leaders at various periods. For the first twenty years of the party's existence its two outstanding leaders were Eugene V. Debs (1855-1926) and Morris Hillquit (1869-1933). Debs's life and a selection from his writings and speeches are to be found in: Debs, *Walls and Bars* (Chicago, 1927, 248 pp.); *Debs: His Life, Writings and Speeches* (Chicago, 1908, 515 pp.), with a biography by S. M. Reynolds; *Speeches of Eugene V. Debs* (intro. by Alexander Trachtenberg; New York, 1928, 95 pp.); David Karsner, *Debs: His Authorized Life and Letters* (New York, 1919, 244 pp.), and *Talks with Debs in Terre Haute* (New York, 1922, 221 pp.); and *Writings and Speeches of Eugene V. Debs* (intro. by A. M. Schlesinger, Jr.; New York, 1948, 486 pp.), taken largely from socialist periodicals. Of the four full-dress biographies of Debs, Ray

Ginger's life, *The Bending Cross* (New Brunswick, N.J., 1949, 516 pp.), is probably the best. McAlister Coleman, *Eugene V. Debs: a Man Unafraid* (New York, 1930, 345 pp.), suffers, as does H. T. Schnittkind, *The Story of Eugene V. Debs* (Boston, 1929, 204 pp.), from straining for lyrical effect. F. R. Painter, *That Man Debs and His Life Work* (Bloomington, Ind., 1929, 209 pp.), suffers from the opposite defect of being prosaic and humdrum. Irving Stone continues the sympathetic tradition with *Adversary in the House* (Garden City, N.Y., 1947, 432 pp.), a fictionalized account of the crusader for brotherhood as adversary in the house of American capitalism with an adversary, his wife, in his own house. See also H. M. Morais and William Cahn, *Gene Debs; the Story of a Fighting American* (New York, 1948, 128 pp.), which squares Debs's theory with communism; and *The Debs Case* (Chicago, 1919, 132 pp.), a history of the Debs trial for sedition in 1918.

The most important works of Hillquit, for long the acknowledged party theoretician, are his previously cited *History*, his *Socialism in Theory and Practice* (New York, 1909, 361 pp.), his debate with John A. Ryan, the liberal Catholic clergyman, which is published under the title, *Socialism, Promise or Menace?* (New York, 1914, 270 pp.), and *From Marx to Lenin* (New York, 1921, 151 pp.). Hillquit's autobiography, *Loose Leaves from a Busy Life* (New York, 1934, 339 pp.), published shortly after his death, contains much valuable material on the history of the party down to the split of 1919. On the practical political achievements of this early period up to 1913, see Ethelwyn Mills, *Legislative Program of the Socialist Party* (Chicago, 1914, 64 pp.), a record of the work of socialist representatives in various state legislatures between 1899 and 1913; and for an estimate of the position and importance of the Socialist Party of the United States at the outbreak of World War I, in comparison to the socialist parties of other countries, see J. W. Hughan, *American Socialism of the Present Day* (New York, 1911, 265 pp.), with a very useful bibliography, and W. E. Walling, ed., *The Socialism of To-day* (New York, 1916, 642 pp.).

Other socialist writers active in this early period (particularly 1910-1920) include Louis B. Boudin, A. M. Simons, John Spargo, Upton Sinclair, W. J. Ghent, and William English Walling, whose works reflect the crises and problems of the party's history. Boudin, *The Theoretical System of Karl Marx* (Chicago, 1907, 286 pp.), is an important contribution to the orthodox side of the orthodox-revisionist controversy in Marxian theory. A. M. Simons, as editor of the *International Socialist Review*, published much material on the relation between socialism and syndicalism, assuming until 1912 the same friendly attitude to syndicalism as is found in Walling's *Socialism as It Is* (New York, 1912, 452 pp.) and Spargo's *Syndicalism, Industrial Unionism, and Socialism* (New York,

1913, 243 pp.). Walling's other important work, *The Larger Aspects of Socialism* (New York, 1913, 406 pp.), represents an early attempt to re formulate the philosophy of socialism on a pragmatic rather than on the traditional materialistic basis. Ghent's *Socialism and Success* (New York, 1910, 252 pp.) is equally valuable for its critique of the Spencerian interpretation of the doctrine of the survival of the fittest. Upton Sinclair, *The Industrial Republic: a Study of the America of Ten Years Hence* (New York, 1907, 284 pp.), reflects the early socialist optimistic hope for a quick socialist victory, while Spargo's *Americanism and Social Democracy* (New York, 1918, 325 pp.) expresses the opposition of the minority which broke with the party in 1917 on the question of supporting the war. See also in the latter connection Boudin's *Socialism and War* (New York, 1916, 267 pp.). Spargo's *Socialism* (rev. ed., New York, 1909, 349 pp.) was a widely read defense of the socialist philosophy written many years earlier when the author was still a party member.

Among the briefer expositions by socialists for the not yet convinced, see H. N. Casson, *The Red Light* (Lynn, Mass., 1898, 147 pp.), a light satire in harmony with Social Democratic Party standards; J. E. Cohen, *Socialism for Students* (Chicago, 1910, 153 pp.), first published in the *International Socialist Review* (Nov. 1908-July 1909), and C. C. Hitchcock, *The Socialist Argument* (Chicago, 1912, 174 pp.), Kerr publications. I. B. Cross, *The Essentials of Socialism* (New York, 1912, 152 pp.), is a good, broadly conceived summary, written at the peak of party success by a nonsocialist sympathizer. R. F. Hoxie, "The Rising Tide of Socialism," *Journal of Political Economy*, XIX (Oct. 1911), pp. 609-631, maps the centers of socialist strength and attempts to analyze the causes of its growth. H. F. Griffin, "The Rising Tide of Socialism," *Outlook*, C (Feb. 24, 1912), pp. 438-448, further attests to the growing public awareness of socialist gains. A short but important article by H. L. Slobodin, "The State of the Socialist Party," *International Socialist Review*, XVII (Mar. 1917), pp. 539-541, ascribes the party's decline not to the unpopularity of its antiwar position, but to the rejection of its revolutionary wing after 1912. Bertram Benedict, "The Socialist Movement in Great Britain and the United States," *American Political Science Review*, XVIII (May 1924), pp. 276-284, briefly contrasts the failure of American socialism with British Labour Party success.

For further biographical material on the party between 1900 and 1920, V. L. Berger, *Voice and Pen of Victor L. Berger: Congressional Speeches and Editorials* (Milwaukee, Wis., 1929, 753 pp.), J. H. Maurer, *It Can Be Done* (New York, 1938, 374 pp.), and Hillel Rogoff, *An East Side Epic; the Life and Work of Meyer London* (New York, 1930, 311 pp.), comprise the speeches and reminiscences of three of the party's most important practical politicians. C. E. Russell, *Bare Hands and Stone*

Walls: Some Recollections of a Side-Line Reformer (New York, 1933, 441 pp.), is the autobiography of an early socialist journalist who later became an apostate. Oscar Ameringer, *If You Don't Weaken* (New York, 1940, 476 pp.), recollections told with humor by the editor of the *American Guardian*, is indispensable for the history of the party in the Middle West. Also illustrative of the populist-tinged socialism of this region are G. D. Brewer, *The Fighting Editor; or, Warren and the Appeal* (2nd ed. rev. and enl., Girard, Kan., 1910, 211 pp.), the life of Fred D. Warren; the autobiography of Julius A. Wayland, editor of *Wayland's Monthly* (Girard, Kan., 1899?-1915?) and a communitarian at the Ruskin Co-operative Colony before joining the party, *Leaves of Life; a Story of Twenty Years of Socialist Agitation* (Girard, Kan., 1912, 260 pp.); and H. H. Quint, "Julius A. Wayland, Pioneer Socialist Propagandist," *Mississippi Valley Historical Review*, xxxv (Mar. 1949), pp. 585-606. Useful material on the history of radicalism among intellectuals is contained in Max Eastman's autobiography, *Enjoyment of Living* (New York, 1948, 603 pp.). The autobiography of R. M. Lovett, *All Our Years* (New York, 1948, 373 pp.), describes an intellectual who remained an independent radical.

Since about 1925 the principal spokesmen for the party have been Norman Thomas and Harry W. Laidler. Thomas was the party's presidential candidate from 1928 to 1948; Laidler has been for many years the executive director of the League for Industrial Democracy. The titles of Thomas' major writings on current events reflect the growing pessimism of the socialist movement in recent years. *America's Way Out: a Program for Democracy* (New York, 1931, 324 pp.), written at the depth of the great depression of 1929-1932, outlined the socialist solution to social problems. *The Choice before Us: Mankind at the Crossroads* (New York, 1934, 249 pp.), continued the argument of the earlier book, this time addressed to the growing threat of totalitarian fascism and communism. *Socialism on the Defensive* (New York, 1938, 304 pp.), still more urgently called public attention to the accelerating danger of war and fascism and examined Popular Front strategy. Thomas opposed American entry into World War II in *We Have a Future* (Princeton, N.J., 1941, 236 pp.), and in *What Is Our Destiny* (Garden City, N.Y., 1944, 192 pp.) analyzed the issues of the war and the peace to follow. After the war his *Appeal to the Nations* (New York, 1947, 175 pp.) prophesied even more pessimistically the devastating results of imperialism, international anarchy, and diplomacy grounded in fear. *A Socialist's Faith*, announced for 1951, summarizes Thomas' views after forty years of public life. Among Laidler's more important works are his already cited *Social-Economic Movements*, his earlier but still well-known *Socialism in Thought and Action* (New York, 1920, 546 pp.), and his *American So-*

cialism, Its Aims and Practical Program (2nd ed., New York, 1937, 330 pp.).

Perhaps nothing indicates so clearly the declining prestige of the party as the public abandonment of its program by early followers and sympathizers. Notable instances of these are: Manya Gordon, *How to Tell Progress from Reaction* (New York, 1944, 320 pp.), an attack upon the idea of government ownership, and Louis Waldman, *Labor Lawyer* (New York, 1944, 394 pp.), the autobiography of a former right-wing socialist who left the party in 1936.

Topic 10.   The Communist Party, and the Left and Right Communist Opposition

The Communist Party, which originated in the left-wing split from the Socialist Party in 1919, has in recent years been the most vocal and most widely publicized of all the American Marxian groups. This has resulted from (1) its early support in the 1920's of an aggressive revolutionary movement on the Bolshevik pattern, calling for ideological clarity and rigid party discipline, and accepting as its ideal the dictatorship of the American working class and the sovietizing of American industry; (2) its insistence upon an international outlook and its undeviating adherence to the policies of the Third International (as imposed by the Comintern's "21 points" of 1920) up to the time that organization was dissolved in 1943; and finally (3) its ruthless policy of "ruling or wrecking" any other organization with which it is associated. The party has also been notoriously characterized by frequent and abrupt changes of the "party line." See PART I, Topic 4, for the international connections of the American communist parties.

From a revolutionary point of view the earliest years of the party (1919-1932) were probably the most significant. Once the young party had sloughed off its early romantic assumption that to be revolutionary it must operate underground, and had emerged in 1921 as a legal political organization—the Workers (Communist) Party—it was able (despite the social apathy of the period, despite the party's own vacillation on such important matters as trade-union policy, and, above all, despite the bitter internal struggles with which it was rent) to create a small but genuinely militant revolutionary movement, which, if not always programmatically clear, was often effective. This is illustrated internally by its development of a disciplined and professional revolutionary leadership and by its creation of a flourishing party press, and externally both by its organization of the great textile strikes at Passaic, New Jersey, and Gastonia, North Carolina, in 1926-1927, and by its active participation in the Sacco-Vanzetti and the Scottsboro agitations.

After 1929, however, the party became progressively more monolithic in structure and more opportunist in policy. In 1928, following the lead of Stalin, it expelled the Left or Trotskyist opposition over the question of "permanent revolution." In 1929, following the same lead, it expelled the Right or Lovestoneite opposition because of the latter's theory that American capitalism is still unripe for revolution. This not only weakened the party in regard to numbers but delivered it wholly into the hands of the Foster-Browder faction, which from then on committed the party completely to following the turns of Russian foreign policy. From this came the party's anti-Fascist crusade of the early and middle 1930's, its abrupt reversal of this stand with the signing of the Moscow-Berlin pact of 1939, and its return to the earlier position once more after Germany attacked Russia in 1941. A later turn in the party line was the decision under Browder in 1943 to disband as a political party entirely and to make common cause with progressive American capitalism. When the war was over and Russia was no more in immediate danger, Browder was expelled and the party revived under Foster.

Of the two opposition groups, neither of which has ever been able to attract more than a handful of followers, the Right opposition under the leadership of Jay Lovestone and Benjamin Gitlow grew progressively nonrevolutionary until its final disbanding in 1940. During the latter years of its existence it established a considerable number of connections in the trade unions. The Trotskyist group, on the other hand, has remained active and has exerted an influence out of all proportion to its size. Thus, although it existed at first as a mere opposition faction—the Communist League of America—it created, under the leadership of Cannon, Shachtman, and Abern, its own party press and successfully penetrated the working-class movement at some strategic points, for example in the great Minneapolis teamsters' strike of 1934 which the party itself organized and led, and in the unemployed league movement which had sprung up almost spontaneously during the early years of the depression. In 1934 it gave up considering itself an opposition faction of the Comintern and supported the call for a new international. A. J. Muste and other leaders of the old Conference for Progressive Labor Action had built up the American Workers Party out of unemployed groups. The Musteites and Trotskyists fused in 1934 to form the Workers Party, which entered the Socialist Party in 1936 as a left-wing fraction. Although required to apply for admission as individuals and to give up their press and separate organization they ignored these conditions. They used the new alliance to promote the hearings of the Dewey commission in Mexico City, which absolved Trotsky of the Stalinist charge that he assisted in Fascist plots against Russia. The Trotskyist fraction wrecked the Socialist Party organization before it was expelled in 1937. It reorganized as the Socialist Workers Party and exists today, a series of small nuclei in the large cities. Besides these maneuverings, at least a dozen minor splits took place in the thirties, overshadowed by the expulsion of the Shachtman faction in 1940 for its hostile attitude toward the Soviet state. The minority continued to publish the *New International* and organized the Workers Party. In 1941-1943 eighteen S.W.P. leaders were tried, convicted, and imprisoned for violating the Smith Act in advising insubordination in the armed forces and advocating violent revolution. Behind this charge was the antagonism of the Teamsters Union to a strong Trotskyist local in Minneapolis. Within a year after their release in 1945 the leaders split again and most of the minority joined the Workers Party. Subsequent negotiations for the reunion of Shachtmanites and Cannonites did not bear fruit.

The best available survey of Communist Party history, from a hostile point of view, is James Oneal and G. A. Werner, *American Communism; a Critical Analysis of Its Origins, Development and Programs* (new ed., New York, 1947, 416 pp.). An introductory reading from communist sources should include the Report of the Central Committee to the party's national conventions in 1934 and 1936. The first of these is reprinted in Earl Browder, *Communism in the United States* (New York, 1935, 352 pp.), pp. 21-93, and the second in the same author's *The People's Front* (New York, 1938, 354 pp.), pp. 19-64.

There is no comprehensive history of the Communist Party, although a history can be pieced together from published sources. Lenin, *A Letter to American Workers* (New York, 1934, 23 pp.), an appeal written in 1918, was influential in converting the Socialist Party's left wing to bolshevism. *Stalin's Speeches on the American Communist Party, Delivered in the American Commission of the Presidium of the Executive Committee of the Communist International, May 6, 1929* (New York, 1931, 39 pp.) expresses the party's policy following the expulsion of the Lovestone faction. Primary sources are the *Reports* and *Resolutions* of the party's national conventions, and the collections of speeches and reports of Earl Browder and other leaders. See also *Campaign Book; Presidential Elections, 1940* (New York, 1940, 128 pp.), and the party press. The *Internationalist* (started in Boston in 1917 and, after a few numbers, continued in New York as the *New International*) spoke for the socialist Left. The independent *Liberator* (New York, 1918-1924) merged with the *Labor Herald* (Chicago, 1922-1924) and *Soviet Russia Pictorial* (New York, Chicago, 1919-1924) to form the *Worker's Monthly*, later the *Communist* (Chicago, New York, 1924- , title varies), a theoretical organ, while the weekly *New Masses* (New York, 1926-1948), superseded by the monthly *Masses & Mainstream* (New York, 1948-), served as a literary magazine. The *Daily Worker* (Chicago, New York, 1922-), with its Sunday edition, the *Worker*, continued after World War II as a news and propaganda outlet. The *Party Organizer* (New York, 1927-1938) is indispensable for an inside view of communist tactics.

Among the autobiographies of loyal Communist Party leaders, two by W. Z. Foster are the most important. *From Bryan to Stalin* (New York, 1937, 352 pp.) traces Foster's wanderings from Bryanism through the Socialist Party and the I.W.W. to the Communist Party. He has been a member and leader since 1921, and in 1924, 1928, and 1932 its presidential candidate. *Pages from a Worker's Life* (New York, 1939, 314 pp.) is less a connected story than a series of impressions of persons and events scattered over many years. Joseph Freeman, *An American Testament; a Narrative of Rebels and Romantics* (New York, 1936, 678 pp.), is particularly valuable for its handling of the years 1917-1924, and for its philosophical analysis of the mood and attitude of the young poets and radicals who joined the party then. See also the reminiscences by E. R. Bloor, *We Are Many* (New York, 1940, 319 pp.), and E. G. Flynn, *Debs, Haywood, Ruthenberg* (New York, 1939, 48 pp.).

Exposés by two prominent party "renegades" have appeared since the outbreak of World War II. Benjamin Gitlow's autobiography, *I Confess; the Truth about American Communism* (New York, 1940, 611 pp.), in spite of its exaggerated air of recantation and general breast-beating, is valuable for its circumstantial account of party policies and personalities, 1919-1935. The less turgid, less personal, but no less violently anticommunist and circumstantial sequel, *The Whole of Their Lives* (New York, 1948, 387 pp.), condenses his earlier work and continues his story down to 1945. Gitlow argues that the Communist Party as an underground movement operates more efficiently. Less informative but equally confessional is L. F. Budenz, *This Is My Story* (New York, 1947, 379 pp.), by a Roman Catholic who returned to his church. Budenz writes like a salvaged criminal of the years 1935-1945, during which he was editor of the *Daily Worker* and prominent in party councils. His most recent work is *Men without Faces: the Communist Conspiracy in the U.S.A.* (New York, 1950, 305 pp.). See also Fred Beal, *Proletarian Journey* (New York, 1937, 352 pp.), and J. B. Matthews, *Odyssey of a Fellow Traveler* (New York, 1938, 285 pp.).

Among books dealing with alleged communism in relation to the Department of State are Alistair Cooke, *A Generation on Trial; U.S.A. v. Alger Hiss* (New York, 1950, 342 pp.); Ralph de Toledano and Victor Lasky, *Seeds of Treason; the True Story of the Hiss-Chambers Tragedy* (New York, 1950, 270 pp.); and Owen Lattimore, *Ordeal by Slander* (Boston, 1950, 236 pp.). Whittaker Chambers' own story, *Witness*, has been announced for 1951. Angela Calomiris, *Red Masquerade* (Philadelphia, 1950, 284 pp.), relates the experiences of an undercover agent of the F.B.I. who joined the Communist Party and later served as a witness for the government in the trial of eleven top American communists. Hede Massing, *This Deception*, announced for 1951, is the story of the first wife of Gerhart Eisler, herself a former Soviet agent who in the second trial of Alger Hiss claimed that she had known him in 1935 as a leader of an underground group. The autobiography of Elizabeth Bentley, the former communist courier who played an important role in the Hiss case, will also be published in 1951 under the title *Out of Bondage*.

The most prominent spokesmen for the party—excluding the leaders of the Left and Right opposition—have been William Z. Foster and Earl Browder, the latter of whom was the party presidential candidate in 1936 and 1940. Foster's most important work since becoming a communist is *Toward Soviet America* (New York, 1932, 343 pp.), a tract analyzing the crisis of American capitalism as expressed in the great depression and the role of the Communist Party in that crisis. Browder's writings have been more voluminous and reflect to a most exact degree the many fluctuations in the party line between 1928 and 1946. His articles, speeches, and reports as secretary of the party have been collected in four volumes: *Communism in the United States* (New York, 1935, 352 pp.), covering 1932-1935; *The People's Front* (New York, 1938, 354 pp.), covering 1936-1937; *Fighting for Peace* (New York, 1939, 256 pp.), covering 1938-1939; and *The Second Imperialist War* (New York, 1940, 309 pp.), covering 1939-1940. Other works belonging to this same period are: *What Is Communism?* (New York, 1936, 254 pp.), *The Way Out* (New York, 1941, 255 pp.), *Victory—and After* (New York, 1942, 256 pp.), and *Teheran: Our Path in War and Peace* (New York, 1944, 128 pp.), all by Browder. Of the above works, all written before 1936 are anti-Roosevelt in tone, all written between 1936 and 1939 are pro-Roosevelt and support a policy of international collective security, all written between 1939 and 1941 condemn World War II as "imperialistic," and all written after 1941 interpret World War II as "liberationist." To judge from what point of view the party has turned, see Browder's series of six articles, "Report on Russia," *New Republic*, cxv (Aug. 5-Sept. 9, 1946). Browder's analysis of communist strategy after both World Wars, *World Communism and U.S. Foreign Policy* (New York, 1948, 55 pp.), while no longer speaking officially for the party, is important as the expression of an ex-leader employed by the Soviet Union as its American book agent. See also, on party leaders, M. J. Olgin's campaign pamphlet, *That Man Browder* (New York, 1936, 23 pp.); George Spiro (George Marlen, pseud.), *Earl Browder, Communist or Tool of Wall Street* (New York, 1937, 493 pp.), representative of the attitude of a Trotskyist splinter group, the Leninist League; and the polemic by the Socialist Labor Party leader, Arnold Petersen, *W. Z. Foster, Renegade or Spy?* (New York, 1932, 40 pp.). A sketch of the current party, "The U.S. Communist Party," by A. M.

Schlesinger, Jr., appeared in *Life*, xxi (July 29, 1946), pp. 84-96. Foster's answers to twenty-three questions most commonly asked about the party appeared in the *New York Herald Tribune* with comment by Bert Andrews, "How U.S. Communists Look at Current Issues" (Jan. 11, 1948), pp. 1, 38-41. See also Joseph Barnes, "The Foreign Policy of the American Communist Party," *Foreign Affairs*, xxvi (Apr. 1948), pp. 421-431.

Oneal and Werner, *American Communism* (cited above), is an attempt to cover the course of communist history from its origins in the I.W.W. and the Socialist Party to the end of World War II. The period to 1924 consists of the thirteen chapters of Oneal's first edition (New York, 1927, 256 pp.) scarcely revised in the light of later published sources, and the nine chapters added by Werner are a series of essays rather than a narrative. The disjointed whole, expressing the violent antagonism of right-wing democratic socialists, does not fill the need for a detailed and comprehensive history of the party. Some of the obstacles to the success of American communism's pro-Soviet policy appear in Meno Lovenstein, *American Opinion of Soviet Russia* (Washington, 1941, 210 pp.). In such a climate of opinion objective views are impossible. In addition to the treatments cited in the General Reading, partial accounts range from J. P. Cannon, *The History of American Trotskyism* (New York, 1944, 268 pp.), pp. 1-59, to Jay Lovestone, *Pages from Party History* (New York, 1929?, 36 pp.), both covering the early period, with Alexander Bittelman, *Fifteen Years of the Communist Party* (New York, 1934, 52 pp.), and *Milestones in the History of the Communist Party* (New York, 1937, 92 pp.), expressing the orthodox Stalinist view. For an opposing view see "The Communist Party," *Fortune*, x (Sept. 1934), pp. 69-74, 154, 156, 159-160, 162. Eugene Lyons, *The Red Decade; the Stalinist Penetration of America* (Indianapolis, Ind., 1941, 423 pp.), is an avowed polemic on the postdepression period by a once sympathetic Moscow correspondent, and Martin Dies, *The Trojan Horse in America* (New York, 1940, 366 pp.), is more tendentious and less discriminating on the Popular Front (pp. 1-304). A. R. Ogden, *The Dies Committee* (2nd rev. ed., Washington, 1945, 318 pp.), and William Gellermann, *Martin Dies* (New York, 1944, 310 pp.), are critical of Dies and the work of the Special House Committee for the Investigation of Un-American Activities, of which he was chairman.

Material on the Right opposition led by Lovestone can be obtained from the files of the group's official organ, *Workers Age* (New York, 1932-1941), which superseded *Revolutionary Age* (New York, 1929-1932); *Class Struggle* (New York, 1931-1937), edited by Albert Weisbord, who was expelled with the group but later headed his own splinter group, the Communist League of Struggle; and *Young Spartacus* (New York, 1931-1935), published by the National Youth Committee of the Communist

League of America (Opposition). Incidental references may also be found in some of the works mentioned above, especially Gitlow's autobiography. See also an early official statement, *The Crisis in the Communist Party . . . Statement of Principles of the Communist Party (Majority Group)* (New York, 1930, 77 pp.); Will Herberg, "The Crisis in Communism; the Viewpoint of the International Communist Opposition," *Modern Monthly*, vii (June 1933), pp. 283-288; B. D. Wolfe, *What Is the Communist Opposition?* (New York, 1933, 38 pp.); and Jay Lovestone, *Soviet Foreign Policy and the World Revolution* (New York, 1935, 31 pp.), and *People's Front Illusion* (New York, 1937, 86 pp.), also by Lovestone. The group has produced no general history, nor any important nonperiodical works, except Benjamin Gitlow's *I Confess* (cited above).

There is no such deficiency in Trotskyist literature. Cannon, *The History of American Trotskyism*, cited above, by the first organizer and principal leader, surveys (pp. 60-256) the group's development from 1928 to 1937. In addition, the group has had a very active press publishing among other periodicals, the *Militant* (New York, 1928-1934), the *New Militant* (New York, 1934-1936), the *Socialist Appeal* (Chicago, New York, 1934-1941), the *Militant* (New York, 1941-), the *New International* (New York, 1934-), and the *Fourth International* (New York, 1940-). The last two journals mentioned are among the most important journals of theoretical Marxism to appear in America in the last decade, and the former, Cannonite to 1940, is particularly useful for reprinting in its department, "Archives of the Revolution," Marxian documents difficult to procure otherwise.

The program of the "Musteite" party, with which the Trotskyists fused just before entering the Socialist Party in 1936, is in *Toward an American Revolutionary Labor Movement; Draft Program of the American Workers Party* (rev. ed., New York, 1934, 46 pp.). *Labor Age* (New York, 1913-1933, title varies), superseded by *Labor Action* (New York, 1933-1934), spoke for the Conference for Progressive Labor Action (1929-1934), an organization of militant trade unions and unemployed led by Muste. It merged into the Trotskyist *New International*. A sample Stalinist attack before the Trotskyists' "French turn" into the Socialist Party is M. J. Olgin, *Trotskyism: Counter-Revolution in Disguise* (New York, 1935, 160 pp.). *The Case of Leon Trotzky* (New York, 1937, 617 pp.), the transcription of the Mexico City hearings of the preliminary commission of inquiry into the charges made against Trotsky in the Moscow trials, under the chairmanship of John Dewey, testifies to Trotskyist influence in the Socialist Party. The essential document on the formation of the Socialist Workers Party is the pamphlet entitled *Declaration of Principles and Constitution* (New York, 1938, 31 pp.). J. P. Cannon published *The Struggle for a Proletarian Party* (New York, 1943, 302 pp.), documents relating to the internal struggle within the party in 1940 over the question of whether the Soviet Union should continue to be defended as a workers' state after the Moscow-Berlin pact of 1939. This book, taken in conjunction with Trotsky's *In Defense of Marxism* (New York, 1942, 211 pp.), defends the majority's affirmative answer to this question and gives the reasons for the subsequent expulsion of the Shachtman-Burnham minority faction. Max Shachtman, *The Fight for Socialism* (New York, 1946, 182 pp.), states the principles and program of the Workers Party, and Albert Goldman, *The Question of Unity between the Workers Party and the Socialist Workers Party* (Long Island City, N.Y., 1947, 93 pp.), rehearses the postwar negotiations for reunion. The subject matter of both works was discussed by these writers in the *New International*.

Topic 11. The I.W.W.

The "Wobbly" movement of the Industrial Workers of the World was the most colorful and most clearly indigenous of all American socialist revolutionary movements. Its suspicion of politics, its contempt for intellectuals and ideologies, and its preference for violence and "direct action at the point of production"—even its ideal of one big union embracing all workers whether manual or white-collar, skilled or unskilled— suggest dominant American traits emphasized nowhere else so clearly in the radical movement. Thus although the I.W.W. was syndicalist in orientation its syndicalism was one which owed very little to the syndicalist movement abroad.

Organized in 1905 by militant trade unionists drawn chiefly from the Western Federation of Miners, the first three years of the organization's history were largely devoted to factional quarrels requiring solution before a definite program could be decided upon. Thus at the second annual convention in 1906 the unskilled workers, under the leadership of Daniel De Leon of the Socialist Labor Party and Vincent St. John of the radical wing of the W.F.M., succeeded in wresting control from the skilled workers' faction led by Charles O. Sherman of the United Metal Workers International Union. Similarly, at the fourth convention in 1908, the combination of De Leon and St. John, which had successfully liquidated the Sherman faction two years before, divided itself over the question of political action, De Leon arguing against the exclusion of political action from the I.W.W. program entirely, St. John, who was anarchist rather than socialist in orientation, standing for "direct action" of an economic character only. As a result, the split of 1906 alienated the W.F.M., which eventually withdrew from the I.W.W. in 1908, while the unseating of De Leon in 1908 led to the formation of a small rival organization known as the "Detroit I.W.W." up to 1915 and as the Workers International

Industrial Union after that date. But also as a result of these defections the parent organization as last achieved both a homogeneous membership—the "Bummery" as its foes called it—and also at the same time ideological clarity, being definitely committed thereafter to a straight anarcho-syndicalist program of direct action.

Both during and after this early period, however, the organization never deviated from its policy of militant industrial unionism. Under the leadership of St. John and Big Bill Haywood it directed the great strikes at Goldfield, Nevada, in 1907, at McKees Rocks, Pennsylvania, in 1909, and at Lawrence, Massachusetts, in 1912, and, besides this, participated in numerous free-speech and civil-rights struggles, such as the Moyer-Haywood-Pettibone case of 1907, the San Diego free-speech fight of 1912, and the bloody battles at Everett and Centralia, Washington, in 1916 and 1919, respectively. At the same time it continued to advocate and was accused of practicing constant industrial sabotage in the form not only of strikes and work stoppages but of refusing to enter into any kind of wage agreement or contract between employer and employed.

The movement was shattered during the decade after 1914 more thoroughly than was the Socialist Party. Both suffered for their antiwar stand, but the Wobblies, even less respectable, were singled out for special reprisals during the red scare of 1919. Haywood, St. John, and others were tried on 10,000 counts in Chicago and sentenced to heavy fines and long imprisonments. When a number of leaders, including Haywood himself, jumped bail and fled to Russia, the organization's reputation was severely weakened among many of its own followers. Both the I.W.W. and the Socialist Party faced competition from the new Communist Party, but the I.W.W. felt this competition more strongly because it seemed to have more in common with the new revolutionaries. Without either of these handicaps, the I.W.W. would still have disintegrated, for it was an anachronism. The Wobblies were hit-and-run revolutionaries, at their best in a strike situation uncompromisingly opposed to the bosses. The industrial unionism which could bargain for a contract and be responsible for its fulfillment had a future. The I.W.W. had none, for it was neither organized for nor interested in the business negotiations which became an increasingly important function of union organizations. After the 1924 split within the organization itself over the long smoldering question of a more or less decentralized party structure, the I.W.W. continued to shrink. At the end of World War II it was only a shadow of its former self.

The best historical and sociological study of the movement down to 1917 is P. F. Brissenden, *The I.W.W.: a Study of American Syndicalism* (2nd ed., New York, 1920, 438 pp.). This is supplemented by J. S. Gambs, *The Decline of the I.W.W.* (New York, 1932, 269 pp.). Both studies include excellent bibliographies which are nonduplicating and which together give a fair sample of the enormous number of periodical articles, governmental reports, and books dealing with various phases of the movement. They also contain lists of I.W.W. periodicals other than those cited below (Brissenden, pp. 395-403; Gambs, pp. 249-250).

The *Proceedings* of the I.W.W. national conventions (New York, 1905-1907, 1912-1936, 4th to 6th, 9th, not published) and the *Official Proceedings* of the Western Federation of Miners while it was still a member of the I.W.W. (1905-1907) are sources of primary importance. See also, in addition to the reports of the various governmental bodies investigating radical activity cited in the General Reading, section 3C, the hearings of Gompers, Hillquit, St. John, and Ettor in the U.S. Commission on Industrial Relations, *Industrial Relations: Final Report and Testimony* (Washington, 1916, 11 vols.), II, pp. 1443-1579. The most important of the I.W.W. publications has been *Industrial Solidarity* (Chicago, etc., 1909-1931), called variously: *Solidarity* (1909-1917), *Defense News Bulletin* (1917-1918), *New Solidarity* (1918-1920), *Solidarity* (1920-1921), and *Industrial Solidarity* (1921-1931). See also the *Industrial Worker* (Seattle, Wash., etc., 1916-1918, 1919-) and *Proletario* (New York, Philadelphia, 1897-1946·), an I.W.W. organ after about 1913, at one time edited by Arturo Giovannitti. The only foreign-language publications still issued by the I.W.W. are the Hungarian weekly, *Bérmunkás* (Chicago, etc., 1912- , title varies); and the Finnish daily, *Industrialisti* (Duluth, 1917-).

The following are representative samples of the voluminous pamphlet literature. T. J. Hagerty, *Economic Discontent and Its Remedy* (Terre Haute, Ind., 1902, 47 pp.), is by a renegade priest influential in determining the early organizational structure of the I.W.W. The speeches and editorials of Daniel De Leon on industrial unionism (cited in Topic 8) defend the "political" members who were driven out at the 1908 convention. *Industrial Socialism* (Chicago, 1911, 64 pp.), by W. D. Haywood and Frank Bohn, outlines the program of those who continued within the organization to favor some political action. Vincent St. John, *Industrial Unionism and the I.W.W.* (New Castle, Pa., n.d., 15 pp.), expresses the point of view of the extreme antipolitical faction. E. V. Debs, *Industrial Unionism* (1905; New York, 1911, 22 pp.), is a plea for one big union by the Socialist Party leader. Another statement by Debs, as epitomized by W. E. Trautmann, is *From Capitalism to the Industrial Commonwealth* (Chicago, n.d., 58 pp.). Also on industrial unionism are A. E. Woodruff, *The Evolution of Industrial Democracy* (Chicago, n.d., 40 pp.), a criticism of the socialist cooperative commonwealth as an "apocalyptic vision"; J. J. Ettor, *Industrial Unionism; the Way to Freedom* (Chicago, 1912, 22 pp.); and W. E. Trautmann, *Industrial Unionism the Hope of the Workers* (Pittsburgh, Pa., 1913, 64 pp.). On sabotage see W. E. Trautmann, *Direct Action and Sabotage* (Pittsburgh, Pa., 1912, 43 pp.), and E. G. Flynn, *Sabotage; the Conscious Withdrawal of the Workers' Industrial Efficiency* (Cleveland, Ohio, 1916, 31 pp.). An I.W.W. pamphlet, *An Open Letter to President Harding from 52 Members of the I.W.W. in Leavenworth Penitentiary Who Refuse to Apply for Individual Clemency* (Chicago, 1922, 28 pp.), has evidence by Wobblies caught in the postwar red scare. See additional titles in PART III, Topic 7.

The outstanding autobiography of a participant is W. D. Haywood, *Bill Haywood's Book* (New York, 1929, 368 pp.). Haywood was one of the most able and colorful Wobbly leaders, often excoriated by the movement after his flight to Russia in 1921. Other personal reminiscences giving "inside" views of the I.W.W. are Ralph Chaplin, *Wobbly* (Chicago, 1948, 435 pp.), E. G. Flynn, *Debs, Haywood, Ruthenberg* (New York, 1939, 48 pp.), and M. H. Vorse, *A Footnote to Folly* (New York, 1935, 407 pp.). Alexander Berkman, *The Bolshevik Myth* (New York, 1925, 319 pp.), the Russian diary (1920-1921) of an anarchist leader, reflects the general disappointment with the course of the Bolshevik revolution felt by many anarchists and syndicalists who were deported or fled to Russia at the end of World War I. The concluding chapter of Berkman's journal, rejected by the publisher, according to the author, on "literary" grounds, was published separately as *The "Anti-Climax"* (Berlin, 1925, 29 pp.). For the relationship between American conservative syndicalism and the I.W.W. see D. D. Lum's pamphlet, reprinted by the A.F.L., *The Philosophy of Trade Unions* (1892; Washington, 1914, 19 pp.), and the general reference works on anarchism, Topic 12, below.

Since throughout most of its career the I.W.W. recruited from the class of unskilled, itinerant, and seasonal workers, it is not surprising to find the general histories of the movement written primarily by outsiders. Two brief sketches by members, however, are Vincent St. John, *The I.W.W.: Its History, Structure and Methods* (rev. ed., Chicago, 1917, 32 pp.), written from the point of view of the faction in favor of direct action, and the I.W.W. pamphlet, *Twenty five Years of Industrial Unionism* (Chicago, 1930, 79 pp.), a collection of articles by various authors. In addition to Brissenden and Gambs (cited above), other good and sometimes sympathetic accounts by scholars who observed the Wobblies in action are found in J. G. Brooks, *American Syndicalism: the I.W.W.* (New York, 1913, 264 pp.); R. F. Hoxie, *Trade Unionism in the United States* (New York, 1917, 426 pp.), chap. 6; Carleton Parker, *The Casual Laborer and Other Essays* (New York, 1920, 199 pp.); M. D. Savage, *Industrial Unionism in America* (New York, 1922, 344 pp.), pp. 143-201, including the I.W.W.'s Canadian rival, the One Big Union; and D. J. Saposs, *Left Wing Unionism* (New York, 1926, 192 pp.), pp. 132-174.

For critical appraisals of the I.W.W. philosophy as compared with the philosophy of political socialism, see John Spargo, *Syndicalism, Industrial Unionism and Socialism* (New York, 1913, 243 pp.), which is sympathetic in tone, and both James Oneal, *Sabotage: or Socialism vs. Syndicalism* (St. Louis, Mo., 1913, 32 pp.), and Robert Hunter, *Violence and the Labor Movement* (New York, 1914, 388 pp.), which are more severe in their indictment.

The policy of the I.W.W. has always been oriented toward violence, and much of its history centers in the long series of strikes and civil liberty trials in which it was involved. For the Goldfield strike of 1907 see U.S., Special Commission on Labor Troubles at Goldfield, Nevada, *Papers Relative to Labor Troubles at Goldfield, Nev.* (60th Cong., 1st Sess., House Doc. 607; Washington, 1908, 30 pp.); for the textile strike at Lawrence, see U.S. Bureau of Labor, *Report on Strike of Textile Workers in Lawrence, Mass., in 1912* (62nd Cong., 2nd Sess., Senate Doc. 870; Washington, 1912, 511 pp.), and U.S. Congress, House, Committee on Rules, *The Strike at Lawrence, Mass.* (62nd Cong., 2nd Sess., House Doc. 671; Washington, 1912, 464 pp.). The material on the Everett and Centralia riots is voluminous, but see especially W. C. Smith, *The Everett Massacre, a History of the Class Struggle in the Lumber Industry* (Chicago, 1920?, 302 pp.); A. L. Strong, "Everett's Bloody Sunday," *Survey*, xxxvii (Jan. 27, 1917), pp. 475-476; Federal Council of Churches, *The Centralia Case* (New York, 1930, 50 pp.); and Ralph Chaplin, *The Centralia Conspiracy* (3rd ed., Chicago, 1924, 143 pp.). On the sedition trials and deportations of 1918-1920 see Harrison George, *The I.W.W. Trial . . . By One of the Defendants* (Chicago, 1918, 208 pp.); C. M. Panunzio, *The Deportation Cases of 1919-1920* (New York, 1921, 104 pp.); and P. F. Brissenden, *Justice and the I.W.W.* (Chicago, n.d., 31 pp.). A connected account of many of these strikes and trials is given in Louis Adamic, *Dynamite* (New York, 1931, 452 pp.).

The relation of American to French syndicalism is discussed in PART III, Topic 7. The I.W.W. demand for one big industrial union is referred to in PART IV, Topic 5. The I.W.W. songs and poetry, which express the Wobbly spirit better than any orthodox history, are discussed in PART VI, Topic 6.

Topic 12. American Individualist, Mutualist, and Communist Anarchism

The anarchist tradition is as old in America as it is in Europe. Beginning with seventeenth-century antinomian tendencies, and continuing in the religious anarchism of the nineteenth century closely allied with communitarianism, it first became a distinctive movement with the activity of Josiah Warren. A musical and mechanical genius, Warren was attracted to Owen's New Harmony, continued his communitarian career in Indiana and Ohio, and finally founded the anarchist community of Modern Times, Long Island, New York. He advocated a cooperative nonprofit system of labor and commodity exchange similar to Proudhon's scheme for a national cooperative bank. Henry Thoreau, who is sometimes considered one of the first American individualist anarchists, belonged to an already developed current of "higher-law" theory, of which the Quakers are notable examples. His doctrine of civil disobedience attracted attention because of his importance as a writer, and because he put his theory into practice on a specific issue, the payment of taxes for the war with Mexico. Toward the end of the nineteenth century the individualist anarchists, led by Benjamin R. Tucker, tended toward mutualism, and in the twentieth century, the mutualists became in many respects a libertarian segment of the cooperative movement. Because individualist anarchism was not a foreign importation, like most forms of American socialism, foreigners such as Tolstoy and Gandhi borrowed from Americans at the same time that American anarchism was being changed by foreign events and theories (see PART I, General Reading, pp. 39-42, and PART I, Topic 10).

American communist anarchism, on the other hand, was as much the result of foreign influence as the contemporary forms of socialism. It is most notably represented in the group involved in the Chicago Haymarket affair, and in those who afterwards made New York their headquarters under the leadership of Johann Most or, more important, Emma Goldman. But before the German and Russian immigrants had definitely assumed the leadership of the movement, and before the anarchist case of 1886 had frightened the American public, a few European exiles began to publish and agitate. The Sacco-Vanzetti case rivaled the Haymarket affair in publicity and surpassed it in the support received from nonradicals. Consequently, the bulk of the literature referring to this case is concerned with civil liberty (see PART IV, Topic 7).

The best introduction to the movement is E. M. Schuster, *Native American Anarchism* (Northampton, Mass., 1932, 202 pp.), which emphasizes the individualists and traces the major variations from Anne Hutchinson and the Quakers down to Tucker, Goldman, and others. Warren's activities and the ideas of his school are sympathetically discussed by William Bailie, *Josiah Warren, the First American Anarchist* (Boston, 1906, 134 pp.). The role of the anarchists accused of inciting the bomb-thrower at the Haymarket meeting, and the temper of the times, are analyzed in Henry David, *The History of the Haymarket Affair* (New York, 1936, 579 pp.), with a detailed bibliography, pp. 545-561, and bibliographical footnotes. Emma Goldman's autobiography, *Living My Life* (New York, 1931, 2 vols.), is a highly personal and vivid account of her life as a revolutionary. For a fresh point of view, popularly written, on Thoreau, Tucker, and Goldman as representatives of American anarchism who lived beyond the enunciation of their theories and saw world events change their perspectives, see C. A. Madison, "The Anarchists," in his *Critics & Crusaders* (New York, 1947, 572 pp.), pp. 157-237.

Warren defended his views in his two most important works, *Equitable Commerce* (New Harmony, Ind., 1846, 90 pp.; 5th ed., published as Pt. 1 of *True Civilization; a Subject of Vital and Serious Interest* [Princeton, Mass., 1875, 117 pp.], Pt. 2 never published), and *True Civilization an Immediate Necessity* (Boston, 1863, 184 pp.). See also his *Periodical Letters* (Modern Times, N.Y., 1854-1858). Thoreau's famous essay, "Resistance to Civil Government," appeared first in *Aesthetic Papers* (ed. by E. P. Peabody; Boston, 1849, 248 pp.), pp. 189-211, and was reprinted elsewhere as "Civil Disobedience" and "On the Duty of Civil Disobedience." His essential criticism of the contemporary state and society was incorporated into *Walden* (New York, 1937, 732 pp.). Equally scornful of socialism with Warren and Thoreau, but placing more emphasis on banking and currency reform, was W. B. Greene, author of *Equality* (West Brookfield, Mass., 1849, 74 pp.), *Mutual Banking* (West Brookfield, Mass., 1850, 94 pp.; a later edition is cited in General Reading, p. 99), *The Sovereignty of the People* (Boston, 1868, 35 pp.), and *Socialistic, Communistic, Mutualistic, and Financial Fragments* (Boston, 1875, 271 pp.). Mutualistic anarchism was elaborated by Warren's disciple, S. P. Andrews, in *The Science of Society* (1851-1853; 3rd ed., New York, 1854, 2 vols. in 1).

After the Civil War, the most important spokesman of individualistic anarchism was Benjamin R. Tucker, editor of *Liberty* (Boston, etc., 1881-1908). The best summary of Tucker's position is "State Socialism and Anarchism," in *Individual Liberty* (ed. by C. L. S.; New York, 1926, 294 pp.), pp. 1-19, an abridgement of *Instead of a Book* (New York, 1893, 512 pp.), a collection of articles which originally appeared in *Liberty*. An example of American influence upon European anarchism is the role of Benjamin Tucker in the development of the German anarchist, John Henry Mackay. This influence is established in T. A. Riley's well-documented note, "New England Anarchism in Germany," *New England Quarterly*, xviii (Mar. 1945), pp. 25-38. Lysander Spooner, whose career overlapped those of Warren and Tucker, contributed to the literature of the movement with many occasional pamphlets and treatises, such as *Poverty: Its Illegal Causes and Legal Cure* (Boston, 1846, 108 pp.), *An Essay on the Trial by Jury* (Boston, 1852, 224 pp.), *No Treason* (Boston, 1867-1870, 3 pts.), and *A Letter to Grover Cleveland* (Boston, 1886,

110 pp.), reprinted from *Liberty*. *Trial by Jury* was abridged as *Free Political Institutions; Their Nature, Essence and Maintenance* (ed. by Victor Yarros; Boston, 1890, 47 pp.). The *Word*, edited by E. H. Heywood (Princeton, Mass., 1872-1893), was largely a personal organ friendly to labor and social reforms. See Heywood's discussion of property, *Yours or Mine* (Boston, 1869, 22 pp.), and his many brochures reprinted from the *Word*. Other expressions of individualistic anarchism at the turn of the century are Victor Yarros, *Anarchism; Its Aims and Methods* (Boston, 1887, 30 pp.); W. H. Van Ornum, *Why Government at All?* (Chicago, 1892, 368 pp.), published by C. H. Kerr; F. D. Tandy, *Voluntary Socialism* (Denver, Colo., 1896, 228 pp.); and J. L. Walker, *The Philosophy of Egoism* (Denver, 1905, 76 pp.). Van Ornum proposed to abolish government by electing legislators who would vote against every bill until all laws were annulled. Tandy expressed Proudhonian ideas, while Walker drew principally from Stirner. See the contemporary evaluation by H. L. Osgood, "Scientific Anarchism," *Political Science Quarterly*, IV (Mar. 1889), pp. 1-36, the first half of which is devoted to the ideas of Proudhon. See also J. A. Labadie, *Essays* (Detroit, Mich., 1911, 60 pp.), and the Labadie collection of materials on labor, socialism, and anarchism in the University of Michigan Library. In the twentieth century, anarchist mutualism produced such works as C. T. Sprading, *Freedom and Its Fundamentals* (Los Angeles, 1923, 255 pp.), and the anthology, *Liberty and the Great Libertarians* (Los Angeles, 1913, 540 pp.), by the same author; C. L. Swartz, *What Is Mutualism?* (New York, 1927, 238 pp.); and other titles in PART IV, Topic 6.

Communist anarchism began in America with the little-read and voluminous publications of two Frenchmen. Joseph Déjacque printed his work, "L'Humanisphère; utopie anarchique," in Volumes 1-2 (1858-1859) of his journal, *Libertaire* (New York, 1858-1861), because he could not get enough subscribers to publish it separately. It appeared as a book at Brussels in 1899. Claude Pelletier, a proscribed Forty-eighter and connected with the First International as well as in touch with the Icarians of Iowa, expressed his ideas of "atercratie" (anarchist socialism) in *Dictionnaire socialiste* (New York, 1874-1876, 3 vols.) and other writings. See also the single number of the first English-language anarcho-communist publication, *An-Archist; Socialistic-Revolutionary Review* (Boston, Jan. 1881).

Chicago was an early center of Socialistic Labor Party strength because of the support received from anarchists such as Albert R. Parsons. In 1883 these anarchists, and others like them, organized an American branch of the so-called "Black International." See the *Plan of Organization, Method of Propaganda and Resolutions, Adopted by the Pittsburgh Congress of the "International Working-Peoples Association,"* October

14th . . . 16th, 1883 (Pittsburgh, Pa., 1883). The letter of Burnette G. Haskell, leader of the West Coast International Workingmen's Association, to the anarchists Labadie and Spies proposing the union of communist anarchists and libertarians is reproduced and commented on by C. M. Destler, "Shall Red and Black Unite? An American Revolutionary Document of 1883," in Destler's essays, *American Radicalism, 1865-1901* (New London, Conn., 1946, 276 pp.), pp. 78-104. A group of Chicago anarchists published the *Alarm* (Chicago, etc., 1884-1889, 1915-1916), with Parsons as first editor, succeeded by Dyer D. Lum after Parsons' arrest. In New York an autonomous group maintained the *Anarchist* (New York, 1889-1895) in German. Their theoretical position is summed up in Parsons, *Anarchism; Its Philosophy and Scientific Basis* (Chicago, 1887, 200 pp.); and Lum, *The Economics of Anarchy; a Study of the Industrial Type* (New York, 1890, 59 pp.), and the same author's *The Philosophy of Trade Unions* (1892; Washington, 1914, 19 pp.), reprinted by the A.F.L. The syndicalist cast to Lum's thought is indicated by his position as a constructive trade-union worker in New York during the radical period of A.F.L. history.

Probably the most important sources on the Haymarket affair are: August Spies and A. R. Parsons, *The Great Anarchist Trial; the Haymarket Speeches as Delivered on the Evening of the Throwing of the Bomb . . . May 4, 1886* (Chicago, 1886, 16 pp.); *August Spies' Autobiography; His Speech in Court and General Notes* (ed. by N. V. Spies; Chicago, 1887, 91 pp.); L. E. Parsons, comp., *The Famous Speeches of the Eight Chicago Anarchists in Court . . . Oct. 7, 8, and 9, 1886* (7th ed., Chicago, 1910, 121 pp.); and D. D. Lum, *A Concise History of the Great Trial of the Chicago Anarchists in 1886* (Chicago, 1886, 191 pp.).

Of the New York group, Johann Most, Alexander Berkman, and Emma Goldman are the outstanding representatives. Most, who came to the United States in 1882, bringing with him his weekly magazine, *Freiheit* (London, New York, 1879-1910), was a prolific writer. Among his most important works are: *Die freie Gesellschaft* (New York, 1884, 85 pp.), and *The God Pest* (New York, n.d., 18 pp.). Many of his writings first appeared in *Freiheit*. For biographies of Most, see his own *Memoiren* (New York, 1903-1907, 4 pts.), Rudolf Rocker, *Johann Most; das Leben eines Rebellen* (Berlin, 1924, 482 pp.), and Ernst Drahn, *Johann Most; eine Bio-Bibliographie* (Berlin, 1925, 20 pp.). Emma Goldman and Alexander Berkman, Russian immigrants deported during the red scare of 1919, were close associates who edited *Mother Earth* (New York, 1906-1917), superseded by *Mother Earth Bulletin* (New York, 1917-1918). Goldman's most important articles in the first years of her editorship are collected in *Anarchism and Other Essays* (New York, 1910, 277 pp.). Berkman, after fifteen years in prison for attempted assassination of Henry

Clay Frick during the Homestead strike of 1892, reported his experiences in *Prison Memoirs of an Anarchist* (New York, 1912, 512 pp.), and summarized his philosophy in *Now and After; the A B C of Communist Anarchism* (New York, 1929, 300 pp.). A general European survey of American anarchism in the late nineteenth century is Paul Ghio, *L'Anarchisme aux États-Unis* (Paris, 1903, 196 pp.). For a minor figure before World War I, see Alexander Berkman, ed., *Selected Works of Voltairine de Cleyre* (New York, 1914, 480 pp.), with a biographical sketch by Hippolyte Havel, and Sadakichi Hartmann's friendly criticism, "Voltairine de Cleyre," *Mother Earth*, x (Apr. 1915), pp. 92-96.

Pamphlets such as Bartolomeo Vanzetti, *Background of the Plymouth Trial* (Boston, 1926, 38 pp.), unclassifiable polemics such as C. E. S. Wood, *Too Much Government* (New York, 1931, 266 pp.), and the periodicals, *Freedom; a Journal of Constructive Anarchism* (New York, 1919), *Road to Freedom* (Stelton, N.J., 1924-1932), superseded by *Freedom; an Anarchist Monthly* (New York, 1933-1934), and *Vanguard* (New York, 1932-1939), are among the varying sources on the declining phase of anarchism after World War I.

For surveys of labor crises which include communist anarchist activities in the United States, see Louis Adamic, *Dynamite* (New York, 1931, 452 pp.), and Samuel Yellen, *American Labor Struggles* (New York, 1936, 398 pp.). E. F. Dowell, *A History of Criminal Syndicalism Legislation in the United States* (Baltimore, 1939, 176 pp.), deals with the laws inspired by the anarchist doctrine of violence; and J. H. Dolsen, *The Defense of a Revolutionist by Himself* (San Francisco, Calif., 1920?, 112 pp.), is a sample account of a trial for criminal syndicalism. See also Topic 11; PART I, Topic 8, and PART III, Topic 7, on syndicalism; PART IV, Topic 7, on civil rights; and PART V, Topic 7, on anarchist theories of the status of women and the family.

Topic 13. Christian Socialism

In one sense Christian socialism in America may be said to trace its continuous lineage back through Oneida, the Fourierists, and the Shakers to the religious communistic sects of the seventeenth century. This topic, however, deals with the Christian socialism of the late nineteenth and twentieth centuries, certain characteristics of which distinguish it from its earlier forms. The religious communists had been tinged with adventism, which customarily led them to retreat from the world in order to prepare themselves spiritually for, or actually to participate in, the millennium. Their communism was incidental to the main purpose of seeking salvation in otherworldly terms. The modern Christian socialists, properly so-called, are a post-Marxian phenomenon, and their thought is conditioned by the dominance of scientific socialism in the modern world. From

1880 to the present there have appeared small but articulate groups of Christian socialists who have given direct expression to the religious idealism which permeates much of American socialist thought in recent times.

Unlike the older religious communists the Christian socialists believe that social reorganization is an integral part of the effort to live a Christian life and to inaugurate a Christian society according to the principles of Jesus. Where the former groups had reverted to the practices of the primitive Christians the latter have rediscovered the social teachings of Christ. With the growth of the country and the spread of industrialism the Protestant churches had become largely identified with the middle and upper classes and accustomed to defend, at least implicitly, their economic and social attitudes. The late nineteenth-century Social Gospel movement, of which the Christian socialists constitute the left wing, arose out of the gospel ethic of brotherly love and self-sacrifice in revolt against this class alignment of Protestantism. Although they clung to the Christian revelation of salvation and belief in heavenly immortality, at times the Christian socialists have nevertheless tended to identify the Kingdom of God with a worldly order. They deny the older Protestant teaching that Christianity is an otherworldly religion concerned only with mediation between the individual and his God.

Christian socialists have never attempted to form a distinct party of their own, although they have contributed such leaders as Herron and Thomas to the Socialist Party and aided in the formation of one of its antecedent organizations, the Brotherhood of the Cooperative Commonwealth, the aim of which was in part "to usher in . . . the Kingdom of God Here and Now." The characteristic organizations of Christian socialism have been such associations as the Society of Christian Socialists, formed in 1889, the Christian Socialist Fellowship, formed in 1905, the Church Socialist League (Episcopal, 1911-1924), and the contemporary Fellowship of Socialist Christians. These groups have confined themselves largely to the sponsorship of lectures and publications.

H. F. May, *Protestant Churches and Industrial America* (New York, 1949, 297 pp.), especially pp. 73-79, 148-265, provides the best orientation to late nineteenth-century Christian socialism as the left-wing minority of Protestant social Christianity, which itself was the left-wing minority of American Protestantism. May relates the progressive to the conservative Protestants and both to industrial capitalism. He finds no direct correlation between theological and social radicalism. A more detailed account of the Christian socialists can be found in James Dombrowski, *The Early Days of Christian Socialism in America* (New York, 1936, 208 pp.). For the relation of the Roman Catholics to socialism a comparable work is lacking; but consult J. A. Ryan, "Socialism and Religion," in the debate between Morris Hillquit and Ryan, *Socialism: Promise or Menace?* (New York, 1914, 270 pp.), pp. 186-199. Key statements by Christian socialists are Rev. Eliot White, "The Christian Socialist Fellowship," *Arena*, XLI (Jan. 1909), pp. 47-52; and A. T. Mollegen, "The Common Convictions of the Fellowship of Socialist Christians," *Christianity and Society*, VIII (Spring 1943), pp. 22-28.

Periodicals were the chief agency for circulating Christian socialist ideas. Among them were *Dawn* (Boston, 1889-1896), ed. by W. D. P. Bliss; *Kingdom* (Minneapolis, Chicago, 1894-1899), ed. by H. W. Gleason but influenced chiefly by G. D. Herron; *Social Crusader* (Chicago, 1898-1901), published by the Social Crusade; *Social Gospel* (Commonwealth, Ga., etc., 1898-1901), published by the Christian Commonwealth Colony; *Social Forum* (Chicago, 1899-1900), mouthpiece of the Social Reform Union of Buffalo; *Christian Socialist* (Danville, Ill., 1903-1916), ed. by E. E. Carr for the Christian Socialist Fellowship; *World Tomorrow* (New York, 1918-1934, title varies), ed. by Norman Thomas for the Fellowship of Reconciliation; and *Christianity and Society* (New York, 1936- , title varies), published by the Fellowship of Socialist Christians. *Arena* (Boston, etc., 1889-1909) published many articles by members of the movement. Edward Silvin, *Index to Periodical Literature on Socialism* (Santa Barbara, Calif., 1909, 45 pp.), lists over a hundred titles on Christian socialism and the attitude of the Roman Catholic Church toward socialism.

During the rise and fall of the Socialist Labor and Socialist Parties before World War I, the idealist reaction to Marxism took many forms. One of the earliest sympathizers with labor and socialism was R. H. Newton, rector of All Souls Church, New York. See his gradualist, mutualist definition of socialism in "The Religious Aspect of Socialism," in his *Social Studies* (New York, 1887, 380 pp.), pp. 259-296, and further comment in other articles of this collection, "Communism," pp. 297-355, and "A Bird's-Eye View of the Labor Problem," pp. 1-81. Austin Bierbower, *Socialism of Christ, or, Attitude of Early Christians toward Modern Problems* (Chicago, 1890, 202 pp.), made extreme analogies quite unacceptable to most contemporary Christian socialists, especially in reference to violent revolution. Paul Monroe, "English and American Christian Socialism, an Estimate," *American Journal of Sociology*, I (July 1895), pp. 50-68, criticizes the Christian socialists' vague ameliorative doctrine and contrasts them with Marxian socialists. Laurence Gronlund, "Christian Socialism in America," *Christian Register*, LXVIII (June 13, 1889), p. 380, and N. P. Gilman's article with the same title in the *Unitarian Review*, XXXII (Oct. 1889), pp. 345-357, were much more sympathetic. A. J. Abell, *The Urban Impact on American Protestantism, 1865-1900* (Cambridge, Mass., 1943, 275 pp.), pp. 75-81, puts Christian socialism in its metropolitan context. H. C. Vedder, *Socialism and the Ethics of Jesus* (New York, 1912, 527 pp.), asserted that socialist, anarchist, and Christian doctrine agreed on ends but used complementary means. Rev. F. M. Sprague, *Socialism from Genesis to Revelation* (Boston, 1893, 493 pp.), searched Scripture for texts against the Social Darwinians. The Collectivist Society published Discipulus (pseud.), *The Socialism of Jesus; a Lesson Learned* (New York, 1903, 40 pp.), the fourth in a series of pamphlets. Bouck White, head resident of Trinity House, New York, and minister of the working-class Church of the Social Revolution, wrote a life of Jesus and a study of the parables: *The Call of the Carpenter* (Garden City, N.Y., 1911, 355 pp.); *The Carpenter and the Rich Man* (Garden City, N.Y., 1914, 339 pp.). I. S. J. Tucker, *Out of the Hell-Box* (New York, 1945, 179 pp.), a kaleidoscopic autobiography, refers briefly (pp. 86-107) to the author's short antiwar Christian socialist experience. See also W. M. Brown, *Communism and Christianism Analyzed and Contrasted from the View-point of Darwinism* (Galion, Ohio, 1920, 184 pp.), by the former Episcopal bishop of Arkansas.

R. B. Y. Scott and Gregory Vlastos, eds., *Towards the Christian Revolution* (Chicago, 1936, 254 pp.), a symposium by members of the United Church of Canada, relates Christian socialist ideas and program to philosophical and scriptural background and to the challenge of Marxism.

For characteristic statements of Christian socialism in the 1890's see W. D. P. Bliss, *What Is Christian Socialism?* (Boston, 1890, 48 pp.; pamphlet reprint of article in *Dawn*, i, No. 9 [Jan. 15, 1890], pp. 1-3; No. 10 [Feb. 1890], pp. 1-3), and P. W. Sprague, *Christian Socialism; What and Why* (New York, 1891, 204 pp.). The development of G. D. Herron's thought from a vague Christian social reformism to thoroughgoing socialism may be traced in his writings, *The New Redemption: a Call to the Church to Reconstruct Society According to the Gospel of Christ* (New York, 1893, 176 pp.), *The Christian Society* (Chicago, 1894, 158 pp.), and *Why I Am a Socialist* (Chicago, 1900, 31 pp.).

Examples of Christian socialism in the twentieth century are J. S. Wilson, *How I Became a Socialist and Other Essays* (Berkeley, Calif., 1912, 9 pts. in 1 vol.), the speeches of a Methodist reconciling socialism with the Bible; E. H. Crosby, *Golden Rule Jones* (Chicago, 1906, 62 pp.), a biographical sketch of a reform mayor of Toledo; J. H. Holmes, *The Revolutionary Function of the Modern Church* (New York, 1912, 264 pp.); V. D. Scudder, *Socialism and Character* (Boston, 1912, 430 pp.); H. F. Ward, *The New Social Order; Principles and Programs* (New York, 1920, 384 pp.), and *Which Way Religion?* (New York, 1931, 221 pp.).

Less positive in their socialist aspirations were a group of Social Gospelers who identified Christianity with a socialized order but who distinguished their ideals from the program of secular socialism. For bibliographical references to the wider Social Cospel movement see Dombrowski, *The Early Days of Christian Socialism*, pp. 195-201, and the footnotes in C. H. Hopkins, *The Rise of the Social Gospel in American Protestantism, 1865-1915* (New Haven, Conn., 1940, 352 pp.). Hopkins has prepared a comprehensive, unpublished bibliography of Social Christianity. Lyman Abbott, *Christianity and Social Problems* (Boston, 1896, 370 pp.), urged progressive political reforms which would preserve the best elements of individualism in a cooperative and Christianized society. Washington Gladden, *Christianity and Socialism* (New York, 1905, 244 pp.), urged the peaceful evolution of vague Christian socialism. The chief theologian of socialized Christianity was Walter Rauschenbusch, although he was less concerned with practical measures for reform than with its theoretical justification. His theology is discussed in Topic 8 of PART III, and the theology at the base of the Fellowship of Socialist Christians is referred to in the succeeding Topic 9. See also PART V, Topic 9, on the socialist sociology of religion.

The Roman Catholic attitude toward socialism is discussed by Father Ryan in the debate with Hillquit, cited above, and from the socialist point of view, in an article signed "By a Leading Socialist," "Why the Catholic Church Opposes Socialism," *Arena*, xxxvii (May 1907), pp. 520-524. Representative expressions of the critical Catholic attitude toward socialism, tempered with criticism of capitalism at the same time, are F. W. Howard, "Socialism and Catholicism," *Catholic World*, lxv (Sept. 1897), pp. 721-727; Bernard Vaughan, *Socialism from the Christian Standpoint* (New York, 1912, 389 pp.); J. C. Husslein, *A Catholic Social Platform* (New York, 1919, 16 pp.); J. C. Harrington, *Catholicism, Capitalism or Communism* (St. Paul, Minn., 1926, 445 pp.); J. D. Callahan, *The Catholic Attitude toward a Familial Minimum Wage* (Washington, 1936, 137 pp.); and Father Ryan's autobiography, *Social Doctrine in Action* (New York, 1941, 297 pp.). *Socialism and the Labor Problem* (Bellevue, Ky., 1900, 40 pp.) is a sample of the writing of Thomas McGrady, socialist priest who later withdrew from the priesthood. He collaborated with Frank Bohn in *The Catholic Church and Socialism* (Chicago, 1913, 31 pp.). William Clancy, *Catholicism and Socialism* (Bridgeport, Conn., 1912, 35 pp.), states the layman's point of view that a Catholic can be a socialist. G. H. Dunne, S.J., "Socialism and Socialism," *Commonweal*, xliii (Nov. 23, 1945), pp. 134-139, asserts that the Church can get along with nondoctrinaire democratic socialists.

Characteristic of a large segment of American Christianity which believes that socialism is anti-Christian is E. R. Hartman, *Socialism versus Christianity* (New York, 1909, 263 pp.).

PART III
The Doctrinal Basis of American Socialism

For discussion in Volume 1 relevant to this Part (PART III) of the Bibliography, see especially Chapters 7 and 8; also Chapters 3, 4, 5, 6, 9, and 10.

General Reading

PARTS I and II treat American socialism and its European backgrounds historically; PARTS III-VI are analytical and comparative. PART III presents the literature concerning the philosophical postulates of American socialism and their relation to the philosophical postulates of the American tradition.

No matter how practical its program, every social creed rests consciously or unconsciously upon a set of general beliefs about the nature of the world and of man. The socialist creed is no exception. Each form of socialism implies an answer to the question of the ultimate naturalistic or supernaturalistic basis of existence; a theory of history; a conception of the ideal of conduct which should govern human behavior before and after the realization of the socialist goal; and beyond this, a theory of the ultimate perfectibility or imperfectibility of man's moral, intellectual, and physical nature. It even implies methodology insofar as it assumes that certain rules of inquiry and certain modes of social action are absolutely essential in the acquisition of truths and in the implementation of its practical program. Together these assumptions comprise what may be called a "socialistic metaphysic," a philosophical *Weltanschauung* which helps distinguish socialism from capitalism and the different varieties of socialism from one another.

The three principal varieties of American socialism (early religious communism, nineteenth-century secular communitarianism, and twentieth-century Marxism) all had this *Weltanschauung* diversely formulated. To what extent is the universe spiritually or materialistically grounded? What is the general character—the determinants and "direction"—of human history? What is the ultimate basis of human knowledge and conduct and how is this related to man's role in history? The answers of representative thinkers to these fundamental questions are explicit or implicit in the following selections: Shakers, *A Summary View of the Millennial Church, or United Society of Believers (Commonly Called Shakers)* (Albany, N.Y., 1823, 320 pp.), pp. 195-235, 258-284; Étienne Cabet, *Voyage en Icarie* (3rd ed., Paris, 1845, 600 pp.); and L. B. Boudin, *The Theoretical System of Karl Marx* (Chicago, 1907, 286 pp.).

There is no general history or analysis of the religious and philosophical bases of American socialism. Even the standard treatises on American philosophy and theology slight the subject, some of them not even mentioning socialist creeds by name. See, for example, H. W. Schneider, *A History of American Philosophy* (New York, 1946, 646 pp.), which includes the pre-Marxians in a short chapter, "Frontier Faiths and Communities," pp. 144-159, and disposes of the Marxians with casual references, pp. 206-207, 566-567.

The works that follow include a selection of (1) the more important socialist "classics" (both European and American) which have been influential in defining or determining the American socialist philosophical attitude; (2) commentaries on those works which have been influential in the same respect; and (3) works of a comparative nature attempting to draw a critical or friendly parallel between the presuppositions of the socialist creed and those of the dominant American creed.

1. Early Religious Communism

Among the early religious communist groups, one of the most important doctrinal sources is, of course, the Bible. This was not only because all of these groups were Christian schismatic sects, but also because they could find in the theocracy of the old Kingdom of Israel, in the intimations of communism in the organization of the primitive Christian church, and more especially in the apocalyptic books of the Old and New Testaments, sacred authority for their own social experiments. Almost every group, however, supplemented the Bible with its own theological writings, often voluminous enough to appall even the most eager student. The pietistic and "inspirationist" groups were constantly admitting new additions to divine truth revealed by their own leaders and members, for they held God's revelation to be continuous.

Their frequent use of mystical language and their often fantastic cosmologies baffle the interested student. The Ephrata Brotherhood, the Rappites, and the Shakers, among the earlier sects, exhibited strong doctrinal affinities—often unconsciously—with the mystical tradition of Neoplatonism represented most strikingly since the Reformation in the writings of Jakob Böhme, Gichtel, and Swedenborg. The later and more indigenous sects, though less mystical in approach, evolved equally fantastic theories of their own, e.g., the Mormons' mythical history of the ten "lost" tribes of Israel.

The central teachings of the group at EPHRATA are contained in the writings of its founder and chief prophet, Conrad Beissel. Not all of Beissel's works have been preserved, but of those which remain the following are the most interesting from the point of view of doctrine. *Mystyrion Anomias; the Mystery of Lawlessness* (1728; tr. by Michael Wohlfahrt; Philadelphia, 1729, 32 pp.) is a dialogue defending seventh-day Sabbatarianism. *A Dissertation on Man's Fall* (tr. by Peter Miller; Ephrata, Pa., 1765, 37 pp.), the English version of Beissel's *Göttliche Wunderschrift*, a mystical history of God's relation to his creation, reveals Beissel's indebtedness to Böhme. *Erster Theil der Theosophischen Lectionen* (Ephrata, Pa., 1752, 432 pp.), is a selection of miscellaneous testimonies read by Beissel at the Sabbath services of the Cloister, with proverbs and poems appended. To these should be added Johannes

Hildebrand's anti-Moravian tracts, *Mistisches und kirchliches Zeuchnüss der Brüderschaft in Zion* (Germantown, Pa., 1743, 44 pp.), and *Schrifft-mässiges Zeuchnüss von dem himmlischen und jungfraülichen Gebäh-rungs-Werck* (Germantown, Pa., 1743, 20 pp.), particularly the latter, which restates the argument of Beissel's *Wunderschrift* more lucidly than the original. See also *Chronicon Ephratense* (1786; tr. by J. M. Hark; Lancaster, Pa., 1889, 288 pp.), an early account of Beissel's religious development by Brother Lamech and Brother Agrippa, two members of the Ephrata Brotherhood. For further material on the theology of Ephrata see O. W. Seidensticker's *Ephrata: eine amerikanische Klostergeschichte* (Cincinnati, Ohio, 1883, 141 pp.), and, above all, J. F. Sachse's monumental study, *The German Sectarians of Pennsylvania, 1708-1800, a Critical and Legendary History of the Ephrata Cloister and the Dunkers* (Philadelphia, 1899-1900, 2 vols.), *passim*. W. C. Klein, *Johann Conrad Beissel, Mystic and Martinet: 1690-1768* (Philadelphia, 1942, 218 pp.), although highly critical, is particularly valuable for its account of Beissel's intellectual background.

The basic teachings of the AMANA community, or the Community of True Inspiration, are summarized, according to B. M. H. Shambaugh, the modern historian of the group, in (1) The Apostles' Creed, (2) "The Twenty-four Rules for True Godliness," and (3) "The Twenty-one Rules for the Examination of Our Daily Lives"—all of which are printed in full in Mrs. Shambaugh's *Amana That Was and Amana That Is* (Iowa City, Iowa, 1932, 502 pp.), pp. 233-244. These documents emphasize the group's adherence to the central doctrines of Christianity and to the pietistic ideal of austerity in conduct and simplicity in religious worship. They also imply the most distinctive dogma of the group that divine inspiration did not cease with the prophets and apostles but that the divine commandments continue to be revealed from time to time through new prophets. This dogma was first elaborated in the writings of Eberhard Ludwig Gruber (d. 1728)—who, together with Johann Friedrich Rock (d. 1749), founded the society in 1714—particularly in his *Bericht von der Inspirations-Sache* (Amana, Iowa, 1884, 23 pp.) and his *Kennzeichen der Göttlichkeit der Wahren Inspiration* (Amana, Iowa, 1884, 8 pp.). This dogma is also elaborated in the community catechism, *Catechetischer Unterricht von der Lehre des Heils* (Amana, Iowa, 1872-1875, 2 vols.), particularly in the section entitled "Das Gnadenwerk der Inspiration."

The new revelations themselves—important as the origin of such community decisions as the resolve to migrate to America in 1845 and to establish a communistic mode of life—are voluminous, but have been carefully preserved by the society. Forty-two volumes of these revelations covering the period 1714-1749 were published under the general title of *Sammlungen* (n.p., 1743-1789), and for the period of the "new awakening," 1823-1883, fifty-eight more were published under the general title, *Jahrbücher der Wahren Inspirations-Gemeinden oder Bezeugungen des Geistes des Herrn* (Vols. 1-2 published in Germany, 1842; Vols. 3-21, Ebenezer, N.Y., 1849-1863; Vols. 22-58, Amana, Iowa, 1866-1884).

Another source of information regarding the doctrinal teachings of the group are the "testimonies" of its prophets, of which the most important are: Barbara Heinemann, *Kurze Erzählung von den Erweckungs-Umständen* (Amana, Iowa, 1885, 60 pp.), and Christian Metz, *Tagebücher* (ed. by Gottlieb Scheuner; Amana, Iowa, 1875, 926 pp.). Metz, Barbara Heinemann, and Michael Krausert were the leaders of the great awakening of 1817. Metz and Heinemann led the migration to America and helped institute communism at Ebenezer and Amana. For the early history of the group, see *Historischer Bericht von der Gründung der Gebets-Versammlungen und Gemeinden* (Amana, Iowa, 1900-1926, 7 vols.), by Gottlieb Scheuner, Metz's "Scribe" and successor as leader of the community, and Metz's own *Historische Beschreibung der Wahren Inspirations-Gemeinschaft* (Buffalo, N.Y., 1863, 189 pp.), a history of the community between 1714 and 1845. Mrs. Shambaugh's work cited above not only covers the external history of the group but offers a detailed analysis of its religious doctrines as well (pp. 195-280).

Uniting the pietism and inspirationism of the Amana group with the mystical doctrine of both Beissel and the Shakers that man's fall from grace is a result of the separation of the male and female principles which can be overcome only by the practice of celibacy, the RAPPITES, or Harmonists, produced no comparably extensive doctrinal literature because of their lack of interest in proselytizing. One of the Harmony Society's few original works is *Thoughts on the Destiny of Man, Particularly with Reference to the Present Times* (Harmony, Ind., 1824, 96 pp.), a disquisition preaching the goodness of the ascetic life ruled by reason and religion and looking forward to a millennium in which all men will live in perfect love and harmony after the model already established by the Rappites. Even this pamphlet was written only because of the pressure of outside requests for information about the teachings of the group. For the most part the community was satisfied with oral instruction and with the study of non-Rappite theological works whose doctrines it approved. Thus the writings of Böhme were much admired, while the Böhmist tract, *Hirten-Brief an die wahren und ächten Freymäurer alten Systems* (Pittsburgh, Pa., 1855, 288 pp.), an esoteric account of the biune nature of Adam and of the Fall, was republished by the society itself and distributed to each of its members. For a brief description of the basic teachings of the group by an outsider see Aaron Williams, *The Harmony Society at Economy, Penn'a.* (Pittsburgh, Pa., 1866, 182 pp.). See also in this connection R. F. Lockridge, *The Labyrinth:*

a History of the New Harmony Labyrinth (New Harmony, Ind., 1941, 94 pp.).

The SHAKERS were more articulate about their beliefs, especially during the first half century of their existence. The most important work is B. S. Youngs, *Testimony of Christ's Second Appearing, Exemplified by the Principles and Practice of the True Church of Christ* (4th ed., Albany, N.Y., 1856, 631 pp.), often referred to as "the Shaker Bible." The pattern of the book is historical, tracing the history of the workings of God from patriarchal times to the fulfillment of the prophecy of Christ's second coming in Ann Lee and her church and offering Biblical proof of all the central Shaker teachings. Other standard treatises on Shaker doctrine are *Testimonies of the Life, Character, Revelations and Doctrines of Our Ever Blessed Mother Ann Lee and the Elders with Her* (Hancock, Mass., 1816, 405 pp.; 2nd ed., Albany, N.Y., 1888, 302 pp.); John Dunlavy, *The Manifesto; or A Declaration of the Doctrines and Practice of the Church of Christ* (Pleasant Hill, Ky., 1818, 520 pp.); S. Y. Wells, ed., *Testimonies Concerning the Character and Ministry of Mother Ann Lee* (Albany, N.Y., 1827, 178 pp.); and Philemon Stewart, *A Holy, Sacred and Divine Roll and Book; from the Lord God of Heaven to the Inhabitants of Earth* (Canterbury, N.H., 1843, 402 pp.). Shorter treatments of more limited subjects include William Leonard, *A Discourse on the Order and Propriety of Divine Inspiration* (Harvard, Mass., 1853, 88 pp.), which also contains discourses on the necessity of communism and on the second advent; F. W. Evans, *God Is God* (Mount Lebanon, N.Y., 1885?, 13 pp.), which includes brief expressions by Shakeresses on the primacy of the spiritual and on confession; and H. C. Blinn, *Advent of the Christ in Man and Woman* (East Canterbury, N.H., 1896, 16 pp.). Shakers, *A Summary View of the Millennial Church, or United Society of Believers (Commonly Called Shakers)* (Albany, N.Y., 1823, 320 pp.), focuses upon Shaker history and doctrine since the establishment of the church by Mother Ann, while F. W. Evans, *Shakers: Compendium of the Origin, History, Principles, Rules and Regulations, Government and Doctrines of the United Society of Believers in Christ's Second Appearing* (New York, 1859, 189 pp.), is a shorter summary of Shaker teachings by one of its most distinguished elders.

In answer to widespread attacks by those who believed that Shaker practices were antithetical to prevailing American institutions, the Shakers produced *A Brief Exposition of the Established Principles and Regulations of the United Society Called Shakers* (Albany, N.Y., 1830, 23 pp.), in which they demonstrated that Shakerism was compatible with a society based upon religious freedom and democratic individualism. See also Fayette Mace, *Familiar Dialogues on Shakerism* (Portland, Me., 1837, 120 pp.); G. A. Lomas, *Plain Talks upon Practical Christian Religion*

(Shakers, N.Y., 1880?, 24 pp.); G. B. Avery, *Sketches of "Shakers and Shakerism"; Synopsis of Theology* (1883; Albany, N.Y., 1884, 50 pp.); and A. G. Mace, *The Aletheia: Spirit of Truth* (Farmington, Me., 1899, 135 pp.). The most sophisticated treatment of Shaker theology is H. L. Eads, *Shaker Sermons: Scripto-Rational; Containing the Substance of Shaker Theology* (Shakers, N.Y., 1879, 222 pp.). The following works are characteristic of Shaker devotional literature: Paulina Bates, *The Divine Book of Holy and Eternal Wisdom* (Canterbury, N.H., 1849, 2 vols. in 1); F. W. Evans, *Tests of Divine Inspiration* (New Lebanon, N.Y., 1853, 127 pp.).

The MORMONS, or the Church of Jesus Christ of Latter-Day Saints, were organized upon the *Book of Mormon* (1830; Salt Lake City, Utah, 1920, 568 pp.), which Joseph Smith, the founder of the church, is believed to have translated from Reformed Egyptian with miraculous aid and which traces the alleged migrations of the lost tribes of Israel to pre-Columbian America. Subsequent revelations vouchsafed to Smith regarding the practical organization and teachings of the church were gathered together in *The Doctrine and Covenants* (Salt Lake City, Utah, 1911, 542 pp.) and became a standard Mormon guide. The most popular collection of Smith's writings—as distinct from his revelations proper—was edited by J. E. Talmage under the title, *The Pearl of Great Price; a Selection from the Revelations, Translations, and Narrations of Joseph Smith* (Salt Lake City, Utah, 1902, 103 pp.), while a somewhat larger selection, emphasizing theological teaching, is to be found in E. F. Parry, ed., *Joseph Smith's Teachings: a Classified Arrangement of the Doctrinal Sermons and Writings of the Great Latter-Day Prophet* (Salt Lake City, Utah, 1912, 192 pp.). For other statements of Mormon theology and its practical applications, see the compilation of Mormon sermons and addresses covering many years entitled *Journal of Discourses* (Liverpool, 1854-1885, 26 vols.), and the *Discourses of Brigham Young* (2nd ed., Salt Lake City, Utah, 1926, 760 pp.), edited by J. A. Widtsoe. A discussion of Mormon theology by a twentieth-century leader of the church may be found in J. E. Talmage, *The Philosophical Basis of "Mormonism"* (Salt Lake City, Utah, 1916, 48 pp.).

For the religious thought of the ONEIDA COMMUNITY, the writings of John Humphrey Noyes comprise an elaborate exposition of his Perfectionism. His most important publications at Putney are *The Way of Holiness; a Series of Papers Formerly Published in the Perfectionist* (Putney, Vt., 1838, 230 pp.); *A Treatise on the Second Coming of Christ* (Putney, Vt., 1840, 32 pp.); and *The Berean; a Manual for the Help of Those Who Seek the Faith of the Primitive Church* (Putney, Vt., 1847, 504 pp.). *Bible Communism* (Oneida, N.Y., 1848), in its later edition (Brooklyn, 1853, 128 pp.), incorporated material from the first three

Annual Reports of the Oneida Community (1849-1851). J. H. Noyes, *Confessions . . . Part I. Confession of Religious Experience, Including a History of Modern Perfectionism* (Oneida Reserve, N.Y., 1849, 96 pp.), and George Cragin, ed., *Faith-Facts* (Oneida Reserve, N.Y., 1850, 40 pp.), summarize the development of Perfectionist doctrine up to the second stage of their experiment. For Noyes's later writings on theology, see especially *Salvation from Sin, the End of Christian Faith* (Wallingford, Conn., 1869, 48 pp.; also Oneida, N.Y., 1876, 48 pp.).

The most important early twentieth-century treatment of Noyes's beliefs is G. W. Noyes, ed., *The Religious Experience of John Humphrey Noyes* (New York, 1923, 416 pp.), a new collection of the founder's early writings with comment. B. B. Warfield, *Perfectionism* (New York, 1931, 2 vols.), II, pp. 219-333, a reprint of "John Humphrey Noyes and His 'Bible Communists'," *Bibliotheca Sacra*, LXXVIII (Jan.-Oct. 1921), pp. 37-72, 172-200, 319-375, views the whole Perfectionist position as a Pelagian heresy, and the Oneida experiment in particular as instructive but unedifying—one of the unwholesome products of excessive religious excitement. See also Frederic Platt's article, "Perfection (Christian)," in *Encyclopaedia of Religion and Ethics*, James Hastings, ed., IX (1917), p. 735, and the article by R. B. Taylor, "Communistic Societies of America," *ibid.*, III (1911), pp. 785-786. The titles discussed in PART II, Topic 4, especially the Perfectionist periodicals, contain additional material.

2. The Secular Communitarians

The philosophic attitude of the secular communitarians of the early and middle nineteenth century forms a natural bridge between those of the early religious communists and those of Marxian socialism, which was to follow. Where the religious utopians were supernaturalistic and the Marxians naturalistic, the secular communitarians had ethical and humanitarian interests. Where the religious postulated the rule of God in history and the Marxians the rule of material forces, the secular communitarians emphasized the role of man as an agent with free choice and as a rational being who could be persuaded by model and precept. Where the religious leaned toward the esoteric and the symbolic in their philosophic interpretation of the world and the Marxians toward the special logic of the dialectic, the secular communitarians relied on reason in the eighteenth-century sense of that term. All three of these traits are reflected in their doctrinal literature.

The ICARIANS, like the Bellamyite Nationalists, were launched by a book. Étienne Cabet's *Voyage en Icarie* (3rd ed., Paris, 1845, 600 pp.), first published in 1840, described an imaginary communist utopia, a highly centralized and uniform society, that aroused great interest among Frenchmen. Although Cabet's social and religious views were unorthodox, he himself believed them to be in the true Christian tradition, and wrote *Le Vrai christianisme suivant Jésus-Christ* (Paris, 1846, 636 pp.) in this spirit. For a Catholic opinion of his work see S. A. Piotrowski, *Étienne Cabet and the Voyage en Icarie* (Washington, 1935, 158 pp.), where Cabet's claims to Christian affiliation are summarily dealt with. The formulation of Cabet's views in actual practice in America are described in *Realization of Communism: Brief History of Icaria; Constitution, Laws, and Regulations of the Icarian Community* (Icaria [Corning], Iowa, 1880, 42 pp.). See also the commentaries by Paul Carré, *Cabet: de la démocratie au communisme* (Lille, 1903, 152 pp.), and J. J. Prud-hommeaux, *Icarie et son fondateur, Étienne Cabet* (Paris, 1907, 688 pp.).

The chief writings of Robert Owen, founder of the OWENITE New Harmony community, for the first stage of his thinking (1813-1821), have been gathered in *A New View of Society & Other Writings* (Everyman's Library, No. 799; intro. by G. D. H. Cole; London, 1927, 298 pp.). Owen's rationalistic religious views are announced in *The New Religion; or, Religion Founded on the Immutable Laws of the Universe* (London, 1830, 11 pp.); in his controversy with the American religious leader Alexander Campbell, *Debate on the Evidences of Christianity* (2nd ed., Cincinnati, Ohio, 1829, 2 vols. in 1; see also Owen's edition, cited in PART II, Topic 5); in *The Book of the New Moral World* (London, 1836-1844, 7 pts.); and in "Oration Containing a Declaration of Mental Independence," delivered at New Harmony, July 4, 1826, and published in *New-Harmony Gazette*, i (July 12, 1826), pp. 329-332. Owen's conception of the socialized society of the future is presented in his *Lectures on the Rational System of Society* (London, 1841, 188 pp.); and in *The Revolution in the Mind and Practice of the Human Race* (London, 1849, 171 pp.).

The fundamental doctrines of the FOURIERIST ASSOCIATIONISTS were derived from the *Oeuvres complètes* (2nd ed., Paris, 1841-1845, 6 vols.) of the founder of the movement, Charles Fourier. It was through the medium of his American disciples, therefore, that Fourierism was preached in this country. Associationism thus acquired more of an indigenous character than the earlier Owenite movement. Americans were more concerned with Fourier's theories of social reorganization than with his philosophy of history. Albert Brisbane, *Social Destiny of Man; or, Association and Reorganization of Industry* (Philadelphia, 1840, 480 pp.), and Parke Godwin, *A Popular View of the Doctrines of Charles Fourier* (New York, 1844, 120 pp.), are the standard introductions to Fourierism. Brisbane also wrote *Theory of the Functions of the Human Passions* (New York, 1856, 160 pp.), in which he reviewed Fourier's thesis that the good society should afford the means of harmonious correlation of human instincts or "passions." The strong religious flavor which permeated American Fourierism is suggested in the "Resolutions" offered at the general convention of Associationists by William H. Channing, April 4, 1844, reproduced in J. R. Commons and others, eds., *A Documentary History of American Industrial Society* (Cleveland, Ohio, 1910-1911, 10 vols. and supp.), vii, pp. 188-202. Henry Edger, who sampled Fourierist and other American projects and then became a devotee of Comte and a member of Josiah Warren's anarchist community of Modern Times, Long Island, represents a unique example of the complete acceptance of positivism in American communitarianism. See his work, *The Positivist Calendar . . . with a Brief Exposition of Religious Positivism* (Modern Times [Thompson], N.Y., 1856, 103 pp.). After the collapse of the Associationist movement Brisbane returned to the teachings of the master in order to obtain wider circulation for his ideas. In *General Introduction to Social Sciences* (New York, 1876, 2 pts. in 1), Brisbane (Pt. 1, 112 pp.) sketched Fourier's stage theory of history and referred briefly to his cosmological idea of universal harmony and belief in immortality.

3. *Marxian Socialism*

Just as the Bible constituted a central ideological authority for the early religious communists, so also the writings of Marx—and more recently of Lenin, Trotsky, and Stalin—have played a similar role among the Marxian socialists. Indeed, if anything, the authority of Marx has been even more absolute. The religious communists often freely supplemented, or even superseded, the revelations of the Bible with revelations of their own; but American Marxists, with a few notable exceptions, have shown little comparable disposition toward originality in their treatment of Marx. For the most part, they have confined themselves to pure exposition and explanation of the Marxian system, or, at the most, to following deviations, such as revisionism and syndicalism, previously worked out abroad.

The two most important periods in American Marxism, as far as philosophic theorizing is concerned, are the periods between 1890 and 1912 and between 1929 and 1938, each of which was quite different in inspiration, character, and output. By 1890 Marxism had triumphed over communitarian and Lassallean socialism. The philosophic activity of the first period was chiefly confined to nonacademic writers, who recognized for the first time the radically materialistic implications of Marxism. They also sought a rationale for reform more effective than humanitarianism. The result was a philosophical literature, nontechnical in character, and given over primarily to exposition or defense, or to attempts to "reconcile" the Marxian philosophy with other prevailing philosophies of the period.

The most important expositions of the time were L. B. Boudin, *The Theoretical System of Karl Marx* (Chicago, 1907, 286 pp.), and the brilliant articles on the labor theory of value, the class struggle, and other aspects of Marxist philosophy contributed to the *People* by Daniel De Leon between 1893 and 1914. Both Boudin and De Leon were "orthodox" or antirevisionist Marxists. Boudin replied ably both to Bernstein and other European revisionists, whose orientation tended to be neo-Kantian, and to Böhm-Bawerk and other defenders of capitalism. De Leon's work is noteworthy for its ability to state Marxian theory in the simple dramatic terms intelligible to uneducated workers. See also for original works on the Marxian dialectic Dietzgen's essays cited in the general reference works, PART II, above, and Ernest Untermann's *Die logische Mängel des engeren Marxismus, Georg Plechanow et alii gegen Josef Dietzgen . . .* (Munich, 1910, 753 pp.). However, since Dietzgen's work was produced long before he settled in America permanently, it belongs to American Marxist literature only by courtesy. Another work by Untermann, *Dialektisches; volkstümliche Vorträge aus dem Gebiete des proletarischen Monismus* (Stuttgart, 1907, 142 pp.), testifies more to the industry than to the insight of the American translator of Marx. See also Untermann's translation of Antonio Labriola, *Socialism and Philosophy* (1898; Chicago, 1944, 260 pp.).

Of the more important revisionist statements of the period Laurence Gronlund, *Our Destiny, the Influence of Socialism on Morals and Religion* (London, 1891, 170 pp.), and Morris Hillquit, *Socialism in Theory and Practice* (New York, 1909, 361 pp.), deserve special notice, the former because it was one of the first American attempts to ground Marxian socialism on an evolutionary rather than a catastrophic or revolutionary theory of history, and the latter because it defends the official gradualistic philosophy of the Socialist Party at that time. To these should also be added W. E. Walling, *The Larger Aspects of Socialism* (New York, 1913, 406 pp.), which tries to fuse socialism with the pragmatic philosophy of the day and thus anticipated the revisionist movement of the 1930's led by Sidney Hook (see below), and V. G. Simkhovitch, *Marxism versus Socialism* (New York, 1913, 298 pp.).

One of the most fruitful sources of philosophic inquiry during the period was the socialists' concern with Herbert Spencer's Social Darwinism, whose evolutionism they wished to defend but whose individualistic ethic they wished to reject. Thus A. M. Lewis' *Evolution, Social and Organic* (4th ed., Chicago, 1908, 186 pp.), and R. R. La Monte, *Socialism, Positive and Negative* (Chicago, 1907, 150 pp.), stress the affinity of Darwinism and Marxism in regard to their naturalism, their developmental approach, and so on; and, together with Ernest Untermann, *Science and Revolution* (Chicago, 1905, 195 pp.), and Anton

Pannekoek, *Marxism and Darwinism* (tr. by Nathan Weiser; Chicago, 1912, 58 pp.), go on to argue that Spencer's individualistic conclusions are inconsistent with his evolutionary premises. Discussion of the problem is also to be found in Lewis, *Ten Blind Leaders of the Blind* (Chicago, 1909, 198 pp.), a critical evaluation of Kant, Comte, Carlyle, Stirner, Ely, George, and others; and in the files of the *International Socialist Review* (Chicago, 1900-1918). For a brief summary of the discussion as a whole, see Richard Hofstadter, *Social Darwinism in American Thought, 1860-1915* (Philadelphia, 1944, 191 pp.), chap. 6; and for an important European source to which American socialists turned for guidance on the question see Enrico Ferri, *Socialism and Modern Science (Darwin-Spencer-Marx)* (tr. by R. R. La Monte; New York, 1900, 213 pp.).

R. W. Sellars, *The Next Step in Democracy* (New York, 1916, 275 pp.), one of the few books on socialism at this time by a professional philosopher, argues that socialism is a species of democracy. See also in this connection E. R. A. Seligman, *The Economic Interpretation of History* (New York, 1902, 166 pp.), a critical examination by another professional scholar of the materialistic approach to history, including the Marxian variant.

Other socialist discussions at this time of a philosophical or religious nature are to be found in the literature of the Bellamy Nationalists and the Christian socialists. These were alike in opposing the Marxian philosophy with a socialism founded upon a spiritualized metaphysic, Bellamy turning for this purpose to the romantic and theosophic philosophies of the past and the Christian socialists to the social gospel of traditional Christianity. Bellamy's chief philosophical writings have been collected by A. E. Morgan in *The Philosophy of Edward Bellamy* (New York, 1945, 96 pp.), which includes Bellamy's longest philosophical work, "The Religion of Solidarity"; but equally important as far as the practical application of the philosophy is concerned are his two utopian novels: *Looking Backward, 2000-1887* (Boston, 1888, 470 pp.) and *Equality* (New York, 1897, 412 pp.), particularly the former. The most detailed examination of Bellamy's philosophy is A. E. Morgan, *Edward Bellamy* (New York, 1944, 468 pp.). For the Christian socialist theology, which seems to have consisted mainly of an appeal to traditional Christian doctrines as an authority for a practical program of socialistic reform, see the works cited in Topic 8 and in PART II, Topic 13. In addition, Henry Vedder, *Socialism and the Ethics of Jesus* (New York, 1912, 527 pp.), argues that socialism and Christianity are ethically allied in their common interest in the brotherhood of man; John Spargo, *Marxian Socialism and Religion* (New York, 1915, 187 pp.), goes even further to argue that socialism and Christianity are compatible metaphysically as well as ethically.

The conservative opposition to Marxian philosophy as philosophy largely took the form during this period of ignoring it altogether or merely denouncing it as atheistic. Serious criticism of the Marxist position in general was thus usually restricted either to the criticism of its economic and political theories exclusively or to apologies which, while admitting the defects of the existing practices of capitalism, claimed that they could be remedied without going to the lengths of socialism. Typical of such works were J. B. Clark, *Social Justice without Socialism* (Boston, 1914, 49 pp.), W. G. Sumner, *What Social Classes Owe to Each Other* (New York, 1883, 169 pp.), and N. P. Gilman, *Socialism and the American Spirit* (Boston, 1893, 376 pp.), the last of which is particularly valuable for the reflective and conciliatory spirit in which it is written. For works which attempted to stand outside the socialist-capitalist controversy and to view it objectively as a more local illustration of the workings of a universal law of history, see Henry Adams, *Mont Saint Michel and Chartres* (Washington, 1904, 355 pp.), *The Education of Henry Adams* (1906; Boston, 1918, 519 pp.), and *The Degradation of the Democratic Dogma* (intro. by Brooks Adams; New York, 1919, 317 pp.), and, more especially, Brooks Adams, *The Law of Civilization and Decay* (1895; new ed. with intro. by C. A. Beard; New York, 1943, 349 pp.).

The second period of heightened philosophic activity in American Marxian socialism occurred in the late years of the 1920's and in the early years of the 1930's. Unlike that of the first period, the philosophic discussion of Marxism during this period was more technical, more comprehensive, and more professional in character. American theorists, as before, had the benefit of earlier and more searching European discussion. Students of the earlier period had concentrated mainly on Marxian economic theory and treated its philosophic foundations and implications in purely general terms. The new generation of students conceived of Marxism as a philosophy of history, a theory of society, and a unique mode of investigation with implications for art, science, religion, and, indeed, all branches of theoretical inquiry. This was partly the result of a more intensive study of the entire corpus of Marx's work—not merely *Capital*. The growing interest among intellectuals in the theory of history and of society had by this time, furthermore, extended itself to Marxism. The new discussion was also more original in the sense that the best of it was carried on independently of European inspiration and moved in the direction of creating a new kind of revisionism in its attempted fusion of Marxism with the instrumentalist philosophy of Dewey.

These new interests first became manifest in such works of the early and middle 1920's as A. S. Sachs, *Basic Principles of Scientific Socialism*

(New York, 1925, 201 pp.), which explained Marxian economic theory in the wider terms of its foundations in the Marxian theory of the dialectic, the materialist conception of history, and the class struggle; and in Max Eastman, *Marx and Lenin: the Science of Revolution* (New York, 1927, 267 pp.). The latter, although popularly written, was significant for its attack upon Marxian philosophy conceived as an absolute metaphysic and for its attempt to reformulate that theory in terms of a science or art of revolution.

Eastman's work was also important in inaugurating, and to a large extent instigating, the serious study of Marx by writers and critics which was to characterize American literature for the next two decades. The pattern set during Eastman's editorship of the *Masses* (New York, 1911-1917) of attempting to trace the theoretical relationship of art and literature to politics, philosophy, psychology, and aesthetics became the model not only for the *Liberator* (New York, 1918-1924), the immediate successor of the *Masses*, but for such later periodicals as V. F. Calverton's *Modern Quarterly* (Baltimore, 1923-1940) and the *Partisan Review* (New York, 1934-). This literary interest in Marxism also manifested itself philosophically in the publications of the Critics Group, a series of Marxian statements on art, literature, and aesthetics. Perhaps the most ambitious of all were such works as Kenneth Burke, *Attitudes toward History* (New York, 1937, 2 vols.), a comparative study of the Marxian with other interpretations of history, and Edmund Wilson, *To the Finland Station* (New York, 1940, 509 pp.), an examination of the history of the philosophy of history from Michelet to Lenin.

Along with this literary trend—so important in developing the aesthetic implications of Marxism—professional scholars in philosophy, science, and theology also developed a serious philosophical interest in Marxism at this time. The scientific interest was manifest in the founding of *Science & Society* (New York, 1936-), a review devoted to the Marxian interpretation of the methods and discoveries of the various branches of the natural and social sciences; while the philosophic interest, although restricted to a relatively narrow circle of professional philosophers, was even more articulate, resulting in the publication of such works as: T. B. Brameld, *A Philosophic Approach to Communism* (Chicago, 1933, 242 pp.), an examination of the communist theory of the relation of the individual to the forces of the environment; Howard Selsam's two works: *What Is Philosophy? A Marxist Introduction* (New York, 1938, 192 pp.), and *Socialism and Ethics* (New York, 1943, 223 pp.); and A. D. Winspear, *The Genesis of Plato's Thought* (New York, 1940, 348 pp.), a scholarly attempt to reinterpret the Platonic philosophy from the Marxian point of view. Selsam is also responsible for the *Handbook of Philosophy, Edited and Adapted by Howard Selsam from the Short Philosophic*

Dictionary by M[ark M.] *Rosenthal and* P[avel F.] *Yudin* (New York, 1949, 128 pp.), based on a book published in Russia in 1939.

The most significant publication on Marxian philosophy by a professional philosopher, however, was Sidney Hook, *Towards the Understanding of Karl Marx* (New York, 1933, 347 pp.), a defense of the instrumentalist approach to Marxism developed earlier by Walling and Eastman (see above), but argued this time on the ground that the authority for this approach may be found in Marx himself. Hook has attempted to document this thesis in detail in his later historical study, *From Hegel to Marx* (New York, 1936, 335 pp.), and to defend it as a workable social philosophy in the symposium *The Meaning of Marx* (New York, 1934, 144 pp.), in which John Dewey, Morris R. Cohen, and other professional philosophers express dissenting views.

Marxism as a general view of life also came to the fore in the theological discussion of the period, particularly in the writings of Reinhold Niebuhr, Niebuhr's heightened sensitivity to the moral shortcomings of capitalist society and his sympathy for the Marxian indictment of that society are balanced on the one hand by a continued allegiance to the central Christian dogmas and on the other by his search for a synoptic theory of history capable of doing justice to both positions. This is the unifying thread binding together Niebuhr's long list of publications (see Topic 9) culminating in his Gifford lectures, *The Nature and Destiny of Man: a Christian Interpretation* (New York, 1941-1943, 2 vols.), probably the most considered, systematic, and comprehensive statement of his views. Another expression of the recent Christian attitude toward Marxism—this time from the Roman Catholic point of view—may be found in Ross Hoffman, *Tradition and Progress and Other Historical Essays in Culture, Religion, and Politics* (Milwaukee, Wis., 1938, 165 pp.). For the Marxist reaction to the Christian socialism of Niebuhr, see the widely publicized attack by Sidney Hook and others, "The New Failure of Nerve," *Partisan Review*, x (Jan./Feb.–Sept./Oct. 1943), pp. 2-57, 134-177, 248-257, 321-344, 473-481.

The contribution of the political leaders of American Marxism to the philosophic discussions of the period has been remarkably slight. Neither Browder, Foster, nor Thomas seems to have much relish or capacity for philosophic speculation. The leaders of schismatic sects, although more active in this regard, have tended to dissipate their speculative energies in factional disputes. This tendency is illustrated in Trotsky, *In Defense of Marxism* (New York, 1942, 211 pp.), and J. P. Cannon, *The Struggle for a Proletarian Party* (New York, 1943, 302 pp.), where a discussion of the nature and value of Marxian dialectics is submerged in personal recriminations. Notable exceptions to the above generalization are: Albert Weisbord, *The Conquest of Power* (New York, 1937, 2 vols.), an historical and theoretical comparison of leading socialist ideologies with the ideology of liberalism and fascism; and many of the articles which have been contributed to the *New International* (New York, 1934-) and the *Fourth International* (New York, 1940-).

Non-Marxists paid increasing attention to Marxist philosophy, and to the philosophical bases of Russian communism in particular, after Soviet strength was generally recognized following World War II. The clearest exposition of all the main aspects of Soviet thought is G. A. Wetter, *Il materialismo dialettico sovietico* (Turin, 1948, 431 pp.). Also see John Somerville, *Soviet Philosophy; a Study of Theory and Practice* (New York, 1946, 269 pp.). For further literature see Wetter and Somerville as well as the bibliographical lists attached to C. J. McFadden, *The Metaphysical Foundations of Dialectical Materialism* (Washington, 1938, 206 pp.), and F. S. C. Northrop, "Russian Communism," in *The Meeting of East and West; an Inquiry Concerning World Understanding* (New York, 1946, 531 pp.), pp. 220-253, 503. McFadden criticizes Marxian epistemology from the Roman Catholic point of view as positing an erroneous concept of free will and failing to posit an adequate metaphysical source of truth. In *The Coming Defeat of Communism* (New York, 1950, 278 pp.), James Burnham tells how he believes the threat of world communism can best be overcome.

Special Topics

ACCEPTANCE of the socialist point of view, as of any other inclusive social creed, involves the further acceptance, consciously or unconsciously, of a definite philosophic interpretation of the world. This interpretation differs from socialist to socialist depending upon the specific variety of socialist ideology embraced. However widely these interpretations may vary among themselves they all agree on certain fundamentals which serve to differentiate them as a class from the philosophy of capitalism and other social ideologies.

The following topics are designed to clarify some of these common fundamental assumptions of socialism, to indicate how they enter into different types of socialist doctrines, and, above all, to establish a comparison between them and the philosophical presuppositions of American democracy. Probably the most central assumptions of the socialist philosophy have to do with the nature of the process of history. As David Bowers also suggests in Chapter 7 of Volume 1, they are summarized in the beliefs (1) that history is not cyclical but exhibits a "direction" culminating in the perfecting of man (Topic 2), (2) that the perfection of man depends primarily upon the perfection of the social order (Topic 4), and (3) that a perfect social order is historically inevitable (Topic 3). Socialist philosophies are also usually in agreement in claiming a special type of insight or knowledge into the nature of the world which helps justify their confidence in the ultimate truth of their own beliefs. Just as in the philosophy of history they have not always been able to agree on whether the determining factors in historical progress are material or spiritual (Topic 1), so here they have not always been able to agree on whether this special insight is grounded in mystical inspiration or dialectic analysis (Topic 5). From these general assumptions about the nature of history and the discovery of truth, there follow certain other socialist assumptions about the role of the intellectual in history (Topic 6).

The following topics are also concerned with the comparative analysis of American socialist philosophy as an integrated theoretical system in relation to other philosophic systems, both socialist and democratic. Topic 7 compares a typical American socialist system with its European variants, while Topic 8 compares another with its democratic analogues. Topic 9, finally, is concerned with the fusion of socialist and democratic ideologies as illustrated, for example, in the Christian philosophy of Reinhold Niebuhr.

Topic 1.   Socialist Materialism and American Idealism

By definition, Marx and Engels sought to classify all philosophy as either "materialistic" or "idealistic"—depending on whether mind was cosmically construed as the by-product and creature of matter or matter the by-product and creature of mind—and then went on to argue that a truly socialistic philosophy will always conceive the world materialistically.

Whatever the merit of these two contentions, it is clear that Marx's own materialistic conception of the world, which he called dialectical or historical materialism, creates a sharp contrast between Marxist philosophy and the idealism both of the American democratic philosophy and of the philosophic standpoint of most of Marx's own socialist predecessors. American intellectual history has by no means been free of philosophical materialism. This is evident, for example, in the materialism of the Southern medical schools after the Revolution and in the minor but belligerent tradition of religious agnosticism as represented in the writings of Ethan Allen, Robert Ingersoll, and others. The dominant American attitude, because of its roots in Puritanism and in the natural-law philosophy of Locke, has nevertheless been prevailingly, if often vaguely and superficially, supernaturalistic in tone. Thus where Marx consistently posits the reign of material force in history, the typical American thinker posits the rule of God (as in Edwards) or the rule of an impersonal moral order (as in Franklin), or, at the very minimum, the possibility of an ever increasing control of nature by human intelligence (as in Dewey). But Marx's materialism offers just as sharp a contrast with the world view of his predecessors, the communitarians. The religious communitarians uncritically interpreted the cosmos in the familiar theistic terms of traditional Christian theology, while the followers of Fourier, Owen, and Cabet confidently assumed that the world was governed by a rational beneficent providence which saw to it that the rational and the good eventually triumphed.

Marx's materialism was revolutionary even within the socialist tradition, and it was a successful revolution. Almost all contemporary socialist philosophy makes at least a bow in the direction of the materialistic theory of history. It is with Marx's theory, accordingly, that this topic is primarily concerned. More specifically, it aims to (1) analyze the fundamental presuppositions of this materialism, (2) examine the Marxian contention that it represents a new type of materialistic philosophy, and (3) contrast it as a philosophic interpretation of the world with the interpretations implicit in the American philosophy of democracy and in the utopian philosophy of past socialism. As an introduction, read: Friedrich Engels, *Ludwig Feuerbach and the Outcome of Classical German Philosophy* (ed. by C. P. Dutt; New York, 1941, 95 pp.), chaps. 2 and 4, one of the classic statements of historical materialism; J. E. Talmage, *The Philosophical Basis of "Mormonism"* (Salt Lake City, Utah,

193

1916, 48 pp.), pp. 6-29, an outline of Mormon theology which may be taken as typical of the religious utopians' reliance upon a biblical cosmology. Mormonism, of course, was less socialistic than the other religious groups discussed in this volume. Emerson's essay "The Over-Soul" in *Essays* [First Series] (Boston, 1841, 303 pp.), pp. 219-245, expresses in the language of transcendentalism, and William James, "The Will to Believe" in *The Will to Believe and Other Essays* (New York, 1897, 332 pp.), pp. 1-31, in the language of pragmatism, the continuing American faith in an overarching spiritual order. Read, in addition, George Santayana, "The Genteel Tradition in American Philosophy" in *Winds of Doctrine* (New York, 1913, 215 pp.), chap. 6, a brilliant if hostile summary of American idealism, and, for a more sympathetic account, R. H. Gabriel, *The Course of American Democratic Thought* (New York, 1940, 452 pp.), chaps. 2 and 28. The first of these chapters in Gabriel describes the American faith in the mid-nineteenth century, and the second, that faith three-quarters of a century later.

For additional authoritative statements of historical materialism see: Engels, *Herr Eugen Dühring's Revolution in Science* (1877; tr. by Emile Burns and ed. by C. P. Dutt; New York, 1935, 364 pp.); and Lenin's *Materialism and Empirio-Criticism* (*Collected Works*, XIII; tr. by David Kvitko and Sidney Hook; New York, 1927, 342 pp.), also translated by A. Fineberg (Moscow, 1947, 391 pp.). On Lenin see Anton Pannekoek, *Lenin as Philosopher; a Critical Examination of the Philosophical Basis of Leninism* (New York, 1948, 80 pp.). See also for a source book of Marx's and Engels' pronouncements on historical materialism, *Über historischen Materialismus (Ein Quellenbuch)* (ed. by Hermann Duncker; Berlin, 1930, 2 vols.). The expository and critical literature on historical materialism is extensive, but the better-known works include: G. V. Plekhanov, *Fundamental Problems of Marxism* (ed. by D. B. Goldendach [Ryazanov, pseud.]; tr. by E. and C. Paul; London, 1929, 145 pp.), and *Essays in the History of Materialism* (tr. by Ralph Fox; London, 1934, 287 pp.), the same author's treatment of Holbach, Helvetius, and Marx. Jonathan Kemp's introduction to his edition of selections from Diderot, *Diderot, Interpreter of Nature* (tr. by J. Kemp and J. Stewart; New York, 1938, 358 pp.), pp. 1-34, claims this *philosophe* as the spiritual ancestor of Marxian dialectical materialism and humanism. For further references see Joseph Stalin, *Dialectical and Historical Materialism* (London, 1941, 32 pp.), a reprint of chap. 4, sec. 2, of *History of the Communist Party of the Soviet Union*, important as the statement of the Soviet leader; A. A. Zhdanov, "On the History of Philosophy," *Political Affairs*, XXVII (Apr. 1948), pp. 344-366, a speech delivered by the secretary of the Central Committee of the Russian Communist Party with profound effects on the party line everywhere;

II. F. Mins, Jr., *Materialism, the Scientific Bias* (New York, 1934, 120 pp.) and two Latin American examples, Enrique Ruiz Guiñazú, *Interpretación económica de la historia; teoría del materialismo histórico* (Buenos Aires, 1912), a pamphlet, and Virgilio Dominguez, *El materialismo histórico* (Mexico, D.F., 1933, 255 pp.). Especially valuable is G. A. Wetter, *Il materialismo dialettico sovietico* (Turin, 1948, 431 pp.), an objective account by a Jesuit which—as already mentioned on p. 191—includes excellent discussion of the Russian background.

Typical expositions of historical materialism by American Marxists are to be found in Ernest Untermann, *Die logische Mängel des engeren Marxismus* (Munich, 1910, 753 pp.), and A. S. Sachs, *Basic Principles of Scientific Socialism* (New York, 1925, 201 pp.), chaps. 2 and 3. See also PART I, General Reading, p. 39. English Marxist discussions of idealism include John Lewis, *Marxism and Modern Idealism* (London, 1944, 43 pp.), and Maurice Cornforth, *Science and Idealism; an Examination of "Pure Empiricism" and Modern Logic* (New York, 1947, 267 pp.), a critique of logical positivism. J. M. Murry, *The Defence of Democracy* (London, 1939, 315 pp.), claims that Marxism is a secular theology which should have developed into Christian socialism, but has not realized that its political idealism stems from religious idealism.

For a systematic exposition and critique of materialist philosophy in general, see, for a sympathetic account, Sidney Hook's article, "Materialism," *Encyclopaedia of the Social Sciences*, x, pp. 209-220, and, for a critical account, F. R. Tennant's article of the same title in *Encyclopaedia of Religion and Ethics*, James Hastings, ed., viii, pp. 488-492. The standard history of philosophical materialism is F. A. Lange, *History of Materialism* (3rd ed., tr. by E. C. Thomas; London, 1890, 3 vols.).

For the American tradition of non-Marxian materialism see Woodbridge Riley, *American Philosophy: the Early Schools* (New York, 1907, 595 pp.), which examines among other things the beginnings of philosophic materialism in America in the writings of Colden, Priestley, Cooper, Buchanan, and other thinkers of the revolutionary period. And for the history of agnosticism and free thought in America in the eighteenth century see B. T. Schantz, "Ethan Allen's Religious Ideas," *Journal of Religion*, xviii (Apr. 1938), pp. 183-217, E. P. Link, *Democratic-Republican Societies, 1790-1800* (New York, 1942, 256 pp.), and G. A. Koch, *Republican Religion: the American Revolution and the Cult of Reason* (New York, 1933, 334 pp.), which also emphasizes Allen. Albert Post's penetrating study, *Popular Freethought in America, 1825-1850* (New York, 1943, 258 pp.), and Sidney Warren, *American Freethought, 1860-1914* (New York, 1943, 257 pp.), are complementary works for the nineteenth century. See also Charles Knowlton, *Elements of Modern Materialism* (Adams, Mass., 1829, 448 pp.).

There exists no general philosophic or historical treatment of the theoretical bases of communitarianism save such as are to be found in the standard histories of socialism and communism in Europe and America already cited in PART I, General Reading, pp. 4-6, and in PART II, General Reading, pp. 93-94. These treatments, however, are inadequate on detail and should be supplemented by a direct study of the special histories and chief theoretical writings of the various utopian groups involved. The more important references to the latter, particularly in their American phases, have also been cited above in PART III, General Reading. See also two Mormon statements, P. P. Pratt, *The Millennium and Other Poems, to Which Is Annexed a Treatise on the Regeneration and Eternal Duration of Matter* (New York, 1840, 148 pp.); and Orson Pratt, *Absurdities of Immaterialism* (Liverpool, 1849, 32 pp.); and the exposition by the mutualist anarchist, C. T. Sprading, *The Science of Materialism* (New York, 1942, 189 pp.).

Studies of the American democratic spirit and its idealistic philosophic presuppositions are numerous. Among the more famous of these, particularly for the origin of the democratic ideology and its history during the early national period, are C. L. Becker, *The Heavenly City of the Eighteenth Century Philosophers* (New Haven, Conn., 1932, 168 pp.), and *The Declaration of Independence* (New York, 1922, 286 pp.), both of which together deal with the eighteenth-century background of the American democratic ideology and with its manifestation in the Declaration of Independence; Alexis de Tocqueville, *Democracy in America* (ed. by Phillips Bradley; New York, 1946, 2 vols.); and Henry Adams, *History of the United States of America* (New York, 1889-1891, 9 vols.), particularly Vol. 9, chaps. 8-10. For later periods see Lord Bryce's commentary, *The American Commonwealth* (new ed., New York, 1931-1933, 2 vols.); N. P. Gilman, *Socialism and the American Spirit* (Boston, 1893, 376 pp.), particularly chap. 3; George Santayana, *Character & Opinion in the United States* (New York, 1920, 233 pp.), and André Siegfried, *America Comes of Age* (tr. by H. H. and Doris Hemming; New York, 1927, 358 pp.). For surveys of the history of American ideology as a whole see Gabriel's work cited above, V. L. Parrington, *Main Currents in American Thought* (New York, 1927-1930, 3 vols.), R. B. Perry, *Puritanism and Democracy* (New York, 1944, 688 pp.), M. E. Curti, *The Growth of American Thought* (New York, 1943, 848 pp.), and H. W. Schneider, *A History of American Philosophy* (New York, 1946, 646 pp.).

For the idealistic strains in technical as distinct from popular philosophic speculation in the United States see the writings of the great idealistic American philosophers, Samuel Johnson of Kings College (Columbia), Jonathan Edwards, Ralph Waldo Emerson, C. S. Peirce, and

Josiah Royce, as well as Woodbridge Riley, *American Thought* (2nd ed., New York, 1923, 438 pp.), J. H. Muirhead, *The Platonic Tradition in Anglo-Saxon Philosophy* (New York, 1931, 446 pp.), and Floyd Stovall, *American Idealism* (Norman, Okla., 1943, 235 pp.). *Contemporary Idealism in America* (New York, 1932, 326 pp.), edited by Clifford Barrett, discusses the recent resurgence of idealism in American philosophy and includes essays by some of its foremost contemporary exponents. For a brief discussion, mainly historical, of the idealistic philosophy in general, see E. Troeltsch, "Idealism," *Encyclopaedia of Religion and Ethics*, James Hastings, ed., VII, pp. 89-95; and for a longer critical study, A. C. Ewing, *Idealism: a Critical Survey* (London, 1934, 450 pp.).

Topic 2. The Socialist Philosophy of History and the American Idea of Progress

Although Marxists have stressed the importance of a choice between materialism and idealism, an even more crucial problem for any socialist or democratic view of life (as David Bowers has shown in detail in Volume 1) concerns the nature of history: that is, such questions as whether the historic process is progressive; at what goal that progress aims; and whether, whatever the goal is, it is ultimately attainable. Without answers to these three questions no social creed, whether socialist or democratic, can properly formulate its goals, determine its methods, or act with any degree of assurance that its objective will be realized.

Socialist and democratic philosophy have, with some recent exceptions, agreed that history is progressive. They have unanimously rejected all species of the cyclical theory—the theory that history purposelessly and periodically repeats itself—and any interpretation which would suggest that the regressive forces in history ultimately outweigh the forces making for progress. Putting the matter more positively, socialism and democracy are alike in the optimistic assumption that history moves steadily, if not always continuously, toward the single goal of the moral, intellectual, and physical perfection of man, and that this goal is approximable in time. The religious communists have conceived of the predetermined ideal socialist society in terms of the apocalyptic vision of Christ's second coming; the secular communitarians, in terms of a world society composed of completely rational individuals; and the Marxists, in terms of an international classless society. Democracy conceives of the historical future in terms of an indefinite improvement of individual welfare.

As shown in Topics 3 and 4 below, the democratic philosophy of history differs mainly from the socialist conception in its view of what the true goal of history is and its view of what forces will bring about the realization of this goal. Meanwhile, this topic stresses the points at which the two philosophies are in agreement: that history has a goal and that this goal promises an improvement in the life of man superior to anything experienced in the past. Particular emphasis is placed upon (1) the reason for the socialist and democratic faith in historic progress and (2) the degree to which they conceived the goal of progress in secular rather than supernatural terms. Read Carl Becker, "Progress," *Encyclopaedia of the Social Sciences*, xii, pp. 495-499, for a brief summary of the history and philosophic implications of the idea of progress in general; A. A. Ekirch, *The Idea of Progress in America, 1815-1860* (New York, 1944, 305 pp.), chaps. 1, 2, and 9, for the early importance of the idea of progress in America; and both Aaron Williams, *The Harmony Society at Economy, Penn'a.* (Pittsburgh, Pa., 1866, 182 pp.), chaps. 8 and 9, and Fourier, *Selections from the Works of Fourier* (tr. by Julia Franklin; London, 1901, 208 pp.), pp. 17-27, 47-54, for expressions of the typical communitarian faith in progress. Read also *The Manifesto of the Communist Party*, section i, which presents the Marxian sense of the direction of history in a succinct, concrete analysis of the inherent tendencies of the world capitalism in Marx's own day.

The classic study of the idea of progress is, of course, J. B. Bury, *The Idea of Progress* (intro. by C. A. Beard; New York, 1932, 357 pp.). Bury's account suffers, however, because of being restricted too closely to the idea of progress as it was developed in seventeenth-, eighteenth-, and nineteenth-century France, with the result that it tends to exclude from consideration all socialist theorizing about history save that of the Saint-Simonian school. In this connection see Albert Salomon's essay on the Jacobins, Saint Simon, and Proudhon, "The Religion of Progress," *Social Research*, xiii (Dec. 1946), pp. 441-462; and Samuel Bernstein's article, "Saint Simon's Philosophy of History," *Science & Society*, xii (Winter 1948), pp. 82-96. A reinterpretation of the concept as held by French rationalists is Charles Frankel, *The Faith of Reason; the Idea of Progress in the French Enlightenment* (New York, 1948, 165 pp.). It is well to supplement Bury's study, therefore, with such a work as Fritz Gerlich, *Der Kommunismus als Lehre vom tausendjährigen Reich* (Munich, 1920, 275 pp.), which treats of the related concept of "millennium" with special reference to its appearance in the socialist tradition. Another important analysis of the idea of progress may be found in A. O. Lovejoy and George Boas, *Primitivism and Related Ideas in Antiquity* (Baltimore, 1935, 482 pp.), which links the concept of a golden age in the future with the concept of a golden age in the past. For one of the most important eighteenth-century formulations of the theory of progress see Condorcet, *Outlines of an Historical View of the Progress of the Human Mind* (London, 1795, 372 pp.), which argues that general progress depends upon mental progress; and for the influence of Condorcet on subsequent democratic thought see J. S. Schapiro, *Condorcet and the*

Rise of Liberalism (New York, 1934, 311 pp.). *The Belief in Progress* by John Baillie, widely known minister of the Church of Scotland, will be published by Scribner's in 1951.

During the nineteenth century the influence of the idea of progress in America was very great, serving as a weapon against the counterinfluence both of Rousseau's teaching that civilization is equivalent to deterioration and of Malthus' teaching that an expanding population is a threat rather than an aid to civilization. Ekirch, in the work cited above, which deals with the first half of the century, points out as among the more important American explorations of the idea at that time: Nathaniel Chipman, *Principles of Government* (Burlington, Vt., 1833, 330 pp.), Alexander Everett, *A Discourse on the Progress and Limits of Social Improvement* (Boston, 1834, 44 pp.), Alexander Kinmont, *Twelve Lectures on the Natural History of Man* (Cincinnati, Ohio, 1839, 355 pp.), Frederick Grimké, *Considerations upon the Nature and Tendency of Free Institutions* (Cincinnati, Ohio, 1848, 544 pp.), and also such works by more widely known figures as Charles Sumner, *The Law of Human Progress* (Boston, 1849, 48 pp.), and George Bancroft, "The Office of the People in Art, Government, and Religion," in his *Literary and Historical Miscellanies* (New York, 1855, 517 pp.), pp. 408-435. For further references see Ekirch's very full bibliography (pp. 268-299).

American discussion of the idea of progress after the Civil War, usually defined with reference to the new theory of evolution, is fully covered in R. H. Gabriel, *The Course of American Democratic Thought* (New York, 1940, 452 pp.), particularly Pts. 3, 4, 5, and 6, and in Richard Hofstadter, *Social Darwinism in American Thought, 1860-1915* (Philadelphia, 1944, 191 pp.). A typical socialist essay attempting to use evolutionary theory against the social Darwinians is Raphael Buck, "Socialism the Goal of Evolution," *International Socialist Review*, vii (Nov. 1906), pp. 271-282. Among the more important analyses of the concept at this time, those assuming a pessimistic attitude toward the possibility of progress include W. G. Sumner, *Folkways* (Boston, 1907, 692 pp.), and Henry Adams, *The Degradation of the Democratic Dogma* (intro. by Brooks Adams; New York, 1919, 317 pp.), while those taking an optimistic view include L. F. Ward, *Dynamic Sociology* (New York, 1883, 2 vols.), and Edward Bellamy, *Looking Backward, 2000-1887* (Boston, 1888, 470 pp.). These titles, however, are only a sample of the very extensive literature on the subject produced during this period, and for further references consult Hofstadter's excellent bibliography (pp. 177-186).

Sample American socialist expressions of the idea of progress include: *The Divine Afflatus; a Force in History* (Boston, 1875, 46 pp.), a publication by the Shaker Family at Shirley, Massachusetts; J. B. Morman,

The Principles of Social Progress (Rochester, N.Y., 1901, 240 pp.); M. W. Simons, "Some Ethical Problems," *International Socialist Review*, I (Dec. 1900), pp. 336-346; and S. Feinstone, *Social Progress; a Marxian Point of View* (Philadelphia, 1935, 32 pp.). See also Käte Asch, *Die Lehre Charles Fouriers* (Jena, 1914, 179 pp.), pp. 35-64, on Fourier's philosophy of history; Paul Tillich, *The Interpretation of History* (tr. by N. A. Rasetski and E. L. Talmey; New York, 1936, 284 pp.), written by a theologian who later came to the United States and has been sympathetic to Niebuhr's variety of socialist Christianity; G. W. Nasmyth, *Social Progress and the Darwinian Theory* (New York, 1916, 417 pp.), based on Novikov's application of Darwinism to sociology and emphasizing Kropotkin's theory of mutual aid; and the critical survey by A. J. Todd, *Theories of Social Progress* (New York, 1918, 579 pp.), especially chaps. 14-15. Morris Zucker, *The Philosophy of American History* (New York, 1945, 2 vols.), I, contains prolix and poorly organized comments on a great variety of thinkers from an essentially Marxian point of view. His "historical field theory" is based on a variety of social determinism and a belief that society can be progressive.

For additional materials on the socialist theory of history see W. D. Wallis, *Culture and Progress* (New York, 1930, 503 pp.); Georges Sorel, *Les Illusions du progrès* (2nd ed., rev.; Paris, 1911, 340 pp.); Gerlich's work cited above, and also the references to the communitarians in Topic 1 above and to dialectical materialism in Topics 3 and 5 below. Another source for socialist views on history consists of the socialist discussions of the evolutionary theory, references to which may be found in the General Reading for this Part (III), pp. 186-187. This discussion is further developed by the English Marxist biologist, Joseph Needham, in his Herbert Spencer lecture at Oxford University, *Integrative Levels; a Revaluation of the Idea of Progress* (Oxford, 1937, 59 pp.).

Topic 3. *Socialist Determinism and Democratic Voluntarism*

Perhaps the most distinctive feature of the socialist philosophy of history, and the one which most differentiates it from the democratic philosophy, is its emphasis upon historical determinism. The socialist theory holds that the course of history is in large degree causally determined and that whatever is to happen in the future—even the socialist society itself—has to a great extent been already foreordained by events in the past. In attributing this doctrine to socialism, however, two facts should be kept in mind. Historical determinism does not imply, and is not ordinarily understood by socialists to imply, the total inefficacy of the human will. Furthermore, the exact mechanism of this determinism—how it works—is described differently in different socialist philosophies.

With respect to the free will, it is clear that even within a completely deterministic scheme, human volitions, both individually and collectively, may still be important as links in the causal chain comprising that scheme. And this is in fact what many socialists—particularly Marxians—have maintained. Marxian theory assumes that the determinants of history are entirely in this world. It does not concede that human desires can manipulate or alter the course of history, yet asserts that these desires still constitute means by which history evolves through the class struggle. Pre-Marxian socialists, with their less materialistically conceived cosmology, paradoxically attached less importance to man's will in history than the Marxians. The religious communists, under the influence of Christian eschatology, assumed that divine providence alone could bring the millennium; secular communitarian philosophy viewed progress as caused partly by divine purpose and partly by human will.

The various socialist theories of historical determinism differ principally on three questions: (1) the degree or pervasiveness of this determinism, particularly as it affects the human will; (2) the way in which—granting it has any role at all—the human will enters into the historical process; and (3) the character of historical change itself, whether teleological or mechanical, evolutionary or catastrophic. For example, as regards the question of the degree to which history is determined, where the Marxists clearly argue for a complete determinism extending to the psychical as well as the physical sphere, the pre-Marxian socialists usually either declare for a modified determinism or leave the matter undecided. Thus the religious communists inherited the unwillingness of Christian theology to accept either horn of the traditional dilemma of either denying God's omnipotence or holding him responsible for the evil in the world. They usually tried to effect a compromise by maintaining that while man in some measure determines his own fate, God overrules human volition to the extent of guaranteeing that goodness shall eventually triumph. And this position, which is difficult to define precisely, is more or less duplicated in the position of the secular communitarians insofar as the latter tried to assume both freedom of will and the overarching power of a beneficent providence working toward the creation of a world society.

Again, socialist philosophers have differed on the character or form of man's participation in the evolution of history. Where Marxism defines that participation in terms of the self-interest of the individual or class concerned, and this self-interest in terms of underlying physical causes, the pre-Marxians defined man's historical role in fundamentally spiritual terms. For example, instead of conceiving man as essentially self-centered and as contributing to historical development only through conflict with other wills in the medium of the class struggle, the pre-Marxians usually envisaged man as capable of being moved by the love of God or the

201

love of man, and as contributing, therefore, most significantly to the march of history through the exercise of cooperation, example, and persuasion.

Finally, socialist philosophers differ in their general description of the character of historical change itself. Some, as in the case of the pre-Marxians, interpret historical change teleologically as a process governed throughout by divine, providential, or human purpose, acting singly or in combination. Others, particularly the more radical Marxians, repudiate the historical efficacy of purpose entirely and trace all historical changes back to changes in the physical modes of production. Similarly, considerable disagreement exists on the question of the continuity of history. For most of the secular communitarians and the Marxian reformists, historical progress toward the socialist goal is a matter of gradual imperceptible evolution. For other socialists, however, progress toward the socialist goal is supposed to be inherently catastrophic and saltatory. The early religious communists taught that Christ's second coming to establish his kingdom on earth would be or had been abrupt, unexpected, and unannounced. The catastrophic view is also implicit in the Marxian dialectic according to which history moves by the sudden violent resolution of class conflict.

But however widely these socialist theories differ among themselves they all stand in common opposition to the democratic theory. Like the socialist theory itself, the democratic theory of history has evolved through a theistic, a providential, and a naturalistic cycle of its own. At the earliest period, democratic ideology was just as vague as that of the pre-Marxian socialists on the question of human and divine cooperation in history. If we except the determinism of the Calvinist school of Edwards, most of our thinkers up through the Civil War were ready both to attribute an infinite resourcefulness and energy to a democratically organized society of free men and at the same time to assume that somehow or other the destiny of such a society was determined by divine providence, and to make these assumptions, moreover, without feeling called upon to indicate the exact degree and form of cooperation in which the human will and divine providence stand.

Unlike socialist theory, however, American theory in passing beyond its supernaturalistic phase has not become deterministic in outlook. In the philosophy of pragmatism and instrumentalism, which best expresses the contemporary American attitude, that attitude is naturalistic only in the sense of rejecting all divine or providential control over human affairs and of regarding the human will in particular as merely one natural force among others. But this attitude is not naturalistic in the sense that it assumes will to be at the complete mercy of other natural forces. Holding that history is a matter of chance as well as of logic, it conceives of intelligence—scientific and engineering intelligence in particular—

as a pivotal force by which the tendencies of history may be continually remolded and redirected. In other words, as opposed to Marxian determinism, it argues for an "open" future, a future in which almost anything may happen, but which man, if he so chooses, can shape to his own ends.

This topic emphasizes the Marxian form of historical determinism, and contrasts it with corresponding features in the democratic philosophy of history. Read for the Marxian view, N. I. Bukharin, *Historical Materialism* (New York, 1925, 318 pp.), chaps. 1, 2, and 3; and for the American view, William James's two essays, "The Dilemma of Determinism" and "Great Men and Their Environment," both found in James, *The Will to Believe and Other Essays in Popular Philosophy* (New York, 1897, 332 pp.), and John Dewey, *Intelligence in the Modern World* (ed. with an intro. by Joseph Ratner; New York, 1939, 1077 pp.), chaps. 4, 7, and 13.

For further material on dialectical determinism see: Friedrich Engels, *Ludwig Feuerbach* (ed. by C. P. Dutt; New York, 1941, 95 pp.), pp. 42-61, 85-95; and the same author's *Landmarks of Scientific Socialism: "Anti-Duehring"* (tr. and ed. by Austin Lewis; Chicago, 1907, 266 pp.), *passim*, but particularly the section on "Freedom and Necessity"; Marx, *A Contribution to the Critique of Political Economy* (tr. by N. I. Stone; Chicago, 1904, 314 pp.), particularly the "Preface," describing the relation of intellectual history to economic history; G. V. Plekhanov, *The Materialist Conception of History* (New York, 1940, 48 pp.), *The Role of the Individual in History* (New York, 1940, 62 pp.), *In Defence of Materialism* (London, 1947, 303 pp.); and Lenin, *Materialism and Empirio-Criticism* (*Collected Works*, XIII; tr. by David Kvitko and Sidney Hook; New York, 1927, 342 pp.). See also in this connection Hyman Levy, *A Philosophy for a Modern Man* (New York, 1938, 309 pp.), a British attempt to defend dialectical determinism in simple non-Marxian language; L. A. Sánchez, *Dialéctica y determinismo* (Santiago de Chile, 1938, 125 pp.), a Spanish-American Aprista treatment; and Theodore Brameld, *A Philosophic Approach to Communism* (Chicago, 1933, 242 pp.), an examination of the relation between the individual and the environment as postulated by Marx, Engels, and Lenin. Early socialist discussions include Austin Lewis, "The Economic Interpretation of History and the Practical Socialist Movement," *International Socialist Review*, VII (Apr. 1907), pp. 608-622, and Lida Parce, *Economic Determinism; or, The Economic Interpretation of History* (Chicago, 1913, 155 pp.). For more recent discussions see the articles in *Science & Society*: Leo Roberts, "The Meaning of Change in Contemporary Philosophy," I (Winter 1937), pp. 168-193; L. S. Feuer, "The Economic Factor in History," IV (Spring 1940), pp. 168-192, "Ethical Theories and Historical Materialism," VI (Summer 1942), pp. 242-272; and the exchange of notes between Feuer, IX (Summer 1945), pp. 255-260, and Harry Slochower, VIII (Fall 1944), pp. 345-353. See also the survey of

historical philosophies set against an exposition of the historical materialist philosophy of history by Herbert Aptheker, "History and Reality,"
Mainstream, I (Fall 1947), pp. 468-492, to be expanded later into a book.

For other relatively recent descriptions and appraisals of Marxian
determinism see M. M. Bober, *Karl Marx's Interpretation of History*
(2nd ed., Cambridge, Mass., 1948, 445 pp.), particularly chaps. 1-8,
and Sidney Hook, *The Hero in History* (New York, 1943, 273 pp.), chap.
5, which reviews and rejects the deterministic theories of Engels and
Plekhanov; while for further critiques of the doctrine consult Max
Eastman, *Marx and Lenin: the Science of Revolution* (New York, 1927,
267 pp.), and the attack by E. F. Carritt which appeared in *Labour
Monthly* (London), xv (May-June 1933), pp. 324-329, 383-391. For an extended reply to Carritt's objections see L. Rudas, *Dialectical Materialism
& Communism* (Labour Monthly Pamphlets, No. 4; London, 1934, 43
pp.). In the special field of semantics, see the articles of Margaret
Schlauch on the mechanist and nonmechanist theories of the determinants
of linguistic change, "Semantics as Social Evasion," *Science & Society*, vi
(Fall 1942), pp. 315-330, and "Mechanism and Historical Materialism in
Semantic Studies," *ibid.*, xi (Spring 1947), pp. 144-167. In June 1950
Stalin reversed the party line on linguistics by declaring that language
shows historical continuity, does not have a class character, and thus is
not determined by a revolution.

On the question of the inevitability of socialism see Hook, *Towards the
Understanding of Karl Marx* (New York, 1933, 347 pp.), particularly pp.
110-114, which argues that Marx did not really accept the dogma of
inevitability. For a reply to this theory see Max Eastman, *The Last
Stand of Dialectic Materialism: a Study of Sidney Hook's Marxism* (New
York, 1934, 47 pp.), Paul Mattick, *The Inevitability of Communism* (New
York, 1935, 48 pp.), and Hal Draper, "The 'Inevitability of Socialism';
the Meaning of a Much Abused Formula," *New International*, xiii (Dec.
1947), pp. 269-279. Read also in this connection Karl Korsch, *Karl Marx*
(London, 1938, 247 pp.), which rejects dialectical materialism as a universal philosophy but defends it as a working sociological method. The
same author's *Marxismus und Philosophie* (2nd ed., Leipzig, 1930, 160
pp.) and *Die materialistische Geschichtsauffassung* (Leipzig, 1929, 130
pp.), and S. K. Padover, "Kautsky and the Materialist Interpretation of
History," in *Medieval and Historiographical Essays in Honor of James
Westfall Thompson* (ed. by J. L. Cate and E. N. Anderson; Chicago,
1938, 499 pp.), pp. 439-464, are critical studies of Kautsky's Marxism.

Non-Marxian socialist views of the historical process are presented in
B. S. Youngs, *Testimony of Christ's Second Appearing* (4th ed., Albany,
N.Y., 1856, 631 pp.), the Shaker bible and probably the most pretentious
and detailed analysis of history to be produced by any of the religious

communist groups; and Robert Flint's analysis of the French utopian school in his *Historical Philosophy in France and French Belgium and Switzerland* (New York, 1894, 706 pp.). Edmund Wilson, *To the Finland Station* (New York, 1940, 509 pp.), contrasts Marxian theory and the nonsocialist philosophies of history of Marx's day. Charles Bray, *The Philosophy of Necessity, or, The Law of Consequences; as Applicable to Mental, Moral and Social Science* (London, 1841, 2 vols.), was quoted by the American Associationists.

For the specific American criticism of Marxist determinism and for attempts to reformulate Marxism in nondeterministic terms, see John Spargo, *Marxian Socialism and Religion* (New York, 1915, 187 pp.), and W. E. Walling, *The Larger Aspects of Socialism* (New York, 1913, 406 pp.). The first "reconciles" Marxism with a religious interpretation, and the second with a pragmatic interpretation, of history. See also in this connection the works of Eastman and Hook cited above.

Jonathan Edwards' famous attack on freedom of the will entitled *A Careful and Strict Enquiry into the Modern Prevailing Notions of . . . Freedom of the Will* (Boston, 1754, 294 pp.), is a native non-Marxian American defense of determinism. Although Edwards' view did not prevail widely or for long, American faith in free will had to wait more than a century for its classic expression in the philosophies of C. S. Peirce and William James. Peirce's subtle arguments for the existence of genuine chance in history are scattered throughout his *Collected Papers* (ed. by Charles Hartshorne and Paul Weiss; Cambridge, Mass., 1931-1935, 6 vols.), but are also adequately presented in the two shorter compilations: *The Philosophy of Peirce: Selected Writings* (ed. by Justus Buchler; New York, 1940, 386 pp.), and *Chance, Love and Logic* (ed. by M. R. Cohen; New York, 1923, 318 pp.). James's arguments for freedom of the will are presented not only in the essays already cited above but also in chapter 26 of his *The Principles of Psychology* (New York, 1905, 2 vols.), while his defense of an "unblocked" universe—one in which the future is not wholly determined—may be found in such representative works as: *Pragmatism* (New York, 1907, 308 pp.), *A Pluralistic Universe* (New York, 1909, 404 pp.), and, especially, *Some Problems of Philosophy* (ed. by H. M. Kallen; New York, 1911, 236 pp.). John Dewey's equally optimistic view of the possibility of a human control of history is developed in many of his works, which have been conveniently abridged by Joseph Ratner in the volume of selected writings already cited.

Topic 4. The Ideal of Collectivism and the Ideal of Individualism

The socialist philosophy of history is distinguished from its democratic analogue no less by the goal it ascribes to history than by its description of the course by which it assumes that goal is to be reached.

The democratic ideal is individualism; the socialist goal, collectivism. But here again as in the case of socialist determinism two qualifications must be kept in view. The explicit and ideal definitions of these goals approach each other with respect to their ultimate values; they differ most widely with respect to the conditions believed necessary for realizing these values. These conditions themselves are defined differently by different socialist groups.

There are few socialists who would deny that individual welfare is the supreme good. This is no less clear in the Marxist demand for a classless (equalitarian) society than it is in the religious communist's passionate concern for the well-being of his own soul or in the secular communitarian's insistence that society must be based upon voluntary association. Conversely, the democratic ideal by no means excludes all tendencies toward collectivism. For the ideal state as envisaged by democratic theorists would be one in which each individual was not only accorded equal opportunity and equal respect but also one in which an ideal citizen worked collectively and cooperatively for the common good. Indeed, the collectivist implications of democracy are no longer merely in the realm of the ideal; democratic practice in America has actually moved toward more government control. The social theory of the period when the constitution was written, conceiving of the state as the minimum of police power needed to maintain peace and safety, has been matched by the theory of the service state as the proper agent to promote the general welfare where improvement is possible and private enterprise has failed.

What is essentially different in the socialist and democratic ideals, however, is their conception of which of the two—individualism or collectivism—is instrumentally primary. For the radical socialist it is axiomatic that the individual can realize his highest potentialities and satisfactions only within the context of a completely collectivized society, and collectivization becomes for him, accordingly, an indispensable means to the individualist end. For the radical democrat on the other hand—who in this respect resembles the individualist anarchist—it is axiomatic that the individual realizes his highest good only insofar as he remains and acts independently of others. For him, therefore, individualism constitutes not only the *end*—as in socialism—but also the *means* to the good life.

But just as democratic theorists have been unable to defend the practice of unrestrained individualism and have been led to admit the need for at least some degree of collectivized control, so socialist theorists in turn have not always held consistently to the ideal of complete collectivism. Thus while at one extreme some of these theorists have been willing to defend a degree of social planning and control that would effectively penetrate the deepest recesses of the individual's private life—as is illustrated, for example, in the restrictive rules of such early monastic types of socialist communities as the Ephrata Dunkers and the Shakers—at the other extreme many socialists have confined their demands for collectivization to the mere demand for the collectivized control of natural resources and basic industries.

This topic makes no effort to catalogue the various types of socialist collectivism. It attempts rather to explore the literature dealing with the basic presuppositions of the collectivist ideal both in itself and in relation to the presuppositions of individualism. It then examines representative attempts to find a compromise between the two ideals. Read for the individualist ideal Emerson's essay "Self-Reliance" in *Essays* [First Series] (Boston, 1841, 303 pp.), and Warner Fite, *Individualism* (New York, 1911, 301 pp.), pp. 170-182; for the collectivist ideal, Howard Selsam, *Socialism and Ethics* (New York, 1943, 223 pp.), chaps. 4 and 5; and, for a current liberal attempt to fuse the two ideals, John Dewey, *Individualism, Old and New* (New York, 1930, 171 pp.).

The expository and critical literature on the ideals of collectivism and individualism is extensive, and the following selections, therefore, must be considered arbitrary. Marx's and Engels' views on the role of ideals as such may be found among other places in their joint works, *Die heilige Familie* (Frankfurt-am-Main, 1845, 335 pp.) and *Die deutsche Ideologie* (*Gesamtausgabe*, Abt. I, Vol. v; Moscow, 1933, 706 pp.), and in Engels, *Herr Eugen Dühring's Revolution in Science* (1877; tr. by Emile Burns and ed. by C. P. Dutt; New York, 1935, 364 pp.), and *Socialism, Utopian and Scientific* (tr. by Edward Aveling; London, 1892, 117 pp.); while for a rigid materialistic interpretation of Marx's and Engels' views implying that ideals are merely "fetishes" which will disappear except as rules of production in the classless society, see N. I. Bukharin, *Historical Materialism* (New York, 1925, 318 pp.), particularly pp. 238ff. G. V. Plekhanov, *The Role of the Individual in History* (New York, 1940, 62 pp.), denied the Narodnik charge that Marxism would reduce the role of the individual to zero. This conception of the significance and power of morality stands in sharp contrast with the communitarian view, secular as well as religious. Robert Flint, *Historical Philosophy in France and French Belgium and Switzerland* (New York, 1894, 706 pp.), chap. 7, discusses the secular view. See also Étienne Cabet and others, *L'Individualisme et le communisme* (Paris, 1848, 35 pp.). Even most Marxian socialists, either for propaganda purposes or because of their interpretation of the Marxian view, tend to concede the importance and efficacy of those ethical ideals which are compatible with their views of the classless society.

This is evident in Marxian discussions of the individualist and collectivist ideals where the attempt is often made to prove collectivism not only not incompatible with but indispensable to individualism. Early essays on this subject include J. E. Hall, *The Place of Individualism in the Socialist System* (New York, 1888, 16 pp.); Daniel De Leon, *De Leon-Carmody Debate, Individualism vs. Socialism* (New York, 1912, 40 pp.); articles in the *International Socialist Review*, e.g., W. H. Noyes, "The Implications of Democracy," I (Oct. 1900), pp. 193-203, and Warren Atkinson, "The Relation of Individualism to Socialism; Reply to Bryan," VII (July 1906), pp. 19-27; and in the *Arena*, T. E. Will, "Individualism through Socialism," XXXVI (Oct. 1906), pp. 359-363. More ambitious and successful attempts by American socialists are R. W. Sellars, *The Next Step in Democracy* (New York, 1916, 275 pp.), and W. E. Walling, *The Larger Aspects of Socialism* (New York, 1913, 406 pp.), particularly chaps. 8-13. European contributions to this theme include Ellen Key, *Individualism och Socialism* (3rd ed., Stockholm, 1910, 64 pp.), and *Men versus the Man; a Correspondence between Robert Rives La Monte, Socialist, and H. L. Mencken, Individualist* (New York, 1910, 252 pp.). Two collections of essays by an English socialist influential in America are E. B. Bax, *The Religion of Socialism* (3rd ed., London, 1891, 177 pp.), and *The Ethics of Socialism* (3rd ed., London, 1893, 210 pp.). See also E. B. Bax and J. H. Levy, *Socialism and Individualism* (London, 1904, 155 pp.); a volume of essays by Sidney Webb and others published with the same title (New York, 1911, 102 pp.); and more recently, Hewlett Johnson, *Marxism and the Individual* (London, 1943, 32 pp.). Karl Kautsky, *Ethics and the Materialist Conception of History* (tr. by J. B. Askew; Chicago, 1907, 206 pp.), seeks to root the collectivist ideal naturalistically in the animal instinct for mutual aid. For typical American socialist blueprints of a collectivized America which would still attempt to safeguard the individual, see Norman Thomas, *America's Way Out: a Program for Demoracy* (New York, 1931, 324 pp.), and also Harry Laidler, *Socialism in Thought and Action* (New York, 1920, 546 pp.), particularly chap. 5, and the same author's more recent work, *Socializing Our Democracy: a New Appraisal of Socialism* (New York, 1935, 330 pp.). Charles Solomon argues for the same guarantees in his radio debate with another New York lawyer, G. G. Battle, published as *Karl Marx or Thomas Jefferson? A Debate on Individualism-Socialism* (New York, 1931, 30 pp.). For the point of view of a non-Marxist sympathizer, with the theme that individualism receives only lip service from capitalists, see Kirby Page, *Individualism and Socialism* (New York, 1933, 367 pp.). See also the later discussion by the democratic socialist, Sidney Hook, *The Hero in History* (New York, 1943, 273 pp.).

The native American anarchists and communo-anarchists (see PART II, Topic 12) are, of course, at one pole in this discussion. B. M. Tucker, *Instead of a Book* (New York, 1893, 512 pp.), represents the individualist anarchists, and Emma Goldman, *The Place of the Individual in Society* (Chicago, 1940?, 16 pp.), the communo-anarchists.

American philosophical defenses of the contrary ideal of individualism are even more numerous. These extend from the classic definition of the individualistic philosophy found in Emerson and Thoreau—and, before them, in Jefferson and Hamilton—down to John Dewey's attempt to adjust that individualism to the realities of present-day conditions. In the last half-century probably the best purely philosophic defense of individualism is to be found in the writings of William James and Warner Fite. James's discussion of the subject is better known and is to be found, in addition to the essays already cited in this and the previous Topic, in "The Importance of Individuals" in his *The Will to Believe and Other Essays in Popular Philosophy* (New York, 1897, 332 pp.), pp. 255-262; but Fite's *Individualism* (New York, 1911, 301 pp.) and *Moral Philosophy* (New York, 1925, 320 pp.) are equally important and even more rounded statements. See for further philosophic treatments of the individualist ideal N. P. Gilman, *Socialism and the American Spirit* (Boston, 1893, 376 pp.), and H. M. Kallen, *Individualism: an American Way of Life* (New York, 1933, 241 pp.). Josiah Royce, *The World and the Individual* (New York, 1900-1901, 2 vols.), and *The Philosophy of Loyalty* (New York, 1908, 409 pp.), are interesting as attempts to define and defend American individualism in neo-Hegelian terms. For a recent discussion, see Dwight Macdonald, "The Future of Democratic Values," *Partisan Review*, x (July-Aug. 1943), pp. 321-344. More recent is the neo-Thomist position of Jacques Maritain, seeking the middle of the road between anarchism and despotism, in "The Person and the Common Good," *Review of Politics*, VIII (Oct. 1946), pp. 419-455. Maritain distinguishes between two aspects of one reality: the person, which emphasizes spirit, and the individual, which emphasizes matter. He concludes that in different senses the very universe is for the person, and yet the person is for the universal good. References to the individualist and collectivist ideals in their economic, political, artistic, and literary aspects may be found in PARTS IV and VI below.

Topic 5. Dialectic and Experiment

In addition to developing its own philosophy of history socialism has often also developed a theory of insight into history purporting to justify and vindicate socialistic historical generalizations. Among the secular communitarians, for example, this theory usually took the conventional form of asserting confidence in the ordinary canons of inductive and deductive reasoning and thus implied a socialist theory of knowledge in no way distinguishable from other theories of knowledge of the day. Other socialist theories, however, have claimed a special way of knowing which supplants or at least supplements the canons of ordinary reasoning. Thus among the religious communitarians, where this tendency was very pronounced, community beliefs were frequently grounded on some unique vision or experience of the community leader (as in the case of Joseph Smith's "translation" of the book of Mormon), or on the leader's special capacity to interpret the Bible and other mystical writings of the past (as in the case of Conrad Beissel, the founder of Ephrata), or, finally, on a continuing series of special revelations from God vouchsafed to various members of the community from generation to generation (as in the instance of the Amana *Werkzeuge*). These religious theories of knowledge are, however, only extreme examples of the common theory of divine revelation.

Probably the most elaborate and distinctive theory of knowledge developed by socialism, however, is the Marxian dialectic. This was an adaptation of the Hegelian dialectic, whose lineage may be traced back to the mystical Neoplatonism of Porphyry in the third century A.D. Briefly stated, the essence of the dialectic—which according to Marxism is a law of things as well as a law of thought—is the analysis, first, of events in terms of their mutual opposition and, second, of the insights, based on this analysis, into how the opposition will be resolved. For anything whatsoever—idea, thing, event, or historical tendency—there is assumed to be an opposite. Out of the conflict between these opposites a new stage of existence or history will emerge, this stage in turn producing conflicts of its own until superseded by a still newer and more advanced stage, and so on indefinitely. In other words, the method assumes that the concrete situation always embodies real contradictions whose existence may be discerned, and whose resolution—even before it occurs—may be inferentially anticipated by anyone who examines the situation carefully. It is on this assumption, in fact, that orthodox Marxians have usually based their confident prediction of the ultimate evolution of a classless society. It should also be noted, however, that the doctrine of the dialectic—which is in essence a claim to insight into absolute truth—conflicts with the further Marxian doctrine that all thinking is inevitably class conditioned and therefore by its very nature relative to its own time.

Democratic theorists have evolved equally esoteric theories of knowledge of their own, such as the romantic Emersonian theory of intuition. But for the most part American democratic thought has tended to accept the scientific point of view that all knowledge is based on observation and experiment and to fuse this, particularly in recent years, with the assumption that knowledge is not something desirable in itself but valuable merely as a tool for solving the practical problems of everyday life. The result has been, especially in the philosophies of James and Dewey, an attitude of practical experimentalism. This resembles the Marxian dialectic in its exclusive concern for practical rather than abstract issues. It differs from the dialectic in its assertion that all generalizations are tentative and should be held subject to revision upon further experimentation. The dialectician brings to the analysis of concrete problems a general though rigid framework to which he is already convinced the problems in question will conform. The experimentalist in his approach to problems regards all past generalizations—even his own—as nothing absolute in themselves but as mere tools for suggesting hypotheses which may or may not turn out to be applicable. The dialectician's conclusions are conservative and therefore highly self-confident; the experimentalist's conclusions are provisional and therefore malleable.

Since the dialectic is at the core of Marxian science, it is pertinent to inquire whether this central concept has heuristic value in the research of Marxian natural scientists, or whether their contributions have resulted from the method of observation and experiment. Beyond their own scientific work, to what uses have Marxians put the discoveries of others? Finally, what is the socialist criticism of capitalist controlled technology, and the socialist view of the function of technology under socialism?

These are questions which an age of science asks, and yet it is possible to go back of the origin of the Marxian dialectic and modern technology and find answers implicit in the activities of the communitarians. Of all the religiously based groups, only the Perfectionists consciously encouraged the mastery of technology for the benefit of the community. Several young men from Oneida were sent to the Sheffield Scientific School at Yale in order to learn the technique of operating their plants. Most of the other communities were engaged in agriculture on a limited scale, and although they occasionally promised economies and even scientific improvements to result from collective operation, they had no idea of applying science methodically to farming. The introduction of laborsaving machinery and utilities among the Rappites and Shakers, however, showed their recognition in practice of the role of technology in a socialized community. Scientific method, as understood in the early nineteenth century, was either ignored, along with other mundane learning (as by the Rappites); accepted as a tool which in no way affected the supernatural tenets of the group (as by the Perfectionists); or its use was actively encouraged (as by Owen at New Harmony).

Marxian contributions to twentieth-century natural science have been predominantly European. Here two contradictory trends are apparent. There has been a tendency to assert that all science is class science, and that none is sound in which the dialectic does not operate. The extreme expression of this tendency is found among Soviet scientists. On the other hand, the discoveries to the credit of Marxians show no indication that the dialectic has been substituted for the experimental method. Yet these scientists state that dialectical thinking has helped in their research. In the Russian view, dialectic—apparently as a supplementary hypothesis—has been particularly fruitful in genetics. Skeptics maintain that the dialectic to a Marxian scientist is on the same level as God to a religious scientist; neither of them is verifiable experimentally.

The Marxian assumption that all areas of knowledge must fit together has led socialists to be among the first who try to incorporate current scientific discoveries into their system. American socialists, in their debate with the social Darwinians, were quick to appropriate the conclusions of the German biologist Weismann, and his Dutch contemporary Hugo De Vries. Weismann's evidence against the Lamarckians, still holding the theory of the inheritance of acquired characteristics, pointed, in the socialists' opinion, to the need for raising the basis for social selection by collectivist means. De Vries' work in mutation theory led some socialists to the conclusion that revolution is analogous in the social field. Some Marxian borrowings have been from scientific conclusions invalidated by later research, e.g., Engels' dependence on Morgan's anthropology.

The function of technology under socialism has been plain to socialists since Marx: technology is the instrument which under capitalism enslaves and under socialism liberates; only through the collective operation of the technological forces of modern society can man achieve the control of nature and of his own destiny.

This topic contains selections contrasting the Marxian dialectic with radical experimentalism, as well as comparisons and evaluations. A few titles are added to represent what little has been written on the relation between socialism and technology. Read for the experimentalist position: John Dewey, *How We Think* (Boston, 1910, 224 pp.), chap. 6, a description of the tentative experimental way in which thought actually works; *The Philosophy of Peirce: Selected Writings* (ed. by Justus Buchler; New York, 1940, 386 pp.), chaps. 2 and 4, a defense of the scientific method and an attempt to show that even this method cannot give certainty; and William James, *Pragmatism* (New York, 1907, 308 pp.), lecture 2, James's famous defense of the practical attitude as a tool for inquiry. Read for the dialectic method: A. S. Sachs, *Basic Principles of Scientific Socialism* (New York, 1925, 201 pp.), chap. 1; M. M. Bober, *Karl Marx's Interpretation of History* (2nd ed., Cambridge, Mass., 1948, 445 pp.), chap. 2; and G. V. Plekhanov, "Dialectic and Logic," in his *Fundamental Problems of Marxism* (London, 1929, 145 pp.), pp. 111-123. Sidney Hook's four essays in *Reason, Social Myths and Democracy* (New York, 1940, 302 pp.), Pt. 2, "Science and Mythologies of Reason," pp. 181-279, a comprehensive and trenchant analysis of the dialectic from the experimentalist standpoint, treat Engels' idea of its place in natural science, its use by certain contemporary European scientists, the history of the concept in philosophy, and the related idea of class science. A recent statement of the dialectical materialist position is M. C. Cornforth, *In Defence of Philosophy against Positivism and Pragmatism* (London, 1950, 276 pp.).

For a discussion of the difference between the Hegelian dialectic and the Marxian dialectic see Sidney Hook, *From Hegel to Marx* (New York, 1936, 335 pp.), Pt. 3 of chap. 1, and Herbert Marcuse, *Reason and Revolution; Hegel and the Rise of Social Theory* (London, 1941, 431 pp.), pp. 273-322, 398-401. For Marx's and Engels' own description of the method see, among other places, Engels, *Landmarks of Scientific Socialism: "Anti-Duehring"* (tr. and ed. by Austin Lewis; Chicago, 1907, 266 pp.), chap. 7, his introduction to *Socialism, Utopian and Scientific* (tr. by Edward Aveling; London, 1892, 117 pp.), and his *Dialectics of Nature* (tr. and ed. by Clemens Dutt; New York, 1940, 383 pp.), a translation of his essays and notes. Other important descriptions of the method by orthodox Marxians include: Plekhanov's essay just cited; Lenin, *Materialism and Empirio-Criticism* (*Collected Works*, XIII; tr. by David Kvitko and Sidney Hook; New York, 1927, 342 pp.); N. I. Bukharin, *Historical Materialism* (New York, 1925, 318 pp.), particularly chaps. 3-8; V. Adoratsky, *Dialectical Materialism; the Theoretical Foundation of Marxism-Leninism* (New York, 1934, 96 pp.); August Thalheimer, *Introduction to Dialectical Materialism; the Marxist World-View* (tr. by G. Simpson and G. Weltner; New York, 1936, 253 pp.); and David Guest, *A Textbook of Dialectical Materialism* (ed. by T. A. Jackson; New York, 1939, 107 pp.). See also such works of the British Marxian school as J. D. Bernal, *Engels and Science* (London, 1936?, 15 pp.); Hyman Levy, *A Philosophy for a Modern Man* (New York, 1938, 309 pp.); Hyman Levy and others, *Aspects of Dialectical Materialism* (London, 1935, 154 pp.), discussions of the Society for Cultural Relations; and T. A. Jackson, *Dialectics; the Logic of Marxism and Its Critics* (London, 1936, 648 pp.). For a bibliography of Marxian treatments of the dialectic both in itself and in its implications for the natural and social sciences and for art, see the list compiled by Angel Flores appearing serially in the Critics Group's *Dialectics* (New York, 1937-1939?), beginning with issue No. 2. There is scarcely anything but periodical material by American Marxians. V. J. McGill, "An Evaluation of Logical Positivism," *Science & Society*, I (Fall 1936), pp. 45-80, suggests that this school may eventually come to dialectical materialism. William Gruen's article, "What Is Logical Empiricism?" *Partisan Review*, VI (Winter 1939), pp. 64-77, answered its question thus: logical empiricism is an ally of revolutionary Marxism in clearing away dogmas without operative significance. Other articles on this subject include Jerome Rosenthal, "What Is Dialectical Materialism?

Science or Mental Healing?" *Modern Monthly*, ix (May-June 1935), pp. 147-159, 232-243, 256, and his brief comments, "On the Soviet Philosophic Front," *ibid.*, x (Dec. 1936-Apr. 1937); and V. J. McGill, "Dialectical Materialism and Recent Philosophy," *Science & Society*, vi (Spring 1942), pp. 150-163. Somewhat unorthodox were both participants in the exchange between Edmund Wilson, "The Myth of the Marxist Dialectic," *ibid.*, vi (Fall 1938), pp. 66-81, and William Phillips, "The Devil Theory of the Dialectic," *ibid.*, pp. 82-90. Will Herberg pointed out the ambivalence arising out of the habit of dialectical thinking in "Semantic Corruptions," *New Europe*, v (July-Aug. 1945), pp. 8-11. Max Eastman, *Marx and Lenin: the Science of Revolution* (New York, 1927, 267 pp.), particularly chap. 12, is adversely critical, and Sidney Hook, *Towards the Understanding of Karl Marx* (New York, 1933, 347 pp.), particularly chaps. 8-10, attempts to restate the Marxian method. A thorough recent discussion of dialectical materialism, including developments in Soviet Russia, is G. A. Wetter, *Il materialismo dialettico sovietico* (Turin, 1948, 431 pp.). This contains a useful bibliography.

The experimentalist method of Dewey is discussed in many of his works. For a more technical description of the character of this method see his *Essays in Experimental Logic* (Chicago, 1916, 444 pp.), and *Logic: the Theory of Inquiry* (New York, 1938, 546 pp.); while for its relation to the scientific method and its cultural significance generally, see Dewey's *Reconstruction in Philosophy* (New York, 1920, 224 pp.), and *The Quest for Certainty* (New York, 1929, 318 pp.). For Dewey's own application of the method in morals and education, where it has proved especially fruitful, see his *Democracy and Education* (New York, 1916, 434 pp.), his textbook, *Ethics* (rev. ed., New York, 1938, 528 pp.), written with J. H. Tufts, and, what is perhaps his most significant contribution to social philosophy, *Human Nature and Conduct* (New York, 1922, 336 pp.). For a brief critical review of the more important philosophical theories of knowledge—which does not, however, discuss the Marxian theory—see W. P. Montague, *The Ways of Knowing* (London, 1928, 427 pp.). Sociological theories of knowledge are mentioned in PART V, General Reading.

In addition to the titles cited in the General Reading for this Part (III), pp. 186-187, 189, these European surveys of science and socialism should be noted: Louis Denayrouze, *Le Socialisme de la science* (Paris, 1891, 118 pp.); Edward Carpenter, *Modern Science; a Criticism* (Manchester, 1885, 75 pp.), an attack on the belief in the infallibility of natural laws by an English socialist with anarchist tendencies; O. G. S. Crawford, "The Dialectical Process in the History of Science," *Sociological Review*, xxiv (Apr.-July 1932), pp. 164-173; J. D. Bernal, *The Social Function of Science* (New York, 1939, 482 pp.); J. B. S. Haldane, *The*

Marxist Philosophy and the Sciences (New York, 1939, 214 pp.); and Paul Langevin, mathematical physicist, "Science and Action," *Science & Society*, XI (Summer 1947), pp. 209-224. Soviet science is represented in the papers contributed by Russian delegates to the second International Congress of the History of Science and Technology, held at London in 1931, published under the title, *Science at the Cross Roads* (London, 1931, 233 pp.). See also K. A. Timiryazev, *Nauka i demokratiya* [*Science and Democracy*] (Leningrad, 1926, 432 pp.).

For summaries of nineteenth-century European socialist and social Darwinian applications of evolutionary theory to social questions, and further references, see Ludwig Woltmann, *Die Darwinsche Theorie und der Sozialismus* (Düsseldorf, 1899, 397 pp.), pp. 32-176, and Gaston Maury's bibliography in his dissertation, *Darwinisme et socialisme* (Rennes, 1899, 142 pp.), pp. 5-10. Woltmann finds socialist principles entirely compatible with natural and moral law, while Maury agrees, with reservations. See also Serge Podolinski, "Le Socialisme et la théorie de Darwin," *Revue socialiste*, No. 3 (Mar. 20, 1880), pp. 129-148, and H. E. Ziegler's "scientific refutation" of Bebel, *Die Naturwissenschaft und die socialdemokratische Theorie* (Stuttgart, 1893, 252 pp.).

The principal scientific work of European interbellum Marxists is referred to in Sidney Hook's attack on their "mythologies" cited above (p. 212). See also chapters 7-12 in Joseph Needham, *History Is on Our Side* (New York, 1947, 226 pp.), especially pp. 211-219; *Science in Soviet Russia*, edited by Needham and J. S. Davies (London, 1942, 65 pp.); J. G. Crowther, *The Social Relations of Science* (New York, 1941, 665 pp.), by the science correspondent of the *Manchester Guardian*, his third favorable account of Soviet science; and Eric Ashby, *Scientist in Russia* (London, 1947, 206 pp.). *Science & Society* has contained numerous articles, e.g., in mathematics, Hyman Levy, "Probability Laws—a Methodological and Historical Survey," I (Winter 1937), pp. 230-240; and in biology and physics, three speeches by the Soviet scientists, Vavilov, Lysenko, and Polyakov, "Genetics in the Soviet Union," IV (Summer 1940), pp. 183-233, and Joseph Needham, "Evolution and Thermodynamics," VI (Fall 1942), pp. 352-375, with comment by A. J. Lotka, VIII (Spring 1944), pp. 161-171. T. D. Lysenko, *The Science of Biology Today* (New York, 1948, 62 pp.), the presidential address at the summer 1948 session of the Lenin Academy of Agricultural Sciences in the U.S.S.R., and *The Situation in Biological Science* (New York, 1949, 636 pp.), the stenographic report of the proceedings of this session, document the battle in which the "reactionary idealist Morganists" were defeated by the faction of Lysenko. For other accounts of this purge in genetics see Julian Huxley, *Soviet Genetics and World Science* (London, 1949, 244 pp.); Conway Zirkle, *Death of a Science in Russia* (Philadelphia, 1949,

319 pp.); and G. S. Counts and N. P. Lodge, *The Country of the Blind* (Boston, 1949, 378 pp.). Also consult John Langdon-Davies, *Russia Puts the Clock Back: a Study of Soviet Science and Some British Scientists* (London, 1949, 160 pp.). For the Soviet emphasis on the importance of environment in psychiatry see Joseph Wortis, *Soviet Psychiatry* (Baltimore, 1950, 313 pp.), a book which members of the American Communist Party are expected to read.

The pre-Marxians contributed no writing specifically on science and technology. See, however, the references to science in the literature of PART II, especially Topic 5, and the example of a follower of Proudhon who was also a mathematician: W. B. Greene, *An Expository Sketch of a New Theory of the Calculus* (Paris, 1859, 88 pp.), and *Explanation of the "Theory of the Calculus"* (Boston, 1870, 12 pp.). *The Theory of the Calculus* (Boston, 1870, 90 pp.). The organicist Edmund Montgomery wrote occasionally in favor of Bellamyite Nationalism. See examples such as "Nationalization of All Means of Industry the Only Remedy," *Twentieth Century*, III (Nov. 21, 1889), pp. 310-312, and the list of Montgomery's writings appended to M. T. Keeton's article in the *Journal of the History of Ideas*, "Edmund Montgomery—Pioneer of Organicism," VIII (June 1947), pp. 309-341.

The American Marxian socialist contribution to the controversy over natural and social evolution was of minor importance. Notable, however, for their use of biological evidence against the social Darwinians were G. C. Stiebeling, *Sozialismus und Darwinismus* (New York, 1879, 45 pp.); Herman Whitaker, "Weissmannism and Its Relation to Socialism," *International Socialist Review*, I (Mar. 1901), pp. 513-523, and "Natural Selection, Competition and Socialism," *Arena*, XXIV (Aug. 1900), pp. 129-144; W. T. Mills, *The Struggle for Existence* (Chicago, 1904, 640 pp.); H. G. Wilshire, "The Mutation Theory Applied to Society," in the second edition of his editorials, *Socialism Inevitable* (New York, 1907, 337 pp.), pp. 250-260; Michael Fitch, *Universal Evolution* (Boston, 1913, 310 pp.); and J. H. Moore, *The Law of Biogenesis; Being Two Lessons on the Origin of Human Nature* (Chicago, 1914, 123 pp.).

The important discussions of science and socialism took place after 1929 in the United States. The outstanding experimental scientist who was a member of the early Socialist Party, C. P. Steinmetz, did not, as one might expect, discuss technology directly in *America and the New Epoch* (New York, 1916, 228 pp.). He was sympathetic toward the great corporations, like the General Electric Company for which he worked, as efficient institutions. B. J. Stern, "The Frustration of Technology," *Science & Society*, II (Winter 1937), pp. 3-28, took the opposite position that the capitalist corporation resists innovation. See also Giorgio de Santillana, "Positivism and the Technocratic Ideal in the Nineteenth Century," in the festschrift for George Sarton, *Studies and Essays in the History of Science and Learning* (New York, 1946, 594 pp.), pp. 247-259, which includes the French utopians. The only extended discussions growing out of studies in genetics were by M. A. Graubard, *Man, the Slave and Master; a Biological Approach to the Potentialities of Modern Society* (New York, 1938, 354 pp.), and other works by Graubard cited in PART V. See also D. J. Struik's Marxian approach to mathematics, "Concerning Mathematics," *Science & Society*, I (Fall 1936), pp. 81-101, "On the Sociology of Mathematics," *ibid.*, VI (Winter 1942), pp. 58-70, and "Marx and Mathematics," *ibid.*, XII (Winter 1948), pp. 181-196. J. S. Allen, *Atomic Energy* (New York, 1949, 95 pp.), issued by International Publishers, reflects the line of the Communist Party. The same firm has announced that it will publish Allen's *The Atom Bomb Business* in 1951.

One of the answers to Hook on classless science, Eliseo Vivas, "A Note on the Question of 'Class Science,'" *Marxist Quarterly*, I (Oct.-Dec. 1937), pp. 437-446, agrees that science *seeks* a universal point of view, but asserts that the two theories—the mind as active in the knowing process, and the historical determination of categories of inquiry—are incompatible.

Topic 6. Socialism and the Role of the Intellectual

All varieties of socialism have been compelled in the struggle for survival to formulate more or less detailed theories in order to distinguish their movement from competing radicalisms, as well as from the majority opinions of their day. One definition of the intellectual excludes those leaders whose ideas have depended on supernatural and mystical assumptions and cannot be verified by the scientific method. This definition is too broad to be useful, for it would exclude from the intellectual classification all religious socialists and all secular socialists—including many Marxians—with a strong utopian element in their thought (see PART I, Topic 6). The definition of the socialist intellectual as the leader who has constructed socialist theory is the one used here.

This topic concentrates upon the implied paradox in Marxism. It is both a revolutionary movement of the working class traditionally concerned with instrumental thought and direct action—and unaccustomed to verbalized and speculative theory—and a highly rationalized, articulated, and comprehensive ideology. While Marxians have insisted that labor be educated in their doctrine in order to perform its class-conscious revolutionary function, most leaders in the Marxian tradition, beginning with Marx himself, have been middle-class intellectuals. Thus the very nature of Marxism made it almost inevitable that occasional revolutionists would become impatient with the elaborate theoretical structure of Marxism and "anti-intellectualism" would crop out sporadically.

Two types of literature are reviewed here: that dealing with the conflict between rivals for leadership who have resorted to calling their opponents petty-bourgeois intellectuals, and that on the anti-intellectualist element of syndicalism (see Topic 7). On the conflict of socialist intellectual elites, see either of two books by Max Nomad, the principal American student of this subject, *Rebels and Renegades* (New York, 1932, 430 pp.), which has an excellent bibliography, or else *Apostles of Revolution* (Boston, 1939, 467 pp.). The best introductions to syndicalist anti-intellectualism are John Spargo, "Anti-Intellectualism in the Socialist Movement; a Historical Survey," in his *Sidelights on Contemporary Socialism* (New York, 1911, 154 pp.), pp. 67-106, written near the climax of the American movement, and Albert Weisbord, *The Conquest of Power* (New York, 1937, 2 vols.), I, pp. 269-333, with a later perspective.

The Marxian doctrine tied revolution explicitly to the historical process. The abortive revolutionary movements in France during Marx's lifetime led him to conclude that the time was not ripe, and that successful revolution must await the process of economic change which would inexorably bring capitalism to the point of collapse where the proletariat could seize power. Among Marx's contemporaries, both the mutualists following Proudhon and the anarchist disciples of Bakunin were dissatisfied with this analysis, and attacked Marx as a bourgeois intellectual betrayer of the working class. Max Nomad treats the more important of these controversies in his article, "Marx and Bakunin," *Hound & Horn*, VI (Apr.-June 1933), pp. 381-418. See also the materials in the General Reading of PART I on Marx, Bakunin, and Proudhon.

At the end of the nineteenth century, anti-intellectualism appeared in French syndicalism. Richard Humphrey, *Georges Sorel*, announced for 1951 by the Harvard University Press, is an investigation of Sorel's anti-intellectualism. In *Reflections on Violence* (tr. by T. E. Hulme; London, 1915, 299 pp.) Georges Sorel was consciously anti-intellectual in prescribing myths of revolutionary violence and the general strike as unifying slogans for the masses, while not believing in their efficacy himself. For the elite, a rationalized system was necessary, but not for the masses. See also Sorel's characterization of utopians, both pre-Marxian and Marxian, as intellectualists in "Y a-t-il de l'utopie dans le marxisme?" *Revue de métaphysique et de morale*, VII (Mar. 1899), pp. 152-175. The reasons for Sorel's distinction are apparently to be found in the differences between syndicalist theory and orthodox Marxism. Contrast, for example, the plea of Paul Lafargue, Marx's son-in-law, for professionals to join the socialist movement, *Socialism and the Intellectuals* (tr. by C. H. Kerr; Chicago, 1900, 22 pp.), a speech to Paris students, also found in translation in the *International Socialist Review*, I (Aug. 1900), pp. 84-101, and in Lafargue, *The Right to Be Lazy* (tr. by C. H. Kerr; Chicago, 1907, 164 pp.), with such syndicalist writings as Hubert Lagardelle, "The Intellectuals and Working Class Socialism," *International Socialist Review*, VII (June 1907), pp. 721-730, VIII (July-Aug., Oct. 1907), pp. 33-41, 94-103, 213-219; Édouard Berth, *Les méfaits des intellectuels* (Paris, 1914, 333 pp.); and A. Cartault, *L'Intellectuel* (Paris, 1914, 311 pp.). Marx himself made the famous statement in the *Communist Manifesto* that brain workers had become "paid wage laborers" of the bourgeoisie, but he was elsewhere not consistent, sometimes referring to the intellectuals as part of the proletariat and sometimes as petty bourgeois.

In the United States, A. D. Lewis, in *Syndicalism and the General Strike* (London, 1912, 319 pp.), favored the anti-intellectualism of Sorel, Berth, and other French syndicalists. W. E. Walling, in *Progressivism— and After* (New York, 1914, 406 pp.), pp. 220-246, and in other writings emphasized the split between skilled and unskilled labor, and attacked the Fabians and the orthodox for abandoning socialism and appealing to the labor aristocracy and "minor professionals" against the unskilled, who alone could achieve real solidarity. For the Fabian position, see Walling's references to the articles by the Webbs, and G. B. Shaw's Fabian Tract No. 146, *Socialism and Superior Brains* (London, 1912, 23 pp.). For German orthodox social-democratic views, see the discussion of "Intelligenz" by Kautsky and others in *Neue Zeit*, XIII (1895), August Bebel, *Akademiker und Sozialismus* (2nd ed., Berlin, 1906, 27 pp.), Max Adler, *Der Sozialismus und die Intellektuellen* (1910; 4th ed., Vienna, 1923, 104 pp.), and Sozialdemokratische Partei Deutschlands, *Protokoll über die Verhandlungen des Parteitages . . . abgehalten zu Frankfurt a. M.* (Berlin, 1894, 190 pp.), especially pp. 65-85. See also the translation of an excerpt from an article by Kautsky in *Neue Zeit*, XXII, Pt. 1 (1903), pp. 99-101, "The Intellectuals and the Workers," *Fourth International*, VII (Apr. 1946), pp. 125-126. John Spargo continued his opposition to anti-intellectualism in *Syndicalism, Industrial Unionism and Socialism* (New York, 1913, 243 pp.), pp. 46-85, and W. J. Ghent, in *Socialism and Success* (New York, 1910, 252 pp.), pp. 129-176, expressed the same view.

The contest for leadership between the college educated and the experience educated is common to most branches of the modern socialist movement and is decided by the composition of the constituency and the skills and character of the protagonists. The concern of Eugene V. Debs for social justice, and his relative lack of concern for the theoretical foundations of the movement he represented, may partially account for the Socialist Party successes under his leadership. See, for example, the discussion in the *International Socialist Review*, XIII (Aug.-Oct. 1912), pp. 163-172, 276-277, 372, over the choice of Mahlon Barnes as Debs's campaign manager that year, and W. E. Walling, "Shall the Socialist

Party Govern Itself?" *ibid.* (Apr. 1913), pp. 755-759. The dogmatic and academic Daniel De Leon, who captured the leadership of the Socialist Labor Party, repelled and expelled followers by his insistence on the niceties of dogma. See the expression of his dislike for academic political economists in *Marxian Science and the Colleges* (New York, 1932, 94 pp.), and his editorial defining the intellectual as one who does not support the Socialist Trade and Labor Alliance—hence does not understand unionism —reprinted from the *Daily People* of March 19, 1905, in *Industrial Unionism* (New York, 1920, 79 pp.), pp. 21-25. The same attitude—more representative of a widely held sentiment than in the case of De Leon, who may have had a personal basis for his feeling—appears in G. R. Kirkpatrick, *Think—or Surrender* (Pittsburgh, Pa., 1916, 96 pp.), chap. 4.

Outside the United States the discussion continued in the pattern set by a little-known Polish-Russian revolutionary thinker ten years an exile in Siberia, Waclaw Machajski (A. Wolski, pseud.). His works include *Umstvennyi rabochy* [*The Intellectual Worker*] (Geneva, 1904-1905, 3 pts.), excerpts of which have been translated and published in V. F. Calverton, ed., *The Making of Society* (New York, 1937, 923 pp.), pp. 427-436; and such pamphlets as *Rabochaya revolyutsiya* [*The Workers' Revolution*] (Moscow, 1918). Further discussion of the subject is found in the work of Robert Michels, particularly his *Political Parties* (1911; tr. by E. and C. Paul; New York, 1915, 416 pp.), and of Pareto. See also the little-known work of E. Lozinsky, *Chto zhe takoe, nakonets, intelligentsiya?* [*What is the Intelligentsia?*] (St. Petersburg, 1907, 259 pp.), and P. L. Lavrov's discussion of the "debt" owed by the intellectuals to the masses in the fourth of his *Lettres historiques* (tr. by Marie Goldsmith; Paris, 1903, 328 pp.). Most significant was the discussion by Henri de Man, active for Belgian workers' education but alienated from the social democrats during World War I, in *The Psychology of Socialism* (tr. by E. and C. Paul; New York, 1927, 509 pp.), pp. 195-237, and *Die Intellektuellen und der Sozialismus* (Jena, 1926, 37 pp.). The new totalitarianism, communist and Fascist, shifted the focus of debate for others, such as W. Drabovitch, *Les Intellectuels français et le bolchévisme* (Paris, 1938, 219 pp.). Drabovitch took exception to statements by L. von Mises in *Socialism* (tr. by J. Kahane; New York, 1936, 528 pp.), p. 508, that the intellectuals are the backbone of Marxian socialism. D. P. Mirsky, *The Intelligentsia of Great Britain* (tr. by Alec Brown; New York, 1935, 237 pp.), claimed that British intellectuals had Fascist tendencies. See also Karl Popper, *The Open Society and Its Enemies* (rev. ed., Princeton, N.J., 1950, 732 pp.), pp. 410-442; Julien Benda, *The Treason of the Intellectuals* (tr. by Richard Aldington; New York, 1928, 244 pp.); and two general works, W. Y. Elliott, *The Pragmatic Revolt in Politics* (New York, 1928, 540 pp.), especially pp. 33-44, and Max Horkheimer, *Eclipse of Reason*

(New York, 1947, 187 pp.), an attack on both the neo-Thomists and the logical positivists.

After World War I the appearance of increasing numbers of "the new middle class" stimulated new union and socialist efforts to recruit them, and forced a reformulation of the labor and socialist attitude toward the brain worker. Samples of this literature are George Soule, *The Intellectual and the Labor Movement* (New York, 1923, 33 pp.), a pamphlet published by the League for Industrial Democracy; and H. E. Cory, *The Intellectuals and the Wage Workers* (New York, 1919, 273 pp.), expressing Marxian or Christian-socialist opinions which the author later claimed to have repudiated soon after the book was published. The standpoint of the A.F.L., hitherto as much a stronghold of anti-intellectualism as the I.W.W., was expressed in two articles by Samuel Gompers in the *American Federationist*, " 'Intellectuals' Please Note," xxiii (Mar. 1916), pp. 198-199, against paternalistic experts in social welfare, and "College Men and the American Labor Movement," xxix (Mar. 1922), pp. 212-215.

The American treatments of communism and the intellectual, 1917-1948, followed three chief themes. In the fifteen years after the Russian Revolution, the tendency among radicals was to hail the opportunity for professionals created by the expansion of Soviet state functions, and to add that the intellectuals as a class would disappear as culture became socialized. This attitude is represented in S. J. Rutgers' essay, "The Intellectuals and the Russian Revolution," in Lenin and others, *The New Policies of Soviet Russia* (Chicago, 1921, 127 pp.), pp. 65-127. The communists have, of course, maintained this point of view. Evidence, however, of the suspicion with which party regulars have eyed their professional converts is recorded in Richard Wright, "I Tried to Be a Communist," *Atlantic Monthly*, Vol. 174 (Aug. 1944), pp. 61-70, (Sept. 1944), pp. 48-56.

The problem arose again among the Trotskyists. Although the principal discussion turned on the members' attitude toward Russia and was conducted in terms of the dialectic, it was bound up with the sociological question of leadership. V. F. Calverton had asserted that the American intellectual never becomes a thoroughgoing revolutionary in "Revolt among American Intellectuals," *New Masses*, iv (Apr. 1929), pp. 3-5. The conflict a decade later, in which the Cannonites expelled James Burnham from the Socialist Workers Party as a "bourgeois intellectual," is recorded in J. P. Cannon, *The Struggle for a Proletarian Party* (New York, 1943, 302 pp.), particularly pp. 18-31. The position of the Burnham-Shachtman opposition is quoted, *ibid.*, pp. 281-285. See also W. F. Warde's similar attack, "From Revisionism to Social-Chauvinism; I. The Degradation of Sidney Hook," *Fourth International*, iii (June 1942), pp. 174-178.

Warde stigmatized the "lost generation," including Hook, Burnham, Dwight Macdonald, Lewis Corey, Edmund Wilson, and Louis Hacker, as intellectuals who never really accepted dialectical materialism. Hook, Macdonald, and others in "The New Failure of Nerve" series (*Partisan Review*, 1943), lumped Trotskyists with others who had appealed to faith. Burnham generalized the question of power and the intellectual elite in *The Managerial Revolution* (New York, 1941, 285 pp.).

Burnham had returned to the main double theme which became an increasing preoccupation during and after World War II: the perpetual success of the intellectual in power aggrandizement, and the rivalry among the intelligentsia at the expense of the masses, with the resulting proletarian antagonism. Max Nomad, the principal writer on this subject, has contributed numerous essays, including "Masters—Old and New," in V. F. Calverton, ed., *The Making of Society* (New York, 1937, 923 pp.), pp. 882-893; and also the essays, "I. Civil and Cultural Liberties in Russia, II. Prophecies That Came True," *Twice a Year*, v-vi (1940-1941), pp. 494-511; "Permanent Class Struggle or Utopia?" *Modern Review*, ii (Jan. 1948), pp. 28-33; and two chapters, "Communism" and "The Evolution of Anarchism and Syndicalism," in *European Ideologies*, ed. by Feliks Gross (New York, 1948, 1075 pp.), pp. 49-100, 327-342. See also Arthur Koestler, "The Intelligentsia," *Partisan Review*, xi (Summer 1944), pp. 265-277.

For the sharpest attack on Marxism as anti-intellectualist because of the "religious" or philosophical nature of its assumptions, see Max Eastman, *Marxism; Is It Science?* (New York, 1940, 394 pp.), which contrasts the scientific attitude with the various religious and philosophical aspects of Marxian theory: the dialectic; historical materialism; the class struggle; the economics of *Capital*; utopianism. He concludes with a criticism of Sidney Hook's attempt to Americanize Marx by the identification of "dialectic religion" with Dewey's pragmatism. For a statement of the role of intelligence as conceived by the liberal tradition see John Dewey, "Science and the Future of Society," in Joseph Ratner, ed., *Intelligence in the Modern World; John Dewey's Philosophy* (New York, 1939, 1077 pp.), pp. 343-363.

For the anti-intellectualism of pre-Marxian socialism see H. L. Eads, *Discourses on Religion, Science, and Education* (South Union, Ky., 1884, 15 pp.), which counsels the acceptance of truth wherever found, but adds, "nothing merely intellectual can benefit the spirit" (p. 6).

See also PART IV, Topics 4 and 5, and PART V, Topic 4.

Topic 7. French and American Syndicalism

The purpose of this topic is to suggest a comparative study of two phases of a common revolutionary tradition appearing in France and in the United States. While syndicalist theory in both countries emphasizes certain characteristic doctrines and tendencies such as belief in direct industrial rather than political action, sabotage, industrial unionism, and suspicion of theory, American syndicalism of the I.W.W. is generally considered to be the most indigenous form of native radicalism. It should be significant to inquire wherein the history of the I.W.W. displays any important differences from French syndicalism.

Some of the more obvious differences relate to the place of syndicalism in the national labor movements of France and the United States. Syndicalist theories were first set forth between 1894 and 1904, particularly in the Confédération Générale du Travail, the French counterpart of the American Federation of Labor. While syndicalist theories were held by an important part of French labor, the American trade unions under Gompers were pursuing a policy of seeking limited gains within the framework of capitalism. The anarchist scare of 1886 and the bitter strikes of 1877 and 1893 influenced American labor to shun the label of radical, to discourage socialist penetration, and to practice business unionism pure and simple. Since American unions were organized more on a craft basis, dual unionism became a feature of the labor situation whenever the I.W.W. entered the scene.

The rise of the I.W.W., organized in 1905 around a nucleus of the Western Federation of Miners and other western unions, might seem to be a natural result of the spread of syndicalist ideas out of France. The American organizers, however, had for the most part little knowledge or understanding of the European theories and their membership was native American. Bill Haywood and W. Z. Foster did confer with French syndicalists in 1910, but found many differences in origin and theory between the two movements.

Revolutionary syndicalism declined in France and the United States under pressure of war patriotism, by defection to communism, and in the face of industrial rationalization, which outmoded its methods; but the result in the two countries was different. In France the C.G.T. adopted a more reformist policy. In the United States the defections to the Bolsheviks made greater inroads in I.W.W. leadership. The remnant were crushed by the criminal syndicalism laws of 1917-1920, which had no French parallel in stringency. Their last appearance in a prominent role was in the Seattle general strike of 1919, but even here their role was that of scapegoats in a movement started and run by the conservative unions.

Read J. A. Estey, *Revolutionary Syndicalism* (London, 1913, 212 pp.), pp. 1-161, and J. G. Brooks, *American Syndicalism; the I.W.W.* (New York, 1913, 264 pp.), pp. 12-32, 61-178, by way of introduction.

Since this study approaches from a different point of view the materials already investigated in earlier parts, look first at references to anarchism (PART I, General Reading, pp. 39-42), French syndicalism (PART I, Topic 8), the I.W.W. (PART II, Topic 11), and syndicalist anti-intellectualism (in Topic 6 above).

General works including a study of syndicalism are A. T. F. Clay, *Syndicalism and Labour* (London, 1911, 230 pp.); Bertrand Russell, *Proposed Roads to Freedom; Socialism, Anarchism and Syndicalism* (New York, 1919, 218 pp.); R. L. Mott, "The Political Theory of Syndicalism," *Political Science Quarterly*, xxxvii (Mar. 1922), pp. 25-40; W. Y. Elliott, *The Pragmatic Revolt in Politics; Syndicalism, Fascism and the Constitutional State* (New York, 1928, 540 pp.); and Albert Weisbord, *The Conquest of Power* (New York, 1937, 2 vols.).

From the mass of literature on French syndicalism, with its publication peak just before World War I, see the following titles in addition to those cited in PART I, Topic 8: Georges Yvetot, *A.B.C. syndicaliste* (Paris, 1911, 72 pp.); Félicien Challaye, *Syndicalisme révolutionnaire et syndicalisme réformiste* (Paris, 1909, 156 pp.); Gäetan Pirou, *Proudhonisme et syndicalisme révolutionnaire* (Paris, 1910, 422 pp.); Anton Acht, *Der moderne französische Syndikalismus* (Jena, 1911, 185 pp.), a judicious study in heavy style; Georges Guy-Grand, *La Philosophie syndicaliste* (2nd ed., Paris, 1911, 237 pp.), which relates the movement to the thought of Marx and Nietzsche, and to anti-intellectualism, antinationalism, and mysticism; A. B. Zévaès, *Le Syndicalisme contemporain* (Paris, 1911, 358 pp.), one of the more detailed studies; Fabian Ware, *The Worker and His Country* (London, 1912, 288 pp.), which shows accurate knowledge and strong sympathy for the French syndicalists; Gustav Eckstein, "Der Syndikalismus und seine Lebensbedingungen in Frankreich," introduction to Paul Louis, *Geschichte der Gewerkschaftsbewegung in Frankreich* (tr. by Hedwig Kurucz-Eckstein; Stuttgart, 1912, 317 pp.), pp. 11-94; J. P. Wirz, *Der revolutionäre Syndikalismus in Frankreich* (Zurich, 1931, 214 pp.); and Robert Bothereau, *Histoire du syndicalisme français* (Paris, 1945, 127 pp.). For later developments in French syndicalism see Roger Picard, *Le Mouvement syndical durant la guerre* (Paris, 1927, 306 pp.); Léon Jouhaux, *Le Syndicalisme et la C.G.T.* (Paris, 1920, 243 pp.); and Maxime Leroy, *Les Techniques nouvelles du syndicalisme* (Paris, 1921, 209 pp.).

Among the pamphlets and books on the I.W.W. by outsiders, those by rival socialists, and the communists who were in a sense their heirs, are prominent. Daniel De Leon, *The Preamble of the Industrial Workers of the World* (New York, 1905?, 48 pp.), was later published with the title, *Socialist Reconstruction of Society* (New York, 1938, 64 pp.). Hans Bötcher, *Zur revolutionären Gewerkschaftsbewegung in Amerika, Deutschland und England* (Jena, 1922, 236 pp.), includes the I.W.W.

W. Z. Foster, a former "Wobbly," discussed the dual unionism of the I.W.W. and the communists in "Old Unions and New Unions," *Communist*, VII (July 1928), pp. 399-405. See also Louis Levine, "The Development of Syndicalism in America," *Political Science Quarterly*, XXVIII (Sept. 1913), pp. 451-479, and Hubert Devillez, "L'Évolution du syndicalisme et des partis ouvriers aux États Unis," *Revue politique et parlementaire*, CLXII (Jan. 1935), pp. 3-29.

Among the contributions of American anarchists and anarcho-syndicalists to the philosophy of industrial and revolutionary unionism are pamphlets privately printed by E. H. Heywood of Princeton, Mass.: *The Labor Party* (New York, 1868, 20 pp.) and *The Great Strike* (Princeton, Mass., 1878, 23 pp.); Emma Goldman, *Syndicalism, the Modern Menace to Capitalism* (New York, 1913, 14 pp.); D. D. Lum, *The Philosophy of Trade Unions* (1892; Washington, 1914, 19 pp.); and V. S. Yarros, *Our Revolution* (Boston, 1920, 251 pp.). For purposes of illustration a few more "Wobbly" writings are noted. *Syndicalism* (Chicago, 1913?, 47 pp.), by E. C. Ford and W. Z. Foster, defends the policy of "boring from within" with reference to French syndicalist experience. Justus Ebert, formerly associated with the Socialist Labor Party, contributed two tracts on the philosophy of the I.W.W., *The Trial of a New Society* (Cleveland, Ohio, 1913, 160 pp.), and *The I.W.W. in Theory and Practice* (2nd ed., Chicago, 1922?, 124 pp.). W. E. Trautmann, *Industrial Union Methods* (Chicago, 1912, 29 pp.), and jointly with Peter Hagboldt, *Hammers of Hell* (Chicago, 1921, 338 pp.), deal with labor struggles in the Pittsburgh area, 1902-1909. The two writers also collaborated on *Riot* (Chicago, 1922, 338 pp.). See also Edward Hammond, *Two Kinds of Unionism* (New Castle, Pa., 1912, 4 pp.), an early leaflet; and Vincent St. John, *Why the A.F. of L. Cannot Become an Industrial Union* (Cleveland, Ohio, n.d., 4 pp.).

The American Civil Liberties Union statement, *The Truth about the I.W.W.; Facts in Relation to the Trial at Chicago, by Competent Industrial Investigators and Noted Economists* (New York, 1918, 55 pp.); D. F. Callahan, "Criminal Syndicalism and Sabotage," in U.S. Bureau of Labor Statistics, *Monthly Labor Review*, XIV (Apr. 1922), pp. 803-812; and G. W. Kirchwey, *A Survey of the Workings of the Criminal Syndicalism Law of California* (Los Angeles, 1926, 47 pp.), are sample studies of the legal pressure which helped destroy the I.W.W. as an effective revolutionary organization.

Topic 8. *The Theological Background of Christian Socialism*

During the greater part of the nineteenth century, when the Protestant churches were identifying themselves with the middle and upper classes in the cities, evangelical Protestant theology emphasized certain patterns of thought consistent with the justification of economic individualism. The traditional teaching of the sinfulness of man and his need for salvation were conceived entirely in individual terms. The competitive order was held to be natural to the sinful world. Inequality of possessions assured a place for the charity and stewardship with which men of wealth were supposed to be charged. The Social Gospel movement (PART II, Topic 13) broke with this aspect of traditional Protestantism, with its insistence that the churches must concern themselves with social problems. At first largely ethical in character, the Social Gospelers emphasized the social teachings of Jesus, and organized settlement work and promoted reform organizations. Gradually, however, new notes began to appear in theological writing, culminating with the theology of Walter Rauschenbusch in which personal and social salvation are identified.

The balance between the old personal and the new social salvation was clear to Rauschenbusch, but his concentration on the new led liberal theologians who followed him to neglect individual piety. His concern for the Kingdom within the church as contrasted with the church as an institution led them to neglect the constant rebuilding of the church as the institutional repository through which piety and the Social Gospel could become effective. Later orthodox theologians have criticized his followers' pantheism or humanism and incorrectly imputed the same lack of emphasis on God's transcendence to Rauschenbusch. The Barthian overemphasis in the opposite direction, on the initiative of God in cleansing the sin of man, was one attempt to redress the balance. Another attempt, led by John C. Bennett and Walter M. Horton, among others, sought to retain the theological achievements of the Social Gospel while recovering its implicit theism. The theology of contemporary Christian socialists is distinguished from that of previous generations by this change of emphasis.

Of the three theological foundations of the gospel of the Kingdom—the Atonement, God as creator, and the Incarnation without its ecclesiastical and sacramental connotations—the evangelistic Rauschenbusch was preoccupied with the love of Christ as shown in the Atonement. But love is primarily a principle of personal relations. Recent evangelicals have shied away from the Social Gospel because the gospel still meant for them the good news of the forgiveness of personal sin. The contribution of Gregory Vlastos has been to redefine love in terms of mutuality—cooperative activity and community of interest—and so identify it with justice and make it applicable to social ethics.

The Anglo-Catholics made the Incarnation their central doctrine and it led them into the Social Gospel. Whereas the Atonement concentrates only on the birth and death of Christ, the Incarnation concerns Christ's whole life on earth. If the Incarnation shows the significance of every man for God, the Christian's duty is to change the society which obliterates this significance. This rediscovery of the Incarnation has spread to American theologians concerned with social salvation.

God as creator is an important theme in the theology of Bennett and Horton. They explore the ways in which God works in society and define the limits of his creativity. To Bennett these limits are the logical structure of reality, the moral character of God, the determinateness of his creation and human freedom.

The way the doctrines of salvation and the Kingdom of God are interpreted in the Social Gospel distinguishes it from the older individualistic theology, as the literature of this topic indicates. See first the most important theoretical justification of socialized Christianity: Walter Rauschenbusch, *A Theology for the Social Gospel* (New York, 1917, 279 pp.), especially pp. 77-94, 119-120, 129-279. See also J. C. Bennett, *Social Salvation* (New York, 1935, 222 pp.), pp. 3-10, 33-39, 87-95, 141-143, 169-216; A. T. Mollegen, "The Meaning of Prophetic Religion," *Radical Religion*, IV, No. 3 (Summer 1939), pp. 17-21; and Paul Ramsey, "A Theology of Social Action," *Social Action*, XII (Oct. 15, 1946), pp. 4-34. R. H. Gabriel, "Protestantism Moves toward Humanism and Collectivism," in *The Course of American Democratic Thought* (New York, 1940, 452 pp.), pp. 308-330, is the most penetrating summary of the intellectual trends in American Christian socialism.

V. P. Bodein, *The Social Gospel of Walter Rauschenbusch and Its Relation to Religious Education* (New Haven, Conn., 1944, 168 pp.), pp. 158-163, contains a full list of writings by or about Rauschenbusch. Among the more important titles are Rauschenbusch's remarks on the relation of theology to religion reported in the Baptist Congress, *Annual Session*, XXII (1904), pp. 89-92; C. H. Hopkins, "Walter Rauschenbusch and the Brotherhood of the Kingdom," *Church History*, VII (June 1938), pp. 138-156; A. C. McGiffert, "Walter Rauschenbusch; Twenty Years After," *Christendom*, III (Winter 1938), pp. 96-109; Bodein (cited above), pp. 100-134; and W. A. Mueller, "The Life, Work and Gospel of Walter Rauschenbusch," *Religion in Life*, XV (Autumn 1946), pp. 529-540. The development of Rauschenbusch's theology is discussed in D. R. Sharpe, *Walter Rauschenbusch* (New York, 1942, 463 pp.), pp. 116-140, 191-355, with frequent quotations from Rauschenbusch's writings, by a former pupil and confidential secretary.

Little noticed because of the fame of Rauschenbusch was H. C. King, *Theology and the Social Consciousness* (New York, 1902, 252 pp.).

The theological controversy over the Social Gospel can be represented by the following titles: A. M. Singer, *Walter Rauschenbusch and His Contribution to Social Christianity* (Boston, 1926, 136 pp.); Shailer Mathews, "The Development of Social Christianity in America during the

Past Twenty-five Years," *Journal of Religion*, vii (July 1927), pp. 376-386, a bibliographical essay, and *The Atonement and the Social Process* (New York, 1930, 212 pp.); W. A. Visser 't Hooft, *The Background of the Social Gospel in America* (Haarlem, 1928, 187 pp.); and Valdemar Ammundsen, *Social Kristendom* (Copenhagen, 1931, 218 pp.). Visser 't Hooft, following the criticism of the Dutch fundamentalist Burggraaff, attacked the Social Gospel and its liberal theology, but from the Barthian point of view. The Danish bishop Ammundsen defended Rauschenbusch against Visser 't Hooft.

The economic crisis following 1929 was a turning point in American theology. While Reinhold Niebuhr was turning from liberal to crisis theology (see Topic 9), other American theologians were revising their estimates of man's capacity to overcome evil. W. M. Horton, *Realistic Theology* (New York, 1934, 207 pp.), and J. C. Bennett, *Social Salvation* (New York, 1935, 222 pp.), are outstanding examples of this trend. An abbreviated reprint of Horton's work and his *A Psychological Approach to Theology* (New York, 1931, 279 pp.), were published later as *Theology in Transition* (New York, 1943, 186 and 196 pp.). Essays by Bennett contributing to the theology of the Social Gospel are "The Social Interpretation of Christianity," *The Church through Half a Century* (ed. by S. M. Cavert and H. P. Van Dusen; New York, 1936, 426 pp.), pp. 113-131, and "The Christian Ethic and Political Strategy," *Christianity and Crisis*, i (Feb. 24, 1941), pp. 3-6. Sample studies by other theologians are F. J. McConnell, *The Christian Ideal and Social Control* (Chicago, 1932, 174 pp.); H. Richard Niebuhr, William Pauck, and F. P. Miller, *The Church against the World* (Chicago, 1935, 156 pp.), especially Pt. 3 by Niebuhr, "Toward the Independence of the Church"; J. B. Thompson, "Prolegomena to a Proletarian Theology," *Radical Religion*, i (Autumn 1936), pp. 11-18; H. Richard Niebuhr, *The Kingdom of God in America* (Chicago, 1937, 215 pp.), showing more the historical approach of Paul Tillich than a systematic theology; and J. C. Schroeder, "Personal Religion and the Social Gospel," *Religion in Life*, vii (Spring 1938), pp. 258-266. Illustrative of the sharpened interest in the subject with the coming of World War II are D. C. Macintosh, *Social Religion* (New York, 1939, 336 pp.); F. E. Johnson, *The Social Gospel Re-examined* (New York, 1940, 261 pp.); Gregory Vlastos, "Religious Foundations of Democracy; Fraternity and Liberty," *Journal of Religion*, xxii (Jan., Apr. 1942), pp. 1-19, 137-155. Paul Tillich, "Marxism and Christian Socialism," *Christianity and Society*, vii (Spring 1942), pp. 13-18, is a theological criticism and appreciation of Marxism, and his "Man and Society in Religious Socialism," *Christianity and Society*, viii (Fall 1943), pp. 10-21, discusses man's variable or permanent nature, utopianism, man's finite freedom in society, and the balance of spiritual and material forces in historical existence. See

228

also C. D. Kean, *Christianity and the Cultural Crisis* (New York, 1945, 211 pp.).

Topic 9. The Christian Socialist Philosophy of History of Reinhold Niebuhr

Reinhold Niebuhr is a significant figure in the American socialist tradition in that his thought represents the renaissance of traditional Christian social thinking on the one hand joined with trenchant criticisms of liberal and Marxian theories on the other. Niebuhr's theology is based upon the conviction that the gospels contain not only the record of divine revelation but also the most profound insights into the problems of human life. He is able to analyze contemporary issues in the light of these insights with a vividness and relevance which has won many adherents in an age of deep uncertainty and confusion.

His thirteen years' pastorate among Detroit automobile workers forced contemporary issues upon him. From practical experience of the problems of social ethics in the ministry he was called in 1928 to the chair of Christian ethics at Union Theological Seminary. By a spiral or dialectical process, in which he subjected each school of thought which influenced him most to violent criticism, Niebuhr has turned gradually from social problems to their theological foundations. European theologians hail him as the American interpreter of the theology of Barth and Brunner, although he criticizes their systems too. His fame rests also on his style of preaching: a blunt challenge to traditional beliefs and an emphasis on the permanent tension between the historical and the transcendental.

Christianity teaches, according to Niebuhr, that man is suspended between nature and the supernatural, participating in both. He is an animal subject to all of the passions of animal life. But he is also man, aware of his kinship with God, and constantly attempting to raise himself above the natural order. Two tendencies have dominated the Christian tradition in recent times, Niebuhr believes. Both are errors, although each contains a measure of partial truth. One is the Christian dualism exemplified in monasticism and the pietistic sects which repudiates the sinful world in the effort to achieve salvation. This view is both too pure and too pessimistic. The other is the modern monistic or pantheistic tradition, which finds God immanent in the natural process and which gives rise to the familiar dogmas of evolution and liberal progress.

Much of Niebuhr's criticism is leveled against this liberal Christian tradition. His reputation arises partly from the sympathetic response of intellectuals to his dissection of contemporary democratic individualism and of the religious attitudes underlying it. Fundamentally Niebuhr maintains that rationalism, and the liberal Christianity associated with it, is too optimistic in its view of the perfectibility of human nature and of social progress. Its optimism has blinded it to the demonic in human nature, has led it to an unwarranted faith in education as a perfector of rational processes, and, most important, has prevented it from understanding the economic and class basis of power, so that in its democratic political form rationalism clings to dogmas which are largely devoid of meaning in the modern world. Nevertheless, he concedes that democratic rationalism and the capitalist economy associated with it have discovered or at least exploited individualist values in many spheres that contribute to the permanent enrichment of human culture.

Marxian socialism grows directly out of liberal rationalism. While it develops the rationalist tendencies of liberalism to greater extremes it also introduces a new mythology which is peculiarly its own. Much of the Marxian criticism of liberal individualism Niebuhr finds to be true. It has uncovered and analyzed the nature of the class struggle for economic and political power. It has sharpened our perceptions of the nature of social change through the atrophy and disintegration of aggregates of social and economic power leading to violent struggles which belie the liberal conception of unilinear and gradual social change. Marxism's essentially ethical critique of economic individualism he finds unassailable, for it conforms to the Christian view that power corrupts and that justice demands at least a rough equalization of economic power in an industrial civilization. But its extreme rationalism emerges in the notion of a pseudo-scientific historical dialectic, and in the belief that a socialized state will socialize and harmonize the wills and appetites of individuals. Likewise he labels as myths the Marxian assumptions that in the historical future the class dictatorship of the proletariat will transform itself into the classless society, and that in this society the state will wither away.

A true political theory, Niebuhr concludes, must be realistically socialist with respect to the sources of economic and political power. It must be based upon the assumption that man desires both justice and power. It must assume that all actual institutions are necessarily corrupt in part; and it must be prepared to face the ferment resulting from the inevitable aspirations of the individual.

Niebuhr's conception of the role of spiritual and material forces creative of change in social institutions can be drawn from his writings cited in this topic. His analysis of social change can then be contrasted with that of liberalism and Marxism. His latest and most comprehensive formulation of his philosophy of history is *Faith and History; a Comparison of Christian and Modern Views of History* (New York, 1949, 257 pp.). The following passages are also cited which indicate the development of these ideas in the previous fifteen years: *Beyond Tragedy; Essays on the Christian Interpretation of History* (New York, 1938, 306 pp.), pp. 3-24; *Reflections on the End of an Era* (New York, 1934, 302 pp.), pp. 3-61, 77-

83, 99-136, 229-239; *Moral Man and Immoral Society* (New York, 1941, 284 pp.), pp. 169-199; *Christianity and Power Politics* (New York, 1940, 226 pp.), pp. 141-158. For a discussion of Niebuhr as a Christian revolutionary from the point of view of an orthodox English theologian, see D. R. Davies, *Reinhold Niebuhr; Prophet from America* (London, 1945?, 94 pp.), pp. 58-94. J. C. Bennett, "The Contribution of Reinhold Niebuhr," *Religion in Life*, vi (Spring 1937), pp. 268-283, represents an evaluation by an American theologian still strongly influenced by religious liberalism.

The chronological approach is particularly valuable in tracing the evolution of Niebuhr's thought. His first book, *Does Civilization Need Religion?* (New York, 1927, 242 pp.), outlines most of the characteristic ideas later developed. *Leaves from the Notebook of a Tamed Cynic* (Chicago, 1929, 198 pp.), illustrates the impact of modern industrial and urban problems on Niebuhr as he noted them in a diary kept during his parish ministry. *An Interpretation of Christian Ethics* (New York, 1935, 244 pp.), the Rauschenbusch memorial lectures delivered at Colgate-Rochester Divinity School in the spring of 1934, still focuses on social ethics but has richer expository sections on the Christian dogmatic tradition. "Christian Politics and Communist Religion," in *Christianity and the Social Revolution* (ed. by John Lewis, Karl Polanyi, and D. K. Kitchin; New York, 1936, 526 pp.), pp. 442-472; *Do the State and Nation Belong to God or the Devil?* (London, 1937, 45 pp.); *Why the Christian Church Is Not Pacifist* (London, 1940, 47 pp.); and *Europe's Catastrophe and the Christian Faith* (London, 1940, 46 pp.), apply the tensions of dialectical theology to political theory and supplement his *Christianity and Power Politics* (cited above). A recent work by Niebuhr amplifying his view that democracy is a permanently valid political theory through its reconciliation of liberty and order is *The Children of Light and the Children of Darkness; a Vindication of Democracy and a Critique of Its Traditional Defence* (New York, 1944, 190 pp.). For an extended statement of Niebuhr's theological position see his Gifford lectures, 1939, published as *The Nature and Destiny of Man* (New York, 1941-1943, 2 vols.). *Discerning the Signs of the Times* (New York, 1946, 194 pp.) is a collection of sermons which do not disclose new elements in his thought, although the focus of his concern has shifted with events.

Niebuhr is a prolific writer of articles in religious periodicals. The following samples are characterized by repeated criticisms of the groups with which he sympathizes: "The Confession of a Tired Radical," *Christian Century*, xlv (Aug. 30, 1928), pp. 1046-1047 (a revolt against the liberals' feigned confession of their sins to bolster their group loyalty by invidious comparison with other groups, thus perpetuating group conflict); "After Capitalism—What?" *World Tomorrow*, xvi (Mar. 1, 1933), pp. 203-205 (political liberalism is useless; fascism is inevitable but will eventually lose to socialism "because of the inexorable logic of history"); "A New Strategy for Socialists," *World Tomorrow*, xvi (Aug. 31, 1933), pp. 490-492 (the weaknesses of Marxism drive the middle classes toward fascism); and "The Church and Political Action," *Christian Century*, li (Aug. 1, 1934), pp. 992-994 (the church cannot transcend the class struggle until it espouses it). As editor of *Christianity and Society* (New York, 1936- , entitled *Radical Religion*, 1936-1940), the quarterly of the Fellowship of Socialist Christians, Niebuhr has exerted his influence against the utopian and liberal tradition of Christian socialism. See his article, "The Creed of Modern Christian Socialists," *Radical Religion*, iii (Spring 1938), pp. 13-18. This statement has since been reformulated.

In addition to the studies by Davies and Bennett cited above, George Hammar, *Christian Realism in Contemporary American Theology* (Uppsala, 1940, 364 pp.), although attempting to deal with all the principal trends in relation to their tradition, considers Niebuhr the leading American theologian and discusses his ideas in greatest detail. For a sharp attack upon Niebuhr from the secular Marxian humanist point of view see Sidney Hook, "The New Failure of Nerve," *Partisan Review*, x (Jan.-Feb. 1943), pp. 2-17, and succeeding articles in this controversy.

PART IV

Economic and Political Aspects
of American Socialism

For discussion in Volume 1 relevant to this Part (PART IV) of the Bibliography, see especially Chapters 9 and 10; also Chapter 6, and Chapters 4 and 5.

General Reading

WRITERS on socialism or socialist criticism of capitalism assumed the religious or philosophical doctrines discussed in PART III; but their principal concerns were the problems of production and distribution, and the role of the state in relation to the economic process. Since Marx, discussion of economics and politics by socialists has been the main ingredient of their works. References in the General Reading and Topics for PARTS I and II to the writings of socialist leaders and the official platforms and organs of their parties serve as an introduction to socialist attitudes toward politics and economics. A selection from this material, with additions, is presented here in a new context. For a general introduction, read Sidney Hook, *Towards the Understanding of Karl Marx* (New York, 1933, 347 pp.), pp. vii-xii, 1-63, 187-321; P. M. Sweezy, *Socialism* (New York, 1949, 276 pp.), in the Economics Handbook Series published by McGraw-Hill, by a Marxist who is also a professional economist; M. R. Cohen, "Property and Sovereignty," *Cornell Law Quarterly*, XIII (Dec. 1927), pp. 8-30; and the scholarly essay of Hans Kelsen, *The Political Theory of Bolshevism* (Berkeley, Calif., 1949, 60 pp.), which relates the theory of Marx and Engels to contemporary communism.

1. Pre-Marxian Socialist Theory

The communitarians were not primarily political theorists—much less economists. Their ideas were usually implicit in their plans for operating colonies, and subordinate to religious or ethical doctrine. Yet observers of their communities constantly kept two closely related questions in mind, and devoted considerable space to the discussion of the answers they found: How did communistic or cooperative economic organization affect the physical well-being of the communitarians? What principle of government aided or hindered survival?

Charles Nordhoff, in *The Communistic Societies of the United States* (New York, 1875, 439 pp.), found an answer to the political question in the presence or absence of a strong and respected leader. B. M. H. Shambaugh's *Amana That Was and Amana That Is* (Iowa City, Iowa, 1932, 502 pp.), emphasizes the importance of centralization of authority (pp. 94-104), but as in many other cases, this authority depended not so much on political status—the council of trustees was elected annually— as on the prestige of the elected group as religious leaders. The same was true of the elders in a Shaker Family, in spite of the fact that the deacons had charge of temporal matters. See F. W. Evans, *Shakers: Compendium of the Origin, History, Principles . . . of the United Society of Believers* (New York, 1859, 189 pp.). See also two Shaker pamphlets on government by Elder Evans, *Shaker Reconstruction of the American Government* (Hudson, N.Y., 1888, 8 pp.) and *Two Orders: Shakerism and Republicanism; the American Church and American Civil Government Co-Equal and Separate; the New Heaven and New Earth* (Pittsfield, Mass., 1890, 12 pp.). Although the Oneida, Harmony, and Zoar communities maintained their coherence through the strong personalities of Noyes, Rapp, and Baümeler (see E. O. Randall, *History of the Zoar Society*, in PART II, Topic 1; J. A. Bole, *The Harmony Society*, and J. S. Duss, *The Harmonists*, Topic 1; R. A. Parker, *A Yankee Saint*, Topic 4), the Oneida Perfectionists maintained an unusually high degree of group participation in government. One device which is usually thought of in connection with the moral life of the Community, mutual criticism, performed a democratic function. It provided a channel for the release of repressed conflicts where the weightiest members of the community could sit in informal judgment, at a stage when the problem was still manageable, without dictating the solution (see W. A. Hinds, *Mutual Criticism*, in PART II, Topic 4). On the other hand, New Harmony, the stronger Associationist phalanxes, and the Icarian communities had a much more elaborate democratic structure. While the conditions of their several failures were often economic—matters of personnel, capitalization, or catastrophes—their failure to find a technique for resolving discussion of differences into cooperative action should rank prominently among the rest. For the Associationists see especially *Constitution of the Brook Farm Association for Industry and Education* (2nd ed., Boston, 1844, 20 pp.); the newspaper debate between Horace Greeley and H. J. Raymond, *Association Discussed . . . a Controversy between the New York Tribune and the Courier and Enquirer* (New York, 1847, 83 pp.); and Horace Greeley, *Essays Designed to Elucidate the Science of Political Economy* (Boston, 1870, 384 pp.), especially pp. 81-107, 273-286. For the Icarians, see *Almanach icarien* (Paris, 1843-1852; 1849-1851 not published), edited by Cabet; Étienne Cabet, "History and Constitution of the Icarian Community," *Iowa Journal of History and Politics*, xv (Apr. 1917), pp. 214-286, and *Realization of Communism: Brief History of Icaria* (Icaria [Corning], Iowa, 1880, 42 pp.), attributed to Émile Péron.

The answer to the economic question varies from group to group. In general the socialist colonists faced hardships common to pioneer life. Having survived the first stage of construction, they depended for economic welfare in part on the manufacture of a commodity sold outside the community, such as traps and silk twist at Oneida, and Shaker brooms, seeds, and washing machines, or at least on an agricultural surplus and their service industries, such as the woolen mills, sawmills, gristmills, and tannery at Amana. Planning and accounting for production and a rough rationing system were characteristic. A simple if not ascetic standard of living dictated by their religious beliefs helped balance the budget. Their labor conditions were reported favorably by those used to the wage system. And yet the remarkable fact was how much their methods of labor management and business administration had in common with contemporary capitalist practice.

Early American radical thinkers, although affected by the communist experiments of their day and preceding Marx, nevertheless turned their back on the pilot project method of the communitarians and sought to combat the nascent merchant capitalism with propaganda and political action. Among these, see Langdon Byllesby, *Observations on the Sources and Effects of Unequal Wealth* (New York, 1826, 167 pp.); Paul Brown, *The Radical: and Advocate of Equality* (Albany, N.Y., 1834, 170 pp.); Thomas Skidmore, *The Rights of Man to Property!* (New York, 1829, 405 pp.); William Maclure, *Opinions on Various Subjects* (New Harmony, Ind., 1831-1838, 3 vols.); and Clinton Roosevelt, *The Mode of Protecting Domestic Industry, Consistently with the Desires Both of the South and the North, by Operating on the Currency* (New York, 1833, 48 pp.), and *The Science of Government Founded on Natural Law* (New York, 1841, 113 pp.). Brown and Maclure had been at New Harmony.

Echoes of this type of literature after Marx, utopian in the literary but not in the colonizing sense, appeared in a flood during the last fifteen years of the nineteenth century. The following gave their views of a better political and economic condition of society, usually a mixture of socialist and democratic institutional changes: Henry George, *Progress and Poverty* (New York, 1940, 571 pp.), staking all on the single tax on land; Edward Bellamy, *Looking Backward, 2000-1887* (Boston, 1888, 470 pp.); H. D. Lloyd, *Wealth against Commonwealth* (New York, 1894, 563 pp.); Laurence Gronlund, *The New Economy* (Chicago, 1898, 364 pp.). Less known are Ignatius Donnelly, *Caesar's Column* (Chicago, 1890, 367 pp.), advocating monetary and political reforms, redistribution of property, government ownership, and operation of public utilities; and Jack London, *The Iron Heel* (New York, 1907, 354 pp.), which underlined the power of the ruling capitalists to crush the proletarian revolution, and *War of the Classes* (New York, 1905, 278 pp.), a curious combination of Spencerian Social Darwinism as modified by Benjamin Kidd and second-hand Marxism.

2. Marxian Theory

It is only after Marx, by and large, that any great emphasis was placed on economic theory. Marx and Engels, however, like other socialists, devoted more space to criticism of existing institutions than to outlining future ones (see PART I, General Reading, pp. 34-39). The first distinction which must be kept in mind in dealing with the economic and political aspects of American socialism is that the theory of *socialists* is not necessarily, or even very often, the theory of *socialism*. Marxist writers about socialism, except for the Russians since 1917, were not themselves living in a socialist society. While the purpose of their writing may have been the achievement of such a society, or the prevention of its achievement in the case of anti-Marxist theorists, most of it has been related to the criticism or defense of past or existing institutions. The problems of socialism are treated accordingly, and often are discussed mainly by implication.

Two other features of this body of literature on Marxian economic and political theory need emphasis: the lack of boundaries between European and American thought, and between political and economic thought. A good deal of early American writing by socialists primarily interested in political or trade-union activities is a summary or a repetition of Marx and other European socialists. Their deviations from European theory were on the one hand the unconscious result of concentration on a small part of the Marxian literature, and on the other the result of their American background. After World War I an increasing body of American socialist works consciously deviated from Marxian texts, but was still in close relation with European thinking. The professional criticism or elaboration of Marxian theory has always maintained an international character. The nearer we approach the contemporary scene, the more are theoretical problems common to scholars on both sides of the Atlantic.

Political economy was a division of scholarship first separated from philosophy during the period of mercantilism, when the close connection between the state and economic enterprise was assumed. The laissez-faire school of the nineteenth century, with its theory of the separation of business and state, buttressed by the distinction between public sovereignty and private property inherited from ancient and feudal law, spread the opinions which made it possible to conceive of the separate study of economic man and the problem of power. Separate departments for such study in universities perpetuated the distinction, but it has become increasingly difficult to deal with politics or economics without including the other. It is possible to separate the bibliography of the professional writers, but extremely difficult to classify in the same way the writings of the socialists. They saw a system, with materialist base and ideological superstructure. They proposed another system, or fragments of one, whose influence would cross the boundaries of the subjects set up by the schools. They could not discuss the problem of power without relating it to the goods and services which a capitalist government failed to distribute equitably and which a socialist government would presumably arrange according to ability and need. These selected general readings, therefore, will preserve the compartments created by the professions when dealing primarily with their writings. The special topics treat problems which have both economic and political implications.

The general point of view of the first American Marxist party under Daniel De Leon's leadership is contained in his *Speeches and Editorials* (New York, n.d., 2 vols.), a collection of his most important pamphlets published by the Socialist Labor Party press. The Marxian idea of the state and its role in economics as seen by his British followers is described in William Paul, *The State; Its Origin and Function* (Glasgow, 1918, 209 pp.). Ernest Untermann, translator of part of Marx's *Capital* for C. H. Kerr & Co., Chicago socialist publishers, takes the Socialist Party position in *The World's Revolutions* (Chicago, 1906, 176 pp.). Also representing the orthodox Marxists, but more clearly expressed, is L. B. Boudin, *The Theoretical System of Karl Marx* (Chicago, 1907, 286 pp.).

A. M. Simons, editor of the *International Socialist Review* from 1900 to 1908, J. A. Wayland and Fred Warren, editors of the widely circulated *Appeal to Reason,* and Oscar Ameringer, who edited a variety of Socialist Party papers in the Middle West between 1903 and World War II, principally *Labor World* (Duluth, Minn., etc., 1895-), and *American Guardian* (Oklahoma City, Okla., 1914-1942; 1914-1931 as *Oklahoma Leader*), had perhaps more weight in formulating prewar socialist opinion than the writers of books. Morris Hillquit, who with Ameringer held to the party through World War I, wrote the essentially Kautskyist *Socialism in Theory and Practice* (New York, 1909, 361 pp.; German tr. by Adolf Hepner, 1911), and revealed how the revolutionary ingredients of Marxism were softened in the American environment in "Marxism Essentially Evolutionary," *Current History,* xxix (Oct. 1928), pp. 29-35. John Spargo and W. E. Walling, who broke with the Socialist Party in 1917 over the war issue, were among the leading intellectuals writing on Marxian theory just before World War I. Spargo contributed *Socialism* (rev. ed., New York, 1909, 349 pp.), *Karl Marx; His Life and Work* (New York, 1910, 359 pp.), and *Social Democracy Explained; Theories and Tactics of Modern Socialism* (New York, 1918, 337 pp.). Walling's works, such as *Progressivism—and After* (New York, 1914, 406 pp.), expressed strong syndicalist sympathies. His pragmatic outlook in *The Larger Aspects of Socialism* (New York, 1913, 406 pp.), shows how Marxian views were modified by the American climate of opinion. For other socialist writings in political and economic theory during this period, see J. W. Hughan's bibliography in *American Socialism of the Present Day* (New York, 1911, 265 pp.), pp. 257-265; the unpublished study of D. A. Shannon, *Social and Economic Thought of Eugene V. Debs, the Socialist, 1897-1916* (1946); as well as the references in PART II, Topics 9-11.

After World War I the existence of Soviet Russia gave American Marxians an example of a socialist society with which to compare their theory.

Besides the works of Browder, Foster, and others (PART II, Topic 10),
Anna Rochester, *Capitalism and Progress* (New York, 1945, 111 pp.),
and also Avrom Landy, *Marxism and the Democratic Tradition* (New
York, 1946, 220 pp.), especially pp. 152-188, represent communist opinion. L. C. Fraina, a left-wing socialist who joined the Communist Party
in 1918, published, by authority of the Socialist Propaganda League, *Revolutionary Socialism; a Study in Socialist Reconstruction* (New York,
1918, 246 pp.). Although among the intellectuals supporting Foster in
1932, his critical writing on capitalism since then, under the name of Lewis
Corey, is more moderate and independent of communist or even socialist
doctrine. His chief studies are *The Decline of American Capitalism* (New
York, 1934, 622 pp.), an analysis of the theory of "crisisless" capitalism;
The Crisis of the Middle Class (New York, 1935, 379 pp.), and *The Unfinished Task; Economic Reconstruction for Democracy* (New York, 1942,
314 pp.). Max Eastman, once editor of the *Masses*, took a similar course
farther to the right. Aside from numerous works on Russian communism
and the translation of Marxian classics, he may be represented by his
Marx, Lenin and the Science of Revolution (London, 1926, 267 pp.).
H. W. Laidler and Norman Thomas continue to stand for gradualist
democratic socialism. The essential elements of their program are contained in *The Socialism of Our Times* (New York, 1929, 377 pp.), edited
by Laidler and Thomas; *Socialist Planning and a Socialist Program* (New
York, 1932, 255 pp.), edited by Laidler; Thomas, *America's Way Out; a
Program for Democracy* (New York, 1931, 324 pp.); and Laidler, *Socializing Our Democracy; a New Appraisal of Socialism* (New York, 1935,
330 pp.). See also Haim Kantorovitch, *Problems of Revolutionary Socialism* (New York, 1936, 34 pp.); John Putnam, *The Modern Case for
Socialism* (Boston, 1943, 179 pp.); Roger Payne and G. W. Hartmann,
Democratic Socialism (New York, 1948, 128 pp.). The recent study by
Leo Huberman, *The Truth about Socialism* (New York, 1950, 256 pp.),
is written from a point of view not unsympathetic to Soviet Russia, although Huberman—together with Paul Sweezy, his co-editor on the
Monthly Review—has since been reproved in the Communist Party periodical, *Political Affairs* (May 1951, pp. 34-53, article by Alexander Bittelman, "Where Is the 'Monthly Review' Going?").

Besides the theoretical party organs referred to in PART II, Topics 8-11,
the following independent periodicals contain articles on socialist political
and economic theory: *Partisan Review* (New York, 1934-); *Social Re-
search* (New York, 1934-); *Science & Society* (New York, 1936-);
Marxist Quarterly (New York, 1937); *Marxist Review* (San Francisco,
Chicago, 1937-1940; title varies); *Politics* (New York, 1944-1949); *Modern
Review* (New York, 1947-1950); *Monthly Review*, (New York, 1949-).
Also see the pamphlets issued by the League for Industrial Democracy.

A. ECONOMIC THEORY. Among the recent surveys of economic thought are Erich Roll, *A History of Economic Thought* (New York, 1939, 430 pp.), written with the assumption that economic interests condition economic theories; E. R. Sikes, *Contemporary Economic Systems; Their Analysis and Historical Background* (New York, 1940, 690 pp.); and Eduard Heimann, *History of Economic Doctrines; an Introduction to Economic Theory* (New York, 1945, 263 pp.), which devotes some attention to socialist ideas (pp. 135-167) but practically none to American socialist theories. No one has devoted so much space to nineteenth-century socialist theory as Heinrich Herkner, *Die Arbeiterfrage* (1894; 7th ed., Berlin, 1921, 2 vols.), II, *Soziale Theorien und Parteien*, with full bibliographical references, or Charles Gide and Charles Rist, *A History of Economic Doctrines from the Time of the Physiocrats to the Present Day* (1909; tr. from 2nd ed. by R. Richards; Boston, 1915, 672 pp.), pp. 198-264 (Saint-Simon, Owen, Fourier, and Blanc), pp. 290-321 (Proudhon), pp. 407-514 (Rodbertus, Lassalle, and Marx, Christian socialism); and pp. 558-642 (rent theories, solidarists, anarchists). But this volume likewise finds little to say about any Americans except Henry George. Joseph Dorfman, *The Economic Mind in American Civilization* (New York, 1946-1949, 3 vols.), is in many respects a pioneer study. The first two volumes, covering the period 1606-1865, although often undiscriminating, with confused organization and few critical comments, are nevertheless invaluable for their summaries of a great deal of obscure literature. The third volume treats the more familiar period, 1865-1918. See also A. G. Gruchy, *Modern Economic Thought; the American Contribution* (New York, 1947, 670 pp.), especially chap. 2, which relates Veblen to Marx.

There are occasional references to the ECONOMICS OF SOCIALISM in Marx's writings. Most of them are scattered through Volume 1 of *Capital* (1867; tr. from 3rd German ed. by Samuel Moore and Edward Aveling; London, 1887, 2 vols.); throughout Marx's correspondence with Engels, published in the *Gesamtausgabe* (see PART I, General Reading, p. 34), and in Friedrich Engels and Karl Marx, *Selected Correspondence, 1846-1895* (tr. and ed. by Dona Torr; New York, 1942, 551 pp.); and throughout Marx's *Critique of the Gotha Programme* (New York, 1938, 116 pp.). See also, for the problem of allocation of resources under socialism, Engels, *Herr Eugen Dühring's Revolution in Science* (1877; tr. by Emile Burns and ed. by C. P. Dutt; New York, 1935, 364 pp.; Pt. 2, chap. 10, was written by Marx). See also Leo Rogin, "Marx and Engels on Distribution in a Socialist Society," *American Economic Review*, XXXV (Mar. 1945), pp. 137-143; M. M. Bober, "Marx and Economic Calculation," *ibid.*, XXXVI (June 1946), pp. 344-357; and Henry Smith, "Marx as a Pure Economist," *Economic History*, IV (Feb. 1939), pp. 245-258. Smith concludes that Marx did not think his labor theory of value was really a theory of value

at all. The key to Marx's economics, he says, is neither his Hegelian training, nor his debt to the classical economists, nor his tremendous erudition,
but his common sense, which enabled him to build a rough yet "water-
tight" theory of the business cycle.

For other discussions in the Marxist tradition on the problems of socialism, see Karl Kautsky's lecture, "On the Day after the Social Revolution," published as the second part of the booklet *The Social Revolution*
(tr. by A. M. and M. W. Simons; Chicago, 1903, 189 pp.). See also
Leon Trotsky's work, starting off, perhaps, with his succinct little essay,
Soviet Economy in Danger (New York, 1933, 67 pp.). For Lenin's ideas
on resources allocation, see especially *The State and Revolution* (1918;
rev. ed., Moscow, 1935, 140 pp.). Relevant in this study for the period
immediately after the initial Russian revolution is the work of another
leading Bolshevist theorist, N. I. Bukharin; see his *Building Up Socialism*,
the translation of *Ekonomika perekhodnago perioda* (London, 1926, 66
pp.). Samples of the flood of reports on Soviet economy during the thirties
are those by Emile Burns, *Russia's Productive System* (New York, 1930, 288
pp.), H. F. Ward, *In Place of Profit; Social Incentives in the Soviet Union*
(New York, 1933, 460 pp.), and Michael Polanyi, *U.S.S.R. Economics;
Fundamental Data, System and Spirit* (Manchester, Eng., 1936, 25 pp.).
For a comment on the status of Marxian doctrines in the Soviet today,
see the article "Teaching of Economics in the Soviet Union" (translated
from Russian), *American Economic Review*, xxxiv (Sept. 1944), pp. 501-
530, and the series of comments following it by Raya Dunayevskaya, P. A.
Baran, Oskar Lange, Leo Rogin, and Brooks Otis. Alexander Baykov,
The Development of the Soviet Economic System (Cambridge, Eng.,
1946, 514 pp.), is one of the best general treatments of Soviet economy
extending into World War II. For the point of view of the Fabians in
England see G. D. H. Cole, *Socialist Economics* (London, 1950, 158 pp.),
written at the request of the Fabian Society.

But the most systematic organized discussion of the economics of socialism has come from orthodox economists, not from Marxists. A body of
literature on the subject emerged, through a more or less continuous
polemical development from the end of the nineteenth century, on the
issue of the possibility of rational allocation of resources under socialism.
The essential arguments against this possibility are contained in the collection of essays, edited with introduction and concluding essay by F. A.
Hayek, *Collectivist Economic Planning; Critical Studies on the Possibilities of Socialism by N. G. Pierson, Ludwig von Mises, Georg Halm,
and Enrico Barone* (London, 1935, 293 pp.). For the opposing view, see
first Oskar Lange and F. M. Taylor, *On the Economic Theory of Socialism*
(ed. by B. E. Lippincott; Minneapolis, Minn., 1938, 143 pp.), which in
the following decade was the more widely held of the two views. The

most important essay in this volume is by Oskar Lange, first published in the *Review of Economic Studies*, IV (Oct. 1936), pp. 53-71, (Feb. 1937), pp. 123-142. Later scholarship in related fields indicated that the question was not closed, but was susceptible of treatment on the basis of theories not hitherto advanced by either side.

One of the first to raise the issue was the Austrian economist Friedrich von Wieser. In his most important book, possibly, *Der natürliche Werth* (Vienna, 1889, 239 pp.), tr. by C. A. Malloch as *Natural Value* (London, 1893, 243 pp.), and in "Theorie der gesellschaftlichen Wirtschaft," *Grundriss der Sozialökonomik*, I (1914), pp. 125-444, tr. as *Social Economics* by A. F. Hinrichs (New York, 1927, 470 pp.), von Wieser advanced the proposition that the method of value calculation is essentially the same under communism and under capitalism. He said not only that economic theory would apply to a communist state, but also that "many a theorist has written the theory of value of communism without knowing it." Soon after, Vilfredo Pareto in his *Cours d'économie politique* (Lausanne, 1896-1897, 2 vols.), II, pp. 364ff., made the claim that economic theory is an abstract tool separate from, and to be applied to, any set of institutions, capitalistic or socialistic. The Dutch economist N. G. Pierson became interested in the question and in 1902 wrote the essay which has been translated into English as "The Problem of Value in the Socialist Community" and published in F. A. Hayek, ed., *Collectivist Economic Planning* (cited above), pp. 41-85. Pierson's doubts were so challengingly stated that Karl Kautsky, then the leading Marxian theoretician, felt obliged to reply to them. He did so in a lecture given in Delft on April 24, 1902, "On the Day after the Social Revolution," cited above. Kautsky's lecture is significant as being one of the few programmatic statements by Marxists as to what the economic workings presumably would be in the socialist state. But the first demonstration of how economic principles might be applied to socialism was done by an orthodox economist, Enrico Barone. Barone actually was a military officer, but as a student of Pareto's, following up Pareto's suggestion, he attempted to apply mathematically the concepts of neoclassical economics to the collectivist society. "The Ministry of Production in the Collectivist State," a translation of his article published in Italian in 1908, appears in F. A. Hayek, ed., *Collectivist Economic Planning*, pp. 245-290. Next to show how orthodox economic concepts are applicable to a socialist economy was Gustav Cassel. By no means a socialist himself, Cassel made a considerable contribution to the theoretical formulation of a socialist economics with the developments in *The Theory of Social Economy* (1918; 5th German ed. tr. by S. L. Barron; New York, 1932, 708 pp.).

After World War I these more or less preliminary discussions aroused wider interest. A debate, centered in Germany, was provoked by the critical attacks of Max Weber and Ludwig von Mises. See Weber's principal work, *The Theory of Social and Economic Organization* (tr. by A. M. Henderson and Talcott Parsons; New York, 1947, 436 pp.); also Weber's *Der Sozialismus* (Vienna, 1918, 36 pp.; also published in *Gesammelte Aufsätze zur Soziologie und Sozialpolitik*, Tübingen, 1924). Mises' attack came with the article, "Economic Calculation in the Socialist Commonwealth," published in F. A. Hayek, ed., *Collectivist Economic Planning* (cited above), pp. 87-130, and with his book, *Socialism; an Economic and Sociological Analysis* (1922; tr. by J. Kahane; New York, 1936, 528 pp.). Mises' book, *Bureaucracy* (New Haven, Conn., 1944, 125 pp.), is essentially a recapitulation of certain ideas in the earlier work. For an early criticism of Mises' ideas, see Jacob Marschak's article, "Wirtschaftsrechnung und Gemeinwirtschaft," in *Archiv für Sozialwissenschaft und Sozialpolitik*, LI (1924), pp. 501-520. Adding to the theoretical part of the Weber and Mises argument was the article by Georg Halm called "Further Considerations on the Possibility of Adequate Calculation in a Socialist Community," in Hayek's *Collectivist Economic Planning*, pp. 131-200. Robert Liefmann wrote *Geschichte und Kritik des Sozialismus* (2nd ed., Leipzig, 1923, 182 pp.), but this was mainly an elaboration of the criticism that had already been developed.

Used as an indication of the empirical validity of these theories was the work of Boris Brutzkus, *Economic Planning in Soviet Russia* (tr. from the German by Gilbert Gardiner; foreword by F. A. Hayek; London, 1935, 234 pp.). Part 1 of the book, "The Doctrines of Marxism in the Light of the Russian Revolution," was written in 1920; that is, before Brutzkus, out of sympathy with the economic program, left Russia. This part is an analysis of the problems of "natural" (defined as nonmonetary) socialism; while Part 2, "The Results of Economic Planning in Russia," written in 1934, is a criticism of "monetary" socialism in the light of the intervening history of Russian socialism.

Socialists did not ignore the problem of pricing, and in addition to the discussions of the Russians, the social democrats of other countries outlined answers. Sidney and Beatrice Webb, *A Constitution for the Socialist Commonwealth of Great Britain* (London, 1920, 364 pp.), represented the ideas of the Fabian socialists on the problem of pricing. In the United States, H. W. Laidler wrote an article which set forth the ideas of American socialists of a similar type; see the symposium, *The Socialism of Our Times*, edited by Laidler and Norman Thomas (New York, 1929, 377 pp.).

On the academic side, the replies to the attacks on the possibility of rational calculation in socialism also started to gain momentum around 1929. In that year F. M. Taylor published his presidential address to the forty-first annual meeting of the American Economic Association, "The Guidance of Production in a Socialist State," in the *American Economic*

Review, xix (Mar. 1929), pp. 1-8; reprinted in Lange and Taylor, *On the Economic Theory of Socialism*, cited above, pp. 30-54.

Continuing the reply to the criticism of socialist-planning possibilities, Carl Landauer in Germany published his big work, *Planwirtschaft und Verkehrswirtschaft* (Munich, 1931, 222 pp.). This author's later work, *Theory of National Economic Planning* (Berkeley, Calif., 1944, 189 pp.), opposes the position of Hayek and Robbins that the computational problem of socialist economic administration cannot be solved. Instead of the trial and error solution of the market, state planning provides at least a proximate solution. This idea recurs in Barbara Wootton, *Freedom under Planning* (Chapel Hill, N.C., 1945, 180 pp.). Also in Germany, Georg Klein wrote *System eines idealistischen Sozialismus* (Vienna, 1931, 294 pp.). In England, H. D. Dickinson started the discussion of the economics of socialism with an article called "Price Formation in a Socialist Community," *Economic Journal*, xliii (June 1933), pp. 237-250. The next year A. P. Lerner followed up Dickinson's discussion with his article, "Economic Theory and Socialist Economy," *Review of Economic Studies*, ii (Oct. 1934), pp. 51-61. See also Lerner's later work, *The Economics of Control* (New York, 1944, 428 pp.). In the same line of development, but using the techniques of mathematical economics, was the article by Ragnar Frisch, "Circulation Planning; Proposal for a National Organization of a Commodity and Service Exchange," *Econometrica*, ii (July 1934), pp. 258-336, (Oct. 1934), pp. 422-435.

Lange and Taylor's volume, referred to above, was Volume 2 of the series *Government Control of the Economic Order*, Volume 1 of which (ed. by B. E. Lippincott; Minneapolis, Minn., 1935, 119 pp.; issued with general series title only), consists of a collection of essays on four topics. The question of the necessity of some form of control in the United States is taken up by G. C. Means; the economic limitation of controls is handled by Gerhard Colm; control in foreign countries is discussed by Emil Lederer, Walter Thompson, and Otto Nathan; and the question of the political form necessary to facilitate control is taken up by John Thurston and Arthur Feiler. F. A. Hayek renewed the attack by editing *Collectivist Economic Planning*, cited above, while Lionel Robbins had anticipated many of Hayek's comments in *The Great Depression* (London, 1934, 238 pp.). The debate had also been well summarized by a Harvard undergraduate, W. C. Roper, Jr., *The Problem of Pricing in a Socialist State* (Cambridge, Mass., 1931, 71 pp.). The American A. R. Sweezy contributed "The Economist in a Socialist Economy," in *Explorations in Economics; Notes and Essays Contributed in Honor of F. W. Taussig* (New York, 1936, 539 pp.), pp. 422-433. The leading English advocate of Marxian economics, M. H. Dobb, wrote "Economic Theory and the Problems of a Socialist Economy," *Economic Journal*, xliii (Dec. 1933), pp.

588-598, and, with H. C. Stevens, "Excursus to Chapter Five: on Money and Economic Accounting," in *Russian Economic Development since the Revolution* (New York, 1928, 415 pp.), pp. 166-181. See also two survey articles, Robert Mossé, "The Theory of Planned Economy; a Study of Some Recent Works," *International Labour Review*, xxxvi (Sept. 1937), pp. 371-393, also in *Plan Age*, iii (Oct. 1937), pp. 193-208; and Eduard Heimann, "Literature on the Theory of a Socialist Economy," *Social Research*, vi (Feb. 1939), pp. 88-113. Heimann maintains that the differences between socialist and capitalist economy are in social arrangements and psychological incentives, not in purely economic issues. Later publications include K. Ostrovityanov, "Basic Laws of Development of Socialist Economy," *Science & Society*, ix (Summer 1945), pp. 232-251, and B. P. Beckwith, *The Economic Theory of a Socialist Economy* (Stanford, Calif., 1949, 444 pp.).

The question whether economic planning under socialism does not inevitably entail dictatorship brings the economists and political scientists together in their writings on the subject, and increasingly attracts the attention of writers in diverse fields. Douglas Jay, in *The Socialist Case* (London, 1937, 362 pp.), believes that traditional democratic methods can transfer private unearned incomes to the community and mitigate poverty and inequality without too great a loss of economic freedom. On the journalistic level, W. H. Chamberlin, formerly an ardent sympathizer in the Russian experiment, decided from observations in Germany and Russia that "Socialism cannot be a road to plenty because it cannot be a road to freedom" (p. 227), and reported his disillusionment in *Collectivism; a False Utopia* (New York, 1937, 265 pp.). F. A. Hayek, *The Road to Serfdom* (Chicago, 1944, 250 pp.), drawing from observations of central European social democracy and fascism rather than Anglo-American examples, reached the same conclusion. K. R. Popper, *The Open Society and Its Enemies* (rev. ed., Princeton, N.J., 1950, 732 pp.), especially pp. 274-463, treats the problem of utopian versus piecemeal social engineering against the philosophical background of an attack on historicism. He regards Marx as having developed historicism—the view that through the study of history one can prophesy—in its purest form, out of the philosophy of Plato and Hegel. The corollaries of historicist thinking are Fascist according to Popper. Among the growing literature in defense of democratic planning are Herman Finer, *Road to Reaction* (Boston, 1945, 228 pp.); Wootton, *Freedom under Planning*, cited above; and Ferdynand Zweig, *The Planning of Free Societies* (London, 1942, 267 pp.). A recent investigation of the problem is Karl Mannheim, *Freedom, Power, and Democratic Planning* (New York, 1950, 384 pp.), which was prepared posthumously from the unpublished manuscripts of the famous sociologist, and which calls for a society planned yet democratic. H. W. Laidler has projected a study of the subject. For further materials, see Topic 11.

The Marxian theory of the ECONOMICS OF CAPITALISM is discussed principally in the General Reading of PART I and Topics 1-3 below. For European Marxian theory see first Ludwig Elster, ed., *Wörterbuch der Volkswirtschaft* (4th ed., Jena, 1931-1933, 3 vols. in 5), especially the articles by Carl Grünberg and Henryk Grossmann on leading theorists and on such subjects as "Sozialistische Ideen und Lehren, I: Sozialismus und Kommunismus," III, pp. 272-341, an excellent survey. The *Handwörterbuch der Staatswissenschaften* (4th ed., ed. by Ludwig Elster and others; Jena, 1923-1929, 8 vols. and supp.), has long articles, and is especially valuable for its bibliographies. See also Eugen Dühring, *Kritische Geschichte der Nationalökonomie und des Socialismus* (2nd ed., Berlin, 1875, 595 pp.); *Wiener staats- und rechtswissenschaftliche Studien* (Vienna, etc., 1898-1937), ed. by Hans Kelsen; Felix Meiner, ed., *Die Volkswirtschaftslehre der Gegenwart in Selbstdarstellungen* (Leipzig, 1924-1929, 2 vols.); Karl Kautsky, *The Economic Doctrines of Karl Marx* (tr. by H. J. Stenning; New York, 1936, 252 pp.); A. A. Malinovsky (A. Bogdanoff, pseud.), *A Short Course of Economic Science* (rev. by S. M. Dvolaitsky; tr. by J. Fineberg; London, 1923, 391 pp.); Henryk Grossmann, *Das Akkumulations- und Zusammenbruchsgesetz des kapitalistischen Systems (zugleich eine Krisentheorie)* (Leipzig, 1929, 628 pp.); Natalie Moszkowska, *Das marxsche System; ein Beitrag zu dessen Ausbau* (Berlin, 1929, 190 pp.); John Strachey, *The Coming Struggle for Power* (New York, 1935, 412 pp.); M. H. Dobb, *Studies in the Development of Capitalism* (London, 1946, 396 pp.). The Englishwoman Joan Robinson in *An Essay on Marxian Economics* (London, 1942, 121 pp.) discovered a source of her Keynesian theory which is common to Marxism, and showed both a dissatisfaction with orthodox economics and a brilliant dissection of Marxian theory, in which she found much to praise. See also the Russian communist manual by L. A. Leontyev, *Political Economy; a Beginner's Course* (New York, 1935, 285 pp.), and *Marx's "Capital"* (New York, 1946, 160 pp.) by the same author, which relates the circumstances of the composition of *Capital*, Engels' part, and its significance today. Eugen von Böhm-Bawerk, *Karl Marx and the Close of His System* (tr. by A. M. Macdonald; London, 1898, 221 pp.), is the classic work of the Austrian school to which anti-Marxians have ever since been indebted. See also the criticism of Tugan-Baranovsky, *Modern Socialism in Its Historical Development* (tr. by M. I. Redmount; London, 1910, 232 pp.). For a general comparison of capitalism and socialism see PART I, Topic 5.

Socialist influence in American economic thought began about 1880, says L. H. Haney in "Der Einfluss des Sozialismus auf die Volkswirtschaftslehre," *Archiv für die Geschichte des Sozialismus und der Arbeiter-*

bewegung, III (1913), pp. 463-480. For the American contribution before World War I, see, for example, C. H. Vail, *Principles of Scientific Social-ism* (New York, 1899, 237 pp.); Daniel De Leon, *Vulgar Economy, or a Critical Analyst of Marx Analyzed* (New York, 1914, 53 pp.) and *Marx on Mallock; or, Facts vs. Fiction* (New York, 1908, 31 pp.); W. T. Mills, *The Struggle for Existence* (Chicago, 1904, 640 pp.); Ernest Untermann, *Marxian Economics* (Chicago, 1907, 252 pp.); Frederick Haller, *Why the Capitalist? A Refutation of the Doctrines Prevailing in Conventional Politi-cal Economy* (Buffalo, N.Y., 1914, 277 pp.); and I. G. Savoy and M. O. Teck, *The A B C of Socialism (Including the A B C of Economics)* (Bos-ton, 1915, 140 pp.). Vail was essentially a Christian socialist. The Canadian scholar O. D. Skelton was the object of De Leon's first attack. Mallock, the object of his second, was a widely-read English antisocialist. Mills was preoccupied with refuting the social Darwinians; Untermann was a philosophical disciple of Dietzgen, and produced a muddled effort difficult to read. Haller's book is a series of miscellaneous essays, and Savoy and Teck's, a propaganda text.

For the recent literature, see the report of the opening session of the December 1937 meeting of the American Economic Association, devoted to the significance of Marxian economics, published in the association's *Papers and Proceedings*, a supplement to the *American Economic Re-view*, XXVIII (Mar. 1938), pp. 1-22, particularly the paper by Leo Rogin. During World War II, R. A. Brady published *Business as a System of Power* (New York, 1943, 340 pp.), which shows Marxian influence. W. J. Blech (W. J. Blake, pseud.), *An American Looks at Karl Marx* (New York, 1939, 746 pp.), also published in a text edition as *Elements of Marxian Economic Theory and Its Criticism*, was written by a business-man rather than a professional economist. It has a lively style and a sympathetic approach, but is poorly organized, and is most valuable for its excellent bibliographical material. P. M. Sweezy provided a compre-hensive analysis in *The Theory of Capitalist Development* (New York, 1942, 398 pp.), and a select bibliography. J. A. Schumpeter, *Capitalism, Socialism, and Democracy* (New York, 1942, 381 pp.), makes one of the best defenses of capitalist economy, but concludes that it is on its way to defeat. More than two-thirds of the book is devoted to the history and analysis of socialism and its relation to democracy. Schumpeter's work receives attention in Eduard Heimann's article, "Recent Literature on Economic Systems," *Social Research*, XIII (Mar. 1946), pp. 103-116, a bibliographical article. A later survey is S. J. Patel, "Marxism and Recent Economic Thought," *Science & Society*, XI (Winter 1947), pp. 52-65. This Marxian periodical has been curiously weak in articles by Americans on economic theory. See also an obscure variety of doctrinaire exposition, John Keracher, *Economics for Beginners* (Chicago, 1935, 40 pp.).

Among the host of hostile critics of Marxian economics in the United States, see O. D. Skelton, *Socialism; a Critical Analysis* (Cambridge, Mass., 1911, 329 pp.), with a good bibliography. Also see, among others, J. E. Le Rossignol's first attack, *Orthodox Socialism* (New York, 1907, 147 pp.), published in virtually a revised edition as *What Is Socialism?* (New York, 1921, 267 pp.), and his latest, *From Marx to Stalin; a Critique of Communism* (New York, 1940, 442 pp.); H. B. Parkes, *Marxism; an Autopsy* (Boston, 1939, 299 pp.); and J. K. Turner, *Challenge to Karl Marx* (New York, 1941, 455 pp.).

B. POLITICAL THEORY. Samples of Marx's writings which apply particularly to political tactics are his contemporary studies of the French uprising in 1848 and its suppression. See first the following titles by Marx and Engels cited in full in PART I, pp. 36-37: *Die deutsche Ideologie*, the *Communist Manifesto*, and *Critique of the Gotha Programme*. See also, Engels' *Ludwig Feuerbach* (cited above in PART III, Topic 1), and Marx, *The Paris Commune* (New York, 1902, 117 pp.). *Die Klassenkämpfe in Frankreich, 1848 bis 1850* (Berlin, 1895, 112 pp.) was written in 1850. A translation by Henry Kuhn of the Socialist Labor Party was published as *The Class Struggles in France, 1848-1850* (New York, 1924, 207 pp.). The German edition is important for its place in the controversy between the gradualists and the revolutionaries, for Engels' introduction seemed to indicate his shift, at the end of his life, to Bernstein's evolutionary position. *Who Are the Falsifiers?* (New York, 1926, 28 pp.), compiled from the *Weekly People*, is a polemical criticism by the Socialist Labor Party of the communist translation of Engels' introduction on the issue of revolutionary tactics. International Publishers' edition (New York, 1934, 159 pp.), which includes the full text of Engels' introduction, indicates that he had not become a gradualist. *The Eighteenth Brumaire of Louis Bonaparte* (tr. by Daniel De Leon, New York, 1898, 78 pp.; 3rd ed., Chicago, 1913, 160 pp.; tr. by E. and C. Paul, London, 1926, 192 pp.) first appeared in German in *Die Revolution*, edited by Joseph Weydemeyer, at New York in May 1852. Engels' article, "Über das Autoritätsprinzip," edited and translated by D. Ryazanov (pseud.) in *Neue Zeit*, xxxii, Pt. 1 (Oct. 10, 1913), pp. 37-39, originally written against the anarchists in the First International and published in 1873 as "Dell' Autorità," in the Italian publication *Almanaco repubblicano*, agrees with the anarchists on the ultimate end of the state but differs on its interim use. Engels' *Socialism; Utopian and Scientific* (tr. by Edward Aveling; London, 1892, 117 pp.), chapters from *Anti-Dühring*, contains a development of this theme and the theory of the class basis of the state. His *The Origin of the Family, Private Property and the State* (1884; tr. by Ernest Untermann; Chicago, 1905, 217 pp.) applies the evolutionary hypothesis of L. H. Morgan's *Ancient Society* as modified by historical materialism, and incorporates Marx's notes on Morgan, a pioneer American anthropologist. Marx's and Engels' theory of the state, however, does not depend on an anthropology the principles of which have since been considerably modified. It rests on their analysis of historical and contemporary states and appeared piecemeal in their other writings.

A good deal of European Marxian political theory received little attention in the United States before 1930. See, for example, Alfred Jourdan, *Du Rôle de l'état dans l'ordre économique, ou, Économie politique et socialisme* (Paris, 1882, 419 pp.); Anton Menger, *L'État socialiste* (tr. by E. Milhaud; Paris, 1904, 385 pp.); Friedrich Lenz, *Staat und Marxismus* (Stuttgart, 1921, 176 pp.); Hans Kelsen, *Sozialismus und Staat* (2nd ed., Leipzig, 1923, 208 pp.); Max Adler, *Kant und der Marxismus* (Berlin, 1925, 247 pp.); Luigi dal Pane, *Brevi note intorno alla concezione marxistica dello stato* (Faenza, 1924, 196 pp.); Carlo Rosselli, *Socialisme libéral* (tr. by Stefan Priacel; Paris, 1930, 195 pp.; Spanish ed., Buenos Aires, 1944, 169 pp.); and M. van der Goes van Naters, *Socialistische Staatsvernieuwing* (Arnhem, 1937, 122 pp.).

As for non-Marxian political theory, American Fourierists were nearly through their experiments when Victor Considérant, *The Difficulty Solved; or, The Government of the People by Themselves* (London, 1851, 80 pp.), was published in English. Ex-communitarians like Gronlund were probably aware of J. B. A. Godin, *La Gouvernement; ce qu'il a été, ce qu'il doit être et le vrai socialisme en action* (Paris, 1883, 568 pp.), a semi-Fourierist treatise by the founder of a *familistère* at Guise. American anarchists eventually read P. A. Kropotkin, *Law and Authority* (London, 1886, 23 pp.). R. R. La Monte translated Gabriel Deville, *The State and Socialism* (New York, 1900, 45 pp.).

American socialists drew most heavily upon Eduard Bernstein, *Evolutionary Socialism* (1899; tr. by E. C. Harvey; New York, 1909, 224 pp.), and especially the works of Karl Kautsky, who later reacted against bolshevism and shifted toward gradualism. Compare his *The Social Revolution* (1902; tr. by A. M. and M. W. Simons; Chicago, 1905, 189 pp.), *The Road to Power* (tr. by A. M. Simons; Chicago, 1909, 127 pp.), and *The Class Struggle (Erfurt Program)* (1892; tr. by W. E. Bohn; Chicago, 1910, 217 pp.), with *The Dictatorship of the Proletariat* (1918; tr. by H. J. Stenning; Manchester, Eng., 1919, 149 pp.), *Terrorism and Communism; a Contribution to the Natural History of Revolution* (1919; tr. by W. H. Kerridge; London, 1920, 234 pp.), *The Labour Revolution* (1921; tr. by H. J. Stenning; London, 1925, 287 pp.), and *Social Democracy versus Communism* (ed. by David Shub; tr. by Joseph Shaplen; New York, 1946, 142 pp.). The last title contains a selection of Kautsky's writings during the last few years of his life.

The communist reply to Kautsky is most pointed in Trotsky, *Dictatorship vs. Democracy (Terrorism and Communism)* (1920; New York, 1922, 191 pp.), and Lenin, *The Proletarian Revolution and Renegade Kautsky* (1918; New York, 1934, 110 pp.). The twentieth-century Marxian classic in political theory is Lenin, *The State and Revolution; the Marxist Doctrine of the State and the Tasks of the Proletariat in the Revolution* (1917; rev. ed., Moscow, 1935, 140 pp.). See also Lenin, *What Is to Be Done?* (New York, 1929, 175 pp.), reprinted from *The Iskra Period* in Lenin's *Collected Works*, IV, Bk. 2, and *"Left-Wing" Communism; an Infantile Disorder* (New York, 1934, 95 pp.), a translation based upon the text published in Volume 25 of the Russian edition of his *Collected Works*. For Russian political theory see N. I. Bukharin and E. A. Preobrazhensky, *The A B C of Communism* (1919; tr. by E. and C. Paul; London, 1922, 422 pp.), and Stalin's commentary, *Leninism* (1926; London, 1940, 667 pp., and other editions).

An American study, Julian Towster, *Political Power in the U.S.S.R., 1917-1947; the Theory and Structure of Government in the Soviet State* (New York, 1948, 443 pp.), is an authoritative analysis written with scholarly objectivity. Also see Barrington Moore, Jr., *Soviet Politics—the Dilemma of Power* (Cambridge, Mass., 1950, 503 pp.), which stresses the role of ideas in social change. Both authors are noncommunists.

British exposition of revolutionary socialism is summed up in R. P. Dutt, *The Political and Social Doctrine of Communism* (London, 1938, 44 pp.). H. J. Laski, one of the most prolific and shifting of Labour Party theorists, who enjoyed a wide American audience, may be represented by his *Authority in the Modern State* (New Haven, Conn., 1919, 398 pp.); *A Grammar of Politics* (London, 1925, 672 pp.); *Communism* (New York, 1927, 256 pp.), and *The State in Theory and Practice* (New York, 1935, 299 pp.). J. R. MacDonald, *Parliament and Revolution* (New York, 1920, 180 pp.), and *Parliament and Democracy* (London, 1920, 75 pp.), reveal a right-wing socialist's reactions to bolshevism in a postwar world. H. A. Taine, "Socialism as Government," *Contemporary Review*, XLVI (Oct. 1884), pp. 507-531; E. C. K. Gonner, *The Socialist State, Its Nature, Aims and Conditions, Being an Introduction to the Study of Socialism* (London, 1895, 251 pp.); C. E. M. Joad, *Introduction to Modern Political Theory* (Oxford, 1924, 127 pp.), especially pp. 39-123, are additional expositions published in England of the socialist alternatives to the capitalist state. See also R. G. Hawtrey, *Economic Aspects of Sovereignty* (New York, 1930, 162 pp.).

General surveys of political and social theory by Americans do not devote much attention to socialism. W. A. Dunning, *A History of Political Theories from Rousseau to Spencer* (New York, 1920, 446 pp.), devotes one chapter to "societarian" theory (pp. 340-408) with very little on

Marx. J. P. Lichtenberger, *Development of Social Theory* (New York, 1923, 482 pp.), pp. 291-302, discusses Marx as a contemporary of Darwin; G. H. Sabine, *A History of Political Theory* (New York, 1937, 797 pp.), pp. 682-746, discusses Marx and Lenin; and R. M. MacIver, *Community* (London, 1917, 437 pp.), influenced the guild-socialist theory of G. D. H. Cole. Studies of recent thought, such as the symposium edited by J. S. Roucek, *Twentieth Century Political Thought* (New York, 1946, 657 pp.), chaps. 1-2 and *passim*, are not much more detailed; F. W. Coker, *Recent Political Thought* (New York, 1934, 574 pp.), pp. 35-287, is the principal exception. W. Y. Elliott, *The Pragmatic Revolt in Politics; Syndicalism, Fascism and the Constitutional State* (New York, 1928, 540 pp.), devotes a chapter each to guild socialism and to Georges Sorel and the general-strike myth. See also M. H. Lin, *Antistatism* (Washington, 1939, 87 pp.), a comparative study in political philosophy which includes both the communists and the anarchists; and Oscar Jászi, "The Marxian Paradox," in his Oberlin lectures, *Democracy Is Different* (New York, 1941, 230 pp.), pp. 34-55. A brief guide to social theory for the ordinary citizen is Louis Wasserman, *Modern Political Philosophies and What They Mean* (Philadelphia, 1944, 287 pp.). This book is a revision of the author's *Handbook of Political "Isms"* (New York, 1941, 147 pp.), with good selected bibliographies. See also the earlier text by the avowed liberal democrat J. A. Leighton, *Social Philosophies in Conflict; Fascism & Nazism, Communism, Liberal Democracy* (New York, 1937, 546 pp.), especially pp. 56-140, 365-433, which generally agrees with the democratic socialists. William Ebenstein, *Man and the State* (New York, 1947, 781 pp.), a collection of documents, contains useful bibliographies and commentary. A balanced critique by an American philosopher is M. R. Cohen, "Socialism and Capitalism," in *The Faith of a Liberal* (New York, 1946, 497 pp.), pp. 93-109. W. M. Thomas, a specialist in Hindu philosophy, has correlated the ideas of Dewey, Marx, and Sankara, the Hindu classical philosopher, in *A Democratic Philosophy* (New York, 1938, 148 pp.). He concludes that instrumental liberalism, socialism, and scientific theism all contribute to the foundations of democratic theory. Among the histories of American political theory the same neglect of socialist ideas prevails. C. E. Merriam, *American Political Ideas* (New York, 1920, 481 pp.), chaps. 11-12, and E. R. Lewis, *A History of American Political Thought from the Civil War to the World War* (New York, 1937, 561 pp.), are the most useful on socialism.

For the purpose of understanding the economic and constitutional bases of capitalist power, the following will serve as an introduction: Justice H. B. Brown, "The Distribution of Property," American Bar Association, *Report of the . . . Annual Meeting*, xvi (1893), pp. 213-242; A. T. Hadley, "The Constitutional Position of Property in the United States," *Inde-*

pendent, LXIV (Apr. 16, 1908), pp. 834-838; J. R. Commons, *Legal Foundations of Capitalism* (New York, 1924, 394 pp.); A. A. Berle, Jr., and G. C. Means, *The Modern Corporation and Private Property* (New York, 1932, 396 pp.); and David Lynch, *The Concentration of Economic Power* (New York, 1946, 423 pp.).

The only detailed general work by a nonsocialist in America on socialist political theory is S. H. M. Chang, *The Marxian Theory of the State* (Philadelphia, 1931, 230 pp.). This doctoral dissertation in *economics* discards revisionism and the "orthodoxy" of Kautsky and the German social democrats and fits Leninism into the Marxian tradition. Other useful distinctions and comparisons in this treatise are Chang's identification of anarchist and socialist views of the millennial society, his distinction between the monistic historical materialism of Marxians and the more widely accepted, pluralistic, economic interpretation of history, and the dictatorship of the proletariat regarded as a form of state rather than of government. Chang was a Chinese small landowner who participated in Sun-Yat-Sen's revolution. His property was confiscated by the Chinese communists and his mother died as a result of their occupation of Changsha just after he had finished the monograph. Yet his exposition is dehydrated and mechanical; he takes refuge in quotations and limits the expression of his own judgment to a short concluding section; and he deals almost entirely with European theorists. See also A. W. Calhoun, *The Worker Looks at Government* (New York, 1927, 176 pp.), a product of the author's teaching at Brookwood Labor College.

One of the most original native efforts to build a theory of the state as the instrument of the ruling class was Randolph Bourne's unfinished study written just before his death in 1918, "Unfinished Fragment on the State" in *Untimely Papers* (New York, 1919, 230 pp.), pp. 140-230. By training and practice a literary critic, he showed little knowledge of the literature of political theory, Marxian or otherwise. By conviction a philosophical pacifist, he emphasized as Marxians did not the power of the state, its potential totalitarianism, and the essential function of war in the preservation of sovereignty. A discussion of this fragment is found in the first of Max Lerner's Stafford Little lectures at Princeton in 1940, "Randolph Bourne and Two Generations," published in Lerner's *Ideas for the Ice Age* (New York, 1941, 432 pp.), pp. 116-142. Alyse Gregory has a study of Bourne in progress. Thorstein Veblen, "The Socialist Economics of Karl Marx and his Followers," *Quarterly Journal of Economics*, xx (Aug. 1906), pp. 575-595, and xxi (Feb. 1907), pp. 299-322, and M. M. Bober, *Karl Marx's Interpretation of History* (2nd ed., Cambridge, Mass., 1948, 445 pp.), contain treatments of Marxian political theory.

Selected samples of American socialist writings which emphasize politics are G. D. Herron, *The Christian State; a Political Vision of Christ* (New York, 1895, 216 pp.), and *Between Caesar and Jesus* (New York, 1899, 278 pp.); R. W. Sellars, *The Next Step in Democracy* (New York, 1916, 275 pp.); W. T. Mills, *Democracy or Despotism* (Berkeley, Calif., 1916, 246 pp.); Karl Reeve, "De Leonism and Communism," *Communist*, VII (June 1928), pp. 364-373, (Aug. 1928), pp. 500-505, and VIII (Jan.-Feb. 1929), pp. 81-87; M. R. Hillquit and others, "Tactics and Next Steps," in *The Socialism of Our Times*, H. W. Laidler and Norman Thomas, eds. (New York, 1929, 377 pp.), pp. 61-171; Albert Weisbord, *The Conquest of Power* (New York, 1937, 2 vols.); H. Elfenbein, *Socialism from Where We Are* (New York, 1945, 214 pp.); Eduard Heimann, *Freedom and Order* (New York, 1947, 344 pp.), sections of which were first delivered to the Princeton American Civilization Program's conference, 1945-1946, on Socialism and America; and H. W. Laidler, "The Changing Functions of the Modern State," in R. N. Anshen, ed., *Our Emergent Civilization* (New York, 1947, 339 pp.), pp. 75-102.

Special Topics

THE special topics below are organized to fit the Marxian theory of the historical process: its predictions about capitalism, its ideas on how to effect the transition from capitalism to complete socialism, and its relatively few conjectures concerning the nature of socialism after it has been fully established. Since these theories reflect the dialectic of the civilization that is and the civilization that ought to be and of necessity will be, they comprehend all theoretical studies but are essentially preoccupied with the state and the organization of its material basis. The pre-Marxians either did not conceive of such ideas as an evolving economy (Topic 1), or were opposed to political action (Topic 4) and other methods later used by Marxians (Topics 5, 9). Wherever possible, however, the theories implied in pre-Marxian practice will be included. Theories of class structure and of human nature and its motivation figure prominently in the socialist critique of existing society, but will be taken up in PART V.

The ripening of capitalism (Topic 1) has been the subject of by far the most voluminous socialist literature, following the first statement in the *Communist Manifesto* and the first elaboration in Marx's *Capital*. It could be broken down into half a dozen parts: the surplus value theory; the increasing concentration of ownership and/or control; the increasing misery of the workingman; the disappearance of the middle class and consequent increase in the size of the proletariat; the theory of cycles as symptoms of disequilibrium between the consuming power of the working population and the producing power of capital; and theories of the declining rate of return on investments. To the Marxian all these theories make a single pattern. He usually treats them together; in fact, imperialism and war (Topics 2 and 3) fit into the same scheme. His critics are more apt to dissect a single phase of his predictions and disregard the fact that to Marx (though often not to Marxians) these predictions were descriptions of tendencies he saw in contemporary society. Imperialism, because of its practical connection with the domestic politics of those countries where socialists are strong, is most often given separate treatment. Should imperialism be obstructed because of its oppression of colonial peoples or should it be allowed to run its course? What answer should socialists give to those who, like Spengler in his *Man and Technics* (tr. by C. F. Atkinson; New York, 1932, 104 pp.), point to the nationalist independence movements born of the industrialization of colonies? Are all modern wars imperialist? Questions of socialist support of war and the conflict of loyalties between their nation and the workers of the world arose as soon as socialists were faced with the need of formulating political programs. Their decisions have varied with each conflict not only between support and opposition, but between types of support and between active sabotage and neutrality.

Marxian theories of transitional society depend on the assumption of the maturity of productive forces. Yet before capitalism matures there are tasks for the class-conscious revolutionary; and the tactics he uses to accomplish them foreshadow the way he would run the transitional socialist society. Since the socialist revolution is presumed to be of, by, and for the workingmen, socialism's first duty is to enlighten labor (Topic 5). This may take the form of organizing the unorganized, or the unemployed. It may lead to dual unionism and the conflict between craft and industrial organizations. Socialists may seek to control the union bureaucracy, or influence its negotiations with management or its program of political action. They have to state their position on the immigration of competing labor. They write the history of the American labor movement in terms of the class struggle. Throughout all socialist union activities runs a basic conflict of theories. One school enters the labor field for propaganda only; the other, to lay the foundations of "the Industrial Republic."

The same division of theory occurs in the question of the relation of socialism to the cooperative movement (Topic 6). One point of view holds that cooperation contradicts the theory of the class struggle and is therefore a blind alley for socialist activity. But for some American socialists, cooperatives are modern versions of their utopias.

The party (Topic 4) is for most socialists the primary agent for propaganda and for the actual overthrow of capitalism. As a focus for the socialists' social activities the party will be discussed in PART V, Topic 4. In this Part the investigation is directed toward such problems as party organization and control; theories of one-party, two-party, and multiple-party government; the economics of party finance; the importance of dogma and the theory of splits and fusions.

Socialists unite to defend their right under capitalism to attack it (Topic 7), but divide into democratic and communist wings on the question of civil liberties, in the traditional Anglo-American sense, under transitional socialism.

American socialism has always had to compete with liberal reform movements purveying panaceas for the economic problems of currency, taxation, distribution, and decentralization, and proposing mechanisms for more democracy in politics (Topics 8 and 12). Sometimes the socialists borrowed reform planks or supported reform candidates. At other times they opposed their own political and economic theories as part of their total view of capitalist development and crisis. Can the socialist revolution (Topic 9) occur by common consent or must it inevitably resort to violence? When did socialists begin to recognize the attempt at counterrevolution as the period of the bitterest violence? What tactics and strategy have socialists proposed for winning control of the means of production and the state? These are some of the questions to be asked of the socialist theory of revolution.

The dictatorship of the proletariat is considered unavoidable by both communist and socialist critics. Democracy to them is plainly incompatible with the conditions of the period of transition, given the dual tasks of destroying the capitalist state machinery and building a socialist economy. Two topics deal with this avowedly temporary situation. The first (Topic 10) concerns the contention that even though dictatorship and not democracy prevails, there is a degree of equality and freedom, based on economic changes, not found in capitalist democracy. Many socialists create a semantic problem by calling the dictatorship "economic" or "industrial" democracy. It is pertinent to discuss the position of welfare economics in the transitional society at this point, as well as "the right to work," which involves a guarantee against unemployment and a theory of wages.

The constructive business of the transitional society, taken up partly in Topic 10, is conceived of primarily as a planning process (Topic 11). To socialists who intend to retain democracy in full, it becomes necessary to explain how plans will not be jeopardized by changing majorities or pressures. To others not hampered by this condition, there is still the computational problem. What can replace what economists of the Austrian and English schools call the mechanism of the free market, and achieve a satisfactory balance of production and distribution?

The ultimate aim of nearly every variety of American radical has been some kind of society in which the inequalities of opportunity, status, and property have been abolished (Topic 12). Life, liberty, equality, happiness, and command of nature are the familiar symbols of the millennial hope. Even the anarchists, who differ radically from the socialists in their choice of means, unite with them in describing goals. Those most conscious of the charge of utopianism and of desertion of the principle of dialectical materialism prefer to concentrate on immediate problems or admit that conflicts continue and that the dynamic is the struggle with nature or within the personality. Here is the place to analyze the process by which the state is supposed to wither away.

Topic 1. Theories of the Maturing of Capitalism

This topic does not embrace the whole literature of the Marxian analysis of capitalism but rather examines some of the twentieth-century American comments on Marxian predictions. Attention is concentrated on three of them: (1) the theories of the increasing concentration of ownership or control, which results in (2) the increasing misery of the wage earners, and (3) the increasing severity of crises leading to the revolutionary crisis. While these problems are predominantly economic, the Marxian assumption of the class basis of the state must be kept in mind. For the Marxian holds that because the modern state is dominated (whether through the democratic process or not) by the capitalist ruling class, the setting for the socialist revolution is prepared by the evolution of these economic processes. As background for this topic, see the section on Marx and Engels in PART I, pp. 34-39, other European Marxist writings in PART I, especially Topics 5, 8-10, and the General Reading above, pp. 241-249.

An abstract summary of Marx's thesis of this historical tendency of capitalist accumulation is found in *Capital*, I, chap. 32 (Kerr ed.). According to this summary, petty industry was at first a system where labor produced for itself, without cooperation, division of labor, or social utilization of natural resources and power. After a preliminary uprooting of population at the dawn of the capitalist era, there follows the amassing of great property by a few. Labor and the means of production are further socialized, science is applied to industry and agriculture, and capitalist magnates approach monopoly by driving out small capitalists. But monopoly, faced with a working class multiplied and organized by the very exploitive process, becomes outmoded in terms of the improved production methods. The expropriators are expropriated. It was a difficult process to transform diffused private property into monopolized capitalist property, because there were many people to feel the oppression. But with capitalism already resting on socialized production, the expropriation of the few usurpers is relatively quick, easy, and without violence. Drawing chiefly from *Capital*, III, Erich Roll outlines Marx's theory of economic development in his *A History of Economic Thought* (New York, 1939, 430 pp.), pp. 287-295.

As developed in Germany by Rudolf Hilferding, *Das Finanzkapital* (*Marx-Studien*, III; 1910; Vienna, 1927, 477 pp.), and Rosa Luxemburg, *Die Akkumulation des Kapitals* (1913; Berlin, 1923, 493 pp.), the theory of exploitation and accumulation has been applied to conditions a generation after Marx. Hilferding stressed the ultimate banker control of the whole global capitalist network and thus minimized the dangers of prolonged crisis and violent revolution in the transition to socialism. Luxemburg, modifying Marx's exposition of capitalist circulation (*Capital*, II), saw the ultimate downfall of the system where there were no unindustrialized peoples to exploit. To Marx (and to Lenin also) this was not the end, for one group of capitalists could extend production by using the surplus value created by another group. Because of Hilferding's evolutionary thesis and Luxemburg's simplification, theories like theirs were more popular in America than those of Marx himself.

In no uncertain language, Marx referred to the concentration and centralization of ownership as well as control, and to the thorough degradation of the laborers. Marx's opponents have chosen to emphasize the diffusion of ownership of corporate securities and the wide distribution of consumers' durable goods—a case particularly easy to demonstrate in the United States. Marxian rejoinders analyze the percentage of the total means of production, and of the total wealth or income, in the hands of a few. They agree that ownership is less concentrated than control but deny any divorce between them. Some deny that Marx predicted "increasing misery" by referring to his discussion of conditions leading to rising wages and shorter hours. If the anti-Marxian points to the psychology of the workingman as without class consciousness and as emulating the habits of higher income groups, the Marxian reply is to point to peculiar American conditions delaying worker solidarity and to the more class-conscious psychology of the European masses.

Business cycle theory is a twentieth-century development of the science of political economy. The early industrial period was aware of financial "panics" but laid the subsequent "hard times" to a variety of natural calamities such as poor crops, or to wars and other politically-created conditions. That Marx developed a theory of periodic crises at all was a remarkable feat, a feat made possible by the dynamic quality of his theory and by his attempt to embrace the whole of man's nature and history. The classical school of his time, and for some time thereafter, took by contrast a static view of economics and saw the motivations of the market in the psychology of demand. Nevertheless, Marx was concerned first with the long-range trend of capitalism toward its eventual extinction. What produced temporary aberrations were, for example, the need to retool when machines wore out, the destruction of capital goods in wars, and the opening of new colonial markets. The gap between capital accumulated and purchasing power distributed, a gap inevitable according to Marx's wage theory, would always return the system to crisis conditions. Modern elucidation and addition to Marxian theory at this point, more than at any other, has been predominantly European.

Late capitalism is described by theorists in several ways. Those holding most firmly to Marx's evolutionary predictions speak of "ripening conditions." Those who agree with Lenin that conditions even in Great Britain and the United States after 1914-1917 passed the stage where peaceful transformation was possible refer to "the revolutionary situation." Non-Marxian economists who note various unhealthy trends and advocate certain governmental and business remedies write of "the mature economy."

Sample American socialist theorists justifying or modifying Marxian predictions are J. W. Hughan, *American Socialism of the Present Day* (New York, 1911, 265 pp.), pp. 84-117, and L. B. Boudin, *The Theoretical System of Karl Marx* (Chicago, 1907, 286 pp.), pp. 147-229, 235-240.

Boudin attacks revisionism and Miss Hughan defends it, yet both were members of the Socialist Party. In order to compare their theories with those of Marxians writing after the depression of the thirties, read P. M. Sweezy, *The Theory of Capitalist Development* (New York, 1942, 398 pp.), pp. 11-108, 133-134, 145-162, 190-236; also B. D. Wolfe, "New Aspects of Cyclical Crises," *Marxist Quarterly*, i (Jan.-Mar. 1937), pp. 99-114.

On the subject of capitalist concentration there is abundant Marxian and non-Marxian discussion. E. H. Heywood, *Yours or Mine; an Essay to Show the True Basis of Property and the Causes of Its Unequal Distribution* (Boston, 1869, 22 pp.), is one of the earliest native anarchist treatments of the subject. Daniel De Leon in the *Nationalist*, August 1889, pointed out James Madison's thesis of the class basis of politics and his prophecy that "the day will come when our Republic will be an impossibility . . . because wealth will be concentrated in the hands of a few." This essay was later published with an editorial from the *Daily People*, May 4, 1913, on Marx's predictions as scientific and accurately in line with Madison's, as *James Madison and Karl Marx; a Contrast and a Similarity* (3rd ed., New York, 1932, 30 pp.). See also the *De Leon-Berry Debate on Solution of the Trust Problem* (New York, 1915, 40 pp.). An author who signs himself "Marxist," in a revisionist article, "Trusts and Socialism," *International Socialist Review*, i (Oct. 1900), pp. 212-228, comments approvingly on A. T. Hadley's conclusion in "The Formation and Control of Trusts," *Scribner's Magazine*, xxvi (Nov. 1899), pp. 604-610, that full trustification will be followed by nationalization and a struggle between individualism and socialism. He also agrees with C. W. Baker, *Monopolies and the People* (1889; 3rd ed. rev. and enl., New York, 1899, 368 pp.), that Marx's view is obsolete; that the trusts will be socialized not by expropriation but by "the unconscious historical activities of the capitalist class." See also the gradualist theory of S. A. Reeve, a professional engineer influenced by Bellamy, in *The Cost of Competition* (New York, 1906, 617 pp.). On the other hand see B. A. Bouroff's study of the contrasts revealed by the 1890 census, *The Impending Crisis: Conditions Resulting from the Concentration of Wealth in the United States* (Chicago, 1900, 196 pp.), and F. A. Adams, *Who Rules America?* (New York, 1899, 59 pp.). L. B. Boudin attacked the gradualists in "Mathematische Formeln gegen Karl Marx," *Neue Zeit*, xxv, Pt. 1 (1907), pp. 524-535, 557-567, 603-610, primarily a criticism of Tugan-Baranovsky. Other Americans wrote for *Neue Zeit*, such as Jacob Winnen of Chicago, "Die industrielle Entwicklung und die Konzentration des Besitzes in den Vereinigten Staaten," xxv, Pt. 2 (1907), pp. 289-295.

Typical of Socialist Party propaganda, touching concentration of control as well as every other question the public might ask, and soft-pedaling the necessity of any aggressive violence, is F. M. Eastwood, *The Question*

Box; Answers to Questions about Socialism (Chicago, n.d., 63 pp.). In the same period appeared Scott Nearing, *Income; an Examination of the Returns for Services Rendered and from Property Owned in the United States* (New York, 1915, 238 pp.); W. E. Walling, *Who Gets America's Wealth?* (New York, 1916?, 14 pp.), issued as a special supplement to the *Intercollegiate Socialist*, IV, No. 2 (Dec. 1915-Jan. 1916), and Gustavus Myers, *History of the Great American Fortunes* (1910; New York, 1936, 732 pp.). I. M. Rubinow, *Was Marx Wrong? The Economic Theories of Karl Marx Tested in the Light of Modern Industrial Development* (New York, 1914, 62 pp.), was written to answer V. G. Simkhovitch, *Marxism versus Socialism* (New York, 1913, 298 pp.). Chapters 3-4 discuss concentration in industry. The relation of Marxism to Veblen's critical study of capitalist economics has been investigated by L. E. Traywick in the unpublished University of Illinois dissertation, *Parallelisms in the Economic Ideas of Karl Marx and Thorstein Veblen*, abstracted in *United States, 1865-1900*, I (1941/1942), pp. 112-113. See also the comments of one of Veblen's students, W. C. Mitchell, in *The Backward Art of Spending Money* (New York, 1937, 421 pp.).

Recent Marxians have used historical and biographical studies to verify the prophecy of concentration. Avrom Landy, "Marx, Engels and America; Attitude toward America in the Early Period," *Communist*, VI (July-Aug. 1927), pp. 295-309, (Sept.-Oct. 1927), pp. 394-400, calls attention to the prediction that the United States would become the center of world capitalism. L. M. Hacker, "The American Civil War; Economic Aspects," *Marxist Quarterly*, I (Apr.-June 1937), pp. 191-213, develops the thesis that the Civil War was the industrial capitalists' revolution in the United States. Hacker, *The Triumph of American Capitalism; the Development of Forces in American History to the End of the Nineteenth Century* (New York, 1940, 460 pp.), traces the changes in types of American enterprise from colonial times on the basis of an economic theory of history professedly non-Marxian. See also the Marxian study of Eric Williams, *Capitalism & Slavery* (Chapel Hill, N.C., 1944, 285 pp.). Lewis Corey, *The House of Morgan; a Social Biography of the Masters of Money* (New York, 1930, 479 pp.), numerous volumes and essays by Harvey O'Connor, such as *The Guggenheims* (New York, 1937, 496 pp.), and Ferdinand Lundberg, *America's 60 Families* (New York, 1937, 544 pp.), carry on the type of study begun by Gustavus Myers. A supplement, *Who Controls Industry?* (New York, 1938, 32 pp.), was added by Lundberg in answer to critics. Anna Rochester strictly affirms all the Marxian predictions in *Rulers of America; a Study of Finance Capital* (New York, 1936, 367 pp.), published by International Publishers. See especially chapter 8 on class control of the government, chapter 9 on concentration of income and increasing misery, Pt. 2 on financial control of selected industries and the wiping out of small capitalists, and Pt. 3 on crisis. The left-wing view after World War II is represented by the Labor Research Association work, *Trends in American Capitalism* (New York, 1948, 128 pp.). Other essays from the Socialist Party point of view are Scott Nearing, *The One Big Union of Business* (New York, 1920, 32 pp.), published by the Rand School of Social Science, and Irving Lipkowitz, *Monopoly and Big Business* (New York, 1940, 56 pp.), a League for Industrial Democracy pamphlet. See also V. N. Cherkezov, *The Concentration of Capital; a Marxian Fallacy* (London, 1911, 25 pp.), by an anarchist, and *One Thousand Americans* (New York, 1947, 312 pp.), by the unaffiliated leftist George Seldes.

Comment on the effects of monopoly and war is found in N. Ross, "A Note on the Development of Post War Capitalism in the U.S.," *Communist*, viii (Sept. 1929), pp. 512-527; W. Z. Foster, "World Capitalism and World Socialism after Eighteen Months of War," *ibid.*, xx (Mar. 1941), pp. 220-237; and J. S. Allen, *World Monopoly and Peace* (New York, 1946, 288 pp.). The first article justifies Marx's prediction that large capital would eat up small capital by referring to industrial rationalization, mergers, and the decreased purchasing power of farmers. Foster concludes that capitalism has been weakened by war costs, the destruction of property, the disruption of the economic system, and the breaking of the anti-Soviet front. Meanwhile socialism gains strength with the growing power of Russia and the mass discontent in belligerent countries.

From the vast literature by non-Marxians on developments in American business a few titles are cited. C. R. Van Hise, geologist, conservationist, president of the University of Wisconsin, and president of the Chamber of Commerce in 1914, proposed in *Concentration and Control; a Solution of the Trust Problem in the United States* (New York, 1912, 288 pp.) to extend the regulatory powers of public utility and trade commissions and amend the antitrust act to protect the public from patent monopolies and other dangers. W. I. King, a student of the distribution of wealth, prepared a treatise with the assistance of Lillian Epstein, *The National Income and Its Purchasing Power* (New York, 1930, 394 pp.), for the National Bureau of Economic Research. C. F. Ware and G. C. Means, *The Modern Economy in Action* (New York, 1936, 244 pp.), emphasize the divorce of ownership from control, like the Berle-Means study cited in the General Reading (p. 253). A. R. Burns, *The Decline of Competition* (New York, 1936, 619 pp.), studies, among other factors, the increasing rigidities of the price structure. W. L. Thorp, *The Structure of Industry* (Washington, 1941, 759 pp.), is one of a long series of monographs prepared for the Temporary National Economic Committee's investigation of concentration of economic power. C. F. Muller, *Light Metals Monopoly* (New York, 1946, 279 pp.), concentrates on control of the products of aluminum and magnesium. See also David Lynch, *The Concentration of Economic Power* (New York, 1946, 423 pp.), and G. W. Stocking and M. W. Watkins, *Cartels or Competition* (New York, 1948, 516 pp.). J. F. Foster, *Theoretical Foundations of Government Ownership in a Capitalistic Economy*, an unpublished doctoral thesis completed at the University of Texas in 1947, explores the growing problems of state capitalism. Limited agreement with the Marxian theory of the state as class controlled is found in R. G. Hawtrey, *Economic Aspects of Sovereignty* (New York, 1930, 162 pp.). James Burnham, a Trotskyist until just before he wrote *The Managerial Revolution* (New York, 1941, 285 pp.), concluded in that book that the elite of skilled business and governmental administrators already possess economic and political power. See P. M. Sweezy's criticism of Burnham, "The Illusion of the 'Managerial Revolution,'" *Science & Society*, VI (Winter 1942), pp. 1-23. The relation of state, class, and society is discussed briefly in Max Lerner, *Ideas for the Ice Age* (New York, 1941, 432 pp.), pp. 376-385.

Little has been written on the theme of increasing misery alone. A Fourierist pamphlet is Zoé Gatti de Gamond, *Paupérisme et association* (Paris, 1847, 176 pp.). One of the outstanding European contributions is Robert Michels, *La teoria di C. Marx sulla miseria crescente* (Turin, 1922, 244 pp.). Robert Hunter, *Poverty* (New York, 1904, 382 pp.), treats the problems of paupers, vagrants, the sick and injured, women, children, and immigrants; Isador Ladoff, *American Pauperism and the Abolition of Poverty* (Chicago, 1904, 230 pp.), sets forth the maldistribution of wealth revealed by his study of the 1900 census. N. A. Richardson, *Industrial Problems* (Chicago, 1912, 229 pp.), devotes twenty-two pages to the concentration of wealth, twenty-five to moral and political corruption, and ninety-nine (pp. 76-174) to increasing evils of the laborers' lot— unemployment, child labor, sweat shops, disruption of the home, vagrancy, dissipation, the liquor traffic, industrial and international wars. See also A. M. Simons, *Wasting Human Life* (Chicago, 1915, 96 pp.), and Michael Gold's autobiography, *Jews without Money* (New York, 1930, 309 pp.).

Neither do socialists pay much attention to Marx's class theory, except to assume it for other purposes. W. J. Ghent, *Mass and Class; a Survey of Social Divisions* (New York, 1904, 260 pp.), investigates the ethics of wage-earners, the self-employed, traders, capitalists, and retainers as related to the class struggle. Abraham Edel, "The Theory of Social Classes; a Logical Analysis," *Marxist Quarterly*, I (Apr.-June 1937), pp. 237-252, is only a brief introduction to the philosophy of classes. He examines various tests of "fundamental" social divisions, such as color, race, creed, urban-rural. He concludes that the economic basis is the most fruitful hypothesis for explaining diverse social behavior; that the Marxian division meets the test: the difficulty of eradicating the division without changing the structure (mode of production) of society. Lewis Corey, "American Class Relations," *Marxist Quarterly*, I (Jan.-Mar. 1937), pp. 134-143, denies that Marx recognized but two classes. The history of the American Revolution, Jacksonian battles, the Civil War, and populism, he says, clearly shows that a class struggle existed. Marx meant only that in terms of relation to production, different social groups stand to gain or be oppressed under capitalism. Corey aims particularly at A. M. Bingham, *Insurgent America* (New York, 1935, 253 pp.). He feels that Bingham mistakes the admitted American dislike of class lines for their nonexistence. Bingham repeats his point, emphasizing Marx's neglect of the professional and white-collar groups, in *Man's Estate* (New York, 1939, 480 pp.). The growth of the wage-earning class, 1870-1910, is discussed in A. H. Hansen, "Industrial Class Alignments in the United States," American Statistical Association *Quarterly Publication*, N.S., XVII (Dec. 1920), pp. 417-425, and population divisions of 1920 analyzed in a sequel in the Association's *Journal*, N.S., XVIII (Dec. 1922), pp. 503-506. R. G. Hurlin and M. B. Givens discuss the picture a decade later in "Shifting Occupational Patterns," *Recent Social Trends* (New York, 1933, 2 vols.), I, pp. 268-324.

The elementary level of the discussion on Marxian crisis theory before 1918 is illustrated in Mark Fisher, *Evolution and Revolution* (Chicago, n.d., 61 pp.), pp. 31-33; and A. M. Lewis, "The Socialist Theory of Panics," chap. 3 of *Vital Problems in Social Evolution* (Chicago, 1909, 192 pp.). The Stalinist point of view is represented by C. E. Wisden, "Innovations and Business Cycles; a New 'Theory' of Cyclical Crises Reveals Old Bourgeois Bankruptcy," *Communist*, xx (Feb. 1941), pp. 164-177, an essay reviewing J. A. Schumpeter's important *Business Cycles; a Theoretical, Historical and Statistical Analysis of the Capitalist Process* (New York, 1939, 2 vols.). See also *Marxist Study Courses: Political Economy*, Lessons 8-9, "Economic Crises" (New York, 1933, 52 pp., 64 pp.). The best recent American socialist treatment of crisis theory is in Sweezy's *The Theory of Capitalist Development* (New York, 1942, 398 pp.), pp. 133-236. Compare the work of such leading American Keynesians on business cycles as A. H. Hansen. M. A. C. Hallgren, *Seeds of Revolt* (New York, 1933, 369 pp.), argued that a capitalist crisis was inevitable but a proletarian revolution was not if no party was prepared for it. Lewis Corey touched the question in "The Problem of Prosperity," *Marxist Quarterly*, I (Apr.-June 1937), pp. 175-190, and "The Costs of Depression," *ibid.*, I (Oct.-Dec. 1937), pp. 384-393. A. Feiler discussed communism and crises in his article, "The Soviet Union and the Business Cycle," *Social Research*, III (Aug. 1936), pp. 282-303; A. B. Lewis treated the factor of technology in *Labor, Machines and Depressions* (New York, 1939, 31 pp.). Among the many writers predicting a serious depression following World War II,

Fritz Sternberg, *The Coming Crisis* (New York, 1947, 280 pp.), allowed for the alternative of an atomic war and based his theory on a Marxism revised in the light of the economic developments of the war period. Marxian crisis theory has been more European than American, as indicated by the references in B. D. Wolfe's article, "New Aspects of Cyclical Crises," *Marxist Quarterly,* i (Jan.-Mar. 1937), pp. 99-114. Beyond his citations, see Henryk Grossmann, *Das Akkumulations- und Zusammenbruchsgesetz des kapitalistischen Systems* (Leipzig, 1929, 628 pp.), and "Die Wert-Preis-Transformation bei Marx und das Krisenproblem," *Zeitschrift für Sozialforschung,* i (1932), pp. 55-84; Max Seydewitz and others, *Die Krise des Kapitalismus und die Aufgabe der Arbeiterklasse* (Berlin, 1930, 188 pp.); John Strachey, *The Nature of Capitalist Crisis* (New York, 1935, 400 pp.); Eugen Varga, *The Great Crisis and Its Political Consequences; Economics and Politics, 1928-1934* (London, 1935?, 175 pp.); R. P. Dutt, *Fascism and Social Revolution; a Study of the Economics and Politics of the Extreme Stages of Capitalism in Decay* (New York, 1935, 318 pp.); Léon Sartre, *Esquisse d'une théorie marxiste des crises périodiques* (Paris, 1937, 148 pp.), and M. H. Dobb, *Political Economy and Capitalism* (London, 1937, 359 pp.).

In all the more recent Marxian discussions of "the great crisis" of the thirties, writers imply that conditions are ripe for the change to socialism. The question whether capitalism is "mature" or not agitates, in a quite different manner, the professional non-Marxians. They have been concerned with the declining rate of population increase, tendencies toward price rigidities, savings overbalancing new investment, chronic unemployment, and the role of wages in a fluctuating economy. J. M. Blair, *Seeds of Destruction; a Study in the Functional Weaknesses of Capitalism* (New York, 1938, 418 pp.), and G. W. Edwards, *The Evolution of Finance Capitalism* (New York, 1938, 429 pp.), concluded that the critical hour for security capitalism had arrived. Oskar Morgenstern investigated one aspect, "Unemployment; Analysis of Factors," in the American Economic Association *Papers and Proceedings,* liii (1940), pp. 273-293. G. W. Terborgh attempted to explode the "stagnationist" notion of A. H. Hansen and others in *The Bogey of Economic Maturity* (Chicago, 1945, 263 pp.). For his continued debate with Hansen see the *Review of Economic Statistics,* xxviii (Feb. 1946), pp. 13-17, (Aug. 1946), pp. 170-172, and for a summary of a theory which receded in importance during the boom after World War I, see E. W. Swanson and E. P. Schmidt, *Economic Stagnation or Progress; a Critique of Recent Doctrines on the Mature Economy* (New York, 1946, 212 pp.).

The link between the theory of the mature economy and the Marxian theory of the revolutionary situation is their agreement that investment opportunities are declining. Their explanations differ. On the other hand, socialists differ among themselves as to exactly what conditions have to be fulfilled. An exchange of views on this question by Eduard Heimann and Sidney Hook, both of whom have individual rather than party interpretations of Marxism, is found in *Social Research*, beginning with Heimann's "The 'Revolutionary Situation' and the Middle Classes," v (May 1938), pp. 227-236, and followed by Hook's reply (Nov. 1938), pp. 464-471, and Heimann's rejoinder, pp. 471-473.

Topic 2. *Imperialism and International Capitalism*

Empire, as a type of government which subjects the people of one territory to the power of another, is as old as civilization. The United States faced imperial problems in the management of its western lands and dependent Indians. It bought Alaska, its first noncontiguous territory, in 1867. Socialist comment on nineteenth-century territorial and annexationist questions is not emphasized in this study. Only after defeating Spain and acquiring Hawaii in 1898 was the country faced with the possession of remote territories having alien inhabitants, and with strong socialist criticism of such possession. The "new imperialism" of Europe had at last involved America. At the same time previous diplomatic efforts to extend American trade, especially in the Orient, were redoubled.

The subject divides chronologically into three parts. From 1898 to 1914 most socialist discussion focused on the question of American imperialism. During the second period, from World War I to 1933, American socialists echoed the detailed world-wide analyses of European socialist writers. The third phase of the argument was conditioned by the rise and defeat of central European fascism. Was the imperialist age over? Did fascism introduce a new type of state or a variation of the old imperialism? Were the victors imperialist? What effect did international monopoly combinations have on capitalist competition?

The discussion of the first period was on the whole crude, vague, and unorthodox. Beyond relating the growth of trusts to foreign trade or conquest as a safety valve against domestic crisis and for increased profits, socialists had no elaborate theory, because they had little American experience to evaluate. Some made connections between free silver or transportation and imperialism; most condemned jingoism and militarism as part of the same capitalist disease.

In the 1920's socialists adhered to the main outline of the Marxian accumulation and breakdown theory, and fitted Lenin's *Imperialism* into the earlier interpretations of Hilferding and Luxemburg (see Topic 1). Only a few writers attempted to formulate a cyclical theory applicable to precapitalist empires. All agreed, however, that the advent of socialism would end the spiral. They assumed that the lack of new fields to conquer, plus the revolt of colonial peoples, would send capitalism into a tailspin for lack of undeveloped areas to exploit. The age of imperialism would soon be succeeded by the age of socialism. Questions of the nature of colonial industrialization and liberation received particular attention.

This easy optimism was shaken by the growth of nazism. Critics of Marxism pointed out that the nationalist and militaristic characteristics explained by Marxians as part of the superstructure of advanced capitalism were now the distinguishing features of autarchy, a new form of state more collectivistic than capitalist. They repeated with new emphasis what earlier anti-Marxians had said, that the psychological and political elements of expansionism preceded the economic, and were not only means to the end of national advantage but ends in themselves. If imperialism were the result of the need to find outlets for surplus capital, how could the Marxians explain the lack of correlation between British foreign investment fluctuations and British political efforts to paint the map red, or the fact that exported capital went primarily to rival empires and independent states? If imperialism were territorial control for the benefit of a nation's foreign trade—and to remove the idea of territorial control would make imperialism a vague unmanageable concept—what could Marxians say to the fact that trade had followed the price list, and not the flag?

The communists declined to accept their opponents' legalistic definition of imperialism. To them, imperialism was a stage in world economy dominated by monopoly capitalism in several countries, each striving to secure the most favorable world market for its industrial products and the widest sphere for the investment of its surplus capital. This severe competition resulted in such cutthroat practices as dumping, truces in the form of international cartels, territorial division of "unoccupied" parts of the world, and wars of redivision precipitated by the have-nots. Nationalism and militarism (see Topic 3), with roots deeper than capitalism, served first to free the bourgeoisie from feudal restraints and then to oppress less developed peoples and combat imperialist rivals. Since the vast majority had little economic interest in empire, only political and psychological symbols could evoke their support. Marxians considered the question of priority between annexation and investment or trade as irrelevant as the fact of economic penetration without annexation. Three forms of annexation were advantageous to monopoly capital without antecedent capital export or commodity exchange: (1) annexation might be protective to avoid the disadvantages of discrimination which might follow annexation by a rival; (2) it might anticipate the discovery of economic values to the empire; and (3) it might be for strategic purposes. Fascism was the form of capitalist imperialism which sought the redivision of the world. Its leaders had merged the state with monopoly capital and diverted the continuing conflicts which they could not abolish without general expropriation. The fact that eventual full employment and high production still failed to benefit labor because of the emphasis on guns instead of butter justified the conclusion that fascism was a palace revolution and not a social revolution.

The comparable Soviet emphasis on war preparation was explained as a temporary necessity resulting from capitalist encirclement. World War II was really three different kinds of war in one: the conflict between Western capitalism and fascism was just as imperialist in 1945 as it had been in 1939, China's battle was for national liberation, while Russia fought to preserve socialism. Communists did not emphasize these distinctions at the time.

Non-Stalinist socialists in the third period had varying theories. In general they lumped all totalitarian states together as the most virulent imperialists. They expected the defeat of fascism and the liberation of colonies to make possible the growth of democratic society into a socialist commonwealth. Many of them felt Marx's predictions were too remote and general to permit their thorough application to new conditions.

For a comparison of the Marxian and non-Marxian theories of 1900 with the 1930's, see, for the early period, C. A. Conant, "The Economic Basis of 'Imperialism,'" *North American Review*, Vol. 167 (Sept. 1898), pp. 326-340, the conclusions of an American financial expert anticipating J. A. Hobson's classic, *Imperialism, a Study* (New York, 1902, 400 pp.), and H. L. Boothman, "Philosophy of Imperialism," *International Socialist Review*, i (Oct.-Nov. 1900), pp. 229-244, 286-303. For the thirties, compare W. L. Langer, "A Critique of Imperialism," *Foreign Affairs*, xiv (Oct. 1935), pp. 102-119, and P. M. Sweezy, *The Theory of Capitalist Development* (New York, 1942, 398 pp.), pp. 237-363, 375-378.

Marx and Engels had no explicit theory of imperialism which predicted war as the inevitable result of capitalist development, although it has been deduced from the theory of historical materialism. Two works by Marx, *Secret Diplomatic History of the Eighteenth Century* (ed. by E. M. Aveling; London, 1899, 96 pp.), and *The Story of the Life of Lord Palmerston* (ed. by E. M. Aveling; London, 1899, 78 pp.), will help the student compare Marx's views on eighteenth- and nineteenth-century imperialism with those of his followers on later developments. Among these later views, outstanding were the major works of Rudolf Hilferding and Rosa Luxemburg (see Topic 1), Karl Kautsky, *Sozialismus und Kolonialpolitik* (Berlin, 1907, 80 pp.), Lenin's classic, *Imperialism, the Highest Stage of Capitalism* (1917; new ed., New York, 1939, 128 pp.; also in *Collected Works*, xix), and N. I. Bukharin, *Imperialism and World Economy* (New York, 1929, 173 pp.). For special problems, see T. A. Jackson, *Ireland Her Own* (London, 1946, 443 pp.), a history of the Irish question; Emil Lederer, "Von der Wissenschaft zur Utopie (Der Sozialismus und das Programm 'Mittel-Europa')," *Archiv für die Geschichte des Sozialismus und der Arbeiterbewegung*, VII (1916), pp. 364-411, on imperialism and central European economic union; and two articles by Hilferding, thoroughly revising his early views, "State Capitalism or Totalitarian State Economy," *Modern Review*, I (June 1947), pp. 266-271 (tr. by Nina Stein), and "The Modern Totalitarian State," *ibid.*, I (Oct. 1947), pp. 597-605. The latter is a translation and condensation of three articles published in the *Neuer Vorwärts* between 1936 and 1939, stating that the imperialism of finance capital ended with World War I, and that the state has taken control of the economy for the purpose of war.

L. J. Ragatz, *The Literature of European Imperialism, 1815-1939* (Washington, 1944, 153 pp.), has no comparable parallel in the American field. B. J. Hovde, "Socialistic Theories of Imperialism Prior to the Great War," *Journal of Political Economy*, XXXVI (Oct. 1928), pp. 569-591, E. M. Winslow, "Marxian, Liberal, and Sociological Theories of Imperialism," *Journal of Political Economy*, XXXIX (Dec. 1931), pp. 713-758, and Hannah Arendt, "Expansion and the Philosophy of Power," *Sewanee Review*, LIV (Autumn 1946), pp. 601-616, can, however, serve as general introductions.

After expressing itself against empire during the first years of the century, American socialism turned to the domestic issues of industrial conflict, the trusts, and the reform of political democracy. They returned to the subject with the opening of the European war. Daniel De Leon's lectures, "Plebs Leaders and Labor Leaders" and "The Warning of the Gracchi," delivered in 1902 and published as *Two Pages from Roman History* (1903; New York, 1943, 93 pp.), compared Rome at the conclusion of her Italian expansion and on the eve of overseas conquests to the contemporary situation in the United States, but were primarily concerned with pointing out the strategic errors of Roman labor in domestic politics. See also Lucien Sanial, *Territorial Expansion . . . With Statistics on the Growth of Socialism in America* (New York, 1901?, 24 pp.).

One of the most violent and prolific anti-imperialists was the anarchist utopian writer M. I. Swift. Within two years he wrote *Anti-imperialism* (Los Angeles, 1899, 64 pp.), published by the *Public Ownership Review*; and *Imperialism and Liberty* (Los Angeles, 1899, 491 pp.).

Some of the peripheral writings, either by conservatives supplying arguments for the socialists or by allied radicals, were W. M. Harvey, *Coin on Money, Trusts and Imperialism* (Chicago, 1899, 184 pp.), populist; magazine articles by Andrew Carnegie, "Imperial Federation," "Americanism versus Imperialism," and "Distant Possessions: the Parting of the Ways," reprinted in *The Gospel of Wealth, and Other Timely Essays* (Garden City, N.Y., 1933, 287 pp.); and several works by Brooks

Adams. Carnegie's disavowal of territorial imperialism and his concern for international peace have been frequently cited to show the lack of connection between capitalism and militarism, and—by socialists—to illustrate the hypocrisy of capitalist propaganda. Brooks Adams propounded a geopolitical theory of imperial cycles based on a complex of mines, trade routes, and financial centers. He surveyed the course of the "social cyclone" from Egypt to the United States and predicted a shift from an Atlantic-oriented to a Pacific-oriented civilization. His "law" that civilizations succeed according to their endowments of natural energy for the exploitation of natural resources was a distinctive hypothesis and his belief in the natural selection of corporation managers was conservative Social Darwinism; but his free-silver ideas, his criticism of government by finance capital, and his fundamentally economic interpretation of history were close to the ideas held by many of his socialist contemporaries. His position is developed in *The Law of Civilization and Decay* (1895; new ed. with intro. by C. A. Beard; New York, 1943, 349 pp.); *America's Economic Supremacy* (1900; New York, 1947, 194 pp.); *The New Empire* (New York, London, 1902, 243 pp.); and "War as the Ultimate Form of Economic Competition," U.S. Naval Institute *Proceedings*, xxix (Dec. 1903), pp. 829-881. E. F. Brown, *Socialism or Empire, a Danger* (Omaha, Neb., 1906, 229 pp.), although concerned with the domestic problem of railroad control, shows Adams' identification of imperialism with transportation and his free-silver bias. See also Thorstein Veblen's works, e.g., *Imperial Germany and the Industrial Revolution* (New York, 1939, 343 pp.) and *Absentee Ownership* (New York, 1923, 445 pp.).

Imperialism almost disappeared as an issue in the socialist press during the Taft administration. Even in 1913, F. Murray's "Capitalist Development and Industrial Revolt in Africa," *International Socialist Review*, xiv (Oct. 1913), pp. 200-209, never once used the term "imperialism" in his survey of the European penetration of South Africa, and stressed the class struggle on the Rand in a syndicalist manner. The symbol soon returned to active circulation, as the following sample articles indicate: F. C. Howe, "Dollar Diplomacy and Financial Imperialism under the Wilson Administration," American Academy of Political and Social Science, *Annals*, lxviii (Nov. 1916), pp. 312-320; and S. J. Rutgers, "The Left Wing: Economic Causes of Imperialism," *International Socialist Review*, xvii (July 1916), pp. 29-32.

To socialists after 1918, American imperialism had matured. I. St. J. Tucker, at the end of his brief Christian socialist period, attempted to show a direct line of succession from the Pharaohs to Wilson in *A History of Imperialism* (New York, 1920, 404 pp.), and asserted, like Brooks Adams, "Empire is a matter of transportation." The official Socialist Party pamphlet by James Oneal, *Labor and the Next War* (Chicago, n.d., 40 pp.), related imperialism and war. Meanwhile in Germany J. A. Schumpeter elaborated Hobson's suggestion that imperialism is a sociological atavism, the legacy of the dead hand of precapitalist society, and denied any connection between expansionist militarism and capitalism in *Zur Soziologie der Imperialismen* (Tübingen, 1919, 76 pp.). Another random sample of the vast German contribution was J. Hashagen, "Marxismus und Imperialismus," *Jahrbücher für Nationalökonomie und Statistik,* cxiii (Sept. 1919), pp. 193-216. The influence of British Fabians on American gradualists led the latter to accept a meliorist tapering off of colonial rule, to sympathize with the Soviet Union as defensive and not imperialist, and to trust the League of Nations to temper capitalist conflicts. For the British position see William Irvine, "Shaw, War and Peace, 1894 to 1919," *Foreign Affairs,* xxv (Jan. 1947), pp. 314-327; the works of L. S. Woolf, especially *Imperialism and Civilization* (New York, 1928, 182 pp.); and T. F. Tsiang, *Labor and Empire* (New York, 1923, 220 pp.). In the United States, Scott Nearing, although more impatient than the typical gradualist, was the most prominent contributor to this theme. His *The American Empire* (New York, 1921, 266 pp.) was followed by *Dollar Diplomacy* (New York, 1925, 353 pp.), written in collaboration with Joseph Freeman and translated into German by the Nazis (Heidelberg, 1943, 345 pp.), and later by *The Twilight of Empire; an Economic Interpretation of Imperialist Cycles* (New York, 1930, 349 pp.). In *Dollar Diplomacy* the authors deny the existence of any boundary between economic penetration and political interference.

The communists followed the theories of Lenin and Bukharin. Max Shachtman, "Limitations of American Imperialism," *Communist,* vi (Mar. 1927), pp. 25-31, predicted a crisis of overproduction and the outbreak of imperialist conflict in China. This article was never concluded as his Trotskyist faction at that time fell out of favor. O. Kuusinen, "A Leninist Analysis of the Colonial Problem," *ibid.,* viii (Jan.-Feb. 1929), pp. 3-30, rejected the theory of decolonization, that imperialist policy promotes reform through deliberate industrialization of colonies. The treatment of "Imperialism" in *Marxist Study Courses: Political Economy,* Lessons 10-11 (New York, 1933, 64 pp., 52 pp.), was intended to provide Communist Party members with answers to "bourgeois, social-fascist and other anti-Leninist theories." It is valuable for its discussion of lesser-known theorists like Braunthal, Sternberg, Grossmann, and Hurland, as well as Kautsky, Hilferding, Luxemburg, Trotsky, and Bukharin. It asserts that imperialism is not only the latest but also the highest and last stage of capitalism.

The professional students of imperialism adopted a pluralist causation theory, emphasizing both ideas and interests, and expected internationalism or the power politics of federated international combinations to follow the age of empires. P. T. Moon, *Imperialism and World Politics* (New

York, 1926, 583 pp.), reflects the optimism of the twenties, and W. L. Langer, *The Diplomacy of Imperialism, 1890-1902* (New York, 1935, 2 vols.), and L. L. Ragatz, *March of Empire* (New York, 1948, 92 pp.), the grimmer outlook of the period of international cartels and fascism. Among Jacob Viner's articles touching on imperialism, see for example, "International Finance and Balance of Power Diplomacy, 1880-1914," *Southwestern Political and Social Science Quarterly*, IX (Mar. 1929), pp. 407-451, and "The Economic Problem," in *New Perspectives on Peace*, edited by G. B. de Huszar (Chicago, 1944, 261 pp.), pp. 85-114. Grover Clark, *The Balance Sheets of Imperialism; Facts and Figures on Colonies* (New York, 1936, 136 pp.), published by the Carnegie Endowment for International Peace with a popular edition entitled *A Place in the Sun* (New York, 1936, 235 pp.), argued that colonies do not pay; that only a few private interests profit. R. P. Dutt, *World Politics, 1918-1936* (New York, 1936, 389 pp.), attacking these interpretations from the Marxian hypothesis that "every act of monopoly-capitalism becomes essentially an act of politics" (p. 87), stated the central world problem as collective organization—an organization possible only after the unification of world economy under socialism. P. M. Sweezy's *The Theory of Capitalist Development*, cited above, mentioned this thesis. A. M. Bingham, in *Man's Estate* (New York, 1939, 480 pp.), attacked the Marxian prediction that the rate of profit would tend to fall and lead to imperialist capital export. He held that pre-1914 tendencies no longer applied because of the decline of foreign commerce and the rise of autarchy. Economic drives to war, he wrote, were as dominant in collectivist as in capitalist economy. The common anti-Soviet identification of tsarist expansionism with Soviet foreign policy is illustrated by Eric Hass's pamphlet, *Stalinist Imperialism* (New York, 1946, 48 pp.).

World War II found imperialism still a living issue although writers had announced its death for years. During the period of the Russo-German agreement, American communists denounced the imperialist war, as in Peter Wieden, *New Aspects of Imperialism* (New York, 1941, 40 pp.), and Gil Green, "How the British Empire Is Conjured Away," *Communist*, XX (Apr. 1941), pp. 319-332. Indicative of the change in policy was the cancellation of the rest of Green's series on "de-imperialism" after the June 1941 attack on Russia. A sample of their postwar views is George Marion, *Bases & Empire: a Chart of American Expansion* (New York, 1948, 199 pp.). W. E. B. Du Bois, whose Marxism is submerged and modified by his preoccupation with the race question, stated the demand for colonial liberation and racial equality as the only secure basis for a permanent peace in *Color and Democracy; Colonies and Peace* (New York, 1945, 143 pp.). Scott Nearing returned to the subject with *The Tragedy of Empire* (New York, 1945, 168 pp.). He rejected the Soviet alternative to the evils of imperialism because of the danger of corruption through greed, nationalism, and the love of power. Although equally sympathetic with the pacifist anarchist theory of decentralism, he felt that a transition period of centralization could not be avoided, and therefore advocated world federation as a compromise.

Pertinent to the discussion of Anglo-American imperialism is the Marxist mestizo reaction to "the Yankee peril." The classic expression is Manuel Ugarte's *The Destiny of a Continent* (1923; ed. by J. F. Rippey; tr. by C. A. Phillips; New York, 1925, 296 pp.), followed by a movement culminating in the Peruvian Aprista program of the middle thirties (see PART I, General Reading, pp. 30, 31). For other writings on this theme, see, for example, Horacio Blanco Fombona, *Crímenes del imperialismo norteamericano* (Mexico, D.F., 1927, 144 pp.), and P. E. Muñiz, *Penetración imperialista (minería y aprismo)* (Santiago de Chile, 1935, 158 pp.).

Topic 3. Nationalism, Internationalism, and War

The socialists' ultimate allegiance to their idea of the good society, like that of other religious or secular groups to the Kingdom of God or to some philosophy of social organization, has tended to cause a variety of rearrangements in their hierarchy of loyalties. Insofar as they have claimed to be determinists or scientific observers of social dynamics, their theory would of course have no ethics of loyalty. Questions of allegiance would not arise, except as socialists conceive of their own ideologies as being determined. The role of free will is not, however, completely ruled out in socialist theory, and in practice it assumes much greater importance than in theory.

We are concerned here with the choices socialists have made when faced with the conflict between loyalty to nation and loyalty to class or socialist community. The question may be broken down into three parts: (1) What kind of patriotism, if any, have socialists professed? (2) What sort of world organization have they found compatible with socialism? (3) How have their loyalties been revealed by the test of war?

The pre-Marxian socialists, in their absorption with community problems, relegated these questions to the background, yet nearly all expressed a theory of the relation between their settlements and the world of nations. The Marxian answers were corollaries of the Marxist theory of capitalist development. Marxism related nationalism and war to the problem of imperialism (Topic 2). Its concepts of the role of coercion and patriotism, in turn, provided the basis for its theories of evolution and the transitional society.

The utopian socialists, recognizing their deviation from the American pattern of individualism, took pains to be law-abiding citizens and called their critics' attention to the common elements of their religious or political heritage. The Shakers and Perfectionists emphasized their origin out of American revivalism. The Anabaptist heritage of the German pietists in particular was a strong element in the dominant American Protestantism, but the bond was noted by outsiders rather than by the German communists themselves. Secular utopians sanctified the principles of the Declaration of Independence and professed to be merely perfecting the relationship of democratic ends and means. Owenite and Associationist ideas of property were capitalistic. Owen's outlook was more in keeping with the radicalism produced by the new industrial order, as it was formed by his industrial experience; while the Fourierists conformed to the prevailing agrarian orientation of American society. World order for most religious socialists was simply the universal fruition of the Kingdom of God, of which their communities were the first fruits. The secular humanitarians, although reticent on the subject, developed the outlines of a theory of a congress of nations on the American federal principle. Nonresistance was a tendency among the religious, although all but the Hutterites were divided on the subject. The Fourierists suggested the substitution of constructive armies for public works in the place of military forces.

The four Internationals (see PART I, Topics 3-4) are sufficient evidence of the Marxian position that the workers have no country. One interpretation of this statement from the *Communist Manifesto* is that the workers would have countries when they seized power, but had none while the capitalists ruled. Marx's followers have tended to follow the more obvious interpretation. Nevertheless, Marxians have supported the nationalist movements in colonies, and also have frequently taken sides in favor of a more democratic, or less oppressive, state. The chief problem of world order was whether or not socialism was a necessary prerequisite. The national question within a socialist state has been met by granting subordinate cultural autonomies. Marx and Engels had the utmost scorn for absolute pacifism and held a Christian theory of the just war. If, on analysis of each historical situation, it is evident that a war will relieve the oppressed, whether they be chattel slaves, serfs, wage slaves, or colonists, the war is just and deserves support. If it is merely a conflict between equally oppressive powers, it is unjust. On the borders of Marxism and religious socialism were a number of eclectic or mixed theories, some making pacifism a primary tenet, and others focusing on nationalism or world federation.

American Marxists have often related nationalism, war, and world government to imperialism and revolution (for example, Nearing's *The Tragedy of Empire*, Topic 2), but there is no really balanced account treating all phases with equal thoroughness. On the utopian socialists the literature is scanty. Consequently, introductory information must be obtained from a number of sources. Read the 1854 constitution of the Practical Christian Republic in Adin Ballou, *History of the Hopedale Community* (ed. by W. S. Heywood; Lowell, Mass., 1897, 415 pp.), pp. 397-410, for a variety of utopian theory which exhibits at once the religious socialists' tendency toward nonresistance in extreme form, the utopians' dissociation from national life, and the secular socialists' inclusion of world government in their system of thought. The classic expression of American Nationalist socialism is in Edward Bellamy's utopian novel, *Looking Backward, 2000-1887* (Boston, 1888, 470 pp.), and in the publications of the Nationalist movement which this novel inspired. Read also for the opinion of Socialist Party members, Alexander Trachtenberg, ed., *The American Socialists and the War* (New York, 1917, 48 pp.); J. W. Hughan, *A Study of International Government* (New York, 1923, 401 pp.), pp. 254-283, 356-379; Norman Thomas, *What Is Our Destiny* (Garden City, N.Y., 1944, 192 pp.), pp. 32-50, and *The Challenge of War; an Economic Interpretation* (New York, 1923, 36 pp.); for the communist point of view, V. J. Jerome, "Marx and National Wars," *Communist*, xxii (Mar. 1943), pp. 211-221; and for the official Socialist Labor Party position stated by its national executive committee, *Workers of the World, Unite! Declaration on the Dissolution of the Communist International* (New York, 1943, 31 pp.).

NATIONALISM. The classic analysis of the concept of nationalism is Lord Acton's conservative essay, "Nationality," in *The History of Freedom and Other Essays* (ed. by J. N. Figgis and R. V. Laurence; London, 1907, 638 pp.), pp. 270-300. S. F. Bloom, *The World of Nations; a Study of the National Implications in the Work of Karl Marx* (New York, 1941, 225 pp.), is the only extensive treatment of Marx and the national question, but it fails to show the development of Marx's thought and makes questionable generalizations from implicit rather than expressed ideas. He concludes that Marx, although no nationalist, took national differences into account. Kautsky, *Nationalität und Internationalität* (*Neue Zeit: Ergänzungshefte*, No. 1; Stuttgart, 1908, 36 pp.), and Stalin, "The October Revolution and the National Question," originally appearing in *Pravda* in 1918 and available in Emile Burns' *A Handbook of Marxism* (New York, 1935, 1087 pp.), pp. 810-821, are the best brief European Marxist expressions on the subject. See also the famous French antimilitarist statement by Gustave Hervé, *My Country Right or Wrong* (tr. by Guy Bowman; London, 1910, 270 pp.); the extended analysis of the question of Austro-Hungarian nationalities by Otto Bauer, *Die Nationalitätenfrage und die Sozialdemokratie* (*Marx-Studien*, ii; Vienna, 1907, 576 pp.); Henri de Man, *Nationalisme et socialisme* (Paris, 1932, 100 pp.); the collection of Stalin's writings and speeches, *Marxism and the National and*

Colonial Question (New York, 1935?, 304 pp.); Dona Torr, ed., *Marxism, Nationality and War* (London, 1941, 2 pts.); and Rudolf Rocker, *Nationalism and Culture* (tr. by R. E. Chase; New York, 1937, 574 pp.). Rocker's publication was financed by the Kropotkin Society in Los Angeles and contains a good book list (pp. 539-548).

M. E. Curti, *The Roots of American Loyalty* (New York, 1946, 267 pp.), contains a good selective bibliography of the general literature on American nationalism (pp. 249-256) and discusses the socialists' critique of patriotism (pp. 207-211). J. H. Noyes, *History of American Socialisms* (Philadelphia, 1870, 678 pp.), pp. 21-29, points out the American characteristics of the utopians. Emma Goldman, *Patriotism; a Menace to Liberty* (New York, 1908?, 16 pp.), expresses the sentiment common to communist anarchists.

The Nationalist movement in the United States, inspired by Edward Bellamy's *Looking Backward, 2000-1887* (cited above), claimed to seek socialism in one country. Socialists like Laurence Gronlund in "Nationalism," *Arena*, I (Jan. 1890), pp. 153-165, hailed the Nationalists' proposal to nationalize monopolies and end "planlessness" and their refusal to adopt such "un-American ideas" as the class struggle. J. R. Bridge, "Nationalistic Socialism," *ibid.*, pp. 184-195, asserted that the Bellamyite state would not be autocratic but in the American cooperative and democratic tradition. See also the *New Nation* (Boston, 1891-1894), Nationalist organ; Rabbi Solomon Schindler, "What Is Nationalism?" *New England Magazine*, N.S., VII (Sept. 1892), pp. 53-61; and *Edward Bellamy Speaks Again!* (Kansas City, Mo., 1937, 249 pp.). The Christian socialist *Arena* (Boston, etc., 1889-1909), besides supporting the Nationalists, published articles and stories preaching patriotism during the Spanish-American War, such as H. E. Foster, "The Decadence of Patriotism and What It Means," *Arena*, XIX (June 1898), pp. 740-751.

The *Masses* (New York, 1911-1917) consistently lampooned the hundred-per-cent Americans from 1916 until it was forced to suspend publication. See especially "Do You Believe in Patriotism?" VIII (Mar. 1916), pp. 12-13—the answers of a dozen socialists and sympathizers that they believed in a variety that was not chauvinist—and short articles in succeeding issues by John Reed and Max Eastman, as well as cartoons by Art Young and Maurice Becker. I. St. J. Tucker, *The Geography of the Gods; a Study of the Religions of Patriotism* (Chicago, 1919, 150 pp.), and *The Chosen Nation* (Chicago, 1919, 45 pp.), the latter a polemical poem written during the author's trial for conspiracy to obstruct the draft, maintained the iconoclastic attitude of the *Masses*. Norman Hapgood, ed., *Professional Patriots* (New York, 1927, 210 pp.), collected evidence on the war period to deliver a final blow at those who exploited patriotic sentiment for private gain. James MacKaye, *Americanized Socialism; a*

Yankee View of Capitalism (New York, 1918, 191 pp.), by a New England mining engineer who supported American participation in World War I, is an interesting rationalistic argument that socialism is efficient democracy. Leon Samson, *Toward a United Front; a Philosophy for American Workers* (New York, 1933, 276 pp.), develops the theme of Americanism as a false substitute symbol for socialism. Representative of the Socialist Labor Party is Eric Hass, *The Americanism of Socialism* (New York, 1941, 45 pp.).

The communists, especially since 1935, have supported their slogan, "Communism Is Twentieth-Century Americanism," with historical articles identifying the current conservatives with the unpopular Tories or conservatives of other periods. Frank Meyer and Robert Strong, "The Treason of Reaction in America's Second War of Independence," *Communist*, xx (July 1941), pp. 635-651, is an example. To the hecklers' perennial question, "Why don't you go back where you came from?" Granville Hicks answered with *I Like America* (New York, 1938, 216 pp.). Typically anticommunist is the publication of the American Legion's National Americanism Commission, *Isms; a Review of Alien Isms, Revolutionary Communism and Their Active Sympathizers in the United States* (2nd ed., Indianapolis, Ind., 1937, 287 pp.). The communists could agree with Hans Kohn's conclusion in "The Nationality Problem and the Soviets," *Revolutions and Dictatorships* (Cambridge, Mass., 1939, 437 pp.), pp. 145-178, that Soviet patriotism is not modern nationalism, yet Soviet culture is a complex of nationalities.

The special subject of the Jews as a nationality and socialism, treated in Section 3-F of PART I, General Reading, evoked American discussion first among Jewish urban labor, especially after Poale Zion was organized in the United States in 1905. See the pertinent sections of Herz Burgin, *Die Geschichte fun der yidisher arbeiter Bewegung* (New York, 1915, 935 pp.), in Yiddish, published by the United Jewish Trade Unions. Since 1930 the communists and Trotskyists have contributed many publications to this subject. Alexander Bittelman, *Program for Survival; the Communist Position on the Jewish Question* (New York, 1947, 63 pp.), is by the editor of *Political Affairs* and general secretary of the Morning Freiheit Association, publishers of the Yiddish daily, *Morning Freiheit* (New York, 1922-). This pamphlet states the views of American communists just before the establishment of the state of Israel. They not only supported an "independent and democratic State of Arabs and Jews" with free admission of European Jewish displaced persons, but also named the countries of eastern Europe, especially Poland, as alternative asylums. For other Stalinist views see the occasional articles in the *Communist*; Earl Browder and others, *The Meaning of the Palestine Partition* (New York, 1937, 32 pp.); and *Jewish Life* (New York, 1937-1938), a monthly published by the Communist Party's New York State Jewish Buro. *Jewish Life* (New York, 1946-) is a monthly "magazine for the Progressive Jew." The Shachtmanite Trotskyists discuss the national question as it relates to Zionism in their "Marxism and the Jewish Question" issue of *New International*, III (Nov. 1946), pp. 259-261 (editorial), and pp. 264-272 (including the Workers Party resolution of May 1946).

INTERNATIONALISM. In addition to the materials on internationalism in PART I, Topics 3-4, see the following socialist treatments outside the United States: Eugenio Forni, *L'internazionale e lo stato* (Naples, 1878, 520 pp.); Gabriel Deville, *Socialism, Revolution and Internationalism* (1893; tr. by R. R. La Monte; Chicago, 1907, 64 pp.); Gustave Hervé, *L'Internationalisme* (Paris, 1910, 178 pp.); Enrique del Valle Iberlucea, *La cuestión internacional y el Partido socialista* (Buenos Aires, 1917, 256 pp.); and Franz Borkenau, *Socialism, National or International* (London, 1942, 172 pp.). Borkenau represents the significant shift of many democratic socialists away from the "utopian internationalism" of the social democrats before 1914, and toward working for world unity through Anglo-American "superimperialism." The Fourierist and Saint-Simonian outlook on world society has been described by J. L. Puech, *La Tradition socialiste en France et la Société des nations* (Paris, 1921, 228 pp.). Adin Ballou, *Practical Christian Socialism* (Hopedale, Mass., 1854, 655 pp.), put the Fraternity of Communal Nations at the peak of his social pyramid, and similar hierarchies of confederation are suggested in Fourierist and Icarian sources (see PART II, Topics 6-7). V. C. Woodhull (Mrs. J. B. Martin), an unorthodox American member of the First International, based her proposal, "Constitution of the United States of the World," *Woodhull & Claflin's Weekly*, IV (Feb. 10, 1872), pp. 11-15, on the United States constitution.

A statement of the early Socialist Party internationalism is found in its 1904 platform, Section 2, printed in John Spargo, *Socialism* (New York, 1906, 257 pp.), pp. 243-244. See also H. W. Laidler's survey, "Socialism and Internationalism," in *Socialism in Thought and Action* (New York, 1920, 546 pp.), pp. 247-282; and PART II, Topics 8-9, 11. I. St. J. Tucker, *Internationalism; the Problem of the Hour* (Chicago, n.d.; five lectures paged separately), contrasted the German, British, and American nationalisms with the Russian Revolution and labor's internationalism, and trusted only in a socialist world federation. "Socialism and the Terms of Peace," Academy of Political Science, *Proceedings*, VII (July 1917), pp. 289-293, a 1917 address by Meyer London, socialist congressman, urged disarmament and the elimination of the concept of "national honor" which prevented many international disputes from being referred to the Hague Tribunal. The international aspects of the Socialist Party schism after World War I are revealed in the debate between James Oneal (affirmative) and Robert Minor (negative), *Resolved: That the Terms of the Third International are Inacceptable to the Revolutionary Socialists of the World* (New York, 1921, 32 pp.). Norman Thomas, *What Is Our Destiny* (Garden City, N.Y., 1944, 192 pp.), pp. 51-137, rejected the possibility of "peace through police," questioned the World Federalists' American analogy, and expressed his only hope in a socialist world order. He later gave qualified support to the present organization in *A Socialist Looks at the United Nations* (Syracuse, N.Y., 1945, 51 pp.). International socialist aims for the postwar world are outlined in L. L. Lorwin, *Economic Consequences of the Second World War* (New York, 1941, 510 pp.), chaps. 15-16, 20.

The pacifist socialists relate their position on war to international political and economic problems. From 1918 to 1934 the *World Tomorrow* was the vehicle for expressing the position of the Fellowship of Reconciliation, pacifist organization with a Christian socialist or anarchist leadership. Its place was taken by *Fellowship* (New York, 1935-). A typical article is W. E. Orchard, "The Basis for Internationalism," *World Tomorrow*, v (Nov. 1922), pp. 329-331. See also Scott Nearing, *The Next Step; a Plan for Economic World Federation* (Ridgewood, N.J., 1922, 175 pp.), and his *United World; the Road to International Peace* (New York, 1945, 265 pp.). M. Q. Sibley reviews contributions to the problem of enlarging the scope of the community in his article, "Modern Universalism," in Joseph Roucek, ed., *Twentieth Century Political Thought* (New York, 1946, 657 pp.), pp. 219-244.

The communist view is expressed by Max Weiss, "Lenin and Proletarian Internationalism," *Communist*, xx (Jan. 1941), pp. 18-34. See also PART II, Topic 10.

WAR. An excellent study by Edmund Silberner, *The Problem of War in Nineteenth Century Economic Thought* (tr. from the French by A. H. Krappe; Princeton, N.J., 1946, 332 pp.), interprets the subject broadly but limits its field to English, French, and German writings. Book 3 (pp. 213-279) is illuminating on Saint-Simon, Owen, the Fourierists, Marx, and Engels. Sample twentieth-century socialist points of view outside the United States are expressed in the following: Karl Kautsky, *Sozialisten und Krieg; ein Beitrag zur Ideengeschichte des Sozialismus von den Hussiten bis zum Völkerbund* (Prague, 1937, 702 pp.), a general history; Karl Liebknecht, *Militarism* (1907; tr. by Savel Zimand; New York, 1917, 178 pp.), parts of a 1906 lecture by a social democrat who later became a Spartacist leader; G. Zinoviev and V. I. Lenin, *Socialism and War* (1918; New York, 1930, 48 pp.), reprinted from Lenin's *The Imperialist War*; Silvano Fasulo, *I Socialisti e la guerra (da Crimea all' Isonzo)* (Forli,

1918, 72 pp.), and Achille Loria, *The Economic Causes of War* (1912; tr. by J. L. Garner; Chicago, 1918, 188 pp.), Italian; Bjarne Braatoy, *Labour and War; the Theory of Labour Action to Prevent War* (London, 1934, 216 pp.), by a Norwegian social democrat; the Labour Party pamphlet, *War and Socialism* (London, 1932, 11 pp.), and the writings of the party's pacifist minority, such as J. M. Murry and George Lansbury; and J. A. Dawson, comp., *Socialism and War; the Marxist Attitude to Nazism; the State* (Melbourne, Australia, 1943, 79 pp.), representative of the position of the American Workers Socialist Party.

All the religious communists except the Mormons had pacifist tendencies, although the German groups contributed both members and material aid to the Union side in the Civil War. See scattered references in the literature of PART II, Topics 1-4, such as R. A. Parker, *A Yankee Saint* (New York, 1935, 322 pp.), pp. 210-211. The Shakers were the most outspoken and consistently pacifist, as indicated by *A Declaration of the Society of People (Commonly Called Shakers) Shewing Their Reasons for Refusing to Aid or Abet the Cause of War and Bloodshed, by Bearing Arms, Paying Fines, Hiring Substitutes, or Rendering Any Equivalent for Military Services* (Albany, N.Y., 1815, 20 pp.); S. Y. Wells (Philanthropos, pseud.), *A Brief Illustration of the Principles of War and Peace* (Albany, N.Y., 1831, 112 pp.); and F. W. Evans, *The Conditions of Peace* (Mt. Lebanon, N.Y., 1890, 6 pp.). See also Julia Neal, "While the People Were at War," a chapter on the South Union Family during the Civil War, in *By Their Fruits* (Chapel Hill, N.C., 1947, 279 pp.), pp. 177-197.

American radical movements before the Civil War often had common leaders but the extreme wings—the peace movement and the utopian socialists—were not often served by interlocking directorates. Adin Ballou was active in both, yet his *Christian Non-Resistance* (Philadelphia, 1846, 240 pp.), an integral part of his communal theory, was too radical for the peace movement. His treatise was an expansion of a pamphlet, *Non-Resistance in Relation to Human Governments* (Boston, 1839, 24 pp.).

After the Civil War another group of nonresistant communists appeared —the Hutterite Mennonites—and have since settled about fifty *Brüderhöfe* on the great plains of the United States and Canada. For these communities see B. W. Clark, "The Huterian Communities," *Journal of Political Economy*, XXXII (June-Aug. 1924), pp. 357-374, 468-486; and L. E. Deets, *The Hutterites; a Study in Social Cohesion* (Gettysburg, Pa., 1939, 64 pp.). Other pacifist sects with Anabaptist backgrounds have mutualist tendencies, submerged by Americanization. See, for example, J. W. Fretz, "Mutual Aid among Mennonites," *Mennonite Quarterly Review*, XIII (Jan., July 1939), pp. 28-58, 187-209, which does not deal with the Hutterites.

The preparedness campaign of 1916 brought a flood of socialist writing on war. Before this, G. R. Kirkpatrick's *War—What For?* (West LaFayette, Ohio, 1910, 349 pp.), sought to focus labor's attention on the class war instead of the international struggle for markets. In *Darrow-Lewis Debate; "The Theory of Non-Resistance"* (Chicago, 1910, 48 pp.), the skeptical C. S. Darrow, author of *Resist Not Evil* (Chicago, 1903, 179 pp.), defended Tolstoyan anarchism on the ground that labor was too weak to use violence, and the socialist A. M. Lewis pointed out Darrow's confusion of nonresistance with nonviolent resistance and expressed the orthodox Marxian view of class struggle and revolution. Sample books of the war period are A. L. Benson, Socialist Party candidate for president in 1916, *A Way to Prevent War* (Girard, Kan., 1915, 180 pp.), proposing a popular referendum; L. B. Boudin, *Socialism and War* (New York, 1916, 267 pp.); F. C. Howe, *Why War* (New York, 1916, 366 pp.); John Spargo, *Americanism and Social Democracy* (New York, 1918, 325 pp.), expressing the prowar socialists' position; and Thorstein Veblen, *An Inquiry into the Nature of Peace and the Terms of its Perpetuation* (New York, 1917, 367 pp.). See also D. A. Shannon's unpublished master of philosophy thesis at the University of Wisconsin (1946), *Anti War Thought and Activity of Eugene V. Debs, 1914-1921.* Randolph Bourne's unfinished study (cited in General Reading, p. 253) on the state as inevitably involved in war expressed a determinism similar to Emanuel Kanter, *The Evolution of War; a Marxian Study* (Chicago, 1927, 123 pp.), a Kerr publication, and to J. F. Carter, *Man Is War* (Indianapolis, Ind., 1926, 398 pp.). Scott Nearing's pacifism is implicit in all his writing. *War; Organized Destruction and Mass Murder by Civilized Nations* (New York, 1931, 310 pp.) was the most comprehensive of his three works directly on the subject. J. W. Hughan, *Three Decades of War Resistance* (New York, 1942, 24 pp.), was published by the War Resisters League, a secular pacifist organization with strong socialist or anarchist tendencies. See also K. E. Boulding, *The Economics of Peace* (New York, 1945, 278 pp.), a Keynesian treatise; Milton Mayer and others, *Conscience and the Commonwealth* (New York, 1944, 32 pp.), and articles in *Politics* (New York, 1944-1949), July 1944-July 1946.

Democratic socialists protested the use of soldiers against strikers or in an imperialist war, but the revolutionary syndicalists completely repudiated militarism together with the state that employed the army. Sorel discussed the general strike in *Reflections on Violence*, but actually this weapon was considered nonviolent as far as the participants were concerned. That Sorel was right in terms of results is illustrated in Jack London's short story, "The Dream of Debs," *International Socialist Review*, IX (Jan.-Feb. 1909), pp. 481-489, 561-570. He described the tremendous wave of violence and brutality unleashed by the disciplined general strike of one big national union.

The noninterventionism of American leftists in the thirties was expressed by such men as A. M. Bingham in *Beware of Europe's Wars* (New York, 1937, 31 pp.); and the Revolutionary Workers League pamphlet, *The Workers' Answer to Boss War* (Chicago, 1937, 22 pp.). Arguments of twenty years before were rehearsed in the *Socialist Review* (New York, 1932-1940; title varies), for example, in Theodore Dan, "Socialism and War," VI (Sept. 1937), pp. 10-13, opposing the Popular Front, and Sidney Hook, "Thoughts in Season," VI (May-June 1938), pp. 6-7, 16, concluding, "Collective security means war and war means Fascism." See also Oscar Ameringer, *Bread or Lead; Production for Use or Production for Destruction* (Norman, Okla., 1940, 52 pp.); Daniel De Leon, *Capitalism Means War* (New York, 1941, 32 pp.); and John West, *War and the Workers* (New York, 1935, 47 pp.), Shachtmanite. The communists followed this line, as expressed by V. J. Jerome, *Intellectuals and the War* (New York, 1940, 63 pp.), and Earl Browder, *The Second Imperialist War* (New York, 1940, 309 pp.), a collection covering the period from March 1939 to May 1940, during the life of the Russo-German pact. Their shift is revealed in Browder's publications after 1941, viewing the war as liberationist, e.g., *Teheran* (New York, 1944, 128 pp.). The essential Marxist position that war can be abolished only after world communism has abolished capitalism and national sovereignty is expressed in Alex Bittelman, *Revolutionary Struggle against War vs. Pacifism* (New York, 1932?, 48 pp.), which echoes Zinoviev's and Lenin's pamphlet cited above (p. 279).

After World War II the so-called Stockholm peace petition as well as various world peace congresses were directed by communists. The Conference for World Peace held at the Waldorf-Astoria Hotel in New York in March 1949 by the National Council of the Arts, Sciences and Professions, was strongly supported by communists although not all participants were communists or fellow travelers. For the proceedings of this conference see *Speaking of Peace: Cultural and Scientific Conference for World Peace* (New York, 1949).

Topic 4. Socialist Political Action

The communitarians felt no need for a political party and expected that their ideas would be spread by writings and by the success of their communities. When the Marxists rejected all such limited experiments the alternative was to organize for political or economic action throughout existing society, coupled with propaganda to awaken class consciousness. Socialist aims were revolutionary whether they chose violent or nonviolent means to transform capitalist society. The bibliographies of PART II, Topics 8-10, should be consulted for an introduction to the history of the American socialist parties, particularly the numerous discussions of tactics in the periodicals cited. In the present topic, the purpose is to examine the theories of the function of parties both before and after the revolution. In PART V, Topic 4, their organizational structure is investigated from the sociological point of view.

To some socialist groups, the party has been primarily an instrument for the education of the public, and labor in particular, in the ideas of socialism. Some have concentrated on winning elections in a few districts so that socialists might be represented in state legislatures and Congress and have wider opportunities for propaganda. Some have supported limited reforms for the same purpose, since these reforms would serve to illustrate the advantages of even partial collectivization and control, while greater democracy would expand the field for propaganda. Parties were also considered as institutions for training the leaders of the revolution. This training of the vanguard is what communists call "propaganda" and socialists "education." Mass work (see PART V, Topic 5) is termed "agitation" by the communists and "propaganda" by the socialists. Those who believed that socialism could capture the government by the ballot differed over the conditions under which the socialists should assume power. One group emphasized an immediate program of reforms short of socialism. Their opponents insisted on a socialist platform, and on taking over administrative control only when the country was ready for a social revolution.

Few socialists ever saw the need of more than one party to represent labor. But from the beginning splits predominated over fusions until there are now over half a dozen political organizations with socialist aims. Splits have arisen because of disagreements about the purpose of a socialist party, as outlined above. They have arisen also as the result of personal loyalty to factional leaders and of contests between the foreign-language groups and those who would Americanize the parties. Dissatisfaction with the position of various parties on current domestic issues, war, Soviet Russia, activity in the labor and cooperative movements, and control of the party presses, has produced further division. Viewed from the point of view of a single party, these divisions were the work of *factions*, but one of these factions might be a *fraction* of another party, a group organized and disciplined for the purpose of carrying out the other party's policies. Fusions have been of two kinds: they have attempted to build a mass party including nonsocialists, like the British Labour Party or the Cooperative Commonwealth Federation of Canada, or else they have sought to join two socialist groups. Except for the original Socialistic Labor Party, formed by the union of Lassalleans and Marxians, and the Socialist Party which was established by the fusion of western social democrats with eastern bolters from the Socialist Labor Party, neither type of fusion has had much lasting success in this country.

Socialist parties have generally sought to achieve a solid core of wage-earning members, particularly in industry, but the actual complexion of their membership has been far from this ideal. Labor unions, once recognized as bargaining agents, become increasingly committed to seeking limited gains within the existing industrial framework, and increasingly unwilling to support a socialist program which they fear will jeopardize these gains, even though it ultimately promises more. The urban middle class, the professional intellectuals, and even some well-to-do "angels" have made themselves useful in socialist organizations. Special campaigns have been repeatedly pushed to recruit farmers, students, and minority groups with special grievances. The result is a heterogeneous membership with a high turnover, for the common interests of the members are not durable and their hopes of patronage are limited to the few party offices.

The organization of socialist parties is one clue to their ideas of party government in the transitional society. The principle of democratic centralism followed by the communists and their offshoots—full discussion before reaching a policy decision by majority vote, subject, however, to review by higher authority and strict obedience to the executive in carrying the policy into effect—corresponds to their theory of the character of one-party rule in the proletarian dictatorship. The tendency is rule from the top down. Self-criticism, initiative, full participation, and full discussion are directed toward the details of the accepted faith as formulated by the leaders, and its application to immediate situations. A close parallel to democratic centralism can be seen in the sections of the Icarian constitution of 1850 on liberty and on respect for law, and in the 1855 regulations of their general assembly. The subordinate position of their Iowa colony until 1856 was similar to the subordination of non-Russian communists to the Communist Party of the Soviet Union.

In the absence of any significant body of democratic socialist theory on the place of parties in a socialist state one might conclude that the gradualists expected party organizations to continue after a socialist electoral victory, with the capitalist parties in the minority. The opposition of democratic socialists to the one-party system of totalitarian governments implies the same conclusion. It is nevertheless strange that the social democrats have not dealt directly with the theory concerning the function of parties after the revolution when they have admitted the continuation of conflict even in the "higher" stage of socialism. Even if they are resigned to a position as third-party propagandists of ideas to be carried out by a major party they still have need for such a theory. Like the framers of the American Constitution they have assumed when discussing the socialist state that "faction" would end with the consummation of the revolution, and have somehow conceived of the administration of things as replacing the rule over men. The attempt to reconcile popular control with modern bureaucratic tendencies has been made by G. D. H. Cole and others in Great Britain, where the problem is immediate. In the United States, however, few socialists have faced the conflict between the oligarchical tendencies within their own parties and their fundamental belief in government from the bottom up.

Read Morris Hillquit, *Socialism Summed Up* (New York, 1913, 110 pp.), pp. 44-75, on the methods and program of gradualist socialism at the peak of its popularity; and Laurence Gronlund, *The Co-operative Commonwealth* (1884; rev. and enl. ed., Boston, 1890, 304 pp.), pp. 167-201, for the theory that parties will be unnecessary under socialism. For an exposition of Communist Party activities and discipline read M. Jenks's manual, *The Communist Nucleus; What It Is—How It Works* (New York, 1928, 61 pp.), and J. Peters, *The Communist Party; a Manual on Organization* (New York, 1935, 127 pp.), pp. 23-35. The Peters manual has been republished under hostile auspices as *Secrets of the Communist Party Exposed! The Secret Communist Party Manual on Organization* (Columbus, Ohio, 1947, 63 pp.). On factions, splits, and fusions, read in J. P. Cannon, *The History of American Trotskyism* (New York, 1944, 268 pp.), an account of the functions and problems of that party. William Isaacs, *Contemporary Marxian Political Movements in the United States, 1917-1939* (New York, 1942, 49 pp.), consists of chapters on communist principles, strategy, and tactics taken from his unpublished doctoral study.

One of the most important European treatments of socialist parties and their organization is Robert Michels, *Political Parties; a Sociological Study of the Oligarchical Tendencies of Modern Democracy* (1911; tr. by E. and C. Paul; New York, 1915, 416 pp.). Michels investigates the leadership of European social democratic parties and concludes that the oratorical skill, political trickery, intellectual ability, and technical competence of a small number of men brought them to the top and kept them there. In this connection, see PART III, Topic 6. Most important for communist theory is *Lenin on Organization* (Chicago, 1926, 235 pp.). See also Eduard Bernstein, *Von der Sekte zur Partei* (Jena, 1911, 76 pp.), and Otto Bauer, *Die illegale Partei* (Paris, 1939, 205 pp.).

Many American studies have related third parties and pressure groups, including the socialists, to American party government. Particularly useful are S. A. Rice, *Farmers and Workers in American Politics* (New York, 1924, 233 pp.), and Nathan Fine, *Labor and Farmer Parties in the United States, 1828-1928* (New York, 1928, 445 pp.). See also C. N. Fay, *Labor in Politics* (4th ed., Cambridge, Mass., 1921, 288 pp.), representing the American aversion to class parties; Robert Hunter, *Labor in Politics* (Chicago, 1915, 202 pp.), a Socialist Party publication; M. R. Carroll, *Labor and Politics* (Boston, 1923, 206 pp.), and a sample treatment in a college text, V. O. Key, Jr., *Politics, Parties and Pressure Groups* (New York, 1942, 814 pp.), pp. 68-101, 273-293. Seba Eldridge, *Political Action* (Philadelphia, 1924, 382 pp.), accepting the class-struggle theory, concludes from his analysis of the nature of man in society that labor cannot reach its goals through liberalism. R. F. Hoxie, "The Socialist Party and American Convention Methods," *Journal of Political Economy*, xx (July 1912), pp. 738-744, points out that the Republicans would have nominated Roosevelt instead of Taft in 1912 if they had used the socialists' democratic and representative methods.

Socialist theories of political action before De Leon can be found in the abundant but little-known pamphlet and periodical sources dealing with the controversies between the Lassalleans, Marxians, reformers, and anarchists before 1895, and in the general labor histories of the period (see PART II, General Reading, pp. 97-104; PART II, Topic 8; and Topic 8 below). E. H. Heywood, an individualist anarchist, was among the first to advocate independent labor politics, in *The Labor Party* (Worcester, Mass., 1868, 19 pp.).

The Socialist Labor Party (see again PART II, Topic 8), although primarily an educational society in the twentieth century, maintained throughout a political front. De Leon's theoretical justifications of party activity, published as editorials in the *People*, have been reprinted in pamphlet form. *As to Politics* (1906-1907; New York, 1935, 117 pp.), argues against the I.W.W. syndicalist objection to any form of political activity. *Woman's Suffrage* (New York, 1909, 48 pp.), also published with the title, *The Ballot and the Class Struggle*, told the suffragettes that they would have to wait for the social revolution before they had a vote that would mean anything. *Berger's Hit and Misses* (New York, 1911, 104 pp.), later published as *Revolutionary Socialism in U.S. Congress; "Parliamentary Idiocy" vs. Marxian Socialism* (New York, 1931, 104 pp.), lectured the socialist congressman for not using his position for propaganda. See also A. Rosenthal, *The Differences between the Socialist Party and the Socialist Labor Party* (Brooklyn, 1908, 44 pp.), and De Leon, *Party Ownership of the Press* (New York, 1931, 32 pp.). De Leon stated his views of a proposed merger of the Socialist Labor Party and the Socialist Party in an address, *Unity* (New York, 1908, 27 pp.).

The Socialist Party at the very outset of its career sought to preserve universal solidarity at the same time it was creating a new socialist sect. G. D. Herron called for solidarity in an address published by the *International Socialist Review*, "A Plea for the Unity of American Socialists," I (Dec. 1900), pp. 321-328. A survey of Socialist Party campaign handbooks will indicate both how much gradualism dominated the program of that party and to what degree its propaganda was successful in inducing major parties to adopt certain planks. Even before the party was organized, W. T. Mills foreshadowed the gradualist approach in *Evolutionary Politics* (Chicago, 1898, 255 pp.). See also John Spargo, *Shall the Unions Go into Politics?* (New York, 1903, 32 pp.); J. S. Crawford, *Political Socialism; Would It Fail in Success?* (3rd ed., Cherokee, Iowa, 1911, 110 pp.); and W. J. Ghent, ed., *The Tactics of Socialism* (Girard, Kan., 1916, 64 pp.). Illustrative of the pamphlet literature on the Socialist Party record in communities of their greatest strength are Ethelwyn Mills, *Legislative Program of the Socialist Party* (Chicago, 1914, 64 pp.), including a survey of socialist activities in state legislatures, 1899-1913; Evans Clark and Charles Solomon, *The Socialists in the New York Board of Aldermen* (New York, 1918, 48 pp.); and August Claessens and W. M. Feigenbaum, *Socialists in the New York Assembly* (New York, 1918, 96 pp.).

Morris Hillquit and others in "Tactics and Next Steps," in H. W. Laidler and Norman Thomas, eds., *The Socialism of Our Times* (New York, 1929, 377 pp.), pp. 59-171, show that the party still planned for the possibility of eventual victory, but J. F. Carter, "Marx on the Half-Shell," in his *American Messiahs* (New York, 1935, 238 pp.), pp. 155-171, characterizes Thomas as having silently transformed an insignificant minority party into a powerful educative force supplying the New Deal with its specific policies. The autobiographies of party leaders and organizers like Oscar Ameringer, *If You Don't Weaken* (New York, 1940, 476 pp.), pp. 227-427, and Morris Hillquit, *Loose Leaves from a Busy Life* (New York, 1934, 339 pp.), and others cited in PART II, Topic 9, contain details on recruiting, financing, and policy formation. Paul Porter, *Which Way for the Socialist Party?* (Milwaukee, Wis., 1937, 47 pp.), a pamphlet for discussion in party branches, has comments on sectarianism, the Popular Front, and the class composition of the party. Opposition to the united front is expressed in the symposium edited by Abraham Cahan, *Hear the Other Side* (New York, 1934, 71 pp.). Scott Nearing, *Democracy Is Not Enough* (New York, 1945, 153 pp.), grounded in a philosophy of popular participation, is more concerned with the maintenance of local councils in the face of increasingly centralized government than with a theory of the future place of socialist parties.

The following pamphlets represent the repeated efforts to start a "mass party" like the La Follette Farmer-Labor Party of 1924, but led by a particular socialist "vanguard": John Pepper, *For a Labor Party* (2nd ed., New York, 1923, 68 pp.), and Earl Browder and Jack Stachel, *How Do We Raise the Question of a Labor Party?* (New York, 1935, 24 pp.), communist; *Why a Labor Party?* (New York, 1934, 16 pp.), Lovestoneite; *Toward an American Revolutionary Labor Movement* (rev. ed., New York, 1934, 46 pp.), American Workers Party; H. W. Laidler, *Toward a Farmer-Labor Party* (New York, 1938, 55 pp.), a League for Industrial

Democracy publication, with a good book list; and Joseph Hansen, *American Workers Need a Labor Party* (New York, 1944, 44 pp.), Trotskyist.

The cause of the split between communists and socialists in 1919 is described in the *Manifesto and Program of the Left Wing Section, Socialist Party, Local Greater New York* (New York, 1919, 14 pp.), and Morris Hillquit, *The Immediate Issue* (New York, 1919?, 15 pp.). In addition to the Peters and Jenks manuals cited above, see the monthly *Party Organizer* (New York, 1927-1938), *Party Building and Political Leadership* (New York, 1937, 127 pp.) by W. Z. Foster and others, and numerous articles. Autobiographies are again useful for the communists, such as Benjamin Gitlow, *I Confess* (New York, 1940, 611 pp.), pp. 283-333, the strictures of a Right deviationist who had held high party offices during the twenties. See also Joseph Freeman, *An American Testament* (New York, 1936, 678 pp.), pp. 292-321; W. Z. Foster, *Pages from a Worker's Life* (New York, 1939, 314 pp.), chap. 7; and other references in PART II, Topic 10.

Anton Pannekoek and others, "The Role of the Party," *Modern Socialism*, I (1941-1942), Nos. 2-4, is a discussion between Abraham Ziegler, the editor, a former member of the Socialist Labor Party who has renounced sectarianism in all forms, and supporters of the "power-vanguard" idea and democratic socialism. Max Shachtman, "Footnote for Historians," *New International*, IV (Dec. 1938), pp. 377-379, lists a dozen schismatic Trotskyist groups "playing revolution." Shachtman, "Five Years of the Workers Party," *New International*, XI (Apr. 1945), pp. 73-81, recounts the history of the Trotskyist minority after its expulsion by the Cannonite faction. The short story by Isaac Rosenfeld, "The Party," *Kenyon Review*, IX (Autumn 1947), pp. 572-607, illustrates splits, factions, press control and propaganda, socials and demonstrations.

Topic 5. *Socialist Labor Agitation*

The emancipation of the working class, according to Marxism, must be the work of the working class itself. But the conviction of a large part of American labor has been that by individual effort a man can achieve a higher status. The ideology of the American open-class system and the sociological aspects of socialist participation in trade-union activity will be investigated in PART V. The student is referred again to PART II, General Reading, and to the titles dealing with socialist labor activities in Topics 8-11.

Before socialism appeared in the United States, some of the wage-earning class had given up the idea of individual advancement. They copied the combinations of the industrial capitalists and organized to improve their position under capitalism. To revolutionize the point of view of labor, socialists have alternately tried organizing rival unions and "boring from within" existing unions. In either case, the policy of their opponents—whether rival socialists or business union leaders—has been labeled "class collaboration." They have not scrupled to uncover the evils of their opponents' labor racketeering, bureaucracy, and faulty strike strategy while they have simultaneously agitated among the unorganized against the evils of capitalist exploitation. In general they have laid the evils of jurisdictional disputes to the craft form of organization and have favored industrial unionism. In recent years some gradualist socialists have concluded that all organized labor is revolutionary, since organization increases the collective power of labor to modify the economic order in its own interests. Thus they discount the divorce of socialist labor leaders from their parties because all union activity still promotes the movement in the long run.

Socialists working among labor have had to face a number of special issues. They have had to reconcile their belief in the ultimate free movement of population with organized labor's hostility to immigration. They have had to decide upon which part of the employed population to concentrate their efforts. They have tried to convince the middle class that it is part of the proletariat. They have tried to create sympathetic attitudes among the churches. When required to explain how labor would manage an industrial republic they have drawn on the theories of syndicalism and guild socialism. They have attacked labor conscription as involuntary servitude and therefore violating the thirteenth amendment. They have defended their theory of the class struggle by writing their own histories of American labor.

In order to compare the policies which the principal socialist parties have adopted to revolutionize the labor movement, read the following selections from the writings of their leaders: for the Socialist Labor Party, Daniel De Leon, *The Burning Question of Trades Unionism* (1904; New York, 1921, 43 pp.), and Eric Hass, *Socialist Industrial Unionism; the Workers' Power* (New York, 1940, 62 pp.); for the Communist Party, W. Z. Foster, *Misleaders of Labor* (Chicago, 1927, 336 pp.), pp. 9-42, 271-336; and for the Socialist Party, Norman Thomas, *America's Way Out; a Program for Democracy* (New York, 1931, 324 pp.), pp. 251-277. For a summary read Sidney Lens, *Left, Right and Center; Conflicting Forces in American Labor* (Hinsdale, Ill., 1949, 445 pp.), written from the point of view of an American trade unionist who believes that "above everything else labor needs its own independent political party."

The communitarian literature is almost devoid of reference to American labor organization, except for sympathetic references in the *Harbinger* and other Fourierist periodicals to local workingmen's organizations, for Icarian connections with the First International, and for occasional leaflets such as *Capital and Labor; What Is in a Name? Wail of a Striker* (Mt. Lebanon, N.Y., n.d., 11 pp.), by the Shaker Elder F. W. Evans.

Marxian periodicals have published many of the comments of Marx and Engels on American labor. For example see A. Landy, "Engels on the American Labor Movement," *Communist*, vii (May 1928), pp. 307-313, and "Unpublished Letters of Karl Marx and Friedrich Engels to Americans," tr. and ed. by L. E. Mins, *Science & Society*, ii (Spring 1938), pp. 218-231, (Summer 1938), pp. 348-375. See also S. A. Dridzo (A. Lozovsky, pseud.), *Marx and the Trade Union* (New York, 1935, 188 pp.); V. I. Lenin, *Should Communists Participate in Reactionary Trade Unions?* (New York, 1920?, 14 pp.); and Rosa Luxemburg, *The Mass Strike, the Political Party and the Trade Union* (1906; tr. by P. Lavin; Detroit, 1920?, 93 pp.).

Among the socialist interpretations of American labor history not cited in PART II are H. N. Casson, *Organized Self-Help* (New York, 1901, 211 pp.); Justus Ebert, *American Industrial Evolution* (New York, 1907, 88 pp.), published by the Socialist Labor Party press; and Austin Lewis, *The Rise of the American Proletarian* (Chicago, 1907, 213 pp.). The best special study issued by International Publishers is Karl Obermann's excellent biography, *Joseph Weydemeyer* (New York, 1947, 160 pp.).

Studies of unions in particular industries where socialist or communist influence has been strong include L. L. Lorwin, *The Women's Garment Workers* (New York, 1924, 608 pp.); James Oneal, *A History of the Amalgamated Ladies' Garment Cutters' Union, Local 10* (New York, 1927, 450 pp.); D. M. Page, *Southern Cotton Mills and Labor* (New York, 1929, 96 pp.); Lawrence Rogin, *Making History in Hosiery* (Philadelphia, 1938, 31 pp.); and R. O. Boyer, *The Dark Ship* (Boston, 1947, 306 pp.), the last a history of the National Maritime Union by a communist sympathizer. International Publishers issued a Labor and Industry Series between 1927 and 1940, containing book-length tracts on individual industries, one of the best of which is H. B. Davis, *Labor and Steel* (New York, 1933, 304 pp.); a biennial *Labor Fact Book* (New York, 1931-); and *International Pamphlets* (New York, 1930-1937), with many titles on labor. See also the *Labor Bulletin* (New York, 1936-1938), published by the Labor Research Front, and Ruth McKenney, *Industrial Valley* (New York, 1939, 379 pp.), on the Akron rubber industry and its labor.

A mass of books and pamphlets have appeared on important strikes. See, for example, Benjamin Hanford, *The Labor War in Colorado* (New York, 1904, 48 pp.), socialist; W. C. Smith, *The Everett Massacre* (Chicago, 1920?, 302 pp.), I.W.W.; and, as pro-communist, Albert Weisbord, *Passaic* (Chicago, 1926, 64 pp.); W. F. Dunne, *The Great San Francisco General Strike* (New York, 1934, 79 pp.); William Weinstone,

The Great Sit-Down Strike (New York, 1937, 45 pp.); and Leo Huberman, *The Great Bus Strike* (New York, 1941, 167 pp.). Still another approach is through the autobiographical writings of labor leaders, such as Benjamin Hanford, *Fight for Your Life!* (New York, 1909, 127 pp.). See also the speeches of Luigi Antonini, president of the Italian American Labor Council in New York, *Dynamic Democracy* (New York, 1944, 463 pp.), mostly in Italian.

For the nineteenth-century socialist labor activities, see PART II and the following additional samples. R. Weil, *Die Revolution und die Arbeiter; ein Beitrag zur Lösung der socialen Frage* (New York, 1858, 18 pp.), preached the class struggle at the time the New York Communist Club was organized. N. A. Dunning, *The Philosophy of a Strike* (Chicago, 1888, 8 pp.), published by C. H. Kerr, favored extensive government ownership and operation, and opposed monopolies and immigration. In J. R. Buchanan, *The Story of a Labor Agitator* (New York, 1903, 460 pp.), the author obscures the nature of his involvement in the West Coast International. See also J. Jacoby, *The Object of the Labor Movement* (New York, 1898, 36 pp.).

Socialist Labor Party theory has always concentrated on propaganda directed toward the industrial worker. Daniel De Leon has of course been the leading exponent of Marxian labor theory. His 1898 address to New Bedford textile strikers, *What Means This Strike?* (New York, 1943, 37 pp.), which has been reprinted nearly two dozen times, expounded the labor theory of value and the theory of the reserve army of labor and promoted dual unionism through the Socialist Labor Party's Socialist Trade and Labor Alliance, which merged in 1905 into the I.W.W. See in addition De Leon's debate with Job Harriman at New Haven, Connecticut, *Socialist Trade and Labor Alliance versus the 'Pure and Simple' Trade Union* (New York, 1900, 44 pp.). De Leon's *Two Pages from Roman History* (1903; New York, 1943, 93 pp.) warned against the betrayal of the proletariat by the "pure and simple" trade-union leaders as the Roman plebs was betrayed by its leaders. *Industrial Unionism* (1905-1913; New York, 1920, 79 pp.) and *Socialist Reconstruction of Society* (originally entitled *The Preamble of the Industrial Workers of the World*) (1905; New York, 1938, 64 pp.) show De Leon in harmony with the incipient I.W.W. movement. Karl Dannenberg, *The Road to Power; or, The Constructive Elements of Socialism* (Detroit, 1919, 33 pp.), published by the Workers' International Industrial Union, continues to hold that craft unionism is out of joint with modern centralized industry and describes the form of industrial republic which agrees with the "requirements of economic evolution." Eric Hass, *The Labor Draft; Step to Industrial Slavery* (New York, 1943, 31 pp.), and Arnold Petersen, *Labor Conscription; Involuntary Servitude of Labor* (New York, 1943,

32 pp.), oppose the Austin-Wadsworth National Service Bill and warn against capitalist planning of a labor reserve army through so-called full employment on state public works.

In nearly half a century of Socialist Party activity, its policy has been to work through existing nonsocialist unions wherever permitted, and through industrial unions if possible. The Socialist Party was sympathetic toward syndicalism until 1912 and recently has favored the C.I.O. It has also been more willing to accept members outside the ranks of industrial labor and with a more mixed membership has oftener than not emphasized the general welfare, rather than the class struggle. N. I. Stone's speech to bolters from the Socialist Labor Party in 1900, *The Attitude of the Socialists toward the Trade Unions* (New York, 1900, 23 pp.), was followed by their resolution opposing dual unionism and wooing the A.F.L. See also the columns of the *International Socialist Review's* labor department, edited by M. S. Hayes. L. B. Boudin, "Die politische Lage in den Vereinigten Staaten und die Demokratische Partei," *Neue Zeit*, xxv, Pt. 2 (July 31-Aug. 14, 1907), pp. 591-605, 634-649, 668-684, analyzed the socialists' chances of winning labor from a Democratic Party tied to the solid and conservative South. Austin Lewis, *The Militant Proletariat* (Chicago, 1911, 183 pp.), was another plea to have the unions unite political with economic action. E. V. Debs, *Unionism and Socialism; a Plea for Both* (Terre Haute, Ind., 1904, 44 pp.), and his *Industrial Unionism* (1905; New York, 1911, 22 pp.), as well as W. E. Walling, *Labor-Union Socialism and Socialist Labor-Unionism* (Chicago, 1912, 96 pp.), illustrate socialist leanings toward syndicalism and dislike of dual organization. The testimony of Morris Hillquit, Samuel Gompers, and M. S. Hayes before the Commission on Industrial Relations, published by the Socialist Party as *The Double Edge of Labor's Sword* (Chicago, 1914, 192 pp.), discussed the conflicts of aim and method between the socialists and the A.F.L. and their common quarrel with capitalist management. Walling returned to the theme in *Socialism as It Is* (New York, 1912, 452 pp.), pp. 324-353. See also W. J. Ghent's compilation for the New Appeal Socialist Classics, No. 7, *Socialism and Organized Labor* (Girard, Kan., 1916, 64 pp.).

Since World War I the socialists have used three main types of approach to the labor problem. They have continued to write exposés of labor's wrongs; they have promoted research on labor questions; and they have explored the relation of industrial labor to other groups of workingmen. Among the attacks on injustice under capitalism are M. E. (Tobias) Marcy, *Industrial Autocracy* (Chicago, 1919, 58 pp.); Upton Sinclair, *Letters to Judd, an American Workingman* (Pasadena, Calif., 1926, 64 pp.); and Norman Thomas, *Human Exploitation in the United States* (New York, 1934, 402 pp.).

J. B. S. Hardman, ed., *American Labor Dynamics in the Light of Post-War Developments* (New York, 1928, 432 pp.), is a collection of articles by socialists and others which constitutes a reply to the communist charge of class collaboration, but tries to maintain an analytical rather than a name-calling attitude. The League for Industrial Democracy, an educational and research organization which succeeded the Intercollegiate Socialist Society after World War I, and which, like the British Fabian Society, has issued many pamphlets on labor questions. See, for example, Theresa Wolfson and Abraham Weiss, *Industrial Unionism in the American Labor Movement* (New York, 1937, 51 pp.); Carl Raushenbush, *Fordism* (New York, 1937, 64 pp.); and D. J. Saposs and E. T. Bliss, *Anti-labor Activities in the United States* (New York, 1938, 39 pp.). Other works of a factual or self-critical nature are J. H. Maurer, *It Can Be Done; the Autobiography of James Hudson Maurer* (New York, 1938, 374 pp.), pp. 139-204, describing how labor in Reading, Pennsylvania, became socialist and the author's activities in the Pennsylvania Federation of Labor; also Emanuel Stein and Jerome Davis, eds., *Labor Problems in America* (New York, 1940, 909 pp.); and Will Herberg, "Bureaucracy and Democracy in Labor Unions," *Antioch Review*, III (Fall 1943), pp. 405-417. Two gradualists who take opposite views on the revolutionary character of organized labor are Frank Tannenbaum, *The Labor Movement; Its Conservative Functions and Social Consequences* (New York, 1921, 259 pp.), pp. 113-125, who believes that the mere fact of organization and bargaining with management has revolutionary implications, and Hiram Elfenbein, *Socialism from Where We Are* (New York, 1945, 214 pp.), pp. 81-123, who has no faith in any socialist union activity and predicts that the capitalists themselves will bring about socialism from sheer necessity.

Socialists have sought to define the place of the unemployed, the immigrant, the white-collar worker, and the farmer in the labor movement. On the first group see Brendan Sexton, "Socialists in the Workers Alliance," *American Socialist Monthly*, v (Feb. 1937), pp. 53-58. Morris Hillquit, an immigrant himself, opposed the free migration of labor in "Das Einwanderungsproblem in den Vereinigten Staaten," *Neue Zeit*, xxv, Pt. 2 (July 3, 1907), pp. 444-455, insofar as it meant the influx of cheap union-disrupting labor, and urged that the position of the American socialists as expressed in a resolution on immigration which he had drafted be adopted by the Second International. See also I. A. Hourwich, *Immigration and Labor* (1912; 2nd ed. rev., New York, 1922, 574 pp.), by one of the first economists in the New World to support Marxian theory publicly. F. S. Cohen, *Immigration and National Welfare* (New York, 1940, 40 pp.), opposed exclusion and combated the traditional myths with statistics. R. M. Lovett, *The Middle Class and Organized Labor*

(New York, 1940, 32 pp.), admitted the gap between industrial and white-collar workers and suggested ways of bridging it. No recent socialist attempt to win farmer support can compare with Oscar Ameringer's saucy pamphlet, *Socialism for the Farmer Who Farms the Farm* (St. Louis, 1912, 32 pp.). Ben Halpern, "A Problem in Practical Socialism," *Jewish Frontier*, xii (Oct. 1945), pp. 19-23, calls attention to the way the Palestine Federation of Labor consolidates rural and urban workers by admitting to membership all who do not exploit labor. Jesse Cavileer, "Church and Labor Relations," *Social Action*, x (Oct. 15, 1944), pp. 4-39, comments on the socialist connections of industrial chaplains and churches with working-class membership.

Among the communists, the outstanding spokesman of their "labor front" has been William Z. Foster, who had former connections with the I.W.W. and the A.F.L. *From Bryan to Stalin* (New York, 1937, 352 pp.) is an autobiographical review of his work as a labor organizer and Communist Party executive. He is the author of at least fifteen more books and pamphlets dealing with labor and a frequent contributor to party periodicals on this subject. The more important titles are *The Great Steel Strike and Its Lessons* (New York, 1920, 265 pp.); *The Railroaders' Next Step—Amalgamation* (2nd ed., Chicago, 1922, 63 pp.); *Organize the Unorganized* (Chicago, 1925, 29 pp.); *A Manual of Industrial Unionism, Organizational Structure and Policies* (New York, 1937, 63 pp.), published during the campaign to organize the steel workers; and *American Trade Unionism* (New York, 1947, 383 pp.), selected writings. See also the mass of agitational literature, of which samples are Jay Lovestone, *The Government—Strikebreaker; a Study of the Role of the Government in the Recent Industrial Crisis* (New York, 1923, 371 pp.); M. H. Vorse, *Strike!* (New York, 1930, 376 pp.); Nathaniel Honig, *The Trade Union Unity League Today; Its Structure, Policy, Program and Growth* (rev. ed., New York, 1934, 23 pp.), and a T.U.U.L. organ, *Labor Unity* (Chicago, New York, 1927-1935); L. F. Budenz, *Red Baiting: Enemy of Labor* (New York, 1937, 23 pp.), and *Save Your Union! The Meaning of the 'Anti-Trust' Persecution of Labor* (New York, 1940, 31 pp.); and Anna Rochester, *Why Farmers Are Poor* (New York, 1940, 317 pp.). For ex-communists' and outsiders' observations on communism in unions, see D. M. Schneider, *The Workers' (Communist) Party and American Trade Unions* (Baltimore, 1928, 117 pp.); C. G. Wood, *Reds and Lost Wages* (New York, 1930, 280 pp.); and Benjamin Gitlow, "Storming the Trade Union Fortress," in *I Confess* (New York, 1940, 611 pp.), pp. 334-396. Trotskyist labor activity is described in J. P. Cannon, *The History of American Trotskyism* (New York, 1944, 268 pp.), pp. 118-168, and its chief triumph attacked by W. F. Dunne and Morris Childs, *Permanent Counter-Revolution; the Role of the Trotzkyites in the Minneapolis Strikes* (New

York, 1934, 56 pp.). The Lovestone group contributed *The American Labor Movement* (New York, 1932, 22 pp.), by Jay Lovestone.

Probably the first study of the general strike as labor's weapon is Arnold Roller, *The Social General Strike* (tr. from the German by F. K.; Chicago, 1905, 32 pp.). The special interest of the I.W.W. in the industrial organization and direct action of labor may be represented by the citations in PART II, Topic 11, and PART III, Topic 7, also the following: A. E. Woodruff, *The Evolution of Industrial Democracy* (Chicago, n.d., 40 pp.), and *The Advancing Proletariat* (Cleveland, Ohio, 1914, 32 pp.), which criticize trade unions and discuss the effects of technological change upon labor; Edward McDonald, *The Farm Laborer and the City Worker* (Cleveland, Ohio, n.d., 16 pp.); and *The General Strike for Industrial Freedom* (Chicago, 1933, 48 pp.). See also R. L. Mott, "The Political Theory of Syndicalism," *Political Science Quarterly*, xxxvii (Mar. 1922), pp. 25-40.

Evidence of the more conservative syndicalism of Samuel Gompers in his early career may be found in L. S. Reed, *The Labor Philosophy of Samuel Gompers* (New York, 1930, 191 pp.), and L. L. Lorwin, *The American Federation of Labor* (Washington, 1933, 573 pp.). It is significant that the A.F.L. reprinted D. D. Lum's syndicalist essay, *The Philosophy of Trade Unions* (1892; Washington, 1914, 19 pp.).

Topic 6. Socialism and Cooperatives

The relation of socialism to the cooperative movement has remained ambiguous and fluctuating throughout the life of both movements in the United States. The purpose of this topic is to list references which may clarify this relationship; and to do so by referring to these seven subjects: (1) the ideas of the communitarians about cooperatives; (2) the connections between nineteenth-century cooperatives and socialist organizations and membership; (3) the attitudes of twentieth-century socialist parties toward producers' and consumers' cooperatives; (4) the attitudes of spokesmen for the consumers' cooperative movement toward socialism; (5) cooperation in utopian novels; (6) communal societies since 1890; and (7) socialist aspects of mutualist and decentralist movements.

Robert Owen, the Associationists, and other communitarians (see PART II, Topics 5-7) emphasized the collective organization of production like many of the early American farmers' and workingmen's cooperatives. The pre-Marxians formed *comprehensive* cooperatives, applying the collective principle to most of their activities. On the other hand, the farmer or labor cooperatives of the Protective Unions, the Sovereigns of Industry, the Grangers, the Knights of Labor, and the Wheel and Alliance engaged in *segmental* cooperative ventures with limited objectives in production, marketing, or consumer services. The relationships between former members of American community settlements and the segmental cooperatives, noticed by several writers, has still to be made the subject of a detailed study.

Socialism which has included cooperatives in its program has been revisionist in spirit. A clear case for the effect of the American environment on orthodox Marxism is difficult to establish, but the cooperative movement provides some insight into this question. Like Marxism, both the Rochdale system of consumers' cooperatives and the communitarian system of producers' cooperatives were European contributions. Their success depended on combination with elements of native radical movements (see Topic 8). Cooperation, if it has had objectives beyond first aid to low income groups during depressions, has at most looked toward a gradual expansion of operations until competing business enterprise has been supplanted. Marxism, on the other hand, has always emphasized the class struggle, and has prepared for violent revolution and the dictatorship of the proletariat wherever socialism has met violent opposition. Rochdale cooperatives originated with former Chartists in 1844 and have solicited working-class support, but have insisted on keeping membership open to all classes. These cooperatives attacked the social problem by modifying the system of distribution, whereas Marxians assigned primary importance to the control of the means of production. Since in spite of these differences, we find American socialists supporting cooperatives, we must conclude that their Marxism has been revised. At first when their interest was in producers' cooperatives, the deviation extended only to the substitution of gradualism for sudden revolution. When they used the cooperatives' funds to support their parties or strikes and other union activities their deviation was opportunistic. The conception of cooperatives as "the other blade of the scissors"—the first blade being the political and economic organization of labor—has retained the proletarian outlook of Marxism but indicates a weakening of the Marxian emphasis on production. In emphasizing the general welfare over class welfare, piecemeal extension leading to the cooperative commonwealth, and the central importance of consumers, socialist cooperators have given up most of the essential ideology of Marxism.

The comments of leading cooperators nearly all deny any affinity with socialism, and yet in the eyes of many of their competitors they seek a revolutionary anticapitalist system. To many of the leaders of the cooperative movement the stereotype "socialism" stands for unlimited government ownership, planning, and management. Besides, whatever its nature, socialism is an alien order in the minds of too many Americans for the cooperatives to damage their propaganda by unnecessary association. Cooperatives have four basic attitudes toward socialism. Many members find no connection with socialism because to them their societies aim only to save the consumer money. Others reach the same conclusion on the theory that cooperatives are yardsticks to insure competition in certain economic areas. Many who support this theory also prophesy a mutualist utopia replacing all forms of state control. Their reasoning adheres at least subconsciously to classical economic theory. This school of thought also points to the immediate advantages of the cooperative form as one in which the proponents of radical changes in society and the defenders of the status quo can meet and compromise. The fourth attitude sees cooperatives as one of the ways to achieve socialism by economic instead of political means.

Comprehensive cooperative groups since 1890 have been overshadowed by socialism as a political movement, yet many new communities have been started. To the previous motives of religion and social reform has been added the revolt against the evils of urban society and particularly against the increasingly powerful state. Decentralism begins with moderate proposals to reduce the power of the federal government and bolster the economic and political activities of the small capitalist community. A further development is the mutualism of groups like the Catholic Workers, some Benedictines, and left-wing Protestant pacifists. The pluralist political theory of the 1920's corresponded with the ideas of this movement, even though pluralism sought to reduce the state to the level of other social organizations while inconsistently admitting the primacy of the state as mediator and protector. Pluralists and their unconscious adherents either returned to some idea of sovereignty, theocratic or democratic, or became anarcho-communists. In some of the more recent cooperative communities elements of cooperation, anarchism, and socialism have even been combined in various ways. Thus socialists with anarchist tendencies had been prominent in the settlements at Equality, Burley, and Home in the State of Washington (1898-1906). The Jewish Sunrise Community (1933-1936) had anarchist leaders. Among its members were socialist Zionists who elsewhere in the United States have organized a few of their own cooperative communities (*kvutzoth*) in preparation for colonization in Palestine. As survivals of so-called "utopian" socialism, the modern communitarians have at least attempted to practice what they preach, and still present a defensible case for comprehensive cooperation.

Read W. J. Campbell, *The Consumers' Cooperative Movement—a Factual Survey*, and H. W. Laidler, *Consumers' Cooperation—a Social Interpretation*, both in a pamphlet published by the League for Industrial Democracy (New York, July 1937, 64 pp.), for a brief historical introduction to cooperatives and for the attitude of a leading socialist spokesman. For early socialist connections read C. W. Perky, *Cooperation in the United States* (New York, 1917, 31 pp.), published as Section 2 of the Apr./May 1917 issue of *Intercollegiate Socialist*, and for Socialist Labor

Party criticism of the movement read O. M. Johnson, *The Coöperative Movement* (New York, 1924, 40 pp.). J. P. Warbasse develops the tacit assumptions of an important segment of cooperative leadership in "Cooperation and the State," in his *Cooperative Democracy* (1923; 4th ed., New York, 1942, 285 pp.), pp. 91-151. The first chapter of S. M. Lipset, *Agrarian Socialism—the Coöperative Commonwealth Federation in Saskatchewan; a Study in Political Sociology* (Berkeley, Calif., 1950, 315 pp.), deals with the general background of agrarian radicalism in relation to cooperatives, especially in the United States. On selected modern communal societies read H. F. Infield, *Cooperative Communities at Work* (New York, 1945, 201 pp.), pp. 20-62.

The *Encyclopaedia of the Social Sciences*, "Cooperation," IV, pp. 359-399, contains an extensive summary of the world-wide movement and useful bibliographies, but needs to be supplemented by more recent material. J. E. Johnsen, comp., *Consumers' Cooperatives* (New York, 1936, 297 pp.), a debate manual, has a fuller bibliography and short arguments on both sides, including comment on the relation of cooperation to socialism. The Cooperative League of the U.S.A.'s *Report* (New York, 1918-1926) and *Yearbook* (New York, 1930-), and its monthly, *Consumers' Cooperation* (New York, 1914-), are essential sources, as is the collection of papers and discussions of the sessions of the American Institute of Cooperation, entitled *American Cooperation* (Washington, 1925-). The latter is primarily concerned with farmers' marketing cooperatives and strenuously seeks to avert the stigma of socialism. See also E. S. Bogardus, *Dictionary of Cooperation* (3rd ed., New York, 1948, 94 pp.).

E. C. Rozwenc, *Cooperatives Come to America; the History of the Protective Union Store Movement, 1845-1867* (Mt. Vernon, Iowa, 1941, 151 pp.), is the only study which shows the influence of the pre-Marxian socialists on nineteenth-century cooperatives. For lack of a comparable study of the Sovereigns of Industry use E. M. Chamberlin, *The Sovereigns of Industry* (Boston, 1875, 165 pp.), and John Orvis, *A Plan for the Organization and Management of Coöperative Stores and Boards of Trade* (Mechanicsburg, Pa., 1876), published, according to Lindsay Swift, by the Sovereigns of Industry, and written by a former Brook Farmer who was later attracted to Bellamy's Nationalism. At a different level T. C. Atkeson, *Semi-centennial History of the Patrons of Husbandry* (New York, 1916, 364 pp.), and W. S. Morgan, *History of the Wheel and Alliance, and The Impending Revolution* (St. Louis, 1891, 774 pp.), refer to Granger and populist cooperatives. See also Eugene Richter, *Cooperative Stores; Their History, Organization and Management* (New York, 1875, 131 pp.), an adaptation for American use; William Elder, *Questions of the Day: Economic and Social* (Philadelphia, 1871, 367 pp.), pp. 247-330; R. H. Newton, *Social Studies* (New York, 1887, 380 pp.), pp. 83-129, short historical sketches of cooperative production and distribution in the United States; Herbert Myrick, *How to Coöperate* (New York, 1891, 349 pp.); and lastly Edward Wenning, *Universal Prosperity* (New York, 1894, 114 pp.).

Among European works relating cooperatives to socialism are the following: E. V. Neale, *The Economics of Co-operation* (Manchester, Eng., 1885, 30 pp.), one of many brochures by a former Christian socialist and cooperative official; Patrick Geddes, *Co-operation vs. Socialism* (Manchester, Eng., 1888, 24 pp.); Karl Kautsky, *Consumvereine und Arbeiterbewegung* (Vienna, 1897, 31 pp.); Firmin Verdier, *Le Mouvement coopératif et le socialisme* (Toulouse, 1903, 150 pp.); Émile Vandervelde, *La Coopération neutre et la coopération socialiste* (Paris, 1913, 226 pp.); Sidney and Beatrice Webb, *The Consumers' Co-operative Movement* (London, 1921, 504 pp.); L. S. Woolf, *Socialism and Co-operation* (London, 1921, 129 pp.); M. I. Tugan-Baranovsky, *Sotsialniya osnovy Kooperatsii* [*Social Bases of Cooperation*] (Berlin, 1921, 521 pp.); Axel Gjöres, *Robert Owen och kooperationens uppkomst* (Stockholm, 1932, 236 pp.); Georges Fauquet, *Le Secteur coopératif* (2nd ed., Brussels, 1935, 97 pp.); Antonio García, *Regimen cooperativo y economía latinoamericana* (Mexico, D.F., 1944, 79 pp.), which considers cooperatives adaptable to "subcapitalism," capitalism, socialism, or anarchism; and Noah Barou's study for the Fabian Society, *Co-operation in the Soviet Union* (London, 1946, 123 pp.), his latest product of twenty years' study of the subject.

Professional economists and political scientists in the United States began to study cooperatives in 1888. Five scholars produced a cooperative survey, *History of Coöperation in the United States* (Johns Hopkins University Studies in Historical and Political Science, vi; Baltimore, 1888, 540 pp.), with emphasis on the previous twenty years. Other works before World War I were A. J. Eddy, *The New Competition* (4th ed., Chicago, 1915, 423 pp.), and James Ford, *Co-operation in New England, Urban and Rural* (New York, 1913, 237 pp.), especially pp. 34-47, 72, containing many references to the strength of the movement among socialists. Since 1936 the universities and other research institutions have produced an increasing number of such treatises. J. G. Brainerd, ed., "Consumers' Coöperation," American Academy of Political and Social Science *Annals*, Vol. 191 (May 1937), pp. 1-201, has notable articles on the economic, political, and psychological aspects of the subject. Jacob Baker, a member of the President's Committee of Inquiry on Cooperative Enterprise in Europe, reported his personal conclusions for application in the United States in *Cooperative Enterprise* (New York, 1937, 266 pp.). In the same year the Social Science Research Council published the report of M. A. May and L. W. Doob, a subcommittee of its Committee on Personality and Culture, *Competition and Cooperation* (S.S.R.C. *Bulletin*, No. 25; New York, 1937, 191 pp.). Regional studies of H. H. Turner, *Case Studies of Consumers' Cooperatives; Successful Cooperatives Started by Finnish Groups in the United States, Studied in Relation to Their Social and Economic Environment* (New York, 1941, 330 pp.), and L. C. Kercher, V. W. Kebker, and W. C. Leland, *Consumers' Cooperatives in the North Central States* (ed. by R. S. Vaile; Minneapolis, Minn., 1941, 431 pp.), point to the socialist Finns in Massachusetts and the Lake Superior region as pioneers in the movement. J. I. Kolehmainen's bibliography, *The Finns in America* (Hancock, Mich., 1947, 141 pp.), contains additional references to Finnish cooperatives. I. V. Emelyanov, *Economic Theory of Cooperation; Economic Structure of Cooperative Organizations* (Washington, 1942, 269 pp.), criticizes the emotional socio-reformistic approach of most writers on cooperatives and analyzes all types of cooperatives from the point of view of the orthodox price economist. He concludes that they are aggregates of economic units and not enterprises, and denies the universal validity of Rochdale principles. Arthur E. Albrecht of the College of the City of New York is writing a comprehensive history of cooperatives in the United States.

The proceedings of Socialist Party conventions and their campaign handbooks occasionally give space to the cooperative movement. The phrase, "cooperative commonwealth," used by socialists as early as Gronlund, was used more to distinguish socialism from competitive society than to denote a system based entirely on cooperatives.

The socialist press was often cooperatively organized. The Socialistic Co-operative Publishing Association brought out Lucien Sanial's *The Socialist Almanac* (New York, 1898, 230 pp.) for the Socialist Labor Party, which later changed its policy in favor of a party-owned press. C. H. Kerr & Co., incorporated in 1893, was to become connected with the socialist movement in 1899. See C. H. Kerr, *A Socialist Publishing House* (Chicago, 1904?, 31 pp.), and its annual reports in the *International Socialist Review*. The Masses Publishing Co. carried on the advisory functions of the American Wholesale Co-operative after its dissolution in 1911, keeping in touch with several hundred socialist stores through the *Masses* until Max Eastman and his associates took over the magazine in 1913.

Joseph Cook, *Socialism, with Preludes on Current Events* (Boston, 1880, 307 pp.); Edmond Kelly, *Twentieth Century Socialism* (New York, 1910, 446 pp.); and J. W. Hughan, *American Socialism of the Present Day* (New York, 1911, 265 pp.), have sections on cooperatives. One of S. M. Stallard's *Five Lessons in Socialism* (Fort Scott, Kan., n.d., 31 pp.) was on cooperation; the first, however, was on the class struggle.

After World War I socialist attention focused on the consumer movement. C. E. Warne, *The Consumers' Co-operative Movement in Illinois* (Chicago, 1926, 420 pp.), pp. 28-32, credits the socialists with furnishing the leaders and making the preliminary though unsuccessful experiments. The author of this doctoral thesis was a socialist in the 1930's. The *World Tomorrow* treats the subject frequently, as in Cedric Long, "Consumers' Coöperation," xii (Feb. 1929), pp. 61-64. For Norman Thomas' attitude, see "The Consumer Pays," in *Human Exploitation in the United States* (New York, 1934, 402 pp.), pp. 304-326, and *After the New Deal, What?* (New York, 1936, 244 pp.). In addition to H. W. Laidler's pamphlet cited above (p. 297), his comments are found in "Voluntary Cooperation," in his *Socializing Our Democracy* (New York, 1935, 330 pp.), pp. 149-163, and in "Incentives in a Cooperative Order," *Consumers' Cooperation,* xxii (June 1936), pp. 85-87. Benjamin Wolf urged cooperatives to be the commissaries of the labor army in "Consumers Cooperation, a Neglected Socialist Weapon," *American Socialist Monthly,* v (Oct. 1936), pp. 33-38. Upton Sinclair, who lived in Helicon Home Colony at Englewood, New Jersey, 1906-1907, and described the life in *The Industrial Republic* (New York, 1907, 284 pp.), pp. 259-284, contributed to the flood of cooperative literature which reached a peak in 1936 with *Co-op; a Novel of Living Together* (New York, 1936, 426 pp.). The Socialist Party's *The Commonwealth Plan* (Chicago, 1934, 31 pp.), written by Paul Porter, favored government assistance to cooperatives, with some of the farms cooperatively operated. Seba Eldridge and associates, *Development of Collective Enterprise; Dynamics of an Emergent Economy* (Lawrence, Kan., 1943, 577 pp.), a collaborative work with a piecemeal socialist point of view and consumer orientation, embraces the whole range of American social organization. The section on cooperatives is factual. See also Eldridge's "Collectivism and the Consumer," *Annals of Collective Economy,* vi (Sept.-Dec. 1930), pp. 293-343. The connection of unions and cooperatives is again advocated by Albert Rees, "Labor and the Co-operatives: What's Wrong?" *Antioch Review,* vi (Fall 1946), pp. 327-340.

Of the early literature on the contemporary consumers' cooperative movement the most explicit on its relation to socialism is Albert Sonnichsen, *Consumers' Coöperation* (New York, 1919, 223 pp.), especially pp. 185-204. Sonnichsen had been a Marxist; he organized cooperatives on New York's east side against the opposition of the Jewish daily *Vorwärts,* which feared the diversion of socialist interests, and was later secretary of the Cooperative League of the U.S.A. The following titles are selected from the voluminous literature since 1936: H. M. Kallen, *The Decline and Rise of the Consumer; a Philosophy of Consumer Coöperation* (New York, 1936, 484 pp.); H. A. Wallace, *Cooperation; the Dominant Economic Idea of the Future* (New York, 1943, 16 pp.); John

Daniels, *Cooperation; an American Way* (New York, 1938, 399 pp.); Hector Lazo, *Controlled Competition; Corporate Chains, Cartels and Cooperatives* (Washington, 1939, 77 pp.); J. M. Luck, *The War on Malnutrition and Poverty; the Role of Consumer Co-operatives* (New York, 1946, 203 pp.); and B. B. Fowler, *The Co-operative Challenge* (Boston, 1947, 265 pp.). Fowler, in this and earlier expositions, treats consumer cooperatives as the saviors of free enterprise. Ellis Cowling, *Co-operatives in America; Their Past, Present and Future* (New York, 1938, 206 pp.), connects the founders with Christian socialism but is critical of socialist contributions. See especially the chapter, "Co-operation and Capitalism," pp. 174-188. J. P. Warbasse, in *The Socialistic Trend* (Chicago, 1940, 32 pp.); "Co-operatives to Be Absorbed by the State," *Review of International Co-operation*, xxxvi (May 1943), pp. 65-68; *The Cooperative Way* (New York, 1946, 184 pp.), pp. 66-73, 105-110; and *Co-operative Democracy through Voluntary Association of the People as Consumers* (1923; 5th ed., New York, 1947, 324 pp.), finds socialism a definite hazard to the movement because socialists promote cooperatives and then want the government to take them over. This attitude stems from Warbasse's early belief in philosophical anarchism and activity in the I.W.W.: see his articles in *Mother Earth*, x (1915), and his pamphlet, *The Ethics of Sabotage* (New York, 1913, 12 pp.), reprinted from the *Call*. In the special field of cooperative medicine, see V. J. Tereshtenko, *The Problem of Cooperative Medicine* (New York, 1940, 78 pp.), as well as J. P. Warbasse, *Cooperative Medicine* (4th ed., New York, 1946, 63 pp.).

More than a hundred utopian novels have been written in the United States since Bellamy's *Looking Backward*, many of them combining the principles of cooperation and social Christianity. Among these are E. E. Hale, *How They Lived in Hampton* (Boston, 1888, 281 pp.); F. U. Worley, *Three Thousand Dollars a Year* (Washington, 1890, 104 pp.); Henry Olerich, *A Cityless and Countryless World; an Outline of Practical Cooperative Individualism* (Holstein, Iowa, 1893, 447 pp.); Zebina Forbush, *The Co-opolitan* (Chicago, 1898, 170 pp.); Florence Converse, *The Burden of Christopher* (Boston, 1900, 315 pp.); Bradford Peck, *The World a Department Store* (Lewiston, Me., 1900, 311 pp.); K. C. Gillette, *The People's Corporation* (New York, 1924, 237 pp.); and Hilliard Wilkins, *Altrurian Farms* (Washington, 1931, 95 pp.). Many have little or no plot; some authors like Peck endeavored to found a movement which was essentially paternalist and profit sharing. W. E. Davies, "A Collectivist Experiment Down East: Bradford Peck and the Coöperative Association of America," *New England Quarterly*, xx (Dec. 1947), pp. 471-491, describes this middle-class venture as a link between Bellamyism and the equally middle-class ferment of the progressive era. See the references in this article, and Ralph Albertson, *Little Jeremiads* (Lewiston, Me., 1903, 59 pp.) and *Little Preachments* (Lewiston, Me., 1903, 66 pp.). For other titles, see PART VI, Topics 3 and 6.

L. E. Deets lists 262 cooperative communities actually organized in the United States in "Data from Utopia," *Sociolog*, III, No. 3 (Dec. 1940), a mimeographed publication of Hunter College, New York. Brief accounts of a number of minor colonies founded after 1890, based on interviews with participants and their letters to the author, as well as published materials, are given in W. A. Hinds, *American Communities and Co-operative Colonies* (3rd ed. rev., Chicago, 1908, 608 pp.), pp. 464-590. See also E. S. Wooster, *Communities of the Past and Present* (Newllano, La., 1924, 156 pp.), often inaccurate but including some communities not found elsewhere. In addition to the materials on the Hutterites listed in Topic 3, see J. M. Hofer's unpublished M.A. thesis, *Hutterite Communism* (University of Chicago Divinity School, 1928). C. H. Shinn, "Coöperation on the Pacific Coast," parts 9-10 of *History of Coöperation in the United States* (cited above, p. 299), describes the Kaweah Colony, then existing in what is now the Sequoia National Forest (pp. 464-475). Robert Hine, "A California Utopia: 1885-1890," *Huntington Library Quarterly*, XI (Aug. 1948), pp. 387-405, based on wider research, indicates the role of the principal founder and leader, Burnette G. Haskell (also Pacific Coast International Workingmen's Association leader) and his associates. Among A. K. Owen's numerous publications in connection with his community in Sinaloa, Mexico, see *Integral Co-operation at Work, No. 2* (New York, 1891, 219 pp.). See also Julia Keleher's description of a colony with possible Bellamyite inspiration, founded by a spiritualist, "The Land of Shalam; Utopia in New Mexico," *New Mexico Historical Review*, XIX (Apr. 1944), pp. 123-134; and Isaac Broome, *The Last Days of the Ruskin Co-operative Association* (Chicago, 1902, 183 pp.), by a leader of a minority faction who attacks his opponents' bad management, anarchism, and free love, and lack of regard for education and culture. Stewart Holbrook, "Anarchists at Home," *American Scholar*, xv (Autumn 1946), pp. 425-438, retells the story of a cooperative community on Puget Sound. The Llano Cooperative Colony's prospectus, *Gateway to Freedom* (Leesville, La., 1924, 36 pp.); *Llano Colonist* (Newllano, La., 1921-1937); Sid Young, *The Crisis in Llano Colony, 1935-1936* (Los Angeles, 1936, 93 pp.); and R. C. Brown, *Can We Co-operate?* (Pleasant Plains, N.Y., 1940, 232 pp.), document the failure of a secular community founded on Marxist principles that lasted over twenty years at the same site. Nachman Syrkin, a leading spirit in the American Poale Zion movement, was enthusiastic for cooperatives. Stimulated by him, several Jewish socialist groups were organized in the United States preparatory to colonizing Palestine. See E. A. Norman and J. W. Eaton, "Kvutzoth in America," *New Palestine*, xxxi (June 20, 1941), pp. 7-8, and the files of the *Jewish Pioneer* (New York, 1936) and the *Jewish Frontier* (New York, 1933-).

The movement for return to the land has Franciscan, Tolstoyan, and native American anarchist roots. The anarchist aspect is represented by the works of F. D. Tandy, *Voluntary Socialism* (Denver, Colo., 1896, 228 pp.); C. L. Swartz, *What Is Mutualism?* (New York, 1927, 238 pp.); and C. T. Sprading, *Mutual Service and Cooperation* (Los Angeles, 1930, 127 pp.). See also the scarce pamphlet by E. F. Boyd, *Uncle Sam and Americus . . . a Plan for a New American National Land and Labor Cooperative System* (Cincinnati, Ohio, 1880, 34 pp.); C. T. Fowler's bimonthly, *Sun* (Kansas City, Mo., 1885-1887), devoted to cooperation, and his numerous pamphlets, e.g., *Co-operation; Its Laws and Principles* (London, 1894, 46 pp.); and the Bellamyite work, *The Philosophy of Mutualism* (Boston, 1894, 33 pp.), by Frank Parsons. Wilfred Wellock, a leader in the English community movement, has written *The Way Out: or, The Road to the New World* (London, 1922, 69 pp.), and *A Mechanistic or a Human Society?* (Birmingham, Eng., 1944?, 32 pp.). Catholic personalism has been inspired by the writings of Emmanuel Mounier, e.g., *Révolution personnaliste et communautaire* (Paris, 1935, 416 pp.); *De la propriété capitaliste à la propriété humaine* (Paris, 1936, 137 pp.); and *A Personalist Manifesto* (1936; tr. by monks of St. John's Abbey, Minn.; New York, 1938, 298 pp.). At St. John's Abbey V. G. Michel is a promoter of the cooperative movement. See also for the Catholic decentralist attitude toward cooperatives A. J. Kress, *Capitalism, Cooperation, Communism* (Washington, 1932, 141 pp.); L. R. Ward, ed., *United for Freedom* (Milwaukee, Wis., 1945, 264 pp.); and Ward's *Ourselves, Inc.; the Story of Consumer Free Enterprise* (New York, 1945, 236 pp.), particularly pp. 58-68. See also *Free America; a Magazine to Promote Independence* (New York, 1937-1947), edited by Herbert Agar, Ralph Borsodi, B. B. Fowler, and others; the *Decentralist* (Suffern, N.Y., Apr. 1942-1946), published by the School of Living founded by Borsodi; and the publications of the Rural Settlement Institute (now called Group Farming Research Institute), Poughkeepsie, New York. Borsodi, *Education and Living* (Suffern, N.Y., 1948, 276 pp.), Volume 1 of a projected trilogy, summarizes the American decentralists' program for dealing with the problems of modern life. Emanuel Lasker, *The Community of the Future* (New York, 1940, 294 pp.), advocating noncompetitive self-help cooperatives for the unemployed; J. W. Eaton and S. M. Katz, *Research Guide on Cooperative Group Farming* (New York, 1942, 86 pp.), and Eaton's *Exploring Tomorrow's Agriculture* (New York, 1943, 255 pp.), have a decentralist emphasis with different ideological background.

Decentralism also stemmed from the progressive-movement attack on irresponsible sovereignty controlled by capitalism and buttressed by legalistic constitutional interpretation. See the two treatises by the Jeffersonian progressive J. A. Smith, *The Spirit of American Government* (New York, 1907, 402 pp.), an analysis of the class struggle in the Confederation period, and the posthumously published essays, *The Growth and Decadence of Constitutional Government* (intro. by V. L. Parrington; New York, 1930, 300 pp.). See also the brief for municipal collectivism, federal democracy, and political pluralism by the Christian socialist Bouck White, *The Free City; a Book of Neighborhood* (New York, 1919, 314 pp.).

Decentralism has a pluralist outlook on the state but has not depended on pluralist political theory for its ideas. For comparison see M. P. Follett, *The New State; Group Organization the Solution of Popular Government* (New York, 1918, 373 pp.), the most extended American criticism of pluralism, and Kung-Chuan Hsiao, *Political Pluralism* (New York, 1927, 271 pp.).

Topic 7. Civil Liberties for Socialists

The observance of civil rights in transitional socialist states can now be studied as it appears in the practice of Great Britain, the birthplace of civil liberty, as well as in Soviet Russia. Yet for the purpose of this topic, foreign examples will in general be ignored aside from mention of the fact that the reader interested in the question of civil rights in Russia should consult H. J. Berman, *Justice in Russia; an Interpretation of Soviet Law* (Cambridge, Mass., 1950, 322 pp.), and that some reference to the rights enumerated in the Soviet Constitution is made in Topic 10.

The remainder of this topic concentrates on the American socialists' fight, since 1917, for a broader interpretation of civil rights by the courts and by the people, with special emphasis on freedom of communication. Denied the right of propaganda of the word, socialists are thrown back upon the right of revolution and the propaganda of the deed.

American gradualists have specifically endorsed the full exercise of civil rights under socialism, and have underlined their statements with promises that the socialization of the means of communication will increase the benefits derived from these rights. They claim that if the means of communication are not equally accessible, the exercise of rights is defective. Whether planning involves a necessary contradiction of these promises is reserved for discussion in the next topic.

The socialists who openly avow their intention to restrict civil liberties once they gain power still demand the full benefits of these liberties for themselves under capitalism. The inordinate fears aroused by these groups have led to the popular demand for the abridgment of their liberties. But many have made a bogey out of socialism in general, and especially in times of crisis have favored indiscriminate restrictions of the civil rights of all socialists. Libertarians and gradualists, however, justify the granting of liberty even to its opponents. The judicial process is so slow that any tendency for the Supreme Court to act as a brake on popular emotions locks the doors after the Liberty Bell has been stolen, as Zechariah Chafee puts it.

The line dividing free speech from speech which instigates violation of the law was developed out of the precedents established in cases concerning the nature of criminal attempts. The Supreme Court upheld the Espionage Acts of 1917 and 1918, and also the state laws restricting free speech on the ground that they did not violate the first and fourteenth amendments since the defendants' words were held to be instigating acts. The opinions of Holmes and Brandeis developed a line of reasoning that unless the defendants' words are of such nature and expressed under such circumstances as to create "a clear and present danger" to public safety, they do not constitute criminal action. The phrase was used by Holmes in Schenck v. U.S., 249 U.S. 47 (1919). This point of view, ratified by the court as a limitation upon Congress in Herndon v. Lowry, 301 U.S. 242 (1937), prepared the foundation for a more discriminating control of communication in World War II.

American experience in wartime illustrates the fact that in the last analysis, the defense of liberty rests in the hands of the people. The interpretation of the bill of rights by legislative majorities, juries, prosecuting officials, and lower-court judges has tended to be in harmony with the popular temper, with results beyond recall by higher courts. Hence the struggle by libertarians and all kinds of socialists to enlist popular support for free speech. Hence also the priority given by socialists to freedom from want. They see that when people are frustrated by insecurity and do not release their resulting aggressions against the frustrating conditions, the displacement of their aggressions against minority scapegoats violates civil rights.

The best summary of cases involving socialists between 1917 and 1937, although somewhat tendentious, is Zechariah Chafee, Jr., *Free Speech in the United States* (Cambridge, Mass., 1941, 634 pp.), pp. 36-282, 298-366, 384-398. The author was an active defender of the socialists during the red scare and has long been a member of the faculty of the Harvard Law School. This work is a condensation and revision of the author's previous writings on civil liberties—including *Freedom of Speech* (New York, 1920, 431 pp.), *The Inquiring Mind* (New York, 1928, 276 pp.), and his contribution to the symposium edited by H. M. Kallen, *Freedom in the Modern World* (New York, 1928, 304 pp.)—as well as a new treatment of the developments in the 1930's. His footnote references to cases and to the pertinent literature of legal theory constitute a useful guide to further study.

A minimum selection of comments by American gradualists on the general problem of civil rights under socialism would include John Spargo, *Applied Socialism* (New York, 1912, 333 pp.), pp. 138-162, 275-325, and Norman Thomas, *America's Way Out* (New York, 1931, 324 pp.), pp. 195-211. Zechariah Chafee, Jr., "Liberty under Socialism," *The Inquiring Mind* (New York, 1928, 276 pp.), pp. 226-231, a book review of Oliver S. B. Brett Esher's *A Defence of Liberty* (London, 1920, 251 pp.), agrees with Esher in classifying socialists with conservatives who want to control men, as opposed to liberals who want to free them. See also H. F. Ward, *Democracy and Social Change* (New York, 1940, 293 pp.), which contains a plea for the political rights of communists.

For treatments of the subject by writers in England see R. E. Dell, *Socialism and Personal Liberty* (London, 1921, 160 pp.); H. J. Laski, *Liberty in the Modern State* (New York, 1930, 288 pp.); Arthur Rosenberg, *Democracy and Socialism* (1938; tr. by George Rosen; New York, 1939, 369 pp.); J. B. S. Haldane, "A Comparative Study of Freedom," in R. N. Anshen, ed., *Freedom; Its Meaning* (New York, 1940, 686 pp.), pp. 447-472; and Michael Polanyi, *The Contempt of Freedom; the Russian Experiment and After* (London, 1940, 116 pp.). Rosenberg, a German exile in Liverpool, analyzed the correspondence of Marx and Engels to show their practical political work from 1845 to 1895 as a continuous fight for democracy. He concluded that wherever democracy based on civil liberties has not been decreed mechanically but has developed out of the life of the working people it has not failed to survive. See also an early Dutch treatment by Henri van Kol (Rienzi, pseud.), *Socialisme et liberté* (Paris, 1898, 267 pp.). For recent antiradical legislation abroad, and especially in Latin America, see the periodical articles by Karl Loewenstein and his monograph, *Brazil under Vargas* (New York, 1942, 381 pp.), pp. 133-234.

An early study of judge-made laws limiting the rights of labor is G. G. Groat, *Attitude of American Courts in Labor Cases; a Study in Social Legislation* (New York, 1911, 400 pp.). In this connection see Pollock v. Farmers' Loan & Trust Company, 157 U.S. 429-654 (1894) and 158 U.S. 601-715 (rehearing), which declared the income-tax law unconstitutional. J. H. Choate's brief and Justice Field's concurring opinion took the attitude that socialism was through this law beginning its assault on capitalism and must be checked at once. L. B. Boudin, "The Supreme Court and Civil Rights," *Science & Society*, i (Spring 1937), pp. 273-309, written at the height of the Supreme Court crisis, declared that the Supreme Court, by its narrow interpretations, had deprived the federal government of the power to protect civil rights. In this frame of mind the Socialist Party has frequently included a plank in its platform calling for the abolition of judicial review of congressional acts. See also Theodore Schroeder, ed., *Free Speech for Radicals* (enl. ed., New York, 1916, 206 pp.), a collection of articles reprinted by the Free Speech League; and Schroeder's *Free Speech Bibliography* (New York, 1922, 247 pp.), especially pp. 87-114.

Attention has been increasingly called to the effects of concentrated control in the communications industry, and of the costs of litigation as barriers to the equal enjoyment of civil rights. On the first point see O. C. Snyder, "Freedom of the Press—Personal Liberty or *Property* Liberty?" *Boston University Law Review*, xx (Jan. 1940), pp. 1-22, and M. L. Ernst, *The First Freedom* (New York, 1946, 316 pp.); and on the second, see PART V, Topic 10.

Besides the court reports themselves, materials on civil-rights cases involving socialists are found in the pamphlet literature of the American Civil Liberties Union, its *Civil Liberties Quarterly* (New York, 1931-), the propaganda of the defense, biographical studies of participants, the reports of legislative investigations, and reviews of cases in law-school journals. See, for example, Justus Ebert, *The Trial of a New Society* (Cleveland, Ohio, 1913, 160 pp.), the case of the I.W.W. leaders of the Lawrence, Massachusetts, strike; *Anarchism on Trial* (New York, 1917, 87 pp.), the speeches of Alexander Berkman and Emma Goldman, reprinted, with additions, from *Mother Earth*, xII (July 1917), pp. 129-163; Harrison George, *The I.W.W. Trial* (Chicago, 1918, 208 pp.); J. T. Doran, *Evidence and Cross-Examination of J. T. (Red) Doran in the Case of the U.S.A. vs. Wm. D. Haywood et al.* (Chicago, 1918?, 151 pp.); Max Eastman, *Address to the Jury in the Second Masses Trial* (New York, 1918, 44 pp.); Scott Nearing, defendant, *The Trial of Scott Nearing and the American Socialist Society* (New York, 1919, 249 pp.); *Hearings before the Special Committee Appointed under the Authority of House Resolution No. 6 Concerning the Right of Victor L. Berger to Be Sworn in as a Member of the Sixty-Sixth Congress* (Washington, 1919, 2 vols.); C. S. Darrow, *Argument of Clarence Darrow in the Case of the Communist Labor Party* (Chicago, 1920, 116 pp.); and C. E. Ruthenberg, *A Communist Trial* (New York, 1921?, 80 pp.), extracts from Ruthenberg's testimony and the defense attorney's closing speech. Morris Hillquit, *Loose Leaves from a Busy Life* (New York, 1934, 339 pp.), pp. 211-273, and biographies of Debs, Gitlow, and Haywood provide personal sidelights on the war trials. The reports of the Lusk Committee (New York, Legislature, Joint Committee Investigating Seditious Activities), *Revolutionary Radicalism* (Albany, N.Y., 1920, 4 vols.), especially III, pp. 2024-2074, not only reprinted much socialist literature which was considered seditious when first published but also collected quantities of data for the purpose of restricting socialist activities. Besides articles on specific cases, law reviews published such general essays as T. F. Carroll,

"Freedom of Speech and of the Press in War Time; the Espionage Act," *Michigan Law Review,* xvii (June 1919), pp. 621-665; E. S. Corwin, "Freedom of Speech and Press under the First Amendment," *Yale Law Journal,* xxx (Nov. 1920), pp. 48-55; and J. P. Hall, "Free Speech in War Time," *Columbia Law Review,* xxi (June 1921), pp. 526-537. G. L. Joughin and E. M. Morgan, *The Legacy of Sacco and Vanzetti* (New York, 1948, 598 pp.), is a review of the impact of the world famous anarchist trial of the 1920's upon American law, society, and literature. See also the congressional reports and hearings of the La Follette Committee (Senate Committee on Education and Labor) on violations of free speech and rights of labor; and the publications of the House Committee on Un-American Activities (formerly Special Committee on Un-American Activities).

From the extensive writings on civil liberties, a few which have special comments on the rights of socialists or their concepts of civil liberties are selected. See first Leon Whipple, *The Story of Civil Liberties in the United States* (New York, 1927, 366 pp.), *passim,* and the Columbia doctoral thesis by J. P. Clark, *Deportation of Aliens from the United States to Europe* (New York, 1931, 525 pp.). Eduard Heimann, *Communism, Fascism or Democracy?* (New York, 1938, 288 pp.), pp. 82-92, explains the socialists' emphasis on equality as opposed in their minds to the liberty to dominate others or the right to accumulate excessive property. *What Is Liberty?* (New York, 1939, 194 pp.), Dorothy Fosdick's attempt to classify definitions of liberty, assembles a mass of illustrations covering civil, economic, and philosophical concepts of liberty but lacks clarity of conclusions. E. H. Sawyer, "The 'Rights of Man' and the Rights of the Worker; a Study of Intolerance in England and the United States," *Vassar Journal of Undergraduate Studies,* xii (May 1939), pp. 149-169, is a sample of college student preoccupation with the problem at the outbreak of World War II. Two lectures on public opinion, labor, and democracy by R. N. Baldwin in Baldwin and C. B. Randall, *Civil Liberties and Industrial Conflict* (Cambridge, Mass., 1938, 137 pp.); and O. K. Fraenkel, *Our Civil Liberties* (New York, 1944, 277 pp.), are the products of American Civil Liberties Union representatives. Fraenkel reasserts the primacy of civil liberties over ethnic, educational, sexual, and economic equality, argues for extending these liberties to those who reject them (pp. 11-20), and denies that such liberties are incompatible with socialism (pp. 257-259). See also George Seldes, *Witch Hunt: the Technique and Profits of Redbaiting* (New York, 1940, 300 pp.), by a radical; Bert Andrews, *Washington Witch Hunt* (New York, 1948, 218 pp.), by a conservative; and Carey McWilliams, *Witch Hunt* (Boston, 1950, 361 pp.), by a liberal. For studies published just after World War II see M. R. Konvitz, *The Constitution and Civil Rights* (New York, 1947, 254 pp.); *Freedom and Experience; Essays Presented to Horace M. Kallen* (ed. by Sidney Hook and M. R. Konvitz; Ithaca, N.Y., 1947, 345 pp.), especially Konvitz on racial discrimination, pp. 46-62, and M. C. Otto on free speech, pp. 78-91; Walter Gellhorn, *Security, Loyalty, and Science* (Ithaca, N.Y., 1950, 300 pp.), one of the Cornell Studies in Civil Liberty; and the monographs dealing with the major agencies of mass communications published by the Commission on Freedom of the Press, a group financed by Time, Inc., and the Encyclopaedia Britannica, e.g., *A Free and Responsible Press* (Chicago, 1947, 139 pp.). The relation of the doctrine of "clear and present danger" to the judicial decisions of the World War I period is reviewed in G. J. Patterson, *Free Speech and a Free Press* (Boston, 1939, 261 pp.), pp. 153-203. The role of Brandeis in developing this doctrine is cited in A. T. Mason, "This Tangled Web of Freedom," *Brandeis; a Free Man's Life* (New York, 1946, 713 pp.), pp. 554-569. See also Holmes's remarks in *Holmes-Pollock Letters* (ed. by M. D. Howe; Cambridge, Mass., 1941, 2 vols.).

All socialist parties gave at least qualified support to the war of 1941-1945. No doubt for this reason, more than because of any popular enlightenment as to the values of civil liberty, the vehemence of earlier attacks on free speech did not recur. Two cases, involving Trotskyists and communists, raised the question of advocacy of violent revolution and employed the test of "clear and present danger" in part of the courts' opinions. In Schneiderman v. U.S., 320 U.S. 118-207 (1943), with Wendell L. Willkie arguing for Schneiderman, the Supreme Court in a 5-3 decision held that Schneiderman's 1927 certificate of naturalization was legal because it was not clear that he advocated violent revolution or was not attached to the principles of the constitution. The opinion of Justice Murphy reviewed communist theories of revolution and proletarian dictatorship and found that they could be interpreted as favoring democratic means to change the government of the United States in 1927. See especially pp. 140-158 of Justice Murphy's opinion, and pp. 187-195 of Chief Justice Stone's dissent. Proceedings had been instituted in 1939, before the communists shifted to support United States involvement in the war. Also see Robert Minor, "The Schneiderman Decision," *Communist*, XXII (Aug.-Sept. 1943), pp. 688-697, 836-851. The question of communist advocacy of violent revolution came up again in the 1949 trial in New York of eleven leaders of the American Communist Party. This case is reviewed in Nathaniel Weyl, *Treason* (Washington, 1950, 491 pp.), a book which also treats the early parts of the Alger Hiss and Judith Coplon cases. Another *cause célèbre* was the deportation proceedings against Harry Bridges, leader of Pacific Coast longshoremen (326 U.S. 135 [1944]): see E. E. Ward, *Harry Bridges on Trial* (New York, 1940, 240 pp.). In this connection see *Stages in the History of the*

Communist Party; a Political Review (New York, 1943, 39 pp.), a section of the "memorandum of law" submitted by lawyers for Bridges to Attorney General Biddle, to refute the argument that the party has been an agent of the U.S.S.R. and has advocated overthrow of the United States government by force. M. R. Konvitz, *The Alien and the Asiatic in American Law* (Ithaca, N.Y., 1946, 299 pp.), discusses the Schneiderman and Bridges cases, but concentrates on the Asiatics. In connection with the deportation proceedings against communists following World War II, and trials under the Smith Act begun in 1948, International Publishers issued Labor Research Association, *The Palmer Raids* (New York, 1948, 80 pp.), edited by R. W. Dunn, an account of counterradical activity in the last generation. The refusal of Hollywood directors, writers, and producers to testify at the hearings of the House Committee on Un-American Activities is discussed in Gordon Kahn, *Hollywood on Trial* (New York, 1948, 229 pp.). See also Robert Myers, "Anti-Communist Mob Action," *Public Opinion Quarterly*, XII (Spring 1948), pp. 57-67, analyzing the riot in Trenton, New Jersey, which prevented Gerhart Eisler from speaking.

In Dunne et al. v. U.S., 138 F. 2d. 137 (1943), the Circuit Court convicted eighteen Trotskyist leaders under the Smith Act for advocating violent revolution, and insubordination in the armed forces. The Supreme Court denied appeal. The testimony of J. P. Cannon is published in *Socialism on Trial* (New York, 1942, 116 pp.); the final argument for the defense is printed in Albert Goldman, *In Defense of Socialism* (New York, 1942, 95 pp.). See also Grandizo Munis and J. P. Cannon, *Defense Policy in the Minneapolis Trial* (New York, 1942, 64 pp.), and frequent reports in the *Fourth International*, II (July 1941), pp. 163-166; (Aug.), pp. 209-217; (Oct.), pp. 227-229, 231-234; (Dec.), pp. 295-298; III (Jan. 1942), pp. 4-9; (Dec.), pp. 355-356; V (Jan. 1944), pp. 3, 8-11; (Feb.), pp. 43-48; and VI (Feb. 1945), pp. 35-36.

Suggestions for bills of rights to be incorporated into national and international constitutions are made by Arnold Brecht, "Democracy—Challenge to Theory," *Social Research*, XIII (June 1946), pp. 195-224, and Hersh Lauterpacht, *An International Bill of the Rights of Man* (New York, 1945, 230 pp.).

Topic 8.   Socialism and American Radicalism or Reformism

To describe the interaction between American socialists and American nonsocialist radicals is to tell the history of attempts to naturalize socialism—and particularly Marxian socialism—in the United States.

The religious communitarians sought to conform to the American tradition insofar as their otherworldly outlook and ways permitted; the liberal communitarians, also of mixed native and foreign origin, capitalized on the native reaction against industrialism. The efforts of both groups to acquire a patriotic protective coloring are mentioned in Topic 3. The pre-Marxians' infection with the myriad manifestations of "ultraism" from respectable temperance and antislavery to the divers schemes for health improvement (see PART II) provided channels for the diversion of their fellow reformers into their own comprehensive movement for a new moral world.

The early workingmen's movements in the United States, by their failures, provided some of the communitarian personnel, especially in the communities of Owen, the Fourierists, and the Icarians. The reverse was also true. After a community had broken up, many leaders, such as Frances Wright, Josiah Warren, Robert Dale Owen, John Orvis, and John Allen, became active in various labor, tax, money, and equal-rights movements. The General Reading of Part II, pp. 97-103, lists the principal materials on the growth of the American labor movement; and the General Reading of PART IV, pp. 235-237, mentions a few of the more radical writers before the Civil War.

The first Marxians in the United States were German exiles of the Revolution of 1848, freethinkers, and preoccupied with the immediate problem of European political reform. Wilhelm Weitling, an editor with Marxian connections, had been disowned before his emigration and concerned himself in the United States with colonization and the reform of currency and banking. Many, like Joseph Weydemeyer and Adolf Douai, supported the radical wing of the Republican Party because of its land and antislavery policies. Although at first cooperating with the followers of Proudhon and Lassalle, the Marxians soon conflicted with the other factions, as their comrades did in Europe. As interest in European politics waned and the immigrants won an economic foothold, a good many gave up their socialism. William H. Sylvis, an American of German ancestry, organizer of the iron molders and leader of the National Labor Union, maintained a lively interest in the First International, but experimented with producers' cooperatives and emphasized monetary reform.

It was only with the triumph of American capitalism after 1865 that discontent, taking its cue from the preoccupation of successful business, concentrated almost entirely upon economic remedies. The half century after 1865, when Marxism was imported through working-class immigrants and spread into the hinterland, is selected to illustrate the cross-currents of socialism and native radicalism, with a minimum sampling of later materials. Political reforms, which sought better representation and free speech, attacked imperialism, and publicized corruption, were derivative. The wave of utopian fiction in the wake of Bellamy's *Looking*

Backward (see PART VI, Topic 3) was the literary manifestation of this radicalism.

As stated in Topic 9, many American radicals were more willing than the Marxians to use violence and to talk revolution. Yet most of their proposals were reformist and mechanistic, and singled out one facet of political economy in their panaceas. It was the function of the Marxians to broaden the scope of their attack to embrace the whole social system (see PART II, Topics 8-9, and PART IV, Topics 4-6).

The three most popular recurrent movements concerned problems of currency, taxation, and monopoly. The organization of cooperatives to combat monopolies is referred to in Topic 6. The alternative, a popular or national monopoly, led from Grangerism through the proposals of Laurence Gronlund, Edward Bellamy, and Henry Demarest Lloyd to the socialism of Eugene Debs. The Greenback movement, with roots deep in the American past, persisted in the free-silver wing of the People's Party and was captured by Bryan in the campaign of 1896. Upholders of Turner's frontier hypothesis have emphasized the agrarian character of radicalism from Greeley to La Follette. Younger scholars have rediscovered relationships between urban labor and the farmers; this has led to studies of the connections between urban American Marxism and populism.

Local socialist groups gave temporary support to Grangers, Greenbackers, and populists, whose principal strength was in the debtor agrarian West and South, with the peak of cooperation in the populist-labor alliances of 1894 in the Middle West under Lloyd's guidance. The climax of nineteenth-century collaboration in the East, however, occurred in Henry George's campaign for mayor of New York in 1886. George's theories grew out of his experience of poverty in the midst of the progress of early California urbanization; hence his emphasis on land reform as a cure for the evils of city growth. Equally in the American idiom and developing a following almost simultaneously, Bellamy's religious Nationalism prepared the ground for greater native acceptance of socialism, but because Nationalism as a distinct movement was short-lived, quickly diffusing into Fabian, Christian socialist, or Socialist Party socialism or progressivism, reference to its literature is limited to titles already cited earlier (PART II, General Reading, p. 103; PART IV, Topic 3). A related factor was the appearance in the late 1880's of a Christian minority sympathetic to socialism. Socialists of German origin had antagonized the vast majority of religious Americans with their freethinking and their attacks on the churches as bulwarks of capitalism (see PART V, Topic 9). The new Socialist Party profited by its neutral contention that religion was a private matter. Political reforms, which sought to achieve more democracy through better representation, free speech, anti-imperialism, and muckraking, were only derivative in this period.

The Socialist Party gained also because of its lenient attitude toward immediate demands. On this issue conflict arose during the preliminary negotiations between the Rochester wing of the Socialist Labor Party and the western Social Democratic Party. The compromise settlement allowed socialists of both meliorist and revolutionary tendencies within the party. It grew from 1901 to 1912 because it captured part of the radical agrarians. James H. Maurer, the Reading socialist, William Z. Foster, Eugene V. Debs, and many others had early affiliations with the Knights of Labor, the populists, and the Bryan Democrats. After their 1912 peak of popular acceptance, socialists closed their ranks, ostensibly to expel un-American advocates of syndicalist violence and sabotage. Actually they lost their most naturalized and militant sections and completed the cycle of intrusion, assimilation, and expulsion previously completed in the Socialist Labor Party under De Leon. Socialist history since World War I has consisted of a series of efforts to master the fresh problems generated in Europe—world war, bolshevism, and fascism—and to weed out the utopian element in native protest. Although the tax, currency, and trust problems are perennial, other programs dealing with national and social security have come to have equal if not greater appeal.

There is so much research in progress on the radicalism of 1865-1915 that the best available introductory material will be soon superseded. For example, Daniel Aaron is investigating the progressive tradition through a study of Theodore Parker, George, Bellamy, Lloyd, Howells, and Veblen, to be published in 1951 by Oxford University Press under the title *Men of Good Hope.* C. M. Destler is preparing a biography of Lloyd; G. R. Geiger is continuing his research on George; and an increasing amount of graduate work in universities is directed into these channels. For fresh but not always profound sketches of the major figures, see Charles Madison, *Critics & Crusaders; a Century of American Protest* (New York, 1947, 572 pp.), pp. 134-154, 194-537. Another collection of papers by a professional historian, C. M. Destler, *American Radicalism, 1865-1901; Essays and Documents* (New London, Conn., 1946, 276 pp.), takes up the thesis of urban influence. See particularly the introductory generalizations, pp. 1-31; also the chapter on the monetary theory of Edward Kellogg, pp. 50-77, and pp. 135-254, preliminary details on the relation of H. D. Lloyd to the populist-labor alliance after the depression of 1893. A collection of extracts illustrating the socialist position on immediate demands was edited by W. J. Ghent for the New Appeal Socialist Classics (No. 9), *Socialism and Social Reform* (Girard, Kan., 1916, 64 pp.).

Among mid-nineteenth-century currency reformers the most influential upon labor leaders and socialists were the individualist anarchists and Edward Kellogg. Stephen Colwell, author of *The Ways and Means of Payment; a Full Analysis of the Credit System with Its Various Modes of Adjustment* (Philadelphia, 1859, 644 pp.), could be classed as an early American Christian socialist; and Victor Considérant, French-American Fourierist, contributed *Three Hundred Millions of Dollars Saved in Specie by the Meaning of a Word; Letter to Secretary McCulloch* (New York, 1867, 16 pp.). Neither author had wide influence among the radicals discussed here.

Kellogg's principal work was *A New Monetary System; the Only Means of Securing the Respective Rights of Labor and Property, and of Protecting the Public from Financial Revulsions* (ed. by M. K. Putnam; rev. ed., New York, 1874?, 374 pp.). This work was first published in 1849 with the title, *Labor and Other Capital; the Rights of Each Secured and the Wrongs of Both Eradicated.* Kellogg's influence on Sylvis can be seen in the latter's article, "What Is Money?" in *Life, Speeches, Labors and Essays of William H. Sylvis* (ed. by J. C. Sylvis; Philadelphia, 1872, 456 pp.), pp. 351-387. Jonathan Grossman, *William Sylvis* (New York, 1945, 302 pp.), pp. 247-256, 269-274, outlines Sylvis' monetary and other reform theories and evaluates him as a labor and reform leader of the late sixties. One modern revolutionary socialist's opinion of Sylvis is expressed by James Sands, "William Sylvis," *Workers Age,* IV (Dec. 14, 1935), pp. 3-4.

Native anarchist theory began with Josiah Warren's experiments with labor notes and time stores, and W. B. Greene's development of Proudhon's ideas on mutual banking. Lysander Spooner wrote over half a dozen pamphlets on credit, currency, and banking in their relations with industry, constitutional law, and freedom between 1843 and 1879. His proposals to base money on real-estate values in *A New System of Paper Currency* (Boston, 1861, 58 pp., 64 pp.), conceived with reference to the banking situation after 1857, had some influence upon the framers of the Civil War banking laws. See also E. H. Heywood, *Hard Cash; an Essay to Show That Financial Monopolies Hinder Enterprise and Defraud Both Labor and Capital; That Panics . . . Will Be Effectually Prevented Only through Free Money* (Princeton, Mass., 1874, 23 pp.); J. K. Ingalls, *Social Wealth; the Sole Factors and Exact Ratios in Its Acquirement and Apportionment* (New York, 1885, 320 pp.); W. H. Van Ornum, *Money, Co-operative Banking and Exchange* (Chicago, 1892, 66 pp.); and W. A. Whittick, *Value and an Invariable Unit of Value* (Philadelphia, 1896, 132 pp.).

American Marxians used the chapter on money or simple circulation in Marx's *A Contribution to the Critique of Political Economy* (Kerr edition, Chicago, 1904, 314 pp.), pp. 73-263, in debates with free-silver populists and Bryan Democrats. An early banking reformer, influenced by Kellogg and incidentally anti-Semitic, was W. H. Gibbs, author of *No Interest for Money, except to the Government* (Lyons, Iowa, 1879, 107 pp.). But the widely circulated work of W. H. Harvey, particularly *Coin's Financial School* (Chicago, 1894, 149 pp.), seduced the radicals after their brief honeymoon with the Marxians. The reactions of the socialists to bimetallism are represented by the following articles: for the Socialist Labor Party, Daniel De Leon, "Money," in Arnold Petersen, *The High Cost of Living; Real Causes Underlying Increased Cost of Commodities Explained* (New York, 1914, 45 pp.), pp. 25-45; for the Socialist Party, Marcus Hitch, "Karl Marx on Money," *International Socialist Review*, I (July 1900), pp. 29-47, urging partial acceptance of the theories of monetary reformers and rejection of Marx's quantity theory; and N. I. Stone, "Karl Marx on the Money Question (A Reply to Mr. Hitch)," *ibid.* (Nov. 1900), pp. 263-274. On socialist monetary theory in the last fifty years see also Frank Parsons, *Rational Money; a National Currency Intelligently Regulated in Reference to the Multiple Standard* (Philadelphia, 1898, 177 pp.); H. G. Wilshire, "Money under Socialism," in his *Socialism Inevitable* (New York, 1907, 337 pp.), pp. 279-281; Lucien Sanial, *General Bankruptcy or Socialism . . . Showing the Futility of Any Legislative "Reform" Having for Its Object to Prevent Panics and the Final Collapse of the Banking Power* (New York, 1913, 19 pp.), prepared from a Socialist Party committee report; E. F. Mylius, *The Socialization of Money* (New York, 1919, 28 pp.); Norman Thomas, "Other Economic Problems for Socialism," in his *America's Way Out* (New York, 1931, 324 pp.), pp. 170-194; D. J. Saposs, "Populism, Socialism and Labor," *American Socialist Quarterly*, II (Autumn 1933), pp. 27-36; G. D. H. Cole, "Socialism and Monetary Policy," *ibid.*, III (Spring 1934), pp. 5-11; and D. P. Berenberg, " 'Pie in the Sky'; a Study of Current Utopian Notions," *ibid.*, IV (Mar. 1935), pp. 52-64. J. E. Reeve, *Monetary Reform Movements; a Survey of Recent Plans and Panaceas* (Washington, 1943, 404 pp.), reviews the schemes proposed between the Wall Street crash and World War II. The trend of thinking in the thirties was to denounce "penny-in-the-slot-brings-paradise" credit and currency schemes, as Cole did, and yet to favor participation in a farmer-labor party which might emphasize these remedies, lest the third party be entirely middle class and reformist. Socialist Party theorists had become Keynesian.

While differences on the money question were pulling Marxians and populists apart, their mutual hatred of monopoly seemed to provide a basis for cooperation, if not fusion. The Marxians of all factions, De Leon as well as Gronlund, realized the urgent necessity of Americanizing their party, although their diverse efforts led to different results.

The briefest sampling of reform and populist tracts includes the following: E. S. Carr, *The Patrons of Husbandry on the Pacific Coast* (San Francisco, 1875, 461 pp.); W. N. Slocum, *Revolution; the Reorganization of Our Social System Inevitable* (1878; new ed., n.p., 1892, 16 pp.); Simeon Stetson, *The People's Power; or, How to Wield the Ballot* (San Francisco, 1883, 63 pp.), by a former temperance lecturer, recommending proportional representation as a panacea; J. H. Keyser, *The Next Step of Progress: How to Break Monopoly . . . A Limitation of Wealth with Graduated Taxation* (New York?, 1884?, 50 pp.); E. A. Allen, *Labor and Capital . . . the Various Organizations of Farmers, Planters, and Mechanics, for Mutual Improvement and Protection against Monopoly* (Cincinnati, Ohio, 1891, 518 pp.); L. C. Hubbard, *The Coming Climax in the Destinies of America* (Chicago, 1891, 480 pp.), a reform campaign text; John Swinton, *Striking for Life; Labor's Side of the Labor Question* (New York?, 1894, 498 pp.), republished as *A Momentous Question* (Philadelphia, 1895, 498 pp.); L. L. Hopkins, *The Coming Trust* (New York, 1900, 154 pp.); and D. C. Reid, *Capital and Profits* (Springfield, Mass., 1914, 221 pp.). See also such autobiographies as Brand Whitlock, *Forty Years of It* (New York, 1914, 373 pp.). For further references, see J. D. Hicks, *The Populist Revolt* (Minneapolis, Minn., 1931, 473 pp.), and F. E. Haynes, *Third Party Movements since the Civil War with Special Reference to Iowa* (Iowa City, Iowa, 1916, 564 pp.), pp. 483-534, especially for references to the periodical press. Other studies of populism and reform, particularly with relation to labor and socialism, include Anna Rochester, *The Populist Movement in the United States* (New York, 1943, 128 pp.), a communist history, especially the concluding section, pp. 120-124; J. G. McDaniel's unpublished Cornell doctoral thesis (1943), *Some Phases of Social Reform in the United States, 1870-1890*; D. L. McMurry, *Coxey's Army; a Study of the Industrial Army Movement of 1894* (Boston, 1929, 331 pp.); and the following articles: Ralph Kauer, "The Workingmen's Party of California," *Pacific Historical Review*, xiii (Sept. 1944), pp. 278-291, on Denis Kearney's anti-Chinese movement, which derailed competing socialists; L. W. Fuller, "Colorado's Revolt against Capitalism," *Mississippi Valley Historical Review*, xxi (Dec. 1934), pp. 343-360; J. M. Klotsche, "The 'United Front' Populists," *Wisconsin Magazine of History*, xx (June 1937), pp. 375-389; G. H. Knoles, "Populism and Socialism, with Special Reference to the Election of 1892," *Pacific Historical Review*, xii (Sept. 1943), pp. 295-304, based too much on De Leonist sources; and James Peterson, "The Trade Unions and the Populist Party," *Science & Society*, viii (Spring 1944), pp. 143-160. The series, "American Movers and Shakers," in the *New Republic*, cxvii (Dec. 22, 1947), begins with the sketch, "Ignatius Donnelly; Apostle of Protest," pp. 20-24, by S. H. Holbrook. Louis Filler, *Crusaders for Ameri-*

can Liberalism (New York, 1939, 422 pp.), is a brief for the muckraker tactic of accurate and pitiless publicity, also used by the socialists with less emphasis on accuracy. See especially chapters 13, 17, and 23. See also on the progressive movement, John Chamberlain, *Farewell to Reform* (New York, 1932, 333 pp.).

The number of former populists in the Socialist Party created a problem of digestion. One method was to advocate the old People's Party planks of government ownership limited to common carriers and city utilities. Details of this position may be found in C. D. Thompson, *Public Ownership* (New York, 1925, 445 pp.). Another was to expose reform-party programs as shams, as in the campaign book of C. E. Russell, *Doing Us Good and Plenty* (Chicago, 1914, 172 pp.), and H. W. Wiley, *The Lure of the Land* (New York, 1915, 368 pp.). On the eve of World War I, party theorists differed as to whether populism had become subordinated to Marxism. See W. E. Walling, "Das neue Agrarprogramm der Sozialdemokratie Amerikas," *Neue Zeit*, XXXI, Pt. 1 (Jan. 10, 1913), pp. 521-530, and A. M. Simons' answer, "Kein Populismus in der amerikanischen sozialistischen Partei," *ibid.* (Jan. 24, 1913), pp. 597-602.

For the sporadic third-party movements since World War I in which socialists participated, see C. E. Russell, *The Story of the Nonpartisan League* (New York, 1920, 332 pp.); K. C. MacKay, *The Progressive Movement of 1924* (New York, 1947, 298 pp.); Upton Sinclair, *I, Candidate for Governor, and How I Got Licked* (Pasadena, Calif., 1935, 215 pp.); and two biographies of H. A. Wallace, Dwight Macdonald, *Henry Wallace; the Man and the Myth* (New York, 1948, 187 pp.), and Russell Lord, *The Wallaces of Iowa* (Boston, 1947, 615 pp.). See also W. B. Hesseltine, *The Rise and Fall of Third Parties; from Anti-Masonry to Wallace* (Washington, 1948, 119 pp.).

The outstanding comparison to be made between socialism and tax-reform ideas focuses on the single-tax movement. Two bibliographies on the subject are R. A. Sawyer, *Henry George and the Single Tax; a Catalogue of the Collection in the New York Public Library* (New York, 1926, 90 pp.), and the Library of Congress *Select List of References on the Single Tax* (Washington, 1913, 15 leaves, mimeographed). *The Writings of Henry George* (New York, 1898-1901, 10 vols.; subsequent editions in 1904 and 1911) include *Our Land and Land Policy . . . Miscellaneous Writings* (1871-1894); *Progress and Poverty* (1879); *Social Problems* (1883); *Protection or Free Trade* (1886); *The Land Question, Property in Land, The Condition of Labor* (1881-1891); *A Perplexed Philosopher; Being an Examination of Mr. Herbert Spencer's Various Utterances on the Land Question* (1892); *The Science of Political Economy* (1898; ed. by Henry George, Jr.); and a biography by his son. Besides G. R. Geiger's biography, *The Philosophy of Henry George* (New York, 1933, 581 pp.), and his essay in land economics, based on George, *The Theory of the Land Question* (New York, 1936, 237 pp.), which represent the religious collectivist wing of the contemporary Georgist school, with a revisionist attitude toward George's original theory, see Anna George De Mille, *Henry George, Citizen of the World* (ed. by D. C. Shoemaker; Chapel Hill, N.C., 1950, 276 pp.), a biography by George's daughter; and C. A. Green, *The Profits of the Earth* (Boston, 1934, 146 pp.), an exposition of Georgist interest theory.

The principal vehicles for the single-tax movement are the *Standard* (New York, 1887-1892), edited by George (1887-1890), W. T. Croasdale (1891), and L. F. Post (1891-1892); the *Public* (Chicago, 1898-1916; New York, 1917-1919), edited by L. F. and A. T. Post (1898-1913), Stoughton Cooley and others (1914-1919); *Land and Freedom* (New York, 1901- ; 1901-1923 as *Single Tax Review*), first edited by J. D. Miller; and the *American Journal of Economics and Sociology* (Lancaster, Pa., 1941-).

The part of Father Edward McGlynn, who was excommunicated by Archbishop Corrigan for founding the Anti-Poverty Society to propagate single-tax reform, but reinstated without recanting in 1892 by the apostolic vicar, is told by Stephen Bell in *Rebel, Priest and Prophet; a Biography of Dr. Edward McGlynn* (New York, 1937, 303 pp.). See also Arthur Preuss, ed., *The Fundamental Fallacy of Socialism; an Exposition of the Question of Landownership, Comprising an Authentic Account of the Famous McGlynn Case* (St. Louis, Mo., 1908, 191 pp.).

The single taxers founded communities like other utopian reformers to which many socialists flocked. The colony in Delaware is described by J. W. Gaskine, "Arden, a Modern 'As You Like It,'" *Independent*, LXXI (Aug. 10, 1911), pp. 299-304. The more successful experiment was at Fairhope, on Mobile Bay, supported by the Fels Foundation. On Fairhope see articles by E. B. Gaston, "Fairhope, the Home of the Single Tax and the Referendum," *Independent*, LV (July 16, 1903), pp. 1670-1677; and H. C. Bennett, "Fairhope—a Single-Tax Colony," *Collier's*, XLIX (Sept. 14, 1912), p. 24.

Laurence Gronlund led socialist critics just after George's united-front mayoralty campaign with *Insufficiency of Henry George's Theory* (New York, 1887, 19 pp.). To George's reply in the *Standard*, II (July 30, Aug. 6, 1887) he rejoined with *Socialism vs. Tax-Reform* (New York, 1887, 35 pp.). George's public debate with the socialist S. E. Shevitch, in October 1887 was reported in the *Standard*, II (Oct. 29, 1887), p. 3. The campaign itself is recorded by L. F. Post and F. C. Leubuscher, *An Account of the George-Hewitt Campaign in the New York Municipal Election of 1886* (New York, 1886, 193 pp.). Post published *Outlines of . . . Lectures on the Single Tax, Absolute Free Trade, the Labor Ques-*

tion, Progress and Poverty, the Land Question, the Elements of Political Economy, Socialism, Hard Times (New York, 1895, 108 pp.) between his editorship of the *Standard* and the *Public*. This work enjoyed three editions to 1912. A. M. Simons, *Single Tax vs. Socialism* (Chicago, 1899, 29 pp.), recapitulated the arguments of Gronlund with less reference to the circumstances of 1886. The writings of other socialists nevertheless showed some borrowings from single-tax theory. Max Hirsch, *Democracy versus Socialism; a Critical Examination of Socialism as a Remedy for Social Injustice and an Exposition of the Single Tax Doctrine* (London, 1901, 481 pp.), is the most important reply to the socialist attacks.

A selection of titles by Georgists indicates that there were still other points in common: A. R. Wallace, *Land Nationalisation; Its Necessity and Its Aims* (2nd ed., New York, 1896, 252 pp.); H. E. Bartholomew, *Henry George; or, The Coming Revolution* (Bath, Pa., 1898, 154 pp.); Henry George, Jr., *The Menace of Privilege; a Study of the Dangers to the Republic from the Existence of a Favored Class* (New York, 1905, 421 pp.); Herbert Quick, *On Board the Good Ship Earth; a Survey of World Problems* (Indianapolis, Ind., 1913, 450 pp.); and Tom Mann, *From Single Tax to Syndicalism* (London, 1913, 112 pp.).

Independent studies since World War I throw additional light on the common and distinct features of the two movements. E. R. A. Seligman, *Essays in Taxation* (10th ed., New York, 1925, 806 pp.), pp. 66-97, is a comprehensive statement of the professional objections to the single tax. In A. N. Young, *The Single Tax Movement in the United States* (Princeton, N.J., 1916, 340 pp.), see especially pp. 9-10, 89-126, 250-256, and 307-312. See also P. A. Speek, *The Singletax and the Labor Movement* (University of Wisconsin *Bulletin*, Economics and Political Science Series, Vol. 8, No. 3; Madison, Wis., 1917, 180 pp.); Ernest Teilhac, *Pioneers of American Economic Thought in the Nineteenth Century* (1928; tr. by E. A. J. Johnson; New York, 1936, 187 pp.), a careful study which labels George's "Socialism" as "pre-Marxian, rationalistic, humanistic and universalistic," according to Geiger; and Sidney Ratner, *American Taxation; Its History as a Social Force in Democracy* (New York, 1942, 561 pp.), which is more concerned with enacted taxes, such as the tariff and the income tax; likewise Helen Tarasov, *Who Does Pay the Taxes?* (intro. by Jacob Marschak; New York, 1942, 48 pp.), supplement 4 to *Social Research*. H. E. Read, *The Abolition of Inheritance* (New York, 1918, 312 pp.), relates his proposal for "cradle equality" with socialism and Georgism without claiming that he has announced a panacea. J. H. Holmes, "Henry George and Karl Marx; a Plutarchian Experiment," *American Journal of Economics and Sociology*, VI (Jan. 1947), pp. 159-167, distinguishes the two leaders on the basis of their opposed attitudes toward religion.

Topic 9. Socialist Theories of Revolution and the American Revolutionary Tradition

Revolution has meant to Marxists the turning point in the development of the modern economic system when the classes led by industrial labor acquire power, if necessary by violence, from the classes dominated by capitalists. Revolution is only the culminating time segment of an evolutionary process. Consequently, the Marxists' criticism of capitalism (Topics 1-3) and their theories of prerevolutionary activity, presumably containing the seeds of socialist organization (Topics 4-8), continually involve their theories of revolution. The major controversy between the revisionists and the orthodox has turned on the issue of the proper tactics for acquiring power. How this power should be used to legalize the collectivist institutions which the Marxists find implicit in capitalist economy is discussed in succeeding topics.

Revolution is illegal if it violates the procedure for change authorized by the fundamental law of any state. Marx and Engels sanctioned the resort to violence and illegality in certain contingencies. Their belief that peaceful and constitutional change was possible in countries like the United States and Great Britain, where political democracy was highly developed, led their followers to draw contradictory conclusions from later developments. Did twentieth-century conditions in democratic countries make a socialist parliamentary victory impossible, or not?

Acts of violence against legal authority created the United States, and violent direct action, from frontier vigilantism to urban industrial warfare, has been endemic. Jefferson and the Southern secessionists were outstanding defenders of the Lockian natural right of revolution, but since the Civil War, those in power have had no use for any revolutionary doctrine. Revolutionary patriots confiscated Tory estates but their successors wrote the protection of private property into the constitution. Socialists can expropriate with or without compensation to private owners. Marxian opinion varies as to whether the present British method of compensation for property taken by right of eminent domain will end capitalism or perpetuate it. So far was the American revolutionary tradition forgotten that even the right to advocate revolution was attacked. The Supreme Court has upheld this right only insofar as no immediate overt act is connected or contemplated—so long as there is no clear and present danger.

The kind of tactics American socialists have proposed depends directly on their answers to the ethical question of the relation of means and ends. At one extreme the communitarians have relied on the propaganda of the word—religious conversion or rational persuasion. In this sense only were they revolutionary: they sought a fundamental reorganization of society by sudden changes in the minds and souls of men. They had

321

little sense of an evolutionary process leading toward any such basic change. Violent revolution was out of the question for most communitarians, either because of the pacifist tenets of their religion (the German pietists and Shakers), or because their founders (Fourier, Owen, and even Cabet, born under Napoleon) had vivid and unpleasant recollections of the French upheaval. At the other extreme, Johann Most and other American anarchist followers of Bakunin proclaimed the propaganda of the deed—direct and violent action. Sporadic theft, counterfeit, sabotage, and assassination frightened millions into indiscriminate attacks on labor in general but brought the revolution no nearer. Between these extremes, the vast majority of socialists sought to combine both methods. Even anarchist terrorism was more verbal propaganda than direct action, and at the other pole, the communitarians expected to convert the world more by their successful practice of community living than by their auxiliary preaching. In describing the tactics of this majority one can speak only of tendencies to justify the means by what is necessary to effect socialism, or to limit the means to those by which socialism would be maintained. Since the first stage of socialism has been viewed both as a political dictatorship and a political democracy, a further differentiation of tactics arises (see Topic 10).

Parliamentary socialists face the possibility, realized by the Spanish Civil War, that their defeated opponents will not acquiesce as a minority under a legitimately elected socialist administration. Socialists, in asserting their right of self-defense, call attention to the history of revolutions, which shows that the major violence occurs in the defense of a new regime and not in the attack on the old. Armed insurrection led by a small disciplined organization has been discussed by American socialists, but there has been no American counterpart of Blanqui's French storm troopers. It is generally assumed by twentieth-century socialists that modern warfare has rendered barricade fighting obsolete as the primary tactic of revolution. Some expect to use the disciplined nucleus or vanguard to divide and obstruct the "class enemies" and prepare for socialist assumption of power in a period of chaos created by war and depression. The general strike, the principal tactic of European syndicalist theory, was accepted by the I.W.W., and used as late as 1919 in Seattle by the A.F.L. Problems of the discipline and endurance of the striking population and the control of the violence of other groups were never solved.

The classic exposition of orthodox Marxian revolutionary theory is Lenin's *The State and Revolution; Marxist Teaching on the State and the Task of the Proletariat in the Revolution* (London, 1919, 124 pp.). Read especially pp. 7-26, 69-85, 106-124, with particular attention to the first stage of the revolution, which Lenin ties almost inextricably with the dictatorship of the proletariat. Max Eastman criticizes Marxist revolutionary theory in "Revolution as a Scientific Enterprise," in Eastman's *Marxism; Is It Science?* (New York, 1940, 394 pp.), pp. 199-272. This work is a revised edition of his book, *Marx and Lenin; the Science of Revolution* (New York, 1927, 267 pp.). The case for peaceful transition to socialism is stated in H. W. Laidler, "Will There Be a Revolution?" in his *Socializing Our Democracy* (New York, 1935, 330 pp.), pp. 82-114. Read also the pair of John Day pamphlets, V. F. Calverton, *For Revolution* (New York, 1932, 28 pp.), and Gilbert Seldes, *Against Revolution* (New York, 1932, 27 pp.), both of which base their arguments on American tradition. Refer again to the citations in PART I, Topics 8-9, and to Eduard Bernstein, *Evolutionary Socialism* (tr. by E. C. Harvey; New York, 1909, 224 pp.), and Rosa Luxemburg, *Reform or Revolution* (tr. by Integer [Herman Jerson]; New York, 1937, 53 pp.).

From the extensive European writing on revolution indicated in the General Reading, pp. 249-251, and in the bibliographies of previous Parts the following works are selected, with additions. Gustave Le Bon, *The Psychology of Revolution* (1912; tr. by Bernard Miall; New York, 1913, 337 pp.), is concerned primarily with the French Revolution. A fresh historical study by a Marxist is Daniel Guérin, *La Lutte de classes sous la Première République; bourgeois et 'bras nus' (1793-1797)* (Paris, 1946, 2 vols.). Émile Pataud and Émile Pouget, *Syndicalism and the Co-operative Commonwealth (How We Shall Bring About the Revolution)* (tr. by Charlotte and Frederic Charles; Oxford, 1913, 240 pp.), is representative of the French syndicalists, and Émile Vandervelde, *Socialism versus the State* (1918; tr. by C. H. Kerr; Chicago, 1919, 229 pp.), of the social democrats. M. J. Olgin, *The Soul of the Russian Revolution* (New York, 1917, 423 pp.), traces the gradual extinction of the intellectuals' allegiance to the tsars over three generations. Curzio Malaparte devotes more space to Fascist than to Marxian tactics in *Coup d'Etat; the Technique of Revolution* (tr. by Sylvia Saunders; New York, 1932, 251 pp.). Heinrich Ehrlich, *The Struggle for Revolutionary Socialism* (tr. by Haim Kantorovitch and Anna Bercowitz; New York, 1934, 62 pp.), by a leader of the Jewish Socialist Party, the *Bund* of Poland, reports on the Labor and Socialist International Conference of 1933, at which the communists were blamed for the rise of Hitler. Kurt Riezler, "On the Psychology of the Modern Revolution," *Social Research*, x (Sept. 1943), pp. 320-336, is also preoccupied with Germany. Barthélemy de Ligt, *The Conquest of Violence; an Essay on War and Revolution* (tr. by Honor Tracy; New York, 1938, 306 pp.), especially pp. 161-173, elaborates the theme, "the more of violence, the less of revolution." Y. O. Martov, *The State and the Socialist Revolution* (tr. by Integer [Herman Jerson]; New York, 1938, 63 pp.), applies the events of twenty years to Lenin's essay.

Guglielmo Ferrero, *The Principles of Power; the Great Political Crises of History* (tr. by T. R. Jaeckel; New York, 1942, 333 pp.), compares legitimacy with revolution or illegitimate government.

In Great Britain authors representing the Labour Party point of view are J. R. MacDonald, *Parliament and Revolution* (New York, 1920, 180 pp.), and R. W. Postgate, *How to Make a Revolution* (New York, 1934, 199 pp.). Postgate, an ex-communist and author and editor of other studies and documents of revolutions, summarizes and evaluates the historical techniques and proposes an improvement on the communist model of a disciplined vanguard within a mass party. British communist writings include Eden and Cedar Paul, *Creative Revolution; a Study of Community Ergatocracy* [Government by Workers] (New York, 1920, 220 pp.). See also H. M. Hyndman, *The Evolution of Revolution* (New York, 1921, 406 pp.), a Marxian survey, in uninspired style, of the rise and fall of slavery, bourgeois revolutions, and socialism; C. D. Burns, *The Principles of Revolution; a Study in Ideals* (New York, 1921, 154 pp.), sketches of Rousseau, Marx, Mazzini, Morris, and Tolstoy with diffident religio-reformist conclusions. T. H. Wintringham, *Mutiny; Being a Survey of Mutinies from Spartacus to Invergordon* (London, 1936, 355 pp.), concludes that revolutions are not made by interested agitators but grow out of class contradictions within the armed forces themselves.

In the western hemisphere outside the United States sample studies are W. D. Herridge, *Which Kind of Revolution?* (Boston, 1943, 162 pp.), by the founder of the New Democracy movement in Canada who urges a bloodless revolution for freedom through total peacetime utilization of resources; and Luis Chico Goerne, *Hacia una filosofía social en el siglo XX; ensayo de sociología política sobre la doctrina de la revolución mexicana* (Mexico, D.F., 1943, 237 pp.), an interpretation of Mexican revolutionary thought from Madero to Camacho by a professor of sociology at the University of Mexico.

American nonsocialist studies of revolution have largely been the result of efforts of sociologists and social psychologists to create a morphology of revolutions in general rather than to delineate the socialist type. The history of this literature begins with C. A. Ellwood, "A Psychological Theory of Revolutions," *American Journal of Sociology*, xi (July 1905), pp. 49-59, and Brooks Adams, *The Theory of Social Revolutions* (New York, 1913, 240 pp.), a prophecy of the collapse of capitalist government with inferences drawn from the functions of American courts. One of the best monographs, clear yet tentative, is L. P. Edwards, *The Natural History of Revolution* (Chicago, 1927, 229 pp.). Edwards' naturalistic definition holds that the distinction between evolution and revolution is misleading. For other definitions of this period see Dale Yoder, "Current Definitions of Revolution," *American Journal of Sociol-*

ogy, xxxII (Nov. 1926), pp. 433-441. P. A. Sorokin, *The Sociology of Revolution* (Philadelphia, 1925, 428 pp.), written soon after the author's exile from the U.S.S.R., analyzes the Russian upheaval. In the third volume of his *Social and Cultural Dynamics* (New York, 1937-1941, 4 vols.), pp. 383-506, Sorokin deals in general and by countries with the fluctuation, duration, and intensity of internal disturbances since the sixth century B.C. E. D. Martin, *Farewell to Revolution* (New York, 1935, 380 pp.), stresses the aspects of crowd psychology and opposes all revolution as ineffectual in solving social problems. Crane Brinton, *The Anatomy of Revolution* (New York, 1938, 326 pp.), is one of the better comparative studies of the last decade, depending somewhat—as do the similar studies—on Edwards. Robert Hunter, *Revolution; Why, How, When?* (New York, 1940, 385 pp.), by a former socialist and communist, is more superficial, covers more movements, but concentrates on the Soviet state as similar to the tsarist state.

Students of government, economics, and even philosophy and literature have recently turned to the subject. Veblen, *The Engineers and the Price System* (New York, 1921, 169 pp.), was taken to indicate that technicians are a peculiarly revolutionary class. S. H. M. Chang, "The Overthrow of the Bourgeois State by Revolution," in his *The Marxian Theory of the State* (Philadelphia, 1931, 230 pp.), pp. 63-87, summarizes Leninist theory. His appendices, pp. 211-222, reproduce documents by A. Trachtenberg and D. Ryazanov (pseud.) showing how Eduard Bernstein, Engels' literary executor, suppressed certain passages in publishing Engels' introduction to Marx's *The Class Struggles in France* to prove that Engels had shifted to Bernstein's revisionist position. Max Lerner, "The War as Revolution," in his *Ideas for the Ice Age; Studies in a Revolutionary Era* (New York, 1941, 432 pp.), pp. 3-26, is a brief sample of the products of World War II.

American socialists of all kinds have either written about specific tactics or contributed innumerable arguments to the orthodox-revisionist debate. An American individualist anarchist favoring revolution was Lysander Spooner, author of *Revolution; the Only Remedy for the Oppressed Classes of . . . the British Empire* (2nd ed., n.p., 1880, 11 pp.). Max Nomad in "The Preacher, Johann Most, Terrorist of the Word," *Apostles of Revolution* (Boston, 1939, 467 pp.), pp. 256-301, shows that Most did not practice the "propaganda by the deed" which he preached, and that he tried to keep his audience even at the cost of changing his tune. "Shall Red and Black Unite? An American Revolutionary Document of 1883," in C. M. Destler, *American Radicalism, 1865-1901* (New London, Conn., 1946, 276 pp.), pp. 78-104, reproduces a letter to Joseph A. Labadie and August Spies from the Pacific Coast revolutionary B. G. Haskell proposing Bakuninist tactics. Theft, another type of direct action, precipitates revolution in M. I. Swift's utopian fantasy, *A League of Justice; or, Is It Right to Rob Robbers?* (Boston, 1893, 90 pp.). See also Swift's *Some Thoughts on the Growing Revolution* (Ashtabula, Ohio, 1891, 16 pp.). Laurence Gronlund, *Ça Ira! or, Danton in the French Revolution* (Boston, 1887, 261 pp.), is a study foreshadowing the author's later Bellamyism. Daniel De Leon's speech, *Reform or Revolution* (1896; New York, 1919, 32 pp.), defines revolution as economic and political organization to change fundamental institutions and reform as superficial doctoring of the same institutions, but does not face the question of change by force or law. Mark Fisher, *Evolution and Revolution* (Chicago, n.d., 61 pp.), typifies the orthodox prewar disavowal of aggressive violence and assertion of the right of defense, and the socialists' use of biological evidence to support their gradualism (see also PART III, Topic 5). Likewise consult S. A. Reeve, *The Natural Laws of Social Convulsion* (New York, 1933, 591 pp.), which contains several chapters of an announced but unpublished work of three volumes on the evolution of social crises, the final product of a writer whose thought was formulated long before.

After World War I the communists took up the orthodox side and pointed most persistently to the American revolutionary tradition and the necessities of the Russian Revolution. An early communist essay, based largely on correspondence from Engels to Sorge and Mrs. Florence Wischnewetsky was Heinz Neuman, *Marx and Engels on Revolution in America* (Chicago, 1926?, 43 pp.). Lincoln Steffens unsuccessfully retold the story of Exodus in *Moses in Red; the Revolt of Israel as a Typical Revolution* (Philadelphia, 1926, 144 pp.) in an attempt to distill his experience of the modern revolutionary situation through historical analogy. The Socialist Party was content with gradualism, but after shedding its right wing in 1936 claimed to be less reformist than the communists. F. C. Howe, *Revolution and Democracy* (New York, 1921, 238 pp.), is noteworthy for its attempt to turn the accusation of sabotage upon the capitalists, as Veblen had done. Scott Nearing and the Labour Research Study Group, *The Law of Social Revolution* (New York, 1926, 262 pp.), is a symposium attempting objectivity. Representative of twentieth-century communitarians was R. C. (Bob) Brown's pamphlet, *Toward a Bloodless Revolution* (Newllano, La., 1933, 14 pp.). The appeal to history is represented by B. D. Wolfe, Jay Lovestone, and W. F. Dunne, *Our Heritage from 1776; a Working Class View of the First American Revolution* (New York, n.d., 23 pp.); Avrom Landy, "The Right of Revolution; an American Revolutionary Tradition," *Communist*, VIII (July 1929), pp. 360-368; and V. F. Calverton, "America's Revolutionary History," in S. D. Schmalhausen, ed., *Recovery through Revolution* (New York, 1933, 504 pp.), pp. 368-390. On the general theme see also articles by

R. M. Lovett and Lewis Corey in the same volume. George Soule, *The Coming American Revolution* (New York, 1934, 314 pp.), deals primarily with contemporary conditions but contains much on the general theory of revolution. J. L. Spivak, also reporting conditions, bases his *America Faces the Barricades* (New York, 1935, 287 pp.) on the exploded theories that revolutions arise directly out of hunger and misery and succeed by street fighting. That "the Communist position on the road to power to-day is blunt reformism" is the thesis of Gus Tyler's article, "People's Government vs. Proletarian Dictatorship," *American Socialist Monthly*, v (Mar. 1936), pp. 20-23. Albert Goldman, a Trotskyist in the Socialist Party, criticizes Felix Cohen, "Socialism and the Myth of Legality," *ibid.*, iv (Nov. 1935), pp. 3-33, as halfway revolutionary in "A Socialist Revolution in Constitutional Garments," *ibid.*, v (May 1936), pp. 22-27, and concludes that revolution has its own legality. L. M. Oak, "Bourgeois and Revolutionary Morals," *Socialist Review*, vi (Mar.-Apr. 1939), pp. 7-9, 17, attacks Aldous Huxley's *Ends and Means* (New York, 1937, 386 pp.) and defends the justification of means by ends. In the symposium ed. by I. D. Talmadge, *Whose Revolution?* (New York, 1941, 296 pp.), see especially the sections by Hans Kohn, Granville Hicks, and R. N. Baldwin. Compare also the shifts in the communist line noted in PART II, Topic 10.

Two books by authors who believe that society is controlled by an elite, whether they are revolutionary socialists or Fascists or conservative capitalists, are Lawrence Dennis, *The Dynamics of War and Revolution* (New York, 1940, 259 pp.), and James Burnham, *The Managerial Revolution* (New York, 1941, 285 pp.). P. M. Sweezy, "The Illusion of the 'Managerial Revolution,'" *Science & Society*, vi (Winter 1942), pp. 1-23, bases his criticism of Burnham on the thesis that control, though more concentrated, is still linked with ownership of contemporary industry. Burnham's "revolution," however, is not primarily the climax struggle for political power, with which this topic deals.

Topic 10. *Political Control and Economic Rights*

When socialists have captured the state their next steps are to maintain their power and at the same time to initiate economic changes which will bring about a socialist society. This topic deals with part of what Marxians have called the lower stage of socialism under the dictatorship of the proletariat. It is limited to the political problem of retaining control of the state, and to that part of the proposed economic changes which relate to labor. The management of the transitional socialist society is treated in Topic 11. Economic rights, without which socialists claim democracy is a sham, are dealt with here. The piecemeal programs of the Socialist Party and kindred groups belong to the lower stage of socialism. Only the long-term goals of socialists, which provide a dynamic by tension between "ought" and "is," are reserved for discussion in Topic 12. Since party control in Marxian theory often applies both before and after the revolution, see also Topic 4. For additional materials on Soviet communism, see the General Reading of PART I, pp. 19-23.

American theorists before 1917 had expressed, at least in general terms, most of the principal ideas about the socialist state and its labor policy. After 1917 these ideas could be compared with conditions in the Soviet Union, which proclaimed itself to be a dictatorship of the proletariat. Discussion of methods to control the displaced capitalists has turned on the interpretation of Marx. One side claims that he was using "dictatorship" as a parallel to contemporary capitalist rule through political democracy and without the usual connotation of the direct tyranny of one man or of an oligarchy. Their opponents counter that Marx recognized the necessity of rule by the proletarian vanguard or even by its leader in the name of the masses. Thus even when protagonists of Soviet dictatorship profess a belief in ultimately greater political liberties, they call authoritarian rule a lesser evil than the economic insecurity of capitalism. At the same time they point to the Soviet constitution of 1936, and to cultural liberties in the Soviet Union, as conditioning its absolutism.

The right to work, guaranteed by article 118 of the 1936 constitution, is regarded as the keystone of Soviet economic rights. Like all rights, it is balanced by the duty of every citizen to maintain labor discipline (article 130). The Russian worker has privileges and obligations like those of the Christian whose service to the divine Dictator is perfect freedom. Soviet theories of full employment, wages, incentives, and social security all stem from the right and duty to work. Americans, who according to a recent public opinion poll are more in sympathy with this collectivist goal than any other, have only begun to evaluate this theory. Among the questions they raise, four stand out. (1) Is not full employment as much a goal of capitalism as it is of socialism? Both depend ultimately on the successful working of each economic system. If the government does not meddle, say the advocates of "free enterprise," capitalists will provide employment. (2) Do not Soviet labor camps and labor reserves, as much as the unemployed on capitalist relief, qualify for Marx's definition of the reserve army of labor? (3) Is not the Stakhanov movement the Russian parallel of the speed-up system? (4) Are labor discipline and wage control a necessary price of the right to work, or merely incidental characteristics of a totalitarian state? American socialists, excluding communists, answer "yes" to the first three and the first half of the fourth question, but with important qualifications, especially of the first. It makes little difference what the employment goal of a perfectly competitive system is, they claim, and they doubt the intention of many capitalists. While they justify the principle of labor discipline they do not sanction the specific means used in Russia.

Opinion about state responsibility for social security likewise differs over methods. It also differs as to what part of welfare legislation is transition and what part must be a permanent function of socialist administration.

The Leninist theory of proletarian dictatorship is expounded in S. H. M. Chang, *The Marxian Theory of the State* (Philadelphia, 1931, 230 pp.), pp. 88-133, 148-180. Arnold Brecht analyzes the possibilities of government under the Soviet constitution of 1936 in "The New Russian Constitution," *Social Research*, IV (May 1937), pp. 157-175, 178-179, 188-190 (the parts omitted deal with civil rights and administrative relationships). Compare this view with that of A. L. Strong, *The New Soviet Constitution; a Study in Socialist Democracy* (New York, 1937, 169 pp.). The U.S.S.R. is the point of reference for the critical articles by B. D. Wolfe, "The U.S. and the U.S.S.R.," and, to a less extent, Lewis Corey, "The Need Still Is: a New Social Order," in *Whose Revolution?* (ed. by I. D. Talmadge; New York, 1941, 296 pp.), pp. 218-248, and 249-273. Jacob Marschak includes a discussion of socialist wage theory in "Wages," *Encyclopaedia of the Social Sciences*, xv, pp. 291-302. Read also H. W. Laidler, *Socializing Our Democracy* (New York, 1935, 330 pp.), pp. 115-148, 181-200, 213-246.

Writings on the dictatorship of the proletariat, both in general and with reference to the U.S.S.R., are *Karl Marx und Friedrich Engels über die Diktatur des Proletariats* (ed. by Ernst Drahn; Berlin, 1920, 39 pp.); Auguste Blanqui, *Critique sociale* (Paris, 1885, 2 vols.), a posthumous work foreshadowing Bolshevik tactics; Karl Kautsky, *The Dictatorship of the Proletariat* (tr. by H. J. Stenning; Manchester, Eng., 1919, 149 pp.); François Perroux, "La Dictature du prolétariat chez les marxistes," *Questions pratiques*, xxiv (July-Sept. 1928), pp. 115-136; Emile Burns, *Capitalism, Communism and the Transition* (London, 1933, 287 pp.); John Strachey, *The Theory and Practice of Socialism* (New York, 1936, 512 pp.), "Socialism and Communism Distinguished," pp. 115-125, "A New Kind of Democracy," pp. 147-159, and "The Dictatorship of the Working Class," pp. 160-167; and E. F. M. Durbin, "The Dictatorship of the Proletariat; a Critique of Communist Political Theory," in his *The Politics of Democratic Socialism* (London, 1940, 384 pp.), pp. 149-231, and appendix, pp. 337-352. Leon Trotsky, in *The New Course* (New York, 1943, 265 pp.), pp. 11-58, and Max Shachtman in the same volume, pp. 121-265, attempt a compromise between democracy and bureaucratism; while Fred Henderson, *The Case for Socialism* (1911; Chicago, 1934, 146 pp.), promises freedom and greater equality throughout the social structure. Arnold Brecht, "Democracy—Challenge to Theory," *Social Re-*

search, XIII (June 1946), pp. 195-224, denies that the term "democracy" can be applied to any state, no matter what "economic basis" is supplied, which permits but one political party. Eugen Varga, former Hungarian cabinet minister under Bela Kun and Soviet editor since 1919, debates this point, as well as the identification of the Stakhanov movement with the speed-up in *Two Systems: Socialist Economy and Capitalist Economy* (tr. by R. P. Arnot; New York, 1939, 268 pp.), pp. 58-70, 222-234. With liberal use of statistics, he discusses unemployment and workers' conditions in chapters 6 and 12. For general treatments of socialist economics, see the General Reading, pp. 241-249, and Emil Lederer, "Socialist Economics," *Encyclopaedia of the Social Sciences*, v, pp. 377-381. See also W. H. Beveridge, *Full Employment in a Free Society* (New York, 1945, 429 pp.). Rudolf Schlesinger, *Soviet Legal Theory* (New York, 1945, 299 pp.), surveys the constitutional framework of the Russian dictatorship, as does Andrei Vyshinsky, *The Law of the Soviet State* (tr. by H. W. Babb; New York, 1948, 749 pp.). Also consult H. J. Berman, *Justice in Russia; an Interpretation of Soviet Law* (Cambridge, Mass., 1950, 322 pp.).

The use of the term "dictatorship" ranges from the Marxist application of the term to capitalist democracy, to claims that the socialist revolution has already arrived in the same democracy, as in W. H. Lyon, *Dictatorship of the Proletariat in the United States; a Tract for the Times* (New York, 1943, 135 pp.). Alfred Cobban, *Dictatorship; Its History and Theory* (New York, 1939, 352 pp.), restricts his definition to the tyranny of one man, but concludes that "all European dictators of the present day are the children of the *Communist Manifesto*" (p. 112). Eduard Heimann, *Communism, Fascism or Democracy?* (New York, 1938, 288 pp.), finds fault with the Marxian identification of the state with class rule (pp. 75-80) and compares the institutions of communism with those of democracy (pp. 138-150). J. A. Schumpeter, *Capitalism, Socialism and Democracy* (New York, 1942, 381 pp.), pp. 210-237, deals with socialist methods of discipline and the problems of transition from a capitalist to a socialist order.

Early American socialists, mindful of the charge of utopianism, nevertheless drew up a number of programs based on capitalist development. Laurence Gronlund, *The Co-operative Commonwealth* (1884; rev. and enl. ed., Boston, 1890, 304 pp.), pp. 103-201, was the earliest attempt, but was later repudiated by both the orthodox and the revisionists. Others include Upton Sinclair, *The Industrial Republic; a Study of the America of Ten Years Hence* (New York, 1907, 284 pp.); J. W. Hughan, *American Socialism of the Present Day* (New York, 1911, 265 pp.), pp. 152-161; and Morris Hillquit, *Socialism in Theory and Practice* (New York, 1909, 361 pp.), chap. 5. The most detailed prognosis, as well as the most thorough in its evaluation of previous socialist writing on the subject, was by the revisionist John Spargo, *Applied Socialism; a Study of the Application of Socialistic Principles to the State* (New York, 1912, 333 pp.), especially pp. 37-86, 163-236. Daniel De Leon, who in his own writings applied Marxian theory primarily to existing conditions, nevertheless adapted Kautsky's ideas to America in his translation, *The Socialist Republic* (New York, 1918, 48 pp.). Frank Tannenbaum, "Comradeship," in his *The Labor Movement* (New York, 1921, 259 pp.), pp. 105-112, discusses the democratic significance of the proletarian "dictatorship"; the latter half of the book, pp. 126-237, describes structural changes in political organization that are possible as a result of labor organization. In contrast to this syndicalism is the pessimistic view of James Burnham. His chapter, "Is Democracy Possible?" in *Whose Revolution?* (cited above), pp. 187-217, states that democrats always become bureaucratic dictators after they gain power.

The right to work was first proclaimed by Louis Blanc. Marx and Engels referred to the obligation to work in the *Communist Manifesto*, and Marx referred to the right to work under capitalism as a miserable sham in *The Class Struggles in France*. "Statement of Essential Human Rights," American Academy of Political and Social Science *Annals*, Vol. 243 (Jan. 1946), pp. 18-26, states that provisions for establishing the right to work are contained in the constitutions of nine countries. In the same issue J. R. Ellingston has an article, "The Right to Work," pp. 27-39. See also P. J. Proudhon, *Le Droit au travail et le droit de propriété* (Paris, 1848, 60 pp.); J. G. Courcelle-Seneuil, *Liberté et socialisme; ou, Discussion des principes de l'organisation du travail industriel* (Paris, 1868, 447 pp.).

Only brief references to this right can be found, such as M. I. Swift, *The Horroboos* (Boston, 1911, 241 pp.), p. 104, and Ernest Riebe, *Crimes of the Bolsheviki* (Chicago, 1919, 48 pp.), pp. 9, 11, 21. Recent American liberal discussion of the unemployment problem emphasizes the social security aspects. Nels Anderson, *The Right to Work* (New York, 1938, 152 pp.), defends work relief; while Abraham Epstein, *Social Security* (L.I.D. Pamphlet Ser.; New York, 1937, 38 pp.), argues for social insurance. Max Ascoli, "The Right to Work," *Social Research*, vi (May 1939), pp. 255-268, and criticism by C. J. Friedrich, Max Lerner, Eduard Heimann, and others, pp. 269-286, is an inconclusive discussion which shuttles between the dangers of labor discipline and the duty of rendering service to society. G. R. Kirkpatrick's last book was vaguely on this theme, with the rhetorical title, *Is Plenty Too Much for the Common People?* (illus. by Art Young; 2nd ed., San Gabriel, Calif., 1940, 312 pp.). A nonsocialist approach to the problem through government guarantees of industrial contracts, following the N.R.A. pattern but neglecting monopoly and price problems, is Mordecai Ezekiel, *Jobs for All through Industrial Expansion* (New York, 1939, 299 pp.). See also J. H. G. Pierson, *Full Employment* (New Haven, Conn., 1941, 297 pp.), and H. A. Wallace, *Sixty Million Jobs* (New York, 1945, 216 pp.).

On the broader aspects of security legislation, see B. N. Armstrong, *Insuring the Essentials; Minimum Wage Plus Social Insurance—a Living Wage Program* (New York, 1932, 717 pp.); I. M. Rubinow, *The Quest for Security* (New York, 1934, 638 pp.); Abraham Epstein, *The Challenge of the Aged* (New York, 1928, 435 pp.), and *Insecurity, a Challenge to America* (1933; 2nd rev. ed., New York, 1938, 939 pp.); G. M. Burnham, *Social Insurance* (New York, 1932, 31 pp.), a communist pamphlet; F. P. Miller, *The Blessings of Liberty* (Chapel Hill, N.C., 1936, 105 pp.), which stresses the need for economic security as well as civil rights; H. W. Laidler, *A Program for Modern America* (New York, 1936, 517 pp.), chaps. 2-4; J. A. Kingsbury, "Health Security for the Nation," *Industrial Democracy*, VI (Oct. 15, 1938), 39 pp.; and H. W. Laidler, ed., *The Third Freedom: Freedom from Want; Symposium* (New York, 1943, 96 pp.). Scott Nearing, *Democracy Is Not Enough* (New York, 1945, 153 pp.), pp. 3-12, 95-100, 124-132, emphasizes the need of broadening democracy to embrace economic as well as political freedoms, which in turn should be balanced by the imposition of certain disciplines. See also Hiram Elfenbein, "How Economic Rights Are Superior to Democratic Rights," *Socialism from Where We Are* (New York, 1945, 214 pp.), pp. 158-160. The position endorsed by the mutualist Catholic Workers, claiming to be neither capitalist nor socialist, is best stated in Étienne Borne and François Henry, *A Philosophy of Work* (1937; tr. by Francis Jackson; New York, 1938, 221 pp.).

On labor discipline and related phases of Soviet labor policy, see Augustine Souchy, *The Workers and Peasants of Russia and Ukraine* (Chicago, 1922, 144 pp.), a report of a syndicalist delegate to the second Comintern congress; M. P. Tomsky, *The Trade Unions, the Party and the State* (Moscow, 1927, 21 pp.); G. M. Price, M.D., *Labor Protection in Soviet Russia* (New York, 1928, 128 pp.); Joseph Freeman, *The Soviet Worker* (New York, 1932, 408 pp.); V. V. Prokofyev, *Industrial and Technical Intelligentsia in the U.S.S.R.* (Moscow, 1933, 85 pp.); Manya Gordon, *Workers before and after Lenin* (New York, 1941, 524 pp.); L. E. Hubbard, *Soviet Labour and Industry* (London, 1942, 314 pp.), whose author has written on other aspects of Soviet economy; L. A. Leontyev, *Work under Capitalism and Socialism* (New York, 1942, 62 pp.); and J. N. Hazard, "The Soviet Government Organizes for Reconstruction," *Journal of Politics*, VIII (Aug. 1946), pp. 248-277. Hazard, professor of public law at the Russian Institute, Columbia University, has written at length on the institutional aspects of the Soviet attempt to provide dwellings for workers in *Soviet Housing Law* (New Haven, Conn., 1939, 178 pp.). That a Soviet intelligentsia has developed which is curbing social security benefits is one of the themes in Salomon Schwartz's publication and research on Soviet labor, a sample of which is "Social Legislation in the Soviet Union," *Jewish Frontier*, vi (May 1939), pp. 15-18.

Topic 11. Socialist Governmental Planning and American Economic Policy

Man as an intelligent creature has always planned. To go no further back than the mercantilist states, we find their economic policies planned as weapons in their diplomatic and military warfare. While classical economic doctrines prevailed, the plans of governments were limited to setting the general and chiefly negative boundaries within which business was allowed to work out its own plans. For example, in the United States, as contrasted with Canada, the public lands were distributed with a minimum of control over their ownership and use, yet with the intention of developing a class of small landholders. In the long struggle over the means of effecting this goal, advocates of disposal to occupants at minimum prices defeated those who favored disposal through middlemen at relatively higher prices. In industry, the plan—or more accurately, program—of Alexander Hamilton to encourage manufacturing with protective tariffs was a continuing thread of government policy until recent times. As business expanded to a national or world scale, each corporation or cartel created a patch of privately planned economy. The responsibility for maximum utilization of social resources in the social interest was somehow left to these partial, uncontrolled businesses whose conflicts were haphazard and whose proper interest was the seeking of profit for their investors.

At first Americans sought through regulation to solve the chief economic problems of their democracy: unemployment, monopoly, and maldistribution of wealth and income. Although the communitarians had practical experience in comprehensive planning on a small scale, their theory must be gleaned from the General Reading cited in Part II. The political socialists, however, proposed a unified national control based upon the social ownership of the instruments of production and distribution. The importance of collective ownership was Marx's emphasis, but Marx's goal was the emancipation of the masses by themselves. As Marx saw history, man had successively freed himself from ecclesiastical authority and political despotism, but economic tyranny remained. Marxists hold that his rationalist and humanist regard for man's personal dignity and intelligence were basic to his belief that society eventually could be planned and organized to promote the general welfare of the dispossessed and depersonalized working classes.

Early American socialists accepted collective ownership uncritically and for the most part neglected the detailed problems of socialist economic administration. On three issues schisms arose among them: (1) whether to approve of planning under capitalism; (2) the extent of immediate and ultimate nationalization after the social revolution; and (3) whether security should be an end or the means to free and creative activity. Before 1917 only the Socialist Party approved of capitalist governmental planning, and then, of course, only if it agreed with the specific ends. To the De Leonists and the I.W.W., as well as a minority of the Socialist Party, planning under capitalism was a concession to buy off the revolution. All groups favored expropriation of all "means of production," but did not agree upon exactly what economic activities were meant by this phrase. They emphasized social securities as means, but did not realize the implications of planning for security.

The consequences of Soviet, Fascist, and New Deal planning have clarified these issues. To the democratic socialists, totalitarian planning, where security is not considered a means to freedom along with the means of political democracy, results in the "security" of the concentration camp. They have hailed and supported, on the other hand, the planning efforts of the New Deal as working in the right direction. On the question of nationalization, their position is scarcely distinguishable from that of capitalists who favor collective organization wherever, for technical reasons, capitalist competition does not work.

Communists base their views on the record of Soviet Russia with justifications of its limitations and reminders that conditions in other countries are different. To them planning under capitalism is a fraud; collectivization of the means of production must be comprehensive; the dictatorship of the proletariat is indispensable to the planned economy; freedom is equated with security.

The opponents of planning argue that totalitarianism is inevitable once a government enters the field of economic planning. They do not believe that the rule of law can continue to operate, and fear the rule of men with power to favor some and hurt others. They also believe that plans and controls involve computational problems beyond the ability of planners to solve, which the "free market" at least imperfectly solved.

On the political level, democratic socialists answer them by distinguishing between bureaucratic commissions to investigate and coordinate and legislative bodies to decide fundamental policy; by denying that general planning means the determination of all the details by an oligarchical planning board; and by proposing a system of agencies at local, regional, national, and world levels. Although they talk of "blueprints," these are conceived as flexible and tentative, to be revised to fit conditions.

The economic questions, such as price and wage fixing (whether a price and wage system as we know it is used or not) have been discussed in England and on the Continent but for the most part have been passed over by American socialists. The latter assume that the techniques of research, adaptation, approximation, and revision already used by partial planners can be redirected for social purposes. They consider this redirection a logical development of the American tradition. They would use the conservation movement, which seeks to plan the use of land and other natural resources, and develop the governmental instruments which have controlled the distribution of money and credit, the oldest of which is taxation.

A concise theoretical discussion of the minimum changes necessary for a planned economy is Carl Landauer, *Theory of National Economic Planning* (Berkeley, Calif., 1944, 189 pp.). Landauer has a short bibliographical essay, "Literature on Economic Planning," in *Social Research*, vii (Nov. 1940), pp. 496-508. To sample the writings on the political issues of planning, referred to in Landauer's last chapter, read F. A. Hayek, *The Road to Serfdom* (Chicago, 1944, 250 pp.), pp. 56-87; B. A. Wootton, *Freedom under Planning* (Chapel Hill, N.C., 1945, 180 pp.), pp. 130-157; and Herman Finer, *Road to Reaction* (Boston, 1945, 228 pp.), pp. 45-67. The state of Socialist Party thought in 1932, alternately holding and rejecting Marxian doctrines and alternately drawn to and repelled by Soviet practice, is illustrated in *Socialist Planning and a Socialist Program; a Symposium* (ed. by H. W. Laidler; New York, 1932, 255 pp.), pp. 105-137. Read also Eugen Varga, *Two Systems: Socialist Economy and Capitalist Economy* (New York, 1939, 268 pp.), pp. 15, 131-142. Refer again to the General Reading, pp. 241-249.

Among the ever-expanding literature on communist and Fascist planning see, for the former, at the beginning of the cycles of five-year plans, R. T. Bye and others, "The Central Planning and Co-ordination of Production in Soviet Russia," *American Economic Review, Supplement*, xix (Mar. 1929), pp. 91-130, and W. H. Chamberlin, *The Soviet Planned Economic Order* (Boston, 1931, 258 pp.). For comprehensive surveys including the recent period, see Gregory Bienstock, S. M. Schwarz and Aron Yugov, *Management in Russian Industry and Agriculture* (ed. by Arthur Feiler and Jacob Marschak; London, 1944, 198 pp.); Charles Bettelheim, *La Planification soviétique* (2nd ed. rev., Paris, 1945, 351 pp.); and Alexander Baykov, *The Development of the Soviet Economic System* (Cambridge, Eng., 1946, 514 pp.). Bienstock, Schwarz, and Yugov find equality of opportunity more an ideal than an achievement. Baykov is concerned with economic structure rather than economic geography.

His fourth section deals with the second and third five-year plans. He concludes with observations on general planning and appends a long bibliography of Soviet public documents. On the background of Nazi planning see W. F. Bruck, *The Road to Planned Economy; Capitalism and Socialism in Germany's Development* (London, 1934, 148 pp.). Studies during and since World War II include the *Over-all Report* by the United States Strategic Bombing Survey (Washington, 1945, 109 pp.), which states that full war production was not achieved by German planning until March 1944. Arthur Schweitzer, "Profits under Nazi Planning," *Quarterly Journal of Economics*, LXI (Nov. 1946), pp. 1-25, found that the Nazis had to retain the high-profit stimulus for maximum production. This resulted in monetary inflation and the failure of the profit-ceiling policy.

English treatments of planning are: G. D. H. Cole, *Principles of Economic Planning* (London, 1935, 435 pp.); Barbara Wootton, *Plan or No Plan* (London, 1934, 360 pp.); L. C. Robbins, *Economic Planning and International Order* (London, 1937, 330 pp.); F. E. Lawley, *The Growth of Collective Economy* (London, 1938, 2 vols.); H. J. Laski, *Will Planning Restrict Freedom?* (Cheam, Eng., 1944, 39 pp.); and John Jewkes, *Ordeal by Planning* (London, 1948, 248 pp.). Contributors on the Continent include Oskar Morgenstern, *The Limits of Economics* (tr. by Vera Smith; London, 1937, 160 pp.); Ingvar Svennilson, *Ekonomisk Planering; Teoretiska Studier* (Uppsala, 1938, 207 pp.); Charles Bettelheim, *Les Problèmes théoriques et pratiques de la planification* (Paris, 1946, 349 pp.); and B. V. Damalas, *La Crise du capitalisme et le problème de l'économie dirigée* (Paris, 1946, 327 pp.). See also, for examples from the British Commonwealth: Co-operative Commonwealth Federation, Ontario, *Planning for Freedom* (Toronto, 1944, 180 pp.), and W. G. K. Duncan, ed., *National Economic Planning* (Sydney, Australia, 1934, 217 pp.). With the advent of socialist and communist governments after World War II the literature dealing with their plans expanded rapidly.

An unpublished survey of American free-enterprise planning between the Civil War and World War I is F. W. Johnston's Yale dissertation in history (1938), *The Evolution of the American Concept of National Planning, 1865-1917.*

Among American nonprofessional economists, the Hayek thesis is found, earlier, in C. P. Steinmetz, *America and the New Epoch* (New York, 1916, 228 pp.), pp. 169-176, 217-229, where monarchical and collectivist organization are identified, and in the *Technocracy Study Course* (1934; 5th ed., New York, 1940, 291 pp.), pp. 213-279, which discards democracy in favor of a totalitarian empire of the North American continent. The kernel of Hayek's position is found in his pamphlet, *Freedom and the Economic System* (Chicago, 1939, 37 pp.).

Nonsocialist planners since 1930 whose writings have not been limited to economic issues include George Soule, *A Planned Society* (New York, 1932, 295 pp.); F. D. Roosevelt, *Looking Forward* (New York, 1933, 279 pp.), chap. 2; Max Ascoli and Fritz Lehmann, eds., *Political and Economic Democracy* (New York, 1937, 336 pp.); and John Dickinson, *Planned Society* (Williamsburg, Va., 1943, 34 pp.). J. A. Schumpeter, *Capitalism, Socialism and Democracy* (New York, 1942, 381 pp.), pp. 167-302, serves as a balanced evaluation. See also the April 1944 issue of the *Journal of Legal and Political Sociology* devoted to "Planned Economy and Law."

On the economic side, see the following, also by nonsocialists or non-party socialists: U.S. National Resources Planning Board publications, and those of its predecessor, the National Resources Committee; J. G. Smith, *Economic Planning and the Tariff; an Essay on Social Philosophy* (Princeton, N.J., 1934, 331 pp.); C. F. Ware and G. C. Means, *The Modern Economy in Action* (New York, 1936, 244 pp.), pp. 196-208; G. M. Peterson, *Diminishing Returns and Planned Economy* (New York, 1937, 254 pp.), pp. 161-234; C. D. Baldwin, *Economic Planning, Its Aims and Implications* (Urbana, Ill., 1942, 188 pp.); L. L. Lorwin, *Time for Planning* (New York, 1945, 273 pp.); and A. P. Lerner and F. D. Graham, *Planning and Paying for Full Employment* (Princeton, N.J., 1946, 222 pp.).

Works by those identified with socialism are not sufficiently explicit before 1917 to warrant special mention here. With the growing popularity of planning slogans, socialists declared that they had long been talking about the same thing. The following selection of titles is limited to the last fifteen years: Eduard Heimann, "Planning and the Market System," *Social Research*, i (Nov. 1934), pp. 486-504; H. W. Laidler, *Socializing Our Democracy* (New York, 1935, 330 pp.), pp. 20-48; *An Economic Program for American Democracy*, by seven Harvard and Tufts economists (New York, 1938, 91 pp.); H. W. Laidler, "Social Planning and Democracy," *Socialist Review*, vi (July-Aug. 1938), pp. 6-7, 16; Eduard Heimann, *Communism, Fascism or Democracy?* (New York, 1938, 288 pp.), pp. 80-97, 164-170, 260-284; Lewis Corey, *The Unfinished Task; Economic Reconstruction for Democracy* (New York, 1942, 314 pp.); and C. E. Ayres, "The Significance of Economic Planning," in Seba Eldridge and associates, *Development of Collective Enterprise* (Lawrence, Kan., 1943, 577 pp.), pp. 469-481. Communist opposition to capitalist planning is expressed in Earl Browder, *Is Planning Possible under Capitalism?* (New York, 1933, 16 pp.), and Alex Bittelman, "Government Intervention in the National Economy," *Communist*, xxⅢ (Oct. 1944), pp. 893-910.

Democratic socialists endorse existing local and regional planning. One of the best surveys is R. A. Stevenson and R. S. Vaile, *Balancing the Economic Controls* (Minneapolis, Minn., 1935, 96 pp.). See also Thomas Adams, *Outline of Town and City Planning; a Review of Past Efforts and Modern Aims* (New York, 1935, 368 pp.), and Findlay MacKenzie, ed., *Planned Society, Yesterday, Today, Tomorrow* (New York, 1937, 989 pp.). Planning local government is discussed in relation to the socialist administration of Milwaukee in D. W. Hoan, *City Government; the Record of the Milwaukee Experiment* (New York, 1936, 365 pp.), pp. 247-263. To illustrate the relation of regional planning to local, national, and international economic policies see the literature on the Tennessee Valley Authority, particularly D. E. Lilienthal, *TVA—Democracy on the March* (New York, 1944, 248 pp.); Herman Finer, *The T.V.A.—Lessons for International Application* (Montreal, 1944, 289 pp.); G. R. Clapp, "The Administrative Resources of a Region; the Example of the Tennessee Valley," in *New Horizons in Public Administration* (University, Ala., 1945, 145 pp.), pp. 79-95; also M. H. Satterfield, "TVA—State—Local Relationships," *American Political Science Review*, xl (Oct. 1946), pp. 935-949; and J. S. Ransmeier, *The Tennessee Valley Authority* (Nashville, Tenn., 1942, 486 pp.).

Topic 12. The Classless Society and American Social Ideals

Communism, the higher stage of socialism, was assumed by Marx and Engels to be the next synthesis of the historical dialectic. They discussed the classless society little and then only in passing. When not committing themselves to the logical dilemma of asserting that the dialectical process would cease to operate upon the achievement of communism, they supposed that the process would continue within the individual. For the most part, however, Marxians have denied the possibility of any historical finality. The new society would be marked by profound psychological, economic, and political changes. Man's thought and behavior patterns would be radically altered; productive abundance would make possible the abolition of certain basic kinds of division of labor, upon which classes depend; the control of persons would be replaced by the administration of things. As long as men remain enslaved to natural and historical pressures they develop habits of conflict which divide them. As they learn to choose those forms of social organization which enable them to master both nature and history, they may ascend into the realm of liberty. Classes are based on the scarcity of vital necessities. Were there no fear of poverty, nor lack of opportunity to exercise talents, the psychological drives for security and status through ownership, position, or power would wither. The application of the anarchist slogan, "From each according to his ability; to each according to his needs," encourages the all-round development of the individual. The system of specialists—in mental or manual labor; in rural or urban pursuits—vanishes through a combination of voluntary rotation of function and the reunion of town and country in the garden city. The productive capacity of society is assumed to be greater than the necessity for the present specialization. The productive, distributive, and administrative processes have been simplified; at the same time the broadly-trained man can be even more successful than the specialist in dealing with the interrelated problems of any particular occupation. The administrative process in the classless society is conceived primarily as the simple statistical survey of needs and abilities by the rotating personnel of a central bureau. Marxists hold that with the disappearance of conflicts, the coercive state becomes unnecessary.

What distinguishes this trinity of social goals—insofar as Marxians slip into the Marxian error of thinking in terms of ultimates—from the utopias which Marxians condemn? All formulations of social goals are utopias; that is, they exist *nowhere* but in the imagination. Man's imagination has been most active during times of social dislocation and crisis. At different times different men have found their social ideals in sharp contrast to actuality, so that almost every period is a time of crisis to one group or another and has produced its utopias. There are also some whose social philosophy creates a perpetual tension with existing society and who consequently are committed to a permanent revolution.

Four aspects of utopian thinking can be distinguished from one another, not absolutely, but according to the degree of emphasis on each. There are utopias of (1) satire, (2) escape, (3) means, and (4) reconstruction. The utopian satire—*Gulliver's Travels* or *Brave New World*—reveals the author's ideal negatively. The utopia of escape includes the type characterized by Marxians as the opium of the people. The elect achieve the blissful state automatically or supernaturally; they cannot work for it. The emphasis on mechanisms or panaceas, such as the Fourierist phalanx or the time-money of Josiah Warren, is in a sense a utopia of escape, but it is an escape which the individual works out by following a prescribed pattern. The utopia of reconstruction is committed to man's application of the scientific or rational method to the materials at hand; to the behavior of man and nature. While the Marxian utopia has strong emphasis on the fourth aspect, the other three can be detected. Marxians also have engaged in satirizing capitalism. Insofar as the inevitability of the classless society enters into Marxian thinking, Marxians too can forget the failures of the moment through their belief in the ultimate triumph of communism. Preoccupation with the devices of party control has the nature of a utopia of means.

Parallels between Christian and Marxian eschatology have often been drawn. The social philosophy of both calls for a permanent revolution against the world as it is. The millennium—the thousand-year reign of Christ on earth, during which Satan is bound—is said to correspond to the dictatorship of the proletariat. The Kingdom of God is compared to the classless society. Of course not all Christians make much of the millennium as a future event, nor do they all believe in the final battle, Armageddon, which has no Marxian parallel. The crucial distinction between these mythologies is their assignment of the role of man. The Christian kingdom is supernatural. It comes beyond history and through God's intervention. In the classless society man can more and more make his own history by applying the science of a nature which includes man.

As the goal of the classless society is liberty, so its distinguishing feature—the means to freedom—is equality. It is obvious from the discussion of abilities and needs, and the free development of talents, that the Marxian concept of equality goes beyond the equality of identity, the dead level of all men. What, then, is the nature of Marxian equalitarianism and how does it compare with American ideas of equality?

The Soviet Union, in spite of frequent Stalinist statements to the contrary, seems to have renounced for the visible future the ideal of the equalitarian classless society. Article 12 of its 1936 constitution, while calling for contributions from each according to his ability, promises rewards to each according to the quantity and quality of his work. Although legal ownership of property has been in large measure abolished, the minority which has power of control over things is just as able to control persons, "for their own good" or otherwise, as if it held title to property.

The American socialists have for the most part referred to the classless society in slogans which cannot be analyzed. They have emphasized it much less than the anarchists and various religious groups.

The anarchist position, which believes in skipping from the revolution directly to the classless society (see PART I, Topic 10), is expressed by Alexander Berkman, "The Social Revolution," in Now and After; the A B C of Communist Anarchism (New York, 1929, 300 pp.), pp. 217-297. John Strachey, The Theory and Practice of Socialism (New York, 1936, 512 pp.), pp. 109-125, 182-206, summarizes Marxian political and economic aspects; and Vernon Venable, Human Nature; the Marxian View (New York, 1945, 217 pp.), pp. 151-213, evaluates the role of human agency in social change as it applies to the problem of achieving the classless society. H. A. Myers, Are Men Equal? An Inquiry into the Meaning of American Democracy (New York, 1945, 188 pp.), opens with a discussion of the philosophical issue of basing social justice on inequality or equality, pp. 1-33, and proceeds to trace the development of American equalitarianism. For the period since 1861, see pp. 98-183. Compare Myers with T. V. Smith, *The American Philosophy of Equality* (Chicago, 1927, 339 pp.), and Herbert Spiegelberg, "A Defense of Human Equality," *Philosophical Review*, LIII (Mar. 1944), pp. 101-124.

The long-range objectives of socialism are related to every aspect of the subject treated in this bibliography; refer particularly, however, to PART I, Topics 6 and 10; PART III, Topics 4, 6, 8, and 9; PART V, Topics 1 and 3; and PART VI, Topic 3. The primary sources for the Marxist-Leninist-Stalinist position are Marx, *Critique of the Gotha Programme* and the introduction to his *The Civil War in France*, and in greater detail in Engels, *Herr Eugen Dühring's Revolution in Science* and *The Origin of the Family*, and Lenin, *The State and Revolution*, all cited in full in PART I; and Stalin, "Some Questions of Theory," in *Leninism* (London, 1940, 667 pp.), pp. 656-657, from Stalin's report to the 1939 congress of the Communist Party of the Soviet Union. One classification of the characteristics of the classless society somewhat different from the one given above is in S. H. M. Chang, *The Marxian Theory of the State* (Philadelphia, 1931, 230 pp.), pp. 133-139, which follows Lenin. M. H. Lin, *Antistatism; Essay in Its Psychiatric and Cultural Analysis* (Washington, 1939, 87 pp.), also issued with the title, *Antistatism, a History of Utopias* (New York, 1941, 87 pp.), is a broadly-conceived and clearly-stated essay linking ancient and modern, communist, liberal, and anarchist political philosophers who have a common antagonism against the coercive state, and suggesting the sources of this antagonism in social and psychological frustrations. Sidney Hook, *Reason, Social Myths and Democracy* (New York, 1940, 302 pp.), pp. 1-40, analyzes ways of belief, the uses of abstractions in social inquiry, and criticizes Karl Mannheim's *Ideology and Utopia*.

For European views on stateless and classless equality, see the sociological study of Célestin Bouglé, *Les Idées égalitaires* (1899; 3rd ed., Paris, 1925, 250 pp.), and the statements of two Continental social democrats, Karl Kautsky, "The Structure of the Future State," in *The Class Struggle* (Chicago, 1910, 217 pp.), pp. 112-126, and Émile Vandervelde, *Socialism versus the State* (1918; tr. by C. H. Kerr; Chicago, 1919, 229 pp.). N. A. Berdyaev, ex-communist and personalist, in *The End of Our Time* (New York, 1933, 258 pp.), inveighed against the principle of equality as one of envy and bitterness. See also the discussion by W. P. Wolgin in the communist journal, *Unter dem Banner des Marxismus*, "Sozialismus und Egalitarismus," III (Feb. 1929), pp. 78-91. The common view that full socialism will bring about the full expression of individuality and complete social equality and justice is expressed by the unorthodox Annie Besant in *Modern Socialism* (2nd ed., London, 1890, 51 pp.), especially pp. 40-51. For other English views see Graham Wallas, *The Great Society* (New York, 1914, 383 pp.), and James Marshall, "Popular

Sovereignty, the Social Compact and the Withering State," in *Swords and Symbols; the Technique of Sovereignty* (New York, 1939, 168 pp.), pp. 73-85.

Among the *Essays* of W. G. Sumner (ed. by A. G. Keller and M. R. Davie; New Haven, Conn., 1934, 2 vols.), is a satirical piece, "The Coöperative Commonwealth," II, pp. 173-194, on the state of affairs after the state has withered away. The same argument that socialism is a return to barbarism, and that greater civilization brings greater distinctions, are found in his papers in *Earth-Hunger and Other Essays* (ed. by A. G. Keller; New Haven, Conn., 1914, 377 pp.), "First Steps toward a Millennium," pp. 93-105, and "The Abolition of Poverty," pp. 228-232. Edward Bellamy, *Equality* (New York, 1897, 412 pp.), a sequel to *Looking Backward*, illustrates the way utopian equalitarianism serves as the agent of liberty. Compare W. D. Howells, "Equality as the Basis of Good Society," *Century Magazine*, LI (Nov. 1895), pp. 63-67. Contemporary Christian socialists, like G. D. Herron, *The Christian State; a Political Vision of Christ* (New York, 1895, 216 pp.), and W. D. P. Bliss, "The Athens of Pericles: the Most Socialistic City of the World," *Arena*, XXXII (Sept. 1904), pp. 287-290, write in similar terms. O. L. Triggs, *The Changing Order* (Chicago, 1913, 300 pp.), emphasizes industrial democracy and its effect on the social superstructure, as do the selections by W. J. Ghent, ed., *Questions and Answers* (Girard, Kan., 1916, 64 pp.), No. 6 of the New Appeal Socialist Classics. See also the selections in Upton Sinclair, ed., *The Cry for Justice* (Philadelphia, 1915, 891 pp.), pp. 833-880.

One looks in vain for optimistic writing of this sort since World War I. After World War II, when socialists did not abandon their goal, they returned to Bernstein's and Gompers' emphasis on the *process* of aiming at an unattainable goal, as in Max Nomad, "Permanent Class Struggle or Utopia?" *Modern Review*, II (Jan. 1948), pp. 28-33. Most writers touching the subject were even more severely critical, for example, Emil Lederer, *State of the Masses; the Threat of the Classless Society* (New York, 1940, 245 pp.), and Solomon Bloom, "The 'Withering Away' of the State," *Journal of the History of Ideas*, VII (Jan. 1946), pp. 113-121. Lewis Mumford incorporates a good deal of Marxian thought into his utopia of reconstruction, buried in masses of historical information in *Technics and Civilization* (New York, 1934, 495 pp.), and *The Culture of Cities* (New York, 1938, 586 pp.). Among the non-Marxian sources of his utopian views are Patrick Geddes, *Cities in Evolution* (London, 1915, 409 pp.), and Ebenezer Howard, *Garden Cities of Tomorrow* (London, 1902, 167 pp.), first issued in 1898 under the title *Tomorrow: a Peaceful Path to Reform*. The most useful edition of *Garden Cities of Tomorrow* (London, 1946, 168 pp.), has an introductory essay by Lewis Mumford and a preface by the editor, F. J. Osborn.

PART V

Sociological and Psychological Aspects
of American Socialism

For discussion in Volume 1 relevant to this Part (PART V) of the Bibliography, see especially Chapters 11 and 12.

General Reading

AMERICAN socialism is here approached from the point of view of those most recently developed studies of man's individual behavior and his social organization. There is overlapping in these two sciences, as social psychology deals with individuals' attitudes toward groups, and sociology sometimes uses evidence about individuals to support its analyses of social relations. Through this comprehensive approach the investigation of socialism can be reviewed as a whole. It is even more difficult than in previous Parts to treat American theory apart from its European background and contemporary development. The historical investigation of socialist types (PART II) again provides subject matter for analysis. Basic religious and philosophical postulates (PART III) are reflected in the problem of fixed or changing human nature, the role of consciousness and knowledge, and the dialectical process. Power is reviewed in the light of class and status and of the psychological roots of radicalism and conservatism; the relations of production are associated with class consciousness and stratification (PART IV). Socialists engaged in psychological and sociological analysis are found to treat artistic creations as part of the social superstructure, according to their class origin, or as propaganda (PART VI).

A general introduction to the fundamental problem of class in Marxian sociology and psychology can be found briefly summarized in R. L. Sutherland and J. L. Woodward's text, "Social Classes," *Introductory Sociology* (2nd ed., Chicago, 1940, 863 pp.), pp. 357-369, and in Max Weber's essay, "Class, Status, Party," in H. H. Gerth and C. W. Mills, eds., *From Max Weber* (New York, 1946, 490 pp.), pp. 180-195 (also found in *Politics*, I [Oct. 1944], pp. 271-278).

There is no general treatment in English of the psychology of socialism by a Marxian; but Henri de Man, who withdrew from his connection with the Belgian social democrats during World War I, has written the standard work on the European movement, *The Psychology of Socialism* (tr. by E. and C. Paul; New York, 1927, 509 pp.). De Man rejected monistic economic determinism and recognized the tendency that workers may adopt bourgeois ideals and may be patriots before they are proletarians. He felt more confidence in the capacity of intellectuals than in workers to effect constructive change. Comments on De Man are Émile Vandervelde, *La Psychologie du socialisme; à propos de trois livres récents: Karl Kautsky—N. Boukharine—Henri de Man* (Brussels, 1928, 48 pp.); E. James, "Un nouveau théoricien du socialisme: Henri de Man," *Revue de métaphysique et de morale*, xxxvi (Mar. 1929), pp. 113-144. A comparable study of American socialism has yet to be written. Representative of the members of the Socialist Party who identified gradualism with Christian democracy is F. J. Melvin, *Socialism as the Sociological Ideal; a Broader Basis for Socialism* (New York, 1915, 216 pp.). American socialist sociology and psychology since 1876 must be pieced together from this, from a few other works of lesser scope and brief articles, and from the fragmentary asides of numerous writers. The liberal communitarians, on the other hand, believed that they had the sound support of social science for their theories. Robert Owen's central concept was environmental character formation, but Fourier's theory of the attractive passions had more explicit psychological and sociological application. See the elaborate formulation of his position in Albert Brisbane, *Theory of the Functions of the Human Passions* (New York, 1856, 160 pp.) and *General Introduction to Social Sciences* (New York, 1876, 2 pts. in 1). Of the latter book, the first part, "Introduction to Fourier's Theory of Social Organization" (112 pp.), is Brisbane's own exposition; the second part is Fourier's *Social Destinies* (158 pp.).

The reason given by some professional sociologists and psychologists why there is so little writing on socialist theory in their fields is that they are concerned with the study of problems of behavior and relationship and not philosophies. Nevertheless, there has recently been more attention paid to Marxian ideas, particularly by sociologist critics.

The following selection of titles deals with (1) general treatments including guides, the most pertinent works of Marx and Engels, and the predominantly European criticism and development of their ideas in general, with a special section devoted to Soviet sociology and psychology; (2) general writings by American socialists; and (3) books related to five major overlapping fields where socialist theories are involved—the problems of knowledge; power and politics; class and status; industrial sociology and psychology; and sex and socialization.

1. General Treatments

A. GUIDES. "Psychology and Marxism; a Bibliography," Angel Flores, comp., in *Dialectics*, No. 4 (1937), pp. 21-24, lists without comment 45 titles, including articles in European Marxist periodicals. No comprehensive bibliography in the field of sociology has been compiled. Good starting points here are the references appended to articles in the *Encyclopaedia of the Social Sciences* such as those on "Class," "Class Struggle," and "Class Consciousness." H. P. Fairchild, ed., *Dictionary of Sociology* (New York, 1944, 342 pp.), will provide preliminary orientation.

B. THE WRITINGS OF MARX AND ENGELS. These deal primarily with the relations of men in groups. Comte had already used the term "sociology" for such studies before their major writings appeared, and Spencer published his system before Engels died, but neither Marx nor Engels described his theories as sociological. They left no single work devoted to psychology but throughout their writings the idea of dialectical materialism serves as a foundation for the socialist approach to psychology.

The *Communist Manifesto* (for full citations of the works of Marx and Engels see the General Reading of PART I, pp. 34-37), although it did not originate the interest group theory of classes and class conflict, gave it its modern emphasis. It is unfortunate that Marx never developed this theory, which was so central to his system. In *Capital* (Kerr ed., III, pp. 1031-1032), his brief preliminary notes for such an analysis were published by Engels. The thesis that the relations of production are the real foundation of the ideological and institutional superstructure is expounded in *A Contribution to the Critique of Political Economy, The German Ideology, Ludwig Feuerbach* (cited in PART III, Topic 1), and most explicitly in *The Eighteenth Brumaire of Louis Bonaparte*, as well as in the published correspondence of Marx and Engels. On the question of changing human nature, Marx stated in criticism of Proudhon, "history is nothing but the continual change of human nature," and in *Capital*, "in changing Nature, man also changes his own nature." Engels in the *Herr Eugen Dühring's Revolution in Science* and *The Condition of the Working Class in England* shows how consciousness is related to the labor process. With regard to the classless society, Marx had in common with the thinkers of the French Revolution, Feuerbach, Stirner, and Nietzsche, the uncompromising feeling that no external purpose should hamper the individual's growth and happiness. Perhaps the most directly social-anthropological work by either Marx or Engels is the latter's *The Origin of the Family*, a treatise projected by Marx and based partly on his critical annotations of L. H. Morgan's *Ancient Society*, which seemed to confirm historical materialism. This book also shows the author's comprehensive acquaintance with the discoveries of other contemporary anthropologists and classical scholars. B. J. Stern, *Lewis Henry Morgan; Social Evolutionist* (Chicago, 1931, 221 pp.), pp. 175-188, treats the interest of Engels and Marx in Morgan. General evaluations are J. L. Gray, "Karl Marx and Social Philosophy," in F. J. C. Hearnshaw, ed., *The Social & Political Ideas of Some Representative Thinkers of the Victorian Age* (London, 1933, 271 pp.), pp. 116-149, and John Somerville, *Methodology in Social Science; a Critique of Marx and Engels* (New York, 1938, 72 pp.). Two notes by Solomon Diamond comment on Marxian psychology: "Marx's 'First Thesis' on Feuerbach," *Science & Society*, I (Summer 1937), pp. 539-544, and "Marx's 'Ninth Thesis' on Feuerbach," *ibid.*, III (Spring 1939), pp. 242-244.

C. GENERAL CRITICISM. This has been predominantly European, and more extensive in the field of sociology. Jules Monnerot, *Sociologie du communisme* (Paris, 1949, 510 pp.), seeks to deal comprehensively with the whole subject of communist sociology, though focused on Marxism. E. Silberling, *Dictionnaire de sociologie phalanstérienne* (Paris, 1911, 459 pp.), has a sociological perspective on Fourierism. Focused directly on Marxian sociology are Pietro Siciliani, *Socialismo, darwinismo e sociologia moderna* (Bologna, 1885, 497 pp.); C. C. A. Bouglé, "Marxisme et sociologie," in his *Chez les prophètes socialistes* (Paris, 1918, 246 pp.), pp. 185-246; Heinrich Cunow, *Die Marxsche Geschichts-, Gesellschafts- und Staatstheorie; Grundzüge der Marxschen Soziologie* (Berlin, 1920-1921, 2 vols.); Mark Abramowitsch, *Hauptprobleme der Soziologie (Probleme marxistischer Lebenserkenntnis)* (Berlin, 1930, 111 pp.); and Hans Freund, *Soziologie und Sozialismus; ein Beitrag zur Geschichte der deutschen Sozialtheorie um 1842* (Würzburg, 1934, 74 pp.), a Basel dissertation. L'Institut International de Sociologie, *Annales*, VIII (Paris, 1902, 327 pp.), contains analyses by several prominent sociologists. The editor of the *Revue internationale de sociologie*, Gaston Richard, contributed *Le Socialisme et la science sociale* (Paris, 1897, 199 pp.). Three outstanding critics of socialism are Vilfredo Pareto, Robert Michels, and Max Weber. For Pareto see *Les Systèmes socialistes* (Paris, 1902-1903, 2 vols.) and *The Mind and Society* (ed. by Arthur Livingston; tr. by Livingston and Andrew Bongiorno; New York, 1935, 4 vols.). Michels' "iron law of oligarchy," although more temperately stated than his label implies, is developed from a study of European Social Democratic parties and set forth in his *Political Parties; a Sociological Study of the Oligarchical Tendencies of Modern Democracy* (1911, tr. by E. and C. Paul; New York, 1915, 416 pp.). See also Michels' "Psychologie der antikapitalistischen Massen-bewegung," *Grundriss der Sozialökonomik*, IX (1926), pp. 241-359; "Historisch-Kritische Einführung in die Geschichte des Marxismus in Italien," *Archiv für Sozialwissenschaft und Sozialpolitik*, XXIV (1907), pp. 189-258; and "Die italienische Literatur über den Marxismus," *ibid.*, XXV (1907), pp. 525-572. On Max Weber, see his own *Wirtschaft und Gesellschaft*, Pt. 1 of which has been edited by Talcott Parsons as *The Theory of Social and Economic Organization* (tr. by A. M. Henderson and Talcott Parsons; New York, 1947, 436 pp.); Karl Löwith, "Max Weber und Karl Marx," *Archiv für Sozialwissenschaft und Sozialpolitik*, LXVII (Mar.-Apr. 1932), pp. 53-99, 175-214, and the preliminary references. Talcott Parsons, *The Structure of Social Action* (New York, 1937, 817 pp.), makes an exhaustive study of Pareto and Weber, with occasional reference to Marx and other social theorists. See also Georges Sorel, *Matériaux d'une théorie du prolétariat* (Paris, 1919, 413 pp.); Gaetano Mosca, *The Ruling Class* (tr. by H. D. Kahn; ed. and rev. by Arthur

Livingston; New York, 1939, 514 pp.); P. A. Sorokin, *Contemporary Sociological Theories* (New York, 1928, 785 pp.); and Karl Mannheim, *Man and Society in an Age of Reconstruction; Studies in Modern Social Structure* (tr. by Edward Shils; London, 1940, 469 pp.), with a bibliographical guide.

Likewise European is the major psychological analysis of socialism. One of the few psychological studies of the pre-Marxians is Georges Dumas, *Psychologie de deux messies positivistes: Saint-Simon et Auguste Comte* (Paris, 1905, 314 pp.). Augustin Hamon, an anarchist himself and expelled from the Second International, wrote *Psychologie de l'anarchiste-socialiste* (3rd ed., Paris, 1895, 322 pp.). Gustave Le Bon's hostile book, *The Psychology of Socialism* (1898; New York, 1899, 415 pp.), asserted that the socialist ideal was low, appealing to the motives of envy and hatred. After Le Bon, Ettore Ciccotti published *Psicologia del movimento socialista* (Bari, 1903, 318 pp.). See also Graham Wallas, *The Great Society; a Psychological Analysis* (New York, 1914, 383 pp.). With an emphasis comparable to Robert Owen's, Henry Sturt concluded in *Socialism and Character* (London, 1922, 214 pp.), that socialism must be constructive and character-building. Pierre Naville, at one time editor of *La Lutte de classes*, and student of eighteenth-century materialism, brought out *Psychologie, marxisme, matérialisme* (Paris, 1946, 207 pp.), just after the close of World War II. Writing as a democratic socialist from Mexico, Victor Serge, "Socialism and Psychology," *Modern Review*, I (May 1947), pp. 194-202, suggested an alternative to the facile explanation of socialist motivation as the product of individual frustration.

Sample treatments of the social and psychological in socialism by professionals in other fields are the following: Georges Politzer, *Les Grandes problèmes de la philosophie contemporaine* (Paris, 1938-) Vol. 1, *La Pensée française et le marxisme*, and Vernon Venable, *Human Nature; the Marxian View* (New York, 1945, 217 pp.), approach the subject as philosophers. The Marxian influence among historians is illustrated in L. M. Hacker, *American Problems of Today* (New York, 1938, 354 pp.). R. L. Worrall, *The Outlook of Science; Modern Materialism* (1933; 2nd ed., London, 1946, 191 pp.), especially the chapter, "Brain and Mind," pp. 136-151, and J. B. S. Haldane's work based on the Muirhead Lectures at the University of Birmingham, *The Marxist Philosophy and the Sciences* (New York, 1939, 214 pp.), pp. 145-206, are the expressions of scientists. M. A. Graubard, a biopsychologist concerned with heredity, has written *Genetics and the Social Order* (New York, 1935, 127 pp.), also "The Science of 'Human Nature,'" in his *Biology and Human Behavior* (New York, 1936, 413 pp.), pp. 294-341, and *Man, the Slave and Master; a Biological Approach to the Potentialities of Modern Society* (New York, 1938, 354 pp.). J. A. Hobson, *Veblen* (London, 1936, 227 pp.), treats the sociological implications of Thorstein Veblen's work against the United States background, and points out his interest in and rejection of Marxism. On this theme, A. L. Harris, "Economic Evolution: Dialectical and Darwinian," *Journal of Political Economy*, XLII (Feb. 1934), pp. 34-79, and A. K. Davis, "Sociological Elements in Veblen's Economic Theory," *ibid.*, LIII (June 1945), pp. 132-149, reach varying conclusions on the place of Marxism in Veblen's thought, Harris holding with Hobson.

American professional sociologists and psychologists have turned occasionally and briefly to examine Marxism. C. H. Page, in *Class and American Sociology; from Ward to Ross* (New York, 1940, 319 pp.), found that L. F. Ward, W. G. Sumner, A. W. Small, F. H. Giddings, C. H. Cooley, and E. A. Ross paid considerable attention to the concept of class, but with no evident borrowing of the Marxian pattern. Small's article, "Socialism in the Light of Social Science," *American Journal of Sociology*, XVII (May 1912), pp. 804-819, however, calls Marx the Galileo of the social sciences. At the same time C. A. Ellwood was applying the tests of psychology to Marxian economics in "Marx's 'Economic Determinism' in the Light of Modern Psychology," *ibid.*, XVII (July 1911), pp. 35-46. In a representative text such as C. A. Murchison, ed., *A Handbook of Social Psychology* (Worcester, Mass., 1935, 1195 pp.), scarcely a reference to socialism can be found. On the other hand, H. E. Barnes and Howard Becker, in *Social Thought from Lore to Science* (Boston, 1938, 2 vols.), I, pp. 637-663, review revolutionary socialism and cite earlier references to the communitarians. See also H. E. Barnes, *Historical Sociology; Its Origins and Development* (New York, 1948, 186 pp.).

D. RUSSIAN SOCIOLOGY AND PSYCHOLOGY. In Russia, sociology and psychology developed in the behaviorist tradition of Pavlov, Bekhterev, and W. A. Wagner, whose work was tolerated under the Soviet state as it never directly contradicted the official dialectical materialism. On this subject the most accessible writings are A. L. Schniermann, "Bekhterev's Reflexological School," in C. A. Murchison, ed., *Psychologies of 1930* (Worcester, Mass., 1930, 497 pp.), pp. 221-242; V. M. Bekhterev, *General Principles of Human Reflexology; an Introduction to the Objective Study of Personality* (tr. from 4th Russian ed. by Emma and William Murphy; New York, 1932, 467 pp.); and Y. P. Frolov, *Pavlov and His School; the Theory of Conditioned Reflexes* (New York, 1937, 291 pp.). The surveys of K. N. Kornilov, "Psychology in the Light of Dialectical Materialism," *Psychologies of 1930* (cited above), pp. 243-278, and G. H. S. Razran, "Psychology in the U.S.S.R.," *Journal of Philosophy*, XXXII (Jan. 3, 1935), pp. 19-24, however, should dispel the notion that the Russians have studied nothing but reflexes. Kolbanovsky engaged extensively in applying Marxism-Leninism to psychology and led the attack on the once-popular pedology. A. R. Luriya ran a controlled psychophysiological experiment charging subjects under hypnosis with artificial complexes and later discharging them, the results of which were published in *The Nature of Human Conflicts; or, Emotion, Conflict and Will, an Objective Study of Disorganisation and Control of Human Behaviour* (tr. and ed. by W. H. Gantt; New York, 1932, 431 pp.). During World War II he headed rehabilitation work at a special hospital. The outstanding contemporary Soviet psychologist is S. L. Rubinstein, author of *Osnovy obshchei psikhologii* [*Foundations of General Psychology*] (Moscow, 1946, 703 pp.). See also his translated articles, "Soviet Psychology in Wartime," *Philosophy and Phenomenological Research*, v (Dec. 1944), pp. 181-198, in "A First Symposium on Russian Philosophy and Psychology," *ibid.*, pp. 157-241; and "Consciousness in the Light of Dialectical Materialism," *Science & Society*, x (Summer 1946), pp. 252-261. In 1948 Rubinstein's work was sharply criticized in Russia: see Joseph Wortis, *Soviet Psychiatry* (Baltimore, 1950, 314 pp.), pp. 261-285.

J. F. Hecker, *Russian Sociology* (New York, 1934, 312 pp.), is chiefly concerned with the nineteenth century. For more details on the recent years see M. M. Laserson, "Russian Sociology," in Georges Gurvitch and W. E. Moore, eds., *Twentieth Century Sociology* (New York, 1945, 754 pp.), pp. 671-702. Lenin's "The Three Sources and Three Component Parts of Marxism," in Karl Marx, *Selected Works* (New York, 1936, 2 vols.), I, pp. 54-59; G. V. Plekhanov, *Essays in Historical Materialism* (New York, 1940, 48 pp., 62 pp.); and N. I. Bukharin, *Historical Materialism; a System of Sociology* (New York, 1925, 318 pp.), all seek to solve the circular argument resulting from the admission that the social superstructure has some reciprocal action upon society's economic base. Russian ethnography ranks high, possibly because of the policy encouraging the self-development of ethnic minorities.

For the Russian attack on health problems through their psychology and their socialized medicine, see Frankwood Williams, *Soviet Russia Fights Neurosis* (London, 1934, 251 pp.); Sir Arthur Newsholme and J. A. Kingsbury, *Red Medicine* (Garden City, N.Y., 1933, 324 pp.), based on an extended visit by two experts on public health organization; and *Socialized Medicine in the Soviet Union* (New York, 1937, 378 pp.), by H. E. Sigerist, for many years eminent historian of medicine at Johns Hopkins University, which is particularly valuable on the organization of medical research and work, though superseded by Sigerist and Julia Older, *Medicine and Health in the Soviet Union* (New York, 1947, 364 pp.). Also see George Borodin's life of Maxim P. Murov, who left medical college in 1917 for active Soviet service, *Red Surgeon* (London, 1944, 224 pp.); and Edward Podolsky, *Red Miracle* (New York, 1947, 274 pp.).

2. General Writings by American Socialists on Sociological and Psychological Problems

A. THE PRE-MARXIANS. American sectarian communities had no explicit Christian sociology or psychology, but were deeply concerned with related problems and wrote about them. Professionals have scarcely begun to analyze either their writings or their behavior. Almost the only study of any of the groups treated in PART II, Topics 1-4, is J. L. Gillin, *The Dunkers* (New York, 1906, 238 pp.), pp. 112-141, on Ephrata.

Once the communities had been established, the major problem was social stability, not social change. Consequently religious radicalism, separated from the conservative world, became the conservatism of the communities. See the brief reference to social control among both sectarians and liberal communities in R. M. MacIver, *Society* (New York, 1937, 596 pp.), pp. 347-351. The socialization of children through vocational and religious training and the maintenance of adult conformity was undertaken in many ways. Members were brought up, as Soviet children are, convinced of the superiority of their own society (see Topic 6). Nevertheless, the competitive spirit almost universally reappeared. The dissidents could and did leave, or concessions were made in the arrangements for labor. In the long run, too much competition was fatal. See M. A. May and L. W. Doob, *Competition and Cooperation* (New York, 1937, 191 pp.), pp. 58-62.

The long-lived communities seem to have constituted villagelike neighborhoods with slight social distance and stabilized status. After the initial expansion there were few recruits. Placement of the grown-up children or reassignment of craftsmen whose trades were abandoned because of the cheapness of manufactured goods were comparatively simple problems. Economic frustration was minimized because there tended to be a surplus of work which had to be turned over to outside wage labor.

A scale of community success could be based on the effective displacement of aggression. In such a scale the sectarian communities appear much more successful than the secular. The Shakers, German pietists, and Perfectionists all had avenues of release through confession and inspirational expression. *Mutual Criticism* (comp. by W. A. Hinds; Oneida, N.Y., 1876, 96 pp.), for example, describes a method of harmonizing the individual with the community by a sort of social behavior analysis, far ahead of the contemporary phrenological technique of examining bumps on the skull. On matters of sex and the family see the writings of Noyes and others about the Oneida Community's complex marriage (PART II, Topic 4).

The liberal communitarians claimed to be social scientists. As environmentalists believing in the natural goodness of human nature they emphasized in theory and practice the importance of education and, in

theory, physical surroundings constructed to encourage human development. The relation of Fourierism to the American social science move
ment is told by L. L. and Jessie Bernard, "The Associationist Phase of
Social Science," *Origins of American Sociology* (New York, 1943, 866
pp.), pp. 59-112, which also relates Owenism to Fourierism. It seems
likely that the American social sciences owe less to the tradition of British
and French rationalism than to the Scottish common-sense philosophy
which dominated American colleges in the middle nineteenth century.
In addition to the works of Albert Brisbane, cited in the introductory
reading, see G. H. Calvert, *Introduction to Social Science* (New York,
1856, 148 pp.). The author had an incidental interest in Fourierism, but
his influence upon the movement was slight. M. E. Lazarus, a homeo-
pathic and vegetarian doctor of Wilmington, N.C., wrote a series of
articles for the *Harbinger*, iv-v (1847), under the heading, "Cannibalism,"
in which he attempted to apply "Natural History to Psychology" (v, p.
103). In at least five volumes published by Fowler and Wells, 1851-1852,
he expanded his mystical mélange of medical and Fourierist theories
to embrace God, man, and the universe, and their interrelations. See
*The Human Trinity; or, Three Aspects of Life; the Passional, the In-
tellectual, the Practical Sphere* (New York, 1851, 141 pp.), and *Passional
Hygiene and Natural Medicine; Embracing the Harmonies of Man with
His Planet* (New York, 1852, 436 pp.). L. L. and Jessie Bernard (cited
above), pp. 274-309, is a discussion of the theories of the communitarian
R. J. Wright, as expressed in his *Principia; or, Basis of Social Science*
(Philadelphia, 1875, 524 pp.). "The Post-Associationist Phase of Social
Science," also in Bernard, pp. 313-386, treats, with bibliographical footnotes, the individualist anarchists and later utopians. Outstanding among
the post-Associationists was Lewis Masquerier (former Owenite, land
reformer with G. H. Evans, and Fourierist), author of *Sociology; or,
The Reconstruction of Society, Government and Property . . . by Organizing All Nations into Townships of Self-Governed Homestead Democracies* (New York, 1877, 310 pp.).

B. The Marxians. It serves no purpose to repeat here general works
by socialists cited in other connections merely because Marxian theory
has strong sociological implications. Parts of these, as well as studies involving the subject matter of psychology, will be referred to in connection with special topics.

Before 1917, psychology was virtually ignored, except for the tendency
to assign it a minor place between biology and anthropology, on Dietzgen's theory that all ideas come from external, natural, and social influences. One exception was M. H. Fitch, *The Physical Basis of Mind
and Morals* (1906; 2nd ed., Chicago, 1908, 414 pp.), a popular treatment

of evolution and ethics. The most serious treatment of stratification by a prewar socialist was W. J. Ghent, *Mass and Class; a Survey of Social Divisions* (New York, 1904, 260 pp.). J. M. Work, *What's So and What Isn't* (1905; New York, 1927, 158 pp.), although written in words of one syllable, devotes more space to psychological and social issues than most answers to the hypothetical red-baiter. See also H. W. B. Mackay's article, "The Historical Study of Sociology," *International Socialist Review*, III (Mar. 1903), pp. 550-558; and two books published by C. H. Kerr & Co., C. K. Franklin, *The Socialization of Humanity; an Analysis and Synthesis of the Phenomena of Nature, Life, Mind and Society through the Law of Repetition; a System of Monistic Philosophy* (Chicago, 1904, 481 pp.), and J. H. Moore, *Better-World Philosophy; a Sociological Synthesis* (Chicago, 1906, 275 pp.). The essay by the executive director of the Socialist Labor Party, Arnold Petersen, *Daniel De Leon; Social Scientist* (New York, 1945, 79 pp.), indicates De Leon's preoccupation with economics and politics rather than sociology.

Up to World War II, A. W. Calhoun, *The Social Universe* (New York, 1932, 170 pp.), and Karl Korsch, "Leading Principles of Marxism; a Restatement," *Marxist Quarterly*, I (Oct.-Dec. 1937), pp. 356-378, were among the few general treatments in English of sociology in terms of Marxism. On a broader scale J. F. Brown, *Psychology and the Social Order* (New York, 1936, 529 pp.), does much the same thing for psychology. Brown uses topology rather than Marxian methods to apply the field theory of Kurt Lewin to political problems, but with similar results. R. L. Gley reviewed current schools of psychology in three 1939 issues of the *Communist*: "Current Trends in American Psychology," XVIII (June), pp. 553-562; "Gestalt Psychology" (July), pp. 657-664; and "Freudism—Psychology of a Dying Class" (Nov.), pp. 1066-1079. The review of Erich Fromm's *Escape from Freedom*, "Psychology versus Marxism," by Abraham Ziegler, in *Modern Socialism*, I, No. 4 (Summer 1942), pp. 5-9, 35-37, rejects all psychology which looks upon the individual rather than the class as of basic importance. See also S. D. Schmalhausen, "A Psychological Analysis of Socialism," *Modern Quarterly*, V (Winter 1928/1929), pp. 61-72.

3. Socialist Theory of Knowledge

The Marxian thesis that intelligence or knowledge is the function of biology or society, and that the economic system determining an individual's mode of life is also the prime determinant of his character structure, has aroused much controversy. In or close to the Marxian tradition are the following articles: Erich Fromm, "Über Methode und Aufgabe einer analytischen Sozialpsychologie," *Zeitschrift für Sozialforschung*, I, No. 1/2 (1932), pp. 28-54, and "Die gesellschaftliche Bedingtheit der psychoanalytischen Therapie," *ibid.*, IV (1935), pp. 365-397; J. M. Lahy, "L'Intelligence et les classes sociales; essai d'une définition objective de l'intelligence," *Journal de psychologie*, XXXII (July 15-Oct. 15, 1935), pp. 543-601; and Hans Speier, "The Social Determination of Ideas," *Social Research*, V (May 1938), pp. 182-205. In *Science at the Cross Roads* (London, 1931, 233 pp.), papers presented to the second International Congress of the History of Science and Technology, B. Hessen goes so far as to say that only proletarian science gives results of social validity. Antonie Pannekoek, "Society and Mind in Marxian Philosophy," *Science & Society*, I (Summer 1937), pp. 445-453, offers an explanation of social lag in the social determination of consciousness and its significance as a factor in precipitating revolution. V. J. McGill, "The Mind-Body Problem in the Light of Recent Psychology," *ibid.*, IX (Fall 1945), pp. 335-361, refers to Soviet studies relating the individual consciousness to history and society, especially the work of Rubinstein. Chapters critical of the Marxian point of view are P. A. Sorokin, "Sociologistic School . . . (Economic School)," *Contemporary Sociological Theories* (New York, 1928, 785 pp.), pp. 514-546, and R. K. Merton, "The Sociology of Knowledge," in Gurvitch and Moore, eds., *Twentieth Century Sociology* (cited above), pp. 366-405. See also the titles discussed in PART III, Topic 5.

4. Socialism and Politics

A compact series of definitions useful for studying the sociology of power, derived from the ideas of Max Weber, is found in an article by Herbert Goldhamer and E. A. Shils, "Types of Power and Status," *American Journal of Sociology*, XLV (Sept. 1939), pp. 171-182. Seba Eldridge, *Political Action; a Naturalistic Interpretation of the Labor Movement in Relation to the State* (Philadelphia, 1924, 382 pp.), applies theories of the conflict of social classes and instinct psychology to the problems of democracy. A. W. Calhoun of Sterling College, Kansas, has completed a manuscript with the title, *American Labor Psychology*, while O. C. Cox of Tuskegee has projected a study of *The Struggle for Power in the United States*, a sequel to his work on caste, class, and race, cited below. Three of H. D. Lasswell's books, *World Politics and Personal Insecurity* (New York, 1935, 307 pp.), *Politics; Who Gets What, When, How* (New York, 1936, 264 pp.), and especially *Psychopathology and Politics* (Chicago, 1930, 285 pp.), illustrate the interest of social psychologists in the question of why individuals become involved in certain political activities. This point of view tends to depreciate the importance of the adult's environment. Solomon Diamond reverses the question in his dissertation, *A Study of the Influence of Political Radicalism on Personality Development* (New York, 1936, 54 pp.; also published in *Archives of Psychology*, No. 203).

A good deal has been published on the psychology of Russian communism and on propaganda. See, for example, John Spargo, *The Psychology of Bolshevism* (New York, 1919, 150 pp.), particularly on the reign of terror; M. J. Olgin, *The Soul of the Russian Revolution* (New York, 1917, 423 pp.), on the transfer of allegiance from the tsars; and René Fülöp-Miller, *The Mind and Face of Bolshevism* (1926; tr. by F. S. Flint and D. F. Tait; London, 1927, 308 pp.). Lenin, *Agitation und Propaganda* (Berlin, 1929, 250 pp.), is a collection from Lenin's works. L. W. Doob, *Propaganda; Its Psychology and Technique* (New York, 1935, 424 pp.), includes (pp. 256-259) the analysis of the biographies of several prominent radicals. He concludes from this analysis that because of a profoundly moving event in each one's adolescence, his rebellion against conservatism and identification with the poor and oppressed can be interpreted as consequent displaced aggression. Alex Inkeles, *Public Opinion in Soviet Russia* (Cambridge, Mass., 1950, 379 pp.), is a valuable study of the theory and practice of propaganda in the Soviet Union, while F. C. Barghoorn, *The Soviet Image of the United States* (New York, 1950, 297 pp.), discusses the aims and techniques of Russian propaganda concerning the United States. H. D. Lasswell and Dorothy Blumenstock, *World Revolutionary Propaganda* (New York, 1939, 393 pp.), is a case study in social psychology of communist activity in Chicago from 1929 to 1934. Additional material on radicalism, socialist political organization, and propaganda is included in Topics 3-5.

5. *Class Conflict and Class Consciousness*

The best survey of class theories is Jean Lhomme, *Le Problème des classes, doctrines et faits* (Paris, 1938, 354 pp.). The latest investigation from the point of view of social psychology is R. T. Centers, *The Psychology of Social Classes: a Study of Class Consciousness* (Princeton, N.J., 1949, 244 pp.). Centers analyzes 1,100 answers to a nation-wide questionnaire given in July 1945. He distinguishes between stratification—the objective result of occupational and income differences—and class, the result of subjective consciousness of these differences. He likewise contends that status, based on prestige, social distance, and associational participation, should not be confused with class, for persons of different status may be conscious of belonging to the same class. Whereas a *Fortune* poll found over 90 per cent of Americans claiming to be middle class, Centers, by giving the subjects a chance to call themselves "working" instead of "lower" class, found 51 per cent who said they belonged to the working class. His general conclusions are that class identification and conservatism-radicalism are almost solely functions of socio-economic stratification; and that his evidence strongly supported the Marxian economic interest group theory of classes. The evidence is clearer for urban than for rural society.

Other early or general studies of classes are Arthur Bauer, *Les Classes sociales; analyse de la vie sociale* (Paris, 1902, 359 pp.); P. E. Fahlbeck, *Die Klassen und die Gesellschaft* (Jena, 1922, 348 pp.), which treats the subject historically; and Paul Mombert, "Zum Wesen der sozialen Klasse," in *Hauptprobleme der Soziologie; Erinnerungsgabe für Max Weber* (Munich, 1923, 2 vols.), II, pp. 237-275. Hans Speier, "Social Stratification," in Max Ascoli and Fritz Lehmann, eds., *Political and Economic Democracy* (New York, 1937, 336 pp.), pp. 255-270, speaks of lower and higher classes in terms of security and social distance. A. W. Kornhauser, "Attitudes of Economic Groups," *Public Opinion Quarterly*, II (Apr. 1938), pp. 260-268, is a pioneer study of Chicago adults which attempts to correlate occupational and income levels with attitudes on political and social issues. Centers' distinction between class and status is made in different language by a Marxian sociologist at Tuskegee, O. C. Cox, *Caste, Class & Race; a Study in Social Dynamics* (Garden City, N.Y., 1948, 624 pp.), pp. 121-313, including bibliography, pp. 283-297. P. A. Sorokin criticizes five prevailing types of class theory in "What Is a Social Class?" in *Society, Culture and Personality; Their Structure and Dynamics; a System of General Sociology* (New York, 1947, 742 pp.), pp. 261-271, and includes general discussions of stratification (pp. 181-310), mobility (pp. 415-444), and revolution and its causes (chaps. 31 and 33). See also Rodolphe Broda and Julius Deutsch, *Das moderne Proletariat; eine sozialpsychologische Studie* (Berlin, 1910, 226 pp.); Jean Muller, *L'Idée de lutte de classes et son évolution depuis le Manifeste communiste* (Paris, 1911, 223 pp.), a University of Paris dissertation; and Robert Michels, "Beitrag zur Lehre von der Klassenbildung," *Archiv für Sozialwissenschaft und Sozialpolitik*, XLIX (1922), pp. 561-593.

The titles below on class consciousness and class conflict are too often characterized by the failure to make their definitions of class clear or generally applicable. Georg Lukács, *Geschichte und Klassenbewusstsein; Studien über Marxistische Dialektik* (Berlin, 1923, 341 pp.), is the most ambitious and discriminating attempt to examine the place of class consciousness in history. He assumes that bourgeois control of culture spreads ideas among the proletariat which raise the problem of false class consciousness. That is, if men were able to understand the situation they would accept a different ideology. In this connection see Karl Mannheim, *Ideology and Utopia* (New York, 1936, 318 pp.), and J. Delevsky, *Antagonismes sociaux et antagonismes prolétariens* (Paris, 1924, 574 pp.). Karl Kautsky, *The Class Struggle (Erfurt Program)* (tr. by W. E. Bohn; Chicago, 1910, 217 pp.), is the standard position held by most orthodox American Marxians. Gustav Schmoller, "Schmoller on Class

Conflicts in General," an excerpt from the sociological chapters of his *Grundriss der allgemeinen Volkswirtschaftslehre* (Leipzig, 1900-1904, 2 vols.), II, pp. 542ff., translated by A. W. Small for the *American Journal of Sociology*, XX (Jan. 1915), pp. 504-531, includes the German social democrats in his discussion of the relations of social classes to the state. An outstanding symposium edited by T. H. Marshall, *Class Conflict and Social Stratification* (London, 1938, 216 pp.), contains chapters by Maurice Dobb, Lionel Robbins, and Brinley Thomas covering mobility, the economic basis, and other aspects. A case study of conflict in the Akron rubber industry is A. W. Jones, *Life, Liberty and Property; a Story of Conflict and a Measurement of Conflicting Rights* (Philadelphia, 1941, 397 pp.). F. D. Wormuth, *Class Struggle* (Bloomington, Ind., 1946, 59 pp.), Indiana University, *Publications*, Social Science Series, No. 4, is a fresh treatment excellent in its analysis of political concepts and has useful references, but confuses class with caste and status.

Other more specialized monographs on class range from Gunnar Landtman's evolutionary, non-Marxian approach in *The Origin of the Inequality of the Social Classes* (Chicago, 1938, 444 pp.), to Emil Lederer, *State of the Masses; the Threat of the Classless Society* (New York, 1940, 245 pp.). Lederer, a former Marxian, makes his peace with the class society and advocates democratic socialism as a bulwark against totalitarianism. See also Lederer and Jacob Marschak, *The New Middle Class* (tr. by Socrates Ellison; New York, 1937, 45 pp.); P. A. Sorokin, *Social Mobility* (New York, 1927, 559 pp.), and G. A. Briefs, *The Proletariat; a Challenge to Western Civilization* (New York, 1937, 297 pp.), especially pp. 172-189 on working-class mobility. Further references are cited in Topics 1-3.

6. Industrial Psychology and Sociology

See first the collaborative work edited by G. W. Hartmann and Theodore Newcomb, *Industrial Conflict; a Psychological Interpretation* (New York, 1939, 583 pp.), first yearbook of the Society for the Psychological Study of Social Issues. The psychological approach to work satisfaction and the productivity of labor has tended to emphasize time and motion study and factors producing fatigue, rather than motivation. The International Conference on Psychotechnics, concerned with vocational guidance and the efficient organization of labor, held nine meetings and published reports between 1920 and 1937. See also I. N. Spielrein, "Zur Theorie der Psychotechnik," in *Prinzipienfragen der Psychotechnik*, by Michael Erdélyi, Otto Lipmann, and others (Leipzig, 1933, 79 pp.), and Henri Wallon, "Psychologie et technique," in Cercle de la Russie neuve, Paris, Commission scientifique, *À la lumière du marxisme*, I (1936), pp. 128-148.

On motivation, Thorstein Veblen's *The Instinct of Workmanship* (New York, 1914, 355 pp.), is rich in insights as well as satire, although few today would regard workmanship as an instinct. F. J. Roethlisberger and W. J. Dixon, *Management and the Worker* (Cambridge, Mass., 1939, 615 pp.), has pertinent chapters on testing the effects of the wage incentive (chap. 6) and the output situation (chap. 18). Roethlisberger has continued in this field with *Management and Morale* (Cambridge, Mass., 1945, 194 pp.). A University of Chicago doctoral thesis of 1930, *Division of Labor; a Study in the Sociology and the Social Psychology of Work Satisfaction*, by W. T. Watson, is published only in abstract form in the University's *Abstracts of Theses: Humanistic Series*, IX (1930-1932), pp. 283-288. W. E. Moore, *Industrial Relations and the Social Order* (New York, 1946, 555 pp.), includes a section, "The Question of Motives," pp. 336-350. See also *Lenin and Stalin on Socialist Competition* (tr. by David Keen; Moscow-Leningrad, 1933, 50 pp.), and *The Secret of Soviet Strength* (New York, 1943, 160 pp.), by Hewlett Johnson, the "Red Dean" of Canterbury. Arthur Kornhauser, "Industrial Psychology as Management Technique and as Social Science," *American Psychologist*, II (July 1947), pp. 224-229, is a provocative note suggesting areas of research hitherto neglected. See further references in Topic 8.

7. Marx and Freud

Psychologists and psychoanalysts attracted to Marxism have sought to coordinate their political and professional ideas. In spite of international communication among scientists the cycle of correlation and Marxian disavowal of the connection between Marx and Freud has been repeated in Germany, France, Great Britain, and, last of all, in the United States. Wilhelm Reich engaged in the original German controversy with "Dialektischer Materialismus und Psychoanalyse," *Unter dem Banner des Marxismus*, III (Oct. 1929), pp. 736-771, although W. Jurinetz had four years before denied any vital agreement between the two thinkers in "Psychoanalyse und Marxismus," *ibid.*, I (Mar. 1925), pp. 90-133. I. Sapir concluded the German attack on the instinctual and individual focus of Freudian psychology with "Freudismus, Soziologie, Psychologie," *ibid.*, III (Dec. 1929), pp. 937-952, IV (Feb. 1930), pp. 123-147. Much of Reich's writing, translated during World War II into English, shows greater anarchist than socialist affinities. See, for example, his key work, *Character-Analysis* (1933; tr. by T. P. Wolfe; New York, 1945, 328 pp.), and "The Masses and the State," and "Work Democracy," in *The Mass Psychology of Fascism* (1933; tr. by T. P. Wolfe; New York, 1946, 344 pp.), pp. 175-340. On a related theme is Erich Fromm, "Sozialpsychologischer Teil," in Institut für Sozialforschung, *Studien über Autorität und Familie* (ed. by Max Horkheimer; Paris, 1936, 947 pp.), a discussion of the conscience of the modern man—the internalization of external social demands. After Fromm came to the United States he published a psychoanalytic study of democracy and totalitarianism, *Escape from Freedom* (New York, 1941, 305 pp.). Another study of fascism with frequent reference to socialism is P. W. Nathan, *The Psychology of Fascism* (London, 1943, 158 pp.). Two English psychoanalysts have studied socialism in the light of their science: Reuben Osbert (R. Osborn, pseud.), *Freud and Marx; a Dialectical Study* (London, 1937, 285 pp.), and J. C. Flügel, *Man, Morals and Society; a Psycho-analytical Study* (New York, 1945, 328 pp.). Osborn has been criticized not for finding dialectical thinking in Freud, but for still emphasizing too much the individual and the leader. Flügel is concerned with radicalism-conservatism. Jack Lindsay, a left-wing writer, believing that dialectical materialism could tell him precisely how far mind can affect conditions, attempted to combine Freud and Marx in *The Anatomy of Spirit; an Inquiry into the Origins of Religious Emotion* (London, 1937, 182 pp.). Close to Lindsay's point of view were Alistair Browne, who contributed "Psychology and Marxism" to the symposium edited by Cecil Day-Lewis, *The Mind in Chains* (London, 1937, 255 pp.), pp. 165-184; and J. D. Bernal, "Psycho-Analysis and Marxism," *Labour Monthly*, xix (July 1937), pp. 433-437. Mention should be made of the work of the Dane Svend Ranulf, especially *Moral Indignation and Middle Class Psychology; a Sociological Study* (Copenhagen, 1938, 204 pp.). Ranulf finds moral indignation a trait typical of the lower middle class. See also R. S. Briffault, *Reasons for Anger* (New York, 1936, 265 pp.), one of his many writings preoccupied with sex, family, and morals, especially the chapter, "The Economic Determination of Intelligence," pp. 51-60. One of the best of many articles by American Marxians since 1930 on the relationships between Freudian and Marxian thought is by a biographer of Freud, F. H. Bartlett, "The Limitations of Freud," *Science & Society*, iii (Winter 1939), pp. 64-105. In subsequent volumes of the magazine the subject recurs frequently, e.g., Cavendish Moxon, "Psychotherapy for Progressives," *ibid.*, xii (Spring 1948), pp. 197-217. The American psychiatrist Joseph Wortis discusses the rejection of Freudianism in Stalinist Russia in his above-mentioned *Soviet Psychiatry* (Baltimore, 1950, 314 pp.), especially pp. 71-102.

Special Topics

Topic 1. The Marxian Theory of Classes

THE theory of stratification based on objective conditions and subjective attitudes, and the theory of warfare between strata in society, as the General Reading (pp. 356-358) has already indicated, have been more assumed than investigated both by Marxians and non-Marxians. This topic is not primarily concerned with the general theory of caste, class, and status, but with its Marxian expression and with the criticism of the Marxian position.

Both sides can be stated briefly. To Marx, class was a group of persons having roughly the same function in production. Since his major writing deals by a highly abstract method with the industrial process, the two classes he is most concerned about are the capitalists and laborers—those who own and have power over machines and those who serve and obey them. Marx recognized other classes, principally the landlords, but his dynamic view of society led him to expect these other classes to decline in importance. Hence the mistake of many of his followers, who believe that the revolutionary crisis has arrived, in referring only to a two-class system. Although function in production is the fundamental criterion, this is closely correlated both with occupation and wealth. The arguments attempting to relate the objective conditions of class with class consciousness have been involved and frequently self-contradictory. To the socialist the obvious gap between working-class "interests" and their recognition is caused primarily by capitalist control of the agencies of propaganda. This control, powerful as it is, they believe will be broken by conditions obtaining under fully developed capitalism.

The critics of Marxian class theory have developed the thesis of continuing class mobility (Topic 2); they have suggested that the relationships of production as expressed in property rights have been modified by collective bargaining; and have sought to demonstrate a much greater degree of complexity in conditions and attitudes of superiority and inferiority. The issue is not, however, whether a minute gradation of status exists, but whether broad classes exist which comprehend several status groups, and if they do, whether the divisions between such classes are the ones Marx assumed. The position of the modern labor union, involved in capitalist industry and operating within an elaborate contractual system, is a phenomenon which cannot be explained by reference to Marx and Engels. Marx favored union organization, but he could not foresee the full consequences of that organization.

Secondary aspects of the subject are the fate of the middle class (dealt with from an economic point of view in PART IV, Topic 1), the time element, and the pejorative connotations of "upper" and "lower" classes. In terms of the control of the industrial process, it is argued that the "new middle class" does or does not carry weight, aside from its salaried position and occupational prestige. Since the "revolutionary situation"—the stage at which capitalism is said to be ripe for transformation into socialism—is a matter for each generation of Marxists to decide on the basis of information which they alone can collect, there are obvious differences of interpretation among the various socialist analysts. The relative importance of their determinist or activist principles conditions their answers. Finally, the concepts of "upper" and "lower" are generally those of non-Marxians. If Marxian socialists use these terms, it is to emphasize the servitude of a proletariat that is not class conscious.

Owen and Fourier were conscious of class distinctions and had no intention of creating a classless society in their communities. Many of their American followers were much more equalitarian, and none wrote anything specifically on class.

Marx's class theory is best presented in his preface to *A Contribution to the Critique of Political Economy* (tr. by N. I. Stone; Chicago, 1904, 314 pp.), pp. 9-15, and in the appendix, pp. 265-312, a sketch which was to have served as an introduction to his main work of analyzing the roots and characteristics of his contemporary society. The student should at the same time review the original expression of the Marxian theory in the *Communist Manifesto*, and read Vernon Venable's commentary on this theory, *Human Nature; the Marxian View* (New York, 1945, 217 pp.), pp. 98-150. Read also W. J. Ghent, *Mass and Class; a Survey of Social Divisions* (New York, 1904, 260 pp.), pp. 37-88, an American socialist revision which finds six functional economic classes; and H. D. Anderson and P. E. Davidson, "Class Consciousness and Political Behavior," in their *Ballots and the Democratic Class Struggle* (Stanford University, Calif., 1943, 377 pp.), pp. 203-285, a non-Marxian criticism.

In addition to the Marxian references already noted, see Marx's *The Class Struggles in France, 1848-1850* (New York, 1924, 207 pp.), and Engels' *Revolution and Counter-Revolution* (ed. by E. M. Aveling; London, 1896, 148 pp.), especially section 1 on Germany at the outbreak of the revolution. Kurt Gentz, "Der Begriff der Klasse bei Marx," *Gesellschaft*, VIII, No. 7 (July 1931), pp. 68-82, asserts that Marx was aware that his theory of the three great classes in capitalist society, as developed in *Capital*, was only approximate.

Socialists have followed the Marxian practice of assuming rather than analyzing the existence of classes. See, for example, the way class is treated in H. G. Wilshire's editorials, "Class vs. Class: Resultant," and "The Two Nations," in *Socialism Inevitable* (New York, 1907, 337 pp.), pp. 207-213, 221-224, and Frank Tannenbaum, *The Labor Move-*

ment (New York, 1921, 259 pp.), especially pp. 45-66. Seymour Deming, *A Message to the Middle Class* (Boston, 1915, 110 pp.), warns the petty bourgeoisie to take sides with the proletariat. Nor is the Socialist Party pamphlet by Ralph Korngold, *Are There Classes in America?* (Chicago, 1914, 34 pp.), much more than a rhetorical question. See also the more analytical treatments of John Spargo, "Classes and Class Conflict," in his *Social Democracy Explained* (New York, 1918, 337 pp.), pp. 158-186; Sidney Hook, "The Class Struggle and Social Psychology," in *Towards the Understanding of Karl Marx* (New York, 1933, 347 pp.), pp. 227-248; and Max Nomad, "Permanent Class Struggle or Utopia?" *Modern Review*, ii (Jan. 1948), pp. 28-33. A. W. Small, "The Church and Class Conflicts," *American Journal of Sociology*, xxiv (Mar. 1919), pp. 481-501, states that class conflict will grow, with devastating results, unless the churches detach themselves from their capitalist class connections and mediate.

Among numerous non-Marxian writings, G. A. Briefs, *The Proletariat; a Challenge to Western Civilization* (New York, 1937, 297 pp.), and Emil Lederer and Jacob Marschak, *The New Middle Class* (tr. by Socrates Ellison; New York, 1937, 45 pp.), deal with particular classes. J. R. Commons, "Is Class Conflict in America Growing and Is It Inevitable?" *American Journal of Sociology*, xiii (May 1908), pp. 756-783, is an early discussion by an institutional economist. The common American adherence to the Jeffersonian ideal of a hierarchy of classes based on talent and condemnation of the pretensions of an aristocracy of wealth and ignorance is exemplified by R. G. White, "Class Distinctions in the United States," *North American Review*, cxxxvii (Sept. 1883), pp. 231-246. James Feibleman, "Liberal Democracy Meets the Class Struggle," *Sociological Review*, xxx (Oct. 1938), pp. 380-399, concludes that the coming of the class struggle to the United States will not be fatal to the democratic form of government if the labor vote is split between the two major parties. George Simpson, "Class Analysis: What Class Is Not," *American Sociological Review*, iv (Dec. 1939), pp. 827-835, discards the Marxian theory and insists that any theory of class must be based principally on objective conditions. Kingsley Davis, "A Conceptual Analysis of Stratification," *ibid.*, vii (June 1942), pp. 309-321, defines man's social position as a complex of all the statuses a society might have. Genevieve Knupfer, "Portrait of the Underdog," *Public Opinion Quarterly*, xi (Spring 1947), pp. 103-114, finds psychological underprivilege, measured in terms of withdrawal from social activity, linked with economic underprivilege—a view held by the American Fourierists. See also Clyde and Florence Kluckhohn, "American Culture: Generalized Orientations and Class Patterns," in the seventh symposium of the Conference on Science, Philosophy and Religion, *Conflicts of Power in Modern Culture* (New York, 1947, 703 pp.), pp. 106-128.

One should mention here the considerable researches of social anthropologists and other students of the social structure of specific communities. The pioneer study was by R. S. and H. M. Lynd, *Middletown, a Study in Contemporary American Culture* (New York, 1929, 550 pp.), an investigation of Muncie, Indiana, which the authors followed up with *Middletown in Transition; a Study in Cultural Conflicts* (New York, 1937, 604 pp.). The four published volumes of the six-volume series on Yankee City (Newburyport, Mass.) by W. L. Warner and others, especially Volume 2, *The Status System of a Modern Community* (New Haven, Conn., 1942, 246 pp.), is the most ambitious project by members of this school, which rejects the two-class concept in favor of a six-class system based on role and status. See also E. L. Anderson, *We Americans; a Study of Cleavage in an American City* (Cambridge, Mass., 1937, 286 pp.), on Burlington, Vermont; E. H. Bell, "Social Stratification in a Small Community," *Scientific Monthly*, xxxviii (Feb. 1934), pp. 157-164; C. W. Mills, "The Middle Classes in Middle-Sized Cities," *American Sociological Review*, xi (Oct. 1946), pp. 520-529; and Carl Withers (James West, pseud.), *Plainville, U.S.A.* (New York, 1945, 238 pp.).

Hadley Cantril, "Identification with Social and Economic Class," *Journal of Abnormal and Social Psychology*, xxxviii (Jan. 1943), pp. 74-80, and a supplementary note by Cantril, J. M. Wallace, Jr., and F. W. Williams, "Identification of Occupational Groups with Economic and Social Class," *ibid.*, xxxix (Oct. 1944), pp. 482-485, found increasing disparity between social class and income group identification as one goes up in social class or down in income group. This type of study has been continued by R. T. Centers and others (see General Reading, pp. 356-357).

Topic 2.   *The Ideology of the American Open Class System; Theory and Evidence*

The Marxian prediction that class structure would become increasingly rigid with the development of capitalism (see PART IV, Topic 1) has had to combat a tenacious belief to the contrary among Americans. It is commonly held that a man or his children can reclassify themselves by using or failing to use existing opportunities. The first section of this topic describes the theoretical formulation of this American belief and the forms of the Marxist attack upon it. An attempt is then made to analyze a representative sample of the evidence for and against increasing rigidity. If there is evidence to support the Marxian theory, when does the rigidifying trend start—during the depression after the Civil War, when the frontier closed, after World War I, or during the great depression of the 1930's?

The theoretical arguments for differential improvement or loss of status started on a moralistic basis. If a man did not succeed in the United States, he was lazy, vicious, or intellectually inferior unless accidental circumstances were patent. Later, the emphasis shifted to pointing out the avenues of opportunity: the widening of the geographical labor market by the American systems of transportation; the free, public educational system which provided for the acquisition of skills; the democratic political system; the relative freedom from ethnic, racial, religious, or sexual discrimination; the promotion system in business; and the existence, even after the close of the physical frontier, of a technological frontier which promised rewards for innovators.

In opposing these arguments, besides stressing the limitations of the opportunities outlined above, Marxians have stressed the overwhelming effect of technological changes in industry, demoting the skilled workman to the position of automatic machine tender. The issue on the question of class mobility, however, is not only whether opportunities for reclassification are disappearing. Marxian literature is full of references to "labor fakirs," "renegades," and "class enemies" who have "betrayed their class" by demonstrating this mobility, as well as to socialist leaders of nonproletarian origin. If Marxian theory denied entirely the possibility of social mobility, instead of predicting that opportunities were declining, it would be a caste and not a class theory. The radical Marxian emphasis on the group, rather than the individual, as the source of social salvation, calls upon the socialist to renounce the admitted possibility of personal success in favor of the collective goal of the class struggle.

On both sides theorists have produced evidence to support their contentions. The evidence ranges from statistics of internal migration, ownership, income, inheritance, and occupation to the less tangible facts of industrial recruiting methods and promotion, and the effects of the organization of capital and labor. Connected with the problem of mobility was the question of aspiration level, recently investigated by social psychologists. Thus the question of class mobility connects indirectly with that of incentives and work satisfaction (Topic 8). The American novel of manners has explored the individual process of changing class or status, but the Marxian novelists referred to in PART VI, Topic 6, have rather tended to imagine situations illustrating class rigidities.

See the classic statement of the open-class theory, W. G. Sumner, *What Social Classes Owe to Each Other* (1883; New Haven, Conn., 1925, 169 pp.), and a recent version by Harold Rugg, "The American Mind and the 'Class' Problem," *Social Frontier*, II (Feb. 1936), pp. 138-142. This is a dissent from G. S. Counts' review of Lewis Corey, *The Crisis of* the *Middle Class* (New York, 1935, 379 pp.), *ibid.*, II (Dec. 1935), p. 89. Read in Corey, pp. 112-193, 244-277. W. F. Ogburn and M. F. Nimkoff, *Sociology* (Boston, 1940, 953 pp.), pp. 306-343, summarize a number of recent studies on class mobility.

One of the earliest reports on the ability of workingmen to get a job and get ahead was by an economics professor, W. A. Wycoff, *The Workers: an Experiment in Reality* (New York, 1897-1898, 2 vols.). Wyckoff worked his way across the continent. See also his *A Day with a Tramp, and Other Days* (New York, 1901, 191 pp.). John Martin's blanket denial of classes and class conflict in the United States and his assertion of the need to tackle each social problem with reference to its own data in "Socialism and the Class War," *Quarterly Journal of Economics*, XXIII (May 1909), pp. 512-527, is representative of the dominant antisocialist point of view. Werner Sombart, *Warum gibt es in den Vereinigten Staaten keinen Sozialismus?* (Tübingen, 1906, 142 pp.), answered his question in part by reference to the prosperous and unorganized condition of the American worker and his chances to rise. P. A. Sorokin, *Social Mobility* (New York, 1927, 559 pp.), especially chapters 16-18, developed a theory of horizontal and vertical movement which some sociologists, e.g., Talcott Parsons, in "An Analytical Approach to the Theory of Social Stratification," *American Journal of Sociology*, XLV (May 1940), pp. 841-862, do not accept. Sorokin has reviewed current changes of stratification in the Atlantic civilization: "War and Post-War Changes in Social Stratification of the Euro-American Population," *American Sociological Review*, X (Apr. 1945), pp. 294-303. Stuart Chase, *The Economy of Abundance* (New York, 1934, 327 pp.), emphasized that the automatic machine process decreases the number of the American industrial proletariat and weakens its power. R. D. McKenzie, *The Metropolitan Community* (New York, 1933, 352 pp.), commented on the eagerness of laborers to conform to middle-class standards. In direct contradiction to Lewis Corey's thesis, A. M. Bingham, *Insurgent America; Revolt of the Middle-Classes* (New York, 1935, 253 pp.), stated that the unwillingness to admit the existence of classes had been and continued to be dominant in the United States. Leon Samson, *The American Mind; a Study in Socio-Analysis* (New York, 1932, 356 pp.), agreed that a new middle class is gaining in power, and in *Toward a United Front; a Philosophy for American Workers* (New York, 1933, 276 pp.), attacked Americanism as a spurious substitute for socialism and criticized the conventional explanation of the backwardness of American labor as expressed in Sombart. Supporting Corey were such books as Clinch Calkins, *Some Folks Won't Work* (New York, 1930, 202 pp.); F. C. Palm, *The Middle Classes Then and Now* (New York, 1936, 421 pp.); and Zalmen Slesinger, *Education and the Class Struggle* (New York, 1937, 312 pp.).

It is hard to select from the mountain of publication providing evidence directly or indirectly on the degree of rigidity or flexibility of the American social system. Hubert Langerock, American correspondent of the European Socialist Press Service, examined the rigidities developed by specialization in "Professionalism; a Study in Professional Deformation," *American Journal of Sociology*, xxi (July 1915), pp. 30-44, and concluded that professionalism hinders the growth of democratic socialism. G. T. W. Patrick, *The Psychology of Social Reconstruction* (Boston, 1920, 273 pp.), and R. A. Freeman, *Social Decay and Regeneration* (London, 1921, 345 pp.), described the working class as having been transformed from a group of skilled men fairly satisfied with fairly good conditions into the masses of unskilled, dissatisfied men under decidedly unfavorable conditions. Josiah Wedgwood, *The Economics of Inheritance* (London, 1929, 276 pp.), pointed out not only the perpetuation of unequal opportunities but the effects of taxation on the inheritance of property. "Industrial Classes in the United States in 1930," a survey by T. M. Sogge in the American Statistical Association *Journal*, xxviii (June 1933), pp. 199-203, can be compared with the detailed report of the U.S. Census Bureau, *Sixteenth Census . . . 1940: Population: Comparative Occupational Statistics for the United States, 1870 to 1940* (Washington, 1943, 206 pp.), prepared by A. M. Edwards. The sources of membership in the wage-earning class are traced by W. B. Catlin, *The Labor Problem in the United States and Great Britain* (rev. ed., New York, 1935, 765 pp.). Carter Goodrich, author of *The Miner's Freedom, a Study of the Working Life in a Changing Industry* (Boston, 1925, 189 pp.), has compiled with others *Migration and Economic Opportunity; the Report of the Study of Population Redistribution* (Philadelphia, 1936, 763 pp.), issued by the Industrial Research Department of the University of Pennsylvania Wharton School. This underlines problems which Marxian socialization programs scarcely face. Elbridge Sibley, "Some Demographic Clues to Stratification," *American Sociological Review*, vii (June 1942), pp. 322-330, discusses migration as an avenue of upward mobility and finds that the father's occupation has more to do with a boy's going to college, and thereby raising his status, than his scholastic record in high school. Omar Pancoast, *Occupational Mobility* (New York, 1941, 155 pp.), in spite of its title, is concerned with employment service and related problems as they affect "democratic efficiency." *Youth Tell Their Story*, by H. M. Bell (Washington, 1938, 273 pp.), describes class and occupational mobility, to a large extent downward, during the depression, while Horst Mendershausen, *Changes in Income Distribution during the Great Depression* (New York, 1946, 173 pp.), deals with the same period from a different angle. The best general studies on occupations are by H. D. Anderson and P. E. Davidson: *Occupational Trends in the United States*

(Stanford University, Calif., 1940, 618 pp.), with supplement, *Recent Occupational Trends in American Labor* (Stanford University, Calif., 1945, 133 pp.); and *Occupational Mobility in an American Community* (Stanford University, Calif., 1937, 203 pp.). The last is a case study of San José. W. F. Whyte, ed., *Industry and Society* (New York, 1946, 211 pp.), mentions the tightening of class lines and the power factor in the conflict between management and labor.

Topic 3. Radicalism and Conservatism

Why have some Americans accepted socialist propaganda? What are the characteristics of the American socialist clientele? What psychological types of personality are attracted to American socialism? These are some forms of the question of radical motivation and environment with which this topic deals. It is first necessary, however, to reach a working definition of radicalism and conservatism.

For the purpose of this topic it is not necessary to go beyond the attitude toward fundamental change in society. The radical is for it; the conservative opposed. There are as many points of view toward social change as there are value judgments as to what is fundamental, and therefore important to preserve, transform, or destroy. Marxians say that the control of the instruments of production and distribution is fundamental. According to the more complex status theory of many non-Marxian sociologists, the minute gradations of superiority-inferiority feeling govern the individual's attitudes, often unconsciously, but contentment or discontent with a particular role has not been generally identified with radicalism or conservatism. American students of this subject, since they live in a capitalist society, have tended to call those attitudes which support capitalism conservative and those which challenge it—the attitudes of socialists and communists—radical. In order to place the large number who "split their vote" on specific issues of basic social change, they have tried to construct distribution curves based on questionnaires and other tests.

Some make improper deductions from the definition. To say that the radicals challenge the status quo seems to imply that they are perpetually aggressive. In the world of conflict, aggression consists of living and growing. In the world of mutual aid, where there are neither radicals nor conservatives, survival and growth consist of aggression only against nature or the uncooperative tendencies of the self. Whether the radical or the conservative is the aggressor is a tactical question which depends on the positions held by the antagonists at a given moment. The terms "liberal" and "reactionary" have little contemporary meaning in the radicalism-conservatism scale, for their commonest connotation is that the user is for or against the group he is labeling. Liberalism in the century between Adam Smith and John Stuart Mill made individual liberty a central principle. The goals of twentieth-century American radicals and conservatives, both heirs to the same tradition, give equal prominence to individual liberty. Likewise, the term "reactionary"—one who would return to the old order—has only tactical meaning. It theoretically applies as well to the enemy of deportation as to the enemy of unions. The traditional belief in progress does not affect the definition's basic distinction. Progress was conceived by conservatives to be within the framework of capitalism, and by radicals to be the succession of socialism. Neither does the twentieth century shift to an acceptance of universal change make the conservative any less eager to adjust capitalism in a dynamic society, or the radical any less willing to supplant it.

Given the power conflict, what motivates the radical? The common explanation is that he is or has been frustrated, and displaces his aggression against society. Recent research based on the frustration-aggression hypothesis indicates that no one can grow up in society—least of all modern society—and not be to some degree frustrated. If this is so, why does the frustrated person become a socialist, rather than a follower of Father Divine or the numbers game? A final answer cannot be given, because the evidence of observation and experiment is fragmentary.

Freudian analysis of the problem, while exaggerating the importance of a special set of conditions, and while not clearly corroborated by attitude measurement tests, has made a contribution. To some psychologists of this school, radicalism and conservatism are not two opposing factors, but combine in a single phenomenon. This polarity finds expression in a wide variety of forms, even in the same individual or society. The dialectical conflict between submission to and rebellion against the parent image or its substitutes is said to emerge in the conservative as docility, conventionality, and loyalty to leader, family, class, nation, private property, and religion. In the radical this conflict expresses loyalty to the group, the "classless" society, the international community, and also suspicion of the family, private property, religion, and traditions. Fatherland, Church, and Home, on the one hand, and Liberty, Equality, Fraternity, on the other, are representative symbols of conservatism and radicalism respectively.

A special case of value judgment applied to basic social changes is that of the religious radical. Insofar as the religious goal is eternal— "utopian" in the literal sense of "nowhere," and therefore nontemporal— there is an inevitable tension between the temporal and the eternal, no matter what the fundamental arrangements of temporal society are. The person faithful to an eternal goal must therefore be a permanent revolutionary, unless according to his creed the eternal goal will be gained entirely without man's action, by supernatural means. The institutional re-

369

ligion which Marx called an opiate had in his opinion identified itself with the capitalists or previous ruling classes (see Topic 9). It sought to divert the people from radicalism and exhibited the same conservative characteristics: authoritarian organization, adherence to rituals and conventions, and exaltation of the family. On the other hand, the radical religion which produced the American communal settlements tended to be equalitarian, collectivist, antiritualistic, and in many cases opposed to the monogamous family. This is true whether the "divine discontent" was transmitted through the Calvinist or Anabaptist line. According to the classification of the German sociologist of religion Ernst Troeltsch, religious conservatives have belonged to churches, religious radicals to sects, and those whose groups started as sects but have grown conservative in a society containing divergent religious groups, to denominations.

Scholars in a number of disciplines have explored the life cycle of radicals and radicalism. They have documented the fact that radicals have become "tired"; that revolutions settle down or are overthrown by counter-revolution; that movements initiated by fanatics are taken over and stabilized by compromisers; or that the destructive and constructive processes need different personality types. The Freudian hypothesis that this represents one or another stage in a process of dynamic equilibrium seems justified. It applies with equal force to the cases where a radical in the larger community is a conservative within his own group.

A. B. Wolfe, an economist, made one of the earliest analyses of the mental traits of radicals and conservatives, their origins and manifestations in behavior, *Conservatism, Radicalism, and Scientific Method; an Essay on Social Attitudes* (New York, 1923, 354 pp.). These traits Wolfe considered as obstacles to be overcome in the interest of a broadminded, inquisitive, and workmanlike approach to social problems. For Freudian answers to the questions raised above read J. C. Flügel, " 'Left' and 'Right' as Social Attitudes," in his *Man, Morals and Society* (New York, 1945, 328 pp.), pp. 281-301, by a radical but non-Marxian British psychoanalyst; and H. D. Lasswell, "Political Agitators," in his *Psychopathology and Politics* (Chicago, 1931, 285 pp.), pp. 78-126, by a nonradical. See also Lasswell's list of books, *ibid.*, p. 53n., on the definition of radical-conservative types. The point of view of the socialist is taken by G. W. Hartmann, "How Is Psychology Used in Social Reform?" in J. S. Gray, ed., *Psychology in Use* (New York, 1941, 663 pp.), pp. 592-652.

The pioneer work in the psychological analysis of radicalism-conservatism has been performed in the United States. A critical textbook summary of these investigations up to 1937 is found in Gardner Murphy, L. B. Murphy, and T. M. Newcomb, "Social Attitudes and Their Measurement," in their *Experimental Social Psychology; an Interpretation of Research upon the Socialization of the Individual* (1931; rev. ed., New York,

1937, 1121 pp.), pp. 889-1046. The following graduate theses have bearing on the subject: Helen Pallister, *The Negative or Withdrawal Attitude; a Study in Personality Organization* (Archives of Psychology, No. 151; New York, 1933, 56 pp.); B. Finkel, *Differences in Home, Health, Social and Emotional Adjustments between Matched Groups of Avowed Political Radicals*, unpublished Columbia M.A. thesis, 1935; Solomon Diamond, *A Study of the Influence of Political Radicalism on Personality Development* (Archives of Psychology, No. 203; New York, 1936, 53 pp.); and B. J. Breslaw, *The Development of a Socio-Economic Attitude* (Archives of Psychology, No. 226; New York, 1938, 96 pp.). The socialists in Miss Pallister's group of college women tended not to have withdrawal attitudes, but the numbers were too few for statistical reliability. Diamond found a tendency to introversion at a certain stage of the radical's development, but the personality was transformed into extroversion once the radical became fully taken up in the activities of his group. Breslaw's interviews of about a hundred subjects pointed to the conclusion that political attitudes result from individual experience, not from a particular social factor or combination of social factors. Conservatives experienced more conservative influences than radicals, and among these influences, that of the home was strongest. Social life was more influential than intellectual life.

The periodical literature of the nineteen-twenties is full of reports of similar experiments conducted with a rather narrow group of subjects—students or cooperating intellectuals—and of general theory not based on specific evidence. The subject first became popular during the red scare following World War I. J. S. Shapiro maintained in "The Revolutionary Intellectual," *Atlantic Monthly*, cxxv (June 1920), pp. 820-830, that parlor pinks turned to radicalism for self-expression because they were bored with the traditional leisure time activities of their class. John Spargo, after his wartime break with the Socialist Party, followed the accusations of Gustave Le Bon in explaining *The Psychology of Bolshevism* (New York, 1919, 150 pp.) in terms of psychoneuroses and the mechanisms of crowd behavior. Theodore Schroeder, "Conservatisms, Liberalisms and Radicalisms," *Psychoanalytical Review*, vii (Oct. 1920), pp. 376-384, countered that conservatives were as neurotic and psychotic as radicals. Stewart Paton, "The Psychology of the Radical," *Yale Review*, xi (Oct. 1921), pp. 89-101, seemed to be following Adlerian psychology in describing the radical as a person whose herd, self, and sex "instincts" were out of balance or not satisfied. The title essay of Walter Weyl, *Tired Radicals; and Other Papers* (New York, 1921, 223 pp.), is hostile to ex-socialists, and the second chapter calls the proletariat "the only true revolutionary class." In reviewing the uncritical literature that had so far appeared on the subject, V. S. Yarros, a lifelong radical, called for real studies of radical personalities in "Induction and Radical 'Psychology,'" *Psychological Review*, xxix (May 1922), pp. 237-240. The author of a history of American farmer-labor movements, S. A. Rice, published his conclusions on motivation in the *American Journal of Sociology*: "Motives in Radicalism and Social Reform," xxviii (Mar. 1923), pp. 577-585. He believed that radical behavior results from "altruistic" impulses which provide outlets for tendencies suppressed in other directions. Radicals become "reconditioned" when their old behavior is attached to new stimuli, "tired" when their impulses reacquire normal satisfactions.

The pioneer experimental and quantitative study of "speech reactions" and ideological phenomena, with various correlations, was made by H. T. Moore, "Innate Factors in Radicalism and Conservatism," *Journal of Abnormal and Social Psychology*, xx (Oct. 1925), pp. 234-244. Hereafter, although the experimental approach predominated in the learned journals, a priori generalizations continued, as, for example, W. D. Tait's article, "The Menace of the Reformer," *ibid.*, xxi (Jan.-Mar. 1927), pp. 343-353. W. T. Root, "The Psychology of Radicalism," *ibid.*, xix (Jan.-Mar. 1925), pp. 341-356, performed investigations similar to Moore's, with the conclusion that radicalism is the product of personal discomfort, the result of being in a position to which the radical feels much superior, and that therefore he has a low emotional breaking point. F. H. Allport and D. A. Hartman, "The Measurement and Motivation of Atypical Opinion in a Certain Group," *American Political Science Review*, xix (Nov. 1925), pp. 735-760, concluded from studying the answers of Syracuse freshmen that atypical opinion is accompanied by greater strength of conviction. Quantitative studies up to this time had been the work of social psychologists. G. A. Lundberg's statistical analysis of four sample communities in North Dakota and Minnesota, "The Demographic and Economic Basis of Political Radicalism and Conservatism," *American Journal of Sociology*, xxxii (Mar. 1927), pp. 719-732, and the study by P. A. Sorokin and others of 1,600 radical leaders, over four-fifths of them American, "Leaders of Labor and Radical Movements in the United States and Foreign Countries," *ibid.*, xxxiii (Nov. 1927), pp. 382-411, contributed information on the environmental conditions of radicalism. M. F. Washburn and others repeated the Moore tests and announced the same results in "The Moore Tests of Radical and Conservative Temperaments," *American Journal of Psychology*, xxxviii (July 1927), pp. 449-452. Charles Kassel described "The Natural History of Reform," *Open Court*, xlii (July 1928), pp. 414-424, as the development of heat rather than light from a radical leader. This, he felt, might be necessary in an absolutist state, but only caused trouble in a democracy. A French contribution was G. L. Duprat, "Physiologie du socialisme," *Revue internationale de sociologie*, xxxvii (Nov.-Dec. 1929), pp. 521-568. Radicalism, he said, is as "normal" as conservatism. The excesses of both give the appearance of the class struggle, but their synthesis is superior to either. Jerome Davis continued the type of investigation performed by Lundberg and Sorokin in "A Study of One Hundred and Sixty-three Outstanding Communist Leaders," American Sociological Society Papers, xxiv (1929), pp. 42-55, using Russian subjects. In two articles, "The Study of Social and Political Opinions," Journal of Abnormal and Social Psychology, xxv (Apr.-June 1930), pp. 26-39, and "The Measurement of Social and Political Attitudes and the Related Personality Factors," ibid., xxv (July-Sept. 1930), pp. 149-189, G. B. Vetter of New York University reviewed the inconclusive work of the past decade and reported an experiment of his own.

Some progress was made in the thirties. D. D. Droba found a high correlation between radicalism and pacifism in a test given to University of Chicago students, "Effect of Various Factors on Militarism-Pacifism," Journal of Abnormal and Social Psychology, xxvi (July-Sept. 1931), pp. 141-153. M. C. Krueger, a socialist, found a loss of confidence developing during the first four years of the depression leading, particularly among the intellectuals, to "Economic and Political Radicalism," American Journal of Sociology, xl (May 1935), pp. 764-771. G. W. Hartmann made several contributions: "Homogeneity of Opinion among Liberal Leaders," Public Opinion Quarterly, i (July 1937), pp. 75-78; "The Differential Validity of Items in a Liberalism-Conservatism Test," Journal of Social Psychology, ix (Feb. 1938), pp. 67-78; with Walter Watson, "The Rigidity of a Basic Attitudinal Frame," Journal of Abnormal and Social Psychology, xxxiv (July 1939), pp. 314-335, built around a questionnaire dealing with theism-atheism; and "Frustration Phenomena in the Social and Political Sphere," Psychological Review, xlviii (July 1941), pp. 362-363. Daniel Katz and Hadley Cantril, "An Analysis of Attitudes toward Fascism and Communism," Journal of Abnormal and Social Psychology, xxxv (July 1940), pp. 356-366, found that attitudes bore little relation to the knowledge of fascism or communism among college students in 1939. Robert Chin, An Analysis of Conformity Behavior (Archives of Psychology, No. 289; New York, 1943, 46 pp.), summarized the findings of the Allport school of direct observation studies. R. B. Vance, "Toward Social Dynamics," American Sociological Review, x (Apr. 1945), pp. 123-131, suggested that social integration and crystallization comes at the end of a dynamic period, with the victory of order over change. The idealistic radicals spearhead the unpopular cause, and the businessmen win the fruits of victory. Fritz Wittels, in a psychoanalytical study, "Economic and Psychological Historiography," American Journal of Sociology, li (May 1946), pp. 527-532, distinguished between the hysterical and the obsessed radical, and pointed out the sudden swings between radical and conservative poles which cannot be explained by materialistic reasoning alone. The pull of wife and family on a "progressive" union leader, to make him substitute "business union" principles, is described by A. W. Gouldner, "Attitudes of 'Progressive' Trade-Union Leaders," *American Journal of Sociology*, LII (Mar. 1947), pp. 389-392. P. M. Kitay, *Radicalism and Conservatism toward Conventional Religion; a Psychological Study Based on a Group of Jewish College Students* (New York, 1947, 117 pp.), carried on Hartmann's concern with attitudes toward theism-atheism and other aspects of religious belief. Studies on complementary subject matter are *Prophets of Deceit* (New York, 1949, 164 pp.), by Leo Lowenthal and Norbert Guterman of the Institute of Social Research at New York, which explores the areas of frustration, the leadership and clientele, agitational techniques, stereotypes, and goals of American native Fascists since 1933; and the work in progress by F. X. Sutton of Harvard, tentatively entitled *A Study of Modern Political Radicalism*, which deals with Marxian and especially communist groups since World War I from the point of view of the sociologist. Morris Ernst, counsel for the American Civil Liberties Union, is preparing with David Loth a book on Communist Party clientele based on personally collected case histories of American ex-communists. His evidence to date supports the belief that most American communists come from homes that are upper-class in education and upper-middle-class in income. He draws the conclusion that present-day communism in the United States is a psychological rather than an economic movement.

In spite of the repeated calls for inductive analysis of radical personalities and movements, little of the biographical or historical literature of socialism has emphasized this aspect of the subject. The writers who have paid more attention to it than others include: C. H. Parker, *The Casual Laborer and Other Essays* (New York, 1920, 199 pp.); Nels Anderson, *The Hobo; the Sociology of the Homeless Man* (Chicago, 1923, 302 pp.), which is pertinent to the study of the I.W.W. radical; and the sketches of Americans in Max Nomad's *Rebels and Renegades* (New York, 1932, 430 pp.) and *Apostles of Revolution* (Boston, 1939, 467 pp.). The autobiographical writings of R. S. Bourne touch the subject at several points. See his *History of a Literary Radical and Other Essays* (New York, 1920, 343 pp.), and two essays in *Youth and Life* (Boston, 1913, 365 pp.), "The Mystic Turned Radical," pp. 207-213 (on Maeterlinck), and "For Radicals," pp. 291-310. See also Louis Filler's biography, *Randolph Bourne* (Washington, 1943, 158 pp.). Emma Goldman's character sketch, "Johann Most," *American Mercury*, VIII (June 1926), pp. 158-166, emphasizes the dominant influence of Most's unhappy childhood in making him a radical. J. R. Buchanan, *The Story of a Labor Agitator* (New York, 1903, 460 pp.), and the biographical material cited in PART II provide indirect evidence on the subject. See also material in

Liston Pope, ed., *Labor's Relation to Church and Community* (New York, 1947, 182 pp.), Pt. 3, containing the "spiritual autobiographies" of six labor leaders; and socialist "documentarian" fiction in PART VI, Topic 6.

Fanaticism is popularly identified with radicalism, but has a much wider application as a psychopathological concentration on a single goal which may be social, religious, or trivial. See M. C. Otto, "Fanaticism," *Encyclopaedia of the Social Sciences*, VI, pp. 90-92, with its references, and Eliseo Vivas, "The Fanatic as Type," *Sewanee Review*, XLVII (Apr.-June 1939), pp. 166-174.

Mention should also be made of such sample European contributions as Max Weber, *The Protestant Ethic and the Spirit of Capitalism* (tr. by Talcott Parsons; London, 1930, 292 pp.), which has reference to the "culturally induced discontent" of Protestantism; Rudolf Rocker, *Johann Most, das Leben eines Rebellen* (Berlin, 1924, 482 pp.); René Fülöp-Miller, *Leaders, Dreamers and Rebels; an Account of the Great Mass-Movements of History and the Wish-Dreams That Inspired Them* (1934; tr. by E. and C. Paul; New York, 1935, 464 pp.); and T. A. Jackson, *Charles Dickens; the Progress of a Radical* (London, 1937, 302 pp.).

Topic 4.   Socialist Organization and Activities

As the motivation which draws men into separate socialist organizations is radical (Topic 3), so the efforts of socialists to maintain social control over their membership are conservative. Their history (see PART II) and their principal external activities—propaganda (Topic 5), and agitation in politics, the labor movement, and consumers' cooperatives (PART IV, Topics 5-6)—are analyzed elsewhere. We shall concentrate here on their organization of their own miniature societies and their activities within them. In the United States, the moderate socialists have not maintained intensive, internal organization much beyond the level of full-time, "professional" party officers and workers. Their practices bear more resemblance to those of major parties, although they have a dues-paying membership. This refers to the moderates only in contrast to the tightly knit, almost self-sufficient, organizational structure of the revolutionary socialists, or to the associative communities.

The organization of the latter two types of socialist groups, as well as that of the party workers among the moderates, has corresponded closely to the sect type of religious group. The chief safety valve for such a group is expulsion or voluntary departure from the group. A state church or party, on the other hand, has to temper its administration to its constituents, the whole population. Execution or exile for heresy, in this case, is a much more serious matter.

If the solution of a problem of discipline or power does not require the expulsion of dissidents, what methods of control are used? In general, little coercion is necessary or sanctioned, either because of the avenues of escape or because of the common existence of fundamental principles of belief against its use. One method is to make loyalty to the group exclusive, so that no conflict of loyalties could occur. The confessional or some kind of criticism is a major device for finding out the temper of the membership. The problem of responsibility, whether in the rank and file or in the leadership, has received extensive comment by observers. The lack of public patronage has been partly compensated for by the existence of a promotion ladder within the organization.

Since one of the chief means for maintaining control over a socialist group is criticism or confession, read the Oneida Community pamphlet compiled by W. A. Hinds, *Mutual Criticism* (Oneida, N.Y., 1876, 96 pp.), and compare with J. Peter's comments on self-criticism and discipline in *The Communist Party; a Manual on Organization* (New York, 1935, 127 pp.), pp. 23-35. D. R. Lamson, *Two Years' Experience among the Shakers* (West Boylston, Mass., 1848, 212 pp.), discusses among other things the object and uses of confession. Read also either in H. G. Stetler's case study, *The Socialist Movement in Reading, Pennsylvania, 1896-1936; a Study in Social Change* (Storrs, Conn., 1943, 198 pp.), pp. 29-86, 135-156, or—as an illustration of the amount of activity wasted in internal quarrels—J. P. Cannon, *The Struggle for a Proletarian Party* (New York, 1943, 302 pp.), pp. 1-18, 50-82, 226-240, 257-293.

The official organs of each party devote more space to party organization and activity than to any other topic, except, of course, critical comment on current political and economic events. To take only one example, see the following articles on organization in Volume 15 of the *Communist* (1936): John Dean, "The Socialist Administration in Reading and Our United Front Tasks" (Jan.), pp. 84-88; B. K. Gebert, "Our Tasks in Developing Activity within the Company Unions" (Jan.), pp. 47-57; Beatrice Shields, "Developing Party Cadres in the Chicago District" (Feb.), pp. 165-170; C. A. Hathaway, "Problems in Our Farmer-Labor Party Activities" (May), pp. 427-433; I. Amter, "Organizational Changes in the New York District of the Party" (May), pp. 465-473, and "New Party Organizational Forms Prove Their Value" (June), pp. 537-541; Max Steinberg, "Problems of Party Growth in the New York District" (July), pp. 643-665, a report to the ninth convention of the New York district; and F. Brown, "Building the Party during the Election Campaign" (Oct.), pp. 966-974. Current party leaders contribute frequent authoritative statements, as, for example, W. Z. Foster, "New Methods of Political Mass Organization," *ibid.*, XVIII (Feb. 1939), pp. 136-146. The extreme importance of organized control of party activities among the communists is indicated by their publication of a special journal for party leaders and active members, the *Party Organizer* (New York, 1927-

1938). Sample issues which best illustrate the variety of their activities and plans are IV, No. 2 (Mar. 1931), No. 4 (May 1931); x, No. 8 (Aug. 1937), special number on party building; and XI, No. 5 (May 1938), National Convention Discussion Issue. See also S. Tsirul, *The Practice of Bolshevik Self-Criticism; How the American Communist Party Carries Out Self-Criticism and Controls Fulfillment of Decisions* (New York, 1932, 32 pp.), and a publication of the Communist Party's national committee, *Party Building; a Handbook for Branch Officers* (New York, 1943?, 15 pp.).

The same emphasis, somewhat milder, can be seen in the periodicals of other parties. W. T. Mills, "Political Organization and Propaganda," in his *The Struggle for Existence* (Chicago, 1904, 640 pp.), Pt. 6, and Harold Kelso, *Build for Socialism! A Manual on Organization* (Chicago, n.d., 31 pp.), are representative nonperiodical treatments from the Socialist Party standpoint. Analysis by a nonsocialist may be found in R. F. Hoxie, "The Socialist Party and American Convention Methods," *Journal of Political Economy*, xx (July 1912), pp. 738-744. J. M. Patterson gives a favorable and specific account of the democratic methods of the Socialist Party in "The Socialist Machine," reprinted in the Pocket Library of Socialism, No. 45, pp. 17-24, from the *Saturday Evening Post*, Vol. 179 (Sept. 29, 1906), pp. 5, 19. Daniel De Leon's independent development of the Soviet theory of industrial organization is outlined in *Socialist Reconstruction of Society* (1905; New York, 1938, 64 pp.). *Ideas for Action* (New York, 1946-), a bulletin published by the Citizens' Social Research Council and edited by a group of democratic socialists, publishes information on current problems for the purpose of promoting intelligent democratic action.

In addition to the references in PART IV, Topic 5, see G. W. Hartmann, "The Behavior of Communists in Unions," *Ethics*, L (Apr. 1940), pp. 329-335, which contains an answer by Earl Browder; and C. W. Fountain, *Union Guy* (New York, 1949, 242 pp.), an autobiographical account of an ex-communist automobile worker's fight against communists in his union. Alexander Trachtenberg, *The History of May Day* (New York, 1932, 31 pp.), sketches the development of the Marxian Labor Day. Julian Gumperz, "Zur Soziologie der amerikanischen Parteiensystems," *Zeitschrift für Sozialforschung*, I (1932), pp. 278-310, declares that American politics interferes with popular sovereignty because it does not allow a clear expression of the class struggle. C. W. Mills, *The New Men of Power, America's Labor Leaders* (New York, 1948, 323 pp.), discusses the relationship between labor and the Left after World War II.

Sectarianism has been studied as a phenomenon of religious movements, but not of socialism, in spite of the tendency among nonsocialists to apply religious terminology to Marxism. Ellsworth Faris, "The Sect and the

Sectarian," American Sociological Society, *Papers and Proceedings*, XXII (1927), pp. 144-158, reprinted in *The Nature of Human Nature* (New York, 1937, 370 pp.), pp. 46-60, is a suggestive note which touches on the Shakers, Mormons, and Perfectionists. Factionalism, the parallel of heresy in religious organizations, is the main topic of C. E. Ruthenberg's pamphlet, *From the Third through the Fourth Convention of the Workers (Communist) Party of America* (Chicago, 1926?, 23 pp.). Earl Browder, *Theory as a Guide to Action* (New York, 1939, 15 pp.), emphatically denies that the Communist Party is a sect. He counters that the very idea of a party, whose origin he attributes to Marx and Lenin, is that it leads its members into cooperation with mass organizations. Contrary evidence is presented by Daniel Lang, "It's Hard to Recant," *Twice a Year*, No. 5-6 (1940-1941), pp. 487-493. He points out that communists become so involved in the parochial activities of their local cells, both in business and recreation, that even private disgust at party policy cannot overcome the fear of lost status and the heavy intellectual and emotional investment in the party line. Another side of the picture is the equivalent of German pietist "shunning," visited on the member of doubtful loyalty. This aspect, as well as the psychological circumstances surrounding the confession of a deviationist, is set forth in Richard Wright, "I Tried to Be a Communist," *Atlantic Monthly*, CLXXIV (Aug. 1944), pp. 61-70, (Sept. 1944), pp. 48-56. Additional material on Trotskyist organization is found in J. P. Cannon, *The History of American Trotskyism* (New York, 1944, 268 pp.), and "Letter of Resignation of James Burnham from the Workers Party," in Leon Trotsky, *In Defense of Marxism* (New York, 1942, 211 pp.), pp. 207-211.

Topic 5. *Socialist Propaganda*

The indoctrination of members and potential members of socialist groups in a hostile or indifferent environment, principally through the use of suggestion, in order to control their actions, is what is understood in this topic by the term "propaganda." We are concerned here primarily with the characteristics of the propaganda rather than the structure of the groups engaged in the propaganda (Topic 4). Communists divide their reinforcing and recruiting activities into what they call "agitation"— the simplified presentation of a few issues to the masses—and "propaganda"—the detailed instruction in the Marxian doctrine of already converted communists. "Agitation," therefore, corresponds more nearly to the popular connotation of propaganda, while "propaganda" corresponds to the traditional meaning of education (Topic 6). The Socialist Party, in fact, uses the latter terms.

In either case, a conflict with the prevalent ideology is implied as well as a need for selecting materials which will enforce beliefs and lead to action changing that ideology. As L. W. Doob puts it, propaganda involves both the sociological gun and the psychological ammunition. A knowledge both of the groups to be approached and of their individually-held attitudes and motivations is prerequisite for the propagandist. No less is this understanding necessary for persons who are the objects of propaganda or who attempt to study it. Although there is inevitably some propaganda which finds its mark for everyone who does not seal himself off from all society, a knowledge of the existing types of propaganda—the ability to recognize propaganda when we see it—makes it possible to avoid being influenced by unwanted types.

Marxian propaganda has been directed primarily at the industrial worker because according to Marxian theory the industrial proletariat is bound to be the prime agent of the revolution. Yet Marx and Lenin were aware of the importance of other groups, particularly the farmers (see PART IV, Topic 5). Their followers have sought to influence all groups who have serious grievances against their society, from colonials (see PART IV, Topic 2) to racial and religious minorities (on the Jewish question see PART IV, Topic 3), women (Topic 7 below), and youth. Methods have included the propaganda of deed and word, as other topics (PART IV, Topic 7; PART VI, especially Topic 10) have indicated. Their criticism of every phase of the civilization they seek to change, from the nature of capitalist development to its philosophical and religious postulates and social manifestations, is the negative half of their propaganda. Their criticism of the capitalist system of education is reserved for Topic 6, in connection with the theory and practice of socialist education. On the borderline are labor colleges and night schools, and research organizations like the League for Industrial Democracy, also discussed in Topic 6. These institutions represent and prefigure the socialist theory of education, and at the same time their isolated situation under capitalism gives their teachings a propagandist character.

A. E. Bestor, Jr., "Albert Brisbane, Propagandist for Socialism in the 1840's," *New York History*, xxviii (Apr. 1947), pp. 128-158, is the only study of the methods used by pre-Marxians to spread their doctrines. The equally spectacular efforts of Robert Owen must be gathered indirectly from such sources as "The Diaries of Donald Macdonald, 1824-1826," Indiana Historical Society *Publications*, xiv (1942), pp. 145-379. Studies of revivalism describe the milieu in which Shakers made converts (see PART II, Topic 2). Compare L. W. Doob, *Propaganda; Its Psychology and Technique* (New York, 1935, 424 pp.), pp. 236-268, with the detailed investigation by H. D. Lasswell and Dorothy Blumenstock, *World Revolutionary Propaganda; a Chicago Study* (New York, 1939, 393 pp.). Read also the comments of a veteran propagandist, W. Z. Foster, "The Human Element in Mass Agitation," *Communist*, xviii (Apr. 1939), pp.

346-352, and the results of an experiment with symbols, G. W. Hartmann, "The Contradiction between the Feeling-Tone of Political Party Names and Public Response to Their Platforms," *Journal of Social Psychology*, VII (Aug. 1936), pp. 336-357.

A collection from Lenin's works is *Agitation and Propaganda* (Berlin, 1929, 250 pp.). B. L. Smith, H. D. Lasswell, and R. D. Casey, *Propaganda, Communication, and Public Opinion; a Comprehensive Reference Guide* (Princeton, N.J., 1946, 435 pp.), brings up to date their earlier guide, *Propaganda and Promotional Activities; an Annotated Bibliography* (Minneapolis, Minn., 1935, 450 pp.). Besides the works by Lasswell and others cited in the General Reading, pp. 355-356, see Lasswell's article, "The Theory of Political Propaganda," *American Political Science Review*, XXI (Aug. 1927), pp. 627-631; Svend Ranulf, "Propaganda," *Theoria*, II (1936), pp. 239-256; and Willi Münzenberg, *Propaganda als Waffe* (Paris, 1937, 281 pp.), the last by a German communist youth-movement leader. Recent studies focused on the Fascists but commenting on socialist propaganda are Amber Blanco-White, *The New Propaganda* (London, 1939, 383 pp.); Sergei Chakhotin, *The Rape of the Masses; the Psychology of Totalitarian Political Propaganda* (New York, 1940, 310 pp.); Ellis Freeman, *Conquering the Man in the Street; a Psychological Analysis of Propaganda in War, Fascism, and Politics* (New York, 1940, 356 pp.); and Ivor Thomas, *Warfare by Words* (New York, 1942, 96 pp.). Thomas was a Labour M.P. from 1942 to 1948, but became a Conservative in 1949. See also Bertrand Russell, *Power; a New Social Analysis* (New York, 1938, 315 pp.), on the struggle for control of public opinion. For a right wing view consult the numerous publications on communist propaganda issued by the Committee on Un-American Activities.

The technique of socialist attack and defense is displayed in manuals for speakers, criticism of the capitalist press, and the promotion of the socialist press. Outstanding among socialist attacks upon the bias of the capitalist communications industry is the veteran writer of book-length tracts, Upton Sinclair, author of *The Brass Check; a Study of American Journalism* (Pasadena, Calif., 1919, 445 pp.), and *Upton Sinclair Presents William Fox* (Los Angeles, 1933, 377 pp.). See also John Keracher, *The Head-Fixing Industry* (Chicago, 1935, 27 pp.); George Seldes, *Lords of the Press* (3rd ed., New York, 1939, 408 pp.); and Barrows Dunham, *Man against Myth* (Boston, 1947, 320 pp.). Half of the pamphlet by M. U. Schappes, *The Daily Worker; Heir to the Great Tradition* (New York, 1944, 30 pp.), is devoted to a sketch of the early socialist and labor press. A. M. Lewis, *The Art of Lecturing* (new ed., Chicago, 1908, 107 pp.), and August Claessens, *A Manual for Socialist Speakers* (New York, 1933, 32 pp.), represent handbooks for socialist propagandists. J. W. Jones, speaking from the standpoint of conservative cooperators, *Membership*

Relations of Cooperative Associations (U.S. Farm Credit Administration *Bulletin*, No. 9; Washington, 1936, 111 pp.), shows the necessity of propaganda to promote active membership participation. See also the *List of References on the Red Flag; Its Origin and History* (Washington, 1920, 4 fols.) prepared by the division of bibliography of the Library of Congress.

The first study to use the technique of deliberate intervention into an actual political situation, an Allentown, Pennsylvania, election, was G. W. Hartmann's "A Field Experiment on the Comparative Effectiveness of 'Emotional' and 'Rational' Political Leaflets in Determining Election Results," *Journal of Abnormal and Social Psychology*, xxxi (Apr.-June 1936), pp. 99-114. Hartmann followed this with an experiment made during the 1936 presidential campaign in Altoona, Pennsylvania, "Immediate and Remote Goals as Political Motives," *ibid.*, xxxiii (Jan. 1938), pp. 86-99. The hypothesis that public response to an objective is inversely proportional to the "distance" from it had to be justified on general considerations, for the specific results of the test were negative. (For these two experiments also see Mr. Hartmann's discussion of them to be found in Chapter 12 of the first volume of the present book.) Other investigations of political campaigning are: Ralph Granneberg and R. H. Gundlach, "A Preliminary Study of Political Campaigning," *Journal of Social Psychology*, x (Aug. 1939), pp. 437-439, dealing with the campaign of Senator Bone of Washington; Muzafer Sherif, "The Psychology of Slogans," *Journal of Abnormal and Social Psychology*, xxxii (Oct.-Dec. 1937), pp. 450-461, which discusses both advertising and revolutionary slogans; and Leopold Bellak, "The Nature of Slogans," *ibid.*, xxxvii (Oct. 1942), pp. 496-510, which identifies slogans as battle or rallying cries. See also S. P. Rosenthal, *Change of Socio-Economic Attitudes under Radical Motion Picture Propaganda* (Archives of Psychology, No. 166; New York, 1934, 46 pp.), discussing the reactions of a group which saw the communist newsreel, *Capitalist World*.

The socialist and communist literature directed toward the Negro illustrates the special efforts made to enlist underprivileged groups. Their general answer to the question, "What will socialism do for the Negro?" is that without socialism neither the Negro nor any other workers could emancipate themselves. Yet this propaganda has attracted only a small fraction of the Negro population. These Negroes tend to be of relatively high status because the Negro worker, already handicapped by color restrictions, does not want to be restricted as a red as well as a black.

The Socialist Party at the outset of its career made a bid for the Negro worker, as indicated in two articles with the title, "The Negro Problem," in the *International Socialist Review*, i (Oct. 1900; Feb. 1901), pp. 204-

211 (by A. M. Simons), pp. 464-470 (by C. H. Vail); and Rev. C. H. Vail, *Socialism and the Negro Problem* (New York, 1902, 16 pp.). See also I. M. Robbins, "The Economic Aspects of the Negro Problem," *International Socialist Review*, VIII (Feb. 1908) to x (June 1910); E. V. Debs, *The Negro Workers* (New York, 1923, 31 pp.); Ernest Doerfler, "Socialism and the Negro Problem," *American Socialist Quarterly*, II (Summer 1933), pp. 23-36; M. I. Lamont, "The Negro's Stake in Socialism," *ibid.*, IV (Mar. 1935), pp. 41-51; and Norman Thomas, "The Negro," in his *Human Exploitation* (New York, 1934, 402 pp.), pp. 258-283.

The *Communist* has frequent articles on the subject, for example, John Pepper, "American Negro Problems," VII (Oct. 1928), pp. 628-638; Otto Huiswoud, "The Negro and the Trade Unions," VII (Dec. 1928), pp. 770-775; and J. W. Ford, Negro communist vice-presidential candidate, "The Struggle for the Building of the Modern Liberation Movement of the Negro People," XVIII (Sept. 1939), pp. 817-828. See also Ford, *The Negro and the Democratic Front* (New York, 1938, 222 pp.); Richard Wright, *12 Million Black Voices* (New York, 1941, 152 pp.); Herbert Aptheker, *The Negro People in America* (New York, 1946, 80 pp.), a criticism of Myrdal's *An American Dilemma* (New York, 1944, 2 vols.); *The Negro People and the Communists* (New York, 1944, 23 pp.), by D. A. Wilkerson, manager of the Harlem weekly, the *People's Voice*; and Harry Haywood, *Negro Liberation* (New York, 1948, 245 pp.). For a detailed history of the party line toward the American Negro, written by a noncommunist sociologist, see Wilson Record, *The Negro and the Communist Party*, announced for 1951 by the University of North Carolina Press.

Other general studies dealing with race prejudice and revolts are O. C. Cox, "Race Prejudice and Intolerance—a Distinction," *Social Forces*, XXIV (Dec. 1945), pp. 216-219; C. L. R. James, *A History of Negro Revolt* (London, 1938, 97 pp.); and Herbert Aptheker, *American Negro Slave Revolts* (New York, 1943, 409 pp.), and *To Be Free; Studies in American Negro History* (New York, 1948, 256 pp.). J. S. Allen, *The Negro Question in the United States* (New York, 1936, 224 pp.), to be issued in revised form by International Publishers in 1951, and *Reconstruction; the Battle for Democracy* (New York, 1937, 256 pp.); and Manuel Gottlieb, "The Land Question in Georgia during Reconstruction," *Science & Society*, III (Summer 1939), pp. 356-388, are historical studies of the struggle for landownership and thus for economic as well as civil rights. Additional studies on this subject are S. D. Spero and A. L. Harris, *The Black Worker; the Negro and the Labor Movement* (New York, 1931, 509 pp.); H. R. Cayton and G. S. Mitchell, *Black Workers and the New Unions* (Chapel Hill, N.C., 1939, 473 pp.); and H. R. Northrup, *Organized Labor and the Negro* (New York, 1944, 312 pp.). Eric Williams, *Capitalism & Slavery* (Chapel Hill, N.C., 1944, 285 pp.), is an Oxford dissertation by a Howard University professor on West Indian slavery, with a Marxist point of view. A. L. Harris, *The Negro as Capitalist* (Philadelphia, 1936, 205 pp.), developed the thesis, similar to the Leninist theory of minorities under capitalism, that Negro enterprises, controlled indirectly by white capitalists, could not expand. Roman Catholic counterpropaganda may be represented by J. T. Gillard, *Christ, Color & Communism* (Baltimore, 1937, 138 pp.).

Propaganda directed toward youth has tended to take the form of group activities rather than writings. Both the communists with their Young Communist League and the socialists with their Young People's Socialist League have maintained separate organizations. Sample pamphlets are Robert Danneberg, *Die Jugendbewegung der sozialistischen Internationale* (Vienna, 1910, 71 pp.), dealing with the better-developed European socialist youth movement, and O. V. Kuusinen, *Youth and Fascism; the Youth Movement and the Fight against Fascism and the War Danger* (New York, 1935, 30 pp.).

Topic 6.   Socialism and Education

The socialist definition of education identifies it with propaganda conducted by conservatives of the prevailing capitalist society. In its view, education transmits to the rising generation the fundamental values of the status quo. This may include the teaching of methods for adjusting existing institutions to change, but always within the capitalist framework (see Topic 3).

Education, in a limited sense, is the middle stage of the socialization process, although the whole process is sometimes referred to as education. The first stage occurs in the family (Topic 7), and the third among adults in society (Topic 5). Education is so important to society that its control is primarily, although not solely, political.

Certain aspects of the education process are much alike in different forms of society. The young in any age or place are taught at least the rudimentary means of communication through speaking and writing, reading and listening. They are taught the skills needed to earn a living, although the skills and the agencies for transmitting them change. But public and private morals—how to be a "good" citizen or individual—vary fundamentally with the ideology. It is this latter aspect of capitalist education, naturally, that socialists criticize, more than the methods used in teaching skills and the three R's.

The following are the best available general guides to the selected subjects of communitarian theory and practice; socialist theory and criticism; labor schools; and the communist point of view. American socialist communities did not in general last long enough, nor did they have sufficient numbers to educate, for them to develop an elaborate system of formal education. Nevertheless, education was conceived, particularly by Owenites and Fourierists, as the prime means of building a world of harmony in unity. A. E. Bestor, Jr., in *Backwoods Utopias: the Sectarian and Owenite Phases of Communitarian Socialism in America, 1663-1829* (Philadelphia, 1950, 288 pp.), compares educational ideas of Fourier and Owen and describes the New Harmony experience. Upton Sinclair, the outstanding socialist critic of American capitalist education, focused on the colleges in *The Goose-Step; a Study of American Education* (2nd ed., Pasadena, Calif., 1923, 488 pp.), and on the public school system in *The Goslings* (Pasadena, Calif., 1924, 454 pp.). The latter study illustrates the conflicts of authority created in modern society between the family and the school. T. B. Brameld, ed., *Workers' Education in the United States* (New York, 1941, 338 pp.), the fifth yearbook of the John Dewey Society, includes a selective bibliography, pp. 303-315. A sympathetic exposition of the Marxian-Soviet theory of education is M. J. Shore, *Soviet Education* (New York, 1947, 346 pp.). Its elaborate references and bibliography, pp. 267-339, are useful guides to the Marxian classics and to Soviet sources in Russian. Shore's emphasis on the originality of Marx's proposals to combine mental and manual training, called "poly-technism" as developed in the U.S.S.R., is only one of many indications that he is not acquainted with pre-Marxian socialist educational theory. See also G. S. Counts' and N. P. Lodge's translation of part of the Stalinist textbook on pedagogy for elementary schools by B. P. Yesipov and N. K. Goncharov, *"I Want to Be Like Stalin"* (intro. by G. S. Counts; New York, 1947, 150 pp.).

Among the communitarian groups in the United States, the Shakers had more than a century of experience in education. They gave orphans and children of new members a combination of Shaker doctrine, Bible study, and apprenticeship. Two general essays on the function of education as character development through vocational and religious training are H. L. Eads, *Discourses on Religion, Science and Education* (South Union, Ky., 1884, 15 pp.), and Daniel Fraser, *The Music of the Spheres* (Albany, N.Y., 1887, 75 pp.). The religious emphasis is plain in Mother Lucy Wright, *The Gospel Monitor; a Little Book of Mother Ann's Word to Those Who Are Placed as Instructors and Care-takers of Children* (Canterbury, N.H., 1843, 47 pp.), "Copied by inspiration . . . March 2, 1841"; *A Concise Shaker Catechism* (Shaker Village, Canterbury, N.H., 1850, 40 pp.), based on the Bible and lives of the first Elders; and A. G. Hollister and Calvin Green, *Pearly Gate of the True Life and Doctrine for Believers in Christ* (Mt. Lebanon, N.Y., 1894-1904, 3 pts.; 2nd ed. of Pt. 1, Mt. Lebanon, N.Y., 1896, 255 pp.). Moral guides for the young include *Gentle Manners; a Guide to Good Morals* (3rd ed., East Canterbury, N.H., 1899, 79 pp.), published in earlier editions as *A Juvenile*

Monitor (New Lebanon, N.Y., 1823, 20 pp.) and *A Juvenile Guide* (Canterbury, N.H., 1844, 131 pp.).

Among the German pietists, the Hutterites have had the longest tradition and are among the few communitarians who still exist. Eberhard Arnold, *Children in Community; a Survey of the Educational Work of the Bruderhof Communities* (Ashton-Keynes, Swindon, Eng., 1939), although dealing with the Hutterites in Europe, illustrates the importance of education to their survival. The Perfectionists used much the same methods of vocational and religious instruction as the Shakers and others, but left no special treatises on their educational theories. See, however, Mr. and Mrs. G. W. Noyes, *An Experiment in Home Education* (Oneida, N.Y., 1914, 24 pp.), by former members of the Oneida Community.

The liberal communitarians, although they had no one religion to inculcate, featured education for the free and harmonious life. See first the Owenite literature on education cited in PART I, Topic 2, and PART II, Topic 5. For the influence of Pestalozzi and Philip Emanuel von Fellenberg on the Owenites and others, see C. A. Bennett, *History of Manual and Industrial Education up to 1870* (Peoria, Ill., 1926, 461 pp.), pp. 106-209. Joseph Neef—an assistant of Pestalozzi who taught eighteen years near Philadelphia under the patronage of William Maclure and near Louisville, Kentucky, before joining Maclure at New Harmony—published, in addition to his two treatises cited earlier, *The Logic of Condillac Translated by Joseph Neef, as an Illustration of the Plan of Education Established at His School near Philadelphia* (Philadelphia, 1809, 136 pp.). See also W. S. Monroe, *Joseph Neef and Pestalozzianism in America* (Boston, 1894, 13 pp.), reprinted from *Education*, XIV (Apr. 1894), pp. 449-461. A recent Swiss Labor Party pamphlet by Max Bächlin, *Pestalozzi als Sozial-Revolutionär* (Zurich, 1946, 56 pp.), while no substitute for the standard biographies, brings out the social implications of Pestalozzi's theories. Paul Brown, who taught with Neef at New Harmony, wrote *An Enquiry Concerning the Nature, End, and Practicability of a Course of Philosophical Education* (Washington City, 1822, 394 pp.). Robert Dale Owen, also a teacher at New Harmony, published *An Outline of the System of Education at New Lanark* (Glasgow, 1824, 103 pp.), on the eve of the Indiana experiment. He and Frances Wright, in the Association for the Protection of Industry and for the Promotion of National Education, still made education the key to national reform.

The American Associationists laid more stress upon education than Fourier himself. Brook Farm was started as an Institute for Agriculture and Education, and the semi-Fourierist Northampton Community's formal title was the Northampton Association of Education and Industry. J. S. Dwight, who emphasized music in *A Lecture on Association in Its*

Connection with Education (Boston, 1844, 22 pp.), and in "Integral Education," published in three issues of the *Harbinger* beginning July 17, 1847, p. 89, drew upon Victor Considérant, *Théorie de l'éducation naturelle et attrayante* (Paris, 1844, 194 pp.), as well as Fourier. See also F. Cantagrel, *The Children at the Phalanstery; a Familiar Dialogue on Education* (tr. by F. G. Shaw; New York, 1848, 60 pp.). Also consult two works by the spiritualist L. A. Hine, prominent in the Clermont (Ohio) Phalanx, *A Plea for Harmonic Education* (Cincinnati, Ohio, 1856, pp. 173-205), on technical, manual, industrial, and physical training for the colleges, and *Hine's Political and Social Economy* (Cincinnati, Ohio, 1855-1856, 2 vols.), II, *Science and Man; Being a Vindication of Man's Educational Relations.* The second work had been published previously with the title, *Hine's Progress-Pamphlets* (Cincinnati, Ohio, 1853, 2 vols.).

Besides the influence of the schools of Pestalozzi and Fröbel (the friend of Fourier) upon the communitarians, later Europeans wrote directly on the subject of socialism and education. It is doubtful whether these works were much read in the United States. E. V. Neale, the Christian socialist and secretary (1874-1892) of the English Cooperative Union, published an address, *Association and Education* (Manchester, Eng., 1882, 16 pp.). The French Marxian contribution, to select only one Continental nation, includes Jean Jaurès, *Action socialiste: Ire série* (Paris, 1899, 558 pp.); C. L. Guieysse, *Les Universités populaires et le mouvement ouvrier* (Paris, 1901, 72 pp.); L. Foubert, "Critique socialiste de la liberté d'enseignement," *Revue socialiste,* XXXIV (July 1901), pp. 1-23; Henri Rovel, *Le Droit à la vie et l'éducation* (Paris, 1908, 57 pp.); and Édouard Guyot, *L'Université et l'état moderne* (Paris, 1929, 190 pp.). See also the following British titles: A. P. Hazell, *The Red Catechism* (London, 1910, 16 pp.); Albert Mansbridge, *An Adventure in Working-Class Education; Being the Story of the Workers' Educational Association, 1903-1915* (London, 1920, 73 pp.); J. F. and Winifred Horrabin, *Working-Class Education* (London, 1924, 93 pp.); and Arthur Calder-Marshall, *Challenge to Schools* (London, 1935, 43 pp.), a criticism of English privately endowed schools and their educational psychology. A sample Latin American work is by the Argentinian Marxist, educational psychologist, and "proletarian humanist," Aníbal Ponce, *Educación y lucha de clases* (Buenos Aires, 1936, 296 pp.). See also the official position of the Partido Nacional Revolucionario, Mexico, *La educación socialista* (Mexico, D.F., 1935, 284 pp.).

It is easier to trace European influence through other lines. The early American Marxian Adolf Douai, an Alsatian, was among the first to organize kindergartens in the United States on the principles of Pestalozzi and Fröbel. See Douai, *The Kindergarten* (New York, 1871, 136 pp.), also *Series of Rational Readers* (2nd ed., New York, 1874, 4 vols.). The theories of Francisco Ferrer Guardia, freethinker and anarchist, found acceptance among American socialists and anarchists. The Modern School, at Stelton, New Jersey, and the Ferrer Center in New York were founded before World War I on his libertarian principles modified from Pestalozzi and Fröbel. See Ferrer's book, *The Origin and Ideals of the Modern School* (tr. by Joseph McCabe; New York, 1913, 147 pp.); Joseph Mc-Cabe, *The Martyrdom of Ferrer* (London, 1909, 96 pp.), an account of the Spanish educator's work and his execution in 1909 because of it; and a pamphlet by the principal of the Modern School, W. T. Brown, *How Capitalism Has Hypnotized Society* (Chicago, 191[?], 29 pp.), which attacks the miseducation of workers' children away from class consciousness. The *Modern School; a Monthly Magazine Devoted to Libertarian Ideas in Education* (Ferrer Colony, Stelton, N.J., 1912-1922), included Scott Nearing, Anna Strunsky Walling, and Margaret Sanger among its contributors.

The attitude of early socialists toward the school system was similar to their attitude toward the political system. They had no quarrel with the ideals of American democracy and education; they only wanted these ideals practiced more. The importance of education appears just as great in F. J. Melvin, *Socialism as the Sociological Ideal* (New York, 1915, 216 pp.), as it did to the early Puritans. Socialists attacked on many separate issues. W. E. Walling, *The Larger Aspects of Socialism* (New York, 1913, 406 pp.), pp. 257-320, proposed John Dewey's educational philosophy of instrumentalism. The Christian socialist Jacob Edson urged a fuller realization of Christian ideals in *Education; or, The Coming Man* (Boston, 1884, 32 pp.). John Spargo dealt with such economic problems as child labor and school lunches in *The Bitter Cry of the Children* (New York, 1906, 337 pp.), and compiled *Socialist Readings for Children* (New York, 1909, 132 pp.) for the Woman's National Progressive League. A similar compilation at the elementary level is Nicholas Klein, *The Socialist Primer; a Book of First Lessons for the Little Ones in Words of One Syllable* (Girard, Kan., 1908, 52 pp.).

Although socialists did not want the kind of vocational training that would teach the laborer to be content with his inferior lot, they demanded enough tax-supported education to give a general schooling to all, and especially an understanding of industrial relations, so that leaders of the coming industrial democracy would be developed. On these points see F. T. Carlton, *Education and Industrial Evolution* (New York, 1908, 320 pp.), and C. H. Henderson, *Pay-day* (Boston, 1911, 338 pp.). That Henderson was no strict Marxist is apparent in his later work, *What Is It to Be Educated?* (Boston, 1914, 462 pp.), which recommends a world tour before college at the same time it asks the teacher to recognize that labor is the source of wealth. Like Upton Sinclair, socialists attacked the universities for limiting academic freedom, as in Lightner Witmer, *The Nearing Case* (New York, 1915, 123 pp.), and for neglecting to direct their social scientists toward the solution of problems at their doorsteps or in the world at large, e.g., A. E. Wood, *Some Unsolved Problems of a University Town* (Philadelphia, 1920, 76 pp.), on the Princeton housing, public health, and dependency situation, and R. S. Lynd, *Knowledge for What? The Place of Social Science in American Culture* (Princeton, N.J., 1946, 268 pp.). In this connection see Florian Znaniecki, *The Social Role of the Man of Knowledge* (New York, 1940, 212 pp.), and refer to PART III, Topic 6, for the conflicting views on the role of the intellectual in the socialist movement. Frank Tannenbaum, "Educational Function of the Labor Movement," in *The Labor Movement* (New York, 1921, 259 pp.), pp. 91-104, speaks of the union as the people's university. R. P. Holben, *Poverty with Relation to Education* (Philadelphia, 1923, 208 pp.), not written by a socialist, documents the socialists' charge that capitalism has not supplied equality of opportunity. See also Seymour Deming, *The Pillar of Fire; a Profane Baccalaureate* (Boston, 1915, 223 pp.); Thorstein Veblen, *The Higher Learning in America; a Memorandum on the Conduct of Universities by Business Men* (New York, 1918, 286 pp.); and H. P. Beck, *Men Who Control Our Universities; the Economic and Social Composition of Governing Boards of Thirty Leading American Universities* (New York, 1947, 229 pp.).

Workers' education, both through special schools and extension courses and in the public system, has been a special concern of socialists. Their periodicals contain frequent reports of labor schools, such as George Sirola, "The Finnish Working People's College," *International Socialist Review*, xiv (Aug. 1913), pp. 102-104. Another source is the catalogue or statement of purpose published by each institution, for example, those of the California Labor School, San Francisco, California, the Brookwood Labor College, Katonah, New York, the Rand School of Social Science, New York City, Commonwealth College, Mena, Arkansas, and the string of communist schools in the metropolitan centers. On workers' education in the nineteen-twenties, see W. E. Payne, "Specific Behavior and Formal Education," *Behavior of Conflicting Economic Groups* (Columbus, Ohio, 1930, 231 pp.), pp. 188-217, and on the following decade, Mark Starr, *Workers' Education Today* (New York, 1941, 48 pp.), by the educational director of the I.L.G.W.U. See also Starr's 1946 Inglis Lecture at Harvard, *Labor Looks at Education* (Cambridge, Mass., 1946, 51 pp.). John Dewey and others, *Thirty-Five Years of Educational Pioneering* (New York, 1941, 32 pp.), trace the growth of the League for Industrial Democracy out of the Intercollegiate Socialist Society founded before the first World War. H. C. Black, *Socialism in American Colleges* (National Association for Constitutional Government *Bulletin*, i, No. 4;

Washington, 1920, 46 pp.), aims at this organization and quotes alarmist letters from conservatives connected with colleges. L. A. Wincott, "College in Our Town," *Jewish Frontier*, VIII (Nov. 1941), pp. 16-19, describes C.C.N.Y. as "the Hull House of higher education," an avenue of social mobility, with a group of radical students.

With the depression after 1929, teachers paid increasing attention to Marxian arguments. Even before this, S. D. Schmalhausen had proposed radical changes in *Humanizing Education (a Preface to a Realistic Education)* (New York, 1926, 343 pp.). Members of the Progressive Education Association, disciples of Dewey and often inclined toward Marxism, discussed the educational relationship of instrumentalist and socialist theories in the association's organ, *Frontiers of Democracy* (New York, 1934- ; 1934-1939 as *Social Frontier*). T. B. Brameld, nearest to Marxian orthodoxy of them all, summarizes one controversy, involving R. B. Raup, John Dewey, and W. H. Kilpatrick, in "American Education and the Social Struggle," *Science & Society*, I (Fall 1936), pp. 1-17. Representative of this group are G. S. Counts, *Dare the School Build a New Social Order?* (New York, 1932, 56 pp.), a John Day pamphlet; John Dewey, *Education and the Social Order* (New York, 1934, 14 pp.); Zalmen Slesinger, *Education and the Class Struggle; a Critical Examination of the Liberal Educator's Program for Social Reconstruction* (New York, 1937, 312 pp.); Paul Bixler, "The Professor as Radical," *Antioch Review*, I (Mar. 1941), pp. 95-108; some of the papers presented at the second Conference on the Scientific Spirit and Democratic Faith, published as *The Authoritarian Attempt to Capture Education* (New York, 1945, 152 pp.); and Sidney Hook, *Education for Modern Man* (New York, 1946, 237 pp.). Communist propaganda has not concentrated on this field of criticism. See, however, Grace Hutchins, *Children under Capitalism* (New York, 1933, 23 pp.), and Rex David, *Schools and the Crisis* (New York, 1934, 46 pp.).

Russian education was observed with interest by Western pedagogues, and the experiments of Soviet psychologists and pedologists were reported in American journals. One monograph which presents a black and white contrast, with attention mostly on possibilities for Great Britain, is Beryl Pring, *Education, Capitalist and Socialist* (London, 1937, 280 pp.). Among Russian studies in child psychology note the following: A. R. Luriya, "The Problem of the Cultural Behavior of the Child," *Pedagogical Seminary and Journal of Genetic Psychology*, xxxv (Dec. 1928), pp. 493-506; L. S. Vygotsky, "The Problem of the Cultural Development of the Child," *ibid.*, xxxvi (Sept. 1929), pp. 415-434; A. N. Leontyev, "The Development of Voluntary Attention in the Child," *ibid.*, XL (Mar. 1932), pp. 52-83; and A. S. Salusky, "Collective Behavior of Children at a Preschool Age," *Journal of Social Psychology*, I (Aug. 1930), pp. 367-

378. See also Vera Fedyaevskaya and P. S. Hill, *Nursery School and Parent Education in Soviet Russia* (New York, 1936, 265 pp.), a detailed investigation with numerous illustrations and an extensive bibliography.

The first Russian educational problem was to conquer illiteracy; of almost equal importance was to combine training with industrial production and to create loyalty for the Soviet state. Scientists had to be trained, as well as artists of propaganda. Of the extensive literature at least two titles should be mentioned: *Les Problèmes de l'instruction publique en régime soviétique* (Paris, 1925, 32 pp.), by A. V. Lunacharsky, early head of the educational bureau; and V. A. Zaitsev, *Youth in the Soviet Union* (New York, 1934, 61 pp.). Foreign observers' comments on youth activities include S. N. Harper, *Making Bolsheviks* (Chicago, 1931, 167 pp.), lectures at the University of Chicago, and Klaus Mehnert, *Youth in Soviet Russia* (tr. by Michael Davidson; New York, 1933, 270 pp.), less sympathetic, by a Russian-born German. A. L. Strong, *Children of Revolution; Story of the John Reed Children's Colony on the Volga, Which Is as Well a Story of the Whole Great Structure of Russia* (Seattle, Wash., 1925, 99 pp.); M. G. Rozanov (N. Ognyov, pseud.), *The Diary of a Communist Schoolboy* (tr. by Alexander Werth; New York, 1928, 288 pp.), and *The Diary of a Communist Undergraduate* (New York, 1929, 288 pp.); and *Those Who Built Stalingrad* (New York, 1934, 268 pp.), are sample writings which show the details of the process. The last consists of fourteen stories by the builders themselves, on the theme that the plant has reeducated the workers. Gorky says in the foreword, "A soviet factory is a school of socialist culture, and not a capitalist slaughter-house." Jerome Davis, "Testing the Social Attitudes of Children in the Government Schools in Russia," *American Journal of Sociology*, xxxii (May 1927), pp. 947-952, discovered that professionals in the sciences were rated as high in the U.S.S.R. as in the U.S., but that Soviet children rated ditch diggers and factory laborers above bankers, businessmen, and ministers. See also on political education, Aleksandr Berdnikov and F. Svetlov, *Elements of Political Education* (Chicago, 1926, 320 pp.), and S. N. Harper, *Civic Training in Soviet Russia* (Chicago, 1929, 401 pp.); on technical education, V. Druzhinin, *How Workers Become Engineers in the U.S.S.R.* (Moscow, 1932, 46 pp.), and A. P. Pinkevich, *Science and Education in the U.S.S.R.* (London, 1935, 176 pp.), with emphasis on higher education; and a sample text, M. Ovsyannikova and others, *Social Science; Textbook for Elementary and Middle Schools, Part Three* (tr. by M. Muscatt; ed. by Tom Bell; Moscow, 1935, 158 pp.).

The following are general studies: John Dewey, *Impressions of Soviet Russia and the Revolutionary World* (New York, 1929, 270 pp.), chaps. 4-5; A. P. Pinkevich, *The New Education in the Soviet Republic* (ed. by G. S. Counts; New York, 1929, 403 pp.), a theoretical discussion by a professor of education at Moscow University; N. A. Hans and S. I. Hessen, *Educational Policy in Soviet Russia* (London, 1930, 236 pp.), by two hostile émigrés who had been active in Soviet educational politics; R. D. Charques, *Soviet Education* (London, 1932, 48 pp.), a good popular pamphlet; Thomas Woody, *New Minds; New Men?* (New York, 1932, 528 pp.), a full discussion by an American, with an excellent bibliography; W. C. Trow, ed., *Character Education in Soviet Russia* (tr. by P. D. Kalachov; Ann Arbor, Mich., 1934, 199 pp.), essays by Russians; Beatrice King, *Changing Man; the Education System of the U.S.S.R.* (London, 1936, 319 pp.), with complete, somewhat uncritical, coverage; V. Chemadanov, *Building a New World* (New York, 1936, 47 pp.); and Deana Levin, *Children in Soviet Russia* (London, 1942, 196 pp.), a very favorable report by a teacher in a school for foreigners in Moscow.

Topic 7. Socialism and Women

American socialist theory has criticized both the prevailing institution of marriage and the institutions governing women's activities as individuals in society. In practice, the communitarians tried many forms of marriage; in theory, the Marxians generally promised monogamy under socialism. In theory and practice, almost all socialists have accorded women more prominence in their organizations than in the contemporary world outside, yet the positions of formal leadership—with the notable exception of the Shakers—have been retained by men.

Plato matched the communal property of his republic with the communal family, believing that the survival of separate, monogamous families would destroy communism of property. Only the pietists of Ephrata and the Rappites, Shakers, and Perfectionists followed this line of reasoning to the full denial of the monogamous family. All American communitarians, however, tried to prevent sex relationships from introducing the spirit of individualism and competition. They applied sumptuary regulations, and transferred from the family to the community such activities as meals and recreation. Victorian America, exalting home and family, found the "unnatural" restraints of the Shakers as objectionable as the "licentious" sex mores of the Perfectionists.

Denominational communitarians followed no common pattern regarding the participation of women, and varied from subordination among the Mormons to Shaker equality. Those of pietist backgrounds tended to separate the sexes. The liberal communities applied their cardinal principle of freedom to the position of women, although not all worked it out in the same detail.

Anarchists of all sorts favored full equality and freedom of the sexes. They objected to monogamous marriage because as a religious institution it was permanent, and because as a civil institution it was legally enforced, in each case without recognizing adequate grounds for separation. No group here discussed ran afoul of the law so persistently or received so much notoriety.

Marxians have used any of four principal lines of attack upon the status of women under capitalism. As a wife, woman is to them a domestic slave, bound by custom, religious sanction, and law. As an acquiescent supporter of the patriarchal and authoritarian family system, she appears to be conservative or politically inactive, ready to submit to the totalitarian state. When circumstances permit or force her to earn her own living she becomes the potential equal of man, but socialists point out that under capitalism her wage slavery is even worse than man's. They explain prostitution as one peculiar consequence of her economic oppression, sometimes forgetting its long precapitalist history. Socialists denounce upper-class woman as an oppressor of the proletariat, either when she is a capitalist in her own right or when she bosses domestic servants; and as a misleader of women into woman suffrage reform, which denies the class struggle. Like the anarchists, the socialists have promised liberty and equality for women, both in the family and in society. Prostitution will wither away. Unlike the anarchists, they have tended to postpone or deny, both in propaganda and practice, changes in the conventional relationships.

In spite of their conviction that the reform of women's status is futile apart from socialism, many American Marxians have taken up the cause of feminism, and feminists have become socialists. This common front has benefited the socialist movement, just as in Europe the Marxians profited by their advocacy of democratic republicanism in the nineteenth century. On the other hand, the irregular married life of some American socialist leaders, like that of Engels in England, was seized upon by their opponents, although these irregularities were probably no more frequent than in the population as a whole. Imputation of sexual heresy is an age-old weapon for the slander of enemies. It was used against the Shakers, the Owenites, the Perfectionists, and the anarchists. Socialists have always had to combat the hostile myth that socialism means free love.

This topic must be studied with reference to the framework of the Marxian class system (Topic 1) and with an eye to the function of marriage as a secondary channel of social mobility (Topic 2). It has applications also to theories of radicalism-conservatism (Topic 3) and motivation (Topic 8). In the latter case, some writers influenced by Marxism have stated that work satisfaction is dependent on a satisfactory sexual life. Given the sexual frustration of modern life and the consequent morbidity of sexual interests, socialist discussion of sex is a successful propagandist technique. Women are only one of the "oppressed" minorities toward which the socialists have directed special efforts (Topic 5). Under the influence of Freudian psychology, socialists have recognized the importance of the early socialization of children in the family. Consequently their emphasis on the financial and institutional means of easing the mother's burden under socialism leads directly to their equally strong emphasis on education (Topic 6).

The first citations below suggest gateways to some of the many avenues of study included under the title. Brief selections from the extensive European literature follow. Late Marxian theory in the United States has drawn upon the literature about Soviet women and is cited at the end.

In no communitarian group were questions of sex so central as at Oneida. Although the denial of marriage had pervasive influence in celibate societies, it was only one consequence of their otherworldly outlook. Two pamphlets by J. H. Noyes, *Male Continence* (Oneida, N.Y., 1872, 32 pp.), and *Essay on Scientific Propagation* (Oneida, N.Y., 1875?, 32 pp.), get at the heart of their two experiments, in birth control and eugenics. Both sprang from a condemnation of selfish and exclusive love and from the practical situation of the Community. The two Marxian classics from which both European and American socialists derived their basic arguments were Friedrich Engels, *The Origin of the Family, Private Property and the State* (Chicago, 1902, 217 pp.), especially pp. 35-101, and August Bebel, *Woman and Socialism* (1879; tr. by M. L. Stern; New York, 1910, 512 pp.). Bebel's book was enormously popular. Two earlier translations had appeared in the United States—by H. B. A. Walther in 1886 and by Daniel De Leon in 1904—and the German reprint of 1910 was the fifty-first "edition." Two of the most detailed American discussions of the question included in general defenses of socialism are John Spargo, "Socialism and the Family," in *Applied Socialism* (New York, 1912, 333 pp.), pp. 237-274, and W. E. Walling, "Man, Woman, and Socialism," in *The Larger Aspects of Socialism* (New York, 1913, 406 pp.), pp. 321-372. Avrom Landy, *Marxism and the Woman Question* (New York, 1943, 64 pp.), is a communist summary of the orthodox theory that woman can be emancipated only through the class struggle. It is a polemic directed not against capitalism but against Mary Inman's interpretation of Marx and Engels. The fullest statement of Inman's position is *In Woman's Defense* (Los Angeles, Calif., 1941, 174 pp.), first published serially in the San Francisco daily *People's World*, beginning October 1939. International Publishers has announced for publication *The Woman Question: Selections from the Writings of Marx, Engels, Lenin, Stalin*. The work of the sexologist Wilhelm Reich is a unique example of the combination of Freudian psychology and Marxian sociology. "The Struggle for the 'New Life' in the Soviet Union," in his volume, *The Sexual Revolu-*

tion; toward a Self-Governing Character Structure (1930; tr. by T. P. Wolfe; New York, 1945, 273 pp.), pp. 151-269, asserts that the Soviet abandonment of "work-democracy" was concomitant with the reversion to sexual and social authoritarianism in the nineteen-thirties. This thesis may be tested by examining the citations below on Soviet woman. For other discussions of Freud and Marx, see the General Reading, pp. 359-360.

For the European utopian background see Emilie Schomann, *Französische Utopisten des 18. Jahrhunderts und ihr Frauenideal* (Berlin, 1911, 192 pp.). The works of Owen prominently display his radicalism on the woman question. His British follower during the period when he founded New Harmony, William Thompson, suggested that society give woman pecuniary independence and subsidize motherhood in *Appeal of One Half the Human Race, Women, against the Pretensions of the Other Half, Men, to Retain Them in Political, and Thence in Civil and Domestic Slavery* (London, 1825, 221 pp.). A typical attack upon Owen was Frances Morrison, *The Influence of the Present Marriage System upon the Character and Interests of Females Contrasted with that Proposed by Robert Owen* (Manchester, Eng., 1838, 16 pp.). Fourier's almost equally subversive criticism of marriage was a less prominent part of his work. See *The Position of Woman in Harmony* (London, 1841, 16 pp.), a Fourierist pamphlet by Zoé Gatti de Gamond, whose views on sex were more conservative than Fourier's. See also Marguerite Thibert's dissertation, primarily on Fourierism, *Le Féminisme dans le socialisme français de 1830 à 1850* (Paris, 1926, 377 pp.), especially the bibliography, pp. 341-374; and C. C. A. Bouglé, "Le Féminisme saint-simonien," in his *Chez les prophètes socialistes* (Paris, 1918, 246 pp.), pp. 51-110. The seventh of Étienne Cabet's *Douze lettres d'un communiste à un réformiste sur la communauté* (Paris, 1841-1842, 146 pp.), was also published separately as *La Femme, son malheureux sort dans la société actuelle, son bonheur dans la communauté* (9th ed., Paris, 1848, 31 pp.). Also by Cabet are *Réfutation de 'L'Humanitaire' (demandant l'abolition du mariage et de la famille)* (Paris, 1841, 12 pp.), and *Opinion icarienne sur le mariage; Organisation icarienne, Naturalisation* (Paris, 1855, 31 pp.).

Of the postutopian works, P. J. Proudhon, *La Pornocratie; ou, Les femmes dans les temps modernes* (Paris, 1875, 269 pp.), was contemporary with early American anarchist attacks. Sex was a central theme in the writings of the eccentric English poet and socialist Edward Carpenter, e.g., *Love's Coming of Age* (New York, 1927, 178 pp.). Sample references from English and German gradualism are Ethel (Annakin) Snowden, *The Woman Socialist* (London, 1907, 100 pp.), by the wife of the I.L.P. leader and agitator for women's rights, Philip Snowden, and

H. G. Wells, *Socialism and the Family* (London, 1906, 60 pp.); Karl Kautsky, *Der Einfluss der Volksvermehrung auf den Fortschritt der Gesellschaft* (Vienna, 1880, 195 pp.), on the Malthusian question, and Lily Braun, *Memoiren einer Sozialistin* (Munich, 1909-1911, 2 vols.). While Léon Blum headed the French Popular Front, the book he had written in his youth received its thirty-sixth edition (1937) and was translated into English as *Marriage* (tr. by W. B. Wells; Philadelphia, 1937, 330 pp.). Max Hodann studies sex morality in terms of economics and the class struggle in *Sex Life in Europe; a Biological and Sociological Survey* (tr. by Jerome Gibbs; Newark, N.J., 1932, 242 pp.), and *History of Modern Morals* (tr. by Stella Browne; London, 1937, 338 pp.). Hilary Newitt, *Women Must Choose* (London, 1937, 288 pp.), compares somewhat superficially women's status under fascism, communism, and Western democracy, and concludes that woman's emancipation depends on the emancipation of labor. Ethel Mannin, *Women and the Revolution* (London, 1938, 314 pp.), contains biographical sketches of famous women involved in revolutions, including the Russian revolution. A social democratic pamphlet by Anna Siemsen, *Frau und Sozialismus* (Arbon, 1946?, 52 pp.), appeared in Switzerland shortly after World War II. For Soviet Russia consult Rudolf Schlesinger, ed., *The Family in the U.S.S.R.: Documents and Readings* (London, 1949, 408 pp.), and "Law and the Family," chapter 12 in H. J. Berman, *Justice in Russia; an Interpretation of Soviet Law* (Cambridge, Mass., 1950, 322 pp.), pp. 234-246. See also frequent articles published by socialist periodicals referred to in PART I.

The specific American communitarian literature on women deals with their ideas of marriage. The general materials cited in PART II, Topics 1-7, contain passages on woman's status in society. Among the celibate groups, the Shakers were continually having to explain why they did not believe in marriage, as in the pamphlet by R. W. Pelham, *A Shaker's Answer to the Oft-Repeated Question, "What Would Become of the World if All Should Become Shakers?"* (Boston, 1874, 31 pp.). See also C. E. Sears, *Shakers; a Short Treatise on Marriage* (Rochester, N.Y., 1867, 13 pp.). The liberal communitarian ideals of emancipation in monogamy and voluntary separation were held by Owen's supporter, Frances Wright. See A. J. G. Perkins and Theresa Wolfson, *Frances Wright; Free Enquirer* (New York, 1939, 393 pp.), and R. D. Owen, *Situations* (New York, 1830, 16 pp.), which includes a characteristic attack on the legal disabilities of women. The Associationists translated Victor Hennequin, *Love in the Phalanstery* (New York, 1849, 27 pp.), to prove that Fourierism did not countenance free love, but the pamphlet urged revision of sexual conventions. On the side of plural marriage stood Mormon polygamy, attacked in numerous tracts but defended only by silence after the enunciation of the doctrine. Nels Anderson, "The

Mormon Family," *American Sociological Review*, II (Oct. 1937), pp. 601-608, finds that childbearing was a major Mormon industry, partly for theological reasons and partly because of the surplus of women converts from Europe. J. H. Noyes and George Cragin edited two numbers of the *Spiritual Moralist* (Putney, Vt., 1842) to expound "the principles of spiritual morality, in relation to the intercourse of the sexes" (*Witness*, XIV [May 10, 1842], p. 112). Articles in the Oneida *American Socialist*, II (Nov. 15, 22, 1877), pp. 363-364, 371-372, show that the Perfectionists, like Marx and Engels, were aware of the implications of L. H. Morgan's evolutionary views on the family. They argued that the corporation was necessary for the isolated family accumulating property, and the "combined family" would be necessary under socialism to utilize and distribute property. See also Dr. J. B. Ellis, *Free Love and Its Votaries; or, American Socialism Unmasked* (New York, 1870, 502 pp.), and other references in PART II, Topic 4.

Two writers bridge the modest gap between the mid-century communitarians and the individualist anarchists on the sex question. J. A. Clay, jailed for practicing his central principle of absolute freedom and equality in love, wrote a diffuse and repetitive brief in his own defense, *A Voice from the Prison* (Boston, 1856, 362 pp.). A former resident at the anarchist community of Modern Times, Long Island, Clay criticized existing communitarianism, yet concluded with a call for a new community. T. L. Nichols, M.D., who had been in and out of Fourierism and Modern Times, organized around a water cure his own Ohio community, Memnonia. He wrote two books with interminable subtitles which echo the Fourierist concern with "passional attraction," *Woman in All Ages and Nations* (pref. by S. P. Andrews; New York, 1854, 240 pp.); *Esoteric Anthropology* (New York, 1853, 482 pp.; 2nd ed. entitled *The Mysteries of Man*, New York, 1861, 466 pp.); and with his wife, M. S. Gove Nichols, *Marriage* (Cincinnati, Ohio, 1854, 466 pp.).

Socialists since Owen have been consistently optimistic on the population question, arguing against Malthus that technology and birth control could maintain the balance between birth rate and the means of subsistence. R. D. Owen, while promoting the New York Working Men's Party, published the first American tract on birth control, *Moral Physiology; or, A Brief and Plain Treatise on the Population Question* (1830; London, 1870?, 64 pp.). This revision of articles first published in Owen's *Free Enquirer* was widely circulated in England and the United States. See N. E. Himes, "Robert Dale Owen, the Pioneer of American Neo-Malthusianism," *American Journal of Sociology*, XXXV (Jan. 1930), pp. 529-547.

The anarchists vigorously took up the cause of birth control. E. H. Heywood, at Princeton, Massachusetts, sold Owen's and Noyes's pamphlets and *Sexual Physiology* (1866; 20th ed., New York, 1875, 304 pp.), by R. T. Trall, M.D., another pioneer. Moses Harman, author of the birth control pamphlet, *Right to Be Born Well* (Chicago, 1905, 66 pp.), with E. C. Walker and others, published *Lucifer, the Light-Bearer* (Valley Falls, Topeka, Kan., Chicago, 1880-1907) in the interests of birth control, sexual equality, and freedom. The prosecutions of these groups under the Comstock Law are discussed in Theodore Schroeder, *"Obscene" Literature and Constitutional Law* (New York, 1911, 439 pp.); and *Free Speech Bibliography* (New York, 1922, 247 pp.), also by Schroeder, lists many of their obscure publications. Emma Goldman put *Mother Earth*, which she edited with Alexander Berkman, at the service of the movement, and at one time devoted a whole issue, xi (Apr. 1916), pp. 449-495, to birth control. See also C. L. James, *Anarchism and Malthus* (New York, 1910, 32 pp.), which argues that the economic independence of women will check overpopulation.

The anarchists were vociferous for the natural right of sexual self-government. The first product of the native individualist school, S. P. Andrews, ed., *Love, Marriage, and Divorce, and the Sovereignty of the Individual, a Discussion by Henry James, Horace Greeley, and Stephen Pearl Andrews, Including the Final Replies of Mr. Andrews Rejected by the Tribune* (New York, 1853, 103 pp.), was republished by Benjamin R. Tucker (Boston, 1889, 121 pp.), with an additional interchange between James and Andrews occurring twenty years later. See also Henry Edger, *Modern Times, the Labor Question and the Family* (New York, 1855, 24 pp.), and *Prostitution and the International Woman's League* (New Bedford, Mass., 1878, 24 pp.), the latter reprinted from the *Radical Review*, i (Nov. 1877), pp. 397-418; E. H. Heywood, *Uncivil Liberty* (1870; 80th thousand, Princeton, Mass., 1877, 23 pp.), and *Cupid's Yokes* (Princeton, Mass., 1879, 23 pp.), the basis of numerous prosecutions; and M. L. David, *Monogamic Sex Relations* (Oakland, Calif., 1888?, 24 pp.). Emma Goldman took her stand in the first issue of *Mother Earth*, "The Tragedy of Woman's Emancipation," i (Mar. 1906), pp. 9-18. This and other articles were republished in *Anarchism and Other Essays* (New York, 1910, 277 pp.).

The variants in socialist opinion before the nineteenth amendment gave women the vote in 1920 may be represented by the following works. Mary Earhart, *Frances Willard; from Prayers to Politics* (Chicago, 1944, 417 pp.), illustrates the convergence of native radical, feminist, and socialist movements in the life of a prominent reformer who became a socialist in 1872. *Autobiography of Mother Jones* (ed. by M. F. Parton; Chicago, 1925, 242 pp.), recounts the author's participation in the labor movement since the 1870's. Mrs. Josephine Conger Kaneko edited a monthly, the *Socialist Woman* (Chicago, 1907-1909), continued as the

Progressive Woman (Girard, Kan., etc., 1909-1913), and published works dealing with woman's class struggle. Daniel De Leon and the Socialist Labor Party avoided the subject, although De Leon pointed out in *Woman's Suffrage* (1909; New York, 1914, 48 pp.), that the vote for women was a delusion without socialism. Of the numerous tracts on prostitution, C. B. Chrysler, *White Slavery* (Chicago, 1909, 251 pp.), has the most detailed discussion. V. D. Scudder, "Woman and Socialism," *Yale Review*, N.S., III (Apr. 1914), pp. 454-470, attacked the general subject in the spirit of a muckraker and a Christian socialist. For Kerr's Pocket Library of Socialism, M. W. Simons contributed No. 1, *Woman and the Social Problem* (Chicago, n.d., 31 pp.), and M. W. Kerr, No. 28, *Socialism and the Home* (Chicago, 1901, 32 pp.). Philip Rappaport, *Looking Forward; a Treatise on the Status of Woman and the Origin and Growth of the Family and the State* (Chicago, 1906, 234 pp.), was also a Kerr publication. K. R. O'Hare, *The Sorrows of Cupid* (rev. and enl. ed., St. Louis, Mo., 1912, 267 pp.), was based on her pamphlet, *What Happened to Dan* (Kansas City, Mo., 1904, 63 pp.). See also Max Eastman, "Is Woman Suffrage Important?" in A. B. Wolfe, ed., *Readings in Social Problems* (Boston, 1916, 804 pp.), pp. 466-478; John Spargo, *Socialism and Motherhood* (New York, 1914, 128 pp.), an amplified lecture; A. A. Maley, *Our National Kitchen* (Minneapolis, Minn., 1916, 62 pp.); and two pamphlets by M. S. Lilienthal, translator of Bebel, *From Fireside to Factory* (66 pp.) and *Women of the Future* (31 pp.), both published in 1916 by the Rand School of New York. A typical tirade by the extreme opposition is B. V. Hubbard, *Socialism, Feminism and Suffragism; the Terrible Triplets, Connected by the Same Umbilical Cord and Fed from the Same Nursing Bottle* (Chicago, 1915, 301 pp.). See also socialist and antisocialist fiction on the subject (PART VI, Topic 6).

The first thorough communist study of wage-earning women was Grace Hutchins, *Women Who Work* (New York, 1934, 285 pp.), issued by International Publishers. Hitherto they had used Alice Henry, *Women and the Labor Movement* (New York, 1923, 241 pp.), in their propaganda, and approved of the works of S. D. Schmalhausen, who edited with V. F. Calverton, *Sex in Civilization* (New York, 1929, 719 pp.), and *The New Generation* (New York, 1930, 717 pp.). Aside from numerous pamphlets issued by the American League against War and Fascism, the Workers Library, and other leftist organizations in the nineteen-thirties —such as Dorothy McConnell, *Women, War and Fascism* (New York, 1935, 18 pp.), and Eugene Gordon and Cyril Briggs, *The Position of Negro Women* (New York, 1935, 15 pp.)—their chief contributions were biographical: A. L. Strong, *I Change Worlds* (New York, 1935, 422 pp.), also published in Moscow with the title, *Remaking an American*; E. R. Bloor, *We Are Many* (New York, 1940, 319 pp.); and Alexander Richmond, *Native Daughter; the Story of Anita Whitney* (San Francisco, Calif., 1942, 199 pp.). See also two contributions by authors sympathetic to communism, Dyson Carter, *Sin and Science* (New York, 1946, 216 pp.), by a Canadian chemist and writer on popular science, contrasting Soviet practice with capitalist venereal disease, prostitution, and high divorce rate; and B. J. Stern, "Engels on the Family," *Science & Society*, XII (Winter 1948), pp. 42-64, by the editor of *Science & Society*.

A great deal has been written about Soviet woman, especially since 1930. A. M. Kollontay, Soviet minister to Sweden, wrote a history of the women workers' movement in Russia, and shorter pieces on woman's place in Soviet industry, sexual ethics, and the family. Aside from *Communism and the Family* (London, 1918?, 22 pp.), little of her nonfiction has been translated into English. A sample of her fiction is *Red Love* (New York, 1927, 286 pp.). Isabel de Palencia, *Alexandra Kollontay; Ambassadress from Russia* (New York, 1947, 309 pp.), treats her subject as novelist, propagandist, and feminist as well as diplomat. In 1921 the Russian government published *The Marriage Laws of Soviet Russia* in English (New York, 85 pp.); later, Hsin-wu Chao translated the 1926 Soviet code, *The Code of Laws on Marriage, Family and Guardianship* (London, 1936, 51 pp.). On this subject see H. J. Berman, "Soviet Family Law in the Light of Russian History and Marxist Theory," *Yale Law Journal*, LVI (Nov. 1946), pp. 26-57, amplifying material in his more recent book cited above on p. 395. Other significant books by Russians in English were E. M. Konius, *Protection of Motherhood and Childhood in the Soviet Union* (tr. by Vera Fedyaevskaya; Moscow, 1933, 117 pp.), by the chief physician at the State Research Institute for the Protection of Motherhood and Infancy; G. N. Serebrennikov, *The Position of Women in the U.S.S.R.* (London, 1937, 288 pp.); N. K. Krupskaya, *Soviet Woman, a Citizen with Equal Rights* (tr. by M. Jochel; Moscow, 1937, 76 pp.), a collection of speeches and articles; and T. Serebrennikov, *Women in the Soviet Union* (Moscow, 1943, 63 pp.), which describes the woman's part in World War II. See also the pamphlet by A. L. Strong, *Marriage and Morals in Soviet Russia* (Girard, Kan., 1927, 64 pp.), and Tatyana Chernavin, *We Soviet Women* (tr. by N. Alexander; New York, 1936, 304 pp.), sketches by a woman who left Russia in 1932.

Outstanding among the reports by other Europeans are two books by the Russian-born Austrian F. W. Halle, both translated by M. M. Green, *Woman in Soviet Russia* (New York, 1933, 409 pp.), and *Women in the Soviet East* (New York, 1938, 363 pp.), with good polyglot bibliographies. In S. D. Schmalhausen and V. F. Calverton, eds., *Woman's Coming of Age* (New York, 1931, 569 pp.), see especially the chapter by R. P. Dutt, "Women in the Class Struggle," pp. 550-564. Vera Rapoport, *Schutz der russischen Arbeiterinnen* (Berlin, 1934, 63 pp.), a Berlin dissertation, has a good list of titles.

Aside from such attacks as Samuel Saloman, *The Red War on the Family* (New York, 1922, 178 pp.), the first general book about Soviet women was by the American suffragette Jessica Smith, relief worker in Soviet Russia, and after 1936 editor of *Soviet Russia Today* (which since January 1951 has been replaced by the *New World Review*). Later writers have drawn much from her *Women in Soviet Russia* (New York, 1928, 216 pp.), and added from their own personal observation and study. See especially A. W. Field, *Protection of Women and Children in Soviet Russia* (New York, 1932, 241 pp.), by an American expert on child welfare; *Red Virtue* (New York, 1933, 332 pp.), especially pp. 95-194, by Ella Winter, the wife of Lincoln Steffens, valuable for its comprehensive view of Soviet social relationships and for its bibliography; *Factory, Family and Woman in the Soviet Union* (New York, 1935, 334 pp.), by two Bryn Mawr professors, S. M. Kingsbury and Mildred Fairchild, who deal primarily with women in industry; and Fairchild's article, "The Status of the Family in the Soviet Union Today," *American Sociological Review*, ii (Oct. 1937), pp. 619-629.

Topic 8. *Incentives and Work Satisfaction*

Marx's major criticism of capitalism was that it deprives labor of surplus value. One stock answer to Marxists has been that the profit motive is essential to make the wheels of industry go around. In this classic argument the socialists at first limited themselves to criticism of the evil effects of profit motivation. They pointed out that men, in their eagerness for profits, would often conduct their businesses in socially harmful ways. If profitable, they would often adulterate their goods; limit the quantity to maintain high prices; suppress inventions or offer inferior services. Communitarians, without an articulate economic theory, showed similar criticism by their practices or their propaganda.

At first, when challenged to offer an alternative, socialists simply pointed to the cooperative movement or to the motivations of those who already were working for public or private nonprofit institutions. Few discarded pecuniary incentives entirely, although these played a minor part in many of their communities, and some Marxians believed that money would no longer be necessary in the classless society (see Part IV, Topic 8). Nor did all socialists object to competition, but to the evil effects of capitalist competition. They suggested a variety of incentives: loyalty to community or nation; social or civil pride in public ownership; the ethic or instinct of constructive work; the desire for security, power, self-expression, or a higher income.

These incentives, they claimed, all existed but were not allowed full scope because of the prevalence of the profit motive.

With the development of industrial psychology and sociology and perhaps because of the socialist attack, there has been less emphasis either on the profit motive as essential to industrial production and distribution or on the alternatives as guaranteeing the good life. Students have come to see the relativity of work satisfaction. In a religious age or in a religious socialist community, faith in immortal salvation sustained the believer in the performance of the most menial tasks. Ignorance of technological possibilities has enabled some to endure the dirty work because they could conceive of its being done in no easier way. Modern man, intrigued by the potentialities of the machine age, has actually raised his standards for judging good working conditions. Many recent scholars label as myth the sharp contrasts, made by William Morris and other socialists, between the deadly monotony of standardized and specialized labor and the creative work of independent craftsmen. Although not criticizing either the Marxian (or liberal communitarian) expectation that urban and rural distinctions would disappear under full socialism or the concept of the well-rounded man who controls nature, they view the division of labor as necessary for improvement. Specialization makes it possible for more persons to feel proud of their unique and essential roles in society. Some occupations, such as mining, have always been deadly; modern methods have lightened the burden. While scope for skill has narrowed in the field of industrial labor, the growing service occupations are susceptible to a considerable development of skills.

We have already seen in the General Reading (pp. 358-359) the wide variety of reasons why men work so hard, both in capitalist countries like the United States and in Soviet Russia. In spite of the difference in property law, there are similarities between the speed-up and Stakhanovism, and between the rewards of socialist competition and the rewards of individual initiative. These similarities point to the fact that the universal bureaucratization of industry has changed the conditions for getting ahead. Important differences remain, principally in the type and amount of social recognition afforded and the means whereby social recognition is conveyed to the performer.

On this topic, too, Freudians have made their contribution. Work to them is both a common outlet for aggressive, destructive tendencies and the "normal," constructive result of a satisfactory love life. And play, for the first time possible for the masses under modern technology, is an equally valid form of either sublimation or erotic expression.

For the critical summary by a contemporary sociologist of the complex variables involved in the study of the problems of fatigue, work satisfaction, incentives, and the social significance of the division of labor, read W. E. Moore, "The Worker and the Machine," in his *Industrial Relations and the Social Order* (New York, 1946, 555 pp.), pp. 269-312, with selected references. Read also one of the best direct references to incentives in the literature of communitarianism, Albert Brisbane, *Association; or, A Concise Exposition of the Practical Part of Fourier's Social Science* (New York, 1843, 80 pp.), pp. 40-64. Writers on the sectarian communities have little to say on the subject, but something can be gathered from the standard histories or such biographical writings as Pierrepont Noyes, *My Father's House* (New York, 1937, 312 pp.), pp. 119-124. Compare H. W. Laidler, *Incentives under Capitalism and Socialism* (New York, 1933, 54 pp.), with a noted article by Thorstein Veblen, "The Instinct of Workmanship and the Irksomeness of Labor," *American Journal of Sociology*, IV (Sept. 1898), pp. 187-201, a theme on which Veblen subsequently wrote much. Veblen's article has been reprinted in the collection of his papers edited by Leon Ardzrooni, *Essays in Our Changing Order* (New York, 1934, 472 pp.), pp. 78-96. For an illustration of the influence of the Soviet example on American sympathizers, read H. F. Ward, "Shifting Incentives," *In Place of Profit; Social Incentives in the Soviet Union* (New York, 1933, 460 pp.), pp. 3-107, or *The Soviet Spirit* (New York, 1945, 160 pp.), by the same author.

Among the European socialist writings dealing with incentives, see the following: Karl Kautsky, *The Labour Revolution* (London, 1925, 287 pp.), chaps. 6-7, and *The Social Revolution* (Chicago, 1905, 189 pp.), Pt. 2, "On the Day after the Social Revolution"; R. E. Dell, *Socialism and Personal Liberty* (London, 1921, 160 pp.), chap. 8; J. A. Hobson, *Incentives in the New Industrial Order* (New York, 1923, 160 pp.); Henri de Man, "Workers' Education in Belgium," *International Labour Review*, VI (Oct. 1922), pp. 527-545, and *Joy in Work* (1927; tr. by E. and C. Paul; New York, 1929, 224 pp.); Otto Lipmann, "The Relation between Industrial Production and the Worker's Disposition to Performance in Some Important Branches of Industry," *International Labour Review*, XXIII (June 1931), pp. 835-852; and John Strachey, "Incentives to Work," in his *The Theory and Practice of Socialism* (New York, 1936, 512 pp.), pp. 126-144.

Discussions by American socialists before World War I are found in R. H. Newton, *Social Studies* (New York, 1887, 380 pp.), "Some Causes of Labor's Lack of Interest," pp. 26-40, by a Christian socialist; Laurence Gronlund, *The Co-operative Commonwealth* (rev. and enl. ed., Boston, 1890, 304 pp.), pp. 1-50; J. M. Work, *What's So and What Isn't* (1905; New York, 1927, 158 pp.), pp. 10-16, 19-26, 59-63, 83-84, 95-101; Edmond Kelly, *Twentieth Century Socialism* (New York, 1910, 446 pp.), pp. 36-39, 303-307; John Spargo, *Applied Socialism* (New York, 1912, 333 pp.), pp. 163-236; and R. W. Sellars, "Some Principles of Pecuniary Reward," *The Next Step in Democracy* (New York, 1916, 275 pp.), pp. 178-199. Socialists after the war continued to view the question narrowly, as "alternatives to the profit motive," or a discussion of wages and conditions of work, in the trade-union sense. See, for example, H. F. Ward, *The Profit Motive; Is It Indispensable to Industry?* (New York, 1924, 44 pp.); Stuart Chase, *Waste and the Machine Age* (New York, 1931, 63 pp.), a combination of two earlier pamphlets, and *Poor Old Competition* (New York, 1931, 36 pp.); Warren Atkinson, *Pay and Place under Socialism* (New York, 193[?], 8 pp.).

One group of socialists, who tend to be religious pacifists as well, contrast the evil profit motive with the good socialist motive of service. Among these see P. M. Malin, "Profits, Needs and Democracy," *World Tomorrow*, xiv (Feb. 1931), pp. 51-54; F. J. McConnell, "Economic Incentives in the New Society," in Kirby Page, ed., *A New Economic Order* (New York, 1930, 387 pp.), pp. 343-356; and Kirby Page, *Individualism and Socialism; an Ethical Survey of Economic and Political Forces* (New York, 1933, 367 pp.).

Miscellaneous nonsocialist writings on motivation other than the pecuniary incentive appeared from time to time. One of the earliest of these, Helen Marot, *Creative Impulse in Industry; a Proposition for Educators* (New York, 1918, 146 pp.), though colored by the war, pointed out the need of recognizing the creative potentialities and collectivist realities of industrial enterprise. M. P. Follett, analyst of pluralism and instrumentalist, carried the theme of work satisfaction further in *Creative Experience* (New York, 1924, 303 pp.). Whiting Williams, *What's on the Worker's Mind, by One Who Put on Overalls to Find Out* (New York, 1920, 329 pp.); C. H. Parker, *The Casual Laborer and Other Essays* (New York, 1920, 199 pp.), especially pp. 125-165; and the anonymously published volume, *Four Years in the Underbrush; Adventures as a Working Woman in New York* (New York, 1921, 315 pp.), were firsthand accounts of laboring groups which lacked the stimulus of profits or favorable conditions. More refined and controlled observation of the same type of situation was reported by S. B. Mathewson and others, *Restriction of Output among Unorganized Workers* (New York, 1931, 212 pp.). Typical Freudian treatments are that of Karl Menninger, "Work," in *Love against Hate* (New York, 1942, 311 pp.), pp. 134-166, and that of the English psychiatrist J. C. Flügel, *Men and Their Motives* (New York, 1947, 289 pp.). Following the lead of Veblen, both engineers and economists contributed to the discovery of nonpecuniary motivations in work. See, for example, R. B. Wolf, "Use of Non-Financial Incentives in Industry," *American Society of Mechanical Engineers Journal*, xl (Dec. 1918), pp. 1035-1038, and P. H. Douglas,

"The Reality of Non-Commercial Incentives in Economic Life," in R. G. Tugwell, ed., *The Trend of Economics* (New York, 1924, 556 pp.), pp. 153-188. See also R. G. Tugwell, "The Principle of Planning and the Institution of Laissez Faire," American Economic Association *Papers and Proceedings . . . 1931*, pp. 75-92, and Sydney Chapman, "The Profit Motive and the Economic Incentive," *Economic Journal*, LVI (Mar. 1946), pp. 51-56. The social anthropologists have contributed such reports as M. A. May and L. W. Doob, *Competition and Cooperation* (Social Science Research Council *Bulletin*, No. 25; New York, 1937, 191 pp.).

More strictly sociological and psychological investigations began at least with A. W. Small, "The Sociology of Profits," *American Journal of Sociology*, xxx (Jan. 1925), pp. 439-461, which claims that profits are generically a wage and not, as Marx maintained, parasitic. The Lynds asked the question, "Why Do They Work So Hard?" in *Middletown* (New York, 1929, 550 pp.), pp. 73-89. W. T. Watson's doctoral thesis, *Division of Labor; a Study in the Sociology and the Social Psychology of Work Satisfaction*, abstracted in Chicago University, *Abstracts of Theses, Humanistic Series*, IX (1930-1932), pp. 283-288, broadened the discussion out beyond the elementary matter of profits or service. See also A. R. Heron, *Why Men Work* (Stanford University, Calif., 1948, 197 pp.), and other studies of this type cited in the General Reading.

As in many other controversial aspects of socialism, the Russian example became significant. We refer here to a few of the titles by Russians seeking to explain what made the Soviet citizen work without expectation of profit. B. Markus, "Sotsialisticheskoe sorevnovanie na podyeme [Socialist Competition on the Increase]," *Bolshevik*, Feb. 28, 1931, pp. 27-40, described the vanguard of shock brigadiers. Stalin, "New Conditions—New Tasks in Economic Reconstruction," in *Leninism* (London, 1940, 667 pp.), pp. 368-387, announced a need for more efficient organization of factory labor because of the lack of worker responsibility. Written for the benefit of foreign workers in the U.S.S.R. or for propaganda were E. Mikulina, *Socialist Competition of the Masses* (Moscow, 1932, 64 pp.); A. S. Aluf, *The Development of Socialist Methods and Forms of Labour* (Moscow, 1932, 62 pp.); L. Kaufman, *Why Piece Work in the U.S.S.R.?* (Moscow, 1932, 56 pp.); *Lenin and Stalin on Socialist Competition* (tr. by David Keen; Moscow-Leningrad, 1933, 50 pp.); V. M. Molotov, *The Stakhanov Movement and the Cultural Growth of the Working Class* (Moscow, 1935, 41 pp.); and *Labour in the Land of Socialism* (Moscow, 1936, 239 pp.), verbatim reports of the speeches at the first All-Union Conference of Stakhanovites, held the previous November. In connection with the problem of incentive in the Soviet Union see the bibliography for PART IV, Topic 10. Two Soviet novels translated into English throw light on this subject. The theme of *The*

Little Golden Calf; a Satiric Novel, by Ilya Ilf and Evgeny Petrov (tr. by Charles Malamuth; New York, 1932, 402 pp.), is that no considerable income can be safely, comfortably, or personally spent in the Soviet Union. A. I. Voinova, *Semi-Precious Stones* (tr. by Valentine Snow; New York, 1931, 604 pp.), revolves around the stratagems used by secretaries, state-educated peasants, "loyal" intelligentsia, and true communists to win promotion in the marble trust. See also the following reports by outsiders: T. V. Smith, "Social Intelligence and the Communistic Experiment," *International Journal of Ethics*, XLII (Jan. 1932), pp. 113-131; Joseph Freeman, *The Soviet Worker; an Account of the Economic, Social and Cultural Status of Labor in the U.S.S.R.* (New York, 1932, 408 pp.); Lili Körber, *Life in a Soviet Factory* (1932; London, 1933, 280 pp.); Sidney and Beatrice Webb, "In Place of Profit," in their *Soviet Communism; a New Civilisation?* (London, 1935, 2 vols.), II, pp. 697-804; M. H. Dobb, *Soviet Planning and Labor in Peace and War* (New York, 1943, 124 pp.); and Hewlett Johnson, *The Secret of Soviet Strength* (New York, 1943, 160 pp.). The London edition was published under the title *Soviet Strength: Its Source and Challenge.*

The increasing amount of public ownership of industry in democratic countries after World War II made the U.S.S.R. no longer the only important field for examining the psychology of government-employed labor. Students of nationalized industries did not immediately exploit this subject. A compact article by Victor Alba, "The 'Nationalized' Worker," *Modern Review*, II (Mar.-Apr. 1948), pp. 187-194, based on observation of British, French, Spanish, and Mexican experience, suggests the growth of a sense of group property and a bureaucratic and managerial outlook detrimental to social solidarity. The author holds that this psychology, which capitalism taught the nonpolitical trade union, is more responsible for failure than the sabotage of conservative or communist opposition.

There is a tremendous literature on industrial fatigue and efficiency, which was developed out of studies made in the British munitions industry during World War I. It is significant for this topic only as socialists used the findings to agitate for improved conditions or argued that under socialism this state of affairs would not exist. The earliest study of this kind, however, was by Josephine Goldmark in connection with the movement for improving the working conditions for women, *Fatigue and Efficiency; a Study in Industry* (New York, 1912, 302 pp.; containing also the substance of four briefs in defense of women's labor laws by Louis Brandeis and Goldmark, 591 pp.).

The writings on profit sharing are likewise extensive, beginning with many of the utopian novels of the late nineteenth century. J. F. Lincoln, *Lincoln's Incentive System* (New York, 1946, 192 pp.), reports experience in both depression and war boom years. W. P. Hapgood, *The Columbia*

*Conserve Company, Indianapolis, Indiana; an Experiment in Workers'
Management and Ownership* (Indianapolis, Ind., 1934, 187 pp.), is a
report on one of the more successful producers' cooperatives which
survived for a time in spite of the lack of profit motive for the managers
as a separate group. The bibliography of PART IV, Topic 6, also contains
material on the nonprofit incentives of cooperatives.

Topic 9. Socialist Sociology of Religion

The focus of this topic is on the animus of socialists against the institutions of religion in a class society as obstacles to the propagation of
socialism because of their inevitable ties with the managers of the society's economic life. Earlier topics have treated many kinds of religious
socialists, and referred to the literature which points out that even Marxism might be called a secular religion (PART I, Topics 1-2, 7; PART II,
Topics 1-4, 13; PART III, Topics 8-9; PART IV, Topic 12). The philosophical basis of the conflict between materialism and idealism, determinism
and voluntarism was discussed in PART III, Topics 1 and 3, and the relation of the radicalism-conservatism axis to religion in Topic 3, above.

On the surface the socialist argument is not complicated, but it has a
number of ramifications. In the first place, it includes both communitarians
and Marxians, both of whom have been rationalist and humanist. The
liberal communitarians, heirs of eighteenth-century materialism, were
for the most part either deists or even evangelicals who still had a
fundamental objection to conservative religion. The charge of atheism
has been bandied about from time immemorial, each school of thought
imputing atheism to its opponents and declaring its own system the in-
fallible guide to truth. Consequently, the Owenites and Fourierists won
the reputation of atheists although few of their adherents could properly
be labeled as such; the Marxians after them received the same name, with
more justice.

A second complication is in the direction of the socialist attack, depending on the nature of the conservative opposition or the competition
of native reformers. While usually carried through to blanket all believers in the supernatural with the charge of subservience to the money
power, socialist criticism often concentrated on the Roman Catholic
Church as a power system or Christian socialism as a dead-end trail because of its religious ties. Jewish socialists might concentrate their attacks
on the synagogues. Still another and more sophisticated approach was
that of some communists. While not denying their belief in the ultimate
incompatibility of pie-in-the-sky religion and Marxism, they nevertheless
offered to unite for specific demands which both sides wanted. When
addressed to Roman Catholics, their argument pointed out the similarities

between the two great movements: both proletarian; both oppressed by Fascists and bigots; both international.

In the general secularization of American culture during the century after 1848, secularists and freethinkers held all shades of social opinion. They included the conservative Robert Ingersoll, the longlived periodical, *Truth Seeker,* generally sympathetic with labor and reform but suspicious of socialism, and the German-American Marxist freethinkers. On one point they could all agree with the socialists: on the separation of church and state. This point of view expressed itself in opposition to tax exemption of religious institutions, state aid to parochial schools, Sunday blue laws, religious services and chaplains in public institutions. They united also in their methods of exposing the weakness of the religious position, through studies of primitive religion, with or without the aid of Freudian psychology; criticism of the Scriptures and religious literature; and accounts of the warfare of science and religion.

For a general introduction to the subject by a non-Marxian, see J. M. Yinger, *Religion in the Struggle for Power* (Durham, N.C., 1946, 275 pp.), or Joachim Wach, *Sociology of Religion* (Chicago, 1944, 412 pp.), both with extensive bibliographies. Wach summarizes his main theses in Georges Gurvitch and W. E. Moore, eds., *Twentieth Century Sociology* (New York, 1945, 754 pp.), pp. 406-437. A good review of Owenite and Associationist freethought, with numerous references, may be found in Albert Post, "Scepticism and Socialism," *Popular Freethought in America, 1825-1850* (New York, 1943, 258 pp.), pp. 171-186. For lack of any comprehensive treatment of the Marxian view, see such representative samples as C. T. Sprading, *Science versus Dogma* (Los Angeles, Calif., 1925, 212 pp.), libertarian anarchist; H. M. Tichenor, *Mythologies; a Materialistic Interpretation, Analyzing the Class Character of Religion* (St. Louis, Mo., 1919, 198 pp.), socialist; and Earl Browder's pamphlets, *A Message to Catholics* (New York, 1938, 15 pp.), *Religion and Communism* (New York, 1935, 23 pp.), and another with the same title (New York, 1939, 15 pp.).

Robert Owen himself was an outspoken atheist, always willing to debate his views. See the stenographic report of his encounter with Alexander Campbell at Cincinnati in 1829, *Debate on the Evidences of Christianity* (2nd ed., Cincinnati, Ohio, 1829, 2 vols. in 1); Robert Owen, *The New Religion; or, Religion Founded on the Immutable Laws of the Universe* (London, 1830, 11 pp.); and another debate in which his son, Robert Dale Owen, defended atheism against Origen Bacheler, *Discussion on the Existence of God and the Authenticity of the Bible* (New York, 1832, 2 vols.). Paul Brown, a freethinker, wrote *A Disquisition on Faith* (Washington, 1822, 168 pp.), before coming to New Harmony, and later lectured frequently to freethinkers. The American

Associationists' religious aberration was most often transcendentalism, adventism, Swedenborgianism, or spiritualism. Although they did not follow the French master's anti-orthodox position through, they could still find the same fault with conventional religion, and in spite of their strenuous efforts to dissociate themselves from the Owenites, received the same obloquy. See, for example, C. A. Dana's claim that Fourierism has basically the same goal as true Christianity in "A Lecture on Association in Its Connection with Religion," an extract of which is printed in J. T. Codman, *Brook Farm; Historic and Personal Memoirs* (Boston, 1894, 335 pp.), pp. 312-318, following a similar article by J. S. Dwight, pp. 309-312; orm H. H. Van Amringe, *Association and Christianity, Exhibiting the Anti-Moral and Anti-Christian Character of the Churches . . . and Urging the Necessity of Industrial Association, Founded on Christian Brotherhood and Unity* (Pittsburgh, Pa., 1845, 122 pp.). Étienne Cabet had much the same approach in *Le Vrai christianisme suivant Jésus-Christ* (Paris, 1846, 636 pp.). On the other hand, Lewis Masquerier, who had both an Owenite and Fourierist past, was more outspoken in *The Sataniad . . . in Which Is Shown That His Godship, Satan, Has Been Much Calumniated* (New York, 1877, 27 pp.), published as an appendix to his *Sociology*.

A sampling of early European Marxian secularists who had some influence in the United States should include the following: E. B. Aveling, *Science and Secularism* (London, 1880, 16 pp.); Robert Blatchford, *God and My Neighbor* (1903; London, 1908, 200 pp.); Tom Mann, the syndicalist, *A Socialist's View of Religion and the Churches* (London, 1896, 16 pp.); Chapman Cohen, *Christianity, Slavery and Labour* (1918; 3rd ed., London, 1931, 124 pp.); the Socialist Party of Great Britain pamphlet, *Socialism and Religion* (New York, 1923, 48 pp.), which quotes from the clergy to show their avowed interest in supporting capitalism. See also J. D. Bernal, *The World, the Flesh and the Devil; an Enquiry into the Future of the Three Enemies of the Rational Soul* (New York, 1929, 96 pp.); Jack Lindsay, *The Anatomy of Spirit* (London, 1937, 182 pp.), an attempt to combine Marx and Freud; Joseph Needham, "Science, Religion and Socialism," and "Laud, the Levellers, and the Virtuosi," in his *Time, the Refreshing River* (London, 1943, 280 pp.), pp. 42-91, revisions of two essays in *Christianity and the Social Revolution* (1935). Paul Lafargue, *Social and Philosophical Studies* (tr. by C. H. Kerr; Chicago, 1906, 165 pp.), sought the origins of abstract theological and ethical ideas, as did Heinrich Eildermann, *Urkommunismus und Urreligion; geschichtsmaterialistisch beleuchtet* (Berlin, 1921, 396 pp.).

Among the early German-American Marxians there was a strong current of freethinking. See the publication of the Milwaukee Freidenker Convention, *Blitzstrahlen der Wahrheit* (Milwaukee, Wis., 1872, 38 pp.);

the pamphlets of Adolf Douai, *A B C des Wissens für die Denkenden* (2nd ed., Leipzig, 1875, 29 pp.), and *Antwort an den Bekenner des Theismus* (Leipzig, 1875, 16 pp.); Joseph Dietzgen's works, cited in the General Reading of PART II, and *Die Religion der Sozialdemokratie* (6th ed., Berlin, 1903, 48 pp.); Fritz Schütz, *Das Heil der Völker* (Milwaukee, Wis., 1879-1880, 2 pts.). Sidney Warren, "Socialism and Freethought," in his *American Freethought, 1860-1914* (New York, 1943, 257 pp.), pp. 135-155, a sketch based on somewhat limited sources, emphasizes the mutual distrust between organized secularism and socialism, caused both by the religion of some socialists and the conservatism of some free-thinkers.

The Socialist Labor Party generally agreed with the Socialist Party in allowing religion to be a private concern of members, although Daniel De Leon clearly illustrated the Marxian attitude toward churches as part of the social organization of capitalism. See his pamphlets, *Abolition of Poverty; Socialist versus Ultramontane Economics and Politics* (New York, 1911, 68 pp.), a series of editorials originally published in the *Daily People* under the title "Father Gassoniana"; *Ultramontanism; Roman Catholic Political Machine in Action* (New York, 1928, 80 pp.), selected editorials; and *Anti-Semitism; Its Cause and Cure* (New York, 1921, 26 pp.); also Arnold Petersen, *Superstition, Father of Slavery* (New York, 1939, 30 pp.), and *Theocracy or Democracy?* (New York, 1944, 191 pp.).

The Socialist Party, more thoroughly tinctured with Christian social-ism, nevertheless had its outspoken secularist wing. See, for example, Isador Ladoff, *Socialism the Antichrist* (n.p., n.d., 61 pp.), promising a new rationalist morality out of the collective conscience of socialism and firmly rejecting Christianity as incompatible. This type of propaganda called forth such answers as David Goldstein, *Socialism; the Nation of Fatherless Children* (ed. by M. M. Avery; Boston, 1903, 374 pp.), by a former socialist who disliked the "atheism" and "free love" which he detected among the German-American socialists and who looked to the Roman Catholic Church or the A.F.L. to combat this influence. Other works during the early period are P. E. Burrowes, *Revolutionary Essays in Socialist Faith and Fancy* (New York, 1903, 319 pp.); Charles Meily, *Puritanism* (Chicago, 1911, 153 pp.), a collection of essays attacking the evils of Puritan morality; Oscar Ameringer, *Communism, Socialism and the Church; a Historical Survey* (Milwaukee, Wis., 1913, 63 pp.); Scott Nearing, *Social Religion* (New York, 1913, 227 pp.), from an address to the Friends' general conference in 1910; W. E. Walling, "The Socialist Explanation of Religion," and "Socialism and Religion," in *The Larger Aspects of Socialism* (New York, 1913, 406 pp.), pp. 228-256, 386-391; John Spargo, *Marxian Socialism and Religion* (New York, 1915, 187 pp.);

Seymour Deming, *From Doomsday to Kingdom Come* (Boston, 1916, 110 pp.); and A. M. Lewis, *The Struggle between Science and Superstition* (Chicago, 1916, 188 pp.), popularizing A. D. White's work on the warfare between science and theology.

During the World War I period, H. M. Tichenor, editor of the *Melting Pot* (St. Louis, Mo., 1913-1920), wrote a series of historical exposés. See, in addition to his *Mythologies*, cited above, *The Roman Religion; a Short History of How the Holy Humbug Was Hatched* (St. Louis, Mo., 1913, 64 pp.); *The Life and Exploits of Jehovah* (St. Louis, Mo., 1915, 222 pp.); *The Creed of Constantine; or, The World Needs a New Religion* (St. Louis, Mo., 1916, 189 pp.); and *Tales of Theology; Jehovah, Satan and the Christian Creed* (St. Louis, Mo., 1918, 580 pp.). The same view is expressed in John Keracher, *How the Gods Were Made (a Study in Historical Materialism)* (Chicago, 1929, 59 pp.). Rev. G. W. McPherson, *Socialism and the New Theology* (Yonkers, N.Y., 1921, 32 pp.), a fundamentalist pamphlet, identified modernism and socialism and condemned them. Such frank statements passed into the background during the interbellum period, while the more limited attack on the bonds between institutional religion and capitalism was redoubled. Upton Sinclair, *The Profits of Religion; an Essay in Economic Interpretation* (Pasadena, Calif., 1918, 315 pp.), was the most notable blast from this quarter. See also S. D. Schmalhausen, "An Open Letter to Pope Pius XI from Pope Impious XII," *Modern Quarterly*, vi, No. 1 (Winter 1932), pp. 63-71, a forthright article declaring that the church is the real antichrist, frowned upon by other leftists as in poor taste. A unique example of Marxian scholarship, by an American in India, is W. C. Smith, *Modern Islām in India; a Social Analysis* (1943; London, 1946, 344 pp.). The work combines an intellectual history of Indian religion since the mutiny with an analysis of the effects of capitalist development on Indian politics, and is based on the author's assumption at that time that this history has been a class struggle submerged by the divisive policy of Great Britain.

In addition to Browder's pamphlets cited above, see such other communist writings as Grace Hutchins and Anna Rochester, *Jesus Christ and the World Today* (New York, 1922, 149 pp.); and Bennett Stevens, *The Church and the Workers* (New York, 1932, 31 pp.). A. L. Strong wrote for a University of Chicago doctoral dissertation *A Consideration of Prayer from the Standpoint of Social Psychology* (Chicago, 1908, 118 pp.). L. F. Budenz, a member of the Communist Party who returned to the Roman Catholic Church, is preoccupied with the party's attitude toward religion in *This Is My Story* (New York, 1947, 379 pp.). For the communist relations with the churches in Russia, see PART I, Topic 7, and the critical bibliography in Philip Grierson, *Books on Soviet Russia,*

1917-1942 (London, 1943, 354 pp.), pp. 267-275. Additional titles include N. I. Bukharin, *Finance Capital in Papal Robes; a Challenge* (tr. by M. J. Olgin; New York, n.d., 23 pp.); and N. A. Berdyaev, *The Russian Idea* (New York, 1948, 255 pp.).

Anarchism was much more closely identified with secularism than was socialism. One of Lysander Spooner's earliest writings, *The Deist's Reply to the Alleged Supernatural Evidences of Christianity* (Boston, 1836, 62 pp.), objected to the gospel miracles, the resurrection, and the divinity of Jesus, and asserted that Christianity could not be the true religion because it had not become universal. See also John Badcock, *Slaves to Duty* (Detroit, Mich., 1938, 39 pp.), a London address in 1894, first published by William Reeves; Emma Goldman, *Philosophy of Atheism and The Failure of Christianity; Two Lectures* (2nd ed., New York, 1916, 15 pp.); M. I. Swift, *The Evil Religion Does* (Boston, 1927, 111 pp.); and G. E. MacDonald, *Fifty Years of Freethought; Being the Story of the Truth Seeker, with the Natural History of Its Third Editor* (New York, 1929-1931, 2 vols.), which includes remarks on Stephen Pearl Andrews, but is generally aloof from socialism and anarchism.

Topic 10.   Socialist Theories of Law and Crime

The coercive functions of the state are the same in all forms of class society, but offenses against the state and its citizens are defined differently by socialists and nonsocialists. The subversive and treasonable activity of which socialists who urge revolution are accused in the United States is of course supreme loyalty to socialism; while loyalty to the older ideals is in turn treasonable if implemented with overt expression and action in the Soviet Union. In a socialist economic system, economic failure is a public offense and a crime, whereas it is generally assumed in capitalist countries that the competitive system provides its own sanctions. Offenses against property are crimes under Roman and common law, but still somewhat private in practice, for there must be a complaining witness. In a socialist economy, they are more serious for they become treasonable offenses against the state.

The basic socialist legal theory is simple environmentalist determinism and as such there is little more to be said about it except to trace the forms of expression which this theory has taken. If society is the criminal and there is no devil theory based on the freedom of the individual to sin, there should be no need for cruel punishments, but only such measures as will contain the antisocial activity of the offender until full socialism will take away the occasion for crime and injustice. Nevertheless, the recriminations between the successors of Lenin came close to implicit acceptance of the theory that the leader has great powers for good or evil. Both the official government of the U.S.S.R. and the Trotskyists have heavily stressed the difference that Stalin's succession has made in the destinies of Russia.

Communitarian problems of order were based on voluntarism. Men freely joined and could freely leave the community; or if problems of discipline were too much to cope with, banishment to the outer world solved them. The methods of maintaining order, discussed in Topic 4, were limited to confession, counsel, and the pressure of community opinion. Among the early religious groups, "shunning," or ostracism of those who had too strong ties with the community to be willing to face the world without it, was a powerful means of discipline—so powerful that the mere threat of its application was usually enough. The Oneida Community and the Shakers were the only groups which maintained for any length of time more than one connected group, and they could take advantage of this situation to transfer members within the organization. This could be done either as a therapeutic, in fitting the individual to the size of "family" where he could be most useful, or as a punishment, depriving him of the associations which he desired most. The voluntarism of the communitarians was one with their pacifist tendencies; corporal punishment was virtually unknown, and many, the Associationists in particular, lent their support to the movement for the abolition of capital punishment. For none but the Mormons had any serious quarrel with the law of the land or attempted to set themselves up as independent sovereignties. Their basic antistatism made them inclined to solve their differences out of court, but with many colonies, especially the weaker and nonsectarian ones, breakdown of leadership and morale led to acrimonious lawsuits for possession of the domain. The spirit of their laws was the same spirit which governed their ideas of education (Topic 6), the place of women (Topic 7), and their emphasis on attraction and nonprofit incentives (Topic 8). General literature on formal law among the communitarians is nonexistent; in fact lawyers, if they belonged, did not practice.

The European Marxists faced legal questions in several ways. They were prosecuted by conservative administrations (PART IV, Topic 7), and they theorized from the assumption that capitalist government was the executive committee of its ruling class and that law was part of the superstructure, taking its form from the type of ownership of the means of production. There was also a positivist school of legal sociology in Italy which developed ahead of the rest the implications of the environmentalist view, of which the pioneer was the non-Marxian scholar Lombroso. Review in connection with this subject the materials on social control (Topic 4), political theory in PART IV, especially Topics 9-11, the philosophical concepts of natural and civil law discussed in

PART III, and the general historical references in PARTS I and II dealing with socialist trials and Russian law.

Soviet legal theory has gone through three major phases, corresponding roughly with the amount of fear of foreign intervention. The treatment of White Russians during the period of war communism was violent, and final. From the stabilization of Europe under the treaty of Versailles to the rise of Hitler, Soviet Russia pioneered in the field of penal reform, emphasizing change of motivation and getting along with a minimum of repression and corporal punishment. Typical of the shift back to "old-fashioned" methods were changes in the divorce law and in education (see Topics 6-7). The series of trials for sabotage of the communist system and its betrayal to the enemies of the state ushered in the third period of Spartan discipline. Whether these trials proved that the Old Bolsheviks had been guilty of espionage for the Fascists, or merely (as seems more likely) of opposition to Stalin, the procedure was beyond the comprehension of most Westerners. For the latter were unacquainted with Russian legal procedure, which had none of the English common law tradition, and was not even the same as Roman civil law. They could not understand the intensity of Soviet citizens' involvement in and loyalty to communism.

For general introductions to the modern sociological study of law and crime see N. S. Timashcff, *An Introduction to the Sociology of Law* (Cambridge, Mass., 1939, 418 pp.), especially pp. 367-403, including bibliography; and two essays in Georges Gurvitch and W. E. Moore, eds., *Twentieth Century Sociology* (New York, 1945, 754 pp.), Roscoe Pound, "Sociology of Law," pp. 297-341, particularly useful as a bibliographical guide, and Jerome Hall, "Criminology," pp. 342-365, a succinct summary of the classical and positivist legacies and current problems. American Marxian treatments include G. A. England, *Socialism and the Law; the Basis and Practice of Modern Legal Procedure and Its Relation to the Working Class* (Fort Scott, Kan., 1913, 62 pp.), and L. B. Boudin, *Government by Judiciary* (New York, 1932, 2 vols.), by the prominent constitutional lawyer and Marxian theorist. The best treatises on Soviet law are A. Y. Vyshinsky, *The Law of the Soviet State* (tr. by H. W. Babb; New York, 1948, 749 pp.), prepared by the Russian Translation Project of the American Council of Learned Societies, W. C. Huntington, editor; and Rudolf Schlesinger, *Soviet Legal Theory* (New York, 1945, 299 pp.). An extreme example of doctrinaire Marxism is John Keracher, *Crime—Its Causes and Consequences: a Marxian Interpretation of the Causes of Crime* (Chicago, 1937, 42 pp.). See also the socialist authors in Isidore Abramowitz, ed., *The Great Prisoners* (New York, 1946, xxxvii, 879 pp.), an anthology with selected bibliography.

Not even European socialists have paid much attention to the study of law, although Marx himself made clear, as theories of private property had not, the inherent power relationship involved in the differential control of capital goods. This is pointed out in W. E. Moore, "The Emergence of New Property Conceptions in America," *Journal of Legal and Political Sociology*, I (Apr. 1943), pp. 34-58, in an issue devoted to ideas of property. European works which relate socialism and legal theory include Adolf Dürrnberger, *Der Einfluss socialistischer Postulate auf das Privatrecht* (Vienna, 1893, 75 pp.); Auguste Castelein, *Le Socialisme et le droit de propriété* (Brussels, 1896, 584 pp.); Edmond Picard, *Le Droit pur* (Paris, 1908, 401 pp.); Pierre Moride, "Karl Marx et l'idée de justice," *Revue d'histoire des doctrines économiques et sociales*, II (1909), pp. 169-194; Gioele Solari, *L'Idea individuale e l'idea sociale nel diritto privato* (Turin, 1911, 343 pp.); F. Cosentini, *Il socialismo giuridico* (Milan, 1906, 38 pp.); and Georges Liet-Veaux, *La Continuité du droit interne; essai d'une théorie juridique des révolutions* (Paris, 1943, 467 pp.).

Soviet legal authorities to about 1937 followed Engels' theory that law is a class tool, and that with full socialization there will be no further need for it. Representative of this standpoint were P. I. Stuchka, *Revolyutsionnaya rol sovetskogo prava* [*Revolutionary Role of Soviet Law*] (3rd ed., Moscow, 1934, 158 pp.), and E. B. Pashukanis, *Obshchaya teoriya prava i marksizm* [*General Theory of Law and Marxism*] (3rd ed., Moscow, 1927, 128 pp.). Exponents of this theory were removed and the point of view of Vyshinsky (cited above), emphasizing the immediate necessity of dictatorship against capitalism, with the promise of democracy for the proletariat, took its place. A favorable essay in English on the early period is D. N. Pritt, "The Russian Legal System," in Margaret Cole, ed., *Twelve Studies in Soviet Russia* (London, 1933, 282 pp.), pp. 145-176. H. J. Berman, "The Challenge of Soviet Law," *Harvard Law Review*, LXII (Dec. 1948-Jan. 1949), pp. 220-265, 449-466, advises Americans to profit both by Soviet mistakes and accomplishments, and to answer the Russian challenge by striking a new balance in law between private initiative and social integration. Berman has now published his articles in book form under the title, already cited, *Justice in Russia; an Interpretation of Soviet Law* (Cambridge, Mass., 1950, 322 pp.). For further references see J. N. Hazard and W. B. Stern, *Bibliography of the Principal Materials on Soviet Law* (New York, 1945, 46 pp.).

The socialists of the progressive era combined an elementary class-struggle theory with simple environmentalism in their criticism of social disorganization, political corruption, and the injustice of the courts. They accepted the attack of Judge B. B. Lindsey and H. J. O'Higgins,

The Beast (New York, 1910, 340 pp.), as their own. A. L. Benson, *Our Dishonest Constitution* (New York, 1914, 182 pp.), took up the findings of C. A. Beard on the class origin of the federal constitution. Frank Parsons, a mutualist, contributed *Legal Doctrine and Social Progress* (New York, 1911, 219 pp.).

After 1929, socialists accepted President Roosevelt's attack on the Supreme Court and emphasized the injustices of legal procedure. The essential answer to the argument that planning is a government of men and not of laws is the socialist reply that judges, too, are men. See L. P. Goldberg and Eleanor Levenson, *Lawless Judges* (intro. by M. R. Cohen; New York, 1935, 303 pp.); Arnold Petersen, *The Supreme Court; Watch Dog of Capitalism* (New York, 1937, 46 pp.), a Socialist Labor Party pamphlet; L. B. Boudin, "The Supreme Court and Civil Rights," *Science & Society*, i (Spring 1937), pp. 273-309, and "Is Economic Planning Constitutional? A Re-Examination of the Concept of Public Interest," *Georgetown Law Journal*, xxi (Mar. 1933), pp. 253-434; Harry Slochower, "The Marxist Idea of Change and Law," *Science & Society*, viii (Fall 1944), pp. 345-353; and G. G. Olshausen, "Rich and Poor in Civil Procedure," *ibid.*, xi (Winter 1947), pp. 11-37.

The Marxian school of criminology, which was strongest in Italy, regarded the exploitation of the workers as the greatest crime, and the resulting poverty as the chief cause of the traditional crimes. Greed and poverty alike could only be ended, and crime with them, by a collectivized society guaranteeing peace and plenty. Enrico Ferri, leader of the Italian Socialist Labor Party in the 1890's, was outstanding in a field which included Achille Loria, Gabriel Tarde, Corre, Manouvrier, Pepitone, Andrea Costa, Barbuto, and Battaglia. See his *Criminal Sociology* (1881; tr. from the French ed. of 1905 by J. I. Kelly and John Lisle; ed. by W. W. Smithers; Boston, 1917, 577 pp.), and *The Positive School of Criminology; Three Lectures Given at the University of Naples* (tr. by Ernest Untermann; Chicago, 1906, 125 pp.). See also Filippo Turati, *Il delitto e la questione sociale* (Milan, 1883, 128 pp.).

Samples from other European countries include P. A. Kropotkin, *In Russian and French Prisons* (London, 1887, 387 pp.); Hermann Seuffert, *Anarchismus und Strafrecht* (Berlin, 1899, 219 pp.); Edward Carpenter, *Prisons, Police and Punishment; an Inquiry into the Causes and Treatment of Crime and Criminals* (London, 1905, 153 pp.), essentially anarchist; C. E. B. Russell and L. M. Rigby, *The Making of the Criminal* (New York, 1906, 362 pp.); Robert Blatchford, *Not Guilty; a Defence of the Bottom Dog* (New York, 1918, 166 pp.); and Victor Serge, *Les Hommes dans la prison* (Paris, 1930, 308 pp.), a fictionalized autobiography dealing with French prisons. See also the exposition and criticism of Russian penology by Mariano Ruiz Funes, "El derecho penal de los soviets,"

Revista de criminología, psiquiatría y medicina legal, xv (Nov.-Dec. 1928), pp. 703-796; Helen (von der Leyen) von Koerber, *Soviet Russia Fights Crime* (New York, 1935, 240 pp.), a favorable report of a six months' visit in 1932 by a German penologist; and M. S. Callcott, *Russian Justice* (New York, 1935, 265 pp.), the best available survey.

American socialists made no original contributions in theory. One of the earliest essays was by the non-Marxian radical K. P. Heinzen, *Mankind the Criminal; a Lecture Delivered in Washington, D.C.* (tr. by C. P.; Roxbury, Mass., 1864?, 24 pp.). C. S. Darrow, the famous trial lawyer who defended many socialists and other radicals, subscribed to the socio-economic theory and inclined toward Tolstoyan anarchism. He wrote from his long experience, *Resist Not Evil* (Chicago, 1903, 179 pp.), and *Crime; Its Cause and Treatment* (New York, 1922, 292 pp.). See also his negative argument against A. J. Talley in *Debate; Resolved, That Capital Punishment Is a Wise Public Policy* (New York, 1924, 62 pp.); and biographies by C. Y. Harrison, *Clarence Darrow* (New York, 1931, 380 pp.), and Irving Stone, *Clarence Darrow for the Defense* (Garden City, N.Y., 1941, 570 pp.). More strictly anarchist was Emma Goldman, "Prisons; a Social Crime and Failure," in her *Anarchism and Other Essays* (New York, 1910, 277 pp.), pp. 115-132. The unions have been more eloquent against the competition of convict labor than the socialists, although E. V. Debs wrote "Prison Labor," *Progressive Thought,* i, No. 4 (Apr. 1899), pp. 1-12, and Walter Wilson, *Forced Labor in the United States* (New York, 1933, 192 pp.), prepared under the direction of the Labor Research Association.

American anarchists and socialists have had their share of prison experiences to record. Here again, profound as these experiences have sometimes been, nothing new has been written aside from a documentation of the variations within the American system of treating its rebels. E. V. Debs, incarcerated for contempt of court in the Pullman strike, is said to have gone into prison an industrial union leader and to have come out a nascent socialist, although some scholars label this a myth. In *Walls and Bars* (Chicago, 1927, 248 pp.), he describes his life both during his first sentence and after World War I at Atlanta Penitentiary. Dorothy Johns, sentenced for violating a Los Angeles ordinance regulating street speeches, gives the socio-economic answer in *Victims of the System; How Crime Grows in Jail and City Hall* (Los Angeles, 1908, 20 pp.). Other examples among the socialists are Bouck White, *Letters from Prison* (Boston, 1915, 163 pp.), about Blackwell's Island; Donald Lowrie, *My Life in Prison* (New York, 1912, 422 pp.), about San Quentin, California, and *My Life out of Prison* (New York, 1915, 345 pp.), on the probation system; and K. R. O'Hare, *Prison Letters* (Girard, Kan., 1919, 95 pp.), and *In Prison* (1920; New York, 1923, 211 pp.), a year's term at Jefferson City, Missouri, and the treatment of federal women prisoners there. For anarchist prison literature see J. A. Clay, *A Voice from the Prison* (Boston, 1856, 362 pp.); Alexander Berkman, *Prison Memoirs of an Anarchist* (New York, 1912, 512 pp.), and with Emma Goldman, *A Fragment of the Prison Experience of Emma Goldman and Alexander Berkman* (New York, 1919, 25 pp.); and the pamphlet about the trial of Jacob Abrams and four other anarchists, *Sentenced to Twenty Years Prison* (New York, 1918?, 32 pp.), published by the Political Prisoners Defense and Relief Committee, strongly pro-Bolshevik.

PART VI

Socialist Aesthetic Theory and Practice and Their Effects on American Art and Literature

For discussion in Volume 1 relevant to this Part (PART VI) of the Bibliography, see especially Chapters 13 and 14.

General Reading

ALL varieties of socialist literature and art (in PART VI, "art" is occasionally used inclusively, but is generally meant in the narrow sense excluding the arts which communicate primarily through words) have certain characteristics in common. In all forms of socialism the arts are considered not ends in themselves, but means to other and communal ends—utilitarian, religious, cultural, propagandistic, etc. For this reason the doctrine of "art for art's sake" has never prevailed under socialism, the individual artist being expected to achieve self-expression by devoting himself to social goals. As a result, communally useful arts tend to be stressed, with little or no distinction between craft art and fine art. Paradoxically, however, individualism does play an important part in determining the theories of art peculiar to a given socialism, for they are usually much affected by the individual beliefs and cultural background of the leader or prophet of the group. Thus the relation of the artist to both the community as a whole and to the theories of the prophet need careful investigation.

The various types of socialism in America and elsewhere, while possessing common characteristics in the arts which they fostered, also necessarily differ considerably in their respective attitudes toward the nature and worth of art and literature. In most of the religious communities—and particularly in the pietistic groups—the arts have usually been looked upon as worldly and therefore with considerable suspicion. The Protestant background of the religious socialisms in America has to some degree given rise to fear of "popish" elaboration, so that even those arts useful for communal worship—such as the architecture of the meetinghouse, hymnology, etc.—have been kept very simple in form.

The liberal communitarians, with their romantically optimistic belief in the possibilities of improving society and the individual in this world, have usually given much more importance to the arts and to literature as offering possibilities for the development of the individual through the cultural development of the group. Consequently, the arts have played a much more important role in their theory than in the theories of the religious communists, and a consciously cultural role at that. The belief of the liberal communitarians in the supreme power of reason to move man resulted in an emphasis, in theory, on rationally ordered composition in art, but their theories were rarely carried out in practice.

Nowhere has European Marxist leadership been more advanced than in art and literature. It is therefore pertinent to consider European Marxist aesthetic theory and practice in relation to European artistic tradi-

421

tions, and in relation to the influence of European Marxist arts and literature in the United States.

In Marxian theory and practice, the arts, though stressed, have been
considered subordinate to economic and political problems. As neither
Marx nor Engels ever directly formulated a complete aesthetic, bitter
disputes have developed over the proper interpretation of their scattered
statements applicable to the arts and literature. Nevertheless, Marxians
have all tended to reckon with the central ideas which Marx introduced
into socialism or to which he gave a new meaning: the class struggle,
historical or dialectical materialism, and organicism.

The idea of the class struggle has raised the question of a proletarian
art and literature. Because art for the socialist must have social significance, such questions as the responsibility of the individual artist to
society and the amount of freedom to be allowed him are immediately
raised. These in turn are related to the problem of censorship and of the
relation of art to propaganda.

The Marxian believes in progress toward the classless society, not
the continuous progress of the pre-Marxians, but following an irregular,
dialectical course. What then is the relation between the proletarian arts
of the class struggle and the arts of the classless society? The activist
role of the Marxist in forwarding the historical dialectic accounts for
his emphasizing the arts as propaganda more than his predecessors did.
At the same time the Marxist relies on critical comprehension and assimilation of ancient, feudal, and capitalist tradition. This dualism necessarily raises problems of artistic style. The Marxist today is also faced by
the question as to whether works of art should express the international
values of socialism (as Trotsky believed), or national values (emphasized
by the Stalinists as part of the socialism preceding full communism)
which are more likely to involve the use of traditional and local artistic
forms and media. The mechanistic determinism of Bukharin also influenced art before it was declared anathema by the Stalinists.

The whole problem of modernism and internationalism versus tradition
and national regionalism has been complicated by the belief of most
Marxians that art must be easily comprehended by the masses. Marxian
"modernists," who have followed futurist, cubist, and other international
abstract currents of modern art, have been opposed by Marxians who
insist that art must be more literal in order to be understood and used by
the proletariat. This raises the question as to just what artistic and
literary usefulness is. The emphasis on utility has in general tended
toward types of functionalism or photographic realism, and functionalism
in turn is related to the doctrine of organicism. A work of art, according
to this theory, must grow out of its natural, social, and particular requirements, just as an organism evolves to fulfill its functions in its en-

vironment. While Marxism tends toward functional and organic points of view in art and literature, functionalism and organicism have, of course, many nonsocialist adherents.

There is no single book covering the general subject of socialist art and/or literature in the United States. Nor are there books covering the art or literature of even a single major type of American socialism, whether religious or secular, pre-Marxian or Marxian. The relative lack of attention to socialist aesthetic theory and practice is the result of the absence of a strong American socialist movement and the subordinate position of socialist aesthetics in theory and practice. American individualism and middle-class spirit have limited the direct influence of socialism on the arts in the United States to comparatively small groups, even though its indirect influence has been great.

This General Reading—after an introductory paragraph of material sampling the whole field—will deal first with foreign socialist theory and practice in art and literature where these have influenced the United States. A few of the most comprehensive and representative materials on American socialist literature and art then follow. In order that most writings referring more directly to the United States and specifically to American socialism may be cited in the special topics, the General Reading includes those items whose bearing on American socialist literature and socialist art is either very general or indirect.

1. Introductory Selections

The following six selections will give a taste of the arts and literature of the major types of socialism, both European and American. Edward Deming Andrews, author of several excellent monographs on Shaker arts, treats hymn verse, music, and the dance, arts which—with architecture—were closest to the core of Shaker beliefs, in *The Gift to Be Simple; Songs, Dances and Rituals of the American Shakers* (New York, 1940, 170 pp.). See its selected bibliography, pp. 160-163. Étienne Cabet, *Voyage en Icarie* (1840; Paris, 1845, 600 pp.), not only an example of a nineteenth-century European novel, but the inspiration for the Icarian movement in the United States, refers specifically to the place of the arts under strict communism on pp. 40-51, 123-128, 219-241, and 267-272. William Morris was a central figure in early English socialism and in the arts and crafts movement. Morris' chief writings and lectures on the arts in relation to socialism are most easily consulted in the volume, *On Art and Socialism; Essays and Lectures by William Morris* (ed. by Holbrook Jackson; London, 1947, 335 pp.). American political socialism, as a movement rather than as a realized condition of society, has been strong in the arts of propaganda, particularly in literature. See, however, a collection of socialist cartoons, with autobiographical commentary, by A. H.

Young, *Art Young, His Life and Times* (New York, 1939, 467 pp.), taken from various periodicals for which Young worked. Granville Hicks and others, eds., *Proletarian Literature in the United States* (New York, 1935, 384 pp.), an anthology, tried to select the best writing in the various genres which had been influenced by Marxism in the previous decade. For a sample of American Marxian criticism, see Joseph Freeman's introduction to that volume, pp. 9-28. Although it is unfriendly to Stalinism, Kurt London, *The Seven Soviet Arts* (New Haven, Conn., 1938, 381 pp.), is probably the most useful factual account of the first two decades of the Soviet arts, which influenced leftist artists everywhere especially in the nineteen-thirties.

2. Art, Literature, and Socialism Abroad

A. THE PRE-MARXIANS. It should be noted at once that European pre-Marxian treatments of the arts and literature were in general of minor importance to American communitarians. The sources cited in PART I, Topic 2, are of course literature in the broadest sense, and those of PART I, Topic 6, in particular. The writings of Robert Owen, Charles Fourier, and Étienne Cabet are more immediately connected with a specific art because of their frequent and direct references to community architecture. These references result from the fact that the environment which they conceived to be necessary for successful community life had to be planned and built. Robert Owen described several times the village communities of his "New Plan," but the best description of the architectural layout of such a community as Owen conceived it just before the New Harmony venture is in his "Report to the County of Lanark," submitted May 1, 1820, and published in 1821. This is most accessible in Robert Owen, *A New View of Society and Other Writings* (ed. by G. D. H. Cole; New York, 1927, 298 pp.), pp. 245-298. Owen described various other projects, an important one being *A Development of the Principles and Plans on Which to Establish Self-Supporting Home Colonies* (London, 1841, 79, 47, 12 pp.), illustrated, with plan. In these plans, Owen became the pioneer advocate of group housing, originally motivated by his desire as a benevolent employer to increase the efficiency of his workmen. The contrast between Owen's ideal projects and his community at New Harmony is obvious if his various proposals are compared with the actual architecture of New Harmony as seen in contemporary sketches, made by a French artist, C. A. Lesueur. These sketches, today in the Museum of Natural History at Le Havre, include some fifty-four made in and around New Harmony between 1826 and 1838. Photographs of these are owned by the American Antiquarian Society. See especially R. W. G. Vail, "The American Sketchbooks of a French Naturalist,"

American Antiquarian Society, *Proceedings,* N.S., Vol. 28, Pt. 1 (Apr. 1938), pp. 49-155.

The most important work of Fourier on the subject of housing is his *Cités ouvrières* (Paris, 1849, 39 pp.), originally published in *Phalange.* For brief descriptions of the phalanstery in English, see *Selections from the Works of Fourier* (tr. by Julia Franklin; London, 1901, 208 pp.), pp. 137-154, and a translation of Victor Considérant, "Architecture," in the *Harbinger,* I (Aug. 16-Sept. 6, 1845), pp. 145-147, 161-163, 181-185, 193-196. The fullest expression of Considérant's views on the architecture of the phalanstery is *Considérations sociales sur l'architectonique* (Paris, 1834, xlix, 84 pp.), illustrated. See also his *Destinée sociale* (2nd ed., Paris, 1848-1849, 2 vols.), I, pp. 303-359, with folding illustration of a plan and three views, and *Description du phalanstère et considérations sociales sur l'architect onique* (2nd ed., Paris, 1848, 111 pp.). For Fourier's comments on other arts, such as opera, both in the existing society and in his harmonial order, see his *Oeuvres complètes* (2nd ed., Paris, 1841-1845, 6 vols.), I, pp. 226-236; III, pp. 348-451; and v, pp. 71-84.

One product of the École Sociétaire, which maintained Fourierist principles, was G.-D. Laverdant, *De la mission de l'art et du rôle des artistes* (Paris, 1845, 64 pp.), which appeared originally in the 1845 volume of *Phalange.* The English Christian socialist and cooperator E. V. Neale describes the housing arrangements of J. B. A. Godin's Familistère at Guise in a published lecture, *Associated Homes* (London, 1880, 29 pp.). In addition to Cabet's novel, cited above, see Jules Prudhommeaux, *Icarie et son fondateur, Étienne Cabet* (Paris, 1907, 688 pp.), pp. 126-144, 174-176, for the sources of Cabet's utopianism and other comments. Two obscure titles illustrating the influence of Owenism on other arts are Joseph Marriott, *Community; a Drama* (Manchester, Eng., 1838, 64 pp.); and *Social Hymns for . . . Friends of the Rational System of Society* (Leeds, Eng., 1840, 176 pp.). A recent book which contains some material on socialism (especially utopian socialism) and city planning is Gaston Bardet, *Le Nouvel urbanisme* (Paris, 1948, 336 pp.).

The anarchist P. J. Proudhon, an older contemporary of Marx, was a friend of the painter Courbet, founder of "realism." Proudhon expanded a brief commentary on Courbet's painting "Le Retour de la conférence" into a discussion of art as a social phenomenon, *Du principe de l'art et de sa destination sociale* (Paris, 1865, 380 pp.), incomplete at the time of his death. J. G. Lossier, *Le Rôle social de l'art selon Proudhon* (Paris, 1937, 203 pp.), and J. C. Sloane, "The Tradition of Figure Painting and Concepts of Modern Art in France from 1845 to 1870," *Journal of Aesthetics and Art Criticism,* VII (Sept. 1948), pp. 1-29, discuss Proudhon's theories and his relation to Courbet.

B. Marxian Theory of Art and Literature Abroad. For convenience in discussing Marxian aesthetic theories abroad the subject will be divided into two subsections. The first of these will be devoted to France, England, and Germany, and will deal both with Marxian theories in those countries before the rise of Soviet Russia and with later developments not fundamentally affected by Soviet Russia. The second subsection will consider Soviet art theories and their influence on the Continent and in England.

With Marxism, material on the relation of socialism to aesthetic theory became much more voluminous. The principal passages of Marx and Engels referring to the arts have been brought together in the volume, *Literature and Art, by Karl Marx and Frederick Engels: Selections from Their Writings* (New York, 1947, 154 pp.), with references, intended as the first of a series on the subject. An earlier collection was edited by Jean Fréville, *Sur la littérature et l'art: Karl Marx, Friedrich Engels* (Paris, 1936, 204 pp.). For the ideas of Marx and Engels that new housing for workers was bad insofar as it postponed the revolution by ameliorating the condition of the workers, see *The Communist Manifesto* (first issued in London in 1848), and Engels, *The Housing Question* (1872; London, 1942, 100 pp.). Extracts from the latter are found in Emile Burns, ed., *A Handbook of Marxism* (New York, 1935, 1087 pp.), pp. 338-348. Also consult in Burns "The Programme of the Communist International," p. 998. A Russian analysis of Marx's aesthetic is Mikhail Lifshitz' essay in the Critics Group Series, No. 7, *The Philosophy of Art of Karl Marx* (New York, 1938, 94 pp.). For Engels' opinion of the relation of the artistic superstructure to the economic base consult the note by Kurt Blaukopf, then a civil servant in Palestine, "Frederick Engels and Materialistic Aesthetics," *Modern Quarterly* (London), N.S., i (Summer 1946), pp. 74-77. Other Marxian critics are more concerned with the aesthetics of Marx's followers, although they also refer to the founders.

In considering the period before 1917, it seems clear that socialist art history and theory had developed furthest in France, but during that period French socialism had relatively little reference to the United States and little influence upon American socialist theory. J. M. Gros, *Le Mouvement littéraire socialiste depuis 1830* (Paris, 1904, 322 pp.), was almost the only criticism anywhere to seek to go back of Marx. Other French examples include Paul Hippeau, *Les Fédérations artistiques sous la Commune* (Paris, 1890, 35 pp.); René Doumic, *Le Rôle social de l'écrivain* (Paris, 1896, 20 pp.); and G. F. Renard, *Critique de combat* (Paris, 1894-1897, 3 vols.).

In England, currents of nineteenth-century socialist thought came together in William Morris, whose works are cited in Part I. He contributed to utopian literature *A Dream of John Ball* (London, 1888, 141 pp.) and

News from Nowhere (London, 1891, 238 pp.), the latter first published serially in the Socialist League periodical, *Commonweal*. Of his numerous writings which particularly affected later points of view toward the arts, see *Art and Socialism* (London, 1884, 72 pp.); *Chants for Socialists* (1885; New York, 1935, 22 pp.); "The Socialist Ideal in Art," in Edward Carpenter, ed., *Forecasts of the Coming Century* (Manchester, Eng., 1897, 192 pp.), pp. 62-72, originally published in *New Review*, IV (Jan. 1891), pp. 1-8; *The Art of the People* (Chicago, 1902, 41 pp.); and *Architecture, Industry and Wealth* (London, 1902, 163 pp.). A useful selection of his writings on art is to be found in *William Morris, Artist, Writer, Socialist* (Oxford, 1936, 2 vols.), a collection of unpublished writings, edited with a biographical setting by his daughter, May Morris. For a detailed bibliography of his writings, see Temple Scott, *A Bibliography of the Works of William Morris* (London, 1897, 120 pp.). See also M. R. Grennan, *William Morris, Medievalist and Revolutionary* (New York, 1945, 173 pp.), with a full bibliographical list containing references to Morris studies in the half century after Scott; J. B. Glasier, *William Morris and the Early Days of the Socialist Movement* (London, 1921, 208 pp.); L. E. Grey, *William Morris, Prophet of England's New Order* (London, 1949, 386 pp.); and Margaret Cole, "The Fellowship of William Morris," *Virginia Quarterly Review*, XXIV (Spring 1948), pp. 260-277. A good discussion of Morris' ideas, together with those of John Ruskin, concerning the problem of the relation of art to industry is contained in II. A. Needham, *Le Développement de l'esthétique sociologique en France et en Angleterre au XIXe siècle* (Paris, 1926, 323 pp.).

After Morris, British socialism continued in its predominantly non-Marxian course and had little but pamphlet literature to contribute to the general problems of socialist aesthetics. See, for example, E. A. Phipson, *Art under Socialism* (London, 1895, 16 pp.); Oscar Wilde, *The Soul of Man under Socialism* (Boston, 1910, 63 pp.); J. C. Squire, *Socialism and Art* (London, 1907, 16 pp.); and Henry Holiday, *Art and Individualism* (London, 1910, 22 pp.).

Fabian socialism, of which William Morris did not approve, was nevertheless much influenced by his ideas, as can be seen in the Fabian Tract No. 177 by Arthur Clutton-Brock, *Socialism and the Arts of Use* (London, 1915, 14 pp.), an important document in the history of functionalism and of industrial design. Morris' influence also helped interest the Fabians and the guild socialists in the housing problem, and particularly in the garden-city movement, which originated with Ebenezer Howard's book, *To-morrow; a Peaceful Path to Real Reform* (London, 1898, 176 pp.), republished as *Garden Cities of To-morrow* (London, 1902, 167 pp.). See Dugald Macfadyen, *Sir Ebenezer Howard and the Town Plan-*

ning Movement (Manchester, Eng., 1933, 166 pp.). Howard was strongly influenced by the American Edward Bellamy. Bellamyite ideas of architecture under "Nationalism" and the growth of the garden-city movement in the United States are referred to in Topic 11. Raymond Unwin, the leading garden-city planner, was a Fabian. See his Fabian Tract No. 109, *Cottage Plans and Common Sense* (London, 1902, 15 pp.); and among his later writings, *Nothing Gained by Overcrowding! How the Garden City Type of Development May Benefit Both Owner and Occupier* (London, 1912, 24 pp.), a pamphlet of the Garden Cities and Town Planning Association, and *Housing & Town Planning* (Washington, 1937, 86 pp.). Another important garden-city planner was A. J. Penty, a father of guild socialism who is referred to in PART I, Topics 1 and 9.

Outstanding in GERMANY was Wilhelm Hausenstein, the author of "Versuch einer Soziologie der bildenden Kunst," *Archiv für Sozialwissenschaft und Sozialpolitik,* xxxvi (1913), pp. 758-794, and *Die Kunst und die Gesellschaft* (Munich, 1917, 291 pp.). Hausenstein influenced the Russian critic Bukharin and is suggestive on art as social expression. See also R. Frohme, *Die Arbeiterbewegung eine Kulturmacht* (Berlin, 1910, 32 pp.).

The profound influence of Morris' ideas on the Continent, especially in Germany and Austria, eventually affected American art. For background see especially Nikolaus Pevsner, *Pioneers of the Modern Movement from William Morris to Walter Gropius* (London, 1936, 240 pp.). A considerable number of European artists influenced by Morris were Marxists, notably the architect H. P. Berlage, who built the headquarters of the Dutch Diamond Workers' Union and who justified his return to medieval forms in terms of historical materialism. See his essay, *Over de waarschijnlijke ontwikkeling der architektuur* (Delft, 1905, 38 pp.). See also Pevsner's *Academies of Art* (Cambridge, Eng., 1940, 323 pp.), and Walter Behrendt, *Modern Building* (New York, 1937, 241 pp.), *passim.*

The Continental tradition of housing erected by municipalities—a tradition stemming from the Middle Ages—combined with revisionism, state socialism, and Christian socialism to help encourage the public housing movement. An introduction to the housing question and its literature, focused on Europe, is C. J. Fuchs's article in the *Handwörterbuch der Staatswissenschaften* (4th ed., Jena, 1923-1929, 9 vols.), "Wohnungsfrage und Wohnungswesen," *Ergänzungsband,* pp. 1098-1160.

The Bauhaus was organized in Germany after World War I under the leadership of Walter Gropius. While Gropius himself can best be described as a liberal, and while political activity was banned at the Bauhaus, many members of the faculty and student body were much interested in the social implications of art, but chiefly from a point of view more like that of Morris than Marx though stressing modern industry and technology much more than Morris. The Bauhaus designers led, with other architects of the International Style, in carrying on the development of the type of housing with long parallel rows oriented to the sun. One of these designers, Mies van der Rohe, a nonsocialist who later became head of the Bauhaus, was the director of the influential housing exhibition at Stuttgart in 1928, in which the leaders of the International Style all participated. For the work of the Bauhaus see Walter Gropius, *The New Architecture and the Bauhaus* (tr. by P. M. Shand; New York, 1937, 80 pp.); *Bauhaus, 1919-1928* (New York, 1938, 224 pp.), published by the Museum of Modern Art and edited by Herbert Bayer, Walter Gropius, and Ise Gropius; and László Moholy-Nagy, *The New Vision* (New York, 1938, 207 pp.). Moholy-Nagy was to some degree stimulated by Russian constructivists who had left Russia because of Lenin's disapproval (Topic 12 below). Largely because of its nonnational spirit, the Bauhaus was closed by the Nazis as "bolshevistic" in 1933, after which many of its leading figures eventually came to the United States. Hannes Meyer, a communist who succeeded Gropius briefly as director, had been forced out when his communism became known, and had gone to the Soviet Union, where he spent several years.

With the rise of SOVIET RUSSIA in 1917, the direct influence of Marxism on American art and literature had much increased, and the bibliography for the period is consequently given in more detail. Aesthetic theories stemming from Russia have been known to Americans almost entirely through writings published in English. For this reason, general works on the theory and criticism of art in the U.S.S.R. are cited here with emphasis on those written in English. Two useful bibliographies covering all Soviet arts and literature are *Soviet Literature, Art, Music* (London, 1942, 48 pp.), and Amrei Ettlinger and J. M. Gladstone, *Russian Literature, Theatre and Art; a Bibliography of Works in English, Published 1900-1945* (London, 1947, 96 pp.), by two librarians commissioned by the Anglo-Soviet Public Relations Association. Ettlinger and Gladstone regard their work as a supplement to the references in the bibliography by Philip Grierson [see p. 21 herein] entitled *Books on Soviet Russia, 1917-1942*, and continued by him in the *Slavonic and East German Review*. See also the materials in the illustrated Stalinist periodicals, *Soviet Culture Review* (Moscow, 1931-1934), and *Information Bulletin* (Washington, 1941-), published by the Soviet Embassy, and the sympathetic *Soviet Russia Today* (New York, 1932-1951). General discussions in English include the Socialist Publication Society, *Education and Art in Soviet Russia, in the Light of Official Decrees and Documents* (foreword by Max Eastman; New York, 1919, 63 pp.); René Fülöp-Miller, *The Mind and Face of Bolshevism* (tr. by F. S. Flint and D. F. Tait; London, 1927, 308 pp.), able but hostile; the Soviet twentieth anniversary number of the London *Left Review*, III (Nov. 1937); and P. N. Milyukov, *Outlines of Russian Culture* (ed. by M. M. Karpovich; tr. by Valentine Ughet and Eleanor Davis; Philadelphia, 1942, 3 vols.), Volume 2 of which is on literature and Volume 3 on architecture, painting, and music. The English edition of *International Literature* (Moscow, 1931-), which superseded *Literature of the World Revolution* (Moscow, 1931), contains some of the essential art criticism by Russians, as well as a world coverage both in authors and subject matter, of critical and creative writing. See especially N. G. Chernyshevsky, "Life and Esthetics" (June-Oct. 1935), originally published in 1853; A. V. Lunacharsky, Lenin's commissar of education, "Basic Problems of Art" (Dec. 1935), pp. 43-61, an analysis of Plekhanov's views; "Lenin and Art" (May 1935), pp. 66-71; "Lenin and Literature" (Jan. 1935), pp. 55-83; and A. Lavretsky, "Gorky on Socialist Realism" (Apr. 1937), pp. 87-95. The *Critics Group Series* (New York, 1936-1939, 12 nos.), contains essays by Soviet and earlier Marxian writers on Shakespeare (No. 2), Cervantes (No. 1), Pushkin (No. 4), Balzac (No. 5), and Ibsen (No. 6), as well as G. V. Plekhanov, *Art and Society*, No. 3 (New York, 1937, 93 pp.), and *Literature and Marxism; a Controversy*, by Soviet critics, edited by Angel Flores, No. 9 (New York, 1938, 95 pp.). The pamphlet by Plekhanov includes "French Drama and Painting of the Eighteenth Century" as well as the title essay. E. J. Simmons, ed., *USSR; a Concise Handbook* (Ithaca, N.Y., 1947, 494 pp.), pp. 384-466, with selected bibliographies, contains favorable factual statements of major contemporary developments in all the arts, and John Somerville, *Soviet Philosophy* (New York, 1946, 269 pp.), pp. 116-145, is a good summary of the philosophy of socialistic realism which has prevailed in Russia since the middle thirties. Somerville summarizes, pp. 213-228, the pivotal controversies in the history of Soviet philosophy, which have profoundly affected the arts.

Lenin's attitude toward the arts and literature can best be seen in his own *Materialism and Empirio-Criticism* (*Collected Works*, XIII; New York, 1927, 342 pp.); his essays on Leo Tolstoy in the *Selected Works* (New York, 1935-1938, 12 vols.), XI, pp. 681-691; and "Party Organization and Party Literature," *Dialectics*, No. 5 (1938), pp. 1-5. See also, besides Lunacharsky's essays cited above, Klara Zetkin, *Reminiscences of Lenin* (New York, 1934, 64 pp.); V. P. Polonsky, curator of the Moscow Museum of Fine Arts, "Lenin's Views of Art and Culture," taken from his *Ocherki literaturnogo dvizheniya revolyutsionnoi epokhi* (Moscow, 1928) and translated by Max Eastman, *Artists in Uniform* (New York, 1934, 261 pp.), pp. 217-252; and B. S. Meilakh, *Lenin i problemy russkoi literatury* (Moscow, 1947, 370 pp.). Jean Fréville has edited quotations from both Lenin and Stalin in the collection, *Sur la littérature et l'art: V. I. Lénine, J. Staline* (Paris, 1937, 169 pp.).

Among the leading Soviet theorists at various times were Bukharin, Trotsky, and Gorky. N. I. Bukharin's point of view, later condemned by Stalinists as mechanistic, may be found in *Historical Materialism* (New York, 1925, 318 pp.), pp. 188-203, and the International pamphlet, *Culture in Two Worlds* (New York, 1934, 31 pp.). For Leon Trotsky, see especially his *Literature and Revolution* (tr. by Rose Strunsky; New York, 1925, 255 pp.), and his article dealing with Diego Rivera, who secured a Mexican refuge for him, "Art and Politics," *Partisan Review*, v (Aug.-Sept. 1938), pp. 3-10, translated by Nancy and Dwight Macdonald. V. F. Calverton, "The Sociological Aesthetics of the Bolsheviki," *American Journal of Sociology*, xxxv (Nov. 1929), pp. 383-392, assesses the theories of Trotsky and Lunacharsky on art in a proletarian dictatorship. Socialist realism, generally accepted in Russia after the expulsion of Trotsky, has been particularly well expounded by Maxim Gorky (pseud. for A. M. Peshkov). See his *Culture and the People* (New York, 1939, 224 pp.), essays written between 1927 and 1935, and his report, with others, in *Problems of Soviet Literature; Reports and Speeches at the First Soviet Writers' Congress [1934]* (ed. by H. G. Scott; Moscow, 1935, 278 pp.), as well as his *Autobiography* (tr. by I. Schneider; New York, 1949, 616 pp.), and the biography by A. I. Roskin, *From the Banks of the Volga; the Life of Maxim Gorky* (tr. by D. L. Fromberg; New York, 1946, 126 pp.). Among other important examples of Soviet artistic and literary criticism see M. I. Kalinin, "The Tasks of Soviet Art," V.O.K.S. *Bulletin* (Nov.-Dec. 1940), pp. 3-9, and A. V. Lunacharsky, *Russkaya literatura; izbrannye statyi* (Moscow, 1947, 429 pp.). For the party line in folklore see Y. M. Sokolov, *Russian Folklore* (tr. by C. R. Smith; New York, 1950, 760 pp.). Alexander Romm, *Matisse: a Social Critique* (tr. by Jack Chen; New York, 1947, 96 pp.), is a Marxian interpretation of the famous modern French painter, originally published in Russia in the mid-thirties.

A characteristic example of Russian literary criticism after World War II of special interest to Americans is M. Mendelson, *Soviet Interpretation of Contemporary American Literature* (tr. by D. B. Brown and R. W. Mathewson; Washington, 1948, 28 pp.), originally delivered in Moscow in April 1947 as a public lecture. For the cultural party line after World War II as expounded by A. A. Zhdanov (d. 1948), the secretary of the Central Committee of the Communist Party who led the postwar cultural purges in Russia, see his *Essays on Literature, Philosophy and Music* (New York, 1950, 96 pp.).

Criticism in Europe outside of Russia has felt the strong pull of Soviet standards. The following samples are taken from only three countries, Germany, France, and Great Britain, as being the most important countries whose languages, also, are widely read in the United States.

431

Among examples from GERMANY are Friedrich Muckle, *Das Kulturideal des Sozialismus* (Munich, 1919, 289 pp.); Paul Bekker, *Kunst und Revolution* (Frankfurt-am-Main, 1919, 33 pp.); Heinrich Vogeler, *Proletkult; Kunst und Kultur in der kommunistischen Gesellschaft* (Hannover, 1920, 15 pp.); and Leo Löwenthal, "Zur gesellschaftlichen Lage der Literatur," *Zeitschrift für Sozialforschung*, I (1932), pp. 85-102. Alfred von Martin, in *Sociology of the Renaissance* (London, 1944, 100 pp.; but originally published in Germany in 1932), interprets the art of the Renaissance as determined by economics and social class (pp. 62-65).

In FRANCE, Élie Faure, *L'Art et le peuple* (Paris, 1920, 14 pp.), is in a series issued by l'Université du Peuple; other numbers discuss the program of that institution, Henri Barbusse, and the plastic arts. One of the conclusions of Max Raphael, a student of Greek architecture and of French impressionism and postimpressionism, in *Proudhon, Marx, Picasso; trois études sur la sociologie de l'art* (Paris, 1933, 237 pp.), is that Picasso (who became a communist during World War II) represents the last phase of a decadent bourgeois art. See also Jean Fréville, "What Is the Marxist Approach to Literature?" *Dialectics*, No. 1 (1937), pp. 1-10; and Laurent Casanova, *Le Communisme, la pensée et l'art* (Paris, 1947, 20 pp.).

In ENGLAND, Eden and Cedar Paul wrote one of the few general works appearing before the depression, *Proletcult* (*Proletarian Culture*) (New York, 1921, 159 pp.). G. D. H. Cole, with ties among the Fabians and the Labour Party rather than communists, published his Hogarth lectures, *Politics and Literature* (London, 1929, 160 pp.), with bibliography. R. D. Charques, *Contemporary Literature and Social Revolution* (London, 1933, 195 pp.), was among the first in the thirties to assert the writer's obligation to recognize the class struggle, but did not insist on the use of proletarian subject matter. *Five on Revolutionary Art* (London, 1935, 87 pp.), by Herbert Read, Eric Gill, F. D. Klingender, A. L. Lloyd, and Alick West, is concerned with different aspects of the modern tendency toward abstraction in art, and all the authors but Read regarded it as symbolic of capitalist breakdown. West also contributed *Crisis and Criticism* (London, 1937, 199 pp.), and Klingender later wrote one of the best brief critical summaries, *Marxism and Modern Art* (London, 1943, 52 pp.), with a useful bibliography. He is also the author of *Hogarth and English Caricature* (London, 1945, 16 pp.), *Art and the Industrial Revolution* (London, 1947, 232 pp.), and *Goya: In the Democratic Tradition* (London, 1948, 235 pp.), all written from a Marxian point of view. Another art historian and critic whose writings, published in England, are Marxian in approach, is Frederick Antal: see his *Florentine Painting and Its Social Background* (London, 1947, 388 pp.), and "Remarks on the Method of Art History," *Burlington Magazine*, XCI

(Feb.-Mar. 1949), pp. 49-52, 73-75. Helen Rosenau, *The Painter Jacques-Louis David* (London, 1943, 83 pp.), on art of the era of the French Revolution, is also Marxian in spirit.

Many of the writings of the noted English art critic and poet, Herbert Read, have been published in American editions. He has visited the United States and has had a good deal of influence in this country. Read has been much stimulated by the writings of Ruskin, Morris, Sorel, Kropotkin, and Edward Carpenter as well as by those of Marx. For his ideas on art and politics see especially his partial autobiography, *The Innocent Eye* (New York, 1947, 268 pp.); his Yale lectures, *The Grass Roots of Art: Four Lectures on Social Aspects of Art in an Industrial Age* (New York, 1947, 92 pp.); *The Politics of the Unpolitical* (London, 1943, 160 pp.); *Poetry and Anarchism* (London, 1938, 126 pp.); *Art and Society* (New York, 1937, 282 pp.); *Art and Industry* (1934, 2nd ed., London, 1944, 188 pp.); and *Education through Art* (London, 1943, 320 pp.). See also Henry Treece, ed., *Herbert Read* (London, 1944, 120 pp.), which lists Read's works. George Thomson, professor of Greek at the University of Birmingham, derived the principle of poetry from the rhythms of labor in *Marxism and Poetry* (New York, 1946, 71 pp.). He has also investigated Greek literature from a Marxian point of view in *Aeschylus and Athens; a Study in the Social Origins of Drama* (London, 1941, 476 pp.); likewise in *Studies in Ancient Greek Society: the Prehistoric Aegean* (London, 1949, 621 pp.), which is only the first of a series projected by Thomson. Other British critics influenced by Marxism include J. S. Strachey, *Literature and Dialectical Materialism* (New York, 1934, 54 pp.), reprinted in part from periodicals; Cecil Day-Lewis, ed., *The Mind in Chains* (London, 1937, 255 pp.), essays which deal with music and literature as well as the visual arts; C. S. Sprigg (Christopher Caudwell, pseud.), *Studies in a Dying Culture* (London, 1938, 228 pp.); and Jack Lindsay, *A Short History of Culture* (London, 1939, 408 pp.). Sprigg died at thirty-one, fighting for Loyalist Spain. Typical of the English reaction against proletarian literature at the end of the decade was Harry Kemp and others, *The Left Heresy in Literature and Life* (London, 1939, 270 pp.). Vehicles for Stalinist criticism were the *Left Review* (London, 1934-1938), published by the British section of the Writers' International, and the *Modern Quarterly* (London, 1938-1939, 1945-), revived after World War II. *Polemic* (London, 1945-1947), edited by Humphrey Slater and to which George Orwell was a prominent postwar contributor, held an independent but leftist course. The *Anglo-Soviet Journal* (London, 1940-) and *Soviet Reconstruction Series*, a mimeographed bulletin compiled from Soviet sources, are published by the Society for Cultural Relations with the U.S.S.R., a British organization which includes separate sections on architecture and planning, the theater, and writing.

C. Marxian Practice in Art and Literature Abroad. From the socialist theory of art abroad we turn now to references dealing primarily with socialist practice in art and literature there. While this bibliography cannot comment in great detail on the many examples of European socialist creative arts and literature, it will at least call attention to a few authors and artists, by countries, who have been most influential in the United States. The writers of Great Britain, because they share with Americans a common language and culture, and the artists and writers of the Soviet Union, because of the world influence of communism, have received the most American attention, and will be discussed first. After that, mention will be made of other specific Marxian developments in the art and literature of the Continent, of Latin America, of China, and finally, of the United States.

In England in the period before World War I, most of the socialist "literature" consisted of propaganda in literary form but of only documentary value. J. S. Clarke, *Satires, Lyrics and Poems, Chiefly Humorous* (intro. by Patrick Lavin; Glasgow, 1919, 184 pp.), a Socialist Labour Press publication in the style of Kipling, may be taken to represent these undistinguished materials. G. B. Shaw and H. G. Wells were in a different class, and immensely popular in the United States, apart from their socialism. See E. Strauss, *Bernard Shaw: Art and Socialism* (London, 1942, 126 pp.), by no means definitive, but an introduction to the playwright's works by a Marxian; and H. G. Wells, *Experiment in Autobiography* (New York, 1934, 718 pp.). Independent Labour Party songs, with a Christian socialist ring, formed the staple of American socialist songbooks. Most important among many collections was Edward Carpenter, *Chants of Labour* (1888; illus. by Walter Crane; London, 1905, 99 pp.), with its famous "England Arise!" with words and music by Carpenter. See also William Morris, *Chants for Socialists* (New York, 1935, 22 pp.), issued in 1885 by the Socialist League; J. B. Glasier, ed., *Socialist Songs* (Glasgow, 1893, 94 pp.); and F. W. L. Adams, *Songs of the Army of the Night* (London, 1894, 132 pp.). William Morris, R. J. Derfel (Munullog, pseud.), James Connell, J. L. Joynes, Tom Maguire, and H. S. Salt wrote the words for some of the most popular songs, and the music for these was often taken from evangelical hymns, as in the case of the American I.W.W. Similar songs continued to be published after World War I: for example see Alan Bush and Randall Swingler, eds., *The Left Song Book* (London, 1938, 64 pp.).

English proletarian literature of the nineteen-thirties, and the writing affected by this fashion, was strong in poetry and weak in other forms.

John Sommerfield, *May Day* (London, 1936, 245 pp.), who made the London working class his protagonist, Randall Swingler, *No Escape* (London, 1937, 287 pp.), by an editor of the *Left Review*, and Arthur Calder-Marshall, *Pie in the Sky* (New York, 1937, 477 pp.), for example, do not measure up to the work of contemporary American proletarian novelists. But see George Orwell's satirical novel, *Nineteen Eighty-Four* (New York, 1949, 314 pp.), reviewed by Philip Rahv in the *Partisan Review*, xvi (July 1949), pp. 743-749. The English did contribute critical writing about the novel, such as Philip Henderson, *The Novel Today* (London, 1936, 312 pp.), and Ralph Fox, *The Novel and the People* (New York, 1937, 172 pp.); and also about the theater, for example, R. D. Charques, ed., *Footnotes to the Theatre* (London, 1938, 335 pp.). Sean O'Casey, author of such plays as *The Star Turns Red* (London, 1940, 183 pp.), about a Dublin transport workers' strike in 1913-1914, was a leading "proletarian" dramatist. The group of poets around W. H. Auden (now an American citizen), however, were pre-eminent. See especially W. H. Auden, *Spain* (London, 1937, 12 pp.), and with Louis MacNeice, *Letters from Iceland* (New York, 1937, 269 pp.); Stephen Spender, *Vienna* (New York, 1935, 37 pp.), his first—and not very successful—poetry influenced by leftism; Cecil Day-Lewis, *Overtures to Death and Other Poems* (London, 1938, 62 pp.); and other examples in Auden, *The Collected Poetry of W. H. Auden* (New York, 1945, 466 pp.), Spender, *Ruins and Visions; Poems, 1934-1942* (New York, 1942, 138 pp.), and Day-Lewis, *Selected Poems* (London, 1940, 80 pp.). Spender described his acceptance of communism in *Forward from Liberalism* (New York, 1937, 281 pp.). See also the compilation by Joan Beauchamp, *Poems of Revolt; a Twentieth Century Anthology* (London, 1924, 105 pp.). Spender's autobiography, *World within World*, will be published in 1951. C. S. Sprigg (Christopher Caudwell, pseud.), *Illusion and Reality* (London, 1937, 351 pp.), applied Marxian criticism to his own poems and achieved perhaps the most sensitive and comprehensive concrete expression of English Marxian aesthetic theory. The near-Marxian Philip Henderson contributed the substantial volume, *The Poet and Society* (London, 1939, 248 pp.). In the case of Auden and Spender, but not Day-Lewis, the leftist tincture of their thought had disappeared by World War II. Auden became a citizen of the United States in 1946, as did several others of this group during the war.

As for the practice of art and literature in SOVIET RUSSIA, American interest in it began because of the freedom with which Soviet artists at first experimented in new forms. After socialistic realism became the accepted standard, interest was sustained by curiosity about the arts under communism. And Soviet literature in particular continued to offer clues to the Russian communist's thought and imagination.

The leading descriptions and appraisals of Soviet arts and literature by Americans are Joseph Freeman, Joshua Kunitz, and Louis Lozowick, *Voices of October; Art and Literature in Soviet Russia* (New York, 1930, 317 pp.), pro-Stalinist, by two writers and a painter; and Max Eastman's anti-Stalinist *Artists in Uniform* (New York, 1934, 261 pp.), dealing mainly with literature. H. M. Kallen, "The Arts under Dictatorship," in his *Indecency and the Seven Arts* (New York, 1930, 246 pp.), pp. 100-129, cites the Italian Fascist dictatorship as unfavorable to the development of the arts, the Soviet dictatorship as favorable. In addition there are numerous articles in the American periodicals cited later.

For other general discussions and illustrations of the Soviet arts of design, see Louis Lozowick, *Modern Russian Art* (New York, 1925, 60 pp. and pls.); Geoffrey Holme, ed., *Art in the U.S.S.R.* (New York, 1935, 137 pp.); Jack Chen, *Soviet Art and Artists* (London, 1944, 106 pp.); the special Russian issue of the London *Studio*, cxxvii (Feb. 1944); Louis Réau, *L'Art russe* (Paris, 1945, 138 pp.); C. G. E. Bunt, *A History of Russian Art* (London, 1946, 272 pp.); and Helen Rubissow, *The Art of Russia* (New York, 1946, 32 pp. and 164 pls.). Likewise consult Arthur Voyce, *Russian Architecture* (New York, 1948, 282 pp.), which is especially useful; also the special Russian number of the *Architectural Review*, lxxi (May 1932); *Arkhitektura SSSR* (Moscow, 1933-); and Edward Carter, "Soviet Architecture Today," *Architectural Review*, xcii (Nov. 1942), pp. 107-114, partly reprinted in *Task*, No. 6 (Winter 1944-1945), pp. 38-45, but with different illustrations; T. F. Hamlin, "Style Development in Soviet Architecture," *American Quarterly on the Soviet Union*, Vol. 1, No. 1 (Apr. 1938), pp. 17-31; and Hannes Meyer, "The Soviet Architect," *Task*, No. 3 (Oct. 1942), pp. 24-32, by a former director of the Bauhaus. Two Russian books on public works, civic improvement, and city planning during the first Five Year Plan are L. M. Kaganovich, *The Socialist Reconstruction of Moscow and Other Cities in the U.S.S.R.* (Moscow, 1931, 125 pp.), and T. Kholodny, *Moscow—Old and New* (Moscow, 1933, 116 pp.). Representative of the many reports in periodical literature on Soviet city planning after World War II is "Reconstruction in the U.S.S.R.," *Architectural Review* (London), ci (May 1947), pp. 177-184.

None of the extensive materials on Soviet literature have sufficient detachment nor do they comprehend all the widely scattered and sometimes mutually antagonistic groups into which the Russian literary tradition splintered after 1917. General books on Soviet literature include N. I. Efimov, *Sotsiologiya Literatury* (Smolensk, 1927, 219 pp.); and Gleb Struve, *25 Years of Soviet Russian Literature* (London, 1944, 347 pp.), critical. A revised and considerably expanded edition of Struve's book will be published in 1951 by the University of Oklahoma Press under the title, *Soviet Russian Literature, 1917-50*. Probably the best sympathetic study in English is George Reavey, *Soviet Literature To day* (New Haven, Conn., 1947, 187 pp.). Reavey had previously edited and translated with Marc Slonim, *Soviet Literature; an Anthology* (New York, 1934, 426 pp.). English and American periodicals since 1929 have carried numerous articles on Soviet literature, e.g., Aleksei Tolstoy, "Trends in Soviet Literature," *Science & Society*, vii (Summer 1943), pp. 233-250; "The Soviet Literary Controversy," *Modern Quarterly* (London), N.S., ii (Winter 1946-1947), pp. 74-84, with John Lewis' editorial, pp. 3-15, defending these Russian statements as healthy, democratic criticism; Evgeny Almazov, "On the 'Tendentious' in Literature," *Mainstream*, i (Spring 1947), pp. 199-211; Alexander Rasumovsky, "The Soviet Literary Purge," *Partisan Review*, xv (Mar. 1948), pp. 323-331; and G. S. Counts and N. P. Lodge, *The Country of the Blind* (Boston, 1949, 378 pp.).

Soviet writers are versatile and have a huge public. Konstantin Simonov, for example, is a poet, journalist, novelist, and playwright. His Stalin Prize melodrama, *The Russian Question*, about an American newspaperman who finds that the U.S.S.R. is not belligerent, played in hundreds of theaters at once in 1947. M. A. Sholokhov, who grew up with the revolution, retained popular favor by writing nationalist, collectivist fiction, from *And Quiet Flows the Don* (tr. by Stephen Garry; New York, 1934, 755 pp.), the second part translated as *The Don Flows Home to the Sea* (New York, 1941, 777 pp.), to the war story, *Oni srazhalis za rodinu [They Fought for the Homeland]* (Moscow, 1943, 58 pp.). Other notable writers among a host include the poets Vladimir Mayakovsky, S. A. Esenin, and B. L. Pasternak; novelists translated into English: M. A. Aldanov, Ivan Bunin, Ilya Ehrenburg, Ilya Ilf, Aleksandra Kollontay, Vladimir Nabokov, and Aleksei Tolstoy; and playwrights: Aleksandr Korneichuk and N. F. Pogodin. Two American studies of Soviet poetry are A. S. Kaun, *Soviet Poets and Poetry* (Berkeley, Calif., 1943, 208 pp.), and G. Z. Patrick, *Popular Poetry in Soviet Russia* (Berkeley, Calif., 1929, 289 pp.), an account of peasant verse with translations. For an introduction to the Russian theater see H. W. L. Dana, ed., *Seven Soviet Plays* (New York, 1946, 520 pp.); Huntly Carter, *The New Spirit in the Russian Theatre, 1917-28; and a Sketch of the Russian Kinema and Radio, 1919-28, Showing the New Communal Relationship between the Three* (New York, 1929, 348 pp.); "The Theatre in the U.S.S.R.," *V.O.K.S.*, vi (1934), pp. 1-105, illustrated; Norris Houghton, *Moscow Rehearsals; an Account of Methods of Production in the Soviet Theatre* (New York, 1936, 291 pp.), illustrated, whose last chapter discusses possibilities of a "collective" theater in the United States; N. Y. Efimova, *Adventures of a Russian Puppet Theatre* (tr. by Elena Mitcoff; Birmingham, Mich., 1935, 199 pp.); and H. F. Griffith, ed., *Playtime in Russia* (London,

1935, 249 pp.), essays which cover political, film, musical, and amateur aspects of the drama as well as sport and children's play. H. W. L. Dana, *Handbook on Soviet Drama* (New York, 1938, 158 pp.), contains bibliography not only on the theater in Russia, but opera, ballet, and cinema as well.

The cinema has been for the Russian communists the most useful medium for dissemination of propaganda among the masses. The technical and artistic achievements of the Russian films are very great. S. M. Eisenstein (1898-1948), the outstanding Soviet director, in *The Film Sense* (1942; New York, 1947, 288 pp.), and in the posthumously published *Film Form; Essays in Film Theory* (ed. and tr. by Jay Leyda; New York, 1949, 279 pp.), developed a theory of the integration of sound, color, and picture. For the propagandistic aims of the Russian films, see Paul Rotha, *Documentary Film* (London, 1936, 272 pp.), pp. 97-103. Other general treatments are V. I. Pudovkin, *Film Technique* (tr. by Ivor Montagu; enl. ed., London, 1933, 204 pp.); Pudovkin, *Film Technique and Film Acting* (tr. by Montagu; New York, 1949, 153 pp.); Bryher (pseud.), *Film Problems of Soviet Russia* (London, 1929, 140 pp.); A. Arosev, ed., *Soviet Cinema* (Moscow, 1935, 312 pp.), a V.O.K.S. publication; Dwight Macdonald, "The Soviet Cinema, 1930-1938," *Partisan Review*, v (July 1938), pp. 37-50, (Aug.-Sept. 1938), pp. 35-62; vi (Winter 1939), pp. 80-95; and Thorold Dickinson and Catherine De La Roche, *Soviet Cinema* (London, 1948, 136 pp.). For a Russian account of the motion picture in the Soviet Union, see the outline history by Nikolai Lebedev, *Ocherk Istorii Kino S.S.S.R.* (Moscow, 1947).

Russian leadership in the dance was maintained under the Soviets, and the ballets of Stravinsky and others retained their popularity in the United States, apart from communist content which only some of them had. The best introduction is *The Soviet Ballet* (New York, 1947, 285 pp.); also see Iris Morley, *Soviet Ballet* (London, 1945, 71 pp.).

The only detailed guide in English to Soviet music, whose influence grew in the United States after 1930, is in Nicolas Slonimsky, *Music since 1900* (New York, 1938, 592 pp.). Alan Bush, president of the London Workers Music Association, edited a translation of the *Handbook of Soviet Musicians* (London, 1944, 101 pp.) by Igor Boelza, a professor at the Moscow State Conservatory. Heinz Unger, *Hammer, Sickle and Baton; the Soviet Memoirs of a Musician* (London, 1939, 275 pp.), written in collaboration with Naomi Walford, is a very unfavorable report of a German's experiences as a regular guest conductor in the Soviet Union, 1924-1937. Among the few Russian theoretical works in English are I. I. Kryzhanovsky, *The Biological Bases of the Evolution of Music* (tr. by S. W. Pring; London, 1928, 57 pp.), and, more important for the Marxian sociology of music, S. M. Chemodanov,

"An Economic Approach to Music," *Modern Music*, x (May-June 1933), pp. 175-181. Leading Russian composers living in the U.S.S.R. submitted to strong criticism from the Politburo in the winter of 1948 on account of the "marasmic" westernizing tendencies of their work (see the *New York Times*, Feb. 12, 1948). Sample biographies of this group include: A. A. Ikonnikov, *Myaskovsky, His Life and Work* (New York, 1946, 162 pp.); I. V. Nestyev, *Sergei Prokofiev* (tr. by Roza Prokofyeva; New York, 1946, 193 pp.); and I. I. Martynov, *Dmitri Shostakovich; the Man and His Work* (tr. by T. Guralsky; New York, 1947, 197 pp.). Prokofyev won his fifth Stalin Prize in 1947. Khachaturyan and others at times under criticism are discussed in *Eight Soviet Composers* (London, 1943, 102 pp.), sketches by Gerald Abraham, who had access to scores and programs not then available in the United States. Juri Jelagin, *Taming of the Arts* (tr. by Nicolas Wreden; New York, 1950, 333 pp.), is the life story of a musician in Soviet Russia who came to the United States after the ending of World War II. F. F. Rothe, "Russian Music," *Kenyon Review*, IV (Winter 1942), pp. 48-61, distinguishes three periods in Soviet theory, and comments on the economic elevation of composers and their moral dependence on official patronage. Norman Cazden, "What's Happening in Soviet Music?" *Masses & Mainstream*, I (Apr. 1948), pp. 11-24, defends the 1948 "purge" as against formalism and for democratic accessibility. For the best accounts of this purge in music see Alexander Werth, *Musical Uproar in Moscow* (London, 1949, 103 pp.), and G. S. Counts and N. P. Lodge, *The Country of the Blind* (Boston, 1949, 378 pp.). Virgil Thomson, the noted American composer who is music critic of the *New York Herald Tribune*, is republishing in his book, *Music Right and Left* (announced for 1951), three of his newspaper columns on Soviet Russian music and musical aesthetics. These, entitled "Composers in Trouble," "Soviet Aesthetics," and "Russians Recover," originally appeared in the *Herald Tribune* for February 22 and May 2, 1948, and February 27, 1949, respectively.

For the effects on art of the changing party line under Stalinism see especially the following periodicals: *Sovetskoe Iskusstvo* [*Soviet Art*], *Literaturnaya Gazeta* [*Literary Gazette*], *Sovetskaya Muzyka* [*Soviet Music*], *Arkhitektura SSSR* (cited above), and *Arkhitektura i Stroitelstvo* [*Architecture and Construction*].

In discussing socialist practice in art and literature in CONTINENTAL COUNTRIES other than Russia, we shall illustrate the relation of art and socialism here by examples chosen only from music and literature. Before the development of a sociology of music, in which German scholars pioneered, Wagner wrote several essays drenched with Schopenhauer and the rebellious romanticism of 1848. He argued confusedly that art, particularly his favorite music-drama, must be revolutionary as long as it was dominated and divided by private commercialism and bourgeois fashion, but could be conservative like Greek art once it became public, integrated, and in touch with the *Volk* spirit. See "Art and Revolution," *Richard Wagner's Prose Works* (tr. by W. A. Ellis; London, 1894-1900, 8 vols.), I, pp. 21-65; "The Art-Work of the Future," *ibid.*, pp. 67-248; as well as "Man and Established Society," *ibid.*, VIII, pp. 227-231, and "The Revolution," *ibid.*, pp. 232-238. It is therefore with some justification that George Bernard Shaw was able to find a hint of socialist symbolism in the "Ring" operas and report it in *The Perfect Wagnerite* (1898; New York, 1909, 151 pp.). See also T. W. Adorno, "Fragmente über Wagner," *Studies in Philosophy and Social Science*, VIII (1939), pp. 1-49. Karl Bücher's theory of the origin of music, developed in *Arbeit und Rhythmus* (1896; 6th ed., Leipzig, 1924, 497 pp.), is generally accepted by those few American socialists who are aware of it. An example of later German musicology is E. H. Meyer, *English Chamber Music* (London, 1946, 318 pp.). For a study of the music of the French Revolution see Julien Tiersot, *Les Fêtes et les chants de la Révolution française* (Paris, 1908, 323 pp.). A collection of the poems of Eugène Pottier, including the *Internationale*, set to music by Pierre Degeyter in 1888, is *Chants révolutionnaires* (1887; 3rd ed., pref. by Lucien Descaves; Paris, 1937, 277 pp.). Pottier, soon after his participation in the Paris Commune of 1871, was a refugee in the United States, where he wrote several of the poems in this collection. The composition of the *Internationale* is described in A. B. Zévaès, *Eugène Pottier et "L'Internationale"* (Paris, 1936, 62 pp.).

Since 1917 various Continental writers of Marxian leanings have had considerable influence in the United States. For the novelists among them, see especially Anna Seghers, *The Revolt of the Fishermen* (tr. by Margaret Goldsmith; New York, 1930, 172 pp.); Ernst Glaeser, *The Last Civilian* (tr. by Gwenda David and Eric Mosbacher; New York, 1935, 398 pp.); Arthur Koestler, an ex-communist combining Freudian and Marxian ideas in *Arrival and Departure* (New York, 1943, 180 pp.); and M. A. Nexø, *Pelle the Conqueror* (tr. by Jessie Muir and Bernard Miall; New York, 1917, 2 vols.). Harry Slochower discusses Nexø in "Socialist Humanism," *Three Ways of Modern Man* (New York, 1937, 240 pp.), chap. 3, including correspondence with Nexø in an appendix. Marxian and Freudian criticism of the novel are combined in Nicolas Calas, *Foyers d'incendie* (Paris, 1938, 261 pp.), by a Greek surrealist and follower of André Breton. See also three important articles by Georg Lukács in *International Literature*, "Essay on the Novel" (May 1936), pp. 68-74, "The Intellectual Physiognomy of Literary Characters" (Aug. 1936), pp. 55-83, and "Narration vs. Description" (June 1937), pp. 96-112, (July 1937), pp. 85-98; and another abridged and translated by

L. F. Mins, "Propaganda or Partisanship?" *Partisan Review*, ɪ (Apr.-May 1934), pp. 36-46. Lukács, a Hungarian who has published in several languages and has been called by Thomas Mann "perhaps the most important critic of literature today," is particularly noted for his studies of Goethe, of Balzac, Stendhal, and Zola, and of Nietzsche. The only book in English of Lukács' work is *Studies in European Realism* (tr. by Edith Bone; London, 1950, 277 pp.). One of his most famous works is *Karl Marx und Friedrich Engels als Literaturhistoriker* (Berlin, 1948, 244 pp.). Lukács has recently been attacked by Joseph Revai, the Hungarian Minister of Culture, for overidealizing the role of bourgeois realism in connection with Marxian aesthetics. This attack has been reprinted in *Masses & Mainstream*, ɪɪɪ (Sept. 1950-Oct. 1950), pp. 42-57, 86-96, under the title "Literature & People's Democracy."

For an introduction to Ignazio Silone's works dealing with the problems of fascism and revolution in Italy, consult the article by J. T. Farrell, "Ignazio Silone," *Southern Review*, ɪᴠ (Spring 1939), pp. 771-783. Notable among European communist poets have been Bertolt Brecht and Louis Aragon. See Brecht's *Selected Poems* (tr. by H. R. Hays; New York, 1947, 179 pp.), and Frida Stewart's essay, "Aragon; the Development of a Communist Poet," *Modern Quarterly* (London), N.S., ɪ (Summer 1946), pp. 41-56. The Dutch poets Henriette Roland Holst and Herman Gorter elaborated a new aesthetic based on Marxism which changed the whole orientation of modern Dutch literature. Roland Holst was at one time a communist but resigned before 1931.

In regard to socialist pictorial art on the Continent since 1917, special mention should be made of Pablo Picasso, a convert to communism late in life. As a sample of the many books on Picasso we cite only Paul Éluard, *Pablo Picasso* (tr. by J. T. Shipley; New York, 1947, 168 pp.), by the leftist and surrealist poet. Other references to the visual arts are made in the topics that follow this General Reading.

A list of communist and leftist writers in LATIN AMERICA should include among the poets the Cuban Negro Nicolás Guillen; the Chilean Gabriela Mistral; the Central American Indian diplomat Rubén Darío; the Argentinian Raul González Tuñon; and perhaps most important after Mistral Pablo Neruda. The development of this Chilean diplomat and politician from a vague anarchistic romantic into a communist is described in L. E. Delano's article, "Pablo Neruda; Poet in Arms," *Mainstream*, ɪ (Fall 1947), pp. 424-439. On a similar list of Latin American novelists would appear the Brazilian deputy Jorge Amado; the Ecuadorians José de la Cuadra, Enrique Gil-Gilbert, and Humberto Salvador; the Peruvian César Vallejo, and the Haitian scientist and poet Jacques Roumain. See *Masters of the Dew* (tr. by Langston Hughes and Mercer Cook; New

York, 1947, 180 pp.), by Roumain (1907-1944), and, for contrast, a novel by the Aprista Ciro Alegría, *Broad and Alien Is the World* (tr. by Harriet de Onís; New York, 1941, 434 pp.).

The Mexican fresco painters, such as the communists David Alfaro Siqueiros and Diego Rivera, and José Clemente Orozco (much less influenced by communist sympathies), have had great influence on American mural painting. General information on this school may be found in MacKinley Helm, *Modern Mexican Painters* (New York, 1941, 205 pp.); Carlos Mérida, *Modern Mexican Artists* (Mexico, D.F., 1937, 202 pp.); and Esther Born and Justino Fernández, *The New Architecture in Mexico* (New York, 1937, 159 pp.). Rivera turned Trotskyist and helped find a refuge for Trotsky in Mexico, but applied again for membership in the Communist Party. One of the earliest important publications of his work outside Mexico is *Das Werk des Malers Diego Rivera* (Berlin, 1928, 18 pp.), with text also in Russian. B. D. Wolfe, *Diego Rivera; His Life and Times* (New York, 1939, 420 pp.), has an excellent bibliography and is perhaps the best source for the background of the political beliefs of his school. For the work of Orozco outside the United States, see his *Autobiografía* (Mexico, D.F., 1945, 156 pp.), and Justino Fernández, *José Clemente Orozco* (Mexico, D.F., 1942, 183 pp., 209 pp.), which has the best bibliography on this artist who was never an active party member. See also D. A. Siqueiros, *No hay más ruta que la nuestra; importancia nacional e internacional de la pintura mexicana moderna* (Mexico, D.F., 1945, 126 pp.).

The modern musicians of Latin America, who combine European, Indian, and United States influence, have often been as much politically as musically to the left. Nicolas Slonimsky, *Music of Latin America* (New York, 1945, 374 pp.), includes, with a wealth of detail, discussion of the chief compositions and brief biographies of such musical progressives as Carlos Chávez, conductor of the Orquesta Sinfónica de México, José Pomar and Silvestre Revueltas, also Mexicans, and the Chilean Pablo Garrido. See also V. T. Mendoza, *El romance español y el corrido mexicano* (Mexico, D.F., 1939, 832 pp.), an analysis of a Mexican art-form often used as a vehicle for radical ballads, and on Chávez, the pamphlet published by the music division of the Pan American Union, *Carlos Chávez, Catalog of His Works* (Washington, 1944, xxxii, 15 pp.), with a biographical preface by Herbert Weinstock. Weinstock has translated Chávez' discussion of the music of electrical instruments and radio, *Toward a New Music; Music and Electricity* (New York, 1937, 180 pp.).

The theory of art and literature in communist China has been set in addresses delivered by Mao Tse-tung in 1942 and published under the title of *Problems of Art and Literature* (New York, 1950, 48 pp.).

3. Art, Literature, and Socialism in the United States

With the foreign background in mind, we can now consider socialist art and literature in the United States in some detail. Because there are no general books whatsoever, except for Marxian criticism, on the arts and literature of American socialism or major segments of it, the preliminary citations here on the earlier periods of American socialism will deal mostly with mere occasional references in volumes not concerned primarily with the arts and literature of socialism. In considering Marxian art in the United States, after reference to a few early writings, the principal Marxian periodicals which have devoted considerable space to the arts and literature will first be discussed, and after them, the major examples of American Marxian criticism and literary history. All the writings cited in PART II are themselves, of course, literature if the word is used in its broadest sense.

A. AMERICAN PRE-MARXIAN ART AND LITERATURE. In the general books about American communitarians, and in other books and articles which refer to them, the little about art that can be gleaned refers most frequently to architecture or includes illustrations of buildings. Next to architecture, music receives the most comment.

For the arts and literature of EPHRATA, see the material scattered through J. F. Sachse, *The German Sectarians of Pennsylvania, 1708-1800* (Philadelphia, 1899-1900, 2 vols.), especially I, pp. 141-168, on religious literature, I, pp. 295-304, on costume, and II, pp. 128-160, on music. Sachse discusses his abundant illustrations only incidentally. The section on music was superseded by Sachse's monograph and later work cited in Topic 1, as well as by "Ephrata and the Cloister Music," in *Church Music and Musical Life in Pennsylvania in the Eighteenth Century* (Philadelphia, 1926-1927, 3 vols.), II, pp. 26-84, and other comment, pp. 242-253, published as Volume 4 of the *Publications* of the Pennsylvania Society of the Colonial Dames of America. For the architecture of Ephrata see, among other sources, occasional references in F. A. Fetherolf, *The Art and Architecture of the Pennsylvania Germans* (MS senior thesis, Department of Art and Archaeology, Princeton University, 1935, 68 pp.); Eleanor Raymond, *Early Domestic Architecture of Pennsylvania* (New York, 1931, 11 leaves, 158 pls.); and G. E. Brumbaugh, "Colonial Architecture of the Pennsylvania Germans," Pennsylvania German Society *Proceedings . . . 1930*, XLI, pp. 47-51, pls. 54-72. H. S. Borneman refers to Ephrata in *Pennsylvania German Illuminated Manuscripts* (Pennsylvania German Society *Proceedings*, XLVI; Norristown, Pa., 1937, 58 pp.). The Cloister has been the subject of some poetry and fiction. See Edward Eggleston's short story, "Sister Tabea," in his *Duffels* (New York, 1893, 262 pp.), and references to seven other pieces in the bibliography of E. E. Doll and A. M. Funke, *The Ephrata Cloisters* (Philadelphia, 1944, 139 pp.), pp. 75-77.

The sparse materials on the arts of AMANA include B. M. H. Shambaugh, *Amana That Was and Amana That Is* (Iowa City, Iowa, 1932, 502 pp.), pp. 85-93, on Inspirationist village plans and housing, and pp. 264-268, on psalms and hymn tunes. Shambaugh's monograph, however, is not illustrated. G. Schulz-Behrend, "The Amana Colony," *American-German Review*, VII (Dec. 1940), pp. 7-9, 38, has a few pictures of the architecture, and there are interesting illustrations in the Federal Writers' Project guidebook *Iowa* (New York, 1941, 583 pp.), in the American Guide Series. Charles Nordhoff, *The Communistic Societies of the United States* (New York, 1875, 439 pp.), pp. 25-59, has some wood engravings of Amana. B. M. H. Shambaugh, "Amana Society," *Encyclopaedia of Religion and Ethics*, James Hastings, ed., I (1908), pp. 358-369, gives a good description of the layout of the towns.

As in the case of Amana, there is very little material of any sort on the various RAPPITE settlements. The student is at present limited to brief remarks in standard histories, such as J. S. Duss's discussion of Rappite music in *The Harmonists* (Harrisburg, Pa., 1943, 425 pp.), pp. 158-163, 364-386. J. A. Bole, "The Harmony Society," published serially in *German American Annals*, N.S., II (May-Nov. 1904), also published separately (Philadelphia, 1904, 176 pp.), has numerous but poor illustrations, and his brief treatment of music, pp. 606, 612-613, 618-624, is not duplicated by Duss. Writers' Program, Pennsylvania, *Pennsylvania Cavalcade* (Philadelphia, 1942, 462 pp.), p. 279, contains a drawing of buildings at Economy. Federal Writers' Project, Pennsylvania, *The Harmony Society in Pennsylvania* (Philadelphia, 1937, 38 pp.), contains drawings of Economy, including a plan of the town. Other illustrations of Economy are to be found in Joseph Bausman, *History of Beaver County, Pennsylvania* (New York, 1904, 2 vols.), II, pp. 1004-1030. G. B. Lockwood, *The New Harmony Movement* (New York, 1905, 404 pp.), has illustrations of some Rappite buildings at Harmony, Indiana, now New Harmony. A. E. Bestor, Jr., *Backwoods Utopias: the Sectarian and Owenite Phases of Communitarian Socialism in America, 1663-1829* (Philadelphia, 1950, 288 pp.), pp. 264-265, has material on architecture at Harmony, while K. J. Arndt's article, "George Rapp's Petition to Thomas Jefferson," *American-German Review*, VII (Oct. 1940), pp. 5-9, 35, has a plan of the early settlement at Harmony, Pennsylvania, and a sketch of the Rappite church there. Among illustrated articles on the Rappites see R. F. Lockridge, "American Experiment in Communism," *Travel*, LXX (Dec. 1937), pp. 12-15, etc.

More books have dealt directly and specifically with SHAKER arts than with the arts of any other type of sectarian community (see Topic 1). For general summaries on Shaker art by non-Shakers, see M. F. Melcher, *The Shaker Adventure* (Princeton, N.J., 1941, 319 pp.), pp. 191-226, and Constance Rourke, "The Shakers," in her posthumously published essays, *The Roots of American Culture* (New York, 1942, 305 pp.), pp. 195-237. The best discussion by Shakers of Shaker literature—which is of course mostly religious—is in Anna White and Leila Taylor, *Shakerism: Its Meaning and Message* (Columbus, Ohio, 1904, 416 pp.), pp. 319-347, which also has illustrations of Shaker architecture. For views of western Shaker communities see especially D. M. Hutton, *Old Shakertown and the Shakers* (Harrodsburg, Ky., 1936, 67 pp.), and J. P. MacLean's series of articles in *Ohio Archaeological and Historical Quarterly*, IX-XI, XIII (1900-1904).

As for the MORMONS, W. J. McNiff, *Heaven on Earth; a Planned Mormon Society* (Oxford, Ohio, 1940, 262 pp.), pp. 91-129, mostly on group arts and literature, pp. 130-155, on the theater, and pp. 156-194, on music, is the most thorough treatment accorded any of the sectarian communities in a single general history. McNiff makes good use of a wide range of scattered sources, the most important of which is E. W. Tullidge, *History of Salt Lake City* (Salt Lake City, Utah, 1886, 896 pp. of history, 172 pp. of biographies, and appendix, 36 pp.), especially pp. 735-818. See also the *Discourses of Brigham Young* (2nd ed., ed. by J. A. Widtsoe; Salt Lake City, Utah, 1926, 760 pp.), chap. 21, including passages in which Young encourages the Mormons to participate in arts of social amusement such as the theater, music, and dancing; and chap. 26, where he urges them to build good houses and beautiful cities. F. J. Cannon and G. L. Knapp, *Brigham Young and His Mormon Empire* (New York, 1931, 398 pp.), chap. 20, discusses Young as a patron of art, especially dancing, music, and the theater. R. A. Skidmore, *Mormon Recreation in Theory and Practice: a Study of Social Change* (Philadelphia, 1941, 137 pp.), a University of Pennsylvania thesis, includes treatment of the Mormon theater. Incidental references to the arts and illustrations of Mormon architecture may be found in Nels Anderson, *Desert Saints* (Chicago, 1942, 459 pp.). For a general discussion of the arts in Utah, see Writers' Program, Utah, *Utah* (New York, 1945, 595 pp.), pp. 153-187, one of the American Guide Series.

For the arts of the Perfectionists at ONEIDA see R. A. Parker, *A Yankee Saint; John Humphrey Noyes and the Oneida Community* (New York, 1935, 322 pp.), Pt. 2, chaps. 7-8. Note that, as among the Mormons also, music and the theater were permitted as group arts. Interesting contemporary illustrations of the theater, etc., at Oneida, together with discussion of the museum, the library, theatrical and musical performances, are contained in J. B. Ellis, *Free Love and Its Votaries; or Ameri-*

can Socialism Unmasked (New York, 1870, 502 pp.), an attack on Oneida and three other communities. Occasional references to the industrial arts and illustrations of some of the buildings are to be found in Pierrepont Noyes, *My Father's House: an Oneida Boyhood* (New York, 1937, 312 pp.); and for the picture of a model of the Oneida Community, see the frontispiece of W. A. Hinds, *American Communities* (rev. ed., Chicago, 1902, 433 pp.). Illustrations of the buildings which were used by the group at Putney before moving to Oneida are illustrated in G. W. Noyes, *John Humphrey Noyes: the Putney Community* (Oneida, N.Y., 1931, 393 pp.).

Relatively little has been written about the arts of the secular communitarians. For an OWENITE community see G. B. Lockwood, *The New Harmony Movement* (New York, 1905, 404 pp.), which contains descriptions of the buildings, with illustrations, and only the briefest mention of music. A more recent and definitive work is A. E. Bestor, Jr., *Backwoods Utopias: the Sectarian and Owenite Phases of Communitarian Socialism in America, 1663-1829* (Philadelphia, 1950, 288 pp.): see his index under "Pictures and models of communities," and bibliography, pp. 264-265. The ideas of FOURIER were spread in the United States chiefly through Albert Brisbane's writings, especially *Association; or, A Concise Exposition of the Practical Part of Fourier's Social Science* (New York, 1843, 80 pp.), pp. 19-26, 74-75, and *Social Destiny of Man; or, Association and Reorganization of Industry* (Philadelphia, 1840, 480 pp.), pp. 362-375. See also Parke Godwin's *A Popular View of the Doctrines of Charles Fourier* (New York, 1844, 120 pp.), pp. 52-54, 60. The situation in the phalanxes, which precluded much development of the arts and literature, is described in the literature of PART II, Topic 6. The following books from the large bibliography on Brook Farm contain occasional mention of the arts there: J. T. Codman, *Brook Farm, Historic and Personal Memoirs* (Boston, 1894, 335 pp.), pp. 91-99, 139-141, 150-171; J. V. Sears, *My Friends at Brook Farm* (New York, 1912, 172 pp.), pp. 80-106; and Lindsay Swift, *Brook Farm* (New York, 1900, 303 pp.), pp. 26-39, describing the buildings and grounds, and pp. 53-68, amusements and customs. G. W. Cooke, ed., *The Poets of Transcendentalism* (Boston, 1903, 341 pp.), includes selections from Margaret Fuller, Christopher P. Cranch, John S. Dwight, Charles A. Dana, George W. Curtis, and Thomas W. Higginson—all associated with Brook Farm—as well as Bronson Alcott, who tried his own community and educational experiment, and Thoreau.

The contrast between Cabet's artistic ideals and the arts of actual ICARIAN settlements is discussed and illustrated in Jules Prudhommeaux, *Icarie et son fondateur, Étienne Cabet* (Paris, 1907, 688 pp.), especially pp. 319-321, 333-335, and plate opposite p. 588. See also Mrs. I. G.

446

Miller, "The Icarian Community of Nauvoo, Illinois," Illinois State Historical Society, *Transactions . . . 1906*, pp. 103-107, for discussion of the Icarian auditorium at Nauvoo, Icarian music, and theatrical performances.

B. AMERICAN MARXIAN ART AND LITERATURE. While the general bibliography on American Marxian socialism in connection with the arts and literature is less limited than on pre-Marxism, there are large gaps, and before 1900 there is practically nothing. Only the most important items on specific phases, principally the fiction writers and critics, will be given here. For further information see incidental references in the literature of PART II and occasional articles in the serials cited there, and Topics 4-9, 12 below. For early comments, see R. T. Ely, "Socialism as a Promoter of Art," in his *Socialism . . . with Suggestions for Social Reform* (New York, 1894, 449 pp.), pp. 157-161, and a not very profound discussion by Robert Hunter, "Socialism in Art and Literature," in his *Socialists at Work* (New York, 1908, 374 pp.), pp. 259-293. The *Comrade* (New York, 1901-1905), merged into the *International Socialist Review* (Chicago, 1900-1918), included John Spargo, Algernon Lee, and George Herron on its editorial board, and had several well-known artists as editors and contributors. Among them was Walter Crane, who was connected with William Morris' arts and crafts movement. See also Upton Sinclair, ed., *The Cry for Justice; an Anthology of the Literature of Social Protest* (intro. by Jack London; Philadelphia, 1915, 891 pp.). Daniel De Leon translated a great deal of the work of the French pre-Marxian socialist, Eugène Sue, for the readers of his paper. See the prefatory comments in Sue's *The Mysteries of the People, or History of a Proletarian Family across the Ages* (tr. by Daniel De Leon; New York, 1923, 3 vols.).

Two outstanding socialist writers who began to publish near the turn of the century were Jack London (1876-1916) and Upton Sinclair (1878-). See first *Jack London, American Rebel; a Collection of His Social Writings, Together with an Extensive Study of the Man and His Times* (ed. by P. S. Foner; New York, 1947, 533 pp.), pp. 3-130 being the critical essay of Foner, and Upton Sinclair, *Anthology*, with an introduction by Irving Stone and Lewis Browne (Culver City, Calif., 1947, 352 pp.). A French comment on both writers is Régis Michaud, *Mystiques et réalistes anglo-saxons d'Emerson à Bernard Shaw* (Paris, 1918, 294 pp.), chaps. 6-7. Several of London's novels, cited in Topic 6, are autobiographical; see also the fictionalized biography by Irving Stone, *Sailor on Horseback* (Boston, 1938, 338 pp.), and Sinclair, *American Outpost; a Book of Reminiscences* (Pasadena, Calif., 1932, 280 pp.). Sinclair published one of the first American socialist essays in criticism, *Mam-*

monart; an Essay in Economic Interpretation (Pasadena, Calif., 1925, 390 pp.), a rather crude study in black and white.

After Max Eastman and John Sloan took over the editorship of the *Masses* (New York, 1911-1917) in 1912, it included short articles on Marxian theory and practice representing various shades of leftist and liberal opinion. See Eastman's autobiography, *Enjoyment of Living* (New York, 1948, 603 pp.), covering his first thirty-four years (1883-1917), and Albert Parry, "Fat Lasses for the Masses," in his *Garrets and Pretenders; a History of Bohemianism in America* (New York, 1933, 383 pp.), pp. 281-294. For the group of writers for some of whom the *Masses* often served as a preliminary vehicle, see also the autobiographies of Floyd Dell (1887-), *Homecoming* (New York, 1933, 368 pp.); Ernest Poole (1880-1950), *The Bridge* (New York, 1940, 422 pp.); Hutchins Hapgood (1869-1944), *A Victorian in the Modern World* (New York, 1939, 604 pp.); and Malcolm Cowley (1898-), *Exile's Return; a Narrative of Ideas* (New York, 1934, 308 pp.); and the forthcoming anthology edited with biographical introduction by John Stuart, *John Reed, American Revolutionary*, to be published in 1951 by International Publishers.

The Socialist Party after World War I no longer exercised the attraction of the *Masses* period for those interested in the arts. See, however, the brief remarks by McAlister Coleman and R. M. Lovett in *Socialist Planning and a Socialist Program*, edited by H. W. Laidler (New York, 1932, 255 pp.), pp. 138-149, and Laidler, "Artistic Effort," in his *Socializing Our Democracy* (New York, 1935, 330 pp.), pp. 275-283. G. L. Joughin and E. M. Morgan, *The Legacy of Sacco and Vanzetti* (New York, 1948, 598 pp.), Pt. 3, traces the impact of the anarchist case on American poets, playwrights, and novelists. See also the theory of art and culture expressed in Leon Samson, *The New Humanism* (London, 1930, 320 pp.), pp. 191-201, 273-300. Samson views art as the result of the individual's attempt in a class society to achieve an imaginary solidarity. With the thorough diffusion of humanist values, to be made possible by socialism, he expects art as a separate pursuit to vanish.

The *New Masses* (New York, 1926-1948) was the principal communist literary weekly. Many nonparty members contributed to it. This was also true originally of the *Liberator* (New York, 1918-1924), but the communist tendencies of this periodical increased until in 1922 it was turned over to the Communist Party. Many artistically excellent cartoons have appeared in the *New Masses*, in the *Liberator*, particularly in the early days, and in the *Daily Worker* (Chicago, New York, 1922-). Joseph Freeman, a leading American communist later expelled from the party, was connected with the *Liberator* and the *New Masses*. See the general issues he raises in "Notes on American Literature," *Communist*, VII (Aug., Sept. 1928), pp. 513-520, 570-578, one of the few examples of aesthetic criticism in the principal Communist Party theoretical organ (called *Political Affairs* since 1945). Also see his autobiography, *An American Testament* (New York, 1936, 678 pp.), on the literary and artistic circles in the party during the nineteen-twenties.

A great achievement of the Communist Party in the decade between the stock market crash in 1929 and the signing of the Russo-German pact in 1939 was its capitalizing on the influential leftward movement of writers and artists. Some went so far in their allegiance to the proletariat in the class struggle as to affiliate with the Communist Party. This "proletarian" influence was felt most powerfully in the novel (Topic 6) and drama (Topic 7), rather less in criticism (Topic 4) and still less significantly in poetry (Topic 8) and the arts of design. The more devoted Marxians tried to follow the changes in party line caused by the waning prestige and final ostracism of Trotsky and the increasing power of Stalin. As a result the leftist artists and writers were finally split into many sects, and the record of their dissensions is very complicated.

The opening manifesto of this movement was an open letter to American intellectuals by the League of Professional Groups for Foster and Ford, *Culture and the Crisis* (New York, 1932, 32 pp.). On the editorial committee were Newton Arvin, Sherwood Anderson, Malcolm Cowley, John Dos Passos, Horace Gregory, Granville Hicks, Langston Hughes, Matthew Josephson, Louis Lozowick, Grace Lumpkin, Alfred Kreymborg, Lincoln Steffens, Edmund Wilson, and Ella Winter. From 1929 to 1934, John Reed clubs were organized in the largest cities, and were joined in a national organization, the Revolutionary Writers' Federation, in 1932. The organs of the principal branches were the *Partisan* (Los Angeles, 1933-1934), *Left Front* (Chicago, 1933-1934), *New Force* (Detroit, 1932-?), *Left Review* (Philadelphia, 1934), *Leftward* (Boston, 1932-1933?), and *Partisan Review* (New York, 1934-). Other little magazines included *Blast* (New York, 1933-1934), for proletarian short stories, and *Art Front* (New York, 1934-1937), the Artists' Union magazine, to which Gropper, Lozowick, and Maurice Becker contributed. With the change to the Popular Front against fascism in 1935, the John Reed clubs were less useful to the party than organizations with a wider membership, and for the most part went out of existence. The last issue of the *Partisan Review* under the aegis of the party was for October 1936. In 1935 the first American Writers' Congress, under the chairmanship of Waldo Frank, was held in New York. See its papers and addresses, edited by Henry Hart, *American Writers' Congress* (New York, 1935, 192 pp.), and those of the second congress, also edited by Hart, *The Writer in a Changing World* (New York, 1937, 256 pp.). The attempts of missionaries of the Leninist-Marxist aesthetic to add a political dimension to the lives of the artists employed in the various federal projects under the New Deal through the technique of trade-union organization is briefly discussed in H. M. Kallen, *Art and Freedom* (New York, 1942, 2 vols.), II, pp. 895ff. Among the most useful materials for orthodox Stalinist views on art are the publications of the Critics Group in New York, including its occasional periodical, *Dialectics* (New York, 1937-1939), edited by Angel Flores. Eugene Lyons' polemic, *The Red Decade* (Indianapolis, Ind., 1941, 423 pp.), chaps. 12, 24, and 27, bitterly sums up the methods of communist penetration into cultural organizations during this period and pronounces the effects far-reaching.

After World War II, *Mainstream; a Literary Quarterly* (New York, 1947) was founded to stand for a Marxian, pro-Soviet "socially purposeful realism." It merged with the *New Masses* in March 1948 to form a monthly, *Masses & Mainstream* (New York, 1948-). The staff of the latter is headed by Samuel Sillen; departments have been covered by Sidney Finkelstein (music), Isidor Schneider (theater), Joseph Solman (art), and Joseph Foster (film), and it has published illustrations by a considerable number of well-known artists (see Topic 10). Finkelstein is stimulating in *Jazz; a People's Music* (New York, 1948, 278 pp.), on the social roots of jazz and its relation both to "art" music and commercialism. The year before, Finkelstein had published a more general book, *Art and Society* (New York, 1947, 288 pp.), the first comprehensive theoretical book on art from an orthodox Marxian point of view to be published in the United States. A later book on art from an orthodox viewpoint is Louis Harap, *Social Roots of the Arts* (New York, 1949, 192 pp.). At first praised by the communist press, these last two books were later criticized (in a series of articles and letters in the *Daily Worker* from May to August 1950) as being in some respects "formalistic" and "classless." For these two books had failed to follow adequately the postwar cultural line as established for American communists in V. J. Jerome, *Culture in a Changing World* (New York, 1947, 94 pp.).

Of the independent periodicals devoted to the arts and literature, the *Modern Quarterly* (Baltimore, 1923-1940, title varies) reflected throughout the personality of its editor, V. F. Calverton (1900-1940)—a socialist from 1918, with Trotskyist leanings between 1934 and 1937, but never a communist. See the sympathetic but candid characterizations of Calverton in the final memorial number, XI, No. 7 (1940). The *Partisan Review* during the first two or three years under the editorial board which revived it in December 1937 expressed the Trotskyist point of view. See "The Situation in American Writing—Seven Questions," *Partisan Review*, VI (Summer 1939), pp. 25-51 (Fall 1939), pp. 103-123, an index of the opinion of a number of American writers on the eve of World War II. In 1943, Dwight Macdonald withdrew from the *Partisan Review* and founded *Politics* (New York, 1944-1949). See its cultural articles, generally with an anarchist orientation, indexed in the Winter 1948 issue. The *Partisan Review*, best of the little magazines, continued a democratic socialist policy under Philip Rahv and William Phillips, and became a monthly in 1948. Consult also the cultural articles and reviews in the *Modern Review* (New York, 1947-1950), democratic socialist.

The critics and literary historians who adopted Marxism in the nineteen-thirties felt the need for rewriting the history of American literature. First came V. F. Calverton, *The Liberation of American Literature* (New York, 1932, 500 pp.), followed by Granville Hicks, dealing with the period since the Civil War, *The Great Tradition* (1933; rev. ed., New York, 1935, 341 pp.). Bernard Smith attempted to provide a Marxian interpretation in his *Forces in American Criticism* (New York, 1939, 401 pp.). His last chapter deals with the new Marxian literary criticism and its opponents. Maxwell Geismar projected a series of books working back from his own times, the first two of which were *Writers in Crisis; the American Novel between Two Wars* (Boston, 1942, 299 pp.), and *The Last of the Provincials; the American Novel, 1915-1925* (Boston, 1947, 404 pp.). His best essays were on Ring Lardner and John Dos Passos in the first volume and Sinclair Lewis in the second—writers whose political orientation he found sympathetic. For a criticism of Marxian criticism, see Alfred Kazin, *On Native Grounds; an Interpretation of Modern American Prose Literature* (New York, 1942, 541 pp.), Pt. 3. The first long essay in Marxian criticism was J. T. Farrell, *A Note on Literary Criticism* (New York, 1936, 221 pp.). He and Dos Passos are discussed in George Snell, *The Shapers of American Fiction, 1798-1947* (New York, 1947, 316 pp.), pp. 249-263 (Dos Passos), and pp. 288-300 (Farrell). A sample of fiction by a noncommunist with a Communist Party theme is Willa Gibbs, *The Tender Men* (New York, 1948, 246 pp.).

The literary discussions at the Cultural and Scientific Conference for World Peace, held at the Waldorf-Astoria Hotel in New York in March 1949 under the auspices of the National Council of the Arts, Sciences and Professions, are unfavorably summarized as mainly "Stalinoid" by Dwight Macdonald in "The Waldorf Conference," a special insert in *Politics*, Winter 1949, pp. 32A-32D. For the proceedings of this conference, attended also by many noncommunists, see *Speaking of Peace: Cultural and Scientific Conference for World Peace* (New York, 1949).

Special Topics

Topic 1. Arts and Literature of the Religious Socialistic Communities

AS ALREADY noted, the pietism of the religious communities of German origin was reflected in their belief that the fine arts and belles lettres are too much of the world, and at the same time—as the expression of the ego of individual artists—are insufficiently communal in spirit. Consequently, these groups tended to shun all kinds of art that are not directly useful for the community as a whole, and that smack in any way of worldliness. This pietistic suspicion of the arts was reinforced both by the general Protestant dislike for "popish" images and elaboration, and by the peasant background of most of the members of these groups which brought a lack of interest in any forms of art other than simple peasant handicrafts. Music, involving group rather than solo performances, was particularly approved, as in other forms of socialism, even though among the religious groups the music itself was very largely restricted to hymn tunes. It is significant that such poetry as was produced in these communities consisted primarily of verses for hymns. Except for the Rappites, all frowned on instrumental embellishments. The first music published north of the Rio Grande was at the Ephrata Cloister, where Conrad Beissel and his followers also contributed to theory and notation. The Shakers, drawing from native versions of revival hymns and white spirituals, added their own notation and wove the inspired product into the ritual of the dance.

As the Shaker communities were also pietistic in their beliefs, their arts and literature have many characteristics in common with those of the German groups. However, the Shaker groups were very largely made up of converts from evangelical revivalism who were of Anglo-Saxon descent. Consequently, the Shaker settlements were less completely cut off from the American society by which they were surrounded than were the German groups, and the effect of this on their arts is worth investigating.

In contrast to the pietism of the German communistic groups and even of the Shakers, the background of both the Mormons and the Oneida Community was more directly Calvinistic, and therefore these two groups have shown a Calvinistic aggressiveness in practical affairs of this world. As a result, the arts of both the Mormons and the Oneida Community—though also reflecting a certain Protestant simplicity—have a conscious up-to-dateness in style lacking in the art and literature of the pietistic communities; indeed, their arts can scarcely be told from the average American middle-class arts of the time. The Calvinistic heritage of these groups also helped to make them more aggressive in seeking converts and hence often led them to build large buildings—such as the Mormon tabernacles and temples—which would impress not only the faithful, but outsiders as well, with the success and power of the group, and, in the case of the Mormons, of its state church. Furthermore, the Calvinistic emphasis on the pursuit of the "calling," and thus on business ability, prepared such groups as these to compete in the new industrial arts and crafts.

As all these groups differed somewhat in their respective points of view toward celibacy and family life, the reflection of these different attitudes on the arrangement of their buildings is another subject to be investigated.

Of recent years outsiders have written about the arts of some of the religious groups as a result of new interest in American folklore and in American regionalism. Also the simple utilitarianism of the arts and crafts of these groups, especially those of the Shakers, has appealed to the functionalism of our age.

As noted in the General Reading of this Part, very little has been written directly on the arts and literature of the sectarian communities. The little that has been written by members of these groups has usually been restricted to the subject of religious music; and most of the writings by later students have dealt with a single group of communitarians, the Shakers. On this account the items included in this topic have been restricted to those few which deal *directly* with the subject. All others are cited in the General Reading.

The reader can secure an introductory orientation to the arts of the religious communities in general and the pietistic communities in particular through the excellent monographs of Edward Deming Andrews on the Shakers, notably his *The Gift to Be Simple: Songs, Dances and Rituals of the American Shakers* (New York, 1940, 170 pp.); *The Community Industries of the Shakers* (New York State Museum *Handbook*, No. 15; Albany, N.Y., 1932, 322 pp.); and, with Faith Andrews, *Shaker Furniture, the Craftsmanship of an American Communal Sect* (New Haven, Conn., 1937, 133 pp.). Since the Shakers did not develop a theater, see, as introductory reading to illustrate the interest of one group in the drama, J. S. Lindsay, *The Mormons and the Theatre* (Salt Lake City, Utah, 1905, 178 pp.). There is nothing comparable for the Oneida Perfectionists even though they too were interested in the drama. Rexford Newcomb, *Architecture of the Old Northwest Territory* (Chicago, 1950, 176 pp.), has a section (chap. 15) on the communal architecture of the Mormons, Shakers, Zoarites, Rappites, and similar groups in that region. For more detailed bibliography on the arts of the religious communitarians, see below.

No other pietistic community of German origin has attracted more attention because of its arts than EPHRATA. *Historic American Buildings Survey* (Washington, 1938, 264 pp.), a catalogue of illustrations in the Library of Congress, lists 104 photographs of Ephrata as well as 60 sheets of drawings. For architecture also see H. H. F. Jayne, "Cloisters at Ephrata," *American Magazine of Art*, xxix (Sept. 1936), pp. 594-598, 620-622. For manuscript illumination consult H. S. Borneman, *Pennsylvania German Illuminated Manuscripts* (Pennsylvania German Society *Proceedings*, xlvi; Norristown, Pa., 1937, 58 pp.). A thorough study of the music of the Ephrata Cloister is being completed by the musicologist, Hans T. David. See his articles, "Hymns and Music of the Pennsylvania Seventh-Day Baptists," *American-German Review*, ix (June 1943), pp. 4-6, 36, a good introduction, and "Musical Composition at Ephrata," *ibid.*, x (June 1944), pp. 4-5, based upon the preliminary report of the research project under his direction. This monograph will supplant the earlier treatment by J. F. Sachse, *The Music of the Ephrata Cloister; Also Conrad Beissel's Treatise on Music, as Set Forth in a Preface to the 'Turtel Taube' of 1747* (in Pennsylvania German Society *Proceedings and Addresses*, xii; Lancaster, Pa., 1903, 108 pp.). The earliest-known book with the imprint of Benjamin Franklin was also the first hymnal published for the Seventh Day German Baptists, *Göttliche Liebes und Lobes Gethöne* (Philadelphia, 1730, 96 pp.). The hymnbook, *Zionitischer Weyrauchs-Hügel* (Germantown, Pa., 1739, 792 pp.), is said to have been the first book printed with German type in what is now the United States.

There are no publications of an artistic or literary character by the Inspirationists of AMANA except their religious writings (see PART II, Topic 1, and PART III, General Reading, section 1), and the hymnbook, *Davidisches Psalter-Spiel der Kinder Zions; oder Sammlung von alten und neuen auserlesenen Geistes-Gesängen* (8th ed., Amana, Iowa, 1869, xxviii, 1173 pp. of text, 110 pp. of music).

As in the case of Amana, nothing important of an artistic or literary nature from the three settlements of the RAPPITES, or Harmonists, has been published except their hymnbook, *Harmonisches Gesangbuch . . .* (Allentown, Pa., 1820, 287 pp.), which contains the words for 371 songs, partly original with the Rappites. Two enlarged editions were published at Economy in 1827 and 1889. There exists, however, in manuscript a detailed study of the architecture of Economy, with elaborate illustrations and drawings, by Charles M. Stotz, a Pittsburgh architect engaged in the restoration of Economy.

Other pietist groups had their hymnbooks, for example, *Die Lieder der Hutterischen Brüder* (Scottdale, Pa., 1914, 894 pp.), in modernized German, without music; and the collection prepared for the Swedish community at Bishop Hill, Illinois, by its leader, Eric Janson, *Några Sånger; Samt Böner* (Galva, Ill., 1857).

Although of all the innumerable sectarian groups, the arts of the SHAKERS have aroused the most attention, there is no comprehensive study of Shaker architecture. E. D. Andrews, "Communal Architecture of the Shakers," *Magazine of Art,* xxx (Dec. 1937), pp. 710-715, has pictures of New Lebanon, New York, and Watervliet, New York. For illustrations of the architecture of other Shaker Families see C. E. Robinson (C. R. Edson, pseud.), "Communism," *Manufacturer and Builder,* xxiii-xxiv (1891-1892), and Julia Neal, *By Their Fruits* (Chapel Hill, N.C., 1947, 279 pp.), on South Union, Kentucky. For New Lebanon architecture and other arts see also the *Peg Board,* iv, No. 3 (June 1936), first Shaker number, published by the Lebanon School, New Lebanon; also *Darrow* (New Lebanon, N.Y., 1940, 50 pp.), a Darrow School prospectus. Elizabeth McCausland, "The Shaker Legacy," *Magazine of Art,* xxxvii (Dec. 1944), pp. 287-291, discusses the Shaker round barn at Hancock, Massachusetts, and also some Shaker furniture.

The following articles by E. D. and Faith Andrews were preliminary essays which culminated in their book on furniture (cited above, with other books by Andrews, in the introductory part of this topic): "An Interpretation of Shaker Furniture," *Antiques,* xxiii (Jan. 1933), pp. 6-9; "Craftsmanship of an American Religious Sect," *ibid.,* xiv (Aug. 1928), pp. 132-136; and E. D. Andrews, "The Furniture of an American Religious Sect," *ibid.,* xv (Apr. 1929), pp. 292-296. Also see "Antiques in Domestic Settings: . . . Shaker Home of Mr. and Mrs. Edward Deming Andrews in Pittsfield, Massachusetts," *ibid.,* xxx (Oct. 1936), pp. 162-163; and "Antiques in Domestic Settings: . . . Summer Home of Dr. and Mrs. Edward Deming Andrews in Richmond, Massachusetts," *ibid.,* xxxv (Jan. 1939), pp. 10, 30-32. Another magazine article on Shaker furniture is W. A. Dyer, "The Furniture of the Shakers; a Plea for Its Preservation as Part of Our National Inheritance," *House Beautiful,* lxv (May 1929), pp. 650, 669-673. For Shaker craftsmanship in general consult the catalogue of an exhibition at the Whitney Museum, *Shaker Handicrafts* (New York, 1935, 15 pp.); Benjamin Knotts, "Hands to Work and Hearts to God," Metropolitan Museum of Art, New York, *Bulletin,* N.S., i (Mar. 1943), pp. 231-236; the March 1945 number of *House & Garden;* and two magazine articles, "Worcester: Functionalism of Shaker Craftsmen," *Art News,* xxxvii (Jan. 14, 1939), p. 22, and "Shaker Craftsmanship," *Hobbies; the Magazine for Collectors,* xlviii (Dec. 1943), pp. 40-41. Shaker drawings mostly executed under spiritualistic inspiration during the 1840's and 1850's are discussed by E. D. Andrews, "Shaker Inspirational Drawings," *Antiques,* xlviii (Dec. 1945), pp. 338-341. Additional references on Shaker industries include E. D. Andrews, *The New York*

Shakers and Their Industries (New York State Museum *Circular*, No. 2; Albany, N.Y., 1930, 8 pp.); and Sister Marcia Bullard, "Shaker Industries," *Good Housekeeping*, XLIII (July 1906), pp. 33-37.

In addition to Andrews' monograph on Shaker music and dancing, see Russel Haskell, *A Musical Expositor; or, A Treatise on the Rules and Elements of Music; Adapted to the Most Approved Method of Musical Writing* (New York, 1847, 82 pp.), an instruction book for alphabetical notation, with an appendix of musical rules following p. 46; and *Extract from an Unpublished Manuscript of Shaker History (by an Eye-Witness) Giving an Accurate Description of Their Songs, Dances, Marches, Visions, Visits to the Spirit Land, &c.* (Boston, 1850, 48 pp.). A sampling of Shaker hymnals includes: S. Y. Wells, comp., *Millennial Praises, Containing a Collection of Gospel Hymns, in Four Parts; Adapted to the Day of Christ's Second Appearing* (Hancock, Mass., 1813, 288 pp.), without music; Richard McNemar (Philos Harmoniae, pseud.), comp., *Selection of Hymns and Poems for the Use of Believers* (Watervliet, Ohio, 1833, 180 pp.); *Musical Messenger; a Compilation of Hymns, Slow and Quick Marches, etc.* (Union Village, Ohio?, n.d., 32 pp.), with alphabetical notation; *A Collection of Millenial Hymns, Adapted to the Present Order of the Church* (Canterbury, N.H., 1847, 200 pp.), without music; H. C. Blinn, *A Sacred Repository of Anthems and Hymns* (Canterbury, N.H., 1852, 222 pp.), with alphabetical notation; *Shaker Music: Inspirational Hymns and Melodies Illustrative of the Resurrection Life and Testimony of the Shakers* (Albany, N.Y., 1875, 67 pp.), in conventional notation, including a note on voice production by John Howard (pp. 65-67); *A Collection of Hymns and Anthems Adapted to Public Worship* (East Canterbury, N.H., 1892, 144 pp.), compiled by H. C. Blinn; and Daniel Offord, Lucy Bowers, and M. J. Anderson, comps., *Original Shaker Music, Published by the North Family of Mt. Lebanon* (New York, 1893, 271 pp.), in modern notation.

Among the standard religious writings of the Shakers, perhaps the one which best gives an idea of Shaker literary style is the famous "Shaker Bible," the actual title of which is *The Testimony of Christ's Second Appearing* (Lebanon, Ohio, 1808, 600 pp.), by B. S. Youngs. A well-known late example of Shaker writing which might be considered to have some literary pretensions is Aurelia G. Mace, *The Aletheia: Spirit of Truth* (Farmington, Me., 1899, 135 pp.), written under the pseudonym Aurelia. See also Anna White, comp., *Mount Lebanon Cedar Boughs; Original Poems by the North Family of Shakers* (Buffalo, N.Y., 1895, 316 pp.), and G. A. Brown, *Song and Story* (Pittsfield, Mass., 1902, 188 pp.), other Shaker poems.

The Shakers early became a subject of fiction; Emerson, Melville, and Hawthorne were particularly interested in their doctrines and communal life. As a young man, Nathaniel Hawthorne considered joining a Shaker Family, but a passage (1851) in his *The American Notebooks* (ed. by Randall Stewart; New Haven, Conn., 1932, 350 pp.), pp. 229-230, speaks disparagingly of the sect. Two of his short stories contrast the hopefulness of lovers with the hopelessness of Shaker refugees from the world: "The Canterbury Pilgrims," first published in *Token and Atlantic Souvenir* (1833), pp. 153-166, and later in *The Snow-Image and Other Twice-Told Tales* (Boston, 1852, 273 pp.), and "The Shaker Bridal," in *Twice-Told Tales* (Boston, 1851, 2 vols.), as well as in the various editions of his collected works. Daniel Pierce Thompson, a Vermont editor who wrote minor stories of local color, used a plot similar to that of "The Canterbury Pilgrims" in the title story of *The Shaker Lovers and Other Tales* (Burlington, Vt., 1848, 88 pp.). W. D. Howells used Shaker background in two of his novels: *The Undiscovered Country* (Boston, 1880, 419 pp.), and *The Day of Their Wedding* (New York, 1896, 158 pp.). His observations of the Shakers at Shirley, Massachusetts, during six weeks of the summer of 1875 are recorded in *Three Villages* (Boston, 1884, 198 pp.), pp. 67-113. A modern novel with sympathetic depiction of a generalized Shaker community is L. G. Cameron (Ann George Leslie, pseud.), *Dancing Saints* (Garden City, N.Y., 1943, 307 pp.).

Although McNiff's admirable monograph cited in the General Reading takes up most of the arts of the MORMONS, neither he nor any one else has discussed Mormon architecture as a whole. For one of the most famous Mormon buildings see D. M. McAllister, *A Description of the Great Temple at Salt Lake City* (Salt Lake City, Utah, 1904, 28 pp.). R. F. Burton, *The City of the Saints* (New York, 1862, 574 pp.), has some early views of Salt Lake City as well as a plan of the city. One of the earliest engravings of the temple at Nauvoo, Illinois, was published in *Graham's American Monthly Magazine*, xxxiv (Apr. 1849), and accompanied by a description with comments by Joseph Smith, p. 257. H. M. Beardsley, *Joseph Smith and His Mormon Empire* (Boston, 1931, 421 pp.), also has illustrations of the architecture at the settlement at Nauvoo, Illinois; while a plan of Nauvoo, together with views of the temple at Kirtland, Ohio, and the tabernacle at Salt Lake City, etc., can be found in T. B. H. Stenhouse, *The Rocky Mountain Saints* (London, 1874, 761 pp.).

The two chief Mormon religious books, Joseph Smith, *The Book of Mormon* (Palmyra, N.Y., 1830, 588 pp.), and *Doctrine and Covenants of the Church of the Latter Day Saints* (Kirtland, Ohio, 1835, 257 pp.), may also be cited here as the best-known examples of the Mormon Biblical style.

Because the Mormons were so notoriously a disturbing element in American society and because they were supposed to be a morally degraded sect, fact and fiction about their life and the history of their migrations and settlements soon began to get into print. There is a vast literature about the Mormons which is satiric, melodramatic, sensational, malicious, or salacious, depending on the attitude toward the sect of the particular author. No scholar has attempted to evaluate this mass of writing nor to sift out the very small proportion which has any relation to the cooperative or communal aspects of Mormon society. There is no satisfactory bibliography of this literature.

The following examples will serve to represent the different kinds of writing which exploited the real or imaginary story of the Mormons. (1) Travel books: P. S. Robinson, *Sinners and Saints: a Tour across the States . . . with Three Months among the Mormons* (Boston, 1883, 370 pp.); Mark Twain, *Roughing It* (Hartford, Conn., 1886, 591 pp.), chaps. XIII-XVI. (2) Supposed confessions of reformed Mormons: Maria Ward, *Female Life among the Mormons: a Narrative of Many Years' Personal Experience by the Wife of a Mormon Elder* (New York, 1855, 449 pp.). This exposé, published anonymously and also attributed to Mrs. B. G. Ferris, was translated into French and German and reprinted several times with varying titles. (3) Fiction: Cornelia (Mrs. A. G.) Paddock, *In the Toils; or, Martyrs of the Latter Days* (Chicago, 1879, 301 pp.), and *The Fate of Madame La Tour: a Tale of Great Salt Lake* (New York, 1881, 352 pp.). (4) Poetry: *Mormoniad* (Boston, 1858, 100 pp.). (5) Drama: Joaquin Miller, *The Danites* [i.e., Mormons] *in the Sierras* (Chicago, 1881, 258 pp.), a revised and enlarged edition of *First Fam'lies in the Sierras* (London, 1875, 151 pp.). This play ran for two seasons in New York and was produced in London. (6) Humor: Artemus Ward (Charles F. Browne), *Lecture on the Mormons* (London, 1882, 64 pp.), one of the most famous of this platform comedian's "lectures."

In recent years the regional novelists have rediscovered the Mormons. Vardis Fisher, *Children of God* (New York, 1939, 769 pp.), is an historical novel about the founders, Smith and Young. For a list of other recent novels using Mormon materials, see Writers' Program, Utah, *Utah; a Guide to the State* (New York, 1945, 595 pp.), p. 156.

Like most religious utopian socialists, John Humphrey Noyes of the ONEIDA COMMUNITY was, in general, very suspicious of the arts except when they could be useful for community purposes. In 1869 he declared, "It seems to me that the great condemnation of mere literary art, and indeed of art of any kind insubordinate to religion and science is that it is an enemy to earnestness." Almost the only arts of which he approved—other than industrial arts—were music and drama involving community participation, which he recognized "as another path to communal sharing." It is significant that the only publication specifically devoted to any Oneida art—aside from the many writings by members of the community, in which the aesthetic was subordinated to the theological, missionary, or practical—was the hymnbook, *Favorite Hymns for Community Singing* (Oneida, N.Y., 1855, 32 pp.). This gives some idea of the musical taste of the group soon after it moved from Vermont, although this taste improved steadily.

Topic 2. The Aesthetic Theory and Practice of the Liberal Communitarians

In contrast to the sectarian communities, the liberal and secular communitarianism of Owen, Fourier, Cabet, and their followers was an outgrowth of eighteenth-century romanticism and rationalism—a fact that profoundly affected the points of view of these men toward the arts and literature. Because they thus believed that man is by nature reasonable, good, and indefinitely perfectible, they held that the evil in men is the result of ignorance and of bad social and cultural environment. Consequently, literature and the other arts were to them important for education and for improving the cultural environment.

As man was held to be inherently reasonable, Owen, Fourier, and Cabet all felt that mankind is entirely open to persuasion either through precept or actual example. All three of them, therefore, wrote books and articles elucidating their precepts for the good society and for those arts—particularly architecture—which should play a part in creating the good society. Furthermore, either they or their followers established actual communities supposed to exemplify the good society. However, these hardly lasted long enough for the arts to develop to any great degree. Thus there is first-hand material available on the aesthetic theories of these leaders, but relatively little on the actual exemplification of those theories.

The firm belief of these men in the importance of education as culture tended to lead them to an interest in the best that has been said and done in the past, while at the same time their optimistic belief in progress led them to desire to be up-to-date. The effect of this dualistic point of view on artistic style—especially the architectural styles—suggested in their writings is worthy of study. The pure form of utopianism, an element strong in these movements and by no means absent from Marxism, may be studied in the novels and tracts discussed in Topic 3. Included there also are the satires against Associationism and reference to the "sociality" of Melville.

The student can be directed to no general introductory reading devoted solely to the arts of American OWENISM or ICARIANISM—not even for a single branch of art. The best introductions are the works of the European founders cited in the General Reading, pp. 424-425. These must be read with the understanding that their American disciples both

459

imperfectly understood and incompletely accepted their theories. The summaries and incidental comments referred to in the General Reading, pp. 446-447, are more pertinent to the understanding of the American experiments, but less comprehensive than the European statements. They are no substitute for specific treatment of the arts and literature by these liberal communitarians themselves; or for monographic literature by outsiders on American Owenite and Icarian arts and literature.

Bibliography, then, is scarce on all the arts of these two groups. Yet the amount of music and dancing indulged in by the Owenites was unusual for the frontier, and the Icarians, not far behind in these forms of recreation, were perhaps ahead of the Owenites in amateur theatricals. Josiah Warren, who organized and conducted the New Harmony orchestra and started other communitarian experiments, published late in life an original treatise on musical notation, *Written Music Remodeled and Invested with the Simplicity of an Exact Science* (Boston, 1860, 107 pp.). The preface to this book indicts the music business for working against the interests of music lovers. The introductory explanation of his system is illustrated with twenty-five songs and rounds, a few of which have original music and words extolling the virtues of a society organized according to the principles of Warren's individualist anarchism. An enthusiastic communitarian, Alcander Longley, briefly an Icarian, expounded his musical system of numbers to denote length of sound in *The Phonetic Songster and Simple Phonography* (St. Louis, Mo., n.d., 27 pp.). See also Longley's *Communism . . . with Several Communist Songs, Printed in a New System of Phonetic Figure Music* (St. Louis, Mo., 1880, 108 pp.).

The situation with regard to FOURIERISM is somewhat better, chiefly because of the galaxy of intellectuals and writers connected with Brook Farm or much interested in the progress of this experiment in Associationism. Among such leaders were Horace Greeley, editor of the *New York Tribune* (a great champion of Fourierism); Charles A. Dana, editor of the *New York Sun*; Margaret Fuller; G. W. Curtis, novelist, editor, and reformer; Parke Godwin, journalist and reformer; Isaac Hecker, founder of the Roman Catholic order of the Paulist Fathers; Orestes Brownson, editor and Catholic apologist; Christopher Pearse Cranch, poet, musician, and painter; Theodore Parker, preacher and reformer. Though many of these thinkers and writers in later life repudiated Fourierism, the theories developed at Brook Farm had been a powerful influence in their lives and, through their speaking and writing, on American culture.

Nathaniel Hawthorne's *The Blithedale Romance* (Boston, 1852, 288 pp.), a novel based on his experiences at Brook Farm—before it became Fourierist, however—is an excellent picture of a community of unusual cultivation. There is much literature on Hawthorne in relation to Brook

Farm. The most important titles are listed in the bibliography of L. S. Hall, *Hawthorne; Critic of Society* (New Haven, Conn., 1944, 200 pp.), pp. 184-193. Hall's thesis is that Hawthorne, a materialist individualist reformer, objected to the Brook Farmers' isolation from society and their failure to combine theory and practice. The book is concerned with Hawthorne's criticisms after he left Brook Farm, but pp. 1-67 refer frequently to his Brook Farm experience. See also Émile Montégut, "Un Roman socialiste en Amérique," *Revue des deux mondes*, xvi (Dec. 1, 1852), pp. 809-841, a review of *Blithedale Romance*, and Lina Böhmer, *Brookfarm und Hawthornes "Blithedale Romance"* . . . (Jena, 1936, 94 pp.), with unreliable references. For essays relating other literary figures to Brook Farm, see Karl Knortz, *Brook Farm und Margaret Fuller: Vortrag gehalten im deutschen gesselligwissenschaftlichen Verein von New York am 11. März 1885* (New York, 1886, 29 pp.), and J. T. Flanagan, "Emerson and Communism," *New England Quarterly*, x (June 1937), pp. 243-261.

As regards other arts, John Sullivan Dwight, teacher of German and music at Brook Farm and an enthusiastic Fourierist even after Brook Farm was abandoned, made the most of the limited talent and equipment at Brook Farm to raise musical standards. He shared Fourier's partiality for opera, and his love for the classics from Handel to Beethoven represented the advance guard of musical taste among American intellectuals. See G. W. Cooke, *John Sullivan Dwight; Brook-Farmer, Editor, and Critic of Music* (Boston, 1898, 297 pp.), pp. 48-145, which shows how Dwight's zeal for Associationism harmonized with his love of music. His interest in music led to his starting *Dwight's Journal of Music* (Boston, 1852-1881) which he devoted to the mission of improving popular taste and enlarging the company of American music lovers. Further information on Dwight's musical criticism and educational essays and lectures can be found in the *Dial* and the *Democratic Review*, and also in the *Harbinger*, e.g., "Teachers' Conventions in Boston," v (Sept. 4, 1847), pp. 203-205, and especially "The American Review's Account of the Religious Union of Associationists," in *ibid.*, v (June 19, 1847), pp. 28-30, his defense of the type of music he selected and directed for the meetings of the Boston Religious Union of Associationists.

As might be expected, reports from Fourierist phalanxes in the *Harbinger* (New York, 1845-1849), and reports of visitors, reveal a yearning for the civilized arts which none of the communities were in an economic position to indulge in as much as they liked.

It may be noted here parenthetically that although not a Fourierist, Horatio Greenough, the American sculptor and early functionalist who furnished Emerson with many of his ideas on art, was much interested in Fourier's writings. Greenough himself had participated in events of the revolutionary year 1848, including the popular demonstration that celebrated the advent of liberty in Florence. As he indicated in his essay "Fourier et hoc genus omne," Greenough considered Fourier to be much too theoretical, and said that he himself could not adopt Fourier's "broad humanity," preferring less breadth and more depth. For this essay by Greenough see the *Crayon*, Vol. 1, No. 24 (June 13, 1855), pp. 371-372.

A few modern writers have used liberal communitarianism as material for novels. K. E. Blake, *Hearts' Haven* (Indianapolis, Ind., 1905, 496 pp.); and C. D. (Parke) Snedeker, a descendant of Owen, *Seth Way* (Boston, 1917, 413 pp.), and *The Beckoning Road* (Garden City, N.Y., 1929, 326 pp.), use a New Harmony setting. Floyd Dell's imaginative description of Apple Farm Commonwealth in *Diana Stair* (New York, 1932, 641 pp.), pp. 502-547, shows unusual insight into the crosscurrents of communitarianism and reform.

Topic 3. Socialism and the Utopian Novel

Long before Marxian socialism began to influence American writing, our novelists used the utopia as a device for setting forth social ideas. Our native writers were in the main as much concerned over the great American experiment in democracy as were the rest of their countrymen. Few of them were so belletristic in their aims as Poe. In writing fiction they tended, therefore, to develop social themes. Indeed, the novel during these years was acceptable to many serious readers solely because it could be used in the cause of reform. Since the utopia was by tradition a convenient device for presenting such social themes and since utopian ideas were at this time being made the basis for actual communities in the United States (see PART II, Topics 6-7), the novelists quite naturally presented their theories in utopian guise. Among the early writers of utopian fiction are such important names as Charles Brockden Brown, J. K. Paulding, James Fenimore Cooper, Nathaniel Hawthorne, and Sylvester Judd.

After the Civil War, as the United States was rapidly industrialized, the problems raised by urbanization, political corruption, labor revolt, monopoly, and agrarian discontent found their way into fiction. In the main, the better-known novelists ignored social questions, or if they attempted to deal with them, their approach was timid and reactionary. Novelists of less stature as artists, however, tried to cope with the social ills of their time. In doing so they found the utopian form particularly useful, although as a fictional disguise it was often extremely thin. In the twelve years after the publication of Edward Bellamy's immensely popular *Looking Backward* (1888), over sixty utopian novels appeared, at least fifteen of which were continuations of or replies to Bellamy's picture of an ideal American society. Its popularity was so great that the "Nationalist" movement was organized to establish the kind of social order Bellamy had imagined in his novel, although it diverged a good deal from Bellamy's ideas (see PART II, General Reading, pp. 103-104; PART IV, Topic 3). The most important writer converted to socialism in this period was W. D. Howells. How far he differed from Marxism can best be seen by reading his two utopian novels cited below. It is necessary with both Bellamy and Howells, who were good friends, to understand the native American cast of their socialistic thinking. Neither one, for instance, believed in the eventuality of the revolution. Both foresaw the socialist state as consistent with the possible development of American democracy.

Very different from Howells' and Bellamy's view was that of some Socialist Party writers, especially Jack London. These recognized the class struggle and the necessity of revolution; the danger of conservative counterrevolution; and the use of the general strike and other economic weapons of a class-conscious proletariat. Other gradualist socialists or radicals, more like Howells and Bellamy, made much of political panaceas, the cooperative movement, bimetallism, and the preachings of Christian socialism (see PART II, Topic 13; PART IV, Topics 6 and 8).

A good factual study of American utopian literature from John Eliot's *The Christian Commonwealth* (London, 1659, 35 pp.) to 1942, excellent on the last century, is V. L. Parrington, Jr., *American Dreams; a Study of American Utopias* (Providence, R.I., 1947, 234 pp.). Parrington makes only limited reference to contemporary writers in other genres, and no attempt to link this literature to the communitarians. Compare also the outstanding examples of the utopian novel in each period: J. F. Cooper, *The Crater, or, Vulcan's Peak* (New York, 1847, 2 vols. in 1); Edward Bellamy, *Looking Backward* (Boston, 1888, 470 pp.); and Jack London, *The Iron Heel* (New York, 1907, 354 pp.). Cooper satirizes a society governed by the masses and defends property. Bellamy is wholly optimistic and has faith in the giant corporation if run by the state. London is much more pessimistic. His novel, purporting to be based on a manuscript discovered in the fourth century of the era of brotherhood, describes the terrible struggle during the years 1912 and 1932 between labor and the oligarchs of the Iron Heel. The book ends in 1932 with the triumph of the oligarchy over the social revolutionaries, who secretly plan a second revolt.

The best account of the influence of economic ideas in American fiction is W. F. Taylor, *The Economic Novel in America* (Chapel Hill, N.C., 1942, 378 pp.). The sections of this book devoted to utopian fiction, to Bellamy, and to Howells reveal how the utopian novels are related to the other novels of the time which are concerned with social ideas.

A. B. Forbes has an excellent brief survey, "The Literary Quest for Utopia," *Social Forces*, VI (Dec. 1927), pp. 179-189. C. R. Flory, "The Program of the Utopian Novelists," *Economic Criticism in American Fiction, 1792-1900* (Philadelphia, 1936, 261 pp.), pp. 151-196, is more detailed than Forbes but will be useful chiefly for its synopses of plots. R. L. Shurter, "The Utopian Novel in America, 1888-1900," *South Atlantic Quarterly*, XXXIV (Apr. 1935), pp. 137-144, is an interpretive article limited to a few outstanding examples and based largely on the frontier safety-valve theory. See also Gildo Massó, *Education in Utopias* (New York, 1927, 201 pp.); D. C. O'Grady, "Utopian States and Experimental Colonies," *Revue de l'Université d'Ottawa*, VII (Jan./Mar. 1937), pp. 31-53, whose second section deals with the United States; and J. F. Normano, "Social Utopias in American Literature," *International Review for Social History*, III (1938), pp. 287-299. Normano appends a list covering from 1798 to 1930, and includes many utopian novels not in other bibliographies. At least 150 such novels have been written in the United States, according to the varying definitions of the scholars, and two-thirds of them in the thirty years after 1888, when Bellamy's *Looking Backward* appeared. The Harvard University library has a particularly strong collection on the utopian novel.

For the period before the Civil War, see, in addition to Cooper's *The Crater* (cited above) and Hawthorne's *Blithedale Romance* (cited in Topic 2), Sylvester Judd, *Margaret* (Boston, 1845, 460 pp.), which concludes with the founding of a kind of transcendentalist utopia. J. A. Etzler, *The Paradise within the Reach of All Men, without Labor, by Powers of Nature and Machinery* (Pittsburgh, Pa., 1833, 2 vols. in 1), and its sequel, *The New World; or, Mechanical System* (Philadelphia, 1841, 75 pp.), received H. D. Thoreau's criticism in "Paradise (to be) Regained," *United States Magazine and Democratic Review*, XIII (Nov. 1843), pp. 451-463, abridged in *American Issues* (ed. by Willard Thorp, M. E. Curti, and Carlos Baker; Philadelphia, 1941, 2 vols.), I, pp. 421-426. See also Herman Melville's description of Serenia, controlled by the principles of Christian socialism, and discovered by his world travelers in *Mardi* (New York, 1849, 2 vols.), II, chap. 83. What is said to be the first utopian novel published in the United States is L. S. Mercier, *Memoirs of the Year Two Thousand Five Hundred* (Philadelphia, 1795, 360 pp.).

Scholarly comment on the social outlook of the above writers includes the following articles and monographs. H. H. Scudder, "Cooper's *The Crater*," *American Literature*, XIX (May 1947), pp. 109-126, treats Cooper's novel as a demonstration of Henry C. Carey's economics. See also J. F. Ross, *The Social Criticism of Fenimore Cooper* (Berkeley, Calif., 1933, 117 pp.), and P. J. Brockway, "Sylvester Judd: Novelist of

Transcendentalism," *New England Quarterly*, xiii (Dec. 1940), pp. 654-677. H. S. Canby, "Thoreau and the Machine Age," *Yale Review*, xx (Mar. 1931), pp. 517-531, pictures Thoreau's anarchist and perfectionist opposition to a machine-oriented society, and the socialism it hatched, as that of "an angry woodchuck" turning "on an intervening world" (p. 519). Melville's recognition of the constant debt of the commonalty of mankind to the community—an outlook in decided contrast to Emerson's and closer to Whitman's and to the Associationists' points of view—is the subject of R. E. Watters' article, "Melville's 'Sociality,'" *American Literature*, xvii (Mar. 1945), pp. 33-49.

In the gilded age, T. B. Aldrich, *The Stillwater Tragedy* (Boston, 1880, 324 pp.), and John Hay, *The Bread-Winners* (New York, 1884, 319 pp.), illustrate the conservatism of the few leading novelists who wrote on social themes. H. F. Keenan answered Hay with *The Money-Makers* (New York, 1885, 337 pp.). The principal exception, W. D. Howells, wrote *A Traveler from Altruria* (New York, 1894, 318 pp.), and its sequel, *Through the Eye of the Needle* (New York, 1907, 232 pp.). George Arms, ed., "Howells's Unpublished Prefaces," *New England Quarterly*, xvii (Dec. 1944), pp. 580-591, includes the prefaces to these novels. See also Howells' writings on Shaker themes (Topic 1). For additional information about Howells' interest in social problems beyond what is found in the general studies cited above, consult George Arms, "The Literary Background of Howells's Social Criticism," *American Literature*, xiv (Nov. 1942), pp. 260-276. Arms explores the influence of the *Atlantic Monthly* coterie and of Bjørnstjerne Bjørnson on the literary side of Howells' fiction. Consult also "Further Inquiry into Howells's Socialism," *Science & Society*, iii (Spring 1939), pp. 245-248, Arms's comment on J. W. Getzels, "William Dean Howells and Socialism," *ibid.*, ii (Summer 1938), pp. 376-386, in which he establishes the conclusion that Howells was satisfied to go no farther than the nationalistic socialism of Gronlund's *The Coöperative Commonwealth* (Boston, 1884, 278 pp.). An early study by J. C. Underwood, "William Dean Howells and Altruria," in his *Literature and Insurgency; Ten Studies in Racial Evolution* (New York, 1914, 480 pp.), pp. 87-129, unfriendly to Howells, describes him as the Quaker, not the Puritan reformer. The most exhaustive study of Howells' contemporary, Bellamy, is A. E. Morgan, *Edward Bellamy* (New York, 1944, 468 pp.). See also John Chamberlain, "Minority Report of the Novelists," in *Farewell to Reform* (2nd ed., New York, 1933, 333 pp.), pp. 86-118, which discusses utopian, progressive, and populist writers, and the novels of social criticism.

Other examples of Jack London's utopian writing besides *The Iron Heel* (cited above) are "Goliah," in his *Revolution and Other Essays* (New York, 1910, 309 pp.), pp. 71-116, and "The Dream of Debs,"

International Socialist Review, IX (Jan.-Feb. 1909), pp. 481-489, 561-570, several times republished. "Goliah" is a fantasy in which an American, having discovered how to harness the cosmic energy from the sun, disarms the world with threats and samples of destruction, socializes society for the purpose of "laughter," and rules as a benevolent despot. In "The Dream of Debs" London imagined the chaos resulting from a general strike. Compare this with the more optimistic view of the general strike in F. M. Elliott, "The National Strike," *ibid.,* VII (Jan.-Feb. 1907), pp. 426-432, 462-466.

Of the more obscure utopian writings, one of the earliest was the anonymous *Equality; a History of Lithconia* (1802; Philadelphia, 1947, 86 pp.), perhaps by James Reynolds. The unpublished satire by John Francis Bray, variously called a Ricardian or Owenite socialist and Chartist, *A Voyage from Utopia to Several Unknown Regions of the World* (Brydone, Franco, and Amrico), was written not long before Bray left England for the United States in 1842. Joseph Déjacque, "L'Humanisphère; utopie anarchique," was issued serially in Volumes 1-2 (1858-1859) of the author's own periodical, *Libertaire* (New York, 1858-1861), after he had failed to raise enough subscription money to publish it separately. A later anarchist, M. I. Swift, wrote *A League of Justice; or, Is It Right to Rob Robbers?* (Boston, 1893, 90 pp.), which justified revolution by theft from the capitalists. Radical Freelance, Esq. (pseud.), *The Philosophers of Foufouville* (New York, 1868, 297 pp.), published and copyrighted by G. W. Carleton, is sometimes referred to as a satire on the North American Phalanx. It has little but a New Jersey setting and casual jibes at Greeley and women's rights to connect it with the leading Fourierist experiment. The author ascribes to his "Foufouite" leader views on sex, spiritualism, and adventism which were similar to those of the religious crackpot A. B. Smolnikar, and is primarily concerned with a nativist attack on foreign influence, "ultraism" of all sorts, and the teaching of the classics. T. W. Collens, *The Eden of Labor; or, The Christian Utopia* (Philadelphia, 1876, 228 pp.), by the Roman Catholic financial backer of Jesse H. Jones's Christian Labor Union of Boston, expresses radical monetary theories, rejects the piecemeal reforms of cooperatives and ordinary trade unions, and calls for full Bible communism. Alcander Longley, *What Is Communism? A Narrative of the Relief Community* (2nd ed., rev. and enl., St. Louis, Mo., 1890, 424 pp.), is interesting as a veteran communitarian's potpourri of Fourierist, Icarian, cooperative, Christian socialist, populist, and Marxian principles. See also J. S. Cowdon, *Pantocracy, or the Reign of Justice* (Washington, 1892, 62 pp.); and B. A. Brooks, *Earth Revisited* (Boston, 1893, 318 pp.).

In the twentieth century the utopian novel enjoyed a continued vogue until World War I, and a few have appeared since. Bradford Peck,

The World a Department Store (Lewiston, Me., 1900, 311 pp.), cited in most lists, is notable because its author started a paternalistic cooperative movement which lasted several years. On this movement see W. E. Davies, "A Collectivist Experiment Down East: Bradford Peck and the Coöperative Association of America," *New England Quarterly*, xx (Dec. 1947), pp. 471-491. Upton Sinclair has several times used the utopian form, as in *I, Governor of California, and How I Ended Poverty* (Los Angeles, 1933, 64 pp.). See other examples by socialists, R. A. Dague, *Henry Ashton; . . . How the Famous Cooperative Commonwealth Was Established in Zanland* (Alameda, Calif., 1903, 235 pp.); C. A. Steere, *When Things Were Doing* (Chicago, 1908, 282 pp.); and two by G. A. England, *Darkness and Dawn* (Boston, 1914, 672 pp.), on the socialist reconstruction of America after a supposed catastrophe in 1920, and *The Air Trust* (St. Louis, Mo., 1915, 333 pp.), a satire on monopoly. See also C. P. Gilman, *Moving the Mountain* (New York, 1911, 290 pp.).

Topic 4. Marxian Aesthetic Criticism in the United States

The problems for art to be inferred from Marxian ideology have been described in the General Reading, pp. 422-423, 426-434. Marxian critics maintain that the artist must choose sides in the class struggle so that his creation will promote the cause of the workingman. This is proletarian art; whether the creator is or has been a worker, or whether he chooses the situation of labor for his subject matter, is secondary. After all, both capitalist and Fascist art can sometimes meet these latter qualifications. Questions of organicism and functionalism, national regionalism or internationalism, while they have not been overlooked, have not been resolved. This is partly because non-Marxians in the United States have accepted forms developed in Europe without their Marxian content. Thus we find Marxians criticizing contemporary nonsocialists for romantic functionalism, vague organicism, utopian internationalism, sentimental regionalism, or populist realism—all without the saving grace of the Marxian class point of view.

As the following introductory selections show, there has been much more Marxian literary than art criticism in the United States. An introduction to the ideas of early American socialists may be found in A. M. Simons, *The Economic Foundation of Art* (Chicago, n.d., 20 pp.), No. 47 in Kerr's Pocket Library of Socialism. D. D. Egbert, "Foreign Influences in American Art," in *Foreign Influences in American Life* (ed. by D. F. Bowers; Princeton, N.J., 1944, 254 pp.), pp. 99-125, contains a brief summary of some traditional tendencies in American art, which may be compared and contrasted with the Marxian point of view. For the vogue of proletarian literature and art after 1929, see M. W. Brown, "The Marxist Approach to Art," *Dialectics*, No. 2 (1937), pp. 23-31;

James Burnham, "Marxism and Aesthetics," *Symposium,* iv (Jan. 1933), pp. 3-30; and Philip Rahv, "Proletarian Literature; a Political Autopsy," *Southern Review,* iv (Winter 1939), pp. 616-628. Burnham, while he rejected Marxism and its tendency to oversimplify criticism by reducing it to socio-economic categories, believed that bourgeois criticism was no longer capable of objective and significant judgments. Rahv agreed that the literary modes of the nineteen-twenties had been exhausted, and held the Communist Party, not Marxism, responsible for the excesses and crudities of "proletarian" literature. It was "the literature of a party disguised as the literature of a class" (p. 623). In *A Note on Literary Criticism* (New York, 1936, 221 pp.) J. T. Farrell reviewed the problems involved in a Marxian interpretation of literature and the attempts of leftist critics in America to use Marxism as their guide. See especially the chapters, "The Duality of Literature," "Left-Wing Dualism," "The Literature of the Past in the Present," and "Marx on the Relative Aesthetic Validity of Literature."

In general, materials are sparse before 1917. Among the early examples are Walter Crane, "Why Socialism Appeals to Artists," *Atlantic Monthly,* lxix (Jan. 1892), pp. 110-115; the editorial, "Ideal Art for the People," *Christian Union,* xlvi (Dec. 17, 1892), p. 1164; and C. S. Darrow, *Realism in Literature and Art* (Chicago, 1899, 29 pp.), in Kerr's Pocket Library of Socialism, also published as the fourth essay in *A Persian Pearl, and Other Essays* (1899; Boston, 1931, 160 pp.). Crane expected socialism to release creativity, remove the artists' middlemen, make more money available for art by eliminating waste, and provide leisure for the practice and enjoyment of art.

Socialists and anarchists have both tried to claim Whitman as their own. See Helena Born, *Whitman's Ideal Democracy, and Other Writings,* with a biography of Born by the editor, Helen Tufts (Boston, 1902, xxxvi, 88 pp.), especially the title essay and the chapter entitled "Poets of Revolt," written from the individualist anarchist point of view. Also consult Mila (Tupper) Maynard, *Walt Whitman, the Poet of the Wider Selfhood* (Chicago, 1903, 145 pp.); and W. E. Walling, *Whitman and Traubel* (New York, 1916, 145 pp.), pp. 39-142, on Horace Traubel as one of Whitman's literary executors, poet, socialist, pragmatist, and humanist. In addition, see David Karsner's biography, *Horace Traubel* (New York, 1919, 160 pp.); Walling's references to Traubel's monthly, the *Conservator* (Philadelphia, 1890-1919); and Traubel's *Chants Communal* (Boston, 1904, 194 pp.). J. F. Bozard criticizes Traubel in "Horace Traubel's Socialistic Interpretation of Whitman," *Furman Bulletin,* xx (Jan. 1938), pp. 35-45. See also the long introduction by S. K. Sillen, editor of the anthology, *Walt Whitman: Poet of American Democracy* (New York, 1944, 175 pp.).

The body of American Marxian or leftist criticism of the arts of design and music is limited, and much of it is cited elsewhere, in the General Reading, especially pp. 447-451, and in Topics 9-12. See the view of the art historian and critic Meyer Schapiro, "Nature of Abstract Art," *Marxist Quarterly*, I (Jan.-Mar. 1937), pp. 77-98; the more orthodox theory of Mark Rosenthal, "Relative vs. Absolute Criteria in Art," *Dialectics*, No. 8 (1940?), pp. 15-24; and the review essay by Max Horkheimer, emphasizing the sociology of art, "Art and Mass Culture," *Studies in Philosophy and Social Science*, IX, No. 2 (1941), pp. 290-304. For background material by Americans on aspects of French art directly relevant to socialism, see the following articles: M. W. Brown, *The Painting of the French Revolution* (Critics Group Series, No. 8; New York, 1938, 96 pp.); Oliver Larkin, "The Daumier Myth," *Science & Society*, I (Spring 1937), pp. 350-361, "Courbet and His Contemporaries," *ibid.*, III (Winter 1939), pp. 42-63, and "Courbet in the Commune," *ibid.*, V (Summer 1941), pp. 255-259; and Meyer Schapiro, "Courbet and Popular Imagery," *Journal of the Warburg and Courtauld Institutes*, IV (Apr.-July 1941), pp. 164-191. All but the first essay are concerned with the effect of the upheavals of 1848 and 1871 on two of the intellectuals regarded as using art as propaganda for the revolutionary proletariat.

The spate of literary criticism, mostly in the periodicals cited in the General Reading, pp. 448-451, can only be sampled here. An illustration of ultra-leftism in Marxian criticism is E. A. Schachner's extended survey of poetry and prose definitely influenced by Marxism, "Revolutionary Literature in the United States Today," in the *Windsor Quarterly*, issued at Hartland Four Corners, Vermont, II (Spring 1934), pp. 27-64. Three important essays by *Partisan Review* editors are Wallace Phelps and Philip Rahv, "Problems and Perspectives in Revolutionary Literature," *Partisan Review*, I (June-July 1934), pp. 3-10; William Phillips and Rahv, "Some Aspects of Literary Criticism," *Science & Society*, I (Winter 1937), pp. 212-220; and William Phillips, "The Esthetic of the Founding Fathers," *Partisan Review*, IV (Mar. 1938), pp. 11-21. See also C. I. Glicksberg, "Proletarian Fiction in the United States," *Dalhousie Review*, XVII (Apr. 1937), pp. 22-32; Edmund Wilson, "Marxism and Literature," in *The Triple Thinkers; Ten Essays on Literature* (New York, 1938, 289 pp.), pp. 266-289, reprinted from the *Atlantic Monthly*, CLX (Dec. 1937), pp. 741-750; Herbert Solow, "Minutiae of Left-Wing Literary History," *Partisan Review*, IV (Mar. 1938), pp. 59-62, on shifts in allegiance and the party line; R. W. Steadman, "A Critique of Proletarian Literature," *North American Review*, CCXLVII (Spring 1939), pp. 142-152; L. R. Lind's series with the general title, "The Crisis in Literature," in the 1939 *Sewanee Review*, XLVII, pp. 35-62, 184-203, 345-364, and 524-551; H. B. White, "Materialists and the Sociology of American Literature," *Social Research,* VII (May 1940), pp. 184-200; C. I. Glicksberg, "The Decline of Literary Marxism," *Antioch Review,* I (Winter 1941), pp. 452-462; Harry Slochower, "Freud and Marx in Contemporary Literature," *Sewanee Review,* XLIX (July-Sept. 1941), pp. 316-324; and S. E. Hyman, "The Marxist Criticism of Literature," *Antioch Review,* VII (Winter 1947-1948), pp. 541-568.

Three noted noncommunist but largely Marxian critics have been Max Eastman, V. F. Calverton, and James T. Farrell. Among Eastman's contributions are *The Literary Mind; Its Place in an Age of Science* (New York, 1931, 343 pp.) and *Art and the Life of Action* (New York, 1934, 226 pp.). Calverton's first work on the subject was *The Newer Spirit; a Sociological Criticism of Literature* (intro. by Ernest Boyd; New York, 1925, 284 pp.), a spirited and extreme defense of a mechanical Marxian aesthetics which the author later abandoned. He raised general issues in "Literature and Economics," *Communist,* VI (June, July-Aug. 1927), pp. 225-231, 313-318, and "Leftward Ho!" *Modern Quarterly,* VI (Summer 1932), pp. 26-32. Evaluations of Calverton include A. Stork, "Mr. Calverton and His Friends; Some Notes on Literary Trotskyism in America," *International Literature,* No. 3 (July 1934), pp. 97-124, which also attacks Eastman; C. I. Glicksberg, "V. F. Calverton; Marxism without Dogma," *Sewanee Review,* XLVI (July-Sept. 1938), pp. 338-351; and S. L. Solon, "V. F. Calverton's Quest for Utopia," *American Mercury,* LII (May 1941), pp. 625-630. Farrell, *A Note on Literary Criticism* (New York, 1936, 221 pp.), a hot polemic against the narrow "leftism" which made a fetish of proletarian literature, discusses the pluralism of literature as a fine art and as propaganda. The mood of righteous indignation persists in *The League of Frightened Philistines and Other Papers* (New York, 1945, 210 pp.), *The Fate of Writing in America* (New York, 1946, 32 pp.), and *Literature and Morality* (New York, 1947, 304 pp.). The last includes movie criticism, the philosophy of George H. Mead, and a retrospect of the literary Popular Front. Irving Howe, "James T. Farrell—the Critic Calcified," *Partisan Review,* XIV (Sept.-Oct. 1947), pp. 545-552, remarks that Farrell is almost alone as an American novelist interested in criticism and still associated with the noncommunist Left. He states that Farrell's critical approach is valuable but misapplied.

The wide sweep of the more orthodox view of proletarian literature can be seen in Ezra Pound, "Address to the John Reed Club of Philadelphia," *Left Review,* I, No. 3 (1934), pp. 4-5; and Richard Wright, "I Tried to Be a Communist," *Atlantic Monthly,* CLXXIV (Aug. 1944), pp. 61-70, (Sept. 1944), pp. 48-56, on the tactics of communists in the John Reed clubs and the New Deal cultural projects; E. B. Burgum, "The Promise of Democracy and the Fiction of Richard Wright," *Science & Society,* VII (Fall 1943), pp. 338-352; Earl Browder, *Communism and Culture* (New

York, 1941, 47 pp.), a compilation from his writings and speeches, 1935-1941; Michael Gold, *The Hollow Men* (New York, 1941, 128 pp.), originally a series in the *Daily Worker*; and V. J. Jerome, *Culture in a Changing World; a Marxist Approach* (New York, 1947, 94 pp.). See also Angel Flores, who edited the collection, *The Kafka Problem* (New York, 1946, 468 pp.), but significantly excluded two notable essays by the anticommunists Rahv and Arendt. J. H. Lawson, "Parrington and the Search for Tradition," *Mainstream*, I (Winter 1947), pp. 23-43, suggests that Parrington was on his way toward an orthodox Marxian Americanism. William Charvat, "American Romanticism and the Depression of 1837," *Science & Society*, II (Winter 1937), pp. 67-82, applies historical materialism to the New England transcendentalists. Besides research in American literary history, the more important examples of which are cited in the General Reading, p. 451, see the explorations of the leftist sympathizer B. A. Botkin in native American folklore, especially *Lay My Burden Down; a Folk History of Slavery* (Chicago, 1945, 286 pp.), a selection from the slave narrative collection of the Federal Writers' Project. See also Margaret Schlauch's essays in linguistics in *Science & Society*, cited in PART III, Topic 3.

Topic 5.   American Writers Look at the Soviet Union

The revolution and the establishment of a communist government in Russia won the admiration of many liberal writers all over the world, as well as of radicals of various socialist groups. One American writer, John Reed, was an eyewitness of the revolution and died in the service of the Bolsheviks. Anti-Bolsheviks such as Angelica Balabanoff assert that Reed was disillusioned by the methods of the dictatorship, but Soviet Russia still commemorates him as a hero, and he is buried by the Kremlin. Lincoln Steffens and the American journalist, diplomat, and relief worker, Paxton Hibben, were among the first Americans to realize the tremendous significance of the revolution and to have faith that the Soviet regime would succeed in building a new Russia.

As it became clear that Lenin and his colleagues had triumphed, liberals from many countries flocked to Russia much as they had come to America in the early part of the nineteenth century to study and report on a great experiment in social reorganization. Some were enraptured by what they saw; others were disillusioned. A few have remained faithful to the regime in control, no matter what twists and turns it has made in the course of a quarter century. Others became bitter and vituperative, as only the disappointed idealist can become, made so by successive or particular events which seemed to prove that the revolution had been "betrayed." Especially disturbing to them were the N.E.P. (New Economic Policy), the ostracism of Trotsky, the ascendancy of Stalin, the

Moscow trials, and the Russo-German pact. The selections below are limited to imaginative writers; many other records of American observation and opinion of Russia are cited elsewhere in this bibliography.

John Reed, *Ten Days That Shook the World* (New York, 1919, 371 pp.), was accepted by Lenin as a classic account of the most critical moments of the revolution. The anthology edited by Philip Rahv, *Discovery of Europe; the Story of American Experience in the Old World* (Boston, 1947, 743 pp.), contains excerpts from the recorded reactions of such American visitors to Russia as Reed (pp. 484-513), Steffens (pp. 514-526), and Edmund Wilson (pp. 588-621).

Reed, a free-lance journalist on the eastern front during World War I, collected his reports in *The War in Eastern Europe* (pictured by Boardman Robinson; New York, 1916, 335 pp.). See also his *Daughter of the Revolution and Other Stories* (ed. by Floyd Dell; New York, 1927, 164 pp.); and Granville Hicks's biography, *John Reed; the Making of a Revolutionary* (New York, 1936, 445 pp.). Ernest Poole, interested with W. E. Walling and Howard Brubaker in the plight of the masses, contributed the following sympathetic sketches: *The Village; Russian Impressions* (New York, 1918, 234 pp.); *"The Dark People"; Russia's Crisis* (New York, 1918, 226 pp.); and *The Little Dark Man and Other Russian Sketches* (New York, 1925, 141 pp.). See also his autobiography, *The Bridge* (New York, 1940, 422 pp.), pp. 103-166, 267-329, on the Russia of 1905 and 1918, sympathizing with the Mensheviks. Lincoln Steffens has described the aftermath of the revolution and of the Bullitt mission to Moscow, which he had helped organize and of which he was a member, in *The Autobiography of Lincoln Steffens* (New York, 1931, 884 pp.), pp. 790-802.

For an interesting brief account of the pilgrimages of the liberal writers to Russia, see Louis Fischer, *Men and Politics* (New York, 1941, 672 pp.), pp. 187-203. M. G. Hindus, more the commentator than the novelist, contributed *The Russian Peasant and the Revolution* (New York, 1920, 327 pp.), *Broken Earth* (London, 1926, 287 pp.), *Humanity Uprooted* (New York, 1929, 369 pp.), and *Red Bread* (New York, 1931, 372 pp.). Notable examples of the literary American's reactions are Theodore Dreiser, *Dreiser Looks at Russia* (New York, 1928, 264 pp.); W. D. Frank, *Dawn in Russia; the Record of a Journey* (New York, 1932, 272 pp.); D. M. Page, *Soviet Main Street* (Moscow, 1933, 108 pp.), illustrated observations of Podolsk by an American novelist with communist sympathies; Elias Tobenkin, *Stalin's Ladder; War & Peace in the Soviet Union* (New York, 1933, 308 pp.), enthusiastic (after a ten-months' visit) over the removal of regulations discriminating against the Jews and over Soviet penal reforms; A. L. Strong, *I Change Worlds; the Remaking of an American* (New York, 1935, 422 pp.), also published in Moscow as

Remaking an American, by an expatriate later expelled from the Soviet Union; Edmund Wilson, *Travels in Two Democracies* (New York, 1936, 325 pp.), pp. 150-322, an earlier and milder view than that in his *To the Finland Station,* cited below, but just as bitterly criticized by the Stalinists; Claude McKay, *A Long Way from Home* (New York, 1937, 354 pp.), pp. 151-234, an autobiography of a poet and novelist who was a former member of the *Liberator* staff, and spent 1922-1923 in the Soviet Union, where he attended a Comintern congress; and Erskine Caldwell, *All-Out on the Road to Smolensk* (New York, 1942, 230 pp.), and *All Night Long; a Novel of Guerrilla Warfare in Russia* (New York, 1942, 283 pp.).

The defections of the liberal writers were particularly numerous after the Russo-German pact, and the liberal weeklies at this time were filled with recantations. For a typical example see Granville Hicks, "On Leaving the Communist Party," *New Republic,* c (Oct. 4, 1939), pp. 244-245.

Some writers, earlier sympathetic to the Soviet regime but never affiliated with the Communist Party, turned against communism because they found unendurable the dizzy maneuvers of the Communist Party in America, which tried to follow the party line with a religious fervor. They were disgusted, too, with the factional splits among the American communists. John Dos Passos made this disillusionment the theme of a novel, *Adventures of a Young Man* (New York, 1939, 322 pp.). His hero tries to escape the tyranny of the party by going to Spain to fight for the Loyalist cause, but his death is brought about by the same kind of persecution to which he had been subject at home because he would not hew to the party line.

Edmund Wilson satirized the gyrations of the party in a brilliant little piece, "Karl Marx, a Prolet-Play," in *To the Finland Station* (New York, 1940, 509 pp.), appendix A, pp. 479-483. Anyone who is able to catch all the allusions in this burlesque may consider himself thoroughly conversant with the shifting applications of Stalinist ideology to the rapidly changing international situation and the quarrels and schisms of the Communist Party in the United States during these years.

After World War II, American writers continued to look at Russia, but from a new and generally more distant ideological vantage point. See, for example, the novel by Godfrey Blunden, *A Room on the Route* (Philadelphia, 1947, 327 pp.), and the neutral reportage of everyday life and tourist sights by John Steinbeck, *A Russian Journal; with Pictures by Robert Capa* (New York, 1948, 220 pp.).

Topic 6. Socialist Fiction and the Proletarian Novel

Fiction, since it is the most popular of literary types, has always offered an opportunity for effective socialist propaganda. The utopian novel

(Topic 3) was the dominant form used by socialists until 1900. At its best it combined destructive criticism of existing society with the suggestion of a constructive substitute. The novel of social criticism, suggesting reform but without a blueprint, was popular before the Civil War, and lost ground only relatively during the next generation because of the exploitation of other types by better-known writers like Henry James, Mark Twain, and Howells. By the end of the century, in spite of the Indian summer of utopian fiction which Bellamy's *Looking Backward* introduced, the fiction of social criticism had become the alternative which the socialist writer was inclined to choose; and in this Marxism increased. The novels of Bjørnson, Norris, and Garland sprang from some form of native radical philosophy (see PART IV, Topic 8). The novels of London, Sinclair, and their successors were rooted in Marxism, modified by an elementary understanding of the European theory, by residual ideas inherited from native American radicalism, and by other currents of thought such as racism and Freudianism. The development of socialist fiction consisted in sloughing off reformist and utopian elements until there was nothing left but the implicit Marxian utopia.

In their treatment of subject matter, socialist novelists developed no distinct form. While they tended to imitate the realists and naturalists—and if they submitted to the party line of the nineteen-thirties, sought to create a "socialist realism"—a romantic quality remained in varying strength. Their only common characteristic was the universal acceptance of the basic Marxian idea of the class struggle and its propagandist corollary that their writing should persuade to action. The most useful basis for classifying the novels and short stories selected in this topic is according to their themes, since the bulk of the product has more documentary than literary value. Each group of narratives constitutes an appendix to many of the topics discussed elsewhere in this bibliography, especially in PARTS IV and V.

The indirect control exercised by the Communist Party over the standards of the proletarian novel in the nineteen-thirties sharply distinguished it from the socialist fiction of the previous period. The thirties also witnessed the first socialist literary successes since Bellamy and Ernest Poole. Whereas leftist criticism and poetry were negligible in quality, and the leftist theater was limited to audiences in a few urban centers, hundreds of proletarian novels were published, several were best sellers, and a few have enduring worth. While accepting the two basic characteristics of previous socialist fiction, arbiters of the proletarian novel expanded the Marxian requirements to include a whole political orientation (see Joshua Kunitz, "In Defense of a Term," in the *New Masses*, xxviii [July 12, 1938], sec. 2, pp. 145-147, and the trends in criticism outlined in Topic 4). The true proletarian novel exemplified all the ramifications of communist theory—a theory which received some five distinct applications in the twenty years after 1929. So violent was the 1939 shift to the third application that it shook off most of the writers who had been attracted to the movement. Hence the limitation of the proletarian novel to the decade 1929-1939. Examples are cited below, however, of novels published since 1939 with the revolutionary Marxian approach.

Some have suggested, and others have insisted, that no novel is authentically proletarian unless its author has a first-hand acquaintance with the problems of the working class, and deals with them. He ought to be a member of the proletariat himself or at least to have experienced, like Jack London, the life of the industrial or manual laborer before he starts writing. Objections were raised to this extension of the definition: proletarian origin or status does not guarantee class consciousness, least of all in the United States. It is not what novelists write about but how they treat it that qualifies them as revolutionary writers. Furthermore, there was no precise agreement as to what groups and occupations were included in the term proletarian.

The chief difficulty which the proletarian novelists faced in this country was the fact that the revolution had not yet taken place here. Their substitute was usually "the revolutionary situation," that is to say, a strike. Sometimes, instead of using the contemporary scene, novelists turned to a labor or revolutionary crisis in American history or proletarian uprisings abroad. Most of these novels are equipped with a strike for a climax, and with an industrialist-villain and a strike-leader-hero. The most difficult artistic problem for the proletarian novelist was to find a means for varying this melodramatic formula.

Titles illustrating changes of emphasis in the Marxian novel are Jack London, *Martin Eden* (New York, 1909, 411 pp.); Ernest Poole, *The Harbor* (New York, 1915, 387 pp.); Upton Sinclair, *Boston* (New York, 1928, 2 vols.); Robert Cantwell, *The Land of Plenty* (New York, 1934, 369 pp.); and Howard Fast, *The Last Frontier* (New York, 1941, 307 pp.). *Martin Eden*, Jack London's most autobiographical novel, was intended as an indictment of individualism and a lesson that proletarian solidarity is the value supremely worth living and fighting for. It did not succeed in this aim and has often been cited to prove the opposite. More successful was London's utopian novel—utopian only in the technical sense of having a setting in the future—*The Iron Heel*, cited in Topic 3. *The Harbor*, probably the best of radical fiction up to 1917, achieved immediate popularity. It traces the awakening of an intelligent young man to the realization that social justice depends on a revolutionary reorganization of society. At the climax, a strike of longshoremen and

475

stokers proposing to improve conditions in New York harbor is defeated by ignorant scabs and the combined pressures of the capitalist power structure. *The Harbor* has been translated into German, Dutch, Norwegian, Danish, Swedish, and Russian. Before the Lanny Budd series, perhaps the most compelling of Sinclair's long list of novels spotlighting one evil of American capitalism after another, is *Boston*, an exhaustive social document of the Sacco-Vanzetti case. From the artistic point of view of plot structure, style, unity, and a discriminating exercise of Marxian assumptions, Cantwell's *The Land of Plenty* is one of the best proletarian novels. The setting is a Pacific Coast sash and door factory strike. *The Last Frontier*, a tale of Cheyennes and the Bureau of Indian Affairs in the late nineteenth century, represents Howard Fast's escape from the rigidities of the strike formula into American history, while still maintaining the approach of dialectical materialism. Like Martin Eden, Fast's central character disintegrates morally when he displaces his class antagonisms onto an oppressed minority. The other participants show the same moral disintegration.

The literary histories mentioned in the General Reading, p. 451, deal with the proletarian novel more than with any other form of socialist literature. E. B. Burgum, *The Novel and the World's Dilemma* (New York, 1947, 352 pp.), includes Steinbeck and Richard Wright among the seven Americans in his essays on fifteen novelists between Proust and Malraux, but not Dos Passos or Farrell. The book's chief value is its implicitly Marxian criticism, yet it asks psycho-analytical questions of its material. See also Harlan Hatcher, *Creating the Modern American Novel* (New York, 1935, 307 pp.), pp. 34-57, 72-79, 127-139, 173-179, 249-250, and 262-274; and the following articles: Obed Brooks, "The Problem of the Social Novel," *Modern Quarterly*, vi (Autumn 1932), pp. 77-82; Granville Hicks, "Revolution and the Novel," *New Masses*, xi (Apr. 3-May 22, 1934); Harold Strauss, "Realism in the Proletarian Novel," *Yale Review*, xxviii (Dec. 1938), pp. 360-374; J. T. Farrell, "The Social Obligations of the Novelist," *Humanist*, vii (Sept.-Nov. 1947), pp. 57-63, 114-118; and Charles Humboldt, "The Novel of Action," *Mainstream*, i (Fall 1947), pp. 389-407.

On the basis of this introductory material, we can now trace the development of American proletarian fiction in more detail.

Probably the earliest fiction by an American Marxian is Adolf Douai, *Fata Morgana: deutsch-amerikanische Preis-Novelle* (St. Louis, Mo., 1858, 297 pp.). Douai, also author of *Die wilde Jagd*, published in the *Westliche Post* of St. Louis, Mo., in 1869, was active in the earliest socialist movement, especially as an editor of the *New Yorker Volkszeitung*, 1878-1888. The Christian socialist version of the novel of social criticism has many of the accoutrements of Marxian socialist fiction, but without the class struggle. An example by M. R. Scott, *Ernest Marble, the Labor Agitator* (Newark, Ohio, 1805, 275 pp.), gives the Pullman strike a happy ending. See also Archibald McCowan, *Christ the Socialist* (Boston, 1894, 357 pp.), and the fiction of the socialist priest Father Thomas McGrady.

Jack London and Upton Sinclair stand out among the socialist writers of the period 1903-1917, but there is a great contrast in their production. London filled his restless life with potboilers and adventure stories celebrating the last American frontier, and can only be credited with two socialist novels and an occasional short story such as "The Apostate," *International Socialist Review*, ix (June 1909), pp. 929-945, about a wage slave in a jute mill. Sinclair's mill ground out novel after novel like so many humorless puppet shows mixing reports of social injustice with romance. His earnest and honest sympathy for the laborer, however, shines through. Perhaps for this reason, and because he exposed the seamy side of American capitalism, almost three million copies of his works were circulated in Soviet Russia in the thirty years after 1917. Only Jack London, with over ten million, and Mark Twain surpassed this record (see Robert Magidoff, "American Literature in Russia," *Saturday Review of Literature*, xxix [Nov. 2, 1946], pp. 9-11, 45-46). In addition to the novels of Sinclair cited below, see Joseph Gaer, ed., *Upton Sinclair, Bibliography and Biographical Data* (California Literary Research Project, *Monograph*, No. 6; n.p., 1935, 54 pp.); Floyd Dell, *Upton Sinclair; a Study in Social Protest* (New York, 1927, 194 pp.). The best of London's socialist fiction is reprinted in P. S. Foner, *Jack London, American Rebel* (New York, 1947, 533 pp.), pp. 133-303, but over half of this is taken from *The Iron Heel*. His nonfiction reveals the imperfectly digested sources—Spencer, Benjamin Kidd, and Nietzsche, as well as Marx and Engels—of the contradictory ideas that crop out in his fiction. London was enslaved by ideas later identified with fascism, the glorification of conquest and money, the reversion to the primitive, and racism; and yet, like Jaurès, he prophetically exposed the mistakes of revisionism and warned his comrades not to underestimate the power and implacable enmity of the ruling class. See, for example, *Revolution and Other Essays* (New York, 1910, 309 pp.), which includes "The Yellow Peril" (1904); *War of the Classes* (New York, 1905, 278 pp.), especially "The Tramp," pp. 53-98, "The Scab," pp. 101-147, and his first essay, "The Question of the Maximum" (1898), pp. 151-194; and *The People of the Abyss* (New York, 1903, 319 pp.), a muckraking report of seven weeks' experience in the East End of London which weakened his faith in the revolutionary power of the slum proletariat. See the brief bibliography in Foner, cited above, pp. 529-533, particularly useful for periodical

477

articles about Jack London, and Joseph Noel's personal impressions of him in *Footloose in Arcadia* (New York, 1940, 330 pp.).

The early socialist novel, while it centered in descriptions of contemporary working-class situations, also ventured into history and occasionally focused on the capitalist oppressor. Among Sinclair's earliest works are several general indictments of capitalism, *A Captain of Industry* (Girard, Kan., 1906, 142 pp.), *The Metropolis* (New York, 1908, 376 pp.), and *The Moneychangers* (New York, 1908, 316 pp.). He also uses capitalist heroes who forsake their class, as in *Boston*. See *Oil!* (New York, 1927, 527 pp.), which brings in the Teapot Dome scandal, the Sacco-Vanzetti case, and the American invasion of Siberia, but concentrates on oil production in southern California; and *Little Steel* (New York, 1938, 308 pp.), which ends with the conversion of the capitalist. See also R. W. Kauffman, *The Spider's Web* (New York, 1913, 409 pp.). Progressives like Brand Whitlock exploited the theme of political corruption and legal injustice more extensively.

A variation of the capitalist theme is the socialist version of the immigrant success story. The best of these is Abraham Cahan's novel, *The Rise of David Levinsky* (New York, 1917, 529 pp.). Elias Tobenkin, also a Russian-born American, treats the effects of naturalization in three novels, but in *The House of Conrad* (New York, 1918, 375 pp.), he shows the loss of socialist conviction in the second generation. On the other hand, the heroine of *Comrade Yetta* (New York, 1913, 448 pp.), the first novel of Arthur Bullard (Albert Edwards, pseud.), maintains her socialist idealism throughout.

Most of the socialist novels focus on the workingman. The book that made Upton Sinclair's reputation was *The Jungle* (New York, 1906, 413 pp.), which first appeared serially in the *Appeal to Reason*. Sinclair was surprised when the novel was taken as a blow for pure-food reform rather than as an exposé of vile labor conditions. He was inspired by the nonsocialist Frank Norris, who dealt with wheat production and the evils of wheat transportation and speculation in *The Octopus* (New York, 1901, 652 pp.), and *The Pit* (New York, 1903, 421 pp.), the two completed volumes of a trilogy which was to have been concluded with *The Wolf*, a story of famine. Sinclair also contributed *King Coal* (New York, 1917, 396 pp.), set in the Colorado mines; and *Jimmie Higgins* (New York, 1919, 282 pp.), the story of a socialist worker in wartime. Walter Hurt fictionalized Big Bill Haywood and the Cripple Creek strike of 1903-1904 in *The Scarlet Shadow; a Story of the Great Colorado Conspiracy* (Girard, Kan., 1907, 416 pp.). Hutchins Hapgood, *The Spirit of Labor* (New York, 1907, 410 pp.), probes the sources of radicalism in the life of an actual Chicago labor leader. See also M. E. (Tobias) Marcy, *Out of the Dump* (Chicago, 1909, 123 pp.), and C. R. Walker,

Bread and Fire (Boston, 1927, 302 pp.), an autobiographical account of labor conditions in the steel industry. Frank Harris, *The Bomb* (New York, 1909, 329 pp.), purports to be the bomb thrower's story of the Haymarket affair.

The sex theme, including the problems of the emancipated woman and the plight of the prostitute, was well developed by socialist writers. See F. E. Plummer, *Gracia; a Social Tragedy* (Chicago, 1899, 124 pp.), a girl who went wrong; Hutchins Hapgood, *An Anarchist Woman* (New York, 1909, 308 pp.), in the form of letters revealing the psychology of radicalism among the slum proletariat; Upton Sinclair, *Sylvia's Marriage* (Philadelphia, 1914, 348 pp.), the proverbial bird in the gilded cage, and *Damaged Goods* (Philadelphia, 1913, 194 pp.), his novelized version of Brieux' play, *Les Avariés*, both painting the horrors of venereal disease. In Elias Tobenkin, *The Road* (New York, 1922, 316 pp.), an unmarried mother finds satisfaction in the socialist movement. Floyd Dell, in *Moon-Calf* (New York, 1920, 394 pp.), is equally concerned with the sex and radical experience of his hero, but becomes preoccupied with the marriage question in the sequel, *The Briary-Bush* (New York, 1921, 425 pp.). Max Eastman's inconclusive *Venture* (New York, 1927, 398 pp.), lets his ex-college-boy hero enjoy Greenwich Village Bohemianism, but he finally attaches himself, like Hilda Thorsen in *The Road*, to the cause of labor.

Socialists wrote historical novels, short stories, and stories for children, but the quantity as well as the quality was insignificant. See Edward Bellamy, *The Duke of Stockbridge; a Romance of Shay's Rebellion* (New York, 1900, 371 pp.); Bellamy, *The Blindman's World and Other Stories* (Boston, 1898, 415 pp.), and May Beals, *The Rebel at Large* (Chicago, 1906, 184 pp.), short stories; and Henry Schnittkind, *Alice and the Stork; a Fairy Tale for Workingmen's Children* (Boston, 1915, 95 pp.). See also John Spargo, *Socialist Readings for Children* (New York, 1909, 132 pp.).

Antisocialist novels mocked or moralized at the un-Americanism, free love, and vicious tendencies of socialism. Samples of this type include C. M. (Mrs. Fremont) Older, *The Socialist and the Prince* (New York, 1903, 309 pp.); Thomas Dixon, Jr., *The One Woman; a Story of Modern Utopia* (New York, 1903, 350 pp.), in three editions, and *Comrades* (New York, 1909, 319 pp.), about latter-day communitarians but aimed at all socialists; Cleveland Moffett, *The Battle* (New York, 1909, 303 pp.), a novelized play; and R. A. Wason's farce, *The Steering Wheel* (Indianapolis, Ind., 1910, 399 pp.), in which love triumphs over both socialism and the trusts.

The proletarian novelist had plenty of fresh material to draw upon, both the depressed or unemployed condition of labor, and the drama of labor organization and conflict. If he dramatized the class struggle, he earned the proletarian label. If he recorded the life of the contemporary poor, his product might better be called, as Horace Gregory has called it, the depression novel. Fellow travelers both reported and dramatized, with varying fidelity to the party line. What distinguished them was their unwillingness to affiliate and their eventual deviation from Marxian paths. This topic does not attempt to distinguish sympathizers and fellow travelers from avowed Marxians, since its aim is to sample all kinds of novelists influenced by the leftist movement of which the Communist Party was the spearhead.

The favorite locale of the strike novel was the North Carolina textile region, made famous by the Gastonia strike of the late twenties. Probably the best of these was Olive (Tilford) Dargan (Fielding Burke, pseud.), *Call Home the Heart* (London, 1932, 432 pp.). See also the sequel, *A Stone Came Rolling* (New York, 1935, 412 pp.); Mary (Heaton) Vorse, *Strike!* (New York, 1930, 376 pp.); and Grace Lumpkin, *To Make My Bread* (New York, 1932, 384 pp.) and D. M. Page, *Gathering Storm* (New York, 1932, 374 pp.). In southern proletarian novels an inevitable feature was the solidarity of black and white workers. In *The Shadow Before* (New York, 1934, 389 pp.), also published in Moscow, William Rollins, Jr., transferred Gastonia to the North. Howard Fast, *Clarkton* (New York, 1947, 239 pp.), equally spoiled by wooden types and a heavy burden of propaganda, uses a similar northern setting. At the same melodramatic level are Clara Weatherwax, *Marching! Marching!* (New York, 1935, 256 pp.), winner of the *New Masses* and John Day Company prize for a novel on an American proletarian theme; A. B. Armstrong (pseud.), *Parched Earth* (New York, 1934, 430 pp.), a California fruit-canning town; and Edward Newhouse, *This Is Your Day* (New York, 1937, 313 pp.), an upstate New York farmers' strike. See also Leane Zugsmith, *A Time to Remember* (New York, 1936, 352 pp.), with the moral that department-store workers are proletarian; and William Cunningham, *The Green Corn Rebellion* (New York, 1935, 302 pp.), abortive resistance of Oklahoma socialist farmers against World War I; and least sloganized of all, *In Dubious Battle* (New York, 1936, 349 pp.), John Steinbeck's picture of a California migrant workers' strike told from the viewpoint of a radical sympathizer.

The best novelists sought from the whole history of their generation the social sources of frustration. Eminently successful was Dos Passos' trilogy, *U.S.A.* (New York, 1937, 1471 pp.), consisting of *The 42nd Parallel* (New York, 1930, 426 pp.), *1919* (New York, 1932, 473 pp.), and *The Big Money* (New York, 1936, 561 pp.), a "collectivist" view of American life from 1900 to 1930. Even more sweeping and much more the crusading Marxist was Josephine Herbst, whose trilogy dealing with economic conditions in America since the Civil War won from some critics the title of major American novelist: *Pity Is Not Enough* (New York, 1933, 358 pp.); *The Executioner Waits* (New York, 1934, 371 pp.), the best of the three; and *Rope of Gold* (New York, 1939, 429 pp.). Narrower themes were exploited by J. T. Farrell, in *Young Lonigan; a Boyhood in Chicago Streets* (New York, 1932, 308 pp.); *The Young Manhood of Studs Lonigan* (New York, 1934, 412 pp.); and *Judgment Day* (New York, 1935, 465 pp.), published together as *Studs Lonigan* (New York, 1935, 3 vols. in 1), the social matrix of the gangster; and John Steinbeck, *The Grapes of Wrath* (New York, 1939, 619 pp.), the depression farm problem in Oklahoma and California. Farrell, although the most outspoken and persistent of leftists still, permits the least intrusion of socialist ideology in his novels. See also his inferior Danny O'Neill trilogy, *A World I Never Made* (New York, 1936, 508 pp.); *No Star Is Lost* (New York, 1938, 637 pp.); and *Father and Son* (New York, 1940, 616 pp.). By the most lenient construction, Ernest Hemingway, *For Whom the Bell Tolls* (New York, 1940, 471 pp.), and Dreiser's naturalistic novels might find a place in this topic, for Hemingway's tale of love and guerrilla warfare against fascism travels the road the communists had traveled during the Spanish Civil War, and Dreiser's career led him at last to the Communist Party. See Dreiser, "The Logic of My Life," *Mainstream*, i (Spring 1947), pp. 225-227, an application for membership; also Dos Passos' characterization of Dreiser as a proletarian writer, *Modern Quarterly*, vi (Summer 1932), p. 12. See also J. W. Beach, "Dos Passos, 1947," *Sewanee Review*, lv (July-Sept. 1947), pp. 406-418, and Dos Passos, "The Failure of Marxism," *Life*, xxiv (Jan. 19, 1948), pp. 96-108, for his change of views.

The realistic or naturalistic depression novels, small scale models of the excellent books just cited, were the commonest type of all. Some of them dramatized the organizer; other traced the awakening of class consciousness; others were content to report the fate of the unenlightened. For social documents, see Catharine Brody, *Nobody Starves* (New York, 1932, 281 pp.), and James Steele, *Conveyor* (New York, 1935, 222 pp.), both on automobile workers; Jack Conroy, *The Disinherited* (New York, 1933, 310 pp.), and Tom Kromer, *Waiting for Nothing* (New York, 1935, 187 pp.), not localized; Albert Halper, *The Chute* (New York, 1937, 558 pp.), a Chicago mail-order house, *The Foundry* (New York, 1934, 499 pp.), a Chicago electrotype foundry in 1928-1929, and *Union Square* (New York, 1933, 378 pp.); Tess Slesinger, *The Unpossessed* (New York, 1934, 357 pp.), Greenwich Village radicals; and later examples, Ira Wolfert, *Tucker's People* (New York, 1943, 496 pp.), the numbers racket in Harlem; and Edward McSorley, *Our Own Kind* (New York, 1946, 304 pp.), Irish working class in Providence, Rhode Island. See also the work of the Yiddish proletarian writer Isaac Moishe Nadir collected in *Di neiste Werk fun Moishe Nadir* (New York, 1932, 4 vols.). The road to radicalism is traversed in Jack Conroy, *A World to Win* (New York, 1935, 348 pp.), symbolizing the unity of the workers of hand and brain; Edward Newhouse, *You Can't Sleep Here* (New York, 1934, 252 pp.), a declassed reporter turned agitator for unemployment insurance; Waldo Frank, *The Death and Birth of David Markand* (New York, 1934, 542 pp.); T. A. Boyd, *In Time of Peace* (New York, 1935, 309 pp.); D. M. Page, *Moscow Yankee* (New York, 1935, 292 pp.), romance in a Soviet factory; and Leane Zugsmith, *The Summer Soldier* (New York, 1938, 290 pp.), contrasting liberals who become class conscious though defeated with those who fail in the crisis. Labor organizing is the subject of Thomas Tippett, *Horse Shoe Bottoms* (New York, 1935. 298 pp.), in the coal mines, and Grace Lumpkin, *A Sign for Cain* (New York, 1935, 376 pp.), among southern black and white workers; and in the next decade, Ruth McKenney, *Jake Home* (New York, 1943, 503 pp.), panoramic; and Chester Himes, *Lonely Crusade* (New York, 1947, 398 pp.), west-coast Negro unions. The autobiographical novels of Isidor Schneider, *From the Kingdom of Necessity* (New York, 1935, 450 pp.), and Richard Wright, *Native Son* (New York, 1940, 359 pp.), and *Black Boy* (New York, 1945, 228 pp.), belong to this "documentarian" group. Wright was by 1940 well on his way out of the Communist Party (see his article in the *Atlantic Monthly*, "I Tried to Be a Communist," CLXXIV [Aug. 1944], pp. 61-70, [Sept. 1944], pp. 48-56); his writings as a communist, such as *Bright and Morning Star* (New York, 1941, 48 pp.), appeared mostly in magazines. The best proletarian short stories are in the collections of Erskine Caldwell, *Kneel to the Rising Sun and Other Stories* (New York, 1935, 246 pp.); Ben Field, *The Cock's Funeral* (New York, 1937, 207 pp.), with an introductory commentary on proletarian fiction by Erskine Caldwell; Albert Maltz, *The Way Things Are, and Other Stories* (intro. by Michael Gold; New York, 1938, 218 pp.); and Meridel Le Sueur, *Salute to Spring* (New York, 1940, 191 pp.).

The revolutionary novel dealt occasionally with political themes, especially the threat of native fascism; much more with American history than previous socialist fiction, especially during World War II; and developed as never before a list of books for juvenile readers. Albert Maltz, *The Cross and the Arrow* (Boston, 1944, 448 pp.), is an allegorical detective-story melodrama of a fifth columnist in a German factory, and his *The Underground Stream* (Boston, 1940, 348 pp.) presents a communist organizer staunch against a Fascist automobile official. See also John Dos Passos, *Number One* (Boston, 1943, 303 pp.), one of several novels suggesting the career of Huey Long; J. T. Farrell, *Ellen Rogers* (New York, 1941, 429 pp.), and *Tommy Gallagher's Crusade* (New York, 1939, 91 pp.), reminiscent of Father Coughlin; and Sinclair Lewis,

It Can't Happen Here (Garden City, N.Y., 1935, 458 pp.), a more in-dividualistic approach. Corrupt Pennsylvania machine politics is flayed in Henry Hart, *The Great One* (New York, 1934, 323 pp.). Dalton Trumbo, *Washington Jitters* (New York, 1936, 287 pp.), satirizes the New Dealers, and his *Johnny Got His Gun* (Philadelphia, 1939, 309 pp.), is a fictional contribution on a horror theme to the anti-interventionist movement of 1939-1941. Isidor Schneider, *The Judas Time* (New York, 1947, 361 pp.), published while the author was an editor of *New Masses*, blasts Trotskyist renegades and reveals the parochial life of Communist Party members, filled with talk and endless meetings.

Howard M. Fast, more than other proletarian novelists, has mined American history for materials. See *Conceived in Liberty* (New York, 1939, 389 pp.), the common man at Valley Forge; *The Unvanquished* (New York, 1942, 316 pp.), George Washington and the Revolution; *Citizen Tom Paine* (New York, 1943, 341 pp.); *Freedom Road* (New York, 1944, 263 pp.), almost the only Marxian Civil War novel; and *The American* (New York, 1946, 337 pp.), on Governor Altgeld of Illinois. Meridel Le Sueur in the same period wrote an impressionistic regional history of Minnesota, *North Star Country* (New York, 1945, 327 pp.). A ponderous and hackneyed example of what communists would call infantile leftism applied to historical fiction is George Spiro (George Marlen, pseud.), *The Road; a Romance of the Proletarian Revolution* (New York, 1932, 623 pp.).

Howard Fast has been one of the leading leftist writers of juveniles, e.g., *The Tall Hunter* (New York, 1942, 103 pp.), on Johnny Appleseed; and International Publishers produces a series for adolescents and pre-adolescents, Young World Books, on simple science, class-struggle morals, and adventure.

Topic 7. Theater of the Left

Since 1915 the American theater has experienced a revival of consider-able importance. Encouraged by the organization of the Washington Square Players (1915), the Provincetown Players (1916), and the Theatre Guild (1918), producing groups receptive to new techniques and bold themes, a number of excellent playwrights emerged whose work was not only highly successful as "theater," but possessed enduring literary quality which the earlier American drama could not claim.

During this period the influence of the Soviet theater was important in this country. The American tour of the Moscow Art Theater in 1923 aroused great interest in the new Russian development. These develop-ments were thoroughly studied in Norris Houghton's excellent *Moscow Rehearsals* (New York, 1936, 291 pp.). American playwrights experi-mented with the amazingly varied techniques which the different Russian theater groups had evolved. There was some opportunity to see in this country examples of Soviet drama. The Theatre Guild brought to the stage, for instance, S. M. Tretyakov's *Roar China* (tr. by F. Polyanovskaya and Barbara Nixon; London, 1931, 87 pp.), a play based on Western imperialism in the Orient and first produced by Meyerhold in Russia in 1926.

As the novel moved to the left in the 1930's, so did the theater. The movement was actively aided by various producing agencies, notably the Group Theatre, under the direction of Harold Clurman, and the Theatre Union, which attempted to build up in New York a working-class audience. Several of the playwrights identified with this leftward trend were avowed communists.

In the depth of the depression the Federal Theatre Project was organized (December 1935) under the Works Progress Administration in order to provide relief for the thousands of theater people out of work. Its director, Hallie Flanagan, a member of the Vassar faculty, was intimately acquainted with and was inspired by the achievements of the Soviet theater. In the three and one-half years of its existence the Federal Theatre organized in all parts of the country a program of productions which brought the drama to tens of thousands of citizens who had never seen a play. Though it produced plays of all kinds, many of the original plays written for it were notable for the skill with which they dramatized social questions. Because of the bold way in which these problems were treated, it was not long before the Federal Theatre was accused in Congress of being communistic, and the fight was on to abolish the project by cutting off appropriations. On June 30, 1939, the death blow was dealt, and one of the most successful cultural projects ever undertaken by the federal government was abruptly terminated.

For an introduction to the theater of the left, see the collection edited with an introduction by William Kozlenko, *The Best Short Plays of the Social Theatre* (New York, 1939, 456 pp.). The story of the Federal Theatre Project is told in Hallie Flanagan, *Arena* (New York, 1940, 475 pp.). Harry Taylor, "Toward a People's Theatre," *Mainstream*, 1 (Spring 1947), pp. 239-249, refers to the principal surveys of the American social theater in a brief review of the leading left-wing writers, plays, and theaters since 1926.

An obscure five-act play by the French Proudhonian anarchist Claude Pelletier, *Les Hérétiques révolutionnaires—socialistes du XVᵉ siècle* (New York, 1867, 218 pp.), little read and perhaps never produced, is probably the first "Marxian" drama written and published in the United States. If there were any amateur theatricals among the early Marxian or native radical organizations—and little dramatic activity has so far been uncovered except for some of the utopian communities—research has yet to describe them. This kind of propaganda-recreation material, however, was also used by the labor organizations in which many socialists, such as James H. Maurer, first learned their radicalism.

The socialists did publish and produce for their amateur entertainments a number of "social problem" plays modeled after the drama of Ibsen and Galsworthy. Sample titles are John Spargo, *Not Guilty* (Westwood, Mass., n.d., 29 pp.), a propaganda skit in three acts on the Moyer-Haywood trials; M. C. Wentworth, *The Flower Shop* (Boston, 1912, 117 pp.); C. F. Quinn, *Under the Lash* (Chicago, 1902, 32 pp.); R. E. Dunbar, *Arthur Sonten* (South Bend, Ind., 1913, 103 pp.); F. P. and K. R. O'Hare, *World Peace* (St. Louis, Mo., 1915, 61 pp.), a spectacle drama; and J. R. Cole and Grace Silver, comps., *Socialist Dialogues and Recitations* (Chicago, 1913, 59 pp.). The last included a short play condensed from a scene in Jack London's *The Iron Heel* and other entertainment for socialist meetings. See also Mrs. M. E. (Tobias) Marcy, *A Free Union; a One Act Drama of 'Free Love'* (Chicago, 1921, 64 pp.); I. S. Tucker, *The Sangreal* (Chicago, 1919, 102 pp.), four acts in verse; and the Christian socialist efforts of C. R. Kennedy, such as *The Idol-Breaker* (New York, 1914, 177 pp.), in five acts. Emma Goldman's book of criticism, *The Social Significance of the Modern Drama* (Boston, 1914, 315 pp.), deals with the group of European dramatists from whom these socialist playwrights derived whatever inspiration they had. See also "The Drama, a Powerful Disseminator of Radical Thought," the last chapter in Goldman, *Anarchism and Other Essays* (New York, 1910, 277 pp.). The use of dramatic demonstrations for morale and propaganda purposes in a strike is illustrated in the I.W.W. pageant staged in Madison Square Garden. *Pageant of the Paterson Strike* (New York, 1913, 31 pp.), contains brief program notes and articles on the history of the strike. Participation in this episode helped make John Reed a revolutionary. The socialist poet George Sterling wrote the play *Truth* (Chicago, 1923, 124 pp.), besides his dramatic poems. Representative of socialist interest in the new theater is Harry Waton's Rand School lecture, *The Historic Significance of O'Neill's "Strange Interlude"* (New York, 1928, 61 pp.).

Among the productions of the Provincetown Players were John Reed, "Freedom," in *The Provincetown Plays*, Ser. II (1916), pp. 70-93, and Neith Boyce, "The Two Sons," *ibid.*, Ser. III (1916), pp. 147-169. Among the playwrights who participated in this extraordinary revival, several wrote drama of social protest. Though some of them were sympathetic to socialism, few of them wrote with socialistic propaganda as their chief aim. Notable among the early plays of social content are Eugene O'Neill, *The Hairy Ape* (New York, 1922, 322 pp.), the class frustration of a stoker, and Elmer Rice, *The Adding Machine* (Garden City, N.Y.,

1923, 143 pp.), exposing the mediocrity and emptiness of a white-collar slave. About 1927 the New Playwrights took over the Provincetown Theater and produced such plays as Paul Sifton, *The Belt* (New York, 1927, 193 pp.), on the Ford speed-up; Upton Sinclair, *Singing Jailbirds* (Pasadena, Calif., 1924, 95 pp.), the I.W.W.; and J. H. Lawson, *The International* (New York, 1927, 276 pp.), attacking American imperialism, and *Loud Speaker, a Farce* (New York, 1927, 186 pp.). Also associated in this enterprise were Michael Gold, Em Jo Basshe, Francis Farragoh, and John Dos Passos. See also Lawson's *Processional, a Jazz Symphony of American Life* (New York, 1925, 218 pp.), produced by the Theatre Guild in 1925, a light satire against superpatriotism and conservatism, and *Roger Bloomer* (New York, 1923, 225 pp.), in the same spirit. In addition, consult Martin Flavin, *The Criminal Code* (New York, 1929, 200 pp.), a protest against the American legal system, and Maxwell Anderson and Harold Hickerson, *Gods of the Lightning* in the volume of the same title (London, 1928, 187 pp.), pp. 3-106, a propaganda play on the Sacco-Vanzetti case. Anderson returned to the theme in *Winterset* (Washington, 1935, 134 pp.).

In studying the drama of the radical playwrights of the thirties, the *New Theatre & Film* (New York, 1934-1937), which superseded the *Workers Theatre* (New York, ?-1933) as the organ of the League of Workers Theatres, later called the New Theatre League, is a valuable source. Theatre Union plays between 1932 and 1937 included George Sklar and Albert Maltz, *Peace on Earth* (1933; New York, 1934, 120 pp.), antiwar; Paul Peters and George Sklar, *Stevedore* (New York, 1934, 123 pp.), solidarity between Negro and white longshoremen in New Orleans; Albert Maltz, *Black Pit* (New York, 1935, 108 pp.), a coal strike; Albert Bein, *Let Freedom Ring* (New York, 1936, 170 pp.), based on Grace Lumpkin's *To Make My Bread*, cited in Topic 6; J. H. Lawson, *Marching Song* (New York, 1937, 166 pp.), also a strike. Several of these plays had good runs in London. Other Marxian productions were Morris Levitt, *We Strike, and On the Bowery; Two One-Act Plays* (New York, 1931, 61 pp.); John Wexley, *They Shall Not Die* (New York, 1934, 191 pp.), based on the Scottsboro case and produced by the Theatre Guild; and Michael Blankfort and Michael Gold, "*Battle Hymn*" (New York, 1936, 108 numbered leaves), produced by the Federal Theatre Project's Experimental Theatre, about John Brown. The Negro playwright Theodore Ward dealt with racial problems in *Big White Fog*, first produced by the Federal Theatre in Chicago in 1938; *Our Lan'*, which opened on Broadway in September 1947; and *Shout Hallelujah* (1947), an excerpt of which appeared in *Masses & Mainstream*, I (May 1948), pp. 8-18.

Of the leftist sympathizers among the playwrights, who were not always strict Marxians or even fellow travelers, the outstanding success was Clifford Odets, who reached an early peak in 1935 with *Waiting for Lefty,* the struggle for militant rank-and-file control of a taxi drivers' union, and *Awake and Sing,* awakening class consciousness in a Bronx middle-class family, and the unsuccessful *Till the Day I Die,* all published in *Three Plays* (New York, 1935, 242 pp.). These plays were shown to many working-class groups in the provinces of England and Wales two years later, and were produced in London. One of the best-known plays written for the Federal Theatre was Marc Blitzstein, *The Cradle Will Rock* (1937; New York, 1938, 150 pp.), a musical satire for unionization which had over one hundred performances. Mention should also be made of John Dos Passos' *Fortune Heights* (1933), first played by the Chicago Workers Theatre and published in *Three Plays* (New York, 1934, 298 pp.), pp. 163-298. Typical of contemporary antiwar sentiment was Irwin Shaw, *Bury the Dead* (New York, 1936, 107 pp.). Lillian Hellman veiled her attack on southern industrial capitalism in *The Little Foxes* (New York, 1939, 159 pp.), and fell in with the anti-Nazi spirit in *The Watch on the Rhine* (New York, 1941, 170 pp.). Both plays achieved movie production in spite of any hidden Marxism on the basis of their plots. Hellman's renewed attack, *Another Part of the Forest* (New York, 1947, 134 pp.), portrayed the Hubbard family of *The Little Foxes* twenty years earlier.

There were many other groups: Labor Stage, Inc., an I.L.G.W.U. organization which gave *Pins and Needles* (1937) by Marc Blitzstein, Arthur Arent, and others, with music by H. J. Rome, a three-season success; Workers' Laboratory Theatre; the Theatre of Action; the Theatre Collective; the Artef, a Yiddish collective founded in 1928 and active in the thirties under the direction of Beno Schneider; and such mobile "agitprop" units as the Red Dust Players and Stage for Action. The "agitprop" owed a great deal to the work of the European communists, Piscator and Bertolt Brecht. The Red Dust Players performed in the Oklahoma sharecropper region after the close of the Federal Theatre until suppressed as criminal syndicalists; while the Stage for Action sought audiences among union locals. *Federal Theatre Plays* (New York, 1938, 2 vols.) included Arthur Arent, *One-Third of a Nation* (1938), on housing, and *Power* (1937), on the T.V.A.; and *Triple-A Plowed Under* (1936), all "living newspapers," with no plot in the usual sense but dramatizing a current issue. The producers drew ideas for this form of drama from Aristophanes, the *commedia dell' arte,* and the movies. Many other Federal Theatre productions were reproduced in mimeographed form.

For various aspects of the theater of the left consult: J. H. Lawson, *Theory and Technique of Playwriting* (New York, 1936, 315 pp.); Ben Blake, *The Awakening of the American Theatre* (New York, 1935, 62 pp.), by a founder of the new theater movement; Harold Clurman, *The Fervent Years; the Story of the Group Theatre and the Thirties* (New York, 1945, 298 pp.), by its director; Eleanor Flexner, *American Playwrights, 1918-1938* (New York, 1938, 331 pp.), written from a leftist point of view; J. W. Krutch, "The Drama of Social Criticism," *The American Drama since 1918* (New York, 1939, 325 pp.), chap. 5; Norris Houghton, *Advance from Broadway; 19,000 Miles of American Theatre* (New York, 1941, 416 pp.), especially pp. 244-292, on the people's theater; and E. M. Gagey, *Revolution in American Drama* (New York, 1947, 315 pp.).

Topic 8. Marxism and Poetry

A great imaginative literature using a socialist symbolism has not appeared. Preoccupation with the necessities of life amid the development of the United States, its wars and depressions, has forced men into a literature of protest or defense. There had been no commonly accepted body of symbols, no world cultural center, until New York began to assume this place for half the world toward the middle of the twentieth century. Stable communities like those of the Shakers (see Topic 1) were too small for their isolation to protect them in their unique tradition. The political socialists were forced to feed on the subject matter of capitalist society. Consequently, the examples given in this topic are either evidence of propaganda in verse (see Topic 10) or mediocre attempts by socialists using the old forms and imagery. The poetry which was used in socialist songs is discussed in Topic 9. Unlike the American writers of the proletarian novel, who were acknowledged in England as in advance of their own leftist novelists, American leftist poets were decidedly outranked by Auden and others in England, and by many poets on the Continent—Henriette Roland Holst, Louis Aragon, and Bertolt Brecht in Holland, France, and Germany; Mayakovsky and Esenin in Soviet Russia (see General Reading, pp. 435, 437, 440-441).

To sample the widest variety of poetry by Marxian socialists in the United States at different periods, see the quotations and references to German-American socialist production in W. F. Kamman, *Socialism in German American Literature* (Philadelphia, 1917, 124 pp.), pp. 64-118, which is almost wholly concerned with poetry appearing in periodicals; and the following anthologies: Upton Sinclair, ed., *The Cry for Justice; an Anthology of the Literature of Social Protest* (intro. by Jack London; Philadelphia, 1915, 891 pp.), *passim*; Genevieve Taggard, ed., *May Days; an Anthology of Verse from Masses-Liberator* (New York, 1925, 306 pp.); and Granville Hicks and others, eds., *Proletarian Literature in the United States* (New York, 1935, 384 pp.), pp. 145-208.

Eugène Pottier, composer of the words for the *Internationale*, lived as a refugee at various places between Newark and South Boston in the late eighteen-seventies. See examples of his verse written during this period in *Chants révolutionnaires* (1887; 3rd ed. by Lucien Descaves; Paris, 1937, 277 pp.), pp. 23, 27, 28, 53-55, 82-84, 87-88, 158-160, 203-205, and especially "The Workingmen of America to the Workingmen of France," pp. 205-214, written for the delegation of socialist workingmen to the Philadelphia Centennial Exposition in 1876. See also for this period, M. D. Learned, *The German-American Turner Lyric* (Baltimore, Md., 1897, 58 pp.), which contains a list of poets, some of whom were socialists.

The poetic product of anarchism is thin, and begins—aside from the occasional verse of Thoreau and one or two rhymes of Warren—with the collection published by Johann Most before he left Germany, *Proletarier-Liederbuch* (5th ed., Chemnitz, 1875, 80 pp.). In the same period, J. W. Lloyd wrote *Wind-Harp Songs* (Buffalo, N.Y., 1895, 132 pp.), an anarchist gift book of verse. See also the satirical doggerel and parodies of M. I. Swift, *Advent of Empire* (Los Angeles, Calif., 1900, 143 pp.), including "Possessional," "Chains of Republican Empire," "The Free American Workingman," etc. Arturo Giovannitti, one of the I.W.W. leaders of the Lawrence textile strike of 1912, composed free verse about his jail experience which was ineffective as poetry but revealing as evidence of the state of mind of an imprisoned syndicalist. Some of these poems, such as "The Walker," were printed in Giovannitti's *Arrows in the Gale* (intro. by Helen Keller; Riverside, Conn., 1914, 108 pp.). See also Adolf Wolff, *Songs of Rebellion* (New York, 1914, 98 pp.), distributed by Mother Earth Publishing Association; and C. E. S. Wood, *The Poet in the Desert* (Portland, Ore., 1915, 124 pp.).

The rhymes published in the Socialist Party journals and in separate volumes achieved their circulation primarily as propaganda dealing with the miseries of the poor, the glories of martyrdom, and the class struggle, a pattern followed in much of the proletarian poetry after World War I as well. Examples of this class are C. P. S. Gilman, *In This Our World* (San Francisco, Calif., 1895, 184 pp.); James Allman, *Carmina Noctis* (New York, 1898, 41 pp.); Edwin Markham, *The Man with the Hoe, and Other Poems* (New York, 1899, 134 pp.), with its famous title poem; F. E. Plummer, *Gracia; a Social Tragedy* (Chicago, 1899, 124 pp.); J. R. Cole, comp., *Socialist Songs, Dialogues and Recitations* (Chicago, 1906, 55 pp.); G. H. Gibson, *The People's Hour, and Other Themes* (Chicago, 1909, 137 pp.); W. F. Barnard, *The Tongues of Toil, and Other Poems* (Chicago, 1911, 192 pp.); Covington Hall, *Songs of Rebellion* (New Orleans, La., 1915, 49 pp.); I. S. Tucker, *Poems of a Socialist Priest* (Chicago, 1915, 64 pp.), by the author of several other volumes of poetry; and Ruth Le Prade, ed., *Debs and the Poets* (intro. by Upton Sinclair; Pasadena, Calif., 1920, 99 pp.). The last included verse and prose tributes to Debs in Atlanta prison. See also H. M. Tichenor, *Rhymes of the Revolution* (St. Louis, Mo., 1914, 62 pp.), and Mrs. M. E. (Tobias) Marcy, *Rhymes of Early Jungle Folk* (Chicago, 1922, 124 pp.).

Later verse by those with a more or less definite affiliation with the Socialist Party is of somewhat better quality. Max Eastman, while still in the radical movement, published *Child of the Amazons* (New York, 1913, 69 pp.), and *Colors of Life* (New York, 1918, 129 pp.). His *Enjoyment of Poetry* (1913; New York, 1939, 317 pp.) had no basis in any Marxian aesthetic theory. Upton Sinclair, primarily a novelist with a purpose, also wrote *Hell; a Verse Drama and Photo-Play* (Pasadena, Calif., 1923, 128 pp.). Perhaps the best of the middle generation of socialist poets was George Sterling, who was still developing when he died in 1926. Sterling, part propagandist and part artist, was a California friend of Jack London and Upton Sinclair. See his *Selected Poems* (New York, 1923, 232 pp.), taken from nine volumes published over the previous twenty years, and his evaluation of *Robinson Jeffers; the Man and the Artist* (New York, 1926, 40 pp.). After him, John Wheelwright, author of *Rock and Shell; Poems, 1923-1933* (Boston, 1933, 87 pp.), *Mirrors of Venus; a Novel of Sonnets, 1914-1938* (Boston, 1938, 87 pp.), and *Political Self-Portrait* (Boston, 1940, 99 pp.), is notable. See R. P. Blackmur's introduction to Wheelwright's *Selected Poems* (Norfolk, Conn., 1941, 32 pp.), in the New Directions Poet of the Month series, 1941, No. 6. Of greater stature and promise is Delmore Schwartz, an independent socialist who has borrowed ideas from Marx and Freud, and fashioned his style in the school of Yeats, Eliot, Cummings, and Stevens. The author of *Genesis* (New York, 1943, 208 pp.), he has since published *Vaudeville for a Princess, and Other Poems* (New York, 1950, 106 pp.). See also his *In Dreams Begin Responsibilities* (Norfolk, Conn., 1938, 171 pp.). David Berenberg's narrative poem, *The Kid* (New York, 1931, 79 pp.), was composed during the period when he was active in the Socialist Party. S. A. De Witt, one of the socialist assemblymen suspended from the New York legislature during the red scare after World War I, most closely approached the revolutionary idiom in *Rhapsodies in Red; Songs for the Social Revolution* (New York, 1933, 48 pp.).

The revolutionary poetry of the New Deal era made up in quantity what it lacked in distinction. The little magazine, *Dynamo* (New York, 1934-1936), edited by Sol Funaroff, Herman Spector, and others, devoted itself to revolutionary verse; *Anvil* (Moberly, Mo., 1933-1935), edited by Jack Conroy and others, published proletarian prose and poetry; and other periodicals of the same type showed similar influence. *Anvil* superseded *Rebel Poet* (Holt, Minn., 1931-1932), and merged with the *Partisan Review* in February 1936. The group around the Dynamo Press, then sympathetic to the party line, were responsible for such titles as Herman Spector and others, *We Gather Strength* (intro. by Michael Gold; New York, 1933, 63 pp.); Sol Funaroff, *The Spider and the Clock* (New York, 1938, 64 pp.); Kenneth Fearing, *Poems* (New York, 1935, 62 pp.); Edwin Rolfe, *To My Contemporaries* (New York, 1936, 64 pp.); and Isidor Schneider, *Comrade-Mister* (New York, 1934, 83 pp.). See also Fearing's *Collected Poems* (New York, 1940, 149 pp.), and Genevieve Taggard, *Not Mine to Finish, Poems, 1928-1934* (New York, 1934, 93 pp.), and *Calling Western Union* (New York, 1936, 74 pp.).

Most prominent among the Negro poets who contributed to the communist press was Langston Hughes, whose first collection, *The Weary Blues* (New York, 1926, 109 pp.), preceded the proletarian renaissance, and who continued a prolific production of topical and light verse, such as *Scottsboro Limited* (New York, 1932, 20 pp.), a verse play; *A New Song* (New York, 1938, 31 pp.); and *Shakespeare in Harlem* (New York, 1942, 124 pp.). See his autobiography, *The Big Sea* (New York, 1940, 335 pp.), and Lydia Filatova, "Langston Hughes; American Writer," *International Literature*, 1933, No. 1, pp. 99-107. See also S. A. Brown, *Southern Road* (New York, 1932, 135 pp.).

The Yale Series of Younger Poets, edited by Stephen V. Benét, brought out *Permit Me Voyage* (New Haven, Conn., 1934, 59 pp.) the first work of J. R. Agee; Muriel Rukeyser, *Theory of Flight* (New Haven, Conn., 1935, 86 pp.); and Joy Davidman, *Letter to a Comrade* (New Haven, Conn., 1938, 94 pp.). Agee was an individualist with a Christian socialist strain. Davidman, many of whose early poems appeared in the *New Masses*, and who is also a novelist, was converted from atheism to Presbyterianism in 1948: see D. W. Soper, ed., *These Found the Way; Thirteen Converts to Protestant Christianity*, by Joy Davidman and others, which will be published in 1951 by the Westminster Press. Rukeyser continued to show a groping preoccupation with proletarian themes and ideas in her second volume, *U.S. 1* (New York, 1938, 147 pp.), but not thereafter. Other poetry of the thirties, based on emotions sympathetic to the working class or the experience of unemployed or declassed artists, failed to master language or form or to incorporate the communist framework successfully. See H. G. Weiss, *Lenin Lives* (Holt, Minn., 1935, 31 pp.); Norman MacLeod, *Horizons of Death* (New York, 1934, 64 pp.); S. J. Kunitz, *Intellectual Things* (Garden City, N.Y., 1930, 63 pp.); and Stanley Burnshaw, *The Iron Land* (Philadelphia, 1936, 115 pp.), a long narrative on factory slavery by a self-conscious Marxian which is nevertheless an essentially anarchist protest.

A variety of poets stayed more along the sidelines of the movement. Edmund Wilson's only poetry is contained in *Poets, Farewell!* (New York,

1929, 78 pp.). Carl Sandburg in *The People, Yes* (New York, 1936, 286 pp.), wrote in what communists called the tone of "populist realism" following Whitman, without any background of Marxian social analysis. Among those who have been placed in the tradition of romantic New England anarchism, protesting against restraints of both style and ideology, is e. e. cummings. See, for example, his *Tom*, a ballet based on *Uncle Tom's Cabin* (frontis. by Ben Shahn; New York, 1935, 37 pp.), and other more extreme work. W. C. Williams, an experimenter and individualist, has written a distinctive long poem, *Paterson* (New York, 1946-1951), in which he keeps a collective focus like that of Dos Passos' novels. The penetration of leftist thought into the work of non-Marxian poets is perhaps best illustrated in the work of Archibald MacLeish during the middle nineteen-thirties, such as *Frescoes for Mr. Rockefeller's City* (New York, 1933, 28 pp.), and *Public Speech* (New York, 1936, 40 pp.).

Topic 9.   Marxism and Music

Little work has been done on the relationships between Marxian socialism and music. There are two fruitful approaches: the function of music in socialist groups, and the socialist variants of musical theories. Does music play the same role among socialists as among all other groups of men, or is there special emphasis on the use of songs to maintain allegiance or win recruits? What have socialists contributed to the theory of the folk origin of music; the direct or indirect influence of the social environment upon music as a part of the cultural superstructure? What do they say of the function of music under socialism?

Two streams of European tradition merged into the music which American Marxians used: Continental romanticism and British evangelical Protestantism. From the French they inherited the *Marseillaise* and the *Internationale*—products of the Revolution and the Paris Commune; from the Germans, the poetry of Heine and Freiligrath as set to folk songs or the lyrics of minor composers, popularized by the Lassalleans, and sung by the transplanted Sängerbund and Liedertafel. As other immigrant strains were woven into the American socialist movement, their national songs took a minor place in socialist song collections. The British contribution had its roots in Owenism, Chartism, and the Christian socialism of Kingsley and Maurice, just as the British socialist movement drew more from native sources than from Marx. The principal American modifications of all these ingredients were the revision of the words to fit party doctrine and the simplification of the tunes for mass singing. Generally speaking, up to the "proletarian renaissance" of the nineteen-thirties, the less doctrinaire Marxian groups made greater use of music, and theory was almost entirely neglected.

Since about 1933, a number of American Marxians have taken up the study of music in its relation to capitalism and to the workingman. The effects of mechanical and mass production and centralized management upon the composer, performer, and audience; the function of rhythm in work; the blending of music with the film, the drama, and the dance; and the battles over "modernism" and "socialist realism" have been examined against the general background of dialectical materialism. Some of these essays reached ludicrously oversimplified conclusions, but the more cautious work, exemplified in the writings of Elie Siegmeister and following the leads of earlier European and Soviet theorists, were among the first American studies of the sociology of music. Composers added little to the fund of socialist mass songs, but experimented in the new media and in new art combinations, and their popular and program music tried to meet the demand for "songs with social significance." The musicians' union became powerful, but without recognizable socialist connections, while New York artists joined special organizations sympathetic to communism. Performance, in its new channels, focused on borrowings from Soviet music and from folk songs.

In the following selections are Marxian song collections, twentieth-century theory, and the diversified fields developed after World War I. European and Latin American socialist music is discussed in the General Reading, pp. 434, 438-440, 442, and American communitarian musical theory and practice, pp. 443-447, and Topics 1-2. The most widely circulated radical song collections were the early compilation by C. H. Kerr, *Socialist Songs with Music* (1901; 4th ed., Chicago, 1902, 45 pp.); S. H. Friedman and Dorothy Bachman, eds., *Rebel Song Book* (New York, 1935, 92 pp.); and the I.W.W. *Songs of the Workers* (28th ed., Chicago, 1945, 64 pp.), words only. Elie Siegmeister, *Music and Society* (New York, 1938, 63 pp.), in the Critics Group Series, No. 10, outlines a theory of the social analysis of music which avoids the mechanical formula of direct environmental influence, suggests the continuing social functions of music, and sketches the history of class music in Western society. In his analysis he rejects the traditional rigid compartmentalization of popular, folk, and art music. Siegmeister's pamphlet, which has a useful bibliography, was also published in England (London, 1943, 55 pp.).

The Lassallean wing of the German-American socialists brought romantic songs into their party life, and the friend of Marx and Engels, F. A. Sorge, made his living as a musician. Socialist song collections of the second half of the nineteenth century, however, are exceedingly rare. The compilation of Hermann Schlüter for the German-language section of the Socialist Party, *Sozialistisches Arbeiter-Liederbuch* (Chicago, 190[?], 120 pp.), was a later sample of the variety. This contains the words to seventy-five songs, with indication of the tunes to be used.

For the anarchists, Benjamin Tucker published *Anarchists' March* with words by J. William Lloyd set to the Finnish war song "Björneborgarnes Marsch." For songs of early American radical labor see G. G. Korson's editions of Pennsylvania hard- and soft-coal miners' songs and ballads, *Minstrels of the Mine Patch* (Philadelphia, 1938, 332 pp.), and *Coal Dust on the Fiddle* (Philadelphia, 1943, 460 pp.), words only. Leopold Vincent, comp., *The Alliance and Labor Songster* (Winfield, Kan., 1891, 64 pp.) is a sample populist collection.

Less important than the Kerr collection cited above, and frequently with a strong religious strain, were Ralph Albertson, ed., *Fellowship Songs* (Chicago, 1908), which included words by Markham, Kingsley, Tennyson, Emerson, Whittier, Swinburne, and Havelock Ellis; and H. P. Moyer, *Songs of Socialism for Local Branch and Campaign Work, Public Meetings, Labor, Fraternal and Religious Organizations, Social Gatherings and the Home* (Chicago, 1911, 97 pp.). Platon Brounoff, composer of "The Hand with the Hammer," a Socialist Labor Party song, included it in the collection of his compositions for socialist poems, *Songs of Freedom (Twenty-One)* (New York, 1904, 80 pp.). See John Spargo, "A Socialist Composer and His Art," *Social-Democrat* (London), VI (Jan. 15, 1902), pp. 3-5. Brounoff collaborated with John Spargo to write "The Torch of Liberty" (1905), a popular Socialist Party song up to World War I. Brounoff published, under the pseudonym of B. A. Sharp, *Stolen Correspondence from the "Dead Letter" Office between Musical Celebrities* (New York, 1901, 135 pp.), a series of digs at contemporary musical education, performance, and composition, with thinly veiled reference to the Damrosches, Victor Herbert, Edward MacDowell, and others. I.W.W. songs and poetry, a latter-day folklore, illustrate the sardonic humor, colorful realism, and dramatic spirit of the native American advocates of syndicalism and direct action. The outstanding Wobbly poets were Ralph Chaplin, Joe Hill, and T. Bone Slim, most of whose rhymes have been collected in *I.W.W. Songs* cited above. See also Chaplin, *When the Leaves Come Out* (Cleveland, Ohio, 1917, 55 pp.), and *Bars and Shadows* (New York, 1922, 48 pp.).

After the war, communists published several songbooks: *America Sings* (New York, n.d., 60 pp.); *Songs of Struggle* (New York, n.d., text in English, 28 pp., in Hebrew, 32 pp.); Workers Music League, *Red Song Book* (New York, 1932, 32 pp.); *Songs of the People* (New York, 1937, 64 pp.), with several tunes by Hanns Eisler and words by Bertolt Brecht; *Songs for America* (comp. and ed. by Miriam Bogorad and others; New York, 1939, 64 pp.). Early in the depression, Yorkville German-Americans organized the Prolet-Bühne, which performed for trade unions the mass chants *Scottsboro* and *Tempo, Tempo!*, the latter contrasting Soviet labor with the capitalist speed-up. A sample of leftist contributions to theater music was the *Proletarian Song Book of Lyrics from the Operetta The Last Revolution*, by Michael Gold and J. Ramircz, music by Rudolph Liebich (Chicago, n.d., 18 pp., words only). The Hollywood Theatre Alliance produced the successful musical comedy *Meet the People* (1939), and Labor Stage, Inc., an I.L.G.W.U. group, the long-lived *Pins and Needles* (1937-1940), by Marc Blitzstein, Arthur Arent, and others. In connection with the Popular Front agitation for Loyalist Spain, *Six Songs for Democracy* (1940) was recorded and widely sold by Keynote Recordings; while for the duration of the Nazi-Soviet pact, the Almanac Singers were the best known "agitprop" group, and recorded *Songs for John Doe* against conscription and war. See also the Decca album, *The Lonesome Train*, words by Millard Lampell and music by Earl Robinson; and the words of fifty-three songs in *The Commonwealth Labor Hymnal*, mimeographed by Commonwealth College at Mena (Mena, Ark., 1940, 26 pp.). After World War II, People's Songs, Inc., was organized around members of the former Almanac Singers, Lee Hays (also once connected with Commonwealth College) and Peter Seeger. They published *The People's Songbook* (ed. by Waldemar Hille and others; New York, 1948, 128 pp.); a monthly, *People's Songs* (New York, 1945-), containing over a hundred songs a year, a mixture of "topical" songs and old favorites; the Asch album, *Roll the Union On*, distributed by Disc; film strips, square-dance and music lists, and other materials. People's Songs disbanded in 1949.

Theoretical discussion in this country really opened with two articles in the *Modern Monthly* by Elie Siegmeister, "Social Influences in Modern Music," VII (Sept. 1933), pp. 472-479, and "The Class Spirit in Modern Music," VII (Nov. 1933), pp. 593-598, some of which was incorporated into his Critics Group pamphlet cited above. But one of the first articles to appear in American leftist magazines had been Ernest Bloch, "Man and Music," translated by Waldo Frank and reprinted from the *Seven Arts* in *Mother Earth*, XII (Apr. 1917), pp. 56-60, (May 1917), pp. 85-89. Soon after, F. H. Martens translated R. D. Chennevière's article, "The Rise of the Musical Proletariat," in *Musical Quarterly* (Oct. 1920), pp. 500-509. Sample essays of the thirties are Charles Seeger, "On Proletarian Music," *Modern Music*, XI (Mar.-Apr. 1934), pp. 121-127; Hanns Eisler, "Reflections on the Future of the Composer," *ibid.*, XII (May-June 1935), pp. 180-186, and his leaflet contrasting the Marxian and capitalist functions of music, *The Crisis in Music* (New York, 1936, 10 pp.); Marc Blitzstein, "Coming—the Mass Audience," *Modern Music*, XIII (May-June 1936), pp. 23-29, by a composer for the labor theater and the radio; and Minna Lederman, "No Money for Music," *North American Review*, CCXLIII (Spring 1937), pp. 124-136, on the conservative control of musical institutions and their failure to reward composers adequately.

Minna Lederman edited *Modern Music* (New York, 1924-) for the League of Composers, a group around Aaron Copland. After World War II, Kurt List reviewed current production and wrote such essays as "Fate of the Artist in America," *Modern Review*, ɪ (May 1947), pp. 170-178.

Radical intellectuals had their own reasons for contributing to the folk-song vogue which blossomed in the thirties. It seemed like an avenue of contact with the otherwise inarticulate masses, who, as a matter of fact, preferred current dance music. A number of popular singers with communist sympathies, such as Paul Robeson, have used folk songs for the cause. Siegmeister, who arranged the music for Lawrence Gellert's collection, *Negro Songs of Protest* (illus. by Hugo Gellert; New York, 1936, 47 pp.), for the American Music League, turned during World War II to compiling folk music, such as *Work & Sing; a Collection of the Songs That Built America* (New York, 1944, 96 pp.). See also Siegmeister's *The Strange Funeral in Braddock*, words by Michael Gold (San Francisco, Calif., 1936, 16 pp.), being Vol. 9, No. 4 of *New Music, a Quarterly of Modern Compositions*.

The outstanding American treatment of film music is by Hanns Eisler, *Composing for the Films* (tr. and ed. by George MacManus and Norbert Guterman; New York, 1947, 165 pp.), the result of the Film Music Project, conducted by the composer Hanns Eisler for the New School for Social Research, with the assistance of Theodor W. Adorno, who was directing an investigation of radio music at the same time. Eisler was placed under federal arrest in 1947 on a charge of being an undesirable alien because—according to his lawyer—he once applied for membership in the German Communist Party. He left the country while the case was pending. Eisler at times takes issue with S. M. Eisenstein, author of *The Film Sense* (New York, 1942, 288 pp.), and discusses the work of the other leading European authority, Kurt London, *Film Music* (London, 1936, 280 pp.). Adorno published extensively before leaving Germany, e.g., "Zur gesellschaftlichen Lage der Musik," *Zeitschrift für Sozialforschung*, ɪ (1932), pp. 103-124, 356-378, and "Über Jazz," *ibid.*, v (1936), pp. 235-259, the latter under the pseudonym of Hektor Rottweiler. Examples of his later work include "On Popular Music," *Studies in Philosophy and Social Science*, Vol. 9, No. 1 (1941), pp. 17-48, written with the assistance of George Simpson; "The Radio Symphony," in *Radio Research, 1941* (New York, 1941, 333 pp.), pp. 110-139; and "On a Social Critique of Radio Music," a mimeographed report available at the Office of Applied Social Research, New York.

A leading Marxist critic of music who follows the Communist Party line is Sidney Finkelstein, a contributing editor of *Masses & Mainstream*. See his *Jazz: a People's Music* (New York, 1948, 278 pp.), already re-

ferred to in the General Reading; "What About Bebop?" *Masses &*
Mainstream, Vol. 1, No. 7 (Sept. 1948), pp. 68-76; and his forthcoming
book, *The Meaning of Music*, announced by International Publishers
for 1951.

Marxians contributed little to the theory or performance of the dance,
although the New Dance League of New York, one of the sponsors of
New Theatre & Film (New York, 1934-1937), operated as a leftist-
oriented organization in the thirties. See also Lincoln Kirstein's prediction in his article, "Crisis in the Dance," *North American Review*,
ccxliii (Spring 1937), pp. 80-103, that "the creative theatre of the
future will resemble ballad-opera . . ." (p. 103).

Topic 10. Pictorial Art, Mass Media, and Socialist Propaganda

Although this topic is devoted primarily to propaganda in connection
with Marxian socialism, the points of view toward propaganda of earlier
forms of socialism will first be noted briefly here.

Because the sectarian communities were interested in withdrawal from
the wicked world, in theory at least they were not interested in propa-
gandizing society outside the group. However, the complete celibacy
of some of the groups, notably the Shakers, did encourage them to seek
converts by such means as opening many of their religious services to
outsiders and by issuing tracts explaining their beliefs and aims. If
they did not have converts, the Shakers could not perpetuate their communities. The more aggressive Calvinistic background of the Mormons
and the Oneida Community often led these groups into more worldly
action to obtain converts. For one thing, they did not hesitate to build
large, though relatively simple, buildings to impress outsiders with
their success.

The liberal communitarians, such as Owen and Fourier, believing that
man is rational and hence can be converted both through verbal precepts
and by the actual examples of the good life expressed in socialist communities, made more use of propaganda. It was chiefly literary propaganda, however, as most of the communities did not last long enough
to develop, on any large scale, actual exemplification of the artistic
theories.

Marxism, with its belief that the Revolution, though inevitable, can
be hastened by suitable activity on the part of the proletariat at certain
critical times, has relied much more heavily on propaganda, both to
organize the proletariat and to discourage its enemies, than has any other
form of socialism. More than any other form of socialism, too, Marxism
has maintained that art must have immediate social usefulness, and this
also has increased the emphasis placed on the propaganda value of art.
In fact, Marxists have often tended to equate art and propaganda and

this has been particularly true in Russia or under Russian influence, especially after the expulsion of Trotsky. It should be noted, however, that what is popularly known as "propaganda" is called "agitation" by Communist Party members. For to them the word propaganda does not mean persuading the masses, but the further instruction of convinced party members (see PART V, Topic 5).

Because Marxist propaganda is necessarily intended to appeal to large groups, the propagandist is more interested in forms of art that permit the widest mass appeal—newspaper art, the frescoes favored by the Mexican artists, some of them communists, who have had so much influence on recent American painting, posters, the cinema (highly praised by Lenin as a socialist art form), the radio, the novel (Topic 6), the theater (Topic 7), and poetry (Topic 8).

An introduction to this topic can be obtained from the following reading: A. H. Young, *Art Young, His Life and Times* (New York, 1939, 467 pp.), pp. 262-281, 302-394; Joseph Freeman, *An American Testament* (New York, 1936, 678 pp.), pp. 303-308, 317-319; B. D. Wolfe, *Diego Rivera* (New York, 1939, 420 pp.), pp. 111-130, 157-180, 235-266, 312-376; L. C. Rosten, *Hollywood* (New York, 1941, 436 pp.), pp. 139-162; and Archibald MacLeish, *The Fall of the City* (New York, 1937, 33 pp.).

The newspaper or magazine drawing and the cartoon have been much used to further the socialist cause and the cause of social protest. The English illustrator Walter Crane, who was a follower of William Morris and who was connected with the *Comrade* (New York, 1901-1905), an early socialist periodical, had considerable influence on illustration in this country. After the *Masses* (New York, 1911-1917) came under the editorship of Max Eastman and the artist John Sloan in 1912, it had a socialist editorial policy and for a time was artistically the best illustrated magazine in the country. Its contributors, some of whom were socialists, included such well-known artists as Glenn Coleman, H. J. Glintenkamp, William Glackens, Robert Henri, George Bellows, Boardman Robinson, Maurice Becker, John Sloan, and Art Young. Some of these artists also contributed to the *Liberator* (New York, 1918-1924), and *New Masses* (New York, 1926-1948). Among the leading cartoonists on the *Masses* and the *Liberator* was Robert Minor, whose technique had much influence and who invented a new method of reproduction. For discussion of Minor and of the *Liberator* and the *New Masses* staffs, see Joseph Freeman, *An American Testament* (New York, 1936, 678 pp.), *passim*. Art Young, who worked for all three periodicals, also published many books: see especially his last publication cited above, and *On My Way* (New York, 1928, 303 pp.); *The Best of Art Young* (New York, 1936, 186 pp.); also *The Campaign Primer* (Chicago, 1920, 22 pp.), and *The Socialist Primer* (Chicago, 1930, 22 pp.), pamphlets of cartoons and captions, both published by the Socialist Party. And see Max Eastman, *Heroes I Have Known* (New York, 1942, 326 pp.), pp. 87-104. Among other artists connected with some or all of the above-mentioned periodicals were William Gropper, Boardman Robinson, Stuart Davis, and Louis Lozowick. See also Gropper's illustrations in the anonymous pamphlet, *Bats in the Belfry; Adventures of an Open Minded Worker* (New York, n.d., 24 pp.), *Gropper* (New York, 1938, 59 pls.), and *Gropper, 1941* (New York, 1941, 30 pp.). For Robinson consult his volumes *Cartoons on the War* (New York, 1915, 75 pp.), *Ninety-three Drawings* (Colorado Springs, Colo., 1937, 16 pp., 93 pls.), and Albert Christ-Janer, *Boardman Robinson* (Chicago, 1946, 131 pp.). For Davis see J. J. Sweeney, *Stuart Davis* (New York, 1945, 40 pp.). For Lozowick, who was a member of the original executive board of the *New Masses* and has written on Soviet Russian art, see the biographical statement in *Current Biography . . . 1942* (New York, 1942), pp. 533-534; also Topic 12 below. The fact that the art of these men ranges from the relatively "realistic" to the "abstract," indicates clearly that there is no single style used by artists who have contributed to radical periodicals.

Among the artists whose work has appeared in *Masses & Mainstream* are Philip Evergood, Hugo Gellert, William Gropper, Robert Gwathmey, all of them contributing editors, also Maurice Becker, Ben-Zion, Jack Levine, Ben Shahn, and Max Weber.

Consult William Murrell, *A History of American Graphic Humor* (New York, 1933-1938, 2 vols.), II, *passim*, and G. H. Hutzler, *The American Cartoon* (MS Senior Thesis, Department of Art and Archaeology, Princeton University, 1943, 109 pp.), pp. 46-55, for brief general discussions of the cartoon of social protest.

For communist cartoons see especially the files of the *Daily Worker* (Chicago, New York, 1922-), and the volume, *Red Cartoons from the Daily Worker* (Chicago, 1926, 64 pp.). Among the more prominent cartoonists who have contributed to the *Daily Worker* are Minor, Art Young, Gropper, Burck, and Redfield. Books of cartoons of social protest include Jacob Burck, *Hunger and Revolt* (New York, 1935, 248 pp.), published by the *Daily Worker*, and A. Redfield, *The Ruling Clawss* (New York, 1935, 184 pp.), also consisting of cartoons from the *Daily Worker*. See also Hugo Gellert, *Karl Marx' 'Capital' in Lithographs* (New York, 1934, 60 numbered leaves), with a passage placed opposite each picture; his *Comrade Gulliver: an Illustrated Account of Travel into That Strange Country, the United States of America* (New York, 1935, 43 numbered leaves); his *Aesop Said So* (New York, 1936, 47 pp.); and the pamphlet by an anonymous artist, entitled *The Truth* (New York, 1936, 16 leaves), published by the Labor Chest for the Relief and Liberation of Workers of Europe. The leading cartoonists for the *Weekly People* and Socialist Labor Party pamphlets have been Walter Steinhilber and Milton Herder.

Diego Rivera and in some respects J. C. Orozco—the first a communist and the second for a time a sympathizer—have exercised the art of fresco painting as propaganda and deeply influenced American muralists. The work of their school in Mexico is cited in the General Reading, p. 442. For Rivera's major works in the United States see Diego Rivera and B. D. Wolfe, *Portrait of America* (New York, 1934, 231 pp.), devoted chiefly to Rivera's frescoes on American history at the Lovestoneite New Workers' School, New York, of which Wolfe was director. Also see Detroit Institute of Arts, *Diego Rivera and His Frescoes of Detroit* (Detroit, 1934, 16 pp.); Museum of Modern Art, New York, *Diego Rivera* (New York, 1931, 64 pp.); and for an American publication of some of his Mexican murals in color, *Frescoes of Diego Rivera* (New York, 1933, 24 pp.), published by the Museum of Modern Art. For an American communist attack on Rivera after he had become a Trotskyist, see Robert Evans, "Painting and Politics, the Case of Diego Rivera," *New Masses*, VII (Feb. 1932), pp. 22-25. (According to Rivera's biographer, Wolfe, Robert Evans is the pseudonym of Joseph Freeman, now no longer a communist.) Rivera replied with an attack on Stalinist art in "The Position of the Artist in Russia Today," *Arts Weekly*, I (Mar. 11, 1932), pp. 6-7. Consult also Rivera's articles, "The Revolutionary Spirit in Modern Art," *Modern Quarterly*, VI (Autumn 1932), pp. 51-57; and "What Is Art For?" *ibid.*, VII (June 1933), pp. 275-278, with three photographs by Rivera of his Rockefeller Center murals destroyed by the management because they contained a portrait of Lenin. For American publications by and about Orozco, see, among others, his brochure published by the Museum of Modern Art, *Orozco "Explains"* (New York, 1940, 12 pp.), and *The Orozco Frescoes at Dartmouth* (Hanover, N.H., 1934, 24 pp.).

Rivera had as an assistant on the Rockefeller Center frescoes the American painter Ben Shahn, in whose work he had become interested as a result of paintings by Shahn of Sacco and Vanzetti. See Jean Charlot, "Ben Shahn," *Hound & Horn*, VI (July-Sept. 1933), pp. 632-634, with reproductions of Shahn's Tom Mooney series; J. D. Morse, "Ben Shahn: an Interview," *Magazine of Art*, XXXVII (Apr. 1944), pp. 136-141; A. B. L[ouchheim], "Shahn Feels Deeply and Sees Clearly," *Art News*, XLIII (Nov. 15-30, 1944), pp. 18ff.; J. T. Soby, *Ben Shahn* (New York, 1947, 20 pp.), and Soby, "Ben Shahn," a whole issue of the Museum of Modern Art *Bulletin*, XIV (Summer 1947), Nos. 4-5. In 1951 Harpers is publishing Selden Rodman's *Portrait of the Artist as an American—Ben Shahn: a Biography with Pictures*.

The art of Rivera, Orozco, and other Mexican painters helped to foster a vogue for "social protest" painting that was particularly strong in the United States during the depression of the 1930's. In this kind of painting communist sympathizers such as Gropper were among the leaders, but by no means all the artists involved were either communists or fellow travelers. See Peyton Boswell, *Modern American Painting* (New York, 1940, 166 pp.), pp. 62-63, and S. M. Kootz, *New Frontiers in American Painting* (New York, 1943, 65 pp.), pp. 42-45, for brief accounts of "social protest" and "class struggle" painting.

Hollywood has been aware of the excellence of Russian films, and has attempted at times to imitate their form without permitting any suggestion of social content to seep into the American product. Material on the difficulties Hollywood has experienced in trying to use Russian techniques while avoiding controversial content which would result in accusations of communism made against the movie makers may be found in M. F. Thorp, *America at the Movies* (New Haven, Conn., 1939, 313 pp.), pp. 210-213; L. C. Rosten, *Hollywood* (New York, 1941, 436 pp.), pp. 139-162; and G. S. Watkins, ed., *The Motion Picture Industry* (American Academy of Political and Social Science, *Annals*, ccliv; Philadelphia, 1947, 236 pp.). Perhaps the sharpest American Marxian film critic was H. A. Potamkin, author of *The Eyes of the Movie* (ed. by Irving Lerner; New York, 1934, 31 pp.), with bibliography. Potamkin discusses movies as propaganda and the religious and ethical aspects of film censorship. *Experimental Cinema* (Philadelphia, 1930-1934) was active in trying to get possession of the original footage of Eisenstein's *¡Que Viva Mejico!*, sponsored by Mr. and Mrs. Upton Sinclair, who edited and produced it as *Thunder over Mexico*, leaving out scenes with revolutionary implications. This fight had its origin not only in the desire for pure and uncensored art but also in factional strife among the socialists and communists. See "Eisenstein in Hollywood," in Edmund Wilson, *The American Jitters* (New York, 1932, 313 pp.), pp. 244-253.

For discussion of the question of communism in Hollywood see especially U.S. Congress, House, Committee on Un-American Activities, *Hearings Regarding the Communist Infiltration of the Motion Picture Industry* (Washington, 1947, 549 pp.); and a similar volume to be issued in 1951; also Gordon Kahn, *Hollywood on Trial* (New York, 1948, 229 pp.).

Leftist articles attacking capitalist or Fascist propaganda in mass media include H. H. Horwitz, "Fascist Tendencies in the Film," *Left Review* (Philadelphia), Vol. 1, No. 3 (1934), pp. 16-17; R. L. Neuberger, "Hooverism in the Funnies," *New Republic*, lxxix (July 11, 1934), pp. 234-245; and Herman Schnurer, "Notes on the Comic Strip," *Antioch Review*, i (Summer 1941), pp. 142-155. E. B. Burgum, "Art in War Time; the Revival of the Heroic Tradition," *Science & Society*, vi (Fall

1942), pp. 331-351, contradicts Trotsky's war propaganda with examples from Soviet movies, music, and literature.

The radio industry in America has been especially fearful lest it be attacked for trying to disseminate leftist propaganda. As a result it has made relatively little effort to experiment with radio entertainment which could at the same time teach the people. The Columbia Broadcasting System, just before the war broke out, did invite the poet Archibald MacLeish to write two radio plays which dealt with the Nazi-Fascist menace. These were published after performance: see *The Fall of the City* (New York, 1937, 33 pp.), and *Air Raid* (New York, 1938, 36 pp.). In spite of the industry's caution, much controversy was stirred up in 1950 by the publication of a book, *Red Channels; the Report of Communist Influence in Radio and Television* (New York, 1950, 213 pp.). This was published by the weekly newsletter *Counterattack: Facts to Combat Communism*, issued since 1947 by American Business Consultants, Inc.

Topic 11. Socialism, Housing, and City Planning

Because equalitarianism and humanitarianism have in some degree characterized all forms of socialism, they have all been interested in giving proper housing to the common man. And whenever the housing has been executed on a large scale, it has necessarily raised the question of city planning, so that socialism has had considerable effect on both modern group housing and city planning. But it is, of course, only one factor of many. For philanthropists, enlightened employers desiring greater efficiency among their workmen, companies or individuals seeking investment, states or cities seeking either to combat socialism or to aid it, have also played leading parts in the development of group housing as we know it.

The absence of family life in most of the sectarian communities, because of the prevalence of celibacy, generally made communal housing advisable. Formal city planning was usually avoided, however, both because it was not necessary at such small scale and also because it smacked of worldliness. Only in a few cases did the leader or prophet of a group become interested in the planning of his community to such an extent as to impose a regular layout upon it—as in the case of the Rappites at Harmony and Economy, Pennsylvania, and of the Mormons at Nauvoo, Illinois, and Salt Lake City.

The liberal communitarians, and particularly Robert Owen, began to develop group housing in its modern aspects. To men like Owen and Fourier, whose ideas grew so largely out of Romantic humanitarianism and rationalism, cooperative living in communal groups was the only adequate way of life. The plans for their ideal communities were, how-

502

ever, rigidly formal and in this expressive of the dogmatic and abstract ideals of the leaders. It was primarily with the garden-city movement, as developed by Ebenezer Howard under the influence of Bellamy's *Looking Backward*, of William Morris' *News from Nowhere*, and of the English medieval village, that the informal type of planning, still so influential, received a new impetus. For Howard's concept of the garden city, see the General Reading, pp. 427-428.

Pure Marxists such as Engels have opposed erecting housing until after the revolution on the grounds that it softens the lot of workmen and thereby postpones the revolution. However, gradualists have not been so strict. For example, Fabianism and guild socialism were both important in the development of the garden city, and in Germany social democracy combined with the German tradition of state and municipal social action to play a part in the German development of the sun-oriented row house and superblock. Both the garden city (which answers the Marxist objection to the separation of city and country) and the German row house have influenced American housing developments, particularly since the New Deal. For it was only during the depression that the idea of government sponsored housing became widely accepted in this country, although more on the grounds of giving work to the building trades than on the grounds of housing the lowest income groups.

The bibliography on housing is enormous. A few books are selected below to indicate the fact that socialism was *only one* of many factors encouraging group housing as we know it, but at the same time an important one. Most of the books referred to are neither by socialists nor even specifically about socialism. They are cited to show how the contributions of socialism in a specific field often exert an influence that is indirect and, indeed, frequently not realized by the authors of many books in that field.

By all odds the best introduction to the subject of housing and its history is Catherine Bauer, *Modern Housing* (Boston, 1934, 331 pp.), which unfortunately was published just before the chief developments in housing took place during the New Deal in the United States. See especially pp. 65-116, 176-187, 237-255. Also see the following: Werner Hegemann, *City Planning, Housing* (New York, 1936-1938, 3 vols.), I, pp. 104-116, 213-224; Nathan Straus, *The Seven Myths of Housing* (New York, 1944, 314 pp.), pp. 3-68, 166-214; Henry Wright, *Rehousing Urban America* (New York, 1935, 173 pp.), pp. 29-50, 86-96; Lewis Mumford, *The Culture of Cities* (New York, 1938, 586 pp.), pp. 454-493, also his *City Development* (New York, 1945, 248 pp.); and H. S. Churchill, *The City Is the People* (New York, 1945, 186 pp.), *passim*.

Among the earlier writings see the Bellamyite pamphlet by J. P. Putnam, *Architecture under Nationalism* (2nd ed., Boston, 1891, 64 pp.), and the detailed plans described in other utopian novels cited in Topic 3. W. D. P. Bliss, prominent American Christian socialist, became secretary of Garden Cities of America in 1907, an organization modeled after the British association that built Letchworth. Another persistent advocate was W. E. Smythe, organizer of Homelanders of America, and author of *City Homes on Country Lanes; Philosophy and Practice of the Home-in-a-Garden* (New York, 1921, 270 pp.). The famous Swiss-French architect Le Corbusier (the pseudonym of C. É. Jeanneret-Gris) took over some of the concepts of the garden city for his project for an ideal city, *The City of Tomorrow and Its Planning* (tr. by Frederick Etchells; New York, 1929?, 301 pp.; originally published in book form in 1924 as *Urbanisme*), a book which has had wide influence in the United States. A volume by one of the planners of Radburn, one of the first garden cities in the United States, is Henry Wright, *Rehousing Urban America* (New York, 1935, 173 pp.), a book which also reflects the influence of Continental housing, though not from any directly socialist point of view. Wright's colleague Clarence Stein, the chief architect of Radburn, is a disciple of Ebenezer Howard and of the Fabian city-planner Raymond Unwin, and served as adviser on the Greenbelt towns built under government auspices during the depression. See his authoritative "Toward New Towns for America," *Town Planning Review*, Vol. 20, No. 3 (Oct. 1949), pp. 202-282, and No. 4 (Jan. 1950), pp. 319-418. This will be published in 1951 as a book under the same title by the Liverpool University Press. James Dahir, *Communities for Better Living* (New York, 1950, 321 pp.), by a sociologist, has a useful bibliography and stresses the importance for contemporary planning of the "neighborhood unit," a concept said to have first been proposed by Ebenezer Howard in 1898 although it was foreshadowed in the decentralization urged by Bellamy and William Morris. It is a concept greatly developed by the American social worker, C. A. Perry, in *The Neighborhood Unit*, Monograph I in Vol. 7, *Neighborhood and Community Planning, of the Regional Survey of New York and Its Environs* (New York, 1929, 140 pp.), and formed the basis of Perry's numerous other writings including his *Housing for the Machine Age* (New York, 1939, 261 pp.). The influence of the Bauhaus (see General Reading, pp. 428-429), so important for the arts today, is reflected in Carol Aronovici, ed., *America Can't Have Housing* (New York, 1934, 78 pp.). To this publication of the Museum of Modern Art leading authorities in the field of housing contributed, including Walter Gropius, formerly of the Bauhaus, and the leading British garden-city planner and Fabian, Raymond Unwin.

The influence of the doctrine of organicism on the International Style—a doctrine pervading modern architecture and indirectly fostered by Marxism (see D. D. Egbert, "The Idea of Organic Expression," *Evolutionary Thought in America* [ed. by Stow Persons; New Haven, Conn., 1950, 462 pp.], pp. 336-396)— is reflected in Eliel Saarinen, *The City, Its Growth, Its Decay, Its Future* (New York, 1943, 380 pp.). The Harvard School of Architecture, with which Gropius is now connected, has become the leading protagonist in this country of the ideals of the Bauhaus and of the International Style, which, while certainly not specifically socialist, assimilated into modern architecture some currents to which socialists have contributed. Two important books which represent this same point of view and which deal in whole or in part with housing and city planning are Sigfried Giedion, *Space, Time and Architecture* (Cambridge, Mass., 1941, 601 pp.), and J. L. Sert, *Can Our Cities Survive?* (Cambridge, Mass., 1942, 259 pp.), both issued by the Harvard University Press.

Robert Moses, in "Mr. Moses Dissects the 'Long-Haired Planners,'" *New York Times Magazine*, June 25, 1944, pp. 16-17, 38-39, made a violent attack on the point of view of the foreign planners who have migrated to this country. He was answered by Dean Joseph Hudnut of the Harvard Faculty of Design, "A 'Long-Haired' Reply to Moses," *New York Times Magazine*, July 23, 1944, pp. 16, 36-37.

The continuing flood of American books on the subject of housing and city planning—books ranging from sympathetic to socialism to strongly individualistic in temper—can only be sampled. The point of view of Lewis Mumford, in *The Culture of Cities* (New York, 1938, 586 pp.) mentioned above, is largely that of the scientist-sociologist Patrick Geddes (in whose work cooperation rather than socialism is the ideal). See Meyer Schapiro's review essay, "Looking Forward to Looking Backward," *Partisan Review*, v (July 1938), pp. 12-24, which defends a Marxist view of architecture and society and characterizes Mumford's judgments as "fuzzy organicism." Appearing at the same time and with somewhat the same outlook as Mumford's was *Architecture and Modern Life* (New York, 1937, 339 pp.), by Baker Brownell and the noted architect Frank Lloyd Wright, who, far from being at all socialistic in spirit, is like Thoreau, an American individualist. Wright's project for an ideal town, "Broadacre City," also described in his *When Democracy Builds* (Chicago, 1945, 131 pp.) and many other writings, has some things in common with the garden city and with the decentralism of Ralph Borsodi (see PART IV, Topic 6). Henry Wright, an American pioneer in the field of housing, discusses in *Rehousing Urban America* (cited above) the garden-city type of housing and the German type of row house, among others. See also Werner Hegemann, *City*

Planning, Housing, ɪ (cited above), which includes interesting discussion of housing in relation to Marxism (especially chaps. 8 and 15). For the problems encountered by the New Deal in justifying government built housing to Americans on other grounds than giving work to the building trades during periods of depression, consult Nathan Straus, *The Seven Myths of Housing,* which is also cited above. Charles Abrams, *The Future of Housing* (New York, 1946, 428 pp.), which contains a useful bibliography on American public housing, calls for a national housing agency. Both housing and town planning are the subject of *Building and Planning* (London, 1945, 286 pp.), by G. D. H. Cole, the well-known English socialist with a wide American audience. See also E. T. Peterson, ed., *Cities Are Abnormal* (Norman, Okla., 1946, 263 pp.), with essays by Louis Bromfield, J. J. Rhyne, and other decentralists. Percival and Paul Goodman, *Communitas* (Chicago, 1947, 141 pp.), present modern ideas on city and regional planning, as does also *New Architecture and City Planning* (New York, 1944, 694 pp.), an interesting but uneven symposium edited by Paul Zucker. Compare American experience and theory with John Graham, Jr.'s discussion, *Housing in Scandinavia, Urban and Rural* (Chapel Hill, N.C., 1940, 223 pp.), of mixed and nonprofit types in a partly planned system.

Topic 12. Socialism, Constructivism, and Machine Art

After the revolution in Russia, one form of art which prevailed for a few years was known as constructivism. This was largely an outgrowth of the cubistic "constructions" originated by Picasso just before World War I, but in its Russian form special emphasis was placed on materials and methods of construction developed during the industrial revolution and hence expressive of the proletariat produced by industrialism. Furthermore, constructivism was considered by some artists to be expressive also of the growing industrialization of Russia under the Bolsheviki. Many of the "constructions" were designed, like those of Italian futurism, to suggest movement or to be actually moving in order to express the dynamic qualities of Marxism in general and of Russian revolutionary Marxism in particular. Thus Russian constructivism was thought to have a socially constructive point of view, as opposed to the nihilistically destructive spirit of dada which also had communistic connections.

Within a few years, however, the mechanistic forms typical of constructivist art—which had never met with Lenin's approval—fell into disfavor as a degenerate "kind of formal decoration based on sentimental mechanistic aesthetic," lacking the realistic and social content supposed to typify the art of the socialist masses. Many of the abler artists were unwilling to devote their art solely to the service of the revolution, as they were called upon to do. Hence, although constructivism lingered on for a time in stage design, it gradually disappeared in Russia. A number of constructivists went to Germany and influenced some teachers at the Bauhaus, the German school of art, architecture, and industrial design which has exerted so much influence on modern art in the United States, and which was closed by the Nazis in 1933.

Yet even after many constructivists had been driven from Russia by Lenin's disapproval, there was one kind of machine art which could retain some popularity and which was also popular in the United States. This was the kind of painting in which factory scenes were depicted. One of the first artists to paint such pictures was the American radical, Louis Lozowick. In 1928 an exhibition of Lozowick's work was held at Moscow.

Under Stalin even more than under Lenin, constructivism—including the kind of architecture which became known as the International Style—was rejected in Russia on the grounds that it was too abstract and nonnational as well as too mechanistic in character. Consequently, such art came to be regarded by Stalinists as reflecting both the Left (Trotskyist) and the Right (Bukharinist) oppositions.

As constructivism glorified technology and "the machine," it has had a considerable appeal for the American love of technology, invention, and gadgets. In 1934 the Museum of Modern Art in New York had a solemn exhibition of "machine art," and in 1948 a show of the works of Gabo and his brother, Pevsner, who had left Russia rather than devote their art to the revolution. The "mobiles" and "stabiles" of the American artist Alexander Calder reflect in part the indirect influence of Russian constructivism, but with any Russian revolutionary content omitted, as so often has been the case when imported socialistic forms of art have become popular in the United States. Bibliography on Calder, Pevsner, and Gabo is cited below.

For the general history of constructivism in relation to other abstract forms of modern art, A. H. Barr, Jr., *Cubism and Abstract Art* (New York, 1936, 249 pp.), published by the Museum of Modern Art, is by all odds the best source, and also has good bibliographies. Barr indicates the relation of some abstract art to politics, including socialism, and summarizes the reciprocal influences between Russian and western European art after the revolution. For the work of Alexander Calder, and bibliography on this American artist who best reflects the influence of the forms of constructivism and machine art, see J. J. Sweeney, *Alexander Calder* (New York, 1943, 64 pp.), published by the Museum of Modern Art, and E. S. Coan, "The Mobiles of Alexander Calder," *Vassar Journal of Undergraduate Studies*, xv (May 1942), pp. 1-18. The most complete expression of the tendency to glorify the machine as art is to be seen in *Machine Art*, the catalogue of the above-mentioned exhibition at the Museum of Modern Art (New York, 1934, 115 pp.). Another publication, *Naum Gabo [and] Antoine Pevsner* (intro. by Herbert Read; text by Ruth Olson and Abraham Chanin; New York, 1948, 83 pp.), issued by the same museum in connection with the show of the artists' work mentioned in the preceding paragraph, gives additional bibliography on constructivism. The Museum of Modern Art also published A. H. Barr, Jr., ed., and Georges Hugnet, *Fantastic Art, Dada, Surrealism* (2nd ed. rev. and enl., New York, 1937, 294 pp.), one of the most useful sources for studying dada and its outgrowth, surrealism which likewise has had some connections with communism. Unlike surrealism, dada has had little direct influence on American art.

For favorable views of the early years of Soviet art, theater, and literature, when futurism, of which constructivism was one variety, flourished, see Louis Lozowick, *Modern Russian Art* (New York, 1925, 60 pp.), and Joseph Freeman, Joshua Kunitz, and Louis Lozowick, *Voices of October* (New York, 1930, 317 pp.), especially pp. 265-277. Unfavorable to the Stalinist point of view are Kurt London, *The Seven Soviet Arts* (New Haven, Conn., 1938, 381 pp.), and Max Eastman, *Artists in Uniform* (New York, 1934, 261 pp.). René Fülöp-Miller, *The Mind and Face of Bolshevism* (London, 1927, 308 pp.), especially pp. 89-132, 152-184, contains an excellent though disapproving account of the early years. On constructivism in the Russian theater, the references cited in the General Reading of this Part, pp. 437-438, should also be consulted. For Lenin's lack of approval of Russian futurism see especially Klara Zetkin, *Reminiscences of Lenin* (New York, 1934, 64 pp.), and A. V. Lunacharsky, "Lenin and Art," *International Literature*, May 1935, pp. 66-71. Trotsky's attitude toward futurism as an expression of a revolutionary period is best expressed in his *Literature and Revolution* (tr. by Rose Strunsky; New York, 1925, 255 pp.).

L. M. [El] Lissitsky, *Russland: die Rekonstruktion der Architektur in der Sowjetunion* (Vienna, 1930, 103 pp.), treats constructivist architecture in Russia, while constructivism as an international movement can be studied best in the volume, *Circle; International Survey of Constructive Art* (ed. by J. L. Martin, Ben Nicholson, N. Gabo; London, 1937, 291 pp.). Additional bibliography is given in Barr, *Cubism and Abstract Art* (mentioned above). The influence of the forms of Russian constructivism on the arts of the Bauhaus—which, however, was essentially non-Marxian in its approach to art—can be seen in the volume, *Bauhaus* (ed. by Herbert Bayer, Walter Gropius, and Ise Gropius; New York, 1938, 224 pp.). As this volume was published by the Museum of Modern Art it also reflects American interest in the movement. The late László Moholy-Nagy, who of all the Bauhaus teachers was most influenced by constructivism, published, as head of what was first called the New Bauhaus, in Chicago, *The New Vision*, cited above, and *Vision in Motion* (Chicago, 1947, 371 pp.), which also reflect constructivist influence. Sibyl Moholy-Nagy, *Moholy-Nagy* (New York, 1950, 253 pp.), is a biography of the artist and teacher by his wife who refers to her husband's interest in dada even though he never actually joined the movement.

Thus, as already noted, interest in the machine as art, a tendency closely related to constructivism, is to be found in many artists who are not socialists or communists. This is true of the writings of Le Corbusier (C. É. Jeanneret-Gris) which have had a great influence in the United States, especially his *Towards a New Architecture* (New York, 1927, 289 pp.). This, with its numerous illustrations of now outmoded automobiles and airplanes, reflects the belief of one influential wing of the modern movement in art that "mechanic" forms offer as valid norms of beauty as "organic" forms. Applying this to architecture, Le Corbusier, like the Bauhaus, was led toward the relatively mechanistic and functional, as well as relatively cubistic, kind of architecture now called the International Style. This, of course, has had a very wide influence not only in the United States but in many other countries. And before the International Style was rejected in Stalinist Russia, Le Corbusier designed the building in Moscow now known as the Ministry of Light Industry. The point of view of Le Corbusier and the Bauhaus has further been fostered by the writings of the English anarchist-socialist critic Herbert Read, especially *Art and Industry* (2nd ed., London, 1944, 188 pp.), and "The Nature of Revolutionary Art," in his *The Politics of the Unpolitical* (London, 1943, 160 pp.), pp. 124-131. See also the other writings by him listed on p. 433. Read has an influential, if not wide, audience in this country, where he has often lectured.

In the United States this point of view has perhaps been most clearly reflected in the designs for the buildings to house the United Nations in New York. For a variety of opinions expressed by over thirty American architects and art critics in regard to the building for the United Nations' Secretariat, the first to be completed, see the *Architectural Forum; the Magazine of Building*, Vol. 93, No. 5 (Nov. 1950), pp. 93-112. The general plans for the buildings were prepared by an international board of design of which two of the most influential members were Le Corbusier and the noted Brazilian architect Oscar Niemeyer, for whose work see the American publication *The Work of Oscar Niemeyer* [*Soares*] (New York, 1950, 220 pp.), by Stamo Papadaki. Niemeyer, whose early architecture was admittedly inspired by the architecture of Le Corbusier, is an avowed communist. Thus—perhaps significantly— the United Nations buildings are in the "International Style" and represent both noncommunist and communist points of view toward architecture. Yet it should be emphasized that these buildings could only have been carried out in a country which permits much greater freedom of expression than does Stalin's Russia. For in Russia itself, despite Niemeyer's communism, such a design would be rejected as both "mechanistic" and abstractly "formalistic," and therefore as reflecting the "deviations" of both the Right and the Left, rather than the nationalistic kind of "socialist realism" officially glorified by Communist parties everywhere.

Index to Volume 2

This index combines a subject index and an index of authors and editors. Translators are listed only when the translated books have direct bearing on socialism and related movements, while publishers and periodicals are indexed only when they themselves are the subject of discussion. Books and articles for which no author or editor is known are indexed by title. The reader should also consult the detailed table of contents at the front of this volume.

Aaron, Daniel, 314
Abad de Santillán, Diego, 30, 33, 86
Abbott, Lyman, 173
Abell, Aaron J., 171
Abern, Martin, 154
Abraham, Gerald, 439
Abraham, William H., 69
Abramovitch, Raphael R., 22, 55
Abramowitsch, Mark, 348
Abramowitz, Isidore, 413
Abrams, Charles, 506
Abrams, Jacob, 417
Accumulation of capital, see Capital, concentration of; Capitalism, maturing of
Acht, Anton, 224
Acrelius, Israel, 109
Acton, Lord, 275
Adair, E. R., 44
Adam, Ernst, 70
Adamic, Louis, 164, 169
Adams, Brooks, 188, 199, 269-270, 324
Adams, Charles C., 115
Adams, Francis A., 260
Adams, Francis W. L., 434
Adams, Frederick B., 93
Adams, Grace, 96
Adams, Henry, 188, 196, 199
Adams, Thomas, 338
Adler, Georg, 4
Adler, Max, 8, 99, 219, 250
Adoratsky, Vladimir V., 35, 77, 213
Adorno, Theodor W., 440, 496
Adresse des Icariens de Nauvoo au citoyen Cabet, 139
Aesthetics, see Art; Criticism
Agar, Herbert, 304
Agee, James R., 491
Agitation, 283, 356, 378, 379, 380, 498; see also Propaganda
Agit-prop, 487, 495
Agrippa, Brother, 109, 179
Akselrod, Pavel B., 55
Alarm, 168
Alba, Victor, 405
Albertson, Ralph, 94, 302, 494
Albrecht, Arthur E., 300

Albrecht, H. F., 139
Alcott, Bronson, 96, 446
Alcott House, 96
Aldanov, M. A. (pseud.), see Landau, Mark A.
Aldington, Richard, 220
Aldrich, Thomas Bailey, 465
Alegría, Ciro, 442
Alegría, Fernando, 32
Alexander, N., 399
Alexander, Robert J., 30, 32
Alexander Berkman Fund, 22
Alexandre, Francisco, 33
Alfaro Siqueiros, David, see Siqueiros, David Alfaro
Alhaiza, Adolphe, 49, 50
All-Union Conference of Stakhanovites, 404
Allemagne, Henry R. d', 11
Allen, Catharine, 119
Allen, Edward J., 122
Allen, Emory A., 317
Allen, Ethan, 193, 195
Allen, James S., 217, 262, 382
Allen, John, 312
Allgemeine deutsche Biographie, 114
Allman, James, 489
Allocation of resources, see Planning
Allport, Floyd H., 372
Almanac Singers, 495
Almanach icarien, 236
Almazov, Evgeny, 437
Altgeld, John P., 483
Altruist, 140
Aluf, Aleksandr S., 404
Alvarez del Vayo, Julio, 26
Amado, Jorge, 441
Amana, 106, 107, 108, 111-112 (112, manuscript-sources), 179-180, 210, 235, 236, 444, 454
Amana Society, see Amana
Ambrosini, Gaspare, 53
America Sings, 494
American Bureau of Industrial Research, 97

511

395; *see also* Communism (by countries below); Communitarianism; Leninism; Marxism; Pre-Marxians; Russia; Socialism; Stalinism; Utopian socialism; entries under specific parties

Communism (British), 18, 324; *see also* Socialism (British)

Communism (Latin American), 32-33 (32, bibliography-sources), 73, 442-443

Communism (Russian), 21, 60-61, 77-80; and capitalism, 62-63; doctrinal basis of, 191; and economics, 242; leaders of, 373; political theory, 251; and propaganda, 356; *see also* Bolshevism; Leninism; Russia; Stalinism, Right opposition (Russian); Trotskyism (Russian)

Communism (U.S.): art and literature, 448-450; cartoons, 499; and Debs, Eugene, 150; and drama, 484; and education, 388; and the intellectual, 221; and labor movement, 294-295, 377; and labor parties, 287; and music, 450, 494-497 *passim*; periodicals, party-line, 449-450; and religion, 406-411 *passim*; and revolution, 326; social psychology of, 356; and strikes, 290-291; and women, 393, 398; and World War II, 272; *see also* Communist Party (U.S.); Socialism (U.S.)

Communist, 155, 277

Communist (St. Louis), 140

Communist Club, New York, 291

Communist Information Bureau, 56, 58

Communist International, *see* International, Third (Communist)

Communist International, 58

Communist Labor Party, 308

Communist League of America, 154

Communist League of America (Opposition), 158-159

Communist League of Struggle, 158

Communist Manifesto, 3, 4, 36, 38, 39, 69, 198, 219, 255, 274, 330, 331, 347, 362

"Communist Party, The," 158

Communist Party (British), 18

Communist Party (French), 13

Communist Party (German), 16, 496

Communist Party (Mexican), 33 (bibliography-sources)

Communist Party (Russian), 21, 78, 194, 284, 341; *see also* Bolshevism; Communism (Russian)

Communist Party (U.S.), 153-158; *also* 102, 107, 161, 311, 451, 473; activities and discipline, 285; agitation, 498; art and literature, 448-450; and atomic en-

ergy, 217; and civil liberties, 310; clientele, 374; criticized by Socialist Labor Party, 145; and Dreiser, Theodore, 481; economic and political theory, 240; and farmer-labor-party activities, 376; formation of, 146; and imperialism, 271; in fiction, 483; and internationalism, 279; and Jews, 277-278; and labor movement, 289; and nationalism, 277; and the Negro, 382; and party organization, 288, 376-377; periodicals, 155-156, 240, 288, 376-377, 449-450 (party-line); and planning under capitalism, 337; and proletarian literature, 468, 474-475; and propaganda, 379-380, 498; and psychiatry, 216; and psychology, 354; and religion, 410; and sectarianism, 378; and self-criticism, 376, 377; trial of eleven leaders, 310; and violent revolution, 310; and war, 275; and World War II, 282; and Wright, Richard, 482; *see also* Communism; Communism (U.S.); Workers Party (Communist)

Communist Party Opposition, *see* Right opposition (U.S.)

Communitarianism, 94-97, 106-140; *also* 91, 92, 98, 200, 237; and anarchism, 165, 297; art and literature, 424-425, 443-447; bibliography-sources, 94; and capitalism, 400; and cooperative movement, 295, 296, 297, 303-304; and drama, 484; economic and political theory, 235-237; and education, 383-386; and incentives, 402; and law and order, 412; and marriage, 395-396; and Marxism, 185; and nationalism, 273-274; philosophical bases of, 177, 196; and planning, 333; and political action, 282; and political theory, 250; and revolution, 321-322, 326; and single tax, 319; sociology of, 350; and women, 391-396 *passim*; *see also* Communitarianism, Christian; Communitarianism, liberal; Utopian socialism

Communitarianism, Christian, 107-108; *also* 91-93, 106; and the American tradition, 311; art and literature, 421, 452-459; and city planning, 502; and communitarianism, liberal, 183; and determinism, 201; doctrinal basis of, 178-183; and housing, 502; and idea of progress, 202; and the ideal society, 197; and individualism, 206; and morality, 207; and music, 452; philosophical basis of, 193; and propaganda, 497;